CONTENTS

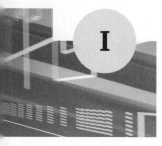

BUSINESS FINANCE 1

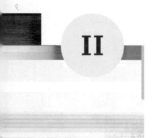

FINANCIAL ACCOUNTING 85

II

BUSINESS ACCOUNTING AND FINANCE

for non-specialists

Australia • Canada • Mexico • Singapore • Spain • United Kingdom • United States

THOMSON

Business Accounting and Finance: For Non-specialists

Copyright © Catherine Gowthorpe 2003

The Thomson logo is a registered trademark used herein under licence.

For more information, contact Thomson Learning, High Holborn House, 50–51 Bedford Row, London WC1R 4LR or visit us on the World Wide Web at:
http://www.thomsonlearning.co.uk

British Library Cataloguing-in-Publication Data
A catalogue record for this book is available from the British Library

ISBN 1-86152-872-8

First edition published 2003

Typeset by LaserScript, Mitcham, Surrey, Great Britain
Printed in Croatia by Zrinski

Book at a Glance

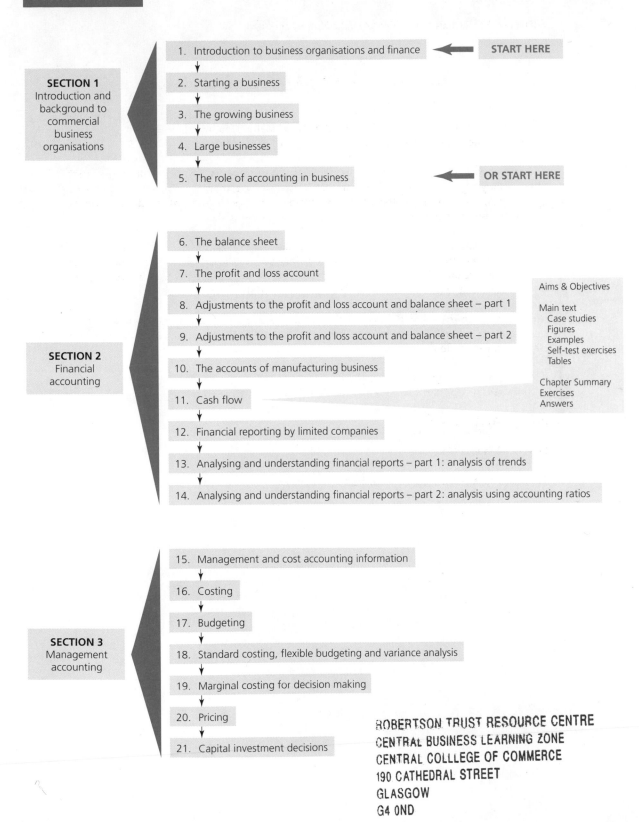

SECTION 1
Introduction and background to commercial business organisations

1. Introduction to business organisations and finance ⟵ START HERE

2. Starting a business

3. The growing business

4. Large businesses

5. The role of accounting in business ⟵ OR START HERE

SECTION 2
Financial accounting

6. The balance sheet

7. The profit and loss account

8. Adjustments to the profit and loss account and balance sheet – part 1

9. Adjustments to the profit and loss account and balance sheet – part 2

10. The accounts of manufacturing business

11. Cash flow

12. Financial reporting by limited companies

13. Analysing and understanding financial reports – part 1: analysis of trends

14. Analysing and understanding financial reports – part 2: analysis using accounting ratios

Aims & Objectives

Main text
  Case studies
  Figures
  Examples
  Self-test exercises
  Tables

Chapter Summary
Exercises
Answers

SECTION 3
Management accounting

15. Management and cost accounting information

16. Costing

17. Budgeting

18. Standard costing, flexible budgeting and variance analysis

19. Marginal costing for decision making

20. Pricing

21. Capital investment decisions

MANAGEMENT ACCOUNTING 395

III

PREFACE

Who is this book aimed at?

The aim of this book is to provide an introduction to business accounting and finance for students who are specialising in some other business discipline, or in a discipline for which some knowledge of business accounting and finance is useful. The book is suitable for students on business and management courses generally, or on more specialised courses such as marketing, human resources management, tourism, hospitality management and information systems. Students outside the business area following courses in engineering, computer science, fashion and fine and applied arts will also find the book a very suitable introduction to accounting and finance.

While the principal intended audience for the book comprises students taking a formal course of instruction at college or university, it is also intended that the book should lend itself to self-study by anyone who is interested in extending their knowledge of basic business accounting and finance. This could include people who are starting, or thinking of starting their own businesses. Also, the book could be useful for people who are already engaged in business but who are aware that they do not quite understand what their accountant is telling them.

The overarching aim of the book is to develop understanding of accounting. It is not, primarily, a book about how to do accounts. Some of the chapters do, indeed, require students to prepare fairly straightforward accounting statements. However, the principal purpose of this approach is to aid understanding; it is often easier to understand how accounting figures hang together if you have had some experience of working them out for yourself.

Special notes for the suspicious

Accounting and finance are often regarded as particularly difficult subjects and lecturers in accounting are often presented with ingrained negative attitudes among their non-specialist students. Below I've tried to challenge some of the most frequently encountered objections that I've met in my career as a lecturer.

'Accounting is boring and it's not relevant to what I'm doing anyway'

Some of you may be struggling to understand why you have to study business accounting as part of your course. If you are a fashion student, for example, you are likely to be much more interested in creative outcomes and in developing your own skills. But people who are successful in making careers in fashion (and other creative endeavours) have to be very much alive to the business environment in which they work. People who have forged successful careers in the creative arts are often surprisingly well-tuned in to all the business and accounting aspects of what they do.

'Accounting should be left to the accountants'

If you are looking forward to a career in, for example, retail management or marketing you may feel that you shouldn't really have to bother with accounting – after all, there are plenty of accountants around to sort out the figures. One of the most important messages of this book is that accounting, on the contrary, is much too important to be left to the accountants. Business managers owe it to themselves to be able to interpret the reports that accountants present to them; they are vital aids to understanding what is going on in the business. Business managers should be able to question accountants from a position of strength about the information that is being presented to them. If they are not sufficiently knowledgeable to do this they risk being quite seriously restricted in their understanding of their business and in their ability to make sound decisions.

It is important to appreciate that accounting is not an exact science. Accounting has emerged in its present day form, after many centuries of development, because there has been a need for it. It is, essentially, about communication between people and so it is vulnerable to all the impediments that hinder proper communication. For example, people sometimes tell lies and accounting can be used, very effectively, to tell lies. Accounting is often imprecise and its imprecision can be easily exploited by the unscrupulous. After studying this book, you should be much more aware of the strengths and limitations of accounting as a means of communication.

'Accounting is all about maths, and I'm no good at maths'

Accounting undeniably involves dealing with numbers. However, the study of accounting rarely involves much beyond simple arithmetic. Specifically, the principal prior skills that this book requires are the ability to add, subtract, multiply, divide and to calculate a percentage. Towards the end of the book you will be required to draw simple line graphs and to calculate compound interest. Most of these are skills that are covered at Key Stages 2 and 3 (for those of you who have come through the UK primary and secondary education system recently). There is nothing in this book (or indeed in many accounting textbooks) that requires knowledge of mathematical techniques beyond GCSE level.

What the study of accounting does involve, however, is the ability to understand what the numbers signify. This is a skill that some students find relatively difficult to acquire. I've written the book with this difficulty in mind; from the early chapters onwards a lot of the exercises and cases are about the messages conveyed by the numbers. It cannot be emphasised too frequently that this book is about developing understanding of accounting information.

'I won't be able to understand all the jargon'

Accounting is no different from many other spheres of fairly advanced human endeavour in that it has its own terminology. Jargon is often baffling to the uninitiated, but, inevitably, some of the jargon simply has to be learned. In this book I have tried to ensure that all unfamiliar terms are fully explained in the most straightforward way possible. There is a glossary towards the end of the book which explains a lot of the more unfamiliar terminology so that you don't have to go hunting back through the book to find the original explanation.

How to use this book: Notes for lecturers and tutors

The book is divided into three parts, each of which is relatively self-contained. The first part is much shorter than the other two and provides general context. Its five chapters provide an introduction to accounting and finance for business. Topics covered include sources of finance for business, business start-ups, some essential facts about companies and the role of accountants in business. Because of time constraints, course tutors may not be able to lecture on these topics, but they may ask students to read these chapters as background material, or may omit them altogether. The important point is to realise that the Part I of the book is helpful to, but not a prerequisite for, understanding ideas introduced later in the book. Chapters within the Part I can be used flexibly. For example Chapter 4 introduces larger companies and their interaction with the financial markets. Lecturers may want to combine study of Chapter 4 with Chapter 21 as a basic introduction to finance at a later stage in the course following study of the management accounting chapters. Chapter 5, which deals with the role of accounting in business, may also be used as a good starting point in the book to precede study of the financial accounting section.

Parts II and III of the book deal, at much greater length, with aspects of financial and management accounting, respectively. From Chapter 6 onwards, most chapters involve the study of some accounting techniques (and therefore the use of some manipulation of figures) but the overall objective is always to encourage understanding of accounting statements.

Chapter structure

All chapters start with Aims and Learning Outcomes. Diagrams and tables aid the narrative explanations and illustrate concepts, and frequent use is made of worked examples.

All chapters, apart from Chapters 1 and 5, contain at least one case study. These are often quite long, highlighting many aspects of the material covered by the chapter. Several of the cases incorporate more general business problems, so as to illustrate the close link between the conduct of a business and the information contained in accounting statements.

At the end of each chapter is an extensive set of exercises so that students can test their knowledge and understanding. Students are often worried and may become demotivated if the end of chapter exercises are too difficult. Therefore, the exercises are designed to test the full range of learning points in the chapter, from simple to complex. If students wish to test their understanding with even more exercises, further examples are provided on the book's dedicated website (see below). About half of the end of chapter exercises contain answers within the book. Answers to the remainder can be supplied by course lecturers who have obtained the Lecturer's Guide (see below).

Supplementary material

In addition to the material presented in the book, a variety of supplementary material is available.

Dedicated website

The website can be found at www.thomsonlearning.co.uk/accountingandfinance/gowthorpe. The lecturer section is password protected and the password is available free to lecturers who confirm their adoption of the book. Lecturers should complete the registration form on the website to apply for their password.

For students and lecturers (open access)

Question bank

This contains supplementary questions for every chapter. Where appropriate, a mixture of multiple choice and longer questions are included.

Links to accounting and finance sites on the web

Including links to the sites mentioned in the book.

For lecturers only (password protected)

- Lecturer's Guide: this includes answers to the end of chapter questions for which answers are not provided in the book.
- Additional questions and answers.
- A bank of multiple choice questions, with answers.
- Additional case studies and solutions.
- Overhead transparencies and PowerPoint presentations to accompany each chapter.

Acknowledgements

My thanks are due to Steve Powell of Coopers & Lybrand (now PricewaterhouseCoopers) for first suggesting many years ago that I might like to try teaching. Thanks also to Angela and Elizabeth Brophy, my first students, and indeed to all the students I taught over 12 years at the University of Central Lancashire, and from whom I learnt so much.

Several people have helped me in the course of developing this book, and I gratefully acknowledge their contributions:

- Andy Humphries of Hugh Baird College, and Nicola Grout-Smith of the University of Central Lancashire who found the time to look at the original proposal for this book. Both made valuable suggestions for its development.
- Ursula Lucas of Bristol Business School for her support and encouragement, and for giving up her time to discuss the direction and content of the book.
- Many of my former colleagues at the University of Central Lancashire with whom I worked and taught on accounting for non-specialist courses, including Rob Bond, Joe Boylan, Terry Deeley, Katy Pilkington, Philip Wallace and Phil Wraith.
- My colleague Laura Spira at Oxford Brookes University for her support and encouragement in this and many other endeavours.

I am also very grateful for the expert guidance of the staff at Thomson Learning:

- Jennifer Pegg who originally commissioned this book and who was so supportive of my proposal.
- Patrick Bond who has given me much useful advice and encouragement.
- Jenny Clapham, Development Manager, Melody Woollard, Development Editor and Paula McMahon, Production Editor, who have guided me through the complex process of publishing a book.

Finally, but not least, I would like to thank all those who have commented on the book.

FIGURES

BUSINESS FINANCE

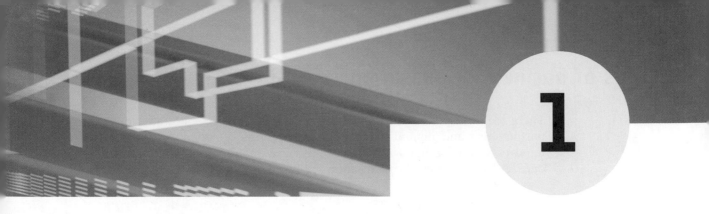

INTRODUCTION TO BUSINESS ORGANISATIONS AND FINANCE

AIMS AND LEARNING OUTCOMES

Aim of the chapter

To introduce the most common forms of business organisation and to discuss the principal sources of finance for those organisations.

Learning outcomes

After reading the chapter and completing the exercises at the end, students should:

- Understand the differences between the sole trader, partnership and company forms of business organisation, including the advantages and drawbacks of each type.
- Know about some of the different sources of business finance available to commercial organisations.
- Know in outline about some important features of the business environment including the various ways in which tax is charged on businesses.

This chapter provides an introduction to the business environment and its financing. It is useful to know about the features discussed in this chapter as a background to the development of more detailed knowledge of accounting and finance in business which occupies most of the book.

The book focuses on the role of accounting and finance in commercial organisations. Accounting is also important for not-for-profit organisations and the public sector, but these are beyond the scope of this book.

Forms of business organisation

There are three common forms of business organisation: sole trader businesses, partnerships and limited companies. Other forms of organisation are encountered occasionally, but we will concentrate in this book on the three common ones. All three types of organisation are run with a view to making profits.

Sole trader businesses

A **sole trader** operates a business himself or herself, keeping any profits that are made (after deduction of tax). This is a useful form of business for certain types of trade or profession. For example, a plumber, carpenter, financial services adviser, tax adviser, writer or night-club singer could each operate as a sole trader business. Each of these offers a service to the public; each receives money in exchange for performance of the service. After deduction of the various expenses that are involved in running the business, any sum that is left over is the profit, all of which can be kept by the sole trader.

Example 1.1 Having finished his apprenticeship, Yasin sets up in business as a plumber. He pays for a listing in *Yellow Pages*, subscribes to a plumbers' trade association, installs a phone in his flat and waits to be contacted by members of the public and other businesses who require plumbing services. If there is a demand for his services (and there almost certainly will be; it is notoriously difficult to find a plumber) he will soon be called upon. Yasin charges fees for his services out of which he must meet business expenses.

What are Yasin's business expenses? They will typically involve: cost of tools, expenses of running a van, telephone bills, advertising (the *Yellow Pages* listing) and small amounts of administrative expense, such as paying for an accountant to sort out his tax affairs.

In order to keep his business affairs in good order, he will need to keep receipts as evidence of his expenses, copies of the bills he makes out to his customers, and bank statements. It is important not to mix up the business income and expenditure with his own personal items. Yasin or his accountant will summarise all the income he has received from customers and all the expenses of running the business on an annual basis. Income less expenses equals the profit of the business.

At an early stage, the tax authorities take an interest in Yasin's business activities. He will have to pay tax based upon the calculation of his profit. Later in the chapter we will examine the tax regime in a little more detail.

Characteristics of the sole trader form of business

The sole trader is the only person responsible for the management of the business. Although he or she may employ other people as the business gets bigger, all the decision making and risk taking involved in the business rests on the shoulders of one individual. If the business runs into financial difficulties or faces other problems, the sole trader is on his or her own in addressing them.

Sole trader businesses tend to remain fairly small. For people who are self-employed in the types of trade or profession mentioned earlier, this form of business can work very well. However, if the business is of a type that is likely to grow very much bigger, the sole trader form of organisation will need to be replaced by a partnership or limited company structure, which allows more than one person to act as manager.

If a sole trader overstretches himself or herself financially, perhaps by borrowing too much, or if losses rather than profits are made, he or she is liable for all the consequences as an individual. For example, a lender would be entitled to pursue repayment of a loan even to the point where the sole trader would have to sell personal property to repay it. In extreme cases, this can result in personal bankruptcy.

The sole trader business is relatively informal and easy to set up. The business does not require registration of a separate legal entity and so it is quite likely that no legal costs will arise. In the initial stages, at least, the principal administrative issues are likely to arise with the Inland Revenue authorities. A competent chartered accountant can mediate between the individual and the Inland Revenue to ensure that the correct amount is paid, and that tax does not become a problem.

Partnerships

A **partnership** is a business run by two or more people with a view to making a profit. Typically, partnerships are fairly small businesses, but there are certain types of business activity in which very large partnerships are operated. Professional partnerships, such as those between solicitors, may develop to be very large businesses indeed. There is a legal restriction limiting the number of partners in most types of partnership to 20; however, professional partnerships (solicitors, accountants, surveyors or architects for example) are exempt from the restriction. The very largest partnerships are such big businesses that people who have barely met each other are in partnership together.

Many different trades and professions may be run through the medium of a partnership; apart from the professions noted above, doctors, pharmacists, business consultants, shopkeepers, builders, hairdressers and almost any other type of trade or business activity could be run via a partnership.

Example 1.2 Winston and Winona are computer games enthusiasts. They both work as local government administrative officers and are bored with their jobs. They decide to start a business selling computer games; they will rent shop premises for retail sales, but will also run a mail order service from the room behind the shop. The business is established as a partnership with a business name of WW Wizard Games. The two partners decide that, as they will both be working full-time in the new business, they will share all the profits from the business equally.

As in the case of Yasin in Example 1.1, it will be necessary to keep some records of the business activities. It makes good sense to do so as it will contribute to good relations with the tax authorities. However, unlike the case of the sole trader, Yasin, there are some legal requirements governing the records that have to be kept by the business, and the way in which the business operates. Partnerships are covered by the Partnership Act 1890. This is a relatively straightforward piece of legislation that sets out a basic structure of legal relationships between partners, minimum record-keeping requirements and ways of resolving disputes between partners. For example, the Partnership Act states that profits will be shared equally between partners unless they make some other agreement between themselves. Winston and Winona have agreed in any case to share profits equally; this is a common arrangement where all partners are contributing equally to the success of the business. However, they could share profits in any way that seems appropriate.

Apart from the basic legal structure set out in the Partnership Act 1890, partners may decide to draw up a formal, legal agreement between them. Typically this would set out the details of the financial and legal arrangements that are to operate; it might, for example, state that Partner A will receive 60% of the profits of the business while Partners B and C each receive 20%. It may also deal with the actions to be taken in the event of a dispute between the partners. Not all partnerships bother to have a formal agreement of this type set up, but it can prove to be very useful if relationships turn sour.

Characteristics of the partnership form of business

The success of a partnership depends to some extent on the quality of the relationships between partners. Sometimes, people who are friends, or who are related to each other, set up a business partnership together. The pressures of running a business can sometimes place an intolerable strain on what has previously been a good relationship. On the other hand, where partnerships work well, they can be highly productive, especially if the partners have a range of skills that complement each other. Winona, in Example 1.2, is perhaps very good at selling over the counter, but lacks the attention to administrative detail that is required to run the mail order side of the business. If Winston is a good administrator, he will complement Winona's skills, and between them they will perhaps be able to run a successful business.

As well as sharing in the running of the business, the partners are likely to be able to command more resources to put into the business. At the start-up stage, each may have savings or other resources (such as equipment) which they can put into the business. If the partnership needs to borrow money, it may be in a better position to do so than the sole trader.

If the partnership loses money, or cannot repay loans, lenders are able to recover money owed by requiring the partners to sell items of property that they own personally. In this respect the partnership is no different from the sole trader, and the partners face the consequence of bankruptcy in the worst cases.

Each partner is liable under the law for the actions of his or her partners. If Winona makes a business decision that turns out badly and the partnership is left owing a large amount of money, both Winona and Winston are liable for the consequences of the decision. Winston could not claim that he knew nothing about the decision; he would still be equally liable with Winona. (It really is important for partners to know and trust each other thoroughly.)

A partnership business is not difficult to set up. However, partners should be prepared to go to the additional trouble and expense of having a clear partnership agreement drawn up with the help of a solicitor. It will make potential disputes in the future easier to resolve.

Limited companies

A **limited company** is a legal arrangement for regulating the ownership of business. A company is regarded as a separate person for the purposes of the law; so, for example, a company, unlike a partnership, can enter into a legal contract. This means that, if the other contracting person sues, he or she sues the company, not the owners of the company. The company itself becomes liable for its unpaid debts, overdrafts and so on.

This legal construction is an extremely important feature of the business world, in the UK and in many other countries. Because the company itself enters into contracts, takes out loans and so on, its owners are protected from any adverse consequences of the action. This is the concept of **limited liability**. It is an extremely useful and helpful device that protects shareholders from personal loss if the business runs into trouble.

Setting up a company (the process of **incorporation**) involves some legal formalities that must be followed strictly. It is therefore more difficult than setting up a sole trader business. However, the difficulties should not be overstated: there are specialist company registration firms, which, for a modest fee, take care of all the formalities. It need cost little more than £150 to set up a company.

After the company is incorporated, there are certain regular legal formalities that must be complied with. More details are given in the following sub-section.

> **Example 1.3** Winston and Winona decide to set up their business as a limited company, rather than as a partnership. The business is registered in the name of WW Wizard Games Limited. They divide ownership of the business between them; each owns exactly 50% of the shares in the business. Winona and Winston are both shareholders. Both are involved in the day-to-day management of the business and, as well as being **shareholders**, are also **directors**.

Characteristics of the limited company form of business

Shareholders are liable only for the amount that they have paid into the company in exchange for shares. This is the maximum amount which they can lose if the company is, for example, sued for not repaying its loans on time.

The legal formalities involved in setting up and running a limited company are more complex than for partnerships and sole traders. The directors of a limited company are responsible for making available to the public a certain amount of financial information about the activities of the company on a regular basis. They must do this via the Registrar of Companies, which is an agency responsible for the collection of data relating to companies. Any member of the public can obtain information about a limited company by visiting one of the offices of the Registrar of Companies or through its website (**www.companieshouse.gov.uk**). Regular filings include accounting information. Information that could remain private in a sole trader or partnership organisation must be made public by limited companies.

In small companies shareholders (who are the owners of the company) and directors (who are responsible for managing it) are the same people. However, in larger companies it is frequently the case that most shareholders have nothing to do with the management of the company. Day-to-day management can be left in the hands of directors who are professional managers. Shareholders in very large companies often have virtually no contact with the company or its managers.

Sole traders, partnerships and limited companies contrasted

When setting up a business from scratch, the founder or founders must consider carefully which form of business organisation is most suitable for them. Usually, it is sensible to take professional advice on the matter as it can be advantageous for tax purposes to choose one form over another. Leaving tax to one side for the time being, the following are the principal advantages and drawbacks of the three different types of organisation.

Sole trader – advantages

- It is easy to start up as a sole trader.
- There are no legal formalities on start-up.
- The sole trader is self-reliant; he or she does not risk getting involved in the personality clashes that can occur where more than one person is managing a business.
- The sole trader does not have to share the profits from the business with anyone else.

Sole trader – drawbacks

- A sole trader bears all of the consequences of legal action against the business for unpaid debts and unfulfilled contracts. His or her personal property may have to be sold to meet business debts.
- A sole trader organisation remains small-scale.
- The sole trader bears the brunt of any losses or business difficulties.
- There is no co-manager with whom problems can be shared.
- If the sole trader is weak in some aspect of business expertise (such as ability to sell, to manage people or to keep track of business records) the business may suffer because there is no one available with complementary skills.

Partnership – advantages

- In a partnership, management is shared and the business can benefit from the complementary skills that the partners bring to it.
- Business decisions do not have to be taken alone.
- Business risks are shared, as are any losses that the business makes.

Partnership – drawbacks

- Partners are responsible in law for the consequences of each other's actions.
- Partners face unlimited liability; they must bear all of the consequences of legal action against the partnership. Their personal property may have to be sold to meet unpaid business debts.
- The profits of the business are shared between all the partners whereas a sole trader keeps all the profits for himself or herself (but note that a partnership business, which combines the skills of two or more people, should be able to generate higher profits than a sole trader).

Limited company – advantages

- The most significant advantage conferred by company status is the limitation of personal liability. Shareholders can invest in a business knowing that they will not be pursued for further contributions once their shares have been paid for.
- The limited company legal structure allows for shareholders to appoint professional managers as directors.
- A limited company's shares can be used to spread the ownership of the business among many people.
- Shares can be sold and bought so that transfer of ownership is relatively easy and straightforward.

Limited company – drawbacks

- Setting up a company requires adherence to a set of strict formal legal requirements, and will sometimes require professional advice.
- Regular filing of financial information with the Registrar of Companies is a legal requirement; this involves additional administration and means that members of the public have access to information that would remain strictly private in a partnership or sole trader organisation.

Finance for business

When starting a business the founder or founders must find a source of finance to pay for the setting-up costs, any equipment that is needed and, probably, for the expenses of the business for the period during which it is getting established. Most established businesses will also require finance from time to time to pay for such items as:

- Buying major items of equipment or land and buildings.
- Expanding the scope of the business (for example, opening new offices or conducting research into new product feasibility).
- Helping the business through difficult periods such as temporary recessions or decreases in sales.

In this section of the chapter we will examine the principal sources of finance that may be available to a business. Some are more appropriate than others for particular purposes.

Existing resources

When a business starts up, the founder(s) will almost certainly make an initial contribution of their own resources. This may be in the form of cash they have saved, or won, or been given. It could be in the form of motor cars or vans, premises or some other item of resource. Such initial contributions are known in accounting terms as **capital introduced**. We will examine financing business start-ups in much more detail in Chapter 2.

Where partners contribute to the setting up of a business, they may contribute unequal amounts depending on the resources they have at their disposal. In such cases, it may be decided between the partners that those who contribute more will receive an extra share of the profits to compensate.

Example 1.4 Jakes, Jones and Jessop form a partnership to conduct legal business. The total capital introduced by the partners is £190 000, constituted as follows:

    Jakes – office building valued at £100 000
    Jones – cash of £50 000
    Jessop – cash of £30 000 plus office equipment valued at £10 000

The partners decide between them that they will allocate a 10% return on each of these contributions out of the profits made by the business, before dividing the profits equally between them. The business makes £49 000 in profits in its first year, which will be allocated between the partners as follows:

	Jakes £	Jones £	Jessop £
10% on Jakes' capital: £100 000 × 10%	10 000		
10% on Jones' capital: £50 000 × 10%		5 000	
10% on Jessop's capital: £40 000 × 10%			4 000

Remaining profit split equally between the partners:
£49 000 − (10 000 + 5 000 + 4 000) = £30 000.

	Jakes £	Jones £	Jessop £
Split equally	10 000	10 000	10 000
Total	20 000	15 000	14 000

The introduction of capital is possible at any point subsequent to the foundation of the business. Whenever the business needs more resources the founders may be able to make a further contribution.

Retained profits

As a business grows it makes profits. The owners of the business usually take out part of the profits as their reward for investing in it. However, they are not obliged to take out all the profits; they may leave some in the business to be invested to produce growth and further profits. The amount of profit left in the business is referred to as **retained profits**. This can be a very good source of funds for further investment as it is not dependent on any outside person or organisation.

Borrowed money

When thinking about potential sources of finance, borrowing may be one of the first possibilities that springs to mind. However, borrowing is not always the most appropriate source of finance for a business. In some circumstances it simply may not be obtainable. Many business start-ups would not be able to borrow money because no organisation would be willing to take the risk of lending it. Lenders need to know that: (a) the money they lend will be paid back eventually; and (b) the business will be able to pay a reasonable rate of interest on the borrowing. In order to do so the business needs to stand a good chance of being profitable.

The cost of borrowing

The cost of borrowing is the interest that must be paid on a regular basis to the lender of the money. Large institutional lenders may agree to lend money to the business but they will expect to receive interest payments on time and without fuss.

The risk/return relationship

Banks and other lenders do not always charge the same rate of interest. They make an assessment of how risky the lending is – i.e. how likely it is that the borrower will fail to repay. If the loan is perceived as more risky than average, the lender will either refuse to lend, or will charge a high interest rate on the lending. Sometimes, it may only be possible to borrow at extremely high interest rates.

Security

Sometimes banks and other lenders will not lend unless the loan is secured. A **mortgage** is a familiar example of a secured loan – familiar because at some point in their lives a lot of people take out a mortgage to buy a house or flat. Businesses often take out commercial mortgages to assist in the purchase of property in the form of real estate.

Overdrafts

Overdraft facilities may be obtainable through the business's bank account. An overdraft is most likely to be made available to a business if it can prove that the extra funds are needed only in the short term and that the business is fundamentally sound.

Example 1.5 Christmas Glitter Limited is an established business making Christmas lights and decorations. The period from July to the beginning of October each year is spent in frantic activity in the factory in order to build up the stocks of goods for sale in the company's three most important trading months – October, November and December. A lot of money is needed in July to October; materials have to be purchased and paid for, and staff costs are heavy because a lot of overtime is worked. At this time of year the business usually requires an overdraft. The company's bank manager is quite happy to provide overdraft facilities during this period because she knows from experience that by mid-November the company will have paid off the loan.

This is an example of a seasonal shortfall in cash, caused purely because of the nature of the business. A short-term facility like an overdraft tides the company over until it starts to generate cash.

It should be noted that an overdraft is a short-term solution. It is technically repayable on demand; this means that the bank can demand immediate repayment of the overdraft at any time. In practice, however, banks rarely demand immediate repayment.

Leasing and hire purchase

When a business makes a large purchase of an item that will be used over the medium to long term, it has to pay out a lot of cash at one time. Sometimes it makes sense to look at alternative ways of financing such a major item.

Under a **leasing** arrangement the business (the **lessee**) pays a regular amount to a **lessor** in exchange for the use of an item such as a piece of machinery. The lease often extends over a period of years. The lessor, usually a financial institution, pays for the machine, which is delivered to the lessee's premises and will, typically, remain there throughout its useful productive life. The lessor organisation is the legal owner of the machine but will probably never even see it. The lessee never owns the machine, but will use it, often for years, in the business.

Short-term leases are sometimes taken out on items such as photocopiers and cars. The items may be replaced regularly and each time this happens a new lease is negotiated. Again, the lessee never actually owns the item in question.

Hire purchase is a similar arrangement to the longer-term leasing described above, with the difference that, once the final agreed payment is made, under the terms of the agreement ownership passes to the purchaser business.

Factoring

Many businesses sell on credit – that is, they supply goods or services for which they are paid after a period of a month or two. The delay in receiving cash can be costly; if it is extended for too long the business may run into difficulties. **Factoring** is a way of speeding up the receipt of cash.

Example 1.6 Noone & Belfast Limited is a business that supplies major retail stores with home furnishings. The stores are slow to pay and sometimes the company has to wait up to three months to receive money that is owed to it.

The directors of Noone & Belfast decide to investigate a factoring arrangement. At the end of most months the company is owed about £200 000 by various stores that have bought goods but have not yet paid for them. The directors approach a factoring company which proposes the following arrangement:

- They will pay Noone & Belfast 80% of the amount owed to them at the next following month end (i.e. £160 000).
- The factoring company will do all of the administration work connected with collecting the debts.
- Each time Noone & Belfast are ready to bill a customer for goods supplied to them the factoring company will pay the company 80% of the amount billed.
- The remaining 20% less a handling charge will be paid over when the factor receives the amount due from the customer.

The advantages of this arrangement for Noone & Belfast are that they receive a one-off large amount of cash (£160 000), and thereafter, they will receive 80% of the invoice value as soon as they bill a customer. They will also be able to devolve most of the administrative work connected with collecting debts to the factor.

In exchange for the cash supplied up-front by the factoring company, and for the administrative work, there will be a handling charge. This could be 2–3% of the total amount billed; obviously the factoring company needs to be able to make a profit out of the arrangement.

Although the arrangement costs money, it may well be worth considering for Noone & Belfast Limited.

Grant finance

Businesses may be able to obtain grants from the government, local authorities or other agencies and funding bodies. Usually, grants would be awarded only in quite specific circumstances. For example, a local authority trying to encourage the growth of local business might allow companies moving into the area a rent-free period in local authority business units. Although this is not a grant of cash it is a saving on the expense of rental, and it may well entice businesses into the area.

Grant finance is very advantageous in that it usually does not have to be repaid. However, there may be strings attached. In the example above, a business taking advantage of the rent-free period might have to undertake to stay in the area for a further minimum period of time of, say, three years.

Financing companies: Share issues

A company (but not a partnership or sole trader business) can raise additional finance by issuing more shares for cash. If the company is doing well, it can offer existing and potential shareholders a sound investment opportunity.

In Chapter 4 we will examine share issues in much more detail.

Financing companies: Venture capital

Medium-sized companies may be able to seek finance from venture capitalists. A venture capital company invests for limited periods in growing companies in order to give them a short to medium-term financial boost. Usually, the venture capitalist buys into the shares in the company, and will often provide management expertise as well.

Example 1.7 Hawthorn and Hayward Limited has been in business for five years, and has experienced very rapid growth during the whole of that period. The company's directors are now looking to expand into European markets and are seeking both additional finance of around £250 000 and specific expertise to help them. They approach a venture capital organisation, Bizexpand, for help.

Bizexpand's adviser explains that his organisation would buy shares in Hawthorn and Hayward in exchange for a cash sum of £250 000. Bizexpand would consequently become a significant shareholder in the company. In addition, one of Bizexpand's specialist staff would take up a directorship in Hawthorn and Hayward. The new director would be appointed because of his or her expertise in opening up European sales markets.

The arrangement is planned to last for between two and three years. At the end of a maximum period of three years, Bizexpand would sell its holding of shares (hopefully at a handsome profit) and the specialist director would move on.

Investment by a venture capitalist can be very helpful to a growing company, because it usually combines a sizeable input of cash together with advice and expertise in areas that will benefit the company.

Short, medium and long-term finance

It is important for businesses to match their needs for finance with the most appropriate form of finance. Using an overdraft to buy a new office building, for example, would be highly inappropriate. Taking out a ten-year commercial mortgage, on the other hand, would probably be the most sensible course.

Table 1.1 categorises the different sources of finance discussed earlier into short-term, medium-term and long-term sources.

Table 1.1 Terms of sources of finance

	Short-term	Medium-term	Long-term
Existing resources	✓	✓	✓
Retained profits	✓	✓	✓
Borrowings	✓	✓	✓
Mortgage			✓
Overdraft	✓		
Short leases	✓		
Long leases and hire purchase		✓	✓
Factoring	✓		
Grant finance	✓	✓	✓
Share issues		✓	✓
Venture capital		✓	✓

Fundamentals of taxation

Taxation is a fact of life for most people and businesses. In this section we will take a brief look at the most common taxes levied on the different types of business which we examined earlier in the chapter.

Income taxes (personal taxation)

Sole traders and partners in business partnerships make profits (they hope) which are chargeable to tax. The tax that is levied is not a specific business tax; it is charged according to the individual's own circumstances at income tax rates.

Example 1.8 Cerise and Cherry are partners in a discounted clothing business. Under their partnership agreement Cerise takes 60% of the profits and Cherry takes 40%. In the tax year 20X5–20X6 the partnership profits are £30 000. Neither partner has any other source of income.

Cerise will be entitled to 60% of the profits: £30 000 × 60% = £18 000
Cherry will be entitled to 40% of the profits: £30 000 × 40% = £12 000

Each partner will include her share of the profits in her personal tax return. Each woman will be liable for income tax on her share less any attributable personal allowances. National Insurance contributions will also be payable.

Corporation tax

As the name implies, this is a tax levied on companies. Directors are paid a salary for working in the company, and they will pay income tax and National Insurance on the amounts they earn (just like any other employee). The company itself, however, is liable to corporation tax on its profits.

The company's profit is calculated (income less expenses = profit) and then corporation tax rates are applied. In recent years in the UK, corporation tax rates have tended to fall. Currently, in the 2002–2003 tax year, the basic corporation tax rate is 30% with a small companies' rate of 19%. The first £10 000 of a corporation's business profits is tax-free.

Capital gains tax

If an item such as an office building is sold at a profit, capital gains tax is likely to be charged. Capital gains tax applies to both individuals and companies, and so would be levied on sole traders, partnerships and limited companies.

Value added tax

Value added tax (VAT) is the UK's principal form of indirect tax; it is a tax on the purchase of goods. As private individuals we frequently pay VAT on goods and services that we purchase; we have no choice in the matter, and because prices are charged inclusive of VAT we do not usually even notice that we are paying the tax.

What about VAT from the point of view of a business? Businesses act as collectors of VAT, which they pay over on a regular basis to the government authority that collects it, the Customs and Excise. The operation of VAT is demonstrated in Example 1.9.

Example 1.9 Palfrey and Bennett Limited is a retail business that sells men's clothing from a series of high street outlets. The company adds a charge of 17.5% (the standard rate of VAT) to all the items that it sells. The company's customers pay the tax.

At the end of the three-month period ending 31 March 20X5, Palfrey and Bennett completes a VAT return. Total sales before VAT for the three-month period are £100 000. VAT at 17.5% is £17 500. The amount of £17 500 is known as output tax.

Palfrey and Bennett has itself, however, paid VAT on the purchases it makes. During the same three-month period it has bought goods totalling £70 000 before VAT. VAT at 17.5% is £12 250. The amount of £12 250 is known as input tax.

The quarterly liability to the Customs and Excise is calculated as follows:

	£
Output tax for the quarter	17 500
Less: Input tax for the quarter	12 250
VAT payable	5 250

The company must complete a VAT return immediately following each quarter. In this case, by the end of April 20X5 it must send the VAT return to the Customs and Excise together with payment of £5250. The Customs and Excise authority is very strict indeed about deadlines.

▶

Each of the businesses supplying Palfrey & Bennett will also be obliged to fill in VAT returns and make payments to the Customs and Excise. People in business often complain about the large administrative burden imposed by accounting for VAT. However, once a business has set up systems to cope with VAT, filling in the VAT return is usually straightforward.

Very small businesses are not obliged to register for VAT. However, if total sales for a year exceed £52 000 or are expected to exceed that amount, it is compulsory to register for VAT.

This section has provided only a very general introduction to the taxation of businesses. For the purposes of this book it is regarded as general background business knowledge. Detailed knowledge of tax is not required for any part of the material that will be covered in the rest of the book. In almost all cases, the exercises ignore the effects of taxation in order to avoid adding an unnecessary layer of complication. However, readers should bear in mind that the effects of taxation can be a significant factor in the real world.

Chapter summary

In this chapter we have examined some general business and finance issues. Students need to understand this background information in order to fully appreciate the context of business accounting.

We looked first at three forms of business organisation:

- sole trader
- partnership
- limited company.

The characteristics of each were described, and then the most significant advantages and drawbacks of each form of business organisation were identified and contrasted.

Next, the chapter examined some of the most significant sources of finance for businesses:

- existing resources
- retained profits
- borrowings (including mortgages and overdrafts)
- leasing and hire purchase
- factoring
- grant finance
- share issues (applicable to limited companies only)
- venture capital (applicable to limited companies only).

Finally, the chapter examined some of the fundamentals of business taxation. The following taxes were identified and briefly described:

- income tax (personal taxation)
- corporation tax
- capital gains tax
- value added tax.

Information about taxation is included as general business background knowledge only. A detailed knowledge of taxation is not required in order to achieve the aims of this book.

The next three chapters will examine various aspects of business finance in more detail and in the context of businesses of different sizes. Chapter 2 is concerned with the start-up of a small business. The case study charts the initial start-up and subsequent development of a sole trader business. Chapter 3 looks at some of the problems and opportunities that face a growing business. The case study deals with financing, staffing and other problems in an established partnership organisation. Chapter 4 examines the financing of limited companies, and extends the basic Chapter 1 coverage into an examination of financing for large businesses via the stock market. The case study deals with a successful company making a decision about stock market flotation.

Internet resources

Some useful websites:

www.3i.com – the website of a very well-known and well established venture capital company.

www.companieshouse.gov.uk – the Registrar of Companies' website, which provides information about all UK companies (most of it at a price, unfortunately).

www.hmce.gov.uk – a comprehensive source of information for anyone who wishes to know more about VAT.

www.inlandrevenue.gov.uk – a very useful source of information about all aspects of personal and corporation tax.

Exercises

The answers to many of the exercises are set out later in this chapter. However, where the exercise number is followed by 'A' the answer is available only to lecturers. Remember that additional exercises (with answers) are available to students on the book's website.

1.1   One of the following statements about the sole trader form of business is correct:

    a) A sole trader has to pay corporation tax.

    b) Sole traders submit annual information to the Registrar of Companies.

    c) The sole trader is entirely responsible for the management of the business.

    d) Because a sole trader business is simple it is not necessary to keep any records.

1.2   One of the following statements about the partnership form of business is correct:

    a) Partnerships are always very small businesses.

    b) Partners are obliged by law to put £50 000 into the business when it starts up.

    c) Partnerships are very difficult to set up because of the amount of information demanded by the government.

    d) Partners are personally liable for the debts of the partnership business.

1.3   One of the following statements about the limited company form of business is correct:

    a) A limited company is a separate person in law.

    b) Limited companies cannot be sued.

    c) It costs a great deal of money to establish a limited company.

    d) Shareholders in a limited company are obliged to act as directors.

1.4A One of the following statements about the limited company form of business is correct:

    a) A limited company must submit information on a regular basis to the Registrar of Companies.

    b) Directors of limited companies are always selected from amongst the shareholders.

c) Limited companies are not eligible to apply for grants.

d) Directors of a limited company are personally liable if the company is sued.

1.5 Select from the following list the most appropriate form of finance for purchasing a new office building:

a) ten-year mortgage loan

b) a loan repayable in six months' time

c) an arrangement with a factoring company

d) hire purchase.

1.6A Select from the following list the most appropriate way of financing the build-up of stocks of Easter eggs in a chocolate business:

a) venture capital

b) overdraft

c) issue of new share capital

d) lease.

1.7 Select from the following list the most appropriate way of financing a new office photocopier:

a) grant finance

b) issue of new share capital

c) lease

d) mortgage.

1.8 You are a small business adviser. A new client, Arnold Tapwood, has come to you for advice. Mr Tapwood explains that he is the sole proprietor of a small building business. One of his friends, Simon, who is a carpenter, has suggested that he and Arnold should join forces in a partnership. Arnold is not sure about the extra legal responsibilities that would be involved in becoming a partnership, and he asks you to explain in outline the required legal formalities.

1.9A Marie Deutsch is a fashion designer who, after graduation with a degree in fashion, obtained a very good job as designer in a lingerie company. She has decided that she would like to leave her job and set up in business with an old friend from college who also trained as a designer. Marie has heard that it is more sensible to set up as a limited company because it would mean that she and her friend would not be personally liable for the debts of the business. However, she says she is sure that there must be some strings attached, and would like you to tell her about any disadvantages in limited company status.

1.10 Geoffrey is a keen dangerous sports enthusiast. He would like to set up in business as a sole trader organising dangerous sports events and activities. His business idea is that people would pay an annual subscription that would allow access to his website and a range of discounts on the fees for dangerous sports events. While he expects the idea to be a winner, because there are so many like-minded enthusiasts, he feels it likely that he will need some start-up finance to equip an office, install a couple of phone lines and pay for some help with administration. He estimates that he will need about £10 000 to get things up and running before the subscriptions start to appear in large numbers.

Geoffrey has just left university with accumulated debts of around £8000 so he has no money to put into the business. His parents refuse to give him any money for the venture. He has come to you for advice on the best ways of financing the start-up.

Answers to exercises

1.1   The only correct statement is c): the sole trader is entirely responsible for the management of the business.

1.2   The only correct statement is d): partners are personally liable for the debts of the business.

1.3   The only correct statement is a): a limited company is a separate person in law.

1.5   Out of those listed the most appropriate form of finance for purchasing a new office building is a ten-year mortgage loan. The correct answer, therefore, is a).

1.7   Out of those listed, the most appropriate form of finance for the new office photocopier is a lease. The correct answer, therefore, is c).

1.8   *Advice to Arnold Tapwood*: It is not difficult to set up in partnership. By contrast with the establishment of a limited company, there is no requirement to submit information to the authorities. However, the partners would be well advised to consider drawing up a partnership agreement, for which they would require legal advice. Although the provisions of the Partnership Act 1890 apply where there is no partnership agreement, in most circumstances it is preferable to have a formal agreement. This would cover areas such as profit-sharing and arrangements in the event of a dispute between the partners.

1.10   Geoffrey will probably find it difficult to finance this business start-up because of its risky nature. He appears to be quite sure that lots of people will want to pay a subscription to his website, but he appears to have nothing but optimism to support this view. It is highly unlikely that a bank would be at all interested in making a loan in the circumstances.

Geoffrey has no existing resources to draw upon and his family have refused to put money into the business. It is remotely possible that grant finance might be available from a specialist organisation, and Geoffrey should explore this avenue. A further possibility is to join forces in partnership with another dangerous sports enthusiast who does have some resources to draw upon.

This appears to be a business proposition that will be very difficult to finance. If Geoffrey cannot find a business partner who is prepared to put some money into the venture, he may have to shelve the idea for the time being. If he gets a job, pays off his debts and saves some cash he might be able to finance the start-up himself at some point in the future.

STARTING A BUSINESS

AIMS AND LEARNING OUTCOMES

Aim of the chapter

To help students to understand some of the key issues – especially those relating to finance – involved in the start-up of a small business.

Learning outcomes

After reading the chapter and its case study, and completing the exercises at the end, students should:

- Know about the most common sources of business finance for start-ups.
- Understand the need for, and the principal elements of, the business plan.
- Know about the most common reasons for business failure.

The discussion relating to the finance of small businesses builds upon and expands the knowledge gained in Chapter 1. It is important to thoroughly understand the issues discussed in this chapter, because they form a foundation for the study of accounting and reporting which is the main focus of this book.

Financing the small business

All businesses have to start somewhere. They mostly start small and are usually based upon a bright idea that occurs to one person, or sometimes, to a small group of people. The idea may be brilliant but impractical in business terms, or it may have occurred to lots of other people so there will be a high level of competition in the market, or it may be so good and original that it is going to make its owner a millionaire.

The basic business idea may arise out of a need for a product or service that cannot, apparently, be found, or cannot be found at the right price.

Example 2.1 Julie has a full-time job. She has two children, aged five and seven, at the village school which closes at 3.15pm each day, two hours before the end of her own working day. Julie cannot be there to collect the children, and no other member of the family is available at that time to help out. After trying various unsatisfactory arrangements for having the children collected, she concludes that the only way to solve the problem is to set up a business to run an After School Club on the school premises, so that the children of working parents can play in properly supervised conditions.

In this example, there is a perceived need for a service that does not currently exist. Provided that the need is shared by a sufficient number of people, and that the service can be provided economically, there is a business opportunity here.

Sources of finance for a new business start-up

In Chapter 1 we examined sources of business finance in outline. Below we look in more detail at some typical sources of finance that might be used to finance the start-up of a new business.

Any business start-up is likely to require an investment of money in order to make it work. Money is needed for some or all of the following:

- purchase of equipment
- supporting the owner and family while the business gets going
- paying for premises
- paying for staff
- expenses like business rates, insurance, running costs of cars, etc.

It can be very difficult to make realistic estimates of some of these costs. Later in the chapter we will begin to look at how to estimate costs. For the moment will assume that some money and/or other kinds of resources are going to have to be contributed to the business in order to get it started. (Other kinds of resources could include, for example, use of a car or van that is already owned by the individual starting the business, or a contribution of free labour by members of the family.)

Where does the money come from?

Existing cash resources

Existing cash resources may be available in the form of savings and windfalls. In fact, the arrival of an unexpected windfall may even provide the impetus for the starting up of a business.

Example 2.2 Tim wins £120 000 on the National Lottery. He has always wanted to have a retail business, but has never had enough spare cash to be able to seriously consider setting one up. Now, because of this windfall, he has enough money in hand to be able to give up his job, and to invest in the lease of premises and the purchase of stock that he needs to get his business off the ground.

This scenario can probably be dismissed as completely unrealistic (although, after all, somebody has to win). More likely is the case where the prospective business person has some savings, or is made redundant and receives a sizeable sum of cash or is conveniently left some money in a will.

Also possible, depending upon the nature of the business, is self-financing through part-time work. In practice, many small businesses are financed in this way.

Example 2.3 Sasha completes her degree in fine art, producing several very good pieces of work at her degree show. Two of the pieces sell, and Sasha is offered an exhibition at a local art gallery. However, even though she may be comparatively successful in her working life as an artist, it is highly unlikely that she will ever earn enough from her work to be able to provide herself with a decent living. Very few artists earn much at all. Sasha takes a job for 15 hours per week in an art materials shop. This pays just enough to allow her to spend enough time producing her work for the exhibition, although she is very hard up indeed.

Family or friends

If the prospective business person has no resources it is possible that his or her family may be prepared to support the business in its early stages. Sometimes this can be through a handy injection of cash, or the loan or gift of an item of equipment. Very often, a supportive partner will agree to cover living costs from his or her salary during the early stages of the business.

It should be clear that the chances of obtaining this kind of financial support will depend upon the previous record and good standing of the individual.

Example 2.4 George wants to start a business supplying animal feed. He needs approximately £25 000 for renting premises, buying a second-hand goods vehicle and enough stock to get the business going. However, he is well known in the family as an unreliable spendthrift with an unfortunate tendency to lie and cheat. He has borrowed small sums of money from his parents and brother in the past and has failed to repay them. In the circumstances they are unlikely to be prepared to lend him anything at all.

Even if finance can be obtained in this way, there may be a downside. If the businessman borrows from his nearest and dearest, and then loses the lot in a reckless business start-up, family relationships can be scarred or even terminated.

Business failure can, and often does, contribute to the breakdown of long-term relationships.

Grant finance

Grants can be an excellent source of start-up finance, as they usually do not need to be repaid. However, they are available only for quite specific purposes and will almost never serve to finance all of the expenses of a start-up. Also, once a grant is given, the granting authority will normally keep quite a close check on the progress of the business.

The chances are high that grant finance will not be available, but it is well worth checking just in case. Grants may be available for quite specific purposes. For example, in areas of high unemployment it may be possible to obtain a grant for employing local people.

In Example 2.1 involving Julie's childcare business (which is a real-life example), grant finance was obtained successfully. The business would have gone ahead without it, but at the time the government was making generous grants available to any business creating additional childcare places, and a grant was obtained to cover the cost of providing equipment and for the first year staffing costs. However, although the grant was 'free' in the sense that a cheque for several thousand pounds was obtained and did not have to be paid back, there were strings attached. The progress of the business was monitored frequently by a local business agency and this involved the keeping of quite detailed monthly accounts, and attending monitoring meetings.

Commercial borrowings

Generally speaking, anyone proposing to start up a small business will be reluctant to borrow money from external sources, such as banks, if it can possibly be avoided. There are several sound reasons for this reluctance. First, banks charge commercial rates of interest on loans. This can add substantially to the costs of a business start-up and can make the difference between potential success and failure.

Secondly, bankers will not lend to just anyone. In fact, they usually will not lend to anyone who does not have a record of success in business. This is not a problem if you are embarking on start-up number ten, with nine successful businesses to your credit, but, realistically, most people without a good track record in business are likely to face a polite refusal when they ask for a start-up loan.

Thirdly, bankers want to know that their loans will be repaid. They will maximise the likelihood of repayment by insisting upon **security** for the loan. This means that an arrangement is made so that, if the loan is not repaid on time, the bank can take an item, or items, of at least equal value from the business or the individual in settlement of the debt. The bank will usually insist upon a legally binding agreement, known as a **charge**, to ensure that the loan gets repaid.

Example 2.5 Des starts up in business with a bank loan of £50 000. He owns his own home, and, to cover its interests, the bank requires a legal charge over Des's house. The business goes bust after two-and-a-half years, still owing the bank the original £50 000 plus £3000 in unpaid interest. Because the bank has the legal charge, the house must be sold to meet the debt, and Des and his family will,

effectively, be evicted and may be made homeless. Bankers are only human, and an individual bank manager may try very hard to find an alternative course of action. Nevertheless, the charge is a legal document, and the bank is quite within its rights to insist upon repayment via the sale of the house. After all, Des went into this with his eyes open; he knew the risks and should be prepared to take the consequences.

If security is not available in any other form, bankers may ask for a guarantee from someone who is sufficiently wealthy to repay the loan if the business fails.

Example 2.6 Suleman wants to borrow £25 000 from the bank for a business start-up. He owns virtually nothing himself, so there is no question of setting up a legal charge as in Des's case. However, his father is a successful businessman who considers it very likely that his son has inherited his business ability. He signs a guarantee for Suleman's loan. If the business fails, still owing the money to the bank, then the bank will require Suleman's father to settle the debt.

This type of arrangement is fine, provided that the guarantor (that's the person giving the guarantee) thoroughly understands the possible consequences if the business fails. In Example 2.6, Suleman's father is an experienced businessman who knows exactly what he is agreeing to when he signs the guarantee. However, there have been unfortunate cases where the guarantor has not understood that he or she stands to lose a very large sum of money if the business goes bad.

A secured loan is less risky, from a bank's point of view, than an unsecured loan. The nature of the loan and the value of the security tends to affect the interest rate. The greater the risk, the higher the rate of interest. Therefore a loan made by a bank on good security will carry a lower interest charge than an unsecured loan.

We are now going to examine an example of a business start-up in an extended case study that divides into two parts. The first part looks at a very low-key start-up requiring little finance.

CASE STUDY 2.1 Business start-up (Part 1)

The idea

Pete has a full-time job as a clerk in a factory office, working from 9.00am to 5.30pm Monday to Friday. Having left school with very few qualifications he has little scope in his present employment for promotion, and his earnings are relatively low. Until recently Pete and his partner, Angie, enjoyed a reasonably good standard of living; she also had a clerical job and the two salaries together allowed them to live comfortably. However, their circumstances have changed recently with the birth of their twin daughters. Angie has her hands full and is unlikely to be able to return to work until the children start school; it is not really worth her while to go back to work in the meantime because childcare for two children would eat up a large proportion of the additional income she could bring in. Besides, she thinks children do better if they have a parent with them full-time.

Pete wants to find a way of earning more money. He and Angie have a mortgage of £45 000 on a flat currently valued at £55 000. They have savings of £3000 kept in a 'rainy day' account on 90-days deposit. The flat looks very small now that there are four in the family but there is no realistic chance of moving to anywhere larger without an increase in income. Given the lack of promotion opportunities in his present job Pete has been looking around at ideas for self-employment. A recent visit to the gardens of a stately home has given him an idea. On the day that he and his family visited, a vintage car rally was taking place and there were large crowds of people around. Pete joined a long queue to buy two cups of coffee from a mobile stand. The refreshments facilities clearly did not match the demand and Pete could see the opportunity to make money.

On the way home he thought it through. He could use the family savings to buy a small mobile coffee stand. If he could borrow his brother's van he could take the stand around at weekends to antiques fairs, car rallies and the like. At the stately home he had paid £1.50 each for the cups of coffee – surely it must be possible to make money?

Financing issues

Peter's business idea is low-key in that it involves very little initial capital outlay, and very little risk. His immediate action plan would look like this:

- Find out about: (a) cost of mobile coffee stand; (b) any charges for setting up a pitch; (c) cost of coffee, cups, sugar etc.
- Discuss plan with: (a) Angie; (b) brother.

One week later

Pete has been busy. The first thing he did was talk the plan over with Angie. She was worried about the possibility of losing their savings, but Pete thinks that there would be very little risk involved. He has also asked his brother, Dave, about borrowing the van. Dave is a plumber and uses the van mostly during the week. He doesn't want to put a lot of extra mileage on the van, and points out to Pete that there will be times – about one weekend in four – when he's on call and will need the van. Pete agrees to pay his brother a reasonable charge for the hire of the van. This will reflect the mileage covered, and also the fact that there will be an additional insurance charge because the van is being used for a business other than plumbing.

Pete has looked at the cost of coffee machines. He cannot afford one of the bigger models, but has discovered he can save some cash by buying a second-hand reconditioned model. This would cost about £2000. For £100 he can buy sufficient coffee, plastic cups and so on to get started, but he doesn't know quite how long they'll last. He does some homework on possible venues, and discovers that the charges for pitches vary quite a lot. However, there is a small garden show due to take place only about 20 miles away, and the organisers are asking only £35 for the pitch that Pete wants.

He talks it through with Angie again. She is still worried. It isn't just the possible loss of the savings; Pete has succeeded in convincing her that if he can't make a go of the business the machine can always be sold on again, and the potential loss is small. She spends all week alone with the twins while Pete is out at work, and she doesn't want to have to cope alone for much of the weekend as well. Pete doesn't really have an answer to this objection, but suggests that she might get her mother or sister to come and stay to take the pressure off. Pete and Angie have an argument over this, but it concludes with her saying that he might as well try it out for a couple of months to see what happens. The next day Pete goes out and buys the coffee machine and arranges to borrow the van from his brother for the day of the garden show.

What are Pete's chances of success?

Factors in Pete's favour include the following:

- He doesn't have to borrow money, and the start-up is very low cost.
- The business idea is simple and will fit in with his existing job.
- He has the support (although not wholehearted) of his immediate family.

Factors working against Pete include:

- He hasn't investigated the business idea thoroughly. What about the competition? Owners of competitor stands might object to a newcomer.
- He hasn't attempted to estimate how much profit the business might make, or thought very clearly about how much he will charge per cup of coffee.
- He should probably have done more research on possible venues.
- Angie may be going to find it very difficult to cope alone at weekends. In addition, Pete doesn't seem to have considered the fact that his plan means that he will see very little of his family, and also that he is committing himself to working six or seven days a week.

Summary

Not all of the above factors relate to finance. We would need to know a lot more (and so would Pete) to be able to assess realistically his chances of success. From a financial point of view, Pete is unlikely (unless he's particularly unlucky or incompetent) to lose a lot of money. However, he should really be thinking more carefully about the business start-up than appears to be the case. It is clear from the case study that Pete's attitude to risk is more relaxed than Angie's. This could be an advantage, up to a point, in that he won't waste time and energy in worrying too much about the progress of the business. However, past a certain point, his attitude could lead to recklessness.

The business plan

Case study 1.1 shows a business start-up that has not been properly thought out. Pete should have produced a **business plan**. If he were seeking financing in the form of a loan or a grant he would certainly have to produce a quite detailed plan. However, even though he is not looking for finance it would be well worth his while to produce a plan. It would help him to clarify his ideas about the business, and give him some idea of its chances of success.

The business plan normally includes most or all of the following elements:

- Description of the business concept.
- Detailed description of the product or service that the business will offer.
- The market for the product or service, including market research and analysis of the competition.
- Profile of entrepreneur. A personal profile detailing relevant experience (including possibly a CV) and an analysis of personal strengths and weaknesses.
- Initial investment required. Type and cost of equipment, premises and similar items.
- Details of other people involved. If the plan is to employ people straight away, details are required of how they will be recruited and how much it will cost to employ them.
- Insurance requirements. Any relevant legal issues.
- Professional advisers. Details of the type of professional advice that may be required and how much it is likely to cost.
- Detailed financial projections. A **budget** will be required for at least the first year, showing the projected **profit** and **cash flow**.

All of these accounting terms will be explained in much more detail later in the book. In the meantime, think of the 'budget' as a statement of anticipated future income and expenses. 'Profit' is the amount left over after all the expenses of a business have been taken away from income. 'Cash flow' is the movement of cash in and out of the business.

Comparing the information in Case study 2.1 with the requirements of the business plan, we can see that Pete has some of the information he needs, but should really do a lot more investigative work before starting the business. The second part of the case study follows Pete's first 18 months of trading.

CASE STUDY 2.1 Business start-up (Part 2)

Pete's business after 18 months

Despite the absence of a proper plan for his business, Pete has managed to muddle through the first 18 months and has succeeded in making some money. He met several unexpected problems and had some bad luck:

- The coffee business is dependent on the weather. At Pete's first venue, the garden show, the temperature was very high and the ice cream vans did excellent business. Pete, on the other hand, had a disappointing day and didn't even manage to cover the costs of the pitch.

- Because Pete hadn't investigated the market he didn't understand how important the position of his pitch would be. The best pitches at a lot of venues are taken by experienced vendors and people like Pete lose out. However, he started attending smaller events and found that he could make more money that way; sometimes his is the only coffee stand, and he has had some excellent days' takings.

- Pete was involved in an accident when driving Dave's van to a venue. The immediate result of this was that he lost a day's takings, but the longer-term problem was that Dave refused to lend him the van again once it was repaired. Pete has therefore had to hire a van and it has cost him a lot of extra money.

- Pete didn't keep proper control over the cash coming in from the business. At the end of each day he put all the banknotes in his wallet, mixed up with his own money, and would use them for spending money. From time to time he would bank any surplus in his and Angie's joint bank account. After several months in business Dave persuaded him to go to see his accountant, Norris. Norris told Pete that he must keep the money from the business separate from his own money, and must count up and record each day's takings. Norris has sorted things out now, but he's just presented Pete with a bill for £550. He tells Pete that £300 of this cost came about through having to sort out the mess that resulted from Pete not keeping proper records.

The new plan

Despite these problems Pete loves running his own business. He really enjoys chatting with the people he meets at the venues, and he and Angie both like having the extra income. He likes the feeling of not having a boss telling him what to do, and he even enjoys the risk and uncertainty of running his own business.

Pete decides that he wants to give up the clerical job and go into full-time self-employment. He decides that he wants to open a coffee shop in the town centre. Pete is more confident now and he's sure he can make a go of it.

There's a small shop to let on the edge of the main town centre shopping area; Pete rings the commercial estate agent who is dealing with the premises and finds that he could take out a five-year lease at a rental of £7500 per year. The shop would need refurbishment, but Pete's brother Dave (who has got over the trauma of having his van wrecked and is now on good terms again) knows a lot of people in the building trade who would do a good job at minimum cost.

Pete gets home from work and tells Angie about his idea. Angie is extremely unhappy about it; she becomes very agitated, loses her temper and starts shouting. She has got used to Pete working most weekends, and the extra money is really useful. If they were careful they could think about moving house sometime next year. She can now see that Pete really wasn't risking much in setting up his coffee business 18 months ago. But now, it seems crazy to her that Pete should even think about giving up his job to take on such a big risk as a proper coffee shop.

Financing issues

Pete has a great deal more to think about this time. He will need to find some external finance for this venture. Norris, the accountant, says that he can help him prepare a business plan to present to the bank manager, and that Pete should start thinking about the type of costs involved in setting up this venture.

Pete comes up with the following list of costs:

- rent
- refurbishment costs
- new equipment (coffee machinery, tables, chairs, crockery and so on)
- insurance
- business rates
- advertising
- wages (he will need to employ somebody else part-time for the busiest times of the week)

▶

- coffee and other catering supplies
- electricity, water and phone bills.

He shows this list to Norris who says 'Well, so far so good, but there are some other things you haven't thought of. What about legal fees for setting up the lease? And I'll be putting in a bill for advice on your business plan, as well as the charges for doing your tax return. Also, if you get a bank loan for the start-up there will be a charge for interest.'

Other issues

Pete has a lot more work to do before he can decide whether or not this new business idea will work out. What about the competition? Are there other coffee shops in the area? Will there be a demand for food or snacks, as well as for coffee? Is the coffee shop really in the right location to attract customers? How much money does the business need to make to cover costs and to ensure that there is enough for the family to live on? Also, how is he going to persuade Angie that it's a good idea? If he can't get her support should he go ahead with the new business?

This second business idea of Pete's is very much more risky than the first. He's managed to make money out of the first business, although he's muddled through rather than following a proper plan. He's made quite a few mistakes, but he's learned something about running a business and has found that he enjoys being self-employed. However, if he takes on this business and it fails, what's going to happen to him and his family?

We'll follow Pete's progress in a future chapter.

Why do businesses fail (and why do some of them succeed)?

It can be quite difficult to estimate the failure rate for businesses. Researchers have estimated that, of every ten businesses started up, only two will still be in existence after five years. Dun and Bradstreet, a business information agency, produces annual figures for business failures (**www.uk.dnb.com**). In each of the three years 1998–2000 the annual rate for the UK excluding Northern Ireland was around 40 000 businesses per year. However, the failure rates vary greatly depending on the business sector, the state of the economy generally and location (business failure appears to be currently more common in the north of England than the south, for example).

Failure factors

The Association of Business Recovery Professionals (**www.r3.org.uk**) regularly surveys failed businesses to find out the reasons why they did not succeed. The main reasons are:

- poor management
- lack of working capital
- lack of long-term finance
- bad debts
- loss of market.

Poor management

As we saw earlier, Pete didn't really understand about managing the money in his business; he could have run into serious trouble with the tax authorities if his brother had not suggested consulting an accountant. His failure to manage properly could have taken many other forms: for example, failing to take out the right kind of insurance. Some people who go into business are brilliant at product ideas, or providing the service that is the basis of the business, but are no good at day-to-day management. They may be both untrained and inexperienced in management.

Lack of working capital

Essentially, lack of **working capital** means running out of money. The bank manager might allow the business to borrow some money on overdraft, but overdrafts always have a limit. Once the limit is reached, closing the business down may be the only option available.

Lack of long-term finance

There is no money to invest in the long-term future of the business. For example, a new machine is required but the business cannot afford to buy it outright and no one will lend the money. In the short term the business may be able to struggle on, but long-term survival is unlikely.

Bad debts

Bad debts are not a problem for a business like Pete's where cash changes hands at the point where the product is purchased. However, if a business supplies on credit (that is, ships the goods to the customer before payment is received) and a big customer will not or cannot pay up, that can result in failure.

Loss of market

This can happen when a competitor business sets up successfully and takes away some of the market share. For example, a florist's business two streets away from a hospital will probably do well. However, if a rival florist opens up in a shop right next door to the hospital this will almost certainly result in a major impact on the existing florist's business.

This list is all very depressing, especially for anyone who is seriously thinking about setting up a business. However, many businesses do succeed and prosper. The factors that tend to lead to success include adequate financing, a cautious approach to risk-taking, existing management experience and sheer good luck.

Chapter summary

This chapter has covered some of the important elements of starting a business. We have seen that financial considerations are just part (although an important part) of the decision to start a business.

We have established a foundation for the study of business finance and accounting. The rest of Part I of the book deals with the financing of larger businesses. After that we will turn to a more detailed study of accounting matters.

Internet resources

Some useful websites:

www.businessadviceonline.org – answers some frequently asked questions about small businesses in the UK.

www.dti.gov.uk – the website of the Department of Trade and Industry containing vast amounts of useful information about all aspects of business in the UK.

www.r3.org.uk – the website of the Association of Business Recovery Professionals.

www.smallbusiness.about.com – provides very useful advice on small business start-ups.

www.startbusiness.co.uk – includes a very useful guide to the contents of a business plan.

www.uk.dnb.com – the Dun and Bradstreet business information website.

Exercises

The answers to many of the exercises are set out later in this chapter. However, where the exercise number is followed by 'A' the answer is available only to lecturers. Remember that additional exercises (with answers) are available to students on the book's website.

2.1   Erika is planning to become a self-employed graphic designer working from a small one-room office in a new development in the middle of town. You are a small business adviser and she has asked you for help in producing her business plan. You decide to prepare a list of questions to ask Erika at your first meeting, based on the major headings that you would expect to see covered in the business plan.

2.2A Ashok has been left £100 000 by his grandma in her will. He plans to start a haulage business and will use part of the money to purchase an HGV. He already has an HGV licence. His wife will run the administration side of the business, initially from home, until they can afford to lease an office. Advise Ashok on the principal types of expense that you think he will face in running his haulage business.

2.3   Ben has a degree in public relations and a huge list of useful contacts in the aerospace business, which he has established over a period of several years while working for Amis & Lovett, a large PR agency. He would like to set up his own PR agency. He plans to employ a new graduate and a secretary immediately in order to avoid being regarded as a 'one-man band'. He is confident that his savings (£45 000) will tide him over the first couple of months while he finds enough work to get started. List the main risks that you see in Ben's plan for the new business start-up.

2.4A Choose any two of the following businesses and, for each, write a list of the main expenses you think would be involved in running them as a profit-making business.

a) Childcare facility catering for children from three months to five years.
b) University café serving light snacks and lunches.
c) Internet-based travel agency.
d) Advertising agency.
e) Firm of estate agents.

Answers to exercises

2.1 Erika: The main points for the business plan, and the related questions, are as follows:

Description of the service to be offered

Is the service highly specialised, or is it a more general design service? For example, the design services offered may be principally focused on, say, company identity and logo designs, or alternatively upon graphic input into advertising material. Or, Erika may be planning to cover a broad range of services, depending upon her talents and interests.

Market for the service

● Who will be the principal customers for the services offered?
● Has Erika investigated the market by carrying out any market research?
● Who are the principal competitors? Are they well established?
● How difficult will it be to break into the market for design services?

Profile of Erika

This will include training and education, relevant experience, age, an analysis of personal strengths and weaknesses, and a current portfolio of her best work.

● Does Erika have the appropriate profile of experience for the work she is planning to do?
● Is her portfolio up to date and does it contain examples of the type of work she will be undertaking to provide as a self-employed designer?

Initial investment required

This will be a particularly important section if Erika is planning to borrow money. Has she prepared a plan of her expenditure and income in the first year to 18 months following her business start-up? Relevant expenditure will probably include the following:

- office rental and business rates
- utilities bills (water, electricity, phone)
- advertising and marketing
- office equipment and computer
- insurance.

Also, how will Erika support herself in the early months of her new business? In this type of business, Erika will need to find the work, do it, submit it and then invoice the client. Under normal commercial arrangements payment will follow about a month later. So, there is a time lag of up to several months between initially being commissioned for the work and finally receiving payment. In the meantime, Erika needs to live off something, and this element must be built into her initial plans.

Detailed financial projections

If Erika is looking for business start-up finance she will need to prepare detailed financial projections in the form of a budget, showing the projected profit and loss and cash flow in the business. Once the business starts she will need to keep business accounting records and submit tax returns. She may need to register for VAT.

- Does Erika have financial management or accountancy skills?
- Will she need an accountant to provide accountancy and tax advice?

Other issues

Will any other professional services be required in the first year or so of the business? For example, Erika may need legal advice in negotiating a lease on her office. Is Erika planning to employ any staff?

2.3   There are several risks attached to Ben's business start up plan:

Risk of not obtaining work

Although Ben has a good contact list, they have all been made through Amis & Lovett, his employers. Much will depend on whether or not any of Amis & Lovett's existing clients will give their work to Ben's agency. If their relationship with Amis & Lovett is good, and they are satisfied with the work, they may be quite happy to stay with the larger agency. However, if they want to stay with Ben, they may be prepared to move their work to his new agency. Ben is taking a big risk.

Risk of running out of money

Even if the work does follow Ben, the nature of the type of service he offers means that he will not start receiving payment for his work for quite some time. He has £45 000 which sounds like a lot, but this may not keep him going for very long. If he has not already done so, he needs to make a realistic plan so that he can budget for the first year or so of his new business.

Risk of employing people

Ben is taking a risk by employing people straight away. He may not have enough work to justify employing anybody in the early months of the business. His employees will expect to be paid at the end of month, whether or not Ben has much work. He would probably be well advised to get the work first, and then employ staff.

3

THE GROWING BUSINESS

AIMS AND LEARNING OUTCOMES

Aim of the chapter

To assist in understanding some of the problems and opportunities that face the growing business, especially those related to finance.

Learning outcomes

After reading the chapter and its case study, and completing the exercises at the end, students should:

- Know about some of the important stages in business expansion.

- Understand some of the problems and opportunities presented by business growth, including issues related to employment, developing the business organisation and moving into new markets.

- Know about the typical money management issues that face the proprietors of successful and growing businesses.

- Appreciate that business growth inevitably involves risk.

Introduction

In Chapter 2 we looked at some of the evidence about business survival. The evidence is not particularly encouraging in that the majority of new businesses will fail. In this chapter we will look at those businesses which survive and, to a greater or lesser extent, prosper. Prosperity and growth bring problems of their own. Sometimes established businesses are simply unlucky: perhaps key staff leave, a competitor offering a cheaper product or service becomes established, or some unforeseen event takes place such as accident or illness of the business proprietor. Sometimes, on the other hand, problems arise that the proprietor(s) of the growing business are simply unable to handle, such as growth that proceeds too rapidly or inability to cope with changing circumstances.

However, although problems may arise, there are also increased opportunities arising from growth. If a business does really well its original owners may be able to sell their stake and realise large amounts of cash. If the original objective in setting up the business was to become seriously rich, such owners achieve their ambition. For owners who decide to remain involved in the business, new opportunities may arise for business expansion. As a business grows and builds up a track record of success it becomes easier for it to borrow money in order to fuel further growth. Often, people who start and run successful businesses thrive on the new challenges and would not choose to give up their involvement even if they were able to retire early with large sums of cash.

In this chapter we will examine the phases of growth from a small to medium-sized business, charting some of the major milestones in business development. Financial management issues are often significant in the development of the growing business, and we will look at several relevant examples.

Stages in business growth and expansion

Employing people

In the previous chapter we examined a sole trader business. Many businesses do not grow past the point where they generate an income for one person and his or her dependants. A self-employed tradesperson, such as a plumber, small builder or garden designer may have no particular need or wish to expand the business to the point where employing another person becomes necessary. However, some business people will see the need for expansion, and employing another person is often the first step towards expansion.

Advantages of employing people in a small business

There is an opportunity to increase the skills base of the business. As we noted in the last chapter, one of the reasons why businesses fail is because of poor management. A sole trader is particularly vulnerable to this type of problem; he or she has to marshal a range of skills including selling abilities, financial management skills, organisational ability, self-discipline and so on. If any one of these is missing the business may fail. One way around the problem of missing skills is to either go into partnership with someone whose skills are complementary, or, in some cases, to employ a person who can contribute skills lacking in the proprietor.

Employing people is likely to increase the volume of trade in goods or services. Two pairs of hands can achieve more than one. If the right person is employed, he or she may be able to contribute to the profitability of the business.

Example 3.1 Kingsley is a self-employed furniture designer who undertakes commissions for the provision of original, well-designed furniture for businesses. He started up in business two years ago, and he has been very successful in generating work. He now has more than he can easily cope with. He is working seven days a week from early morning until late at night and his relationships with friends and family are suffering. Also, he has received some unpleasant letters recently from suppliers, including a threat from the electricity utility company to cut off his supplies unless he pays his bill within seven days.

It is pretty clear that Kingsley needs help. Administering a small business can take a disproportionately large amount of time. While Kingsley may not be ready to take on a full-time administrator, he should examine the possibility of employing a part-timer who can keep control of the paperwork. This would, presumably, free up part of Kingsley's time so that he could get on with more productive work.

The other area in which he probably needs help is in the design work. This is a much more difficult issue to resolve than the administration. People award Kingsley design commissions because they like his work. If he delegates some of the work to an assistant the design values may suffer. Unless Kingsley is prepared to carry on working all hours, he will have to make a decision on whether he keeps the business very small by turning down any commissions that he cannot manage himself, or, alternatively, whether he is prepared to share the design work with someone else. The first course of action involves a risk; if he turns down too much work the supply of commissions may dry up altogether. The second course of action also involves a risk; will the quality of work suffer? Also, does Kingsley have the necessary management skills to control the work of one or more designer employees?

Disadvantages of employing people in a small business

There is a very significant risk attached to employment. If a poor choice of employee is made, the mistake can threaten the survival of the business. Mistakes can be made in employing someone with whom there is a personality clash, or someone who is less competent than they appeared from their CV and the interview. Many employers will make an employment decision which, sooner or later, they come to regret.

Employing people costs money. Many successful small businesses pass through an awkward stage where there is too much work for the sole trader or partners to handle by themselves but where the financial risk of taking on an employee is unacceptable. The business proprietor(s) must be sure that they have the financial resources to pay for employment.

Employing people involves a great deal of paperwork. If staff are employed, the business becomes involved in the administration of pay as you earn (PAYE) and National Insurance contributions (NIC) on behalf of the employee. Detailed records must be kept, and these are liable to be inspected periodically by the Inland Revenue. Business people often complain bitterly about the amount of work they have to undertake as tax collectors on behalf of the government. The amount of administration involved acts, potentially, as a disincentive to employing people. (However, it should be noted, perhaps, that the administrative burden in the UK is probably less than in some other countries. France, for example, imposes a notoriously heavy administrative burden on the employer.)

Example 3.2 Recently, Kelly started a business importing and selling ornamental lamps, vases and similar items to retailers. The business has been ˙successful, making profits of £35 000 in its first year and £38 000 in its second. Kelly has realised that, if the business is going to be able to grow, she will have to employ someone to assist her in selling goods to retailers. The ideal employee would have a good track record in selling and would be able and willing to travel four or five days a week visiting stores.

What financial factors does Kelly need to consider in making a decision about employing an assistant?

- *Salary.* Kelly needs to look carefully at how much she will have to pay in order to ensure the right employee. She needs someone with experience and who is prepared to act on his or her own initiative. Part of Kelly's annual profits will have to go to paying the employee. In addition to the annual salary, there will be the cost of providing transport (presumably an additional car will be required).
- *Employer's National Insurance and administration costs.* The employer must pay employer's National Insurance contributions, and the cost of administering the payroll must be taken into account. Kelly may be able to undertake this herself (the cost of doing this is the time taken up, which could be used on something else), or she may have to pay her accountant a little extra to do it.
- *Balancing costs and benefits.* If Kelly succeeds in employing someone who is good at selling, the benefits could far outweigh the costs of employment. Suppose the total cost of employment is £30 000 per year; provided the employee can generate additional business that makes more than this amount in profit then it makes good business sense for Kelly to employ him or her. There may be other less obvious benefits: if Kelly gets flu and has to spend a week in bed the business, at the moment, grinds to a halt until she is better. If she could depend upon an employee, the business could be kept going more or less as normal.

Developing the business organisation

As a business grows and starts to employ more people, the way in which it is organised becomes more of an issue. There is a tendency in most business organisations to establish manageable units according to the functions they carry out. For example, in a typical manufacturing organisation it may be appropriate to establish separate departments for marketing, production, despatch, design, personnel, accounting and general administration. In the early days of the business only one or two people will be employed in each function, and the business proprietors are likely to retain firm control over all of the operations of the business. However, as the business grows, it becomes increasingly difficult for its owners to control every aspect of its functions. It is important for proprietors to be able to recognise when this stage has arrived, and to be prepared to delegate control to others.

Professional management

People who have started up successful businesses are often very reluctant to concede any part of their control to others. However, in most cases, it eventually becomes necessary to employ professional managers – people who have the experience and knowledge to manage functions such as marketing and personnel. Conflict sometimes ensues between the managers and the founders of the business as they disagree about the right way to manage change and growth.

Communication issues

As the business grows and departmental structures emerge, a range of communication problems can arise. Departments develop their own identities, and can, if not properly managed, become narrow in outlook, fighting territorial battles with other departments to protect their own status. Where this type of 'in-fighting' occurs, the overall objectives of the business tend to be forgotten.

Growth in bureaucracy

As we have already noted in this chapter, a certain amount of unavoidable record-keeping and administration is imposed on businesses by government regulation. As businesses grow and organisational functions separate, the business itself starts to require more complex records. An accounting department is usually required in order to keep the financial records straight. Some kind of authorisation and control procedures are inevitably required, but a great deal of management skill is needed to make sure that the generation of paperwork does not get out of hand. Organisations with excessive administration procedures may ultimately fail because they have become too inwardly focused. For example, staff become demotivated by the requirement to produce what they see as excessive paperwork. Perhaps the need for prompt and thorough organisational reporting starts to take priority over activities such as production quality control and establishing new sales contacts.

Moving into new markets or products

Expansion and growth of a successful business usually involves moving into new areas. Sometimes, this means expanding the range of products and/or services on offer, or new opportunities may arise to expand the market that the business serves. Clearly, there is always a risk involved in taking this kind of action. Some examples of typical business expansion decisions are examined in the following sub-sections.

Borrowing to finance expansion

Expanding a business involves additional costs, which can be substantial. The managers responsible for making the decision on whether or not to expand the business need to think carefully about all of the costs and potential benefits involved. Borrowing is often an attractive option, but the risks should be properly weighed up. The next example looks at a typical expansion decision.

Example 3.3 Lucinda and Lister are sole (and equal) shareholders and directors of L & L Limos Limited, a company that runs a small fleet of limousines for hire for weddings and by celebrities visiting the local area. Each year the business has

gradually expanded its total sales as its reputation for reliability has grown. There is no direct competitor for their service in their own town, and, increasingly often, the firm is asked to undertake business in neighbouring towns and cities. Quite often the directors have to turn business away because all of the available cars are booked. Expanding the fleet and taking on new drivers seems like an increasingly attractive option.

How could this expansion be financed? The following costs would be involved: (a) the purchase or leasing costs of new vehicles; and (b) the employment of drivers, plus related costs. Also, the expansion might incur additional administrative costs (because more bookings would be made, more invoices would be generated and so on), and perhaps additional premises costs. The limos have to be housed securely in garage premises, and it might be necessary to expand the space available.

The directors need to look at the costs involved and think about financing. Several options may be open to them:

- *Investment in new vehicles.* Buying the limos outright involves a substantial capital outlay and it might be preferable to lease the vehicles. However, if the directors want to borrow to finance outright purchase of the new limos they may well be able, as an established business, to obtain a bank loan quite easily. If they do not wish to take the risk of borrowing, they may be able to lend their own savings to the company.
- *Investment in other costs of expansion by using existing resources*. If there is spare cash available in the business, financing the expansion could be a good use for the funds.
- *Financing via a flexible overdraft facility*. The directors need to prepare a cash flow budget that will reveal any points in the year at which short-term finance may be needed to cover shortfalls.

The directors face the risk that they have misjudged the market. If they invest in expansion and the demand for services is less than they thought, they may severely damage the future prospects of the business. Another risk is that, if they borrow money, interest rates could rise and become more of a burden on the business.

Amalgamating businesses to create expansion

Amalgamation of two or more businesses can be an attractive route to growth. For example, the managers of a business may decide that they wish to expand their business to a different city or area of the country. Starting up a new branch from scratch may be difficult, perhaps because the competition is well established. In such circumstances it often makes sense to try to join forces with a similar business in the area. Similarly, where a business wishes to expand the range of services it offers, the least-cost option may be to amalgamate with an established business.

Example 3.4 Linus, Lonsdale & Co is a firm of accountants established about ten years ago by Peregrine Linus and Paula Lonsdale. The business has always made a profit, and in recent years profitability has tended to improve. At a recent society of accountants' local meeting they met a sole practitioner, Liz, who is looking for an

opportunity to merge her practice with another. She finds it difficult to cover the range of services that people expect from an accountant these days, and would like to take her own business into a partnership arrangement with another small practice. She specialises in capital gains tax and inheritance tax advisory services.

Bringing the two firms together would create a larger firm with three partners. If their range of skills is complementary the larger practice could, potentially, provide a better service to clients than at present. Also, a larger firm is in a better position to take on larger businesses as clients.

An amalgamation of businesses like this would probably involve some costs (for example, it might be necessary to enlarge the premises) but these would probably be fairly modest. The combined business could be more effective and better placed to expand in the future.

What risks are involved? The principal risk for the two firms is that the amalgamation does not work because of differences in style between the partners. The three partners must be able to get along harmoniously and, ideally, should have skills that complement each other. In a small firm it is very difficult to ignore major personality clashes.

Takeovers

In the previous example the amalgamation under consideration would involve the owners of the two businesses entering into partnership together. All of them would retain an ownership interest in the expanded firm. Takeovers, by contrast, involve buying out the interests of most, or all, of the existing owners. Where a business decides to attempt a takeover of a limited company (the 'target company'), for example, the shareholders in the target company are approached to see if they are willing to sell their shares. Where there are few shareholders this process can be relatively straightforward. If both buyer and seller(s) are willing, and a suitable price can be agreed, the takeover can go ahead. The result will be an expanded business, but the original holders of the shares will no longer have any financial or other interest in it.

The next example looks at a typical proposed takeover. Some of the business risks involved in takeovers are explored.

Example 3.5 Lupine Leisure Limited is a very successful manufacturer of sportswear. The company has grown rapidly since it was established five years ago, and it has built up a substantial cash surplus. The company's managing director, Lex Lupine, is highly entrepreneurial and is full of ideas for expanding the company's range of interests. The company's goods sell in a competitive market where big discounters and retailers are able to put pressure on suppliers to cut prices. Lex is unhappy with the margins that the company makes. He would like to break through into the retail market so that the company would control not only manufacturing but also the retailing of the products.

The options available to the company are to:

● Finance the opening and management of a small chain of retail stores.
● Acquire a small chain of retail stores (Lex has his eye on a particular chain that he thinks is ripe for takeover).

In both cases the medium-term plan would be to build aggressively upon a smallish local network of stores to expand rapidly into neighbouring areas and, within five years, have nationwide representation. (Lex likes to think big.) When Lex presents the options to the other directors, he points out the advantages of the takeover approach: 'The beauty of it is that we can do this very quickly. We don't have to look around for suitable retail stores, and then arrange leases and employ managers and staff and so on. If we buy the chain it's all set up and in place. We can then concentrate on improving the overall management – we'll keep the decent managers and get rid of the rest – and we'll be in prime position to take up all the profit that's going.'

There are several potential risks in this situation. First, Lex may have misjudged the situation. He is seeking to integrate the supply of goods with their retailing, but the expansion into another area of the supply chain may not work well. The directors of Lupine Leisure are clearly good at running a manufacturing company; they may not have the necessary skills and experience to run a retailer successfully.

Secondly, there is a risk that, because of lack of knowledge, the company could pay too much for the retailer. If the retailer is a takeover target it may be because of some inherent weakness in its operations.

Thirdly, Lex wants to 'keep the decent managers and get rid of the rest'. However, what often happens in such situations is that the managers in takeover targets become concerned about their future prospects in the new, larger organisation. The good managers, who have portable skills and can easily get new jobs, tend to leave. The managers who stay may be the people who cannot easily transfer, perhaps because they are near to retiring age, or because they simply do not have the requisite skills and experience to attract another employer.

Finally, because of the apparent attractions of the scheme to take over the retailer, the directors of Lupine Leisure may not be giving sufficient thought to alternative uses for the company's cash resources.

Making money

As we have seen, the evidence is that most business start-ups do not succeed. However, those that do succeed may flourish and make money for their proprietors. In this section we will look at some of the issues and problems related to money management that arise for the owners of successful businesses.

Extracting cash

How do business people actually take money out of their businesses? We saw in the previous chapter, in the case study concerning Pete, that business resources must be kept strictly separate from personal resources. A business must be able to declare its profits for taxation purposes, and in order to do that, must have an orderly system of record-keeping. The **business entity concept** of accounting describes the necessary separation of the business and its proprietor.

Sole traders and partners in partnerships take money (and sometimes goods) out of the business in the form of **drawings**. Sole traders and partners usually need to take drawings from their businesses to pay their normal living expenses.

Where the business is set up as a company, the situation is slightly different. Directors are employees of the business and usually receive a salary for their work, just like any other employee. Where the directors are also shareholders they receive cash in the form of a **dividend**, which may be paid once or twice annually. Many companies have just one or two shareholders and directors who are the same people. The proprietors of such companies usually receive cash, therefore, in two forms: salaries and dividends. There are tax advantages to be gained by getting the balance of salaries and dividends just right; usually the business's accountant advises on the correct combination.

Managing cash within the business

One way of helping the business to grow is to keep past profits to fund future growth. Most business proprietors, therefore, aim to keep a balance between the amount of cash they remove from the business and the amount that is left in to fund growth. Spare cash in the business should be put to good use to help create future wealth – if it lies more or less dormant in a low interest bearing bank account, it is not being well used. Business proprietors and managers need to manage the position carefully so as to ensure that the business does not run short of cash when it is needed, but also that it is properly used to optimise the overall profitability of the business.

Exit strategies

Although people starting new businesses rarely bother thinking about it, it is important at some stage to start thinking about the most effective way of exiting a business. Serial entrepreneurs, whose principal interest is in start-ups, may be the exceptions to this generalisation; they will often have a vision of the length of time they wish to devote to the business before bailing out and starting on a new venture. However, all proprietors of successful businesses will need at some stage to evolve an exit strategy by addressing some of the following questions:

- When do I want to retire/leave?
- Who should take on the business when I go?
- How am I going to prepare for the transition to new management?
- Should I just sell my stake in the business?
- Is it saleable?
- Who is likely to buy it?

The problem is one of turning business wealth into hard cash which can be taken away by the retiring proprietor. This is more feasible for some kinds of business than for others. Businesses that manufacture or trade in goods, which have machinery, premises and a good brand name may be quite easy to sell. For example, earlier, in Example 3.5, we looked at the possibility of buying a chain of retail shops in preference to setting up shop businesses from scratch. As well as the shops, the fittings, the stock and so on, the retail chain would have a recognised brand name and, probably, some degree of customer loyalty. Factors such as loyalty and brand name are brought together under the general heading of **goodwill** in business terminology. Goodwill refers to all those intangible factors that are hard to quantify, but which add value to a business. Brand names, in particular, are powerful and valuable signifiers of a set of attributes to which customers are attracted.

By contrast, businesses that rely upon the particular skills and expertise of their proprietor may have little value once the proprietor decides to leave the business. In service businesses, there may be little left apart from desks and chairs once the proprietor (along with any remaining cash) is removed. For this type of business there is a particular challenge in building it up to the point where it can be continued without the original founder. The founder of the business may not want to let go of an enterprise that he or she has nurtured from day one, but part of ensuring the business's longer-term survival is to ensure that effective successors are identified and that they are given the space and opportunity to develop the business.

Some of the issues explored in this chapter are examined in the following case study.

CASE STUDY 3.1   A successful business in danger

In this case study we will examine some of the problems that can face even a successful business. The business context is that of a partnership, but some of the problems could also be found in a sole trader or company structure.

Chris and Anwar have been in partnership for over eight years running a computer consultancy business. Both men are in their mid-40s. They first met up almost 30 years ago at Sixth Form College where they studied computing at A level and founded a computer programmer's club. After that, they went to different universities and then gradually lost touch. However, almost ten years ago they met up again at a school reunion and started talking about their dissatisfaction with their respective jobs. At the time Anwar was employed in computer sales; although his job was well paid with high levels of commission, he really felt the time had come to run his own business. Chris had had various programming and consultancy jobs but he, too, was unhappy at the time because of an unsympathetic boss.

A year or so after their chance meeting, Chris and Anwar had taken the plunge into self-employment. Eight years on they remain the sole partners in the business, but now they employ nine consultants, three secretaries and a bookkeeper. The business has been successful and profitable almost from day one; the partners have complementary skills and have continued to work harmoniously together. Anwar is the public face of the firm; he has a 'larger-than-life' personality, is immensely sociable and extrovert, and has been able to build up a huge range of useful contacts in many industry sectors. The firm has never been short of work; in fact, the consultants all have to put in long hours to fulfil the existing contracts. Chris is the details man; he organises the provision of consultancy time to ensure that the contract requirements are met and is in charge of the management of all administrative matters. His technical knowledge is more advanced than Anwar's and he is involved hands-on in every contract the firm takes on. Despite having such different personalities, Chris and Anwar get along very well both personally and in business. They see each other socially, their families get along well and their sons go to the same school.

Now, however, the business has reached its first major crisis. About a year ago, Anwar suffered a fairly serious heart attack. He was advised to cut back on his hours of work, to give up smoking and to lead a much healthier life. It's been a huge struggle, but he's managed to kick the smoking habit; cutting back on work, however, has been much more difficult. Anwar loves his work; he cannot imagine life without it. Chris has encouraged him to leave earlier, to take on less and not to work so much at weekends. The trouble is, though, that the business is so absorbing and there's always so much to do that he hasn't really noticed that Anwar is putting in just as many hours as before.

▶

One morning Anwar doesn't come into the office and Chris gets a phone call from the hospital. Anwar has suffered a much more serious heart attack; he will need major surgery and there is no question of him returning to work for many months. For the first time, Chris is really on his own.

A couple of days later, Marcia, one of the firm's best consultants, drops into Chris's office to tell him that she's leaving. She's got a good offer from one of the business's competitors. The initial salary is less than she's getting at the moment, but she's been promised a partnership position in a year's time. She says she's sorry to have to add to Chris's troubles by leaving at this point, but she has been in negotiations with the rival firm for a couple of months now. Chris tries to persuade her to stay, but Marcia's made her mind up. As she explains: 'The thing is, Chris, I've been here five years, and you and Anwar have never so much as mentioned me joining the partnership. I know I've done well here financially, but I'm still just an employee and I always will be as far as you're concerned.'

Chris is completely taken aback by this development. He really doesn't know what to do. Neither he nor Anwar has ever thought about inviting someone else to join the partnership. They've just assumed that the staff must be happy because they're earning so much money.

There's another problem, too. For the last three or four years, the business has been severely short of office space. The consultants spend most of their time out of the office visiting and working at clients. However, they all need some office space for the time they spend designing and planning solutions to clients' problems, liaising with equipment suppliers, and dealing with general administration. There has been a severe shortage of desk and storage space, and the business records are in a mess. Three months ago, Anwar and Chris started looking around for office premises to buy. Almost immediately they found the perfect solution – a three-storey office block not far from the existing offices. There would be enough space for all the staff on the first two floors, and the third floor could be let to provide some investment income. The purchase is going to be financed partly in cash, and partly by a mortgage secured on the value of the property. The partners are due to exchange legally binding contracts on the office building next week.

Later on Chris starts thinking seriously about the future for the first time. What's going to happen if Anwar doesn't get better, or if he can't return to work full-time? How will he, Chris, manage? He knows he doesn't have the skills or the sheer force of personality to take on Anwar's role as the public face of the firm. He shrinks at the thought of going out actively looking for business. He doesn't enjoy taking people out to lunch, like Anwar does, and he knows that he's no good at selling. He's always been a 'backroom' person.

What about the future of the firm? If Marcia leaves to become a partner elsewhere, perhaps the other consultants will follow her example and go too. What about the new office building? Should he go ahead and buy it on behalf of the firm?

Chris now thinks that perhaps he and Anwar should have thought about this sooner. And another thing: even assuming that Anwar's operation proves to be completely successful, and he's able to return to work full-time, what should they do about the future? One day they'll want to retire from the firm with a large enough amount of money to allow them a very comfortable retirement. What's the firm actually worth? Would he and Anwar be able to sell it?

The worst thing is that, for the first time since they set up the business together, Chris feels that he cannot discuss the business with Anwar. It wouldn't be fair to burden him with the problems when he's so ill.

Chris is very much in need of advice. What action should he take, both immediately and in the medium term?

Case study discussion

The partnership between Chris and Anwar has been very successful up till now; it appears to be based upon a sound working relationship that is enhanced by the partners' complementary skills. Anwar deals with the aspects of the business that require good people skills, while Chris is more of a technician and administrator.

Now, however, the partnership and therefore the business, is in danger. While the immediate problem relates to Anwar's state of health and the question mark over his future contribution to the business, there is an emerging problem with staff that has been building up, it appears, over a long period of time. High salary levels have not, evidently, been enough to keep Marcia committed to the business. She wants to be involved in running the business, and to be entitled to a profit share, and she is prepared to take the risk of leaving in order to put herself in the running for a partnership position. If Marcia feels like this it is quite possible that some of her colleagues feel the same way, and they may also be thinking about leaving.

One major problem that faces Chris is that he cannot take significant decisions without the involvement of his partner. Ideally, he needs to wait until Anwar returns, or at least, is sufficiently well to discuss the problems facing the business. The decision to buy the new premises, however, was taken jointly by them both, and Chris probably ought to go ahead with that. If the basic property investment is sound, it is unlikely that the partnership would lose money in the long run. Chris will probably have to organise the details of the move into the new premises himself, but then he would probably have handled that area of work in any case.

Decisions have to be made in the near future on the following:

- Employing someone to replace Marcia.
- Possibly employing someone to take over parts of Chris's work while he stands in for Anwar.
- Reallocating parts of Anwar's work to other consultants.

In the medium term decisions must be made on the following:

- Creating an employment and incentive structure in the firm that will allow it to retain staff.
- Agreeing on ways in which the ownership of the firm can be spread more widely, with a view to easing the retirement of the two existing partners and allowing them to withdraw the value of their equity from the firm.

If Anwar is unable to return to a full-time role within the business, the problems become even more pressing. Chris knows that he doesn't have the right mix of skills to take his partner's place. If the firm is to survive, he must ensure that Anwar's role in the firm is taken over by someone else. This may mean, ultimately, appointing from outside, merging with another similar firm, or allowing the firm to be taken over.

What is the business worth to Anwar and Chris? The case study is a good illustration of how an apparently successful business could easily fade away as a result of an unforeseen event. This is a service business that depends for its survival on the partners and the quality of the staff they employ. Without the people, the business has very little substance or worth.

▶

If the partners want to be able to take cash out of the business when they retire they need to plan their exit strategy carefully. The strategy will almost certainly involve admitting other people into the partnership. New partners admitted to an established business usually have to buy their way in, either by contributing a share of their salaries over a period of years, or by contributing a lump sum. These contributions compensate the existing partners for giving up part of the ownership and control of the business. If the strategy is managed well it provides several advantages:

- The partners who originally established the partnership are compensated for the share of the business which they transfer to new partners.
- Gradually, the skills base of the partnership can be broadened, making it more resilient to changing circumstances.
- The possibility of joining the partnership provides an incentive for staff.
- The business can survive even if the original partners leave it.

Risk

Risk has been mentioned at several points in this chapter. Each of the business decisions outlined in the examples involves taking a risk; this is an unavoidable factor in running a business. For example, a business may have to make a momentous decision about whether or not to invest several millions of pounds in a new factory. This type of decision clearly involves potentially major risks. Getting it wrong could bring about the downfall of the business.

All business people have to take risks. Sometimes their decisions prove to be wrong. More rarely, the decisions prove to be disastrously wrong. Successful businesses minimise their risks as far as possible, but risk cannot be eliminated. Financial analysis can help business managers to understand the range of possible consequences of their decisions. Later in the book we will examine the financial dimensions of decision making.

Chapter summary

In this chapter we have discussed the problems and opportunities presented by business growth. Specifically, we examined the advantages and drawbacks, and the most significant risks involved in employing people, developing a more complex business organisation and expanding the business into new products and markets.

We examined three approaches to business expansion:

- borrowing to finance expansion
- amalgamating businesses to create expansion
- takeovers.

Next, we looked at the issues involved in making money in a successful business, and ways in which proprietors of businesses actually extract money for their own use, including drawings by sole traders and partners, and dividends and salaries receivable by company shareholders and directors. This section concluded by examining exit and succession management by the proprietors of smaller businesses.

The case study developed several of the issues discussed in the chapter, in particular the problems involved in managing a successful service business constituted as a partnership. The case involves consideration of problems relating to the following areas:

- complementary skills in a partnership
- personnel management
- succession management
- broadening ownership
- exit strategies.

The chapter concluded by considering the element of risk that is inherent in all business decisions.

Exercises

Note: the principal objective of the following exercises is to set students thinking about some of the financial and other issues involved in business growth and development. No specific knowledge of particular types of business is required to answer these questions. Use imagination and common sense to think through the problems.

The answers to many of the exercises are set out later in this chapter. However, where the exercise number is followed by 'A' the answer is available only to lecturers. Remember that additional exercises (with answers) are available to students on the book's website.

3.1 Nancy is a self-employed hairdresser. She runs a salon with the assistance of one untrained employee who takes bookings, tidies and sweeps up, and makes tea and coffee for the clients. Nancy would like to expand the business; this would involve employing a fully trained stylist. There is sufficient space in Nancy's existing premises for another person to work.

Advise Nancy on the costs, risks and potential benefits involved in employing a stylist.

3.2A Norman and Naylor Partners is a business that runs corporate events. Sam Norman and Sally Naylor founded the business about five years ago and it has been very successful. The partners share profits equally. It now employs five full-time staff and calls upon a pool of up to 40 additional staff who can be employed part-time for specific events. Sally is several years older than Sam, and would now like to pull out of the business. She plans to take out her share of the value of the business with a view to buying and running a vineyard in Italy.

Identify the business problems and risks that Sam must deal with as a result of Sally's decision. What are the financial implications (in broad terms) for the partners?

3.3 Oleander Enterprises Limited is a small holiday company run by its two principal directors and shareholders, Libby and Lisa. The company organises exclusive (and expensive) holiday tours of French chateaux. During the four years since it was set up the company has gone from strength to strength. It now employs six people and it makes substantial annual profits. The company has a cash surplus and the directors have been considering ways of using the surplus to expand the business, possibly by starting up operations in new countries. Recently, the directors have been approached by Loretta, the managing director of another holiday company, Oxus Orlando Limited, which organises holiday tours in Turkey. Loretta is the principal director and shareholder of Oxus Orlando. She would like to sell her company and retire on the proceeds.

Advise Libby and Lisa on:

1. The advantages and drawbacks of expanding by buying into another company.

2. The type of information they will require in order to be able to make a decision on whether or not to buy Oxus Orlando.

3.4A Lionel is an experienced chartered surveyor with many years of experience. He is employed by a large property company where he receives a good salary and a performance-related bonus. He has recently been approached by an old friend, Leo, who is one of three partners in a firm of surveyors. The other two partners are nearing retirement age and they have decided that they need to bring in some 'new blood'. The partnership has been in operation for nearly 20 years and has carved out a sizeable niche in commercial property management. Leo tells Lionel that the partnership has been valued by a business valuation specialist at £1 200 000, a figure that includes goodwill of £500 000. If Lionel accepts the invitation to join the partnership he will be required to pay £300 000 in cash for a quarter share of the business. In exchange he will be entitled to 25% of the profits made by the partnership in the future.

1. Explain to Lionel what is meant by the term 'goodwill'.

2. Advise him on the type of information he will need to examine in order to be able to make a decision on whether or not to buy into the partnership.

3. Identify the main elements of risk involved in Lionel's decision.

Answers to exercises

3.1 Nancy: As regards costs, because there is sufficient space for another person to work on the premises, there will be no significant additional premises costs involved. There will be a small additional cost in consumables such as hair products and electricity, but the main cost will be in paying the salary of the new stylist, plus any additional administrative costs. Nancy already employs one person, so presumably she or her accountant already operates a payroll system that makes sure that the employee and the Inland Revenue are paid the correct amounts.

There are two main risks:

1. That there will not be sufficient extra business to keep the new stylist busy. Employing another person does not make financial sense unless the new employee can generate enough additional business to cover the costs of employing him or her;

2. That the new stylist will prove to be unsatisfactory in some way. Perhaps there will be personality clashes with Nancy or with the customers, or perhaps he or she will not produce work of sufficient competence. An employee who turns up late, or not at all, or who is unpleasant to clients will create problems.

As regards benefits, if the appointment of a new stylist turns out well, there could be two main benefits for Nancy and her business:

1. Additional profits could be generated that would increase Nancy's wealth. She could either draw down more money from the business or could invest the profits in further expansion, perhaps by moving to larger premises and employing more staff.

2. The range of services offered could be expanded and improved.

3.3 Oleander Enterprises Limited

Buying into another business

Buying into another company may be advantageous because Libby and Lisa will be buying up an established business with employees who have knowledge of holiday operations in Turkey. They will not need to start from scratch in finding out about a new country.

However, Oxus Orlando is, essentially, a service business which is very dependent upon the quality of its employees. Loretta, the main director, plans to retire, so her expertise will be lost. If the key employees also choose to leave, there may not be much value left in the company, and Libby and Lisa may find out that they have paid too much for the investment.

Information needed

Libby and Lisa need to know:

● The price of the investment in Oxus Orlando, which Loretta wishes to sell. (Note that Libby and Lisa would almost certainly need to have the investment independently valued.)

● What they would get in exchange for the investment (for example, does the business own its own premises?).

● How profitable Oxus Orlando is (they will be able to ascertain this information from the business's annual accounts).

● Details about the employees of the business. How much are they paid, how long have they been in their current jobs and how likely is it that they will stay if the company changes ownership?

4

LARGE BUSINESSES

AIMS AND LEARNING OUTCOMES

Aim of the chapter

To understand the context in which large businesses operate and in particular, the financing of quoted companies and the decision on whether or not to finance expansion of a company via a stock exchange flotation.

Learning outcomes

After reading the chapter and its case study, and completing the exercises at the end, students should:

- Understand the operation of the UK stock market.
- Understand the reasons why companies choose to have their shares publicly quoted, and understand the fundamentals of what is involved in listing.
- Know about the advantages and drawbacks of operating as a listed company.
- Understand the need for information about listed companies, know about the principal sources of information concerning them, and be able to obtain relevant information.

Before we begin, a note about financial jargon. In this chapter we will examine several important aspects of the financing of companies, especially via the issue of shares. This will involve assimilating quite a lot of financial jargon and terminology. Remember to consult the glossary at the end of the book where necessary.

The jargon used in the financial news on television and radio, and in the financial press, can be very off-putting for the novice. However, once some basic items of terminology have been learnt, it soon becomes possible to read and understand the financial news. After a short time, it ceases to be such an effort, and may even, believe it or not, become interesting.

Sources of finance for companies

As explained in Chapter 1, there are many possible sources of finance that businesses may be able to obtain. Some of these, however, are available only where the business is structured as a company.

Issue of shares

Upon the initial formation of a company, ordinary share capital is issued to the first shareholders of the company. In the case of small businesses, the number of shareholders is usually low, often no more than one or two people. As companies grow, they may issue more shares to other people. Private companies (companies with 'limited' after their name) are not permitted to issue shares to the general public or to have their shares quoted on a stock market. Public limited companies (companies with 'plc') after their name, on the other hand, are permitted to issue shares to a wider public. Some plcs are quoted on a stock market and so are able to issue their shares widely to the general public. It is important to note that not all plcs are quoted companies, but that only plcs (and not private companies) may have their shares quoted on the stock market.

The ordinary shares of companies are often referred to as **equity shares**. They have a **nominal value** such as £1.50p or 25p; this is the basic denomination of the share. Shares that are quoted on a stock market have a share price representing a **market value** that is, usually, greater than nominal value. For example, a listed company has 5 000 000 shares with a nominal value of 50p each and a market value of £3.75. This gives the company a total nominal value of 5 000 000 × 50p = £2 500 000; this is the nominal value of its issued share capital. The total market value of the company (its **market capitalisation**) is 5 000 000 × £3.75 = £18 750 000.

Don't worry if this seems confusing at the moment. We will return to the same point later in the book when we examine accounting for limited companies in more detail.

Rights of shareholders

Ordinary (equity) share capital entitles its owners (shareholders) to a vote which they can exercise at the general meetings of the company. Usually, the only general meeting of a company is the annual general meeting (AGM) at which shareholders vote on such matters as appointment of directors, appointment of auditors, and on whether or not to accept the annual accounts that are presented at the meeting. In almost all cases, AGMs are extremely dull affairs, often poorly attended, but occasionally something interesting happens at the AGM of a major company, triggering a report about the AGM in the financial press.

The other principal right of shareholders is to receive dividends. Dividends are paid out to shareholders, often on a regular basis; they constitute the income received by shareholders on their investment. Very large companies usually have two regular payment dates each year for dividends (an interim dividend and a final dividend). The company's directors decide upon the level of dividend to be paid out; it is usually expressed as an amount in pence per share: for example, 'the directors have declared an interim dividend of 5p per ordinary share in issue'.

Benefits of limited company status

The liability of shareholders in companies is limited. That means that, even if the company fails, the shareholders cannot be called upon to contribute any further cash.

Because the capital of limited companies is split up into many shares, it is possible for a shareholder to sell a very small proportion of the total share capital of the company to another person. This can be useful where, for example, the original shareholders of a company have decided that they wish to spread the share ownership more widely, perhaps to other family members.

Usually, if a business becomes really large, a limited company is the only realistic business vehicle for it. It allows for multiple shareholders, each owning perhaps a very small proportion of the total business. Sole traders, for obvious reasons, usually own very small businesses. Similarly, partnerships, except in a few special cases, tend to be small or medium-sized businesses. The special cases tend to be professional firms (such as firms of accountants, lawyers, architects or other professionals) where very large partnerships do exist. In most cases, however, if a business grows to be very large, it will be in the form of a company.

Sometimes, the directors of a company may choose to raise finance by obtaining a listing on the stock exchange. This involves selling shares to a wider public than family, friends and business associates. In the next two sections we look at various aspects of the operation of the UK stock market.

The UK stock market

A stock market is a place where stocks are traded. So, what are the stocks referred to in the term 'stock market'? The UK stock market trades in, principally, the shares of quoted companies. Quoted companies comprise both UK based companies and overseas companies that have a quotation in the UK. The market also trades in British government bonds (these are known as 'gilts' or 'gilt-edged stock') and other types of shares and company bonds (also known as **loan stock** or **debentures**).

So, where is this 'place' where stocks are traded? In former times the principal stock market location in the UK was the trading floor of the London Stock Exchange. This was located in the City of London where the agents of people and organisations wishing to trade in stocks and shares met in person to arrange transactions. This physical location is no longer necessary following the far-reaching reforms and reorganisation of trading implemented over the last fifteen to twenty years. Transactions in shares now take place electronically.

The London Stock Exchange (LSE) is a powerful organisation that regulates the trading in shares and organises their listing. The LSE operates in two principal capacities: as a 'primary market' and as a 'secondary market'.

Primary market

The primary market function allows companies to raise capital via the LSE. In order to exploit the capital raising potential of the LSE new entrants to the market apply for a listing and, if successful, float the company on the stock market. This means that they are entitled to offer shares – either newly issued or existing shares – to the public.

Companies which already have a stock market listing may decide that they need to raise more finance. Such companies can issue more shares and sell them for cash.

Secondary market

The secondary market function allows trading in shares to take place between willing buyers and sellers. This is an extremely useful function providing for liquidity in shares. Liquidity means, in this context, that shares can be bought and sold easily. High liquidity is extremely attractive to investors; it means that they are not tied into their investment over long periods, but can liquidate (turn into cash) their investment whenever it suits them to do so. One of the problems of investing in unquoted companies is that it can be difficult (or downright impossible) to sell the investment to anyone else.

Organisation and operation of the London Stock Exchange

The LSE's market is split into two: the main market and the Alternative Investment Market (AIM).

The main market

The main market is the most important element of the market provided by the LSE. Companies on the main market have a full listing and are subject to the full range of regulation applicable to listed companies. In order to obtain a listing on the main market companies normally have to have been in business for at least three years and to have a full record of accounts for that period.

The Alternative Investment Market (AIM)

AIM is a market that deals in shares of smaller and/or newer companies than those eligible to obtain a full listing. Many relatively small companies choose to obtain a quotation on this market. Investing in these companies is potentially riskier than investing in companies with a full listing because: (a) the business venture may be inherently riskier; and (b) the shares of AIM companies are often relatively illiquid – that is, they may not be traded very often or in very large volumes. This could make a holding of shares in an AIM company relatively more difficult to sell. However, some AIM companies are highly successful; they may move on to a full listing once they have built up a trading record.

Share prices

There are over 2000 UK companies quoted on the LSE at any one time, plus several hundred overseas companies. Although many companies have been listed for years, the list is constantly changing as new companies come to the market (at a rate of some 200–300 per year), and existing companies leave (because they have failed and go into liquidation, or because they are taken over, or because their directors decide to de-list).

Shares in quoted companies have a market price that can fluctuate a great deal. Shares in the larger, better known companies are traded very frequently, and their price can change from minute to minute. It is possible to obtain share prices with a delay of approximately 15 minutes from many sources nowadays. One of the best and most reliable is the LSE's own website (**www.londonstockexchange.com**). Shares in smaller companies, especially those on AIM, may be traded infrequently – i.e. their trading volume is low. Prices for such shares may remain relatively static with long periods of inactivity.

Share prices will tend to rise when a company is doing well, or when some piece of good news is announced (for example, the company has obtained new business or it has sacked an incompetent director). Conversely, bad news often results in a fall in share price. However, sometimes movement in share prices has relatively little to do with individual companies' activities and is the result of general market sentiment. For example, in the early part of 2000 share prices were generally high, but they fell during the middle of the year as the dotcom bubble burst. This 'bursting of the bubble' affected dotcom companies most severely but there was a more general loss of faith in high technology companies and in the market in general. For many individual companies, the drop in their share price had very little, if anything, to do with their activities, but was the result of a downturn in general market sentiment. There was a huge general drop in share prices following 11 September 2001. This affected all companies, but those involved in aerospace, insurance or tourism were particularly badly affected.

Stock market regulation

All companies are subject to regulation. The Companies Acts contain many legal stipulations about, for example, the internal constitutional arrangements for companies, the appointment and remuneration (that is, payment) of directors, the filing of accounts with the Registrar of Companies and the form and content of accounts. In addition there are other sources of regulation, including **accounting standards** which contain detailed requirements about specific items in the financial statements. However, listed companies are subject to another level of regulation in the form of a detailed rule book that used to be controlled by the LSE but is now regulated by the Financial Services Authority (FSA). The rules include, for example:

- A requirement for listed companies to report, via **interim financial statements**, half-yearly as well as annually (and in some specific cases, three-monthly – also known as quarterly – reporting is required).
- A requirement to include, alongside the annual financial statements, a **chairman's statement**.
- Regulations about building up large holdings of shares.
- Regulations about notifying the market of major events or large transactions.

Stock market indices

The FTSE

Anyone who watches television news, or who listens to radio news, will have heard the (usually) brief reports about the financial markets which sound something like: 'Bad news on the financial markets. The Footsie 100 fell 13 points to close at 5345.5.' While the first sentence makes sense, the second sounds like gibberish to the financial novice. Let's pick the important pieces out of the statement. 'Footsie' is the usual verbal reference for 'FTSE' which stands for 'Financial Times Stock Exchange'. The FTSE organisation, which is owned by the London Stock Exchange and the *Financial Times* newspaper, runs a series of indices both for the UK stock market and worldwide.

The FTSE 100 is an index that rises and falls in line with the value of the top 100 listed UK companies. The index started originally with a value of 1000. Each of the 100 constituent companies figures in the index according to the relative size of its capital. The minute-by-minute changes in the value of the 100 companies' share prices are fed into the index calculations. For most interested observers, daily tracking of the index value tells them all they need to know, but it is possible for people and organisations who are deeply involved in investing to find the current value at any time during LSE trading hours.

So, if the index falls by 13 points, it reflects an overall, average fall for the day in the share prices of those companies that make up the index. Some of the companies' share prices may have gone up; some will have fallen; but, overall, the average movement for the day is slightly downwards.

The reported index total (5345.5) is only really helpful to a person who keeps a regular eye on the movements in share prices. The index figure on its own means very little.

Which companies are in the FTSE?

At regular intervals the FTSE committee reviews membership of the FTSE 100; the principal criterion for membership is size, which, of course, fluctuates. The committee also reviews membership of the other principal stock market company classifications, and there are indices for the following:

- FTSE 250 – these are the 250 companies that are next in order of size after the FTSE 100.
- FTSE 350 – these are the FTSE 100 and FTSE 250 together.
- FTSE All-Share – the FTSE 100 and FTSE 250 plus a group of smaller, but still significant companies classified as FTSE SmallCap.
- FTSE Fledgling – these are fully listed companies that do not qualify in size terms for the FTSE SmallCap.
- FTSE TechMark – these are companies listed on the TechMark part of the LSE, which is a separate market introduced in 1999 for shares of high tech companies.

Information about the current values of all of these indices, and the rules that operate for their calculation, can be found at the FTSE website: (**www.ftse.com**).

Flotation and other types of share issue

Floating a company

As noted earlier, between 200 and 300 companies become publicly quoted each year. The process is time-consuming (it can easily take up to a year to organise and carry out) and may deflect directors' attention from running the business. A great deal of professional advice is required in order to conduct a successful flotation. Corporate finance advisers, stockbrokers (usually referred to simply as 'brokers'), lawyers and professional accountants are involved in ensuring that the process is successful.

Flotation for most companies involves a **placing** of the shares. This means identifying prospective buyers (usually institutional investors such as pension schemes, life assurance companies, venture capitalists, investment trusts and asset managers), and arranging to sell a portion of the shares. In the case of a placing, there is no invitation to the general public to buy into the new shares. An **offer for sale**, by contrast, does involve a general invitation to the general public and the institutions to buy shares in the company. It involves preparation of a detailed **prospectus** containing a great deal of information about the history and prospects of the company.

In either case, once the shares are floated they can be bought and sold in the secondary market. However, in most cases of smaller companies coming to the market for the first time, the principal or only buyers of the new shares are likely to be half a dozen or so of the well-known institutional investors.

Other types of share issue

New issues

Once a company has been floated successfully it may issue further blocks of shares in order to raise new capital. If there is sufficient demand for the shares, the new issue is likely to be successful.

Rights issues

It is commonly the case that, where a listed company wishes to raise cash via a new issue of share capital, it will do so via a **rights issue**. A rights issue is an offer to existing shareholders to purchase additional shares. It is usually expressed in terms such as 'a one-for-three rights issue'. This would mean that for every three shares already held in the company, the shareholder could buy one additional share. Taking up the rights issue allows an individual shareholder to retain the same percentage shareholding as before, as the following example illustrates.

Example 4.1 Wendover Household Goods plc has a total issued share capital of £1 000 000 £1 shares, the current market price of which is £5.30 each. It requires a fresh injection of capital to finance the building of a new factory to produce the company's revolutionary range of cleaning products. Wendover's corporate finance advisers tell the directors that the best way of raising the money is via a rights issue. They suggest an issue of one-for-four at £4.40.

An issue of one share for every four held will result in the issue of an additional 250 000 £1 shares. Each of these will be sold for £4.40, resulting in a cash inflow for Wendover of £1 100 000 if all the rights are taken up.

Jeannie Lemmon is one of Wendover's principal shareholders. She holds 170 000 of the issued shares. How much will Jeannie have to pay if she takes up the rights issue? She will have the opportunity to buy 170 000 ÷ 4 = 42 500 shares. She will have to pay, therefore, 42 500 × £4.40 = £187 000 if she decides to take up the rights issue.

As in Example 4.1, it is usually the case that the rights issue price will be pitched below the current market value of the share in order to make it attractive to shareholders. If the rights issue fails (in that existing shareholders do not take up the issue) then it would be possible to try to raise additional capital by a placing or an offer for sale. However, existing shareholders could be assumed to have a particular interest in the company; if they are not interested in investing more money in the company, it is even less likely that outsiders will wish to do so.

Mergers and acquisitions

Where a full-scale effort is made by one company to purchase a majority of another company's shares, this is referred to as a **takeover bid**. What happens is that the bidding company offers to purchase shares from existing shareholders at a stated price. The existing shareholders do not have to accept the offer, so it has to be pitched at a price that will make it sufficiently attractive to induce a large number of the existing shareholders to sell. Takeovers are a common feature of the stock market environment. A **hostile bid** refers to a bid by one company that is rejected by the target company's directors. Not all takeovers, however, are hostile.

The consequences of a successful takeover bid are often far-reaching. The purpose of a takeover, in principle, is to allow a better quality management to take on the control of the operations of the target company. Ideally, takeovers should lead to improved efficiency and better returns for shareholders of the company that is taking over the other. In practice, it appears that takeovers do not always have the desired effect.

Mergers and acquisitions (M&A) is a general term referring to any bringing together of companies either by agreement or as a result of a hostile bid. Both 'mergers' and 'acquisitions' have specific meanings for accountants, but it is beyond the scope of this book to examine those meanings.

To list or not to list?

It may not be easy for the directors of a limited company to decide on whether or not to list. There are advantages and drawbacks.

Advantages of listing

● The principal advantage of listing, of course, is that the company can raise more finance for new projects and investments.
● Listing increases a company's general profile and credibility and may enhance its reputation.
● Listing may allow the founder members of a company to turn their hard work in the past into cash by selling part or all of their holding of shares.
● Listed companies shares can, in most cases, be liquidated easily. Listing is, therefore, likely to increase the pool of potential investors and may increase the value of the company.

A 2001 survey carried out jointly by the LSE and Eversheds (a firm of business lawyers) found that the most popular reason cited for seeking flotation was 'to raise funds' (mentioned by 64% of respondents), followed by 'to increase the company's profile and credibility' (mentioned by 23% of respondents).

Drawbacks of listing

- A listed company is in the public spotlight. Financial journalists are likely to become much more interested in a company's activities once it is listed. This may work to the company's advantage when everything is going well and the publicity is welcome. However, if the company is struggling, or if it is engaged in some controversial activity, publicity may be a major drawback.
- A listed company may become a 'takeover target'. A company can take over another company by buying up a majority of the shares in order to obtain control over it. The directors of the target company usually find themselves in a difficult position in these circumstances and they often lose their jobs.
- There is increased pressure on companies' management to produce consistent and ever-improving results. This pressure may result in short-termism, where investment in the long-term future of the company may suffer in order to produce the kind of short-term results that satisfy City commentators.
- Obtaining a listing is not cheap. A great deal of accounting and legal work must be paid for, plus underwriting costs. The total costs usually amount to at least 10%, and occasionally as much as 20%, of the amounts of cash raised by the flotation.
- The additional layers of regulation are onerous and compliance with them can be very expensive. It is usually necessary to employ additional staff.
- Movements in the company's share price can be worryingly difficult to explain or predict.

In the LSE/Eversheds' survey referred to earlier, the principal drawbacks to being a public company were identified as 'additional reporting requirements and associated costs' (mentioned by 57% of respondents) and 'volatility of share price, often with little correlation to business fundamentals' (mentioned by 18% of respondents).

The role of information in stock markets

Information is the lifeblood of stock markets. People, including those who represent the institutions that buy shares (for example, pension funds and insurance companies), need to have some assurance that they are buying shares that have some underlying value.

Sources of information about listed companies' shares

Published financial statements

All companies, whether listed or unlisted, are required to produce annual accounts for the benefit of shareholders. They are also required to file certain information (although not the full accounts in all cases – there are various exemptions for small and medium-sized companies) with the Registrar of Companies. However, the reporting requirements are more onerous for listed companies. All listed companies must produce an annual report, which has to be made available to interested parties. These are often very long and elaborate documents, running to many pages and involving high quality paper and design work. In addition to the full annual report, listed companies produce interim financial statements, which report results for the six-month period immediately following the year-end.

The reporting requirements mean that investors, potential investors and anyone else who is interested can obtain information about a company at approximately six-monthly intervals. It takes time, however, to compile this information. Most listed companies publish an annual report, at the earliest, some three to four months after the company's year-end.

How reliable is the information? There have been many cases of investors and others being misled by financial statements that were inaccurately or fraudulently prepared. All large companies are required by law to have an annual **audit** of their financial statements carried out by an independent firm of auditors. Although the audit process is not foolproof, and although it in no way guarantees accuracy, it does provide investors with some assurance that the financial statements are fairly stated.

The internet

The internet has emerged in the last five years or so as a very useful source of information about listed companies and their activities. Although not all listed companies have websites (and the law in the UK does not, currently, require them to have websites), most do.

There is no standardisation of content on websites, but, typically, a corporate website includes:

- Information about the activities of the business (this is often very extensive).
- The latest annual and interim financial statements.
- An archive of annual and interim financial statements.
- E-mail contact details.
- A constantly updated share price (sometimes via a link into the stock exchange's own website).
- Links into other useful websites.

A company's website can be a very useful source of information. However, the quality of website construction and content varies enormously. Some are out of date, dull, difficult to access and badly designed.

Many companies listed on stock exchanges outside the UK also have websites. Before the late 1990s it was often very difficult to obtain information about overseas companies; by contrast, nowadays, it can be very easy. Most US companies have extensive websites and it is becoming increasingly common to find good corporate websites among continental European companies.

As well as companies' own websites, there are many other sources of information available nowadays. The Hemscott Group website (**www.hemscott.net**) provides information about all UK based companies listed on the London Stock Exchange, including companies listed on the Alternative Investment Market. Some of the information is available by subscription only, but a large amount is freely available.

The financial press

The best and most extensive coverage of company activity and general financial news available in the UK is undoubtedly provided by the *Financial Times* (FT), which is published six times a week. Anyone who reads the FT thoroughly on a daily basis before long will be a fount of financial knowledge. Most business and accounting students will find that making a conscientious attempt to read the FT fairly thoroughly once a week will add considerably to their general financial knowledge.

Some Sunday papers and broadsheet daily papers (e.g. *The Times* and *The Guardian*) contain good coverage of financial and accounting issues.

The case study for this chapter examines various aspects of the flotation decision.

CASE STUDY 4.1 Going public

The directors of Gropius & Garner Productions plc are about to hold one of the most important board meetings in the company's history. A few months ago the founding shareholders, Brendan Gropius and Amelia Garner, suggested to the board that it was time to think about 'going public', by obtaining a listing on the stock exchange.

Brendan Gropius is the company's managing director, and Amelia Garner, who is a chartered accountant, is the finance director. They founded the company, which produces television commercials and documentaries, nine years ago. Since its foundation, the company has produced strong results; it has grown very rapidly and now employs almost 150 staff. The shares are currently held as follows:

- Bernard Gropius, 40%
- Amelia Gardner, 30%
- Sigmund Gropius (Bernard's cousin), 15%
- Karl-Heinz Muller (Amelia's brother-in-law), 15%.

As well as Bernard and Amelia, Sigmund and Karl-Heinz also hold directorships. There is one further member of the board who does not hold any shares: Judy Segal, who has overall responsibility for the production of commercials and documentaries.

Bernard and Amelia propose that 300 000 of the 700 000 shares currently in issue should be sold. Each director would sell shares in proportion to his or her total shareholding as follows:

Director	Shares currently held	Shares to be sold (3/7)	Shares remaining
Bernard (40%)	280 000	120 000	160 000
Amelia (30%)	210 000	90 000	120 000
Sigmund (15%)	105 000	45 000	60 000
Karl-Heinz (15%)	105 000	45 000	60 000
Total	700 000	300 000	400 000

In addition to the 300 000 existing shares that would be sold, the company would issue a further 200 000. The directors have been advised by their corporate finance advisers that they could probably raise around £10.50 per share on flotation, after taking into account all the costs of issue.

There are two principal reasons for the proposal to obtain a listing:

1. Bernard and Amelia are both paid large salaries for their work as directors of the company. However, they are both interested in selling a substantial part of their shareholding now, while share values in the market generally are high. The sale would allow each of them to realise a substantial amount of cash, which they could then invest elsewhere. They would both like to plan for an early retirement in about 5–8 years time.

2. The company plans to move into children's entertainment programmes because there are very substantial profits to be made from this area of the market in programmes. This will require a substantial investment of resources. Borrowing money to fund the expansion would be a possibility, but both Bernard and Amelia feel that the time is right for a flotation.

Judy Segal, the sole director without a shareholding, is concerned about the proposal. She can see, of course, that her fellow directors all stand to gain substantial sums by selling their shares, but she is not sure that the flotation will be advantageous to the company in the longer term. She would like the company to remain as an independent operator, and she has been alarmed by a spate of recent takeover announcements in the business press. She fears that, once floated, the company could be swallowed up rapidly by one of the bigger companies.

Bernard assures her that there is no particular reason why Gropius & Garner should become a takeover target. The company is well managed and has a good record of producing profits even in difficult times. He can see nothing but advantages from the move.

Discuss the advantages and drawbacks of stock market flotation for the company, taking into consideration the following questions:

● Would the company be at risk of becoming a takeover target?

● Are Bernard and Amelia being unreasonable in wanting to cash in their shares?

● Is Bernard correct in seeing only advantages in the flotation?

Case study solution and discussion

In order to assess the advantages and drawbacks of the proposed flotation, it would be sensible first to assess the financial impact of the deal.

Would the company be at risk of becoming a takeover target?

A company is usually only at risk of becoming a takeover target if more than 50% of the voting shares are available for purchase. This deal involves the issue of a further 200 000 shares. Added to the existing 700 000 shares, this gives a prospective total of shares in issue of 900 000. How many of the shares will be retained by the current directors?

Holdings now (before flotation)	700 000
To be sold on flotation	(300 000)
Retained after flotation	400 000

So, the directors will hold 400 000 of 900 000 shares (i.e. less than half of the issued share capital). If another person or company wished to take over Gropius & Garner it would be technically possible to do so. Judy's concerns are, therefore, realistic in the circumstances.

In total, 500 000 shares will be sold. If the corporate finance advisers' estimates are approximately correct, this would mean that 500 000 × £10.50 could be raised, i.e. £5 250 000. The sale of the shares belonging to the directors will raise 300 000 × £10.50 = £3 150 000 and new capital raised for investment in children's programming will be 200 000 × £10.50 = £2 100 000.

How much money will the directors make?

● Bernard holds 40% of the shares currently in issue, and so he will be entitled to 40% of the proceeds of the directors' shares: 40% x £3 150 000 = £1 260 000.

● Amelia holds 30% of the shares currently in issue, and so she will be entitled to 30% of the proceeds: 30% × £3 150 000 = £945 000.

● Sigmund and Karl-Heinz each hold 15% of the shares currently in issue, and so will each be entitled to: 15% × £3 150 000 = £472 500.

▶

Clearly, all the directors (except Judy) stand to make substantial sums out of the flotation. All will retain large holdings of shares in the business, and so they could potentially make more money out of selling more shares in the future.

Is it unreasonable of Bernard and Amelia to want to sell their shares?
Flotation on the stock market is a common way for founders of company to turn part or all of their investment into cash. As both Bernard and Amelia are thinking ahead to retirement, the proposal to float the company makes perfect sense from their point of view.

Is Bernard correct in only seeing advantages in the flotation?
Because Bernard stands to gain a substantial sum of cash from selling part of his shareholding he is, perhaps, not very likely to dwell on the potential drawbacks of the flotation. However, Judy has pointed out one significant drawback in the form of a potential takeover bid. If the company were taken over the existing management might not be able to hold on to their lucrative directorships. Even if they did, they would find that they no longer have complete control over the company's activities.

Other possible drawbacks include:

● Increased public attention which is not always welcome. Following flotation the company would find itself subject to much more media interest than before.

● The company would have to start producing interim financial statements as well as a full annual report, and there are various other forms of additional regulation that would come into play. A listed company incurs additional costs in complying with regulation.

● There might be pressure from the City to produce better and more consistent results.

Most of these drawbacks are unavoidable. The company could help to minimise the possibility of takeover by floating rather fewer shares than originally intended. If 400 000 of 900 000 shares were to be made available, this would leave a majority in the hands of the four shareholder/directors. The company could, of course, still be vulnerable if one or more of the four were persuaded to sell all or part of their holding.

Chapter summary

The chapter started by examining some aspects of the financing of companies by the issue of shares, including the rights of shareholders, and a brief reprise of some of the benefits conferred by limited company status.

The role of the UK stock market as both a primary and secondary market was then discussed. A brief description of the main market and the Alternative Investment Market was included, followed by an introduction to stock market regulation. The FTSE indices were then briefly described and discussed.

Flotation of companies, new issues in established listed companies and rights issues were described. There are advantages and drawbacks to listing on the stock market, and these were detailed and discussed.

Finally, the important role that information plays in stock markets was flagged, and some of the principal sources of information about companies were described, including published financial statements, various internet resources and the financial press.

The case study examined a company contemplating a listing. This involved assessment of the financial consequences of listing, both in terms of rewarding the company's founders and in raising fresh capital for investment.

Internet resources

Some useful resources:

www.ftse.com – explains the operation of the FTSE indices and reports regularly updated values for the main indices.

www.fsa.gov.uk – the website of the Financial Services Authority.

www.hemscott.net – provides a large quantity of useful information about UK based companies listed on the London Stock Exchange.

www.londonstockexchange.com – provides information about all companies currently listed on the LSE (including current share prices) and about the activities of the exchange itself. For example, at the time of writing, the website contained the LSE/Eversheds' survey report referred to earlier in the chapter.

Links to individual company's websites are often provided through the Hemscott site and through the LSE site referred to above. If there is no obvious link it is worth contacting the company by phone (phone numbers are obtainable from the Hemscott data) to ask if they have a corporate website.

Exercises

The answers to many of the exercises are set out later in this chapter. However, where the exercise number is followed by 'A' the answer is available only to lecturers. Remember that additional exercises (with answers) are available to students on the book's website.

4.1   Ashton Longton plc, a listed company, has issued share capital of £8 000 000 comprising shares of £1 nominal value. The current quoted price per share is £3.85. What is the company's market capitalisation?

4.2A Amery Chorlton plc, a listed company, has issued share capital of £4 000 000 comprising shares of 25p nominal value. The current quoted price per share is 98p. What is the company's market capitalisation?

4.3   The Alternative Investment Market is a market for:

a) companies that do not currently wish to proceed to full listing

b) companies that promote alternative lifestyles

c) British government securities

d) overseas companies without a trading history.

4.4A Interim financial statements are:

a) first drafts of the final financial statements of listed companies

b) provisional financial statements that are awaiting audit

c) half-yearly financial statements produced by listed companies

d) audited financial statements awaiting directors' approval.

4.5   Warminster Toys plc has a total issued share capital of £3 000 000 in 50p shares. The company decides to make a rights issue of one-for-five at a price of £5.42 per share. To take up the rights the holder of 50 000 shares will have to pay:

a) £27 100

b) £135 500

c) £54 200

d) £271 000.

4.6A Willoughby Wooster plc has a total issued share capital of £1 000 000 in 25p shares. The company decides to make a rights issue of one-for-two at a price of £2.70 per share. To take up the rights the holder of 30 000 shares will have to pay:

a) £40 500

b) £10 125

c) £20 250

d) £7 500.

4.7   Yolande Brighton is the managing director of Brighton Bestwines plc, a company that supplies the licensed trade. The company has been very successful but has now reached the point where it needs to expand its warehousing capacity if it is to continue growing. The directors have been contemplating applying for a quotation on the Alternative Investment Market (AIM). The company will issue a further 500 000 shares (it already has 1 000 000 shares in issue). It hopes to be able to sell the shares at around £2.50 each.

The directors have invited you to their board meeting to discuss the flotation. They are keen to raise the finance, but one or two of them are wondering about potential drawbacks to being quoted on the AIM, and they would like you to give them an outline of any possible problems they face. Prepare a list of potential drawbacks for discussion at the meeting.

4.8A Tatiana, a friend of yours, has recently been left approximately £50 000 of listed company investments in her grandmother's will. She has been trying to read the *Financial Times* in order to see what is happening to her investments. She has found some information about three of them:

1. Turtlehammer plc rose to 215p on speculation of a hostile bid from a competitor, but fell back to 210p by the end of the day's trading.

2. The share price of Teddington Tilmain plc has risen by 26p following the announcement that it has obtained an important new export contract.

3. Tolson Tortellini plc has announced today that it is making a rights issue of one-for-four at £2.30.

Tatiana frankly admits that she doesn't understand any of this. She asks you to explain each of the pieces of news in terms that she can understand. She would like to know if any of it is likely to be good news for her. Also, she would like you to tell her if the *Financial Times* is the only source of information about her investments.

Answers to exercises

4.1 Ashton Longton plc: The company has 8 000 000 shares in issue, each valued at £3.85. Market capitalisation is 8 000 000 × £3.85 = £30 800 000.

4.3 The Alternative Investment Market is a market for companies that do not currently wish to proceed to full listing. The correct answer, therefore, is a).

4.5 The rights issue gives the holder of 50 000 shares the right to buy 50 000/5 shares = 10 000 shares. Each new share costs £5.42, so the total amount payable to take up the rights is: 10 000 × £5.42 = £54 200. The correct answer, therefore, is c). (Note that if the issued share capital is £3 000 000 denominated in 50p shares, the total number of shares in issue is 6 000 000. The shareholder in this question holds 50 000 shares of 50p each.)

4.7 Brighton Bestwines plc: Potential drawbacks of quotation on the Alternative Investment Market include:

1. Additional regulation applies to quoted companies; for example, they have to produce additional published financial reports. The additional compliance costs often involve employing more staff to deal with the extra requirements.

2. Although the company could raise the capital it needs, there will be legal and other professional fees involved. These are likely to be around 10% of the amount raised. This means that, for every share sold at the target price of £2.50, approximately 25p will be spent on fees. The percentage could be even higher.

3. Many directors are uncomfortable with the additional attention paid to quoted companies by the media. They may have to start meeting journalists, and there may be additional costs involved if professional public relations advice is required. (Tutorial note: AIM quoted companies are generally subject to rather less attention than companies with a full listing, but financial journalists will obviously take some interest when things go wrong.)

4. The company's share price may fluctuate for reasons that are difficult to explain (because they are related to general market sentiment, or the unpopularity of the industry sector to which the company belongs, for example).

5. There is a potential drawback in allowing other parties to buy shares in that the company may lay itself open to takeover bids. However, in this case the shares issued for sale will amount to only one-third of the total share capital, so the company will be safe from takeover unless and until it issues more shares for sale.

5

THE ROLE OF ACCOUNTING IN BUSINESS

AIMS AND LEARNING OUTCOMES

Aim of the chapter

To understand the reasons why people need accounting information, the nature of accounting information and the role of the accountant.

Learning outcomes

After reading the chapter and completing the exercises at the end, students should:

- Understand why accounting information is produced.
- Be able to identify the principal groups in society who need and use accounting information.
- Know about the principal characteristics and features of accounting information.
- Understand the distinction between financial accounting and management accounting.
- Know about the functions that accountants perform in the production of accounting information.
- Appreciate the reasons why business managers should be able to understand accounting reports.

The need for accounting information

Quite simply, accounting information is produced because people need it. The reasons why they need it vary from one group of people to another. In this chapter we will examine the range of reasons for the production of accounting information and the nature of the information produced by commercial businesses.

First, we will re-examine the three types of business organisation introduced in Chapter 1, considering in each case the range of accounting information that might be required and the purposes for which it is needed.

Sole trader

A sole trader business, because it usually remains small, is not complex in its organisation. There is one manager, the sole trader, who may employ a few staff. The sole trader does not have to make information about the business's profitability generally available. In fact, the only consumers of financial information about the business are the taxation authorities (the Inland Revenue) and, possibly, the Customs and Excise (if the sole trader is registered for VAT).

Annual information

Tax returns to the Inland Revenue have to be made once a year, within the stipulated deadline. The sole trader needs to prepare simple accounting statements to accompany his or her tax return. There will be a statement showing the calculation of profit or loss for the year, and, possibly, a statement that shows the resources owned by the business. These statements are known as the **profit and loss account** and the **balance sheet**.

The profit and loss account shows the revenue for the business for the year, less the business expenses. The remainder is either a profit or loss. The balance sheet is a statement of the resources owned and controlled by the business at a single point in time. It also shows any amounts owed, for example, loans taken out from the bank and payments due to suppliers of goods.

Every business has a year-end date. The profit and loss account is prepared for the year ending on that date, and the balance sheet shows the statement of resources less amounts due on the same year-end date.

Quarterly information

If the sole trader is registered for VAT, a quarterly VAT return will have to be prepared. As explained in Chapter 1, this contains a summary of sale and purchase transactions that have taken place in the quarter, and a calculation of input and output tax, in order to arrive at the net amount payable to the Customs and Excise. Failing to meet Customs and Excise deadlines for submission of the return and the amounts due must be avoided at all costs, so the sole trader business has to be able to keep accounting records sufficiently well to be able to provide the required information quickly.

Accounting information within the business

As well as information provided for external authorities, there will almost certainly be a need for more frequent information to help the sole trader manage the business efficiently, and to assist him or her in making decisions. At the simplest possible level this means keeping an eye on the state of the bank balance.

Example 5.1 Deva runs a small nursery specialising in tender plants. Most of her business is via mail order. Every three months she pays rent for the premises, comprising two glasshouses, a yard and a small office. The quarterly rental is £1500.

Before writing the cheque to the landlord Deva must know whether or not there is enough money in the bank account to cover the £1500 payment. If there is not, the cheque may be returned because of lack of funds (i.e. it bounces). A business manager cannot afford to accumulate unopened bank statements; he or she needs to know how much is in the bank so as to be able to anticipate any difficulties in meeting payments, or to ensure that any surplus is transferred to a high interest account.

At a slightly more sophisticated level, it is usually helpful for most small business owners to understand how the business is doing on a regular basis. A sole trader should keep records of sales and receipts of cash, and of the payment of expenses. From these it should be possible to prepare a simple monthly statement of profitability. This will not be used for reporting outside the business; it is an internal document for the sole trader's own use.

Recording and summarising information

In most cases, sole trader businesses do not employ an accountant. It would be far too expensive, and, besides, because accounting information needs are relatively modest, there would be little point. If the sole trader is equipped with some basic knowledge of record-keeping, has the time to do it, and is sufficiently well organised to keep the records straight, the cheapest and most straightforward option is to do the job himself or herself.

Some sole traders pay a bookkeeper for a few hours a week to keep the records straight. Where staff are employed it is particularly important to keep good records and to make accurate calculations of pay, income tax and National Insurance contributions due. In almost all cases, the sole trader is well advised to use the services of a qualified accountant for assistance with preparing annual financial statements, preparing tax returns and ensuring that the correct amount of tax is paid. Unless some very complex advice is involved, this kind of service can usually be purchased for a few hundred pounds each year.

In summary, the sole trader produces financial information to be used outside the business by the Inland Revenue and, probably, the Customs and Excise. No other external party can require information from the sole trader. Financial information for internal use will be produced as frequently as necessary to provide the sole trader with the information needed to run the business.

Partnership

A partnership, as we have seen in Chapter 1, does not need to make financial information generally available to the public. However, it must, in the same way as the sole trader, prepare annual financial statements that form the basis for tax calculation by the Inland Revenue. Also, quarterly financial information will probably have to be made available to the Customs and Excise in the form of summaries of sales and expenses and input and output tax totals supplied on the VAT return every quarter.

In most respects the information requirements are, so far, very similar to those of a sole trader. However, there is one important difference: in a partnership the annual profit and loss account provides the profit figure that will be split between the partners in accordance with their profit-sharing arrangements. The annual accounts, therefore, take on an additional dimension of importance in a partnership. The partners themselves need to be satisfied that the accounts have been prepared properly and that they present a reasonably accurate profit figure.

Audit

In some cases, the partners may decide to have an **audit** conducted to ensure that the annual accounts are properly prepared and fairly stated. There is no legal stipulation for audit of partnership accounts, but partners may decide, in drawing up the partnership agreement, that an audit should be carried out annually.

So, what is an audit? It is an independent examination, by a properly qualified person, of the financial records and financial statements of an entity. One of the important qualities of a well-conducted audit is that the auditor should be independent of the management of the business he or she is auditing. A partnership requiring an audit would appoint a professionally qualified auditor to conduct the examination of the records and give an impartial opinion on whether or not the annual financial statements have been properly drawn up. The opinion takes the form of an **audit report** which is attached to the financial statements. In addition to providing reassurance to the partners themselves, the fact that an audit has been conducted may be reassuring to the Inland Revenue. However, it should be emphasised that there is no legal requirement for the audit of partnerships (or of sole traders).

Accounting information within the business

We saw earlier in the chapter that sole trader businesses will find it helpful in running their businesses to produce accounting information such as monthly statements of profit. Partnership businesses tend to be larger than sole trader businesses (because more people are involved) and the need for internal accounting information may be greater because of the increased size and complexity of the business. As a business increases in size, its managers will usually find that they need more detailed information to help in decision making.

Example 5.2 Poste, Ponsonby and Peppard is a partnership of solicitors. As well as the three partners, the practice employs three other qualified solicitors and several administrative staff, including a full-time bookkeeper. The partners have a monthly management meeting at which they make decisions on important issues. In order to help them, they have instituted a system of internal financial reports. The bookkeeper prepares the reports, which are confidential, to be seen only by the partners.

The principal reports are:

- profit and loss account for the month
- billings summary for each solicitor for the month
- summary of hours worked by each solicitor for the month
- list of client invoices unpaid.

These reports allow the partners to see whether any of the solicitors are falling behind target in their monthly billings. They also allow for an assessment of profitability so that if, for example, monthly profits are tending to fall, the partners can take stock of the situation and decide whether action is necessary.

The list of unpaid client invoices informs the partners of any clients who are taking an excessively long time to pay. They can then make the necessary phone calls and send out letters to prompt the client to pay up.

Limited company

Accounting information needs within the sole trader and partnership types of business organisation are, essentially, very similar. However, the picture changes when we examine accounting for limited companies.

Provision of financial information outside the business

As we noted in Chapter 1, limited companies are required to publish financial information via the Registrar of Companies. Because everyone has access to the information held at Companies House, the information is potentially available to a very large number of people. In fact, the financial information of most companies remains undisturbed because there are very few people who are interested in it, apart from the shareholders. The company's shareholders are informed, in any case, of the financial condition of the company because they are entitled to receive a full set of annual accounts.

However, it is possible that other groups of people, apart from the shareholders, could be interested in the information. People or organisations who have been asked to lend money to the company are likely to be interested in its financial status. People who are affected by a company's existence (for example, those living near the premises of a chemical company that regularly breaches environmental legislation) may also take an interest. Later in this chapter we will consider the different categories of people who might be interested in a company's financial information.

Companies are required to submit tax returns and VAT returns, and financial reports must be made available to the Inland Revenue and Customs and Excise in the same way as for sole trader and partnership organisations.

Separation of ownership and management

In smaller companies the shareholders and directors are often the same people. Because they are engaged in the day-to-day management of the business, directors who are also shareholders really do not need annual financial information to tell them what is going on. They have access to as much internal financial information as they need.

However, the position is different for shareholders who are not directors. In large companies, most of the shareholders are remote from the activities of the business; they receive dividends and an invitation to the annual general meeting (AGM) of the business, but have no other contact with it. If they are shareholders in a listed company, they will be able to follow movements in the share price by consulting the financial press, but they are not entitled to the regular detailed internal financial information that the directors use in managing the business.

The relationships between the company, the directors and the shareholders are depicted in Figure 5.1. The diagram demonstrates the separation between the ownership of the company and its management. Shareholders appoint directors (who in larger companies are professional managers) to manage the company on their behalf: the directors act as agents of the shareholders, or (to use an old-fashioned term) as stewards on their behalf. The **stewardship** function requires directors to act in the best interests of the company at all times. In order to demonstrate good stewardship, they should report on a regular basis to shareholders – hence the requirement in company law that full annual financial statements are sent to shareholders.

Clearly, where shareholders are remote from the management of their company there is potential for the directors to take action that benefits themselves rather than benefiting the shareholders. This is one of the potential problems of the agency, or stewardship, relationship. For example, a current, and recurring issue, is that of directors' remuneration in very large companies. Criticisms are often voiced in the press of the very large increases in salary and substantial bonuses that directors award themselves. Shareholders are in a position to take action if they do not approve of directors' remuneration packages (via their votes at the AGM) but, in practice, they rarely challenge the directors.

If directors wish to manipulate financial information they are well placed to do so. How can shareholders be sure that the annual financial information they receive has not been distorted in some way? The mechanism that is used in company law is the requirement for audit by an independent auditor. Until recently, all companies, whatever their size, were required to have an audit of their annual financial statements. The requirements have, in recent years, gradually been relaxed by the government so that smaller companies are now exempt from regular audit. However, shareholders in exempt companies can still require an audit if they wish for the reassurance it provides.

Accounting information within the business

With the exception of the very large professional partnerships permitted by law, all larger businesses in the UK are constituted as limited companies. As a company grows in size, its management needs ever larger quantities of internally generated accounting information in order to keep control of the business and to make good quality decisions. Larger companies, especially those involved in the complexities of, say, manufacturing or banking, tend to produce highly complex and sophisticated information for use by management.

Figure 5.1

Separation of ownership and management in a limited company

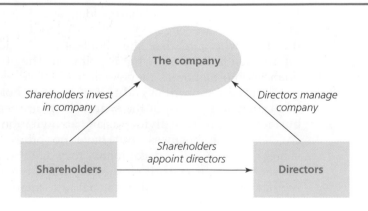

Users of accounting information

Different groups of users of financial information can be identified. In this chapter we have discussed many of them already. Table 5.1 lists the principal user groups and summarises the most likely reasons for their interest.

Table 5.1 Principal groups of users of financial information

User group	Reason for interest in financial information
Shareholders	To assess the performance of management in their role as stewards of the company
	To use the information to make decisions on whether or not to sell the investment in the shares of the company, or perhaps whether to buy more shares in the company
Potential shareholders	To make decisions on whether or not to invest in the shares of a company
Investment analysts	To assess the performance of the company in order to be able to advise their clients on investment strategy
Lenders and potential lenders	To assess the ability of the business to make repayments and to meet regular interest payments
Employees and trade unions	To assess the viability of the business and the extent to which it is likely to be able to: (a) continue to offer employment; (b) increase pay and improve employees' conditions
Suppliers	Where suppliers offer credit terms, they need to be able to assess the likelihood of being paid promptly
Special interest groups	In the case of an environmental activist group, for example: to assess the extent to which the company has set aside funds for environmental clean-up operations
Government: tax collecting agencies	To assist in the assessment and collection of taxes
Government: other agencies	To assist, for example, in the collection of national statistical information
Financial journalists	To obtain information about a company's activities and profitability which will be of interest to the journalist's readers
Academics and students	To assist in the study of business activity
Customers	To assess the likelihood of the business continuing in existence, and continuing to supply the goods or services required by the customers
The general public	Anyone, not covered by any of the categories above, who has an interest in the activities of company

Access to information

As we have seen, access to information about the financial affairs of sole traders and partnerships is strictly limited. Most of the user groups identified in Table 5.1 would not be able to gain access; the exceptions are the government agencies concerned with the assessment and collection of tax, and lenders who are likely to be in a position to be able to demand financial information would not normally be available.

Because company financial statements are made publicly available, however, all these categories of users have access to them. In many cases the user groups are making important decisions on the basis of the information, answering questions such as:

- Should I sell my shares in this company?
- Should my bank be making an overdraft facility available to this company?
- Is the company doing well enough to make it safe for me to carry on working for it?
- How risky is it to supply goods on credit to this company?
- How well are the current management looking after my interests as a shareholder?

Company accounting information is called upon to be useful to a wide range of users in making decisions. In the next section of the chapter we look at the characteristics of useful financial information.

Characteristics of useful financial information

Ideally, financial information produced by businesses should have the following key characteristics:

- *Relevant:* to the decision being made. For example, the information should be prepared shortly after the events being reported so that it is not out of date by the time it is used.
- *Reliable*: the information should be properly prepared and free from error or bias in its preparation.
- *Comparable*: where financial statements from more than one period are concerned, the information should be prepared on the same basis, so that it is comparable.
- *Understandable*: the information in the financial statements should be capable of being understood.

In practice, it is not always possible to achieve information that fulfils all of these characteristics. In large and complex businesses collecting accounting data and processing it into a set of financial statements is a time-consuming process. By the time it is published (usually three to four months after the year-end date in a very large company) circumstances may have changed and the information may be of limited use for decision making. Also, the information that is reported is all historical – i.e. it relates to events that have already occurred. The extent to which past events are a reliable guide to the future is questionable in a fast-changing business environment.

Accounting information should be understandable, but, again, this is not always easily achievable. The financial statements of very complex organisations tend, inevitably, to reflect that complexity. People who are reasonably knowledgeable about business matters should be able to comprehend financial statements, but even their ability to understand is sometimes tested by the complex financial statements of major listed companies.

Financial accounting and management accounting

There are two distinct strands to accounting in organisations. **Financial accounting** refers to the processes and practices involved in providing users external to the business with the information that they need. Companies, because they provide a relatively large amount of information to outside users relative to partnership and sole trader entities, tend to devote substantial resources to financial accounting. This type of accounting is also referred to as **financial reporting**, and both terms are used in this book. **Management accounting** is the accounting that a business organisation carries out for its own internal uses. It assists management in controlling the business and in making decisions.

Both financial and management accounting use information generated by the accounting system of the business. Clearly, the accounting systems of businesses are likely to vary enormously depending upon the complexity and size of the business organisation. However, all accounting systems have certain characteristics in common. The flow of information in an accounting system and its relationship to financial accounting and management accounting is demonstrated diagrammatically in Figure 5.2.

Data and information about events and transactions flow in and out of the business. For example, when a business makes a sale of goods to a customer that it supplies on credit (i.e. the customer is not obliged to pay cash straight away) the events and information flows set out in Table 5.2 take place. At each stage

---

Figure 5.2

The production of financial reports and management accounting reports

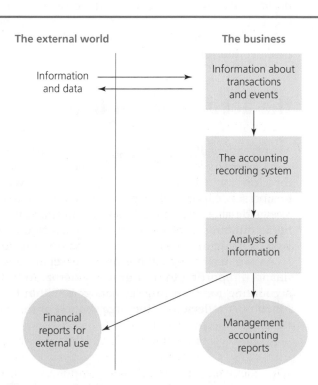

Table 5.2 Events and information flows relating to the sale of goods

Event	Information flow
An order is placed	Data about the nature and quantity of the goods required flows into the business and is recorded
Goods are assembled, packaged and sent out	A record of despatch is produced within the business and is sent out with the goods to the customer
An invoice is raised through the business recording system	The invoice is sent out from the business to the customer – information leaves the business
The customer sends payment	Information is received in the business and is recorded. The cheque is banked – information again flows out of the business

details about the event are 'captured' by the accounting recording system. Periodically, data that shares common characteristics (e.g. all sales invoices) are analysed and the analysis is used to produce reports for both financial and management accounting purposes.

The principal purpose of this book is to assist business and other non-accounting students to understand the important elements of financial and management accounting reports. Therefore, we are not concerned with the details of data capture, recording and analysis for accounting purposes. These areas are the province of accountants. Unless students are so captivated by the accounting and financial understanding they glean from this book that they decide to change direction and become accountants, detailed knowledge of accounting systems really is not necessary. However, it is helpful to have some outline understanding of the way accounting information is gathered in order to produce the reports.

The role of the accountant in business organisations

Many readers of this book will be aiming for a career in business management. In their future lives they will perhaps be sales or production managers, or personnel directors, or chief executives. Perhaps they will at some stage own their own businesses. All of these types of business manager and business proprietor work alongside accountants and use the information, often on a daily basis, produced by accountants. It is therefore important to understand what accountants do, as well as being able to understand and interpret the reports that they produce.

As we have seen, there are two separate strands in business accounting: financial reporting to user groups external to the organisation, and management accounting for reporting to managers within the organisation. This variation in function is reflected in the organisation of the accounting profession and in the training of accountants.

The accounting profession

The accounting profession includes the following types of accountant: independent accounting practitioners and accountants in business.

Independent accounting practitioners work outside industry and business in professional practices. These are the accountants who provide taxation and accounting services to a wide range of businesses. If they are **registered auditors**, they are authorised to carry out the audits of companies and other organisations.

Accountants in business are the accountants with whom business managers work in organisations. Broadly, they are either **financial accountants** or **management accountants**, depending upon whether they specialise in the external or the internal provision of accounting information.

Professional accountants may have one or more accounting qualifications. These days almost all professional accountants have a university degree, although it is not necessarily in accounting or a related subject (the author of this book, for example, is a chartered accountant with a degree in Russian). After university they enter into a period of three or four years training with an employer during which they take some very tough examinations. Not everyone who embarks on accountancy training will manage to qualify because the examinations are so demanding.

The following are the principal professional accounting bodies in the UK which have their own qualification systems:

- ICAEW: the Institute of Chartered Accountants in England and Wales (members have the letters ACA or FCA after their names).
- ICAS: the Institute of Chartered Accountants of Scotland (members have the letters CA after their names).
- ACCA: the Chartered Association of Certified Accountants (members have the letters ACCA or FCCA after their names).

The members of these organisations are found in both professional independent accounting practice and in business. Students of ICAEW and ICAS usually train in professional accountancy firms. Students of ACCA are found in both professional and business environments. Usually those who go into business specialise in financial accounting and reporting rather than in management accounting.

Finally there is CIMA: the Chartered Institute of Management Accountants (members have the letters ACMA or FCMA after their names). As the name of this organisation implies, its members work principally in management accounting, and its students train exclusively in the business environment.

People who have trained as accountants are often found at the most senior levels in business organisations. It is not unusual in the UK to encounter chief executives and senior directors who started their careers as accountants before moving into more general business management.

Why do business managers have to understand accounting reports?

As we have seen earlier in the chapter, and in the four previous chapters in this part of the book, accounting information is necessary to business organisations. To summarise, accounting is used to provide:

- Financial reports about companies for a range of user needs.
- Management reports in all types and sizes of business organisation to assist management to: control business operations; plan for the future; make decisions; and find out how the business is performing.

In business organisations where there is more than one manager, decisions tend to be taken collectively by directors or partners. It is very often the case that accounting information feeds into business decision making. In order to be able to make informed decisions non-financial managers must be able to understand the financial information that accountants present to them.

Accountants occupy a service function in the business, but the service they provide is a very important one. Poor financial reporting and control can be the downfall of an otherwise successful business.

Purpose and organisation of the remainder of this book

The principal purpose of this book is to equip prospective business managers and proprietors with the skills they need in order to be able to understand the information that accountants present to them. The rest of the book is concerned with the acquisition of those skills.

Part II of the book is concerned with financial accounting and reporting. Chapters 6 to 11 inclusive are concerned with various aspects of financial statement preparation. These chapters cover the fundamentals of balance sheets, profit and loss accounts and cash flow statements. Chapter 12 develops further the knowledge of the accounting statements of limited companies acquired in Part I of the book. Chapters 13 and 14 are concerned with understanding the financial reports of businesses.

Part III of the book is concerned with management accounting. Chapter 15 provides an introduction to the objectives of management accounting while Chapters 16 to 18 inclusive develop understanding of the management accounting techniques that allow managers to control the business and to plan for the future. Chapters 19 to 21 inclusive deal with management accounting techniques that assist managers to make decisions.

In many of the chapters students will find that they are learning how to prepare straightforward accounting statements; this may appear at first to run counter to the stated objective of the book. However, most people find that learning something about the preparation of the statements is a useful aid to developing a fuller understanding of their meaning.

Chapter summary

This chapter has provided a framework of information about accounting, which underpins the remainder of the book. First, the need for accounting information was examined in the context of three different types of business organisation: sole trader; partnership; and limited company. Each organisational type needs to make some information available to people or organisations outside the business. In addition, accounting information is needed to assist management in running the business.

The provision of information to outsiders is a much more important issue for limited companies than it is for partnership or sole trader organisations. The general public has access to company financial information through the medium of the Registrar of Companies. As well as filing information at Companies House, companies are also obliged by law to make annual accounting information available to their shareholders. The chapter explained the important issue of the separation between the ownership and management of limited companies, which is especially noticeable in larger companies.

There is a long list of potential users of accounting information: shareholders, potential shareholders, investment analysts, lenders and potential lenders, employees and trade unions, suppliers, special interest groups, the government, financial journalists, academics and students, customers and the public at large.

The chapter went on to discuss the characteristics of useful financial information: it should be:

- relevant
- reliable
- comparable
- understandable.

The distinction between financial accounting and management accounting was described and discussed, and then the role of the accountant in business organisations was described. There are several different professional accountancy qualifications and the main ones were noted.

The chapter concluded with a brief discussion of why business managers need to be able to understand accounting reports.

Exercises

The answers to many of the exercises are set out later in this chapter. However, where the exercise number is followed by 'A' the answer is available only to lecturers. Remember that additional exercises (with answers) are available to students on the book's website.

5.1   One of the following statements about the regulations governing a sole trader business is correct:

a) A sole trader does not need to supply any accounting information about his or her business to anyone.

b) A sole trader must employ an accountant.

c) Sole trader businesses are exempt from completing VAT returns.

d) A sole trader must submit a tax return annually.

5.2A One of the following statements about the regulations governing partnership businesses is correct:

a) Partnerships are obliged to have an annual audit of their financial statements.

b) Partnerships must prepare annual financial statements as the basis for the calculation of tax.

c) At least one of the partners is obliged to hold a bookkeeping qualification.

d) Each partner must submit his or her own VAT return.

5.3 One of the following statements about the regulations governing limited company businesses is correct:

a) All limited companies are obliged by company law to have an annual audit.

b) A limited company must send annual accounts to all of its shareholders.

c) All shareholders have unlimited access to their company's management accounting information.

d) The general public can access information about a company only by applying in writing to the directors.

5.4A Which of the following statements is correct? The stewardship function requires directors of limited companies to:

a) Act at all times in the best interests of the company.

b) Allow shareholders to see detailed accounting records upon request.

c) Hold regular monthly meetings to answer shareholders' questions.

d) Consult the shareholders over particularly difficult management decisions.

5.5 Podgorny & Weaver Limited is involved in the wholesale supply of fashion goods to retailers. The company directors have a monthly meeting to discuss strategy and to make decisions. The directors are presented with the following reports prepared by the company accountant each month:

- List of amounts owed by the retail businesses that the company supplies.
- Summary of the value of fashion goods items currently held in stock.
- Summary of the orders received during the month.
- Profit and loss account for the last month.

Explain how the directors would be able to make use of each of the reports listed in order to improve the management of the company.

5.6A Ponderosa & Smythe plc is a shoe manufacturing business, specialising in children's shoes. The finance director has just received the following letter from a shareholder who has recently bought some shares in the company:

'Dear Mr Pershore
I have just read a most interesting article in the *Financial Times* about the decline in the market for children's shoes. The article suggests that, because of demographic changes, the market will decline by 3–4% each year over the next ten years. In the circumstances I think our company should branch out into women's shoes. I would like the directors to discuss this at the next board meeting. Could you please send me a copy of the sales budget for the coming year, so that I can see whether or not you have taken the declining market properly into account.'

What are the principal points that the finance director should make in response to this letter?

5.7   A group of environmental activists is interested in the activities of Burnip Chemicals plc, a company that has been regularly fined in the past for emitting toxic waste into the river running past the factory premises.

    What kind of information would the activist group be seeking about the activities of the company? To what extent are the annual financial statements likely to be helpful to them?

5.8A Mohsin, a bank manager, is looking at an application for a loan from Boxer Burstall Limited, a local company. The company has included a copy of its most recent annual accounts, which are for the year ending 31 December 20X6. The accounts show that a modest profit has been made in the year. It is now March 20X8.

1. What type of information will Mohsin be looking for from the annual accounts to help him in making a decision on whether or not to lend the money?
2. How relevant is the accounting information that the company has provided to Mohsin's decision?
3. Is Mohsin entitled to request any further information?

Answers to exercises

5.1   The only correct statement is d): a sole trader must submit a tax return annually.

5.3   The only correct statement is b): a limited company must send annual accounts to all of its shareholders.

5.5   Podgorny & Weaver Limited

List of amounts owed by retail businesses

The directors would be able to see if any of the retailers owed very large amounts. If, in addition, the list contained details of the length of time the amounts had been outstanding, the directors would also be able to see if the amounts owing were significantly overdue for payment.

Summary of the value of goods held in stock

It is important for a fashion goods business not to carry excessive stocks of goods that may be about to go out of fashion. The business will lose money if the stock cannot be sold. The directors need this statement to assess the risk of having excess stocks.

Summary of the value of orders received in the last month

The directors need to assess whether the orders received meet their expectations. If the value of orders received is less than expected, the directors need to take action to address the problem.

Profit and loss account for the last month

The directors will be able to assess the performance of the business compared to their expectations, and perhaps, compared to the same month in the previous financial year.

5.7　Burnip Chemicals plc: the activist group would probably be looking for the following types of information:

- Details about the amounts of emissions.
- Details of the sums the company has paid in fines.
- Details of plans for improvements to the factory that will minimise the emission of toxic waste.

A company's financial statements contain principally information about the financial performance and condition of the business. Details about the amounts of emissions during the year are not financial items, and it is quite possible that the company would make no reference to the matter.

The amount of fines paid might be evident from the financial statements. However, the expenses listed in the profit and loss account are summarised information (it would not be feasible to list each individual payment), and the amount paid in fines might well not be evident. Details of planned improvements, similarly, may not be evident from the financial statements. Although annual financial statements can be of interest to activist groups, they do not necessarily provide a full picture. (Tutorial note: some companies voluntarily publish information about their environmental policies and performance in addition to their financial statements, but they are not obliged by law to do this.)

II

FINANCIAL ACCOUNTING

THE BALANCE SHEET

AIMS AND LEARNING OUTCOMES

Aim of the chapter

To enable students to understand how a balance sheet is prepared.

Learning outcomes

After reading the chapter and completing the related exercises, students should:

- Understand the terminology used in a balance sheet.
- Be able to draw up a balance sheet for a sole trader from a list of account balances and explanatory notes.
- Be able to understand and comment on the basic information conveyed by a balance sheet.

Balance sheet basics

A balance sheet is a financial statement that shows the position of a business at a single point in time. It shows the assets, liabilities and capital of a business. We will now look at these three elements in more detail.

Assets

Assets are resources controlled by a business, which it will use in order to generate a profit in the future. Examples of such resources include:

- Cash in the form of notes and coins, and cash kept in bank accounts.
- Amounts of money that people or organisations owe to the business. Such amounts are described in accounting terminology as **debtors.**
- Items bought by the business to sell on to somebody else, or to process or transform in some way to make saleable goods. Such items are known as **stock** or **inventory** (although note that 'inventory' is a term more commonly used in the USA).

Cash, debtors and stock are categorised as **current assets**. This description reflects the fact that they do not remain static for long. For example, debtors usually pay their bills within a short period of time, stock is sold and then replaced, and the business bank account balance changes very frequently.

Items bought (or sometimes leased) by the business, which will be used over a long period of time are known in accounting terminology as **fixed assets**. 'Fixed' implies that the assets stay in the business for a long time (not that they necessarily stay in one position). Examples are buildings (and the land they stand on), which are bought to house the activities of the business, vans and lorries that can be used for transporting goods and people, and computer hardware and software.

Liabilities

Liabilities are amounts that the business is obliged to pay to other people or organisations. Examples of liabilities include:

- Amounts owing to people or organisations that have provided goods or services on credit (i.e. they provide the goods or services without expecting immediate payment); these amounts are known as **trade creditors.**
- Amounts owing to the government in the form of taxation, for example, corporation tax or value added tax (VAT).
- Loans that will have to be repaid in due course to banks or other lenders.

All of these liabilities are known as **creditors**. The convention in drawing up a balance sheet is to subdivide liabilities into two major categories: (a) long-term liabilities (amounts that do not have to be paid for a year or more after the date of the balance sheet); and (b) current liabilities (amounts that are payable within one year of the balance sheet date).

Capital

Capital is the amount invested by the owner(s) of the business. There may be one or more owners: as we have seen in earlier chapters, in a sole trader business all of the capital is invested by a single owner or proprietor. In a partnership the ownership is split between several individuals.

This question tests understanding of the descriptions of the key balance sheet elements of assets and liabilities described above.

George's retail business sells kitchen utensils, crockery and cutlery. The following are descriptions of some of the items in his balance sheet. For each item fill in the adjacent box with 'Asset' or 'Liability'.

Bank overdraft

Computer and printer used to keep the administrative records of the business

Plates and cups in the stockroom

Cash float kept in the till – £100 in various notes and coins

Loan of £20 000 from George's brother

The accounting equation

A key feature of balance sheets is that they balance. Obvious, perhaps, but what does 'balance' mean in this context? At any point in time a business should be able to provide a complete list of its assets and liabilities, each having a monetary amount. The resources available to the business are the total of assets less the total of liabilities. The total of the net resources is owned by the owner(s) of the business.

Therefore, it is possible to express the basic elements of a balance sheet in the following equation:

Assets less Liabilities equals Capital

Or, using arithmetical terms:

Assets − Liabilities = Capital

This is all very abstract and may be difficult to understand at first. An example will help to illustrate the equation.

Example 6.1 Robert is a wholesaler selling gardening tools to garden centres. His balance sheet at 30 June contains details of his assets, liabilities and capital, as follows:

	£
Assets	
Fixed assets (a small warehouse, a van and a computer)	60 000
Stock (gardening tools)	8 000
Debtors (amounts owed to him by garden centres)	4 000
Cash in the business bank account	6 000
Total assets in the business	78 000
Liabilities	
Trade creditors (amounts owed to the firm that supplies Robert's business with gardening tools)	6 000
Other creditors (amounts owed to the bank)	8 000
Total liabilities in the business	14 000
Net assets (total assets less total liabilities)	64 000
Capital (Robert's resources tied up in the business)	64 000

We have a value in this example for each of the three elements of the accounting equation: assets, liabilities and capital. Robert's capital in the business is £64 000. Although assets come to more than that (£78 000) a total of £14 000 will have to be used up in paying liabilities. £78 000 less £14 000 equals £64 000 which is the amount of Robert's capital.

Summarised under the three basic elements, Robert's balance sheet looks like this:

	£
Assets	78 000
Liabilities	14 000
Net assets (assets less liabilities)	64 000
Capital	64 000

It is therefore logically true (Assets − Liabilities = Capital) that:

1. Net Assets = Capital, and that
2. Liabilities + Capital = Assets, and that
3. Assets − Capital = Liabilities.

We can test these three equations by using the figures from Robert's balance sheet:

1. Net Assets = Capital: £64 000 = £64 000
2. Liabilities + Capital = Assets: £14 000 + £64 000 = £78 000
3. Assets − Capital = Liabilities: £78 000 − £64 000 = £14 000.

Next try these two self-test questions:

Self-test question 6.2 (answer at the end of the chapter)

Saqib's balance sheet at 30 September shows the following items:

	£
Fixed assets	30 000
Stock	5 000
Debtors	4 000
Cash held in the business bank account	3 000
Trade creditors	6 000
Saqib's capital	36 000

1. What is the total of assets in the business?
2. What is the total of liabilities in the business?
3. What is the capital of the business?
4. Write down the figures for the basic accounting equation (Reminder: Assets — Liabilities = Capital) in Saqib's business.

Self-test question 6.3 (answer at the end of the chapter)

Amy's balance sheet at 31 August contains total assets of £58 000 and total liabilities of £30 000. Use the accounting equation to find Amy's capital. (Note that if we know two out of the three elements of the accounting equation we can work out the third.)

Example 6.2 We need to supply the missing figure in each of the following incomplete accounting equations.

1. Capital
Assets are £15 000 and liabilities are £3 000. What is capital? Use the accounting equation (Assets — Liabilities = Capital):

$$£15\,000 - £3\,000 = £?$$
$$£15\,000 - £3\,000 = £12\,000$$

Capital is therefore £12 000.

2. Assets
Capital is £6 000 and liabilities are £18 000. What is the total for assets? Use the accounting equation (Assets — Liabilities = Capital):

$$? - £18\,000 = £6\,000$$
$$£24\,000 - £18\,000 = £6\,000$$

Assets are therefore £24 000.

Drawing up a balance sheet

In this part of the chapter we will look at a business start-up example to see how the balance sheet develops from basic transactions. We will use the accounting equation looked at in the previous section and we will be using the accounting terms described earlier in the chapter. Therefore it is important to have gained a basic understanding of what has been dealt with so far in this chapter. It may be helpful to run through it again, and to do some or all of Exercises 6.1 to 6.15 at the end of the chapter, before moving on to the following case study.

CASE STUDY 6.1 Balance sheet basics

Part 1: Business start-up – the first balance sheet

Following completion of her degree course in textiles, Isobel Buchanan was unable to find a job that really used her skills and knowledge. For the last five years she has worked in a clothing firm where she deals with import and export paperwork. She has maintained her interest in textiles, and continues to produce creative work, but the experience of some of her university friends has convinced her that she does not want to face an uncertain future as an independent textile artist or designer.

Recently, however, events have occurred that have encouraged her to think about leaving her employment to set up a new business. Isobel attended a regional training course on changes in the law affecting businesses that import from outside the European Union. At the coffee break she was introduced by a colleague to Ivan, who runs his own importing business. Ivan has been investigating the possibility of importing hand-made rugs and carpets from the Middle East and India where he has several contacts. He does not want to go into the retail business himself and is examining the possibility of selling his goods wholesale to retailers. He has identified an outlet in London, but is also looking for possible selling opportunities in Scotland. Isobel expresses an interest in seeing the samples and she and Ivan arrange to meet the following week.

At the meeting, Isobel is very impressed by the samples; the quality of the work is very fine and the patterns and colour combinations are striking and unusual. She begins to wonder whether she could set up a retail outlet herself in Scotland. She doesn't know anything about business start-ups or finance, but her uncle, Andrew, is an accountant, and she decides to ask his advice.

Andrew has been of the opinion for a long time that Isobel is more likely to make a success of a career in commerce than in the creative arts. Before she went to university he had tried to persuade her to do an HND in finance or a degree in accountancy, but without success. So, when Isobel outlines her business idea to him he is very receptive and listens carefully. To her considerable surprise he offers to provide her with some financial backing in the form of a loan at a commercial rate of interest. Isobel, who had been wondering how she could possibly persuade a bank to give her a commercial loan, is very keen to take up the offer.

Several months pass. Andrew, although wanting to help his niece, is, after all, an accountant. He insists on Isobel producing a reasoned business plan before he will lend the money. She finds this difficult, but at last succeeds in writing a plan that Andrew finds acceptable. Isobel is prepared to risk her own savings of

£10000 (which she has built up over the last five years with a view to putting down a deposit on a flat) but the business plan shows that she will need a great deal more than that. Andrew and his wife pay the legal fees to have a proper loan agreement drawn up. The terms of the loan are that they will lend Isobel £40000 immediately, with a further loan of up to £40000 available if it is needed. The interest rate is variable, tied to commercial bank rates, and is currently at 6%. The £40000 is to be paid off at the rate of £5000 at the end of each financial year over an eight-year period. However, no repayment will be expected in the first three years of the business while it is getting established.

Andrew and his wife Hannah are well off, and have no children of their own. They intend that their four nieces and nephews should be the main beneficiaries of their wills. Although they want, and expect, to have the loans to Isobel repaid, if Isobel loses all or part of the money they intend to deduct the loss from her share of the inheritance. Hannah thinks they should tell Isobel this so that she won't have to worry too much about paying the money back. Andrew, on the other hand, thinks that it will do Isobel good to have to treat the loan as a proper commercial liability; she is more likely to run the business sensibly if she's forced to worry about meeting the repayments.

On 1 March 20X1 Andrew and his wife give Isobel a cheque for £40000 which she puts into a bank account that she has opened for the business. On the same day she makes a bank transfer of £10000 from her own savings account into the business account. Isobel has handed in her notice at work and is ready to take the plunge into self-employment. She decides to name the business 'Buchanan International Designs'.

Case study discussion

Isobel's new business is 'born' on 1 March 20X1 when the first business transactions take place. We can summarise the transactions described above as follows:

1. Isobel starts her business with an injection of £10000, of her own money which she puts into the new business bank account.

2. Isobel borrows £40000 from her uncle and aunt, which she puts into the new business bank account.

Therefore, on 1 March 20X1 a total of £50000 is paid into the bank account.

We can apply some of the terminology from earlier in the chapter to the events of 1 March:

- An **asset** is established – the balance in the business bank account of £50000.
- A **liability** now exists – the £40000 owed to Andrew and Hannah by the business.
- Isobel's **capital** in the business is the amount she has just put into it – i.e. £10000.

Already, we have the three basic accounting equation elements, and it is then a short step to draw up a balance sheet for the business at 1 March 20X1. The accounting equation in this case is:

Asset (£50000) − Liability (£40000) = Capital (£10000)

Using this, we can draw up the following balance sheet.

Buchanan International Designs – Balance sheet at 1 March 20X1

	£
Asset (bank account)	50 000
Liability (loan from uncle and aunt)	40 000
Net assets	10 000
Capital	10 000

This simple balance sheet statement follows certain conventions that are generally accepted as the norm in accounting in the UK and many other countries:

1. It has a heading showing the name of the business and the date of the balance sheet.
2. It is in vertical format – that is, the figures are neatly arranged in a column.
3. It is headed by a £ sign, telling the reader which currency is being used.
4. Assets are stated first, followed by liabilities. Capital is reported last.
5. The key totals are underlined.
6. The balance sheet is that of the business, rather than of Isobel herself. From its beginning the business has a financial existence distinct from Isobel's personal financial affairs.

Later on in this chapter and in subsequent chapters we will encounter many more complex balance sheet statements. Nevertheless, they all will obey these basic conventions.

The next part of the case study gives us some more information about the progress of Isobel's business.

Part 2: Subsequent transactions

While some business start-ups can be run from home (for example, where people are using their skills in consultancy businesses), a retail business will almost always need shop premises. Isobel knows that the location of her premises will be a key factor in her success (or failure), and she spends a long time looking for a small shop in a suitable location which she can afford to rent. The main streets of towns and cities tend to be occupied by major retail chains (e.g. Boots, Next, Marks & Spencer) and it becomes clear to Isobel early on in her search that she cannot afford even a small shop in the city's main shopping streets. Two or three streets away, however, there is a cluster of smaller shops and galleries specialising in selling art and antiques. Isobel finds a basement shop in this area that has almost exactly four years left to run on its lease.

The cost of the lease comprises two elements. First of all, a sum of £10 000 is payable immediately for the purchase of the right to occupy the premises for four years. This is known as a **lease premium**. After that, there is an annual rental of £14 000, which is payable quarterly in arrears (i.e. at the end of each three-month period during which Isobel occupies the premises). At the end of four years, if she is still in business, Isobel will have to leave the premises, or negotiate a new lease with the landlord. On 2 March 20X1 Isobel pays a cheque out of the business bank account for £10 000 for the lease premium.

The shop is in reasonably good condition, but lacks any kind of display facilities. Isobel commissions a carpenter to produce two wall-mounted display racks and some hollow plywood boxes over which goods can be displayed. The racks are installed on 3 March 20X1 and Isobel writes a cheque to the carpenter for £4500.

Another major purchase is the first consignment of rugs and carpets which Isobel buys from Ivan, the importer. A retail business needs sufficient stock in order to start trading; in Isobel's business it is important to have a wide range of designs for customers to select from. Therefore, she has had to allow quite a large amount of money in her initial business plan for stock purchase. The merchandise comes in four main size categories: small rugs, larger rugs and two sizes of carpet. Isobel expects to be able to sell a larger number of the rugs and so her initial purchase is as follows:

	Cost (£)
30 small rugs at £100 each	3 000
10 larger rugs at £300 each	3 000
10 small carpets at £750 each	7 500
10 larger carpets at £1000 each	10 000
Total purchase of stock	23 500

Ivan delivers the rugs and carpets to Isobel on 4 March so that she can get the shop organised and the displays set up prior to the opening on 10 March. He gives Isobel an invoice for £23 500 which will require payment by 1 April.

Case study discussion

Isobel's business is rapidly growing more complex. Each of the three transactions above makes a difference to the basic balance sheet we drew up earlier at 1 March 20X1.

Lease transaction

The initial payment for the lease represents the acquisition of premises. Although Isobel doesn't own them, she has acquired rights over the shop premises that will last for four years. The payment for the lease is regarded as the acquisition of a fixed asset.

So, a fixed asset with a value of £10 000 is acquired, and can now be included in the balance sheet. However, the value of cash in the business changes by an equivalent amount; Isobel has written a cheque for £10 000, which comes out of the business bank account. In summary, fixed assets increase by £10 000 while the bank account asset decreases by £10 000.

This transaction has no effect on liabilities or capital. The balance sheet still balances – all that has happened is that the nature of the assets has changed. We can draw up a balance sheet at 2 March that reflects the effect of the lease acquisition:

Buchanan International Designs: Balance sheet at 2 March 20X1

	£
Fixed assets	
Lease	10 000
Current assets	
Bank account*	40 000
	50 000

▶

	£
Long-term liabilities	
Liability (loan from uncle and aunt)	40 000
Net assets	10 000
Capital	10 000

*The balance on the bank account was £50 000 before Isobel wrote the cheque for £10 000. After she has issued the cheque the bank account balance drops to £40 000.

Some additional descriptions have now been introduced into the balance sheet. The business has acquired a fixed asset so it is worthwhile making the distinction between fixed and current assets. Similarly, it is more informative to describe the liability of the loan as long term; this description tells the reader of the balance sheet that the loan does not have to be repaid in the near future. (Note that the totals for net assets and for capital are £10 000; these amounts are unchanged from the previous balance sheet.)

Part 2 of the case study gives some details about the rental that Isobel will have to pay. However, the rental transactions have not yet taken place and so have no effect on the current balance sheet.

Display racks transaction

When Isobel writes the cheque for £4500 to the carpenter on 3 March she is buying another asset for the business. It is reasonable to assume that the display racks and boxes will be used over a long period of time in the business, and that they are therefore fixed assets. In summary, fixed assets increase by £4500 while the bank account asset decreases by £4500.

We can draw up a balance sheet at 3 March that reflects the effect of the purchase of the display racks:

Buchanan International Designs: Balance sheet at 3 March 20X1

	£
Fixed assets	
Lease	10 000
Display stands	4 500
	14 500
Current assets	
Bank account*	35 500
	50 000
Long-term liabilities	
Liability (loan from uncle and aunt)	40 000
Net assets	10 000
Capital	10 000

*The balance on the bank account was £40 000 before Isobel wrote the cheque to the carpenter for £4500. After she has issued the cheque the balance on the bank account drops to £35 500.

The balance sheet at 3 March looks slightly more complicated. There are two descriptions under fixed assets, each with a cost figure shown. This presentation gives more information than would be the case if the two figures were simply lumped together and shown under the general heading of fixed assets. However, the total for fixed assets (£10 000 + £4500 = £14 500) is shown as a subtotal in the balance sheet, so that the reader of the balance sheet can see very quickly the amount that has been spent on the fixed assets. (Note that the totals for net assets and for capital are £10 000; these amounts are unchanged from the previous balance sheet.)

Stock transaction

On 4 March the business acquires its first consignment of rugs and carpets, the stock with which the business will start trading. If Isobel proves to be successful as a dealer in rugs and carpets the stock will be sold, preferably sooner rather than later, and will be replaced by further purchases. Stock is a current asset because it is not expected to remain in the business for a long period. We can see, therefore, that current assets increase because of this transaction. However, in this case there is no effect (yet) on the bank account, because Ivan does not require Isobel to pay for the goods immediately. He is supplying on credit and does not expect to be paid until a month after delivery. So, what has occurred?

- An asset of £23 500 of stock arises, and current assets in the balance sheet will increase by this amount.
- A liability of £23 500 arises; this is a current liability because it will have to be paid in the near future.

Taking this transaction into account, the balance sheet of the business at 4 March 20X1 is as follows:

Buchanan International Designs: Balance sheet at 4 March 20X1

	£	£
Fixed assets		
Lease		10 000
Display stands		4 500
		14 500
Current assets		
Stock	23 500	
Bank account	35 500	
	59 000	
Current liabilities		
Amount owed to Ivan	(23 500)	
Net current assets (£59 000 − £23 500)		35 500
		50 000
Long-term liabilities		
Liability (loan from uncle and aunt)		(40 000)
Net assets		10 000
Capital		10 000

▶

What's going on here? Why are there so many more figures in this balance sheet compared to the previous one? Don't panic. Most of the changes from the previous balance sheet have been made in order to make the balance sheet statement clearer and more useful to the reader. Starting at the top of the balance sheet at 4 March:

- Fixed assets are the same as before at £14 500.

- Under current assets we now have the new asset of stock. There are now two categories of current asset, so it is helpful to summarise current assets by means of a total figure of £59 000.

- We have now introduced the new category of **current liabilities**; that is, in this case, the £23 500 due to be paid to Ivan in about a month's time.

- It is a convention, when drawing up balance sheets, to show a total for 'net current assets' – that is, current assets less current liabilities. In this balance sheet the total for net current assets is £35 500. Because the balance sheet is getting a little bit crowded with figures at this point, we pull the figures relating to current assets and current liabilities to one side and show them in a separate column. Once the reader gets accustomed to this convention it makes understanding what is going on in the balance sheet very much easier.

- The other change we have introduced is the use of brackets around liability figures in order to emphasise the fact that they are being deducted from assets. It is not strictly necessary to do this, but it may help understanding by creating an obvious distinction between the figures relating to assets and those relating to liabilities.

Note that: the totals for net assets and for capital are £10 000; these amounts are unchanged from the previous balance sheet.

Case study summary

It will take most students quite a while to understand and thoroughly assimilate all the details presented in this case study. It may be necessary to run through it several times and to refer back to it while working on the questions at the end of the chapter. However, it is worth persevering in order to grasp the basic principles, which can then be applied to understanding the balance sheets of very complex businesses.

Each transaction that we have examined makes the balance sheet a little more complicated – and by the end of this stage of the case study the business is only four days old and hasn't even made a sale yet. However, it is not necessary or even useful in practice to spend time at the end of each day drawing up a balance sheet for the business. Balance sheets are drawn up on a periodic basis – at least once a year, possibly as often as once a month, but practically never on a daily basis. We have examined the balance sheet at the end of each of the four days simply in order to make it clear how an individual transaction can change asset and liability balances.

Note, however, that the basic balance sheet totals (£10 000 for net assets and £10 000 for capital) have remained the same at the end of each of the four days. All that has changed is the composition of the assets and liabilities of the business. So, what would it take to alter the balance sheet totals? Let's look at the possibilities. First, the value of capital, and therefore of net assets, could increase. This would happen in either of two situations:

1. The owner (or owners) of the business put some more of their own personal resources into it. In Isobel's case she might, for example, sell her car, and put the money into the business bank account. This would increase net assets and also her capital.

2. The business increases its net assets by making a profit. An organisation run on commercial terms will attempt to make profits. In Isobel's case she will do this by selling rugs and carpets at a price greater than the price she paid for them.

Alternatively, the value of capital, and therefore of net assets, could decrease. This would happen in either of two situations:

1. The owner (or owners) of the business take out some of the resources they have put into it. The owner(s) will want or need to remove some part of the assets (probably in the form of cash). Net assets decrease and so does capital. The removal of the assets is traditionally known as **drawings**. (The issue of owners extracting cash from their businesses is discussed at greater length in Chapter 3.)

2. The business decreases its net assets by making a loss. If goods are sold for amounts that do not, overall, cover the costs of the business, a loss will be made and the net assets, and capital, will be depleted.

In the situation described in the case study, the business has not yet reached the point where it is open for trading. No sales have been made, and, therefore, no profit exists.

At this point we will leave Isobel's business, but we will develop this case study further in a later chapter.

More practice with balance sheets

The case study for this chapter examined a new business start-up to illustrate the basics of preparing a balance sheet. This section applies the knowledge gained from the earlier part of the chapter to established businesses that are preparing balance sheets at the end of an accounting period.

Each business – whether a company, a partnership or a sole trader (like Isobel) – has a year-end date, at which point it prepares its annual accounts. Conventionally, year-ends tend to fall at the ends of months (31 December, 31 March, etc.) but there is no rule about this. It would be quite acceptable to have a year-end of 3 January, for example.

The next example deals with preparing a balance sheet for an established business.

Example 6.3 Dipak has been established for several years in a business selling computers for home use and for small businesses. As well as selling standard systems he also builds PC systems to customers' specifications and sells a limited range of software packages, printers and fax machines. He runs the business from shop premises that he owns on a freehold basis.

Dipak's business has the following balances at its annual year-end, 31 August.

▶

	£
Freehold premises	53 000
Shop fittings and equipment	6 300
Cash	60
Loan from brother (no fixed repayment date)	8 000
Stock of PCs	48 000
Printers, modem cards, etc.	9 650
Bank overdraft	13 750
Debtors (amounts owed by businesses for computers)	5 250
Dipak's capital	99 130
Software	15 000
Creditors (due to suppliers)	16 380

First, we need to establish which categories each of the balances fall into – asset, liability or capital:

	£	Category
Freehold premises	53 000	Asset
Shop fittings and equipment	6 300	Asset
Cash	60	Asset
Loan from brother (no fixed repayment date)	8 000	Liability
Stock of PCs	48 000	Asset
Printers, printer supplies, modem cards, etc.	9 650	Asset
Bank overdraft	13 750	Liability
Debtors (amounts owed by customers)	5 250	Asset
Dipak's capital	99 130	Capital
Software	15 000	Asset
Creditors (due to suppliers)	16 380	Liability

Note: It may be helpful to refer back to the definitions and examples at the beginning of the chapter if any of these classifications are unclear.

Classifying assets

Seven of the items on the list are classified as assets. Which are fixed and which are current? Remember that stock, debtors and cash are categorised as current assets.

The first two items on the list are fixed assets – i.e. freehold premises and the shop fittings and equipment; these have been, and will continue to be, used in the business for a long time.

There are three categories of stock in the list. These will be added together to arrive at the total for stock:

	£
PCs	48 000
Printers etc.	9 650
Software	15 000
Total stock	72 650

As well as fixed assets and stocks, Dipak's business has debtors (amounts owed to the business by customers) of £5250 and cash of £60.

Drawing up the balance sheet

Having done the preliminary work on classification, we can now prepare the balance sheet at 31 August.

Dipak: Balance sheet at 31 August

	£	£
Fixed assets		
Freehold premises		53 000
Shop fittings and equipment		6 300
		59 300
Current assets		
Stock	72 650	
Debtors	5 250	
Cash	60	
	77 960	
Current liabilities		
Bank overdraft	(13 750)	
Creditors	(16 380)	
	(30 130)	
Net current assets (£77 960 − £30 130)		47 830
		107 130
Long-term liabilities		
Liability (loan from brother)		(8 000)
Net assets		99 130
Capital		99 130

Dipak's balance sheet – what does it say?

It should always be remembered that balance sheets are intended to be useful to people as ways of communicating important information about a business. When involved in the difficulties of fitting the figures together and getting the balance sheet to balance it can be difficult to remember that the point of the exercise is to communicate a message.

So what is this balance sheet telling us? We know that Dipak is in business, and we know that he sells computers; that is why the business has stocks of computers, software and so on. But does the business need to have quite so much stock? Let's say the average price that Dipak has paid for a PC is £600. That means that he has approximately 80 systems (£48 000 divided by £600) in stock. How long will it take to sell these items, and will they be out of date soon? Similar questions could be asked about the printers and the software.

Dipak owes his creditors more than £16 000. Presumably they will expect to be paid very soon. How is he going to pay them? The business has a large overdraft with the bank. Will the bank let him borrow more money on overdraft? Even if the debtors were to pay up straight away, there would still be a problem. Does Dipak have more resources of his own that he can put into the business?

Trying to understand this balance sheet leads to asking a lot of questions, which cannot currently be answered. In order to answer the questions we need more information. In the next few chapters we will be looking at other accounting statements that provide more information about businesses.

In the meantime, it is important to bear in mind that the purpose of balance sheets (and accounting in general) is not to provide number puzzles for business students, but is to provide information that actually means something in the context of the real world.

Chapter summary

This chapter has explained the basics of preparing a balance sheet. The main accounting terminology used in the balance sheet has been described, and the accounting equation (Assets − Liabilities = Capital) should by now be familiar.

Students who have worked through this chapter thoroughly should now be able to draw up a balance sheet from a list of balances provided.

The communications aspect of the balance sheet statement has been recognised and discussed, and it should now be possible for students to ask informed questions about the meaning of specific balance sheet statements.

The end-of-chapter exercises follow the answers to the self-test questions. It is important to work through as many as necessary in order to achieve complete understanding of the chapter content, before moving on to the next chapter.

Answer to self-test question 6.1

- Bank overdraft = Liability.
- Computer and printer used to keep the administrative records of the business = Asset.
- Plates and cups in the stockroom = Asset.
- Cash float kept in the till − £100 in various notes and coins = Asset.
- Loan of £20 000 from George's brother = Liability.

Answer to self-test question 6.2

1. The total of assets in Saqib's business is £30 000 (Fixed assets) + £5000 (Stock) + £4000 (Debtors) + £3000 (Cash held in business bank account) = £42 000.
2. There is only one category of liability in the business: trade creditors of £6000. Therefore total liabilities are £6000.
3. Saqib's capital is stated in the question as £36 000.
4. Applying the accounting equation to Saqib's business: Assets (£42 000) − Liabilities (£6 000) = Capital (£36 000).

Answer to self-test question 6.3

Assets − Liabilities = Capital

Therefore, Amy's capital can be calculated as:

£58 000 − £30 000 = £28 000

Exercises

The answers to many of the exercises are set out later in this chapter. However, where the exercise number is followed by 'A' the answer is available only to lecturers. Remember that additional exercises (with answers) are available to students on the book's website.

6.1   Alexander's business manufactures and sells biscuits to supermarkets and grocery shops. Below are descriptions of some of the items in his balance sheet. For each item fill in the adjacent box with 'Asset' or 'Liability'.

Cash kept in a tin in the factory office

Oven

Bank loan, repayable over 5 years

Plastic packaging for biscuits

Flour and sugar

Amounts payable to supplier of dried fruit

6.2   Amir has a consultancy business that he runs from rented offices. The following are descriptions of some of the items in his balance sheet. For each item fill in the adjacent box with Fixed asset, Current asset, Long-term liability or Current liability.

Value added tax (VAT) payable to Customs and Excise

Office computer

m Lomax plc for consultancy
t by Amir

103

ə repaid in three years' time

le to stationery supplier

6.3A   Adrian owns and runs a restaurant. The following are descriptions of some of the items in his balance sheet. For each item fill in the adjacent box with Fixed asset, Current asset, Long-term liability or Current liability.

Restaurant tables

Wages owed to waiter

Bank account containing £3850

Tax bill due to Inland Revenue

Restaurant premises

Mortgage (i.e. loan) from bank to buy restaurant premises

Food supplies in kitchen fridges

Amounts due to baker for bread supplied over the last month

6.4   Brian's balance sheet shows totals for assets of £83 000 and £36 500 for liabilities. Use the accounting equation to find the total for Brian's capital.

6.5   Basil's capital in his business is £43 650. The business assets total £188 365. Use the accounting equation to find the total for liabilities.

6.6A   Bernie's business has liabilities of £63 000. His capital is £28 000. What is the total for assets?

6.7   Brenda's business has fixed assets of £12 000, current assets of £8500 and total liabilities of £17 300. What is Brenda's capital?

6.8A   Bjork's capital in her business is £97 000. The total for current liabilities is £31 000. There are no long-term liabilities. What is the total for assets?

6.9   Brigitte's business has fixed assets of £27 000, current assets of £16 000, current liabilities of £12 000 and long-term liabilities of £10 000. What is her capital in the business?

6.10   Bryony's balance sheet shows the following totals:

	£
Fixed assets	35 840
Current assets	16 500
Current liabilities	12 000
Long-term liabilities	6 000

Which of the following is Bryony's capital in the business?

a) £70 340

b) £1 340

c) £46 340

d) £34 340.

6.11A Bashir's balance sheet shows the following totals:

	£
Capital	68 350
Fixed assets	79 403
Current assets	16 276

Which of the following is the total of liabilities in Bashir's business?

a) £131 477

b) £27 329

c) £5 223

d) £164 029

6.12   Benito's balance sheet shows the following totals:

	£
Fixed assets	39 497
Current assets	26 004
Current liabilities	16 777
Capital	33 058

Work out the missing figure for long-term liabilities. (Hint: first, work out total liabilities using the accounting equation.)

6.13A Benedict's balance sheet shows the following totals:

	£
Current assets	716 237
Current liabilities	426 663
Long-term liabilities	100 000
Capital	1 373 424

What is the total for fixed assets?

6.14   Blanche's balance sheet shows the following totals:

	£
Fixed assets	36 609
Current assets	38 444
Current liabilities	26 300
Capital	39 477

Which of the following is the missing figure for long-term liabilities?

a) £61 876

b) £9 276

c) £15 012

d) £67 612.

6.15   Callum's balance sheet at 31 July shows the following:

	£
Fixed assets	18 337
Stock	12 018
Debtors	365
Cash	63
Bank overdraft	3 686
Creditors	2 999

a) What is the total of assets in the business?

b) What is the total of current assets?

c) What is the total for liabilities?

d) What is Callum's capital?

6.16   Ciera's business has the following balances at 31 December:

	£
Stock	18 600
Creditors	23 700
Cash in bank account	13 000
Long-term loan	20 000
Fixed assets – premises	39 000
Amounts owed by customers	6 500
Amounts owed to Inland Revenue	3 800
Ciera's capital	29 600

Prepare Ciera's balance sheet at 31 December. Use the format shown in the chapter – i.e. start at the top with fixed assets, then work down the page presenting current assets, then current liabilities (remember to show a total for net current assets), then long-term liabilities. Capital is shown at the bottom.

Remember to line up columns of figures neatly, and to use a proper heading for the balance sheet.

6.17A   Carmela's business has the following balances at 18 October:

	£
Amounts due from customers	16 303
Fixed assets – machinery	12 722
Amounts payable to creditors for materials	6 868
Bank balance	6 993
Cash on the premises	120
Amounts payable to the Inland Revenue	396
Long-term loan from sister	1 800
Fixed assets – office computer	1 060
Stocks of goods	17 721

Prepare the balance sheet for Carmela at 18 October. (Note: no figure is given for Carmela's capital – it has to be calculated from the information given above.)

6.18 Dan's balance sheet at 1 May is as follows:

	£	£
Fixed assets		30 000
Current assets		
Stock	15 000	
Debtors	5 000	
Bank account	18 000	
	38 000	
Current liabilities		
Creditors	(16 000)	
Net current assets (£38 000 − £16 000)		22 000
Net assets		52 000
Capital		52 000

(1) On 2 May Dan pays £1500 for an office computer to help him keep the business accounts. (2) On 3 May Dan pays a creditor £3000. Explain how his balance sheet will be affected by the two transactions and show the new balance sheet at 3 May after taking account of both transactions.

6.19A Diana's balance sheet at 28 August is as follows:

	£	£
Fixed assets		13 500
Current assets		
Stock	10 300	
Debtors	1 200	
Bank account	1 000	
Petty cash	600	
	13 100	
Current liabilities		
Creditors	(6 400)	
Net current assets (£13 100 − £6 400)		6 700
Net assets		20 200
Capital		20 200

1. Diana has saved up some money for her holiday, but decides to put it into the business instead. She pays a cheque for £2000 into the business bank account on 29 August.
2. On 30 August the business receives a cheque for £600 from one of its debtors.

Explain how her balance sheet will be affected and show the new balance sheet at 30 August after taking account of both transactions.

6.20 Ernest runs an art gallery. He organises exhibitions at which painters and sculptors show their work. If a piece of art work is sold, Ernest takes a commission of 50% of the selling price. He banks the cash and then pays out what is due to the artists. He held a successful exhibition in November, and is planning the next one for January. Each time he holds an exhibition he pays for advertising and sending out leaflets to people on his mailing list, and also for wine and soft drinks on the opening night of the exhibition. Putting on the exhibition in January will cost him around £4000.

Ernest has the following assets and liabilities at 31 December:

	£
Gallery premises	68 000
Cash at bank	18 600
Amounts payable to artists	16 560
Office equipment	2 260
Amounts payable to printers for publicity material for recent exhibition	1 600
Capital	70 700

1. Prepare Ernest's balance sheet at 31 December.

2. Write a brief assessment of Ernest's business position as shown by the balance sheet.

6.21A Erik has a retail business selling china and glass ornaments from a small shop in a town centre. He has the following balances at his year-end of 30 November:

	£
Freehold premises	16 800
Shop fittings, computer, till, etc.	8 300
Cash – float in till	600
Loan from mother (no fixed repayment date)	2 000
Stock	10 300
Bank overdraft	3 800
Creditors – due to suppliers	3 200
Creditors – due to Customs and Excise for VAT	800
Capital	26 200

Note that the amounts due to suppliers include £2200 owed to one company, Ornamental Glass Products Limited. The company has been waiting for payment for this amount since August and Erik has been rung up on several occasions by the company's chief accountant requesting immediate payment. Erik has an overdraft limit of £4000.

1. Prepare Erik's balance sheet at 30 November.

2. Erik has asked you to advise him on whether he should ask the bank manager for an increase in his overdraft limit. Assess Erik's position at 30 November as shown by the balance sheet.

Answers to exercises

6.1   ● Cash kept in a tin in the factory office = Asset.

● Oven = Asset.

● Bank loan, repayable over five years = Liability.

- Plastic packaging for biscuits = Asset.
- Flour and sugar = Asset.
- Amounts payable to supplier of dried fruit = Liability.

6.2
- Value added tax (VAT) payable to Customs and Excise = Current liability.
- Office computer = Fixed asset.
- Amount due from Lomax plc for consultancy work carried out by Amir = Current asset.
- Bank overdraft* = Current liability.
- Bank loan to be repaid in three years' time = Long-term liability.
- Amount payable to stationery supplier = Current liability

*Tutorial note: some businesses have an almost permanent bank overdraft, which they effectively use as long-term finance. However, a bank overdraft is technically 'repayable on demand', meaning that the bank is entitled to demand repayment at any time. Because of this, bank overdrafts are always classified as current liabilities in the business balance sheet.

6.4   The accounting equation is:

$$\text{Assets} - \text{Liabilities} = \text{Capital}$$

Applying the equation to the information given in the question:

	£
Assets	83 000
Less Liabilities	(36 500)
= Capital	46 500

Brian's capital is £46 500

6.5   In this case we turn the accounting equation around to find liabilities:

$$\text{Assets} - \text{Capital} = \text{Liabilities}$$

	£
Assets	188 365
Less Capital	(43 650)
= Liabilities	144 715

The liabilities in Basil's business total £144 715.

6.7   In this question assets are split into fixed and current assets. However, the basic principle remains the same: (Total assets minus Total liabilities = Capital.

	£
Fixed assets	12 000
Plus Current assets	8 500
= Assets	20 500
Less Liabilities	(17 300)
= Capital	3 200

Brenda's capital is £3200.

6.9   In this question four pieces of information are given. However, the basic accounting equation still holds good.

Total assets = £27 000 (Fixed assets) + £16 000 (Current assets) = £43 000

Total liabilities = £12 000 (Current liabilities) + £10 000 (Long-term liabilities) = £22 000.

Brigitte's capital in the business is Assets − Liabilities, i.e. £43 000 − £22 000 = £21 000.

6.10   Bryony's capital is £34 340 (i.e. answer d)). This is calculated as:

Total assets = £35 840 (Fixed assets) + £16 500 (Current assets) = £52 340

Total liabilities = £12 000 (Current liabilities) + £6 000 (Long-term liabilities) = £18 000

Bryony's capital in the business is Assets − Liabilities, i.e. £52 340 − £18 000 = £34 340.

6.12   Reminder: the accounting equation =

Assets − Liabilities = Capital

or

Assets − Capital = Liabilities

* Assets = £39 497 (Fixed assets) + £26 004 (Current assets) = £65 501
* Capital = £33 058
* Total liabilities therefore = £65 501 − £33 058 = £32 443.

Total Liabilities = Current liabilities + Long-term liabilities

Therefore:

£32 443 = £16 777 + Long-term liabilities

Long-term liabilities therefore = £15 666.

6.14   The missing figure for Long-term liabilities is £9 276 (i.e. answer b). This is calculated as:

* Total assets = £36 609 (Fixed assets) + £38 444 (Current assets) = £75 053
* Capital = £39 477

Therefore:

Total Liabilities = £35 576 (£75 053 − £39 477)

Current liabilities are £26 300, therefore Long-term liabilities = £9 276 (£35 576 − £26 300).

6.15   a) Total assets = £18 337 (Fixed assets) + £12 018 (Stock) + £365 (Debtors) + £63 (Cash) = £30 783.

b) Total current assets = £12 018 (Stock) + £365 (Debtors) + £63 (Cash) = £12 446.

c) Total liabilities = £3 686 (Bank overdraft) + £2 999 (Creditors) = £6 685

d) Callum's capital can be found by using the accounting equation: £30 783 (Total assets) − £6 685 (Total liabilities) = £24 098.

6.16

Ciera's business: Balance sheet at 31 December

	£	£
Fixed assets		
Premises		39 000
Current assets		
Stock	18 600	
Debtors	6 500	
Bank	13 000	
	38 100	
Current liabilities		
Creditors	(23 700)	
Due to Inland Revenue	(3 800)	
	(27 500)	
Net current assets (£38 100 − £27 500)		10 600
		49 600
Long-term liabilities		(20 000)
Net assets		29 600
Capital		29 600

6.18   In transaction (1), Dan is using up £1500 of the amount in the business bank account, but at the same time is increasing fixed assets.

Increase fixed assets by £1500
Decrease bank account by £1500.

In transaction (2), Dan is using up £3000 of the amount in the business bank account, but at the same time is decreasing creditors.

Decrease creditors by £3000
Decrease bank account by £3000.

Dan's business: Balance sheet at 3 May

	£	£
Fixed assets (30 000 + 1 500)		31 500
Current assets		
Stock	15 000	
Debtors	5 000	
Bank account (18 000 − 1 500 − 3 000)	13 500	
	33 500	

	£	£
Current liabilities		
Creditors (16 000 − 3 000)	(13 000)	
Net current assets (£33 500 − £13 000)		20 500
Net assets		52 000
Capital		52 000

Note that the capital in the business has not changed at all between 1 and 3 May.

6.20

Ernest's business: Balance sheet at 31 December

	£	£
Fixed assets		
Gallery premises		68 000
Office equipment		2 260
		70 260
Current assets		
Bank	18 600	
	18 600	
Current liabilities		
Creditors: Payable to artists	16 560	
Creditors: Payable to printers	1 600	
	18 160	
Net current assets (£18 600 − £18 160)		440
Net assets		70 700
Capital		70 700

Once Ernest has paid the artists and the printers (and, presumably, he will have to in the very near future) he will be left with only £440 in the bank. This will not leave him with enough money to pay the costs, which are estimated at £4000, of the exhibition in January. He may be able to obtain the goods and services needed to put on the exhibition on credit (that is, he will not pay for them straight away), but he would be taking the risk that the exhibition is a failure. If it produces no money, or less than the £4000 or so needed to cover essential costs, then Ernest will be in a very difficult position.

He may be able to borrow some money to put the business on a better footing. The only substantial asset the business owns is the art gallery premises. It may be possible to secure a mortgage loan on the property so as to obtain some much-needed cash.

7

THE PROFIT AND LOSS ACCOUNT

AIMS AND LEARNING OUTCOMES

Aim of the chapter

To enable students to understand how a profit and loss account is prepared and how it fits together with the balance sheet.

Learning outcomes

After reading the chapter and completing the related exercises, students should:

- Understand the terminology used in a profit and loss account.
- Be able to draw up a profit and loss account for a sole trader from a list of account balances and explanatory notes.
- Be able to understand and comment on the basic information conveyed by a profit and loss account.
- Combine skills gained as a result of studying Chapters 6 and 7 to draw up a set of financial statements comprising a profit and loss account and balance sheet.

Profit and loss

As noted in the previous chapter, an organisation run on commercial terms will attempt to make profits. In straightforward terms, it does this by selling goods and/or services at prices that will allow it to cover all the expenses of the business, with a surplus remaining.

- **Revenue** (also referred to as 'sales' or 'turnover') is the amount of goods and/or services sold, expressed in monetary terms.
- **Expenses** are the amounts incurred by the business in purchasing or manufacturing the goods sold, and other expenditure on items such as rent and telephone charges.
- **Profit** is the surplus remaining when revenue exceeds expenditure (a desirable state of affairs in a commercial organisation).
- **Loss** is the deficit that occurs when expenditure exceeds revenue (a state of affairs that cannot persist for a long period in a commercial organisation).

The **profit and loss account** summarises the revenue and expenses of an organisation over a period of time. It shows the performance of the business over the period. It gives the reader information showing how well or how badly the business is doing. Note that 'profit and loss account' is the description that is usually used in the UK; however, the term **income statement** is also used, especially internationally.

Categories of commercial activity

Commercial activities can be broadly classified into three types, as follows:

- trading
- manufacturing
- service.

Trading organisations operate as 'middlemen'. Typically, they buy in goods that have been manufactured by another individual or organisation and then sell them on at a higher price to someone else. Isobel's rug and carpet business, which we examined in the case study in the previous chapter, is a trading organisation. Her business has nothing to do with the manufacturing of rugs and carpets; she buys in finished goods and aims to sell them at a profit.

Manufacturing organisations are often complex operations. They manufacture goods that are either sold directly to the public or to trading organisations which then sell them on. For example, a factory manufactures woollen coats which it sells to fashion shops. The factory business sells at prices that cover the various costs of manufacture plus a profit. The shop owners sell at a higher price than they are charged by the factory business, and so they, too, make a profit. By the time the customer in the shop buys the coat, at least two organisations have made a profit on the transaction.

Service organisations sell services rather than goods. For example, a solicitor is not concerned at all with the sale of goods. He or she makes a surplus out of the provision of professional services.

Some organisations have a mixture of activities. Take, for example, a commercial tennis club. It sells annual subscriptions to a range of services such as use of tennis courts and tennis coaching. It also sells a range of shoes and clothing that it buys in from all the well-known sports clothing manufacturers. The club, therefore, operates both trading and service activities.

Profit and loss account for a sole trader

Later, we will examine the financial statements of other types of business. For the moment, however, we will concentrate on drawing up a profit and loss account for a trading business.

The profit and loss account of a trading business splits into two parts: first, the profitability of the buying and selling processes are shown in the trading account, to arrive at a figure of **gross profit**, and then all the other expenses of the business are deducted to arrive at a **net profit**.

The basic layout of the profit and loss account is as follows:

	£
Sales	—
Less: cost of sales	(—)
Gross profit	—
Various expenses	(—)
Net profit	—

First, we will look at the calculation and presentation of the upper part of the profit and loss account to arrive at gross profit. This part of the financial statement is known as the **trading account**.

Example 7.1 Mary has a shop that sells cookers. For the sake of simplicity we will assume that she sells only one type of cooker at a price of £195 each. She buys all the cookers from one manufacturer at a cost of £135 each. Each cooker therefore produces a profit of £60 (£195 less £135). If Mary bought and sold only one cooker the basic trading account information would be as follows:

Mary: Trading account

	£
Sale of cooker	195
Less: cost of cooker	135
Profit	60

The standard terminology used in drawing up a trading account is to describe the deduction for the cost of the goods as **cost of sales**, and the profit shown in the trading account as **gross profit**. We can restate Mary's trading account using this standard terminology:

Mary: Trading account

	£
Sales	195
Less: Cost of sales	135
Gross profit	60

Naturally, if Mary is trying to make a profit out of her business she will hope and expect to sell more than one cooker. If she sells 100 cookers during the course of the month of May 20X2 her trading account will be as follows:

Mary: Trading account for the month ending 31 May 20X2

	£
Sales: 100 cookers @ £195	19 500
Less: cost of sales (100 cookers @ £135)	13 500
Gross profit	6 000

Note that this trading account statement has a proper heading showing Mary's name and the period covered by the statement. It is necessary to show this information so that the reader of the financial statement can be quite sure about the scope of the information covered. Note also the use of the terminology: sales, **cost of sales** and **gross profit**.

Self-test question 7.1 (answer at the end of the chapter)

This question tests the understanding of the key elements of the trading account. Jules sells leather bags from his market stall. The bags are all to the same design but are produced in a range of different colours with slightly different fastenings. During the month of December 20X5 he sells 66 bags at £23 each. He has bought the bags for £14.50 each. Show Jules's trading account for the month.

Movements in stock

In most trading businesses a stock of goods has to be held at all times, so that goods can be displayed and so that there are enough items in stock to satisfy potential demand. For example, in the cooker business outlined above, Mary has found that she needs to have at least five cookers on display at any time in order to show minor differences in styling and colours to her potential customers. Also, she needs to have a further 20 cookers in stock to cope with potential demand. Stock is replaced when necessary in order to ensure that there are always at least 25 cookers on the premises. The factory from which she orders guarantees rapid delivery so Mary does not have to keep a large amount of stock on the premises.

Example 7.2 Let's explore this example further by looking at some transactions during the month of June 20X2. At 1 June Mary has 30 cookers in stock. During June she sells 76 cookers. She orders 35 cookers which are delivered on 10 June and a further 40, delivered on 24 June. How many cookers does Mary have in stock at 30 June? In order to answer this question we can construct a stock movement account:

	Units	£
Opening stock: 30 cookers @ £135	30	4 050
Add purchases: (35 + 40) 75 cookers @ £135	75	10 125
Less: items of stock sold: 76 cookers @ £135	(76)	(10 260)
Closing stock: 29 cookers @ £135	29	3 915

Note that items sold are expressed in terms of the price Mary pays, so that like is compared with like. This account would form part of Mary's business record-keeping but would not be shown as part of the financial statements.

We can use the information about stock movements to draw up a more informative trading account for Mary for the month of June 20X2.

Mary: Trading account for the month ending 30 June 20X2

	Units	£	£
Sales:			
76 cookers @ £195	76		14 820
Cost of sales:			
Opening stock: 30 cookers @ £135	30	4 050	
Add: purchases: 75 cookers @ £135	75	10 125	
	105	14 175	
Less: closing stock: 29 cookers @ £135	(29)	(3 915)	
Cost of sales: 76 cookers @ £135	76		(10 260)
Gross profit for month			4 560

Because this is a simple example we can double check the gross profit. Mary has sold 76 cookers and we know that the gross profit on each is £60.

$$76 \times £60 = £4560$$

so the answer is correct.

Note that the column containing the cost of sales calculation has been pulled to the left-hand side: this is simply to make the trading account easier to read and understand.

Self-test question 7.2 (answer at the end of the chapter)

At 1 January 20X6 Jules has 36 handbags in stock. Usually, January is a poor month for sales. This January is no exception and he sells only 42 bags at £23 each. However, Jules decides to improve the display by buying in several of each of the full range of colours. He buys in total 68 bags in January, at a cost of £14.50 each.

Prepare a stock movement account for Jules, showing the number of units of stock and monetary amounts. Also, prepare a full trading account for the month of January, assuming that all handbags are sold for £23.

Calculating cost of sales

The example of Mary's cooker business has been kept deliberately straightforward in order to illustrate the calculation of cost of sales. However, most businesses, even small ones, would trade in more than one product. It would become very complicated to calculate precise numbers of units in the trading account. It is also unnecessary.

Most businesses have periodic stocktaking, usually to coincide with the date at which the accounts are drawn up. This allows them to keep track of stock, to identify those items that are not selling, to dispose of any damaged items found, and to generally make sure that there have not been any significant losses through poor accounting or theft. Stocktaking identifies the quantities of stock, which can then be valued by reference to how much it cost. Therefore, at the date of the profit and loss account and balance sheet, a valuation of stock is established. Purchases in the period are calculated from delivery records and from the invoices that suppliers send for payment.

Because the stock value at the beginning and the end of the accounting period are established, and because the total purchases are known, it is easy to calculate cost of sales as follows:

	£
Opening stock	—
+ Purchases	—
− Closing stock	(—)
Cost of sales	—

At this point it may be helpful to check this simplified layout against the trading account for Mary in Example 7.2 – note that it shows the same basic components.

Now we will look at Mary's trading account for a one-year period.

Example 7.3 Mary's accounting year ends on 31 October. In respect of the year to 31 October 20X2 she will need information about:

Opening stock on 1 November 20X1
Closing stock on 31 October 20X2
Purchases for the whole year.

At 1 November 20X1 her opening stock value was £4725. At 31 October 20X2 her closing stock value was £6480. During the year she received total purchases of cookers of £153 900. She sold 986 cookers at the normal selling price of £195 and a further 141 at £175 in a special Christmas promotion. This is all the information that is needed to calculate Mary's gross profit for the year.

Mary: Trading account for the year ending 31 October 20X2

	£	£
Sales		
986 cookers @ £195	192 270	
141 cookers @ £175	24 675	
		216 945

▶

Cost of sales

Opening stock at 1 November 20X1	4 725
Add: purchases during year	153 900
	158 625
Less: closing stock at 31 October 20X2	(6 480)
	(152 145)
Gross profit for year	64 800

Calculating net profit

Earlier in this chapter we looked at the basic layout of a profit and loss account, which was as follows:

	£
Sales	—
Less: cost of sales	(—)
Gross profit	—
Various expenses	(—)
Net profit	

The calculation of gross profit has now been covered comprehensively. Provided we know the expenses of the business we can deduct them from gross profit to arrive at the net profit for the period.

Typical business expenses

Expenses vary from one sort of business to another, in both type and importance. For example, one of the main expenses in a road haulier's business will be the costs of fuel and other costs associated with running a fleet of haulage vehicles. By contrast, fuel and motoring costs in a business like Mary's cooker business are likely to be minor.

Expenses could include the following:

- *Cost of premises*: rental, business rates, insurance, electricity, gas, water and repairs.
- *Selling costs and costs of distributing goods*: haulage costs, delivery services, costs of sales' staff salaries and commissions.
- *Administration costs*: telephone, stationery, administrative staff salaries, accountants' and legal fees, computer costs.
- *Finance costs*: bank charges and interest on loans.

In the next example we will continue to look at Mary's business.

Example 7.4 In the year to 31 October 20X2 Mary's business expenses are as follows:

- *Staffing costs*: Mary works in the shop by herself on quieter days, but she employs an assistant for three days per week, and on some extra days in the run-up to Christmas. She pays the assistant £28 per day and he is employed for a total of 165 days during the year to 31 October 20X2.
- *Premises costs*: Mary pays an annual rental for the shop of £17 500, including business rates, any major repair costs and service charges. In addition, in the year to 31 October 20X2 she pays general business insurance of £1350, electricity bills of £1207 and water rates of £795.
- *Administration*: Mary does all of the basic bookkeeping herself, and pays an accountant £585 to produce the final accounts and the tax computation for the Inland Revenue. She spends £103 on stationery, stamps and so on. Her phone bills for the year to 31 October 20X2 come to £312, and she spends £132 on other odds and ends (usually known as 'sundry' expenses) for use in the business. Her membership subscription to the trade association, the Cooker Association of Retailers and Manufacturers (CARM), costs £87 per year.
- *Finance costs*: bank charges total £85. Mary has not borrowed any money so there are no interest charges.

From this information it is possible to complete Mary's profit and loss account to arrive at her net profit for the year, as follows:

Mary: Profit and loss account for the year ending 31 October 20X2

	£	£
Sales (detailed calculation given earlier)		216 945
Less: cost of sales (detailed calculation given earlier)		(152 145)
Gross profit		64 800
Expenses		
Staffing costs (165 days @ £28 per day)	4 620	
Rental of premises	17 500	
Business insurance	1 350	
Electricity	1 207	
Water rates	795	
Accountant's fees	585	
Stationery	103	
Telephone	312	
Sundry expenses	132	
CARM subscription	87	
Bank charges	85	
		(26 776)
Net profit for year		38 024

Note that the expenses are set off in a separate column towards the left hand side of the page; this is to make the statement easier to read.

Mary has made £38 024 out of her business in the year to 31 October 20X2. Out of this she will have to pay tax, but for the sake of simplicity we are going to ignore tax in most of the examples in this book. Ignoring tax, what happens to the £38 024? In the previous chapter we noted that the balance sheet of a sole trader includes a capital account. This account shows the total resources of the owner which are tied up in the business. It includes: capital introduced, plus profits retained in the business, minus drawings, minus any losses made by the business.

So, to answer the question, Mary's net profit of £38 024 goes into her capital account. It is up to her, the owner of the business, to decide how much, if anything, she will withdraw from the business. If it is her only source of income she will almost certainly have to take money out of the business to live on.

In the case study towards the end of this chapter we will examine an example of how the profit and loss account and the balance sheet fit together.

What does the profit and loss account mean?

The profit and loss account and other financial statements are prepared for a purpose; that purpose is to communicate information to people who need to know about the business. So, what information does Mary's profit and loss account communicate? An obvious and important piece of information is that the business is profitable in the year to 31 October 20X2. If this is a typical year, it is possible to draw the general conclusion that the business is currently successful, and may continue to be successful into the future. This general conclusion could be taken a little further by examining gross profit and net profit.

Mary is interested in assessing whether the general trend in her business profitability is upwards or downwards. She supplies the key figures from the profit and loss account for the previous year's trading to 31 October 20X1: sales were £197 535, gross profit was £57 300, expenses totalled £24 904 and net profit was £32 396. This information can be summarised alongside the comparable figures for 20X2:

	20X2	20X1
	£	£
Sales	216 945	197 535
Less: cost of sales	(152 145)	(140 235)
Gross profit	64 800	57 300
Various expenses	(26 776)	(24 904)
Net profit	38 024	32 396

Gross profit analysis

Gross profit is an important element in judging how well or badly a business has performed. However, one isolated figure has little significance on its own. We need to make comparisons between at least two figures.

Comparing two consecutive years

The increase in gross profit is £64 800 − £57 300 = £7500. This is sufficient information to be able to calculate the percentage increase in gross profit from 20X1 to 20X2, as follows:

20X1 gross profit	= £57 300
Increase in gross profit	= £7 500

$$\text{Percentage increase} = \frac{7\,500}{57\,300} \times 100 = 13.1\% \text{ (to one decimal place)}$$

If we were further informed, for example, that the Cooker Association of Retailers and Manufacturers published figures to its members showing that there had been an increase in the gross profit on cooker sales across the UK of 10% between 20X1 and 20X2, we could see that Mary's business has done rather well, and certainly better than average. Mary could achieve this better than average performance by either increasing her sales prices by a rate that is slightly above average, or by negotiating lower prices than average with the supplier, or by a combination of the two factors. As a sole trader, she may well charge higher prices than a large retailer, but customers may be prepared to pay a little more for better service and after-sales advice.

Gross profit margin

'Gross profit margin' is a way of expressing, by means of a percentage, the relationship between gross profit and sales. It simply shows gross profit as a percentage of sales.

Two figures are needed to calculate a gross profit margin: sales and gross profit. Mary's trading account shows both, so we can apply the following formula:

$$\frac{\text{Gross profit}}{\text{Sales}} \times 100 = \text{Gross profit margin } \%$$

In Mary's case:

$$\frac{\pounds 64\,800}{216\,945} \times 100 = 29.9\% \text{ (to one decimal place)}$$

Does this tell us anything useful? Again, not unless we have more information to compare it with. Calculating the comparable ratio for 20X1 uses the gross profit and sales figures for 20X1:

$$\frac{\text{Gross profit}}{\text{Sales}} \times 100 = \text{Gross profit margin } \%$$

$$\frac{57\,300}{197\,535} \times 100 = 29.0\% \text{ (to one decimal place)}$$

To summarise, Mary's gross profit margin in 20X1 was 29.0% and in 20X2 was 29.9%. The gross profit margin in her business has improved. This means that the difference between the selling price and the cost of sales has increased. This may be as a result of selling prices increasing, cost prices reducing, or a combination of the two.

Net profit analysis

We can analyse net profit in the same way as gross profit.

Comparing two consecutive years

Net profit for the year is £38 024, and for 20X1 was £32 396. The fact that it has increased is good news for Mary, but we can extend the analysis further to look at the percentage increase in the same way as we did for gross profit: the increase is £38 024 − £32 396 = £5628.

$$\text{Percentage increase} = \frac{5628}{32396} \times 100 = 17.4\% \text{ (to one decimal place)}$$

The figures for gross profit increased by 13.1% but net profit has increased by an even greater percentage. Why? The answer lies somewhere in the figure for expenses. In 20X1 expenses totalled £24 904, increasing to £26 776 in 20X2, an increase of £1872.

$$\text{Percentage increase} = \frac{1872}{24904} \times 100 = 7.5\% \text{ (to one decimal place)}$$

We could extend the analysis further by looking at the percentage increases and decreases in the separate categories of expense. The basic analysis shows that, although expenses have increased, the level of increase is much lower than the level of increase in gross profit. As a result net profit shows a substantial increase.

Net profit margin

Net profit margin is a way of expressing, by means of a percentage, the relationship between net profit and sales. It shows net profit as a percentage of sales. In Mary's business the net profit margin for 20X2 is as follows:

$$\frac{38024}{216945} \times 100 = 17.5\% \text{ (to one decimal place)}$$

The net profit margin for the previous year, 20X1 is as follows:

$$\frac{32396}{197535} \times 100 = 16.4\% \text{ (to one decimal place)}$$

These calculations show that net profit margin has increased. The conclusion is that, on the basis of the analysis of gross profit and net profit, Mary's business performance seems to have improved substantially.

It is possible to take this type of analysis much further, given more information. In later chapters we will examine more closely the meaning of financial information. However, it is never too soon to start thinking about the information content of financial statements.

Profit and loss accounting in a service business

A service business does not trade in goods and therefore does not need to produce a trading account. In this section of the chapter we will look at the example of a business that supplies services only.

Example 7.5 Tony is a chartered surveyor who supplies property advice services to clients investing in commercial property. He also acts as a commercial property agent, handling the selling of office and retail buildings. He makes commission on

any successful sales. He employs a full-time personal assistant and, in the year to 31 December 20X7 he has employed a student from the local college's estate management course on a day release basis. Other expenses incurred in his business include motor expenses for his large BMW (Tony clocks up around 50 000 miles each year in taking prospective clients to view industrial estates and business parks), entertaining, the cost of office premises, large phone bills for office phone and mobile, and sundries such as professional subscriptions and stationery.

Tony is a sole trader, trading as Aisgarth & Co. He provides the following list of income and expense items from which to draw up a profit and loss account for the year ending 31 December 20X7.

	£
Premises rental	12 570
Electricity bills	2 907
Personal assistant's salary	15 788
Income: commissions on commercial property sales	68 360
Motor expenses	15 370
Office and general insurance	1 003
Professional indemnity insurance (PII)*	1 880
Entertaining	9 351
Telephone charges	3 775
Income: fees for professional advice	23 333
Student's wages	1 200
Sundry office expenses	3 720

*Many qualified professionals, such as surveyors and accountants, are obliged under the regulations of their professional body, to take out special insurance against possible liabilities for professional negligence.

From this list of balances we can draw up Tony's profit and loss account for the year to 31 December 20X7 as follows:

Aisgarth & Co.: Profit and loss account for the year ending 31 December 20X7

	£	£
Fees for professional services	23 333	
Commissions	68 360	
		91 693
Expenses		
Premises rental	12 570	
Electricity	2 907	
Personal assistant's salary	15 788	
Student's wages	1 200	
Motor expenses	15 370	
Insurance	1 003	
PII	1 880	
Entertaining	9 351	
Telephone charges	3 775	
Sundry office expenses	3 720	
		67 564
Net profit for year		24 129

Note that sole traders can trade under a business name, like Tony's. It is quite common for professional businesses like accountants, solicitors and surveyors to trade as 'Something & Co.', even though there is only one sole trader involved.

We can work out a net profit margin figure for Tony's business:

$$\frac{£24\,129}{91\,693} \times 100 = 26.3\%$$

However, in a business like this, the net profit margin may fluctuate quite significantly from one year to another. Expenses are likely to be similar from year to year, but income may vary. Commercial property transactions are usually large, and the commission on a single transaction may amount to many tens of thousands of pounds. However, Tony may have to do a lot of entertaining and travel (both of which, as shown in the profit and loss account, cost the business significant sums) in order to bring off just one deal. Without having other years' results for comparison it is not possible to say whether 20X7 was a good, bad or middling year for Tony.

Preparing the profit and loss account and balance sheet

In this section of the chapter we will prepare the two financial statements for one business in order to demonstrate how they fit together. For this purpose we will look at information in a case study.

CASE STUDY 7.1 Preparing and using accounts

Jimmy Bowden has run a bicycle shop for several years in rented shop premises. He sells new and reconditioned second-hand bikes and also runs a repair service, with the help of a part-time assistant. The business has been moderately profitable and has provided Jimmy with enough to live on. His wife, Sophie, works as a local government officer and between them they have been able to afford to take out a mortgage on a house and go on holiday at least once a year. Jimmy, however, is concerned that his business is in decline. Local parking restrictions near to his shop have increased and people are parking in a multi-storey at the other end of town. Before the restrictions were imposed they used to park in a large free car park in the next street to Jimmy's shop, and so a lot of people would pass his shop on the way into town. This no longer happens and Jimmy thinks that general awareness of the existence of his business has declined. While he still gets a lot of trade from cycling enthusiasts, his sales of children's bicycles have declined and he didn't sell as many as expected just before Christmas. Jimmy suspects that a lot of this trade has been transferred to the bicycle and car maintenance retailing chain store in the town's main shopping centre.

Sales of more expensive bikes to cycling enthusiasts are the more profitable end of Jimmy's business. His stocks of this type of bike are at around the usual level at 28 February, which is Jimmy's year-end. However, the stock room is crammed full of the cheaper bikes reflecting the fact that Christmas sales were lower than expected.

It is now early March 20X5. Jimmy is anxious to get the annual accounts prepared so that he can assess the overall effects of the downturn in trade on his profitability. He is worried about both the immediate and the longer-term future of his business. The business bank account balance at 28 February 20X5 is quite a bit lower than it was at the previous year-end.

Jimmy provides the following list of figures for incorporation into the profit and loss account and balance sheet:

	£
Sales	143 520
Opening stock	9 274
Fixed assets	3 823
Opening capital balance 1 March 20X4	19 776
Cash in the bank account	1 685
Rental expense	16 500
Insurance	2 023
Electricity	2 056
Trade creditors	8 229
Debtors	1 800
Drawings	23 153
Bank interest received	118
Purchases	103 221
Income from repairs services	4 389
Repairs service expenses – bicycle parts	1 317
Administration, finance and sundry expenses	2 278
Assistant's wages	8 902
Closing stock*	16 337

*Jimmy counted and valued the stock on 28 February.

He asks a local business adviser to do two things:

1. Prepare a profit and loss account for the year ending 28 February 20X5 and a balance sheet at that date.

2. Prepare a brief report on the profitability of the business compared to the previous year with some recommendations as to possible courses of action in the future. To help the adviser with this he provides the following information about the year ending 28 February 20X4:

Bicycle sales for the year to 28 February 20X4	£164 728
Gross profit on bicycle sales	£49 418
Gross profit margin	30%
Profit on repairs service	£3 422
Total expenses	£27 263
Interest received	£260
Net profit	£25 837
Net profit margin	15.7%

Case study solution and discussion

Financial statements

First we will prepare the profit and loss account and balance sheet for the business. The list that Jimmy has provided is a jumbled mixture of profit and loss account items and balance sheet items, so a useful preliminary step is to identify a category for each item depending upon whether it goes in the trading account, the rest of the profit and loss account or the balance sheet. For balance sheet items the terminology used in Chapter 6 can be used:

- fixed assets
- current assets
- current liabilities
- long-term liabilities
- capital.

	£	Category
Sales	143 520	Trading account
Opening stock	9 274	Trading account
Fixed assets	3 823	Balance sheet: fixed assets
Opening capital balance 1 March 20X4	19 776	Balance sheet: capital
Cash in the bank account	1 685	Balance sheet: current assets
Rental expense	16 500	Profit and loss account
Insurance	2 023	Profit and loss account
Electricity	2 056	Profit and loss account
Trade creditors	8 229	Balance sheet: current liabilities
Debtors	1 800	Balance sheet: current assets
Drawings	23 153	Balance sheet: capital
Bank interest received	118	Profit and loss account
Purchases	103 221	Trading account
Income from repairs services	4 389	Profit and loss account
Repairs service expenses – bicycle parts	1 317	Profit and loss account
Administration, finance and sundry expenses	2 278	Profit and loss account
Assistant's wages	8 902	Profit and loss account
Closing stock	16 337	Trading account and balance sheet: current assets

Note that closing stock always appears in both the trading account and the balance sheet as a current asset. Stock that remains unsold at the balance sheet is deducted, as we have seen, in arriving at the cost of sales figure. However, it is also an asset of the business, because it can be sold to make money in the following accounting period.

Having categorised all the items the next stage is to pick out those that appear in the trading account, and then prepare the trading account. Then, immediately below it, the rest of the profit and loss account items are listed, ending with net profit. Remember that a heading with the name of the business (in this case Jimmy simply uses his own name – which is common among sole traders) and a description of the financial statement is always required.

Jimmy Bowden: Profit and loss account for the year ending 28 February 20X5

	£	£
Sales		143 520
Less: cost of sales		
Opening stock	9 274	
Add: purchases	103 221	
	112 495	

Less: closing stock	(16 337)	
		(96 158)
Gross profit		47 362
Repairs service: income	4 389	
Repairs service: expenses – bicycle parts	(1 317)	
		3 072
Other income – bank interest received		118
		50 552
Expenses		
Rental expense	16 500	
Insurance	2 023	
Electricity	2 056	
Administration, finance and sundry expenses	2 278	
Assistant's wages	8 902	
		(31 759)
Net profit		18 793

Once all of the balances have been put into the profit and loss account the remainder should all relate to the balance sheet, which can then be prepared.

Jimmy Bowden: Balance sheet at 28 February 20X5

	£	£
Fixed assets		3 823
Current assets		
Stock	16 337	
Debtors	1 800	
Cash	1 685	
	19 822	
Current liabilities		
Creditors	(8 229)	
Net current assets (£19 822 – £8 229)		11 593
Net assets		15 416
Capital		
Opening capital balance 1 March 20X4	19 776	
Add: net profit for the year	18 793	
	38 569	
Less: drawings	(23 153)	
Closing capital balance 28 February 20X5		15 416

The capital account shows the resources committed to the business by the owner. The balance on the capital account increases or decreases in the following ways, noted earlier in the chapter: Capital introduced, plus Profits retained in the business, minus Drawings, minus any losses made by the business. Jimmy Bowden's capital account, as shown in his balance sheet at 28 February 20X5, has been increased by the amount of net profit for the year (calculated in the profit and loss account) and has been decreased by the drawings he has made from the business.

Profitability

Having prepared the profit and loss account and balance sheet for Jimmy's business, it is now possible to address his questions about the profitability of the business. A logical first step is to take the table of figures he provided for 20X4 and slot in the equivalent figures for 20X5:

	20X5	20X4
Bicycle sales for the year	143 520	164 728
Gross profit on bicycle sales	47 362	49 418
Gross profit margin	33%	30%
Profit on repairs service	3 072	3 422
Total expenses	31 759	27 263
Interest received	118	260
Net profit	18 793	25 837
Net profit margin	13.1%	15.7%

Note: calculation of the gross profit margin is as follows:

$$\frac{£47\,362}{143\,520} \times 100 = 33\%$$

Calculation of the net profit margin is as follows:

$$\frac{£18\,793}{143\,520} \times 100 = 13.1\%$$

From this information a report with recommendations can be constructed by the business adviser, as follows:

18 March 20X5

Report to Jimmy Bowden on business profitability based on the financial statements at 28 February 20X5

There has been a substantial decline in sales, gross and net profits and net profit margin between 20X4 and 20X5. The fall in sales is over £20 000, which represents a decline of almost 13%. The effect on gross profit is not quite so significant because the gross profit margin percentage has actually improved. This is presumably because the sales of higher value bicycles to enthusiasts produce better profit margins. There has been a small drop in profitability in the repairs service but this is a fairly insignificant part of the business.

Total expenses have increased from £27 263 to £31 759, an increase of 16.5% which seems high in the context of a low general inflation rate in the economy. A more detailed comparison of expenses would be useful in order to pinpoint the specific expenses that have risen. There may be a need for better control of business expenses.

Net profits have fallen from £25 837 to £18 793, and the net profit margin has fallen from 15.7% to 13.1%. The decline is significant and an action plan should be drawn up to address the problems the business faces.

The business is not under immediate threat. The bank balance at 28 February 20X5 is £1685 and there are no long-term borrowings. But, creditors total £8229, and there could be problems if they start to press for immediate payment. However, because of the good record of profitability in the past, the bank is likely to grant overdraft facilities if they are required. The level of drawings from the business of a little over £23 000 is not justified by the present level of profitability. Closing stock is much higher than opening stock because of the shortfall in Christmas sales.

Recommendations
1. Mr Bowden should consider a campaign of local advertising. This could be allied to a stock clearance sale at discounted prices.
2. The current level of business profitability does not support drawings at the level of £23 000 per year. Mr Bowden should plan for a lower level of personal expenditure until business profitability improves.
3. Business expenses should be considered item by item to identify areas where savings might be possible.
4. If other measures fail, the possibility of moving to new shop premises nearer the centre of town could be considered. Suitable premises should be identified and a business plan and budget drawn up on the basis of the likely increase in sales and expenses if the move were to be made.

Signed: Business adviser

Case study summary

This case study pulls together in one example much of the contents of Chapters 6 and 7. Students should ensure that they thoroughly understand how the figures in the financial statements fit together before attempting the more complex of the questions at the end of the chapter.

In this case study we have been concerned with two major elements of accounting: first, the preparation of financial statements, and, secondly, the significance of the information they convey to the reader. Both elements are important, but for business students, the second element is probably much more useful and relevant to their future careers. All businesses have access to accountants and accounting technical staff who are skilled in producing financial statements. Business students, in their future careers, may never have to draw up the statements themselves, but they will certainly have to be able to understand the financial statements that other people have prepared.

Chapter summary

This chapter has explored the basics of preparing a profit and loss account. Students should now understand the principal components of the profit and loss account, and should be ready to undertake the end-of-chapter exercises.

The chapter has covered not only preparation of the profit and loss account but also has started to consider the information content of the statement. Calculation of changes in certain items has been covered, as have calculations of gross and net profit margin. Students should be able to comment on the basic information conveyed in the profit and loss account.

Finally, the chapter drew upon knowledge and skills gained as a result of studying Chapter 6 to produce both a profit and loss account and a balance sheet from a set of given information.

The end-of-chapter exercises follow the answers to the self-test questions. It is important to work through as many as necessary to achieve complete understanding of the chapter content, before moving on to the next chapter.

Answer to self-test question 7.1

Jules: Trading account for the month ending 31 December 20X5

	£
Sales: 66 bags @ £23	1 518
Cost of sales: 66 bags @ £14.50	957
Gross profit	561

Note: the heading specifying the name of the business and the period covered by the trading account is essential information and must not be omitted.

Answer to self-test question 7.2

Jules: Stock movement account for January 20X6

	Units	£
Opening stock: 36 bags @ £14.50	36	522
Add purchases: 68 bags @ £14.50	68	986
Less: items of stock sold: 42 bags @ £14.50	(42)	(609)
Closing stock: 62 bags @ £14.50	62	899

Note that this account is part of Jules's business records. It is not shown in his financial statements.

Jules: Trading account for the month to 31 January 20X6

	Units	£	£
Sales			
42 bags @ £23	42		966
Cost of sales			
Opening stock: 36 bags @ £14.50	36	522	
Add: purchases: 68 bags @ £14.50	68	986	
	104	1 508	
Less: closing stock: 62 bags @ £14.50	(62)	(899)	
Cost of sales: 42 bags @ £14.50	42		(609)
Gross profit for month*			357

*Check: each bag sold gives a gross profit of £23 – £14.50 = £8.50. If Jules sells 42 bags he expects to make a profit of 42 × £8.50 = £357

Exercises

The answers to many of the exercises are set out later in this chapter. However, where the exercise number is followed by 'A' the answer is available only to lecturers. Remember that additional exercises (with answers) are available to students on the book's website.

7.1   Jackie sells garden furniture in sets comprising a dining table and four chairs. She purchases each set for £75 from the manufacturer and retails a set for £132. At the beginning of June 20X1 Jackie has 30 sets in stock. At 30 June 20X1 the stock room contains 42 sets. She sells 35 sets during the month.

1. How many sets of dining table and chairs has Jackie purchased during the month?
   a) 107
   b) 47
   c) 23
   d) 37.

2. What is Jackie's cost of sales figure for the month?
   a) £4425
   b) £4620
   c) £2625
   d) £1875.

3. What is Jackie's gross profit for June?
   a) £2745
   b) £1425
   c) £6783
   d) £1995.

7.2   Jay's business is shoe retailing. He has bought in a special purchase of 1000 pairs of trainers for £8500. He sells 750 pairs quite quickly at a retail price of £15.50 per pair. Then, in order to clear the stock out of the shop, he reduces the selling price to £12.50 and clears a further 200 pairs. The remaining 50 pairs are put into a bargain bin at a price of £5 per pair and these sell during the shop's autumn sale.

What is Jay's gross profit on this line of trainers? How much gross profit would he have made if he had been able to sell the whole consignment at £15.50 per pair?

7.3A Jin-Ming's mail order business sells trampolines. The selling price is £400 for a standard size trampoline and £550 for a large one. The opening stock at 1 January 20X3 is 6 standard trampolines and 5 large. The cost of the trampolines to Jin-Ming is £260 (standard) and £330 (large). In the year to 31 December 20X3 Jin-Ming sells 30 standard and 17 large trampolines. He could have sold more of the large size but the manufacturer stopped making them part-way through the year. Jin-Ming's purchases for the year totalled £14 880 including the purchase of 12 large trampolines.

a) Draw up Jin-Ming's trading account for the year ending 31 December 20X3.

b) Calculate the gross profit on the sale of large and standard trampolines respectively.

7.4 During the year Jake sells 8000 units of stock at £42.50 each. The gross profit on each unit is £17.50. He purchased stock at a total cost of £197 300 and still had £17 400 in stock at the year-end. What was Jake's opening stock?

7.5 Jethro sells an extensive range of children's toys. He likes to be well informed at all times about the performance of his business. Part of the routine work of his administrative assistant is to draw up a monthly trading account so that Jethro can check on gross profit levels. Information about sales and purchases relating to a three-month period, October–December 20X2, is as follows:

	October	November	December
	£	£	£
Sales	39 370	48 998	56 306
Purchases	37 085	40 830	6 250

Stocks at the beginning of October are valued at £30 863. Stocks at the end of each of the three months are as follows: October £43 258; November 53 190; and December 23 980.

Draw up a trading account for Jethro's business for each of October, November and December 20X2.

7.6A Jodie is a wholesaler of electrical discount goods. She buys in end-of-line and seconds quality stock from manufacturers and sells it on to small electrical retailers. She has to take advantage immediately of any special offers that manufacturers make available; if she does not the manufacturers will sell to one of her competitors. Therefore, her stock levels can fluctuate substantially from one week to the next. The level of sales is not steady from month to month; it depends upon what is in stock and whether there is much demand for the items Jodie currently has in her warehouse.

At the beginning of March Jodie's stock is valued at £93 882 and comprises principally kettles, toasters and dishwashers. An unexpected surge in demand by small retail wholesalers for these items results in a high level of sales in March of £89 907. By the end of March stock has dropped to £34 920. At the end of

April, as the result of a special purchase of electric blankets it has gone up to £82 860 dropping back only slightly to £75 918 at the end of May. Jodie knows that she will find it difficult to dispose of most of this stock before the end of the summer.

Sales for April are £31 241 and for May, £40 270. Purchases for each of the three months are: March £3074; April £65 747; and May £18 911.

a) Draw up trading accounts for each of the three months.

b) Discuss the business and financial problems Jodie would encounter in running this type of wholesaler operation.

7.7 Keith has small shop unit in a town centre selling ready-made sandwiches and a range of cakes, bottled drinks, crisps and similar snack foods, mainly to office workers. At the end of each day any surplus sandwiches and cakes are taken round to the local shelter for the homeless. The only stock kept in the shop are supplies of drinks and snack foods in packets. Anything that has passed its sell-by date is disposed of.

The value of stock in Keith's business is low. Apart from the cost of food, drinks and similar items, his principal business expenses are rental and staff wages. He employs two full-time and a part-time member of staff. His accounting year-end is 31 December.

Information about the business expenses is as follows:

- *Staff costs.* The two full-time members of staff are paid £149 per week each for a five-day week, with four weeks paid holiday in each year. During staff holidays, Keith's wife, Penny, and their daughter Gloria, come in and help out. Penny works for nothing but Gloria is no fool, and insists on payment of £149 for each of the four weeks she works each year. The part-time member of staff is a student who works all day on Saturday for £28. She gets no holiday pay or sick pay, and during the year to 31 December 20X9 has worked 45 Saturdays.

- *Shop rental.* Keith is appalled at the level of shop rental he pays for a very small unit in the town centre. Under his lease arrangement his rental was due to increase on 1 January 20X9; it increased from £17 400 to £25 750 for the year. As a result Keith has had to increase his prices to customers.

- *Other premises costs.* These include the following:

	£
Business rates	2 998
Gas	986
Electricity	1 351
Insurance	1 850
Sundry shop supplies	96

- *Administrative and financial expenses.* The helpful Penny keeps the books of the business, so Keith saves on accountants' fees. He pays the accountant £375 for tax advice. He has also paid a solicitor £220 for advice about resisting the rent increase. Keith has paid bank charges during the year of £360 and bank interest of £284. Phone bills total £382 for the year, stationery was £35 and office sundries were £93.

Keith's sales for the year are £183 600 on which he has made gross profit of £88 128. Draw up Keith's profit and loss account for the year ending 31 December 20X9.

7.8A   Kerry owns the concession to run a souvenir shop at a tourist location near London. She sells souvenir tea towels, cards, biscuits, and various toys and gifts. Kerry's sales for the year to 30 September 20X3 are £121 040. Her gross profit margin is 50%. The business expenses for the year are as follows:

- *Staffing*. The shop is open for ten months of the year with a very busy period from Easter to the end of August. During that period Kerry employs two members of staff at an hourly rate of £5 for as many hours as necessary. The time sheets for hours worked between April and August in 20X3 show the following monthly totals:

	Hours worked
April	120
May	160
June	210
July	280
August	280

- *Premises*. Kerry pays a basic rental of £18 000 per annum for the shop premises to the local authority, which owns the tourist attraction. In addition, she pays a variable contribution calculated at 5% of net profits after taking all other expenses into account. Premises costs other than rental total £4521 for the year.

- *General and administration costs*. These are as follows for the year ending 30 September 20X3:

	£
Bookkeeping and accountancy fees	745
Telephone	415
Sundry charges	169
Insurance	1 200

Prepare Kerry's profit and loss account for the year ending 30 September 20X3.

7.9   Leon runs a retail grocery business dealing in luxury and delicatessen goods. In 20X6 sales are £295 993, with cost of sales at £242 085. The equivalent figures for 20X5 are sales of £287 300 and cost of sales of £235 920. Calculate:

1. Leon's gross profit margin in both years.
2. The increase in sales.
3. The percentage increase in sales.
4. The increase in gross profit.
5. The percentage increase in gross profit.

7.10A   Lulu's sales in 20X3 are £115 399. The following year, 20X4, sales increase by 4.3%. In 20X5 sales are 7.8% higher than they were in 20X3. Gross profit margin in each of the three years is:

20X3: 19.3%
20X4: 21.4%
20X5: 18.7%

Calculate cost of sales for each of the three years, 20X3, 20X4 and 20X5 (working to the nearest £).

7.11 The summarised results of Louise's business for the three years to the end of 20X8 are as follows:

	20X8 £	20X7 £	20X6 £
Sales	291 318	282 400	269 340
Cost of sales	(213 916)	(206 420)	(196 071)
Gross profit	77 402	75 980	73 269
Expenses	(52 394)	(51 720)	(49 270)
Net profit	25 008	24 260	23 999

Calculate the gross and net profit margins for each year and comment briefly on the general trends in the business trading results.

7.12A In 20X8 Lola's net profit margin has fallen to 9.8% from 10.2% in the previous year. Her gross profit margin, on the other hand, has increased from 30.2% to 33.8%. Sales in 20X7 were £148 360 and in 20X8 were £153 062.

From this information prepare summary profit and loss account statements for 20X7 and 20X8 showing sales, cost of sales, gross profit, expenses and net profit. (Work to the nearest £.)

7.13 Madigan & Co. is the trading name of Basil Madigan, a chartered accountant. He runs a small city centre office employing a part-qualified accountant as an assistant and a secretary, both on a full-time basis.

In the year to 31 March 20X5 fees from Madigan's clients total £95 311. The assistant's salary is £19 300 and the secretary is paid £11 150. Basil's one-room office is in a run-down office building at a comparatively low rental of £10 310, which includes energy costs and business rates. There is also an annual service charge (to cover repairs, caretaking and so on) which this year comes to £3790.

Basil pays general insurance of £794, plus professional indemnity insurance (PII) of £1250. Subscriptions and professional registration charges are £952. Business travel expenses (mileage claims for use of own car by himself and his assistant) come to £1863. Entertainment is £342.

Telephone charges are £1103 for the year and other administration charges are £1575. Stationery is £761 and sundry expenses total £715. Basil has made donations to local charities out of the business account to the sum of £120.

Prepare the profit and loss account for Madigan & Co. for the year ending 31 March 20X5.

7.14A Mahbub runs a recruitment agency. The agency's income is earned in the form of commissions from clients who pay a percentage of the first year's salary of new employees recruited by the agency. In the year to 31 December 20X7 the total of commission income earned is £115 900. Mahbub is very pleased with this record level of commission; it is 25% higher than total commissions in the previous year.

Expenses, however, have also increased. Premises costs total £16 506, staff costs are £29 900 and administration costs are £15 981. In the year to 31 December 20X6 the equivalent expenses totals were: premises £13 370; staff costs £28 807; and administration costs £12 773.

From the information given above, prepare Mahbub's profit and loss account for both 20X7 and 20X6. Calculate the percentage increase or decrease in net profit.

7.15   Nellie sells boots from her market stall and also carries out a boot repair service. This activity has never made much of a profit, but some of Nellie's long-standing customers continue to expect the service. Nellie's year-end is 31 May, a time of year when boot sales are low and when she has very little stock on hand. She counts and values her stock on 31 May 20X1 and arrives at a value of £2904.

You are employed in the office of Naylor & Co., Nellie's accountants. Your boss, Nasser, asks you to prepare her accounts for the year to 31 May 20X1. As well as the information about stock, you are given the following list of items as at the year-end date:

	£
Stock at 1 June 20X0	2 672
Stall rental and service charge	3 844
Bank interest received	320
Sundry expenses	313
Saturday assistant's wages	1 200
Repairs income	1 801
Purchases	42 640
Creditors	2 497
Accountant's fees and other administration	862
Insurance	574
Cash at bank	3 422
Drawings	14 257
Repairs expenses	1 742
Motor expenses	1 252
Sales of boots	63 060
Capital at 1 June 20X0	6 060
Fixed assets – display stands	960

Nasser will be having a meeting with Nellie next week to talk about her business. She feels that she is not doing as well as in previous years. Her gross profit for the year ended 31 May 20X0 was £22 831 on sales of £67 760. In addition to preparing the accounts, Nasser would like you to calculate the actual and percentage changes in gross profit and sales between 20X0 and 20X1, and to compare the gross profit margins between the two years. He would also like you to make some preliminary comments on Nellie's business performance.

7.16   Norbert runs a small wholesaling business selling imported Italian coffee machines to retailers. His business is run from a small warehouse with an office at the side on an industrial estate on the edge of a large city. The industrial estate is largely deserted at night and the crime rate is high for theft and criminal damage. Norbert has recently joined a scheme run by the local authority on behalf of tenants of its industrial units; he makes an annual contribution to a fund, which pays for improved lighting and security patrols.

Norbert's accounting year-end is 31 March. He provides you with a list of figures relating to the most recent year which ended on 31 March 20X7. You are required to prepare a profit and loss account and balance sheet from the figures.

	£
Delivery van	5 020
Sales for the year	351 777
Staff costs: storeman's wages	12 090
Electricity	2 821
Cash at bank	3 444

	£
Capital at 1 April 20X6	18 011
Administrative costs	3 810
Opening stock at 1 April 20X6	20 762
Fixed assets in warehouse and office	3 900
Drawings	25 219
Sundry expenses	1 406
Warehouse and office rental	10 509
Insurance	3 909
Debtors	36 623
Water rates	1 226
Security services charge	2 937
Purchases	255 255
Bank charges	398
Creditors	31 950
Delivery expenses	8 630
Part-time admin assistant's wages	3 779

Norbert has counted and valued the coffee machines on the premises at the 31 March 20X7. The total value is £22 446.

Prepare the profit and loss account and balance sheet for Norbert's business for the accounting year to 31 March 20X7.

Answers to exercises

7.1   1. Jackie has purchased 47 sets during June – i.e. answer b). Explanation:

	No. of sets
Opening stock	30
Add: purchases (missing figure)	X
Less: closing stock	(42)
= Sets sold in June	35

The missing figure is 47.

2. Jackie's cost of sales is £2625 – i.e. answer c). Explanation:

	No. of sets	£
Cost of sales:		
Opening stock at 1 June 20X1	30	2 250
Add: purchases during month	47	3 525
	77	5 775
Less: closing stock at 30 June 20X1	(42)	(3 150)
	35	2 625

An even easier calculation is to take the number of sets sold (35) and multiply by the cost price (£75). This gives an answer of £2625.

3. Jackie's gross profit for the month of June is £1995 – i.e. answer d). Explanation:

	£
Sales (£132 × 35 sets)	4 620
Less: cost of sales (see answer 7.1.2)	2 625
Gross profit	1 995

Another way of calculating this is to work out the gross profit on one set (£132 − £75 = £57) and multiply it by the number of sets sold (£57 × 35 = £1995)

7.2   The sales revenue raised through selling the special purchase trainers is as follows:

	£
750 pairs @ £15.50 per pair	11 625
200 pairs @ £12.50 per pair	2 500
50 pairs @ £5 per pair	250
Total sales revenue	14 375

The cost of sales was the purchase price of £8500. There is no opening or closing stock. Gross profit is therefore: £14 375 − £8500 = £5875.

If Jay had managed to sell 1000 pairs at £15.50 the sales revenue would have been £15 500. Gross profit would therefore have been £15 500 less the cost of sales figure of £8500 = £7000.

7.4   We can construct Jake's trading account and use it to find the value of the missing figure of opening stock.

First we put in the total value for sales, and for gross profit. The difference between these two is cost of sales, i.e. £340 000 − £140 000 = £200 000. Then we can work in reverse order through the cost of sales calculation. Because closing stock is £17 400 the total value of opening stock + purchases must be £217 400 (i.e. we deduct closing stock of £17 400 to get cost of sales of £200 000). If the total value of opening stock plus purchases is £217 400 and we know that purchases for the year equal £197 300, then opening stock is the difference between these two figures:

£217 400 − £197 300 = £20 100

The missing figure (X) is £20 100.

Jake: Trading account for the year

	£	£
Sales: 8000 units @ £42.50		340 000
Cost of sales		
Opening stock (missing figure)	X	
Add: purchases	197 300	
	217 400	
Less: closing stock	(17 400)	
		(200 000)
Gross profit: 8000 units @ £17.50		140 000

7.5   **Jethro: Trading accounts for October, November and December 20X2**

	October £	November £	December £
Sales	39 370	48 998	56 306
Cost of sales			
Opening stock	30 863	43 258	53 190
Add: purchases	37 085	40 830	6 250
Less: Closing stock	(43 258)	(53 190)	(23 980)
	24 690	30 898	35 460
Gross profit	14 680	18 100	20 846

7.7   Cost of sales are calculated as follows:

	£
Sales	183 600
Less: gross profit	88 128
= Cost of sales	95 472

Staff costs are calculated as follows:

	£
Full-time staff: £149 × 52 weeks × 2 staff	15 496
Gloria's holiday cover: £149 × 4 weeks	596
Saturday part-time staff: £28 × 45 days	1 260
Total	17 352

Keith: Profit and loss account for the year ending 31 December 20X9

	£	£
Sales		183 600
Less: cost of sales (as calculated above)		95 472
Gross profit		88 128
Expenses:		
Staff costs (as calculated above)	17 352	
Shop rental	25 750	
Business rates	2 998	
Gas	986	
Electricity	1 351	
Insurance	1 850	
Sundry shop expenses	96	
Accountant's fees	375	
Solicitor's fees	220	
Bank charges	360	
Interest	284	
Telephone	382	
Stationery	35	
Sundry office expenses	93	
		52 132
Net profit		35 996

7.9   Leon's trading results are as follows for the two years under review:

	20X6 £	20X5 £
Sales	295 993	287 300
Cost of sales	(242 085)	(235 920)
Gross profit	53 908	51 380

1. Gross profit margin in 20X6 =

$$\frac{53\,908}{295\,993} \times 100 = 18.2\%$$

Gross profit margin in 20X5 =

$$\frac{51\,380}{287\,300} \times 100 = 17.9\%$$

2. The amount of the increase in sales is £295 993 − £287 300 = £8 693
3. The percentage increase in sales is:

$$\frac{8\,693}{287\,300} \times 100 = 3\%$$

4. The amount of the increase in gross profit is £53 908 − £51 380 = £2 528
5. The percentage increase in gross profit is:

$$\frac{2\,528}{51\,380} \times 100 = 4.9\%$$

7.11   The table shows the gross and net profit margins for Louise's business for three years:

	20X8 £	20X7 £	20X6 £
Gross profit margin	$\frac{77\,402}{291\,318} \times 100$ = 26.6%	$\frac{75\,980}{282\,400} \times 100$ = 26.9%	$\frac{73\,269}{269\,340} \times 100$ = 27.2%
Net profit margin	$\frac{25\,008}{291\,318} \times 100$ = 8.6%	$\frac{24\,260}{282\,400} \times 100$ = 8.6%	$\frac{23\,999}{269\,340} \times 100$ = 8.9%

Louise's sales have increased in each of the three years, as have gross profit and net profit. However, the gross and net profit margins have fallen. Gross profit margin has declined from 27.2% in 20X6 to 26.6% in 20X8. Net profit margin is stable in the latest two years, but has declined from 8.9% in 20X6.

7.13   Madigan & Co: Profit and loss account for the year ending 31 March 20X5

	£	£
Fees from clients		95 311
Expenses		
Salaries: assistant	19 300	
secretary	11 150	
Office rental	10 310	
Office service charge	3 790	
Insurance	794	
PII	1 250	
Subscriptions etc.	952	
Business travel	1 863	
Entertainment	342	
Telephone	1 103	
Other administration expenses	1 575	
Stationery	761	
Sundry expenses	715	
Charitable donations	120	
		54 025
Net profit		41 286

7.15   First, categorise the accounting items for Nellie's business:

	£	Category
Stock at 1 June 20X0	2 672	Trading account
Stall rental and service charge	3 844	Profit and loss account
Bank interest received	320	Profit and loss account
Sundry expenses	313	Profit and loss account
Saturday assistant's wages	1 200	Profit and loss account
Repairs income	1 801	Profit and loss account
Purchases	42 640	Trading account
Creditors	2 497	Balance sheet: current liabilities
Accountant's fees and other administration	862	Profit and loss account
Insurance	574	Profit and loss account
Cash at bank	3 422	Balance sheet: current assets
Drawings	14 257	Balance sheet: capital
Repairs expenses	1 742	Profit and loss account
Motor expenses	1 252	Profit and loss account
Sales of boots	63 060	Profit and loss account
Capital at 1 June 20X0	6 060	Balance sheet: capital
Fixed assets – display stands	960	Balance sheet: fixed assets
Stock at 31 May 20X1	2 904	Trading account *and* balance sheet: current assets

Nellie: Profit and loss account for the year ending 31 May 20X1

	£	£
Sales		63 060
Less: cost of sales		
Opening stock	2 672	
Add: purchases	42 640	
	45 312	
Less: closing stock	(2 904)	
		(42 408)
Gross profit		20 652
Boot repairs: income	1 801	
Boot repairs: expenses	(1 742)	
		59
Other income – bank interest received		320
		21 031
Expenses		
Stall rental and service charge	3 844	
Motor expenses	1 252	
Saturday assistant's wages	1 200	
Insurance	574	
Accountant's fees and other administration	862	
Sundry expenses	313	
		(8 045)
Net profit		12 986

Nellie: Balance sheet at 31 May 20X1

	£	£
Fixed assets		960
Current liabilities		
Stock	2 904	
Cash	3 422	
	6 326	
Current liabilities		
Creditors	(2 497)	
Net current assets (£6 326 − 2 497)		3 829
Net assets		4 789
Capital		
Opening capital balance 1 June 20X0	6 060	
Add: net profit for the year	12 986	
	19 046	
Less: drawings	(14 257)	
Closing capital balance 31 May 20X1		4 789

Change in sales: sales have decreased from £67 760 to £63 060, a decrease of £4 700. The percentage change is calculated as follows:

$$\frac{4\,700}{67\,760} \times 100 = 6.9\%$$

Change in gross profit: gross profit has decreased from £22 831 to £20 652, a decrease of £2 179. The percentage change is calculated as follows:

$$\frac{2\,179}{22\,831} \times 100 = 9.5\%$$

Gross profit margins compared:

	20X1 £	20X0 £
Gross profit margin	$\frac{20\,652}{63\,060} \times 100$	$\frac{22\,831}{67\,760} \times 100$
	$= 32.7\%$	$= 33.7\%$

Comments on Nellie's accounts

Sales and gross profits have both fallen between 20X0 and 20X1. The gross profit margin is poorer in 20X1 than in the previous year. We do not have net profit information available. Nellie may be able to pinpoint reasons for the decline in trade, and Nasser needs to make some suggestions as to how she might be able to increase sales in future. For example, a change of suppliers might improve gross profit margin.

Other observations include the fact that the boot repair service is making virtually nothing. Nellie's time could perhaps be better used elsewhere and she may like to consider finally ceasing to offer the service. Nellie's drawings are in excess of the net profit generated by the business. There may be specific reasons why this level of drawings has been made during this recent financial year, but Nellie really should be considering ways of reducing drawings if possible, at least until her trade has recovered to its previous levels.

7.16 First, categorise the accounting items for Norbert's business:

	£	Category
Delivery van	5 020	Balance sheet: fixed assets
Sales for the year	351 777	Trading account
Staff costs: storeman's wages	12 090	Profit and loss account
Electricity	2 821	Profit and loss account
Cash at bank	3 444	Balance sheet: current assets
Capital at 1 April 20X6	18 011	Balance sheet: capital
Administrative costs	3 810	Profit and loss account
Opening stock at 1 April 20X6	20 762	Trading account
Fixed assets in warehouse and office	3 900	Balance sheet: fixed assets
Drawings	25 219	Balance sheet: capital
Sundry expenses	1 406	Profit and loss account
Warehouse and office rental	10 509	Profit and loss account
Insurance	3 909	Profit and loss account

	£	Category
Debtors	36 623	Balance sheet: current assets
Water rates	1 226	Profit and loss account
Security services charge	2 937	Profit and loss account
Purchases	255 255	Trading account
Bank charges	398	Profit and loss account
Creditors	31 950	Balance sheet: current liabilities
Delivery expenses	8 630	Profit and loss account
Part-time admin assistant's wages	3 779	Profit and loss account
Closing stock	22 446	Trading account *and* balance sheet: current assets

Norbert: Profit and loss account for the year ending 31 March 20X7

	£	£
Sales		351 777
Less: cost of sales		
Opening stock	20 762	
Add: purchases	255 255	
	276 017	
Less: closing stock	(22 446)	
		(253 571)
Gross profit		98 206
Expenses		
Staff costs: storeman's wages	12 090	
Warehouse and office rental	10 509	
Insurance	3 909	
Electricity	2 821	
Water rates	1 226	
Security services	2 937	
Delivery expenses	8 630	
Administrative costs	3 810	
Part-time admin assistant's wages	3 779	
Sundry expenses	1 406	
Bank charges	398	
		(51 515)
Net profit		46 691

Norbert: Balance sheet at 31 March 20X7

	£	£
Fixed assets		
Delivery van	5 020	
Fixed assets – warehouse and office	3 900	
		8 920
Current assets		
Stock	22 446	
Debtors	36 623	
Cash	3 444	
	62 513	

Current liabilities
Creditors   (31 950)

Net current assets (£62 513 — £31 950)   30 563

Net assets   39 483

Capital
Opening capital balance 1 April 20X6   18 011
Add: net profit for the year   46 691
                                                     64 702
Less: drawings   (25 219)

Closing capital balance 31 March 20X7   39 483

8

ADJUSTMENTS TO THE PROFIT AND LOSS ACCOUNT AND BALANCE SHEET: 1

AIMS AND LEARNING OUTCOMES

Aim of the chapter

To enable students to understand the use of various accounting adjustments and their effect on the profit and loss account and balance sheet.

Learning outcomes

After reading the chapter and completing the related exercises, students should:

- Understand the treatment in the profit and loss account of complexities such as discounts and returns of goods.
- Appreciate and be able to apply some of the important conventions in accounting for recognition of income and expenses.
- Understand the need for provisions against certain current assets, and be able to make appropriate adjustments to the profit and loss account and balance sheet.

The chapter is divided into the following principal sections:

- Consideration of some additional items that may be included in the profit and loss account – namely, returns of goods, discounts and delivery charges.
- An introduction to some of the main conventions in accounting, including the important principle of matching (accruals).
- Adjustments that may be required in respect of stock and debtors.

Some further complexities in preparing the profit and loss account

In this section we will extend the knowledge gained in the previous chapter to encompass three further items that may be included in the profit and loss account: returns; discounts; and delivery charges.

Returns

The majority of the examples in Chapter 7 involved the purchase and sale of items of stock, and in all cases it was assumed that the transactions were straightforward in that no items were ever returned. However, while transactions are often completed without error or dispute, this is not always the case. A retail customer, for example, may buy a pair of jeans but find, on examining the purchase at home, that the zip is broken. The jeans are taken back to the shop and either a replacement is provided or a refund paid. The same can happen, although usually on a larger scale, with the purchase and sale of items in business. The goods are not what was ordered, the quality level of the goods is insufficiently high, the quantity is wrong, or a combination of any and all of those factors. Where a return of purchased items is made there are implications for the profit and loss account of both the vendor and the purchaser.

> **Example 8.1** John runs a business selling artists' easels and other art equipment. Imran purchases 30 easels from him at a cost of £45 each: total = £1350. The transaction is added to John's sales, and added to Imran's purchases. Upon close examination of the easels Imran discovers that five are missing essential bolts and screws. He decides to return them to John. The effect of this return is that John's sales and Imran's purchases are reduced by the same amount: 5 × £45 = £225.

Where returns are a fairly frequent occurrence, as will be the case in many businesses, a total of items returned is built up during the year and will feature in the list of balances from which the profit and loss account is drawn up. Sales returns must be deducted from sales, and purchases returns must be deducted from purchases in drawing up the trading part of the profit and loss account. Rather than setting these figures off against each other, it is conventional to show the total for sales and then deduct the total for returns.

Discounts

Trade discounts

A trade discount is a special kind of discount given, for example, to long-standing customers, or to customers who purchase a very high volume of goods. This type of discount is normally given via reduced prices, thus resulting in a relatively lower cost of purchases for the recipient. Large businesses are often able by this means to buy goods at lower unit prices than small businesses, and so obtain a competitive advantage. If they pass on the discounts via lower prices to their customers then they may be able to gain market share at the expense of their smaller competitors.

Where discounts like this are given or received, there is no special adjustment to be made in the profit and loss account. The amounts invoiced already reflect the reduction. However, the issue of trade discounts may be relevant when analysing the meaning of profit and loss account statements, especially when comparing one business with another.

Financial discounts

Many businesses trade on credit – that is, they do not demand immediate payment but instead are prepared to wait for a period. The acceptable period varies from one business to another, and will depend upon the norms in that particular industry. A frequently encountered arrangement is to require payment within 30 days of invoice. For example, goods are dispatched to a customer on 15 May and an invoice is sent on 17 May; until the invoice is paid the amount is recorded as a debtor. The invoice specifies that payment should be made within 30 days; it is therefore expected that payment will be received by 16 June. Some customers will pay within the time allowed; others will take longer; and some may not pay at all (a problem we will examine in more detail later in this chapter).

Business people in most trades and professions have to accept the necessity for trading on credit. However, they will seek to minimise the length of time they have to wait for their money, and one way of actively encouraging early payment is to offer an incentive in the form of a discount. The cost of the discount has to be carefully balanced against the benefit of receiving the cash earlier than it would be received if there was no discount.

Example 8.2 Fernando runs a small business manufacturing and selling gloves. His customers are mainly retail businesses, many of which do not pay within his stipulated terms of credit, which are receipt of cash required within 30 days of invoice. In order to encourage earlier payment, Fernando decides to set up a discount incentive. Customers who pay within 30 days are entitled to reduce the invoice amount by 0.5%.

On 1 October he sends an invoice to one of his biggest customers for £3000 with a note about the discount. The value of the sale recorded in Fernando's accounting records on that day is £3000. Thirty days later, a cheque arrives for £2985, i.e. £3000 less 0.5% of the invoice value. The discount is, therefore, £15. How should Fernando record it?

The discount is an expense of Fernando's business – a type of finance charge paid in order to get the money into his bank account sooner than he would have done otherwise. Therefore, it is included as an expense in his profit and loss account. Where a business receives financial discounts, they are included as part of its other income, below the trading account details.

Delivery charges

Some businesses incur the expense of distributing their goods to customers. Typical expenses would include road or rail haulage costs, handling costs and import duties. In some cases the selling business pays such costs and they appear in the expenses section of the profit and loss account. Where the purchasing business pays these costs, they are added to the cost of the purchases and appear in the trading account.

Example 8.3 Brooklyn imports Brazilian footballs in cartons of 100, each carton costing £52. In addition, he must pay import duty of £5 per carton. On 15 August he orders 16 cartons. How much is added in to his total of purchases for the year?

	£
Cost of 16 cartons @ £52 per carton	832
Import duty: 16 cartons @ £5 per carton	80
Total added to purchases for the year	912

So, in summary, accounting for delivery and similar charges varies depending upon whether the selling organisation or the purchasing organisation is paying the cost.

Example 8.4 Bennie runs an art shop that sells all kinds of artists' materials, and also lines in greetings cards, books and office stationery. As well as over-the-counter sales for cash, he also supplies local art colleges and schools with art materials and equipment. This type of sale is made on credit. Bennie requires payment within 30 days, but finds that colleges and schools are slow to pay. During the year to 31 October 20X5 he introduces an early payment discount scheme: all credit customers paying within one month are entitled to deduct 1.25% of the invoice value. Some of the schools and colleges take advantage of the scheme and Bennie allows total discounts of £196 during the year. Other relevant points are:

- Bennie himself receives discounts for early payment from some of his suppliers. The total for the year is £98.
- During the year he buys in some easels from John, but finds them to be faulty. Several sub-standard easels have to be returned to John; the cost of the easels is £853.
- One of the art colleges supplied by Bennie returns to him a large order of paint because it is infested with weevils. The value of the amount returned, at selling price, is £590.
- Generally, delivery charges are included in the price of the goods that Bennie buys. However, he imports a range of fragile pastel sticks from France. He pays a courier firm for special delivery of these items so that they will not be damaged in transit. The total for this type of delivery for 20X5 is £150.

The following is a list of all Bennie's sales and expenses items (including the items described above) for 20X5:

	£
Insurance	2 984
Discounts allowed to colleges and schools	196
Stock at 1 November 20X4	16 037
Subscription to Chamber of Commerce	100
Delivery van expenses	760

	£
Shop rental	18 300
Sales	159 760
Sundry expenses	1 982
Purchases	94 736
Courier service – pastel imports	150
Returns of goods sold to college	590
Electricity and other premises costs	3 598
Assistant's wages	10 920
Discounts received for early payment	98
Returns of easels to John	853
Accountancy fees	570
Stock at 31 October 20X5	18 006

This example is more complicated than any encountered so far. The additional adjustments mean that more items are included in the trading account. As a first step, then, each of the items is classified as belonging either to the trading account or to the rest of the profit and loss account, as follows:

	£	Category
Insurance	2 984	Profit and loss account
Discounts allowed to colleges and schools	196	Profit and loss account
Stock at 1 November 20X4	16 037	Trading account
Subscription to Chamber of Commerce	100	Profit and loss account
Delivery van expenses	760	Profit and loss account
Shop rental	18 300	Profit and loss account
Sales	159 760	Trading account
Sundry expenses	1 982	Profit and loss account
Purchases	94 736	Trading account
Courier service – pastel imports	150	Trading account
Returns of goods sold to college	590	Trading account
Electricity and other premises costs	3 598	Profit and loss account
Assistant's wages	10 920	Profit and loss account
Discounts received for early payment	98	Profit and loss account
Returns of easels to John	853	Trading account
Accountancy fees	570	Profit and loss account
Stock at 31 October 20X5	18 006	Trading account

Several items in the above list are included in the trading account. If we separate them out, we can deal with them first:

	£	Category
Stock at 1 November 20X4	16 037	Trading account
Sales	159 760	Trading account
Purchases	94 736	Trading account
Courier service – pastel imports	150	Trading account
Returns of goods sold to college	590	Trading account
Returns of easels to John	853	Trading account
Stock at 31 October 20X5	18 006	Trading account

Of the above seven items, two relate to sales transactions: £159 760 of sales and £590 of sales returns. These will be presented as follows:

	£
Sales	159 760
Less: sales returns	(590)
	159 170

The remaining items relate to the cost of sales calculation. The basic calculation remains as:

$$\text{Opening stock} + \text{Purchases} - \text{Closing stock}$$

But the calculation of purchases has become a little more complicated.

	£	£
Cost of sales:		
Opening stock		16 037
Add purchases:		
Purchases	94 736	
Add: courier charges	150	
Less: purchase returns	(853)	
		94 033
		110 070
Less: closing stock		(18 006)
Cost of sales		92 064

Note that the detail of the purchases calculation has been pulled over to the left-hand side for greater clarity.

The remainder of the profit calculation follows the same approach as in the previous chapter, so should not be especially difficult. Once all the figures are put together Bennie's profit and loss account looks like this:

Bennie: Profit and loss account for the year ending 31 October 20X5

	£	£	£
Sales			159 760
Less: sales returns			(590)
			159 170
Cost of sales:			
Opening stock		16 037	
Add purchases:			
Purchases	94 736		
Add: courier charges	150		
Less: purchase returns	(853)		
		94 033	
		110 070	
Less: closing stock		(18 006)	
Cost of sales			(92 064)
Gross profit			67 106
Discounts received			98
			67 204

▶

Expenses

Shop rental	18 300
Electricity and other premises costs	3 598
Assistant's wages	10 920
Insurance	2 984
Discounts allowed	196
Accountancy fees	570
Delivery van expenses	760
Sundry expenses	1 982
Chamber of Commerce subscription	100
	(39 410)
Net profit	**27 794**

Note the following:

1. Discounts received are a type of income. However, they are not included in the trading section of the profit and loss account, but are added on to gross profit. This is because the level of discounts received has no bearing on the trading activities of the business; they are received as a result of good financial management.
2. Delivery van expenses are the expenses that Bennie has to pay for running a van to deliver goods to his customers. These costs are obviously not being passed on to customers and therefore have to be paid for out of the proceeds of Bennie's business.
3. Bennie's profit and loss statement looks quite complicated because it has three columns of figures. Figures are indented like this in order to make the statement easier for the reader to understand.

Accounting conventions

Recognition and realisation

Accounting conventions help to determine the amounts at which items should be stated in the financial statements, and, indeed, whether or not those amounts should be included at all.

This section considers the issue of **recognition** of income and expenses. Recognition occurs when items are brought into the accounting statements. In some cases the point at which items should be recognised is straightforward. A sale made for cash is recognised at the point where the exchange of goods for cash takes place. So, for example, in the case of Bennie's art shop all the sales he makes for cash up to closing time on 31 October 20X5 are included in the accounts for that year.

However, Bennie makes both cash sales and sales on credit. At what point should sales on credit be recognised in the accounts? The accounting convention on this point is that income should be recognised at the point at which the goods are supplied or services rendered. So, for example, goods that are delivered to the local art college on 31 October 20X5 with a sales value of £366 are included in Bennie's total sales for the year ending on that date. Goods delivered on the next day (1 November 20X5) will be included in total sales for the next accounting year (the year ending on 31 October 20X6).

It is important to appreciate that this convention (known in accounting terminology as the **realisation** convention) means that the total recorded for sales in an accounting period will not usually be the same as the cash received. The goods Bennie delivers to the art college on 31 October are included in sales at a value of £366. However, payment for these goods will not be received until after the year-end. Any amounts due at the year-end are debtors and will be included as assets in the business's balance sheet.

Similar considerations apply in respect of expenses. In Bennie's case all goods delivered up to the close of business on 31 October 20X5 are included in his total purchases for the year. Bennie has almost certainly not yet paid for all of the purchases. Any amounts still to be paid at the year-end are creditors and will be included as liabilities in the business's balance sheet. So, the total for purchases and expenses recorded in an accounting period will not be the same figure as cash spent.

In summary, accounting income is not the same as cash received, and accounting expenditure is not the same as cash paid.

Matching (accruals)

The matching, or accruals, convention is very important in the calculation of profit. The effects of transactions should be recognised in the accounting period in which they occur, which is not necessarily the period in which they are invoiced or paid. In the last chapter we established the basic foundation for calculating profit:

$$Sales - Expenses = Profit$$

In order to calculate profit with as much precision as possible it is important to match sales and expenses. That means setting off against sales for an accounting period all the expenses that have contributed to making those sales. So, for example, in a business like Bennie's which pays rent, the matching convention requires that one year's rent is matched against one year's sales in working out the profit for that year. If only nine months rent is included the expenses figure will not be large enough and profit will be overstated. If 15 months rent is included the expenses figure will be too large and profit will be understated.

Expenses are recorded as they are paid or when bills are received. When drawing up the year-end accounts it is important to examine the detail of the amounts recorded for expenses to ensure that expenses and income are matched as closely as possible. Note that the **matching** convention is also referred to as the **accruals** convention. The importance of matching is illustrated in the following example.

Example 8.5 Gregory runs a small business supplying leather goods on credit to small shops and market stalls. The business is run from a warehouse on a trading estate. Gregory pays rental for the warehouse, and the usual type of expenses such as insurance and telephone.

Gregory's accounting year-end is 30 June. The annual warehouse rental is paid in quarterly instalments in advance. So, for example, Gregory pays rental on

29 September every year, which will cover October, November and December. Any increases in rental take effect from 1 January in the calendar year.

Gregory has the following rental arrangements with his landlord for 20X6 and 20X7: in 20X6 the total annual rental is £12 000, but in 20X7 there is a substantial increase to £14 400. What is the total of rental expense for Gregory's business in the year ending 30 June 20X7?

Following the matching convention in accounting, Gregory's sales for the year ending 30 June 20X7 must be matched with the expenses that have been incurred in order to achieve those sales. Between 1 July 20X6 and 31 December 20X6 (a period of six months) the cost of the warehouse rental was £12 000/2 = £6000. Between 1 January 20X7 and 30 June 20X7 (a period of 6 months) the cost of the warehouse rental was £14 400/2 = £7200. The total rental expense to be matched against Gregory's sales for the year is therefore £6000 + £7200 = £13 200.

Comprehensive example – matching

In the next example we will look at the adjustments that may be required to the financial statements because of the timing of the recording of expenses. Parts 1 and 2 of the example examine the detail of the adjustments and then, in Part 3, we look at the effect on the accounts overall.

Example 8.6

Part 1

Graham has a consultancy business with a year-end of 31 December. He receives quarterly bills for telephone call charges. At the 31 December 20X6 year-end the total in his account books for his business telephone call charges is £6840. This is the total of three separate payments made during the year:

1. Payment on 13 April 20X6 of £2175 for the bill covering 1 January to 31 March.
2. Payment on 30 July 20X6 of £2444 for the bill covering 1 April to 30 June.
3. Payment on 18 October 20X6 of £2221 for the bill covering 1 July to 30 September.

By 31 December 20X6 Graham has received no bill for the last quarter of the year. This is not surprising as the bill will cover the period up to and including 31 December and so Graham would not expect to receive it until several days after the year-end. However, Graham must include the amount of the final quarter bill in his accounts to 31 December 20X6 so that the total charge for telephone expense reflects all of the charges for calls made in the year. If he fails to include an appropriate amount expenses will be understated and, consequently, profit will be overstated.

In drawing up the accounts, then, Graham must add the appropriate amount to telephone expense. If he receives the bill before he completes the accounts he can make an exact adjustment. If not, he must make a reasonable estimate of the likely cost. Unless the final quarter is unusual in some way, Graham could estimate based upon the previous quarters' bills. An estimate of around £2200 to £2300 would probably be appropriate.

Suppose that Graham receives the bill in good time before the accounts are finished. The total amount of call charges is £2237 for the quarter. Graham adds this to the charges for the first three quarters: £6840 + £2237 = £9077 total telephone expense for the year.

There is another adjustment to be made as well, this time to the balance sheet. The three bills already paid have depleted the bank balance. The new bill will deplete the bank balance at some point in January or February 20X7, but at the date the accounts are drawn up (31 December) the payment transaction has not yet occurred. Graham, therefore, must show the telephone bill as a creditor at the year-end. This particular type of creditor is known in accounting terminology as an accrual, and it is included in the balance sheet under current liabilities.

Part 2

Telephone charges are billed after the calls have been made. The phone company extends credit to its customers, and other utilities companies commonly do the same (unless the customer is known to be very bad at paying up, in which case the companies will insist on payment in advance or via pay meters). Some types of expense, however, may be payable in advance, and matching problems may therefore occur.

Graham pays his business buildings and contents insurance on 1 July each year, in advance. The amount paid on 1 July 20X6 covers the whole year from 1 July 20X6 to 30 June 20X7. Only half of the amount paid, therefore, relates to the year to 31 December 20X6.

At 31 December the balance on Graham's insurance account is £3901, which includes the bill paid on 1 July 20X6 for £2644. Half of this (£1322) relates to the next following accounting year (20X7). This is known in accounting terminology as a **prepayment** – a type of current asset. It will be included in the balance sheet at 31 December 20X6 under current assets of the business.

The total expense for Graham's business insurance for the year comprises £1322 for the second half of the year, plus the amount relating to the first six months of the year:

	£
Insurance expense in Graham's records at 31 December	3 901
Less: amount relating to 20X7	1 322
Insurance expense for inclusion in the 20X6 accounts	2 579

Because we know that the insurance expense relating to the second six months of the year was £1322 we can work out (£2579 – £1322) that the expense for the first six months of the year was £1257.

Part 3 – the full accounts

Next we will look at how the accrual and prepayment adjustments explained above fit into Graham's accounts for the whole year.

The following is Graham's list of balances at 31 December 20X6, before any adjustments for accrual and prepayment items. Each item is identified as to whether it belongs in the profit and loss account or balance sheet:

▶

	£	
Consultancy income	103 907	Profit and loss account
Secretarial assistant's salary	18 742	Profit and loss account
Entertaining expenses	961	Profit and loss account
Fixed assets	3 336	Balance sheet
Cash at bank	12 906	Balance sheet
Travel expenses	1 888	Profit and loss account
Telephone	6 840	Profit and loss account
Interest received	360	Profit and loss account
Debtors	14 820	Balance sheet
Creditors	1 793	Balance sheet
Capital at 1 January 20X6	21 130	Balance sheet
Office premises – rent and other expenses	23 590	Profit and loss account
Sundry office expenses	2 553	Profit and loss account
Insurance	3 901	Profit and loss account
Accountant's fees	772	Profit and loss account
Drawings	36 881	Balance sheet

The adjustments for the accrual and the prepayment must be made before Graham's profit and loss and balance sheet are drawn up.

1. *Accruals adjustment*: £2237 is added to telephone expenses and an accrual for £2237 appears in the balance sheet, included under current liabilities.
2. *Prepayment adjustment*: £1322 is deducted from insurance expenses and a prepayment for £1322 appears in the balance sheet, included under current assets.

Using all of the above information, Graham's accounts can be drawn up:

Graham: Profit and loss account for the year ending 31 December 20X6

	£	£
Consultancy income		103 907
Interest received		360
		104 267
Expenses		
Office premises: rent and other expenses	23 590	
Secretarial assistant's salary	18 742	
Entertaining expenses	961	
Telephone (£6840 + £2237)	9 077	
Travel expenses	1 888	
Sundry office expenses	2 553	
Insurance (£3901 − £1322)	2 579	
Accountant's fees	772	
		(60 162)
Profit for the year		44 105

Graham: Balance sheet at 31 December 20X6

	£	£
Fixed assets		3 336
Current assets		
Debtors	14 820	
Prepayment	1 322	
Cash at bank	12 906	
	29 048	
Current liabilities		
Creditors	1 793	
Accrual	2 237	
	4 030	
Net current assets (£29 048 − £4 030)		25 018
Net assets		28 354
Capital		
Opening capital balance 1 January 20X6	21 130	
Add: net profit for the year	44 105	
	65 235	
Less: drawings	(36 881)	
Closing capital balance 31 December 20X6		28 354

The following should be noted:

1. After the adjustments are made the balance sheet still balances. The first adjustment, for the accrual, is an addition to expenses and a reduction in profits for the year. Consequently, the capital side of the balance sheet is reduced. However, there is a balancing reduction in net assets because we have included a creditor in the form of an accrual. The second adjustment, for the prepayment, is a deduction from expenses and an increase in profits for the year. Consequently, the capital side of the balance sheet is increased, but there is a balancing increase in net assets because we have included a current asset in the form of a prepayment.
2. Note the position of the new items. Prepayments are usually recorded immediately below debtors in the balance sheet list of current assets. Accruals are recorded immediately below creditors as part of current liabilities.

The accounting adjustments that arise because of the matching convention can be difficult to assimilate at first. However, there are several examples at the end of the chapter which will help to reinforce understanding.

Current asset adjustments

In this section of the chapter we will examine the range of adjustments that may have to be made, in certain circumstances, to stock and debtors.

Stock

The value of stock at the year-end is determined by the following calculation:

Number of items in stock × Value of individual items

The number of items is usually established by means of a stocktake carried out on the last day of the year. Value is generally, but not always, cost. As we saw, earlier in the chapter, it may be necessary to add in certain items (such as import duties, for example) to the cost of purchasing goods. Also, it can happen that stock loses some part of its value before it can be sold. This can happen because the stock is accidentally damaged or where, by its nature, it does not hold its value for long.

The fundamental rule to be applied to stock valuation is that stock is valued at the lower of cost and net realisable value. Net realisable value is the amount for which the stock could be sold, less any incidental expenses of sale. The following example illustrates the point.

Example 8.7 Taruni runs a wholesale business dealing in novelty items and toys. Following a massive televised talent show a new band, Neolithic Hamster, has been formed. Its first two releases have done really well, and the band's promoters have rushed out a range of supporting merchandise – T shirts, cuddly hamster toys and so on. This type of merchandise presents a difficult problem for Taruni in judging just how much to keep in stock. While the band remains popular the merchandise will sell very well and there is likely to be a strong demand for it. However, the market for such items is fickle and unreliable because the public tends to grow tired of manufactured bands within a couple of years at most.

Neolithic Hamster, it emerges, has a shorter shelf life than average. After only six months, public interest dwindles to nothing. Taruni has miscalculated her purchasing and is now left with 3000 giant cuddly hamsters. They originally cost her £6.50 each from the manufacturer and she was able to sell them to shops for £9.50 each at the height of the interest in the band. In order to be able to value the hamsters still in stock at her year-end date (31 August) Taruni needs to know whether she will be able to sell them at a price above £6.50, the original cost to her. If so, she will value the stock at cost price – i.e. £6.50 × 3000 = £19 500.

Taruni makes enquiries. Unfortunately, hers is not the only business trying to unload hamsters in a hurry. The promoters misjudged the whole merchandising promotion and arranged for the production of far too many tie-in goods. Finally, in early September, Taruni finds a man who runs several street market stalls. He is prepared to take the hamsters off her hands for a price of £2 each, and he even offers to come and collect them in his van from her warehouse. In the circumstances Taruni feels she has little choice but to accept the offer. It is clear that Taruni will make a loss on the stock. At 31 August the stock items were no longer worth £6.50 each. She must value at the lower of cost or net realisable value – i.e. at the lower of £6.50 or £2.

Sales for the year are £265 331. Opening stock was £42 307, purchases amounted to £165 956 and closing stock, apart from the hamsters, was £19 952. As noted above, if the hamsters are valued at cost the total value is £19 500. If they are value at net realisable value, the total value is £2 × 3000 = £6000.

In the table below we will assess the effect on Taruni's gross profit of valuing the hamsters at cost and at net realisable value.

	Hamsters at cost	Hamsters at net realisable value
	£	£
Sales	265 331	265 331
Cost of sales		
Opening stock	42 307	42 307
Add: purchases	165 956	165 956
Less: closing stock (19 952 + 19 500)	(39 452)	—
Less: closing stock (19 952 + 6 000)	—	(25 952)
	168 811	182 311
Gross profit	96 520	83 020
Gross profit margin	36.4%	31.3%

The difference between the two figures for gross profit is £13 500 – that is, the loss per item of £4.50 × 3000 units of stock. This has been a very costly error in purchasing.

Businesses involved in the sale of fashionable items always face the risk that their stock will go out of fashion before it can be sold. Purchasing in such businesses involves a high level of skill, judgement and experience. However, the risk is likely to be absorbed to some extent by charging high prices for the goods while the fashion still lasts.

Debtors

Earlier in this chapter the issue of income recognition was discussed. The realisation convention in accounting requires that income from a transaction is recognised at the point when the goods are dispatched or when services are rendered. In a commercial environment it is very often the case that there is a time lag between the supply of goods (or provision of services) and the receipt of payment.

Once goods have been dispatched a sales invoice follows. The risk for the business selling the goods, of course, is that the purchaser will subsequently fail to pay for the goods. Businesses can take certain precautions against this happening: for example, they can contract with credit agencies to obtain advice on whether or not to offer credit to prospective purchasers. Larger businesses employ their own credit control staff to investigate credit ratings and to chase up unpaid debts. Nevertheless, even in the best organised businesses unpaid invoices can become a problem.

Debtors in the balance sheet represent the total value of unpaid sales invoices. A business problem arises if some debtors will not, or cannot, pay their debts. There is also an accounting problem to be solved. In order to help ensure that the balance sheet provides information that is useful and reasonably accurate, debtors should be stated at their 'recoverable amount' – that is, the amount that can be expected to be paid within a reasonable time after the balance sheet date.

Accounting adjustments are made to cover, broadly, two eventualities:

1. *Bad debts*. These are debts that will almost certainly not be paid.
2. *Doubtful debts*. These are debts that may not be paid.

Example 8.8 Hilda runs a business that supplies water filter equipment. She allows customers 30 days credit. At her year-end, 31 May 20X9, the total of her debtors list is £38 384. She has problems with two of the debtor balances, as follows:

1. £1200 is owed by Jimbo Associates. Jimbo, head of the business, has disappeared to South America taking with him all the cash that was left in his business and leaving many angry creditors behind. It emerges that police in several countries wish to interview him. His creditors, who include Hilda, are unlikely ever to receive payment. From Hilda's point of view this is a bad debt.

2. Hilda sells goods at a total price of £3985 to a firm, Bernini & Co. on her normal terms of trade which are payment within 30 days of receipt of invoice. Three months pass and by her year end, 31 May, Hilda has still not been paid. For the last month she has rung Bernini & Co every week and every Monday Mr Bernini gives her his personal assurance that the cheque will be in the post by Friday. Hilda is beginning to have doubts about these assurances and intends to threaten Bernini with legal action if the debt is not settled.

There is a difference between the debts described above. In the first case Hilda will never receive the money. In the second case, there is a possibility that Mr Bernini will be sufficiently impressed by the threat of legal action to pay up without further fuss.

How should these debts be recorded in Hilda's accounts? In the first case, the debt has ceased to be an asset. It is a **bad debt** and it should be excluded from the total of debtors. In the second case, it is not clear whether or not the debt can be recovered. Hilda will treat this item as a **doubtful debt**. The appropriate accounting treatment is to make a **provision** against the doubtful debt. The provision is deducted from debtors in the year-end balance sheet. Debtors will be shown as follows at 31 May in Hilda's balance sheet:

	£
Debtors (£38 384 − £1200)	37 184
Less: provision	(3 985)
	33 199

The £1200 due from Jimbo is excluded altogether. The debt due from Bernini remains in the list because it might be recovered in due course, but is deducted from the total in the form of a provision.

The £1200 represents an actual loss of profit. The asset of debtors is reduced and so, consequently, is Hilda's profit. The £3985 is a potential loss of profit. It is recognised, for the time being, as a deduction from profit for the year ending 31 May 20X9.

Next, we will look at how these adjustments fit into Hilda's accounts for the whole year. She has the following list of balances at 31 May 20X9, before making any adjustments to the debtors. Each item is identified as belonging in the trading account, the rest of the profit and loss account or the balance sheet.

	£	Category
Stock at 1 June 20X8	34 401	Trading account
Sundry administration expenses	1 270	Profit and loss account
Cash at bank	1 700	Balance sheet

	£	Category
Drawings	38 380	Balance sheet
Premises costs	26 670	Profit and loss account
Marketing expenses	2 190	Profit and loss account
Travelling expenses	1 630	Profit and loss account
Purchases	281 830	Trading account
Debtors	38 384	Balance sheet
Fixed assets	18 361	Balance sheet
Staffing costs	21 010	Profit and loss account
Telephone	2 620	Profit and loss account
Creditors	34 600	Balance sheet
Capital at 1 June 20X8	49 855	Balance sheet
Sales	389 005	Trading account
Delivery van expenses	2 967	Profit and loss account
Insurance	2 047	Profit and loss account
Stock at 31 May 20X9	35 433	Trading account *and* balance sheet

From the balances and the information about bad and doubtful debts the following accounting statements can be drawn up for Hilda's business.

Hilda: Profit and loss account for the year ending 31 May 20X9

	£	£
Sales		389 005
Cost of sales		
Opening stock	34 401	
Add: purchases	281 830	
	316 231	
Less: closing stock	(35 433)	
		(280 798)
Gross profit		108 207
Expenses		
Premises costs	26 670	
Staffing costs	21 010	
Marketing expenses	2 190	
Delivery van expenses	2 967	
Travelling expenses	1 630	
Telephone	2 620	
Insurance	2 047	
Sundry administration expenses	1 270	
Bad debts	1 200	
Provision for doubtful debts	3 985	
		(65 589)
Net profit		42 618

▶

Hilda: Balance sheet at 31 May 20X9

	£	£	£
Fixed assets			18 361
Current assets			
Stock		35 433	
Debtors	37 184		
Less: provision	(3 985)		
		33 199	
Cash at bank		1 700	
		70 332	
Current liabilities			
Creditors		(34 600)	
Net current assets (£70 332 − £34 600)			35 732
Net assets			54 093
Capital			
Opening capital balance 1 June 20X8		49 855	
Add: net profit for the year		42 618	
		92 473	
Less: drawings		(38 380)	
Closing capital balance 31 May 20X9			54 093

The following should be noted:

1. After the adjustments are made in respect of debtors, the balance sheet still balances. Assets are depleted by the amount of the adjustments, but so is profit. The reduced profit decreases the capital side of the balance sheet by the same total amount.
2. The total for debtors includes the amount owed by Bernini & Co. The debtors total will continue to include this debt until either: (a) it is paid; (b) Hilda concludes that the debt has gone bad.

Let us look at the two possibilities in turn. If the debt is paid by Bernini & Co. the asset of debtor (£3985) will be replaced by the asset of cash. The provision for the doubtful debt would no longer be necessary and it would have to be removed from the accounts. This essentially involves reversing the original adjustment. The provision would cease to exist and profit would be increased by £3985 in the following period.

If Hilda concludes that the debt has gone bad, the provision will prove to have been necessary. The debt would be removed from the list of debtors and the provision would also be removed. We can see from the balance sheet above that the net effect of this adjustment on assets would be nil.

Specific and general provisions

The type of provision for doubtful debts made by Hilda in the case above is 'specific'. That means that the provision relates to a certain specific debt. Sometimes, however, businesses make 'general' provisions against doubtful debts.

Example 8.9 Walter sells goods on credit. Usually the invoices are for small amounts and at any time Walter has about 500 debtors who owe him money. He knows, on the basis of many years' experience, that a few of the debtors will not pay up, but it is not usually possible to identify them specifically. He has calculated that, on average, about 1.5% of the value of debtors will not be paid.

Walter's accountant recommends that at his year-end, 30 September 20X1, he should make a general provision for doubtful debts. The total of debtor balances at that date is £52 250. The general provision is calculated at 1.5% of £52 250, or £784 to the nearest £. Walter's accountant makes the adjustment. Profit for the year is reduced by £784, and debtors are shown in the year-end balance sheet as follows:

	£
Debtors	52 250
Less: provision	(784)
	51 466

At 30 September 20X2 Walter's debtors total is £59 942, and his accountant again advises him to make a general provision of 1.5%, which is £899 (to the nearest £). What accounting adjustment is necessary for this? Walter has £784 recorded as a provision in his accounts. The accounting adjustment to be made at 30 September 20X2 is £899 − £784 = £115. Therefore, £115 is added to the existing provision and is deducted from the profit for the year. Debtors are shown in the year-end balance sheet as follows:

	£
Debtors	59 942
Less: provision	(899)
	59 043

CASE STUDY 8.1   A problem debtor

The case study brings together several of the adjustments examined in the chapter. Richard studied hotel management many years ago at college. After leaving, he spent two years as a sous-chef at a large hotel in London, but soon grew tired of the hectic pace of work. While on holiday in Italy he bought a very stylish pan from a range of well-designed kitchenware. On his return to the UK he decided he would like to buy another pan from the range, but was unable to find a stockist. He made enquiries and discovered that no-one in the UK was currently importing the range. He persuaded his mother to lend him some cash and started a business importing kitchenware, initially only from Italy, but as the business developed, from other countries as well.

The business has been successful. Richard has always managed to make a profit, but he is not very careful with money. He spends a lot, and he has never quite been able to follow his original intention, which was to invest part of the profits in expanding the business. Still, he has always prided himself on being able

▶

to provide a high standard of living for his family. However, more recently Richard has fallen into difficulties. Four years ago his wife, Hermione, discovered that he was having an affair with an Italian sales rep. Horrified and upset, she refused to believe his assurances that the affair was over and that it would never happen again. She turned him out of the house and demanded a divorce. Richard feels that he has done rather badly out of the divorce, under the terms of which Hermione kept the family home, and Richard has had to pay what he considers to be an unreasonably large sum of maintenance for the three children of the marriage. He now lives in a small rented flat.

A few months after the divorce Richard met up, by complete coincidence, with Charlie, a former friend from college, on a train journey to London. After college Charlie spent several years working as a chef in France and Switzerland, but had now returned to the UK to start a private restaurant school. He is delighted to find that Richard deals in high quality kitchen supplies, and promises that he will place all his contracts for equipment with Richard's business. Charlie and Richard discover that they are both keen Formula One enthusiasts and, after that chance meeting, they see each other regularly at races and social events. Because he knew Charlie at college and considers him to be a good friend, Richard is quite relaxed about supplying goods on credit. Charlie explains that he will be a bit short of money for the first few months in the new business, but he will pay Richard whatever he is able to spare: 'Once the business is on its feet, there'll be no problem at all . . .'.

Charlie's business starts up in July 20X3, and Richard supplies all the equipment for the demonstration kitchen in the school at a cost of £23 000. At first the business seems to be doing well, and Charlie is so confident about it that he starts up another, bigger, branch in another city only six months later, in December 20X3. Again, Richard supplies all the equipment, this time at a cost of £27 600, although this time he does say to Charlie that he would like to have some of the debt paid off soon. Charlie has not been able to pay him anything at all in the first few months of his business. As the months go by, Richard notices that he's not seeing Charlie around so much, and even starts to suspect that Charlie is avoiding him.

Richard, in the meantime, has his own money troubles. Hermione has pestered him for extra money to take herself and the children on an exotic cruise. Because Richard still feels guilty about the failure of the marriage he gives in and pays over £7500 out of his drawings from the business. Feeling depressed, Richard decided to cheer himself up by going on a skiing holiday in Colorado with his new girlfriend. Somehow, the drawings from the business seem to be much higher, and, for the first time ever, Richard needs a business overdraft. The bank manager is happy to oblige and, because interest rates are low, Richard is not really worried about it. He knows that his cash position will be back to normal as soon as Charlie pays him.

In late October 20X4 Richard is alarmed to find an article in the trade press about Charlie. Headlined 'Charmer Charlie in closure chaos', the article reports the sudden closure of the restaurant schools. Irate clients, all of whom had paid in advance for courses, have been trying to gain entry to the schools, the doors to which are permanently locked. Richard rings the journalist responsible for the article. Off the record, the journalist confirms that this latest enterprise is not the first business failure that Charlie has experienced. He is notorious in some circles for his ability to charm people into lending him money. Several years ago he started a restaurant business with money that he persuaded friends to contribute. The restaurant was not a success and Charlie went abroad still owing his ex-friends large sums of money. There is some speculation now that the Fraud Squad is interested in Charlie's activities.

Richard rings Charlie on his business telephone line, but the line does not appear to be working. There is no reply from Charlie's mobile phone. In desperation he rings a chef who has been working at one of the schools. The chef is extremely angry. He hasn't been paid for over a month and he has no idea of Charlie's present whereabouts.

Richard is not very good at keeping track of his financial affairs. A bookkeeper maintains the basic records of the business and, once a year, his accountant, Frank, prepares a profit and loss account and balance sheet at 31 December. At this point, in October 20X4, Richard really does not know how the business stands, but he is aware that he is close to the business overdraft limit of £24 000. For the first time in the history of the business his Italian supplier, Giovanni, has rung him asking politely when he is likely to be paid. Richard does not have an immediate answer to the question, but tells Giovanni that he will call him back in a couple of days.

Richard visits Frank with a list of balances prepared by the bookkeeper as at the end of September 20X4. Richard is, by now, extremely anxious and asks Frank to prepare financial statements as at the end of September as soon as possible, and to advise him on the impact there will be upon the business if the money owed by Charlie cannot be recovered. Richard is desperate to have Frank's opinion on whether or not the business can survive.

The list of balances is as follows:

	£
Interest paid and bank charges	1 560
Sales	250 836
Delivery expenses	2 612
Stock at 1 January 20X4	17 881
Creditors	51 760
Discounts allowed	870
Discounts received	183
Import duties related to purchases	1 536
Purchases	140 255
Premises rental and other charges	31 580
Overdraft	23 861
Debtors (including £50 600 owed by Charlie)	93 242
Staff wages	23 391
Administration charges	7 726
Capital at 1 January 20X4	64 084
Drawings	61 760
Fixed assets	8 311
Closing stock at 30 September 20X4	19 870

The bookkeeper sends a note with the balances to say that the telephone bill for the quarter to 30 September 20X4 still needs to be paid and is not included in the total for administration charges above. The bill is for £422. In addition, Frank thinks that it would be sensible to make an accounting adjustment for an accrual for his own fees. He has not sent a bill to Richard for a while and he estimates that about £1300 will be due for tax work already carried out and for the work of preparing these interim accounts. These two items (£422 + £1300) will create a total accrual to be included in balance sheet liabilities of £1722.

▶

Frank prepares financial statements without any adjustment for the amount of the debt due from Charlie, as follows:

Richard: Profit and loss account for the 9 months ending 30 September 20X4

	£	£	£
Sales			250 836
Cost of sales			
Opening stock		17 881	
Add: purchases	140 255		
import duties related to purchases	1 536		
		141 791	
		159 672	
Less: closing stock		(19 870)	
			(139 802)
Gross profit			111 034
Discounts received			183
			111 217
Expenses			
Staff wages		23 391	
Premises rental and other charges		31 580	
Administration charges	7 726		
Add: accrued telephone expense	422		
		8 148	
Accrued accountancy charges		1 300	
Discounts allowed		870	
Interest paid and bank charges		1 560	
Delivery expenses		2 612	
			(69 461)
Net profit			41 756

Richard: Balance sheet at 30 September 20X4

	£	£
Fixed assets		8 311
Current assets		
Stock	19 870	
Debtors	93 242	
	113 112	
Current liabilities		
Creditors	51 760	
Accruals	1 722	
Bank overdraft	23 861	
	77 343	
Net current assets (£113 112 − £77 343)		35 769
Net assets		44 080

Capital

Opening capital balance 1 January 20X4	64 084
Add: net profit for the year	41 756
	105 840
Less: drawings	(61 760)
Closing capital balance 30 September 20X4	44 080

Case study discussion

If the debt from Charlie cannot be recovered it will be treated as a bad debt in Richard's accounts. As explained earlier in the chapter, the appropriate accounting treatment is to deduct the debt from the debtors balance, thus reducing assets, and from profit for the period. The latter adjustment directly affects the capital account.

The effect, in summary, will be as follows. Profit for the nine months to 30 September 20X4 currently stands at £41 756. If Charlie's debt of £50 600 is deducted a loss arises:

$$£41 756 - 50 600 = £8844 \text{ loss}$$

In the balance sheet the debt of £50 600 is deducted from the total debtors of £93 242, leaving a revised debtors balance of £42 642. The revised balance sheet is as follows:

Richard: Revised balance sheet at 30 September 20X4

	£	£
Fixed assets		8 311
Current assets		
Stock	19 870	
Debtors	42 642	
	62 512	
Current liabilities		
Creditors	51 760	
Accruals	1 722	
Bank overdraft	23 861	
	77 343	
Net current liabilities (£62 512 − £77 343)		(14 831)
Net liabilities		(6 520)
Capital		
Opening capital balance 1 January 20X4	64 084	
Less: loss for the year	(8 844)	
	55 240	
Less: drawings	(61 760)	
Closing capital balance 30 September 20X4		(6 520)

▶

Note that the balance sheet now shows net liabilities and that the capital account is negative. The business is insolvent and Richard is in very deep trouble. There is no money available to pay the creditors, and the overdraft limit is virtually reached. The future looks bleak for the business, and for Richard.

Can the business survive this disaster? Looking at the original set of accounting statements before the adjustment is made for the bad debt, we can see that the business is basically profitable. If it could be refinanced there is no reason for it not to continue to be a viable concern. The original balance sheet before adjustment suggests that Richard's spending has got out of hand: the high level of drawings of £61 760 is not sustainable. Even if new sources of finance were to be found, Richard would need to curtail his spending by a significant amount.

How likely is it that further finance would be available? If Richard had any personal assets these could be sold to raise much-needed cash for the business. What we know of Richard's personal life suggests that he is short of assets; he cannot borrow on the security of a house because the family home is now owned by Hermione. If the business is to survive Richard needs urgently to explore other options. Some possibilities might be:

- A personal loan. It is possible that the bank may be prepared to lend Richard some money. However, even if this is the case, there are likely to be stringent conditions attached to any loan.

- A personal loan from a private source. Richard's mother originally lent him the money to start the business. It is possible that she may be willing to make further loans. There may be other relatives or friends who will stand by Richard in his difficulties.

- Financial assistance from Richard's supplier in Italy. For many years Giovanni has been supplying goods to Richard for distribution in the UK. If Richard goes out of business, Giovanni loses his UK outlet and it may be difficult and expensive to establish another. Giovanni may be prepared to, say, go into partnership with Richard in order to keep the distribution outlet open. As the business is basically profitable, it could be to Giovanni's personal benefit to put money into the venture to keep it afloat.

- Legal action against Charlie for recovery of the debt. This should probably be attempted in any case, but the reports of Charlie's former business activities and the fact that he cannot currently be found indicate that it will probably be very difficult to recover any cash.

If Richard cannot obtain fresh finance for the business it will not be able to meet its liabilities. Because he is a sole trader he is personally liable for the debts incurred by the business, and it is quite likely that he will become personally bankrupt. In the circumstances, his panic seems completely justified.

Chapter summary

This chapter has explained the accounting treatment of returns of goods, discounts received and allowed, and of delivery charges.

The concept of income and expense recognition was introduced. The realisation and matching conventions in accounting were dealt with in detail, using a comprehensive example to explain the necessary accounting adjustments.

Adjustments to the value of stock and debtors have been examined in depth. The distinction between the accounting treatment of bad debts and of doubtful debts has been explained, and finally, in the case study, the potential impact of bad debts upon a small business was considered.

A great deal of quite complex material has been covered in this chapter. Students should ensure that they complete as many of the end-of-chapter questions as necessary in order to be sure of completely understanding all the principles and practices described in the chapter.

Exercises

The answers to many of the exercises are set out later in this chapter. However, where the exercise number is followed by 'A' the answer is available only to lecturers. Remember that additional exercises (with answers) are available to students on the book's website.

8.1 Oscar's trading company prepares accounts to 31 December. In the year to 31 December 20X1 the following trading transactions occur:

	£
Sales	72 411
Purchases	53 005
Sales returns	361
Purchases returns	1 860

Stock at 1 January 20X1 was £4182, and at 31 December 20X1 it was £5099. What is Oscar's gross profit for the year?

a) 21 822

b) 18 102

c) 18 824

d) 22 544.

8.2A Olivia's trading company prepares accounts to 31 August each year. In the year ending 31 August 20X4, the following trading transactions occur:

	£
Sales	193 306
Purchases	144 315
Sales returns	1 836
Purchases returns	63

Opening stock at 1 September 20X3 was £16 399 and closing stock at 31 August 20X4 was £17 041. What is Olivia's gross profit for the year?

a) 47 797

b) 51 469

c) 47 860

d) 51 658.

8.3   Omar imports onyx picture frames from India. He prepares accounts to 30 April each year. In the year ending 30 April 20X7 he records the following totals for trading transactions:

	£
Sales	347 348
Purchases	240 153
Import duties	6 043
Sales returns	2 971
Purchases returns	1 800

Omar's opening stock at 1 May 20X6 was £43 730 and his closing stock at 30 April 20X7 was £41 180. What is Omar's gross profit for the year?

a) 97 431

b) 99 773

c) 109 517

d) 91 388.

8.4A   Ophelia imports glass ornaments from Norway. She prepares accounts to 30 June each year. In the year ending 30 June 20X9 she records the following totals for trading transactions:

	£
Sales	83 722
Purchases	65 277
Special charges for safety packaging	604
Sales returns	426
Purchases returns	291

Opening stock at 1 July 20X8 was £5799. Closing stock at 30 June 20X9 was £5904. What is Ophelia's gross profit for the year?

a) 18 084

b) 18 437

c) 18 663

d) 17 811.

8.5   Poppy imports and sells display fireworks. She supplies her customers on credit terms, requiring payment of invoices within 30 days. In order to encourage early payment she offers customers a discount of 0.5% of invoice value for receipt of payment within 30 days.

The following is a list of Poppy's account balances for all sales and expenses items at 28 February 20X2:

	£
Staffing costs	9 777
Opening stock at 1 March 20X1	7 140
Sales returns	3 997
Import duties	9 911
Rental	17 211
Discounts allowed	716
Telephone charges	1 227
Purchases	123 057
Insurance	8 204
Marketing	1 888
Administrative expenses	922
Electricity	1 604
Delivery van expenses	2 107
Sales	220 713
Stock at 28 February 20X2	7 393

Prepare Poppy's profit and loss account for the year ending 28 February 20X2.

8.6A   Paolo trades in promotional goods. His customers order items like mouse mats, biros, playing cards, golf balls and so on, printed with their own logo. Paolo keeps a stock of blank goods. When he receives an order from a customer he sends the plain items of stock to a local printer who adds the customer's logo and address details. The business is run from a shed in Paolo's back garden at home. The shed is supplied with electricity; the cost of the electricity is billed together with Paolo's domestic supply. He estimates that one-sixth of the bill is attributable to electricity used in the shed. His electricity bills for the year to 31 March 20X6 total £3072.

Apart from the electricity, Paolo's records show the following items of sales and expenses for the year:

	£
Discounts allowed to customers	88
Travelling expenses	3 914
Sales	118 242
Opening stock at 1 April 20X5	5 918
Cost of printing	17 291
Telephone	1 671
Mobile phone call charges	419
Purchases	43 947
Discounts received from suppliers	133
Accountancy and tax advice	800
Office sundry expenses	977
Marketing	2 663
Interest received	204
Purchases returns	1 774
Closing stock at 31 March 20X6	4 261

Prepare Paolo's profit and loss account for the year ending 31 March 20X6.

8.7   Per prepares his accounts to 31 January each year. At 31 January 20X4 he has the following balances on electricity and telephone accounts:

	£
Electricity	6 464
Telephone	3 118

Per is due to receive an electricity bill in respect of the three-month period to 31 January 20X4, but it has not yet arrived. By 15 February it has still not arrived and he rings up the electricity company. The customer services representative tells Per that they are having trouble with their computerised billing system, but that the amount of the bill to 31 January 20X4 will be £2350.

The most recent telephone bill received by Per covered the three-month period to 30 November 20X3. Usually Per would expect to spend about £300 per month on phone charges and that seems a reasonable estimate for January 20X4. However, he knows that an unusually large number of calls were made just before Christmas, and he estimates that call charges for December were probably in the region of £420.

a) What amount should be included in Per's profit and loss account for electricity and telephone expenses up to 31 January 20X4?

b) What is the total accrual for electricity and telephone at 31 January 20X4?

c) Where is this amount shown in the balance sheet?

8.8 Pookie's business involves telephone sales, so her business phone bills are high. Her accounting year ends on 31 August, and in the year to 31 August 20X8 she has received bills for phone charges as follows:

Date received	Date paid	Period covered	Amount (£)
9 October 20X7	15 October 20X7	1.7.X7–30.9.X7	9 760
5 January 20X8	15 January 20X8	1.10.X7–31.12.X7	12 666
6 April 20X8	14 April 20X8	1.1.X8–31.3.X8	8 444
8 July 20X8	12 July 20X8	1.4.X8–30.6.X8	9 530

Pookie estimates that her telephone charges for July and August will be two-twelfths of the total of the charges for the 12 months to 30.6.X8.

To the nearest £, what is the telephone expense for inclusion in Pookie's profit and loss account for the year ending 31 August 20X8?

a) £40 400

b) £40 626

c) £47 133

d) £33 667.

8.9A In 20X7 the gas bills for Peregrine's business are received and paid as follows:

Date received	Date paid	Period covered	Amount (£)
4 March 20X7	10 March 20X7	1.12.X6–28.2.X7	841
6 June 20X7	20 June 20X7	1.3.X7–31.5.X7	790
6 September 20X7	15 September 20X7	1.6.X7–31.8.X7	654
9 December 20X7	20 December 20X7	1.9.X7–30.11.X7	752

Peregrine prepares accounts to 31 December each year. He estimates that gas used in December 20X7 would be billed at about £300.

What figure for gas expense should be included in Peregrine's accounts to 31 December 20X7? (Work to the nearest £.)

a) £2 737

b) £3 037

c) £3 057

d) £2 457.

8.10A Parvati's business insurance is paid annually, with the bill running from 1 June to 31 May each year. Her accounting year-end is 31 December. Her insurance transactions over a two-year period are as follows:

Date paid	Amount (£)	Period covered
6 June 20X5	3 724	1.6.X5–31.5.X6
8 June 20X6	4 942	1.6.X6–31.5.X7

Parvati pays the bill for £4942, but queries the large increase over the previous year with the insurance company. The company discovers that it has made a mistake and sends her a refund of £836 on 17 September 20X6.

What is the amount of insurance expense to be included in Parvati's profit and loss account for the year ending 31 December 20X6? (Work to the nearest £.)

a) £5 055

b) £3 883

c) £4 435

d) £3 947.

8.11 Patience pays a subscription to a business trade association annually in advance. The subscription is due on 30 September each year, to cover one year running from 1 October. Patience's accounting year runs to 28 February. The subscriptions paid in September 20X6 and 20X7 are as follows: 20X6 = £644; 20X7 = £796.

What are the amounts included in prepayments for this expense at 28 February 20X7 and 20X8? (Work to the nearest £.)

a) 20X7 = £268; 20X8 = £332

b) 20X7 = £376; 20X8 = £464

c) 20X7 = £376; 20X8 = £332

d) 20X7 = £268; 20X8 = £464

8.12A Paula's business expenses for 31 October 20X1 are summarised as follows:

	£
Insurance	7 280
Phone	2 017
Other expenses	36 470

Examination of the detailed transactions in the insurance account shows the following:

	£
Insurance charges for seven months to 31 May 20X1	2 660
Paid 3 June for one year from 1 June 20X1 to 31 May 20X2	4 620
	7 280

Examination of the detailed transactions in the phone account shows the following:

	£
Bill for period 1 November 20X0–31 January 20X1	690
Bill for period 1 February 20X1–30 April 20X1	627
Bill for period 1 May 20X1–31 July 20X1	700
	2 017

The bill for the three-month period to 31 October 20X1 was not received until after the year-end. The amount of the bill was £696.

What is the total amount of Paula's business expenses for inclusion in her profit and loss account for the year ending 31 October 20X1?

a) £45 767

b) £43 768

c) £43 072

d) £41 825.

8.13   Simon trades in soft furnishings from shop premises in the centre of a small town in northern England. He provides basic summaries of his transactions for his accountant, Bernie, who prepares his final accounts and tax computation. The business year-end is 31 July.

Simon's income and expense transaction totals for the year ended 31 July 20X4, before any necessary year-end adjustments, are as follows:

	£
Delivery expenses	2 490
Opening stock at 1.8.X3	38 888
Income from curtain-making service	6 519
Costs of curtain-making service	2 797
Shop rental	18 750
Business rates	3 510
Assistant's wages	22 379
Insurance	4 478
Electricity	2 064
Travelling expenses	603
Sales	317 342
Telephone	1 035
Purchases	230 133
Discounts received	377
Trade subscriptions	165
Charitable donations	500
Closing stock at 31.7.X4	39 501

Note the following additional information:

1. Of the £4478 included above for insurance, £501 relates to the period after 1 August 20X4.

2. Simon has two very trustworthy assistants working in the shop. As well as wages, he pays each of them an annual bonus of 0.5% of total sales (not including income from the curtain-making service). An accrual needs to be made for this item.

3. Electricity charges of £377 require accrual.

4. Bernie always makes an accrual for his own fees when drawing up Simon's accounts. He estimates that the fee required for the year ended 31 July 20X4 will be £800.

5. In conversation, Simon mentions that he has been having a lot of trouble with the occupants of the shop next door who regularly leave rubbish scattered on the forecourt that serves both shops. Simon has taken legal advice to see whether he can obtain a legal injunction, but he has not yet received a bill from the solicitor for work done. At Bernie's request Simon contacts the solicitor for an estimate of the fees at 31 July 20X4. The solicitor tells Simon that time charges for consultation and correspondence amount to about £350. Bernie and Simon agree that an accrual should be made for this amount.

Prepare a profit and loss account for Simon for the year ending 31 July 20X4 and calculate the totals for accruals and prepayments for inclusion in the balance sheet at that date.

8.14A Sylvester runs a consultancy business, employing two members of staff as consultants and a secretarial assistant. Because he has done an accountancy course, he is able to prepare his own accounting records and statements. He consults an accountant periodically for tax advice. Sylvester's accounting year-end date is 31 January.

In the year to 31 January 20X8 Sylvester has built up the following income and expenditure balances on his accounts:

	£
Staff consultants' salaries	47 090
Secretarial assistant's salary	14 441
Premises expenses – office rental	12 750
Premises expenses – other	4 419
Consultancy fees	239 000
Telephone – office	4 200
Mobile phone	2 419
Entertainment	3 007
Membership subscriptions	1 136
Administration costs	3 422
Sundry expenses	1 620
Electricity	5 187

Note the following additional information:

1. Sylvester pays the two assistant consultants a basic salary plus a bonus based upon performance. The bonus for each consultant for the year ended 31 January 20X8 will be the higher of 10% of total consultancy fees billed in the year and £24 500. The bonus element of salaries must be accrued for at the year-end.

2. £366 of the membership subscriptions relate to the period after 31 January 20X8.

3. Office telephone charges include bills for the 10 months to 30 November 20X7. Phone charges for the business vary very little from month to month and the charges for December and January should be in line with previous months.

4. Sylvester rings his accountant for an estimate of costs in relation to tax advice for the year. The accountant suggests that an accrual of £400 will probably be appropriate.

Prepare Sylvester's profit and loss account for the year ending 31 January 20X8.

8.15   Sharon runs a business selling cards and novelty items from a busy shop in a large shopping centre. She has the following list of account balances at 31 August 20X1:

	£
Administration expenses	8 219
Purchases	224 069
Fixed assets	27 662
Sundry expenses	1 007
Bank charges	1 830
Premises rental (including business and water rates)	68 000
Opening stock at 1 September 20X0	45 517
Sales	464 714
Subscriptions to trade association	818
Electricity	5 337
Property services charge	17 004
Cash at bank	18 712
Interest received	460
Assistants' wages	38 830
Mobile phone	766
Travelling expenses	3 600
Phone – shop	3 234
Drawings	61 300
Insurance	5 237
Creditors	24 165
Opening capital at 1 September 20X0	42 065
Accountant's and solicitor's fees	2 070
Discounts received	1 808
Closing stock at 31 August 20X1	46 522

Note the following additional information:

1. In a normal year Sharon expects to make a gross profit on sales of 50% and a net profit of 16.3%.

2. An accrual of £1307 for property services charges is required at 31 August 20X1.

3. Not all of the £5237 for insurance relates to the year to 31 August 20X1. Sharon estimates that £465 of the charges relate to the next accounting period.

4. Sharon is still waiting for an electricity bill up to 31 August 20X1. She reads the electricity meter at 31 August and on the basis of the reading estimates that further charges of £1107 will have to be accrued for the year.

5. Some phone charges have not been billed by the year-end. An accrual of £200 should be made.

Prepare a profit and loss account for Sharon for the year ending 31 August 20X1 and a balance sheet at that date. Calculate gross and net profit margins and compare them with the expected performance of the business.

8.16   Ted sells belts and accessories to fashion stores around the country, buying in most of his goods from China. Long experience in the business has developed his judgement in purchasing; he needs to be able to judge fashion trends at least six months in advance. Even Ted, however, makes mistakes.

In his accounting year to 31 December 20X5, Ted buys in a range of coordinating accessories in hot pink. By the middle of the year Ted realises that he has misjudged the market. This year's colours are sludgy browns and greens and there is no demand for pink. In total Ted's purchases for the year are £379 322. Of these, £21 900 related to the pink items and £17 750 of the stock remains unsold at the year-end. Ted's sales are £599 790 for the year. Total opening stock (which included no pink items, and which was valued at cost) was £49 071, and total closing stock is £62 222 including the unsold £17 750 of pink items. Ted has had an offer from a discounter of £6000 for all the pink items that remain in stock.

Draw up a trading account that values closing stock at the lower of cost or net realisable value. Calculate Ted's gross profit margin and compare it to the gross profit margin that would have been achieved if the whole of closing stock were valued at cost.

8.17   Ulrich prepares his accounts to 31 July each year. At 31 July 20X1 his debtors list totals £397 700. Included in the list is a debt of £17 000 owing by Gayle Associates. Gayle Associates has recently ceased to trade and Ulrich has been told by Gayle's administrator that there is little likelihood of him ever recovering the £17 000 owing to him.

There is a recession in the general economy and Ulrich is concerned that some of his other debtors could run into difficulties. He decides to make a general provision for doubtful debts of 1% of debtors whose balances have been outstanding for more than three months at 31 July 20X1 (excluding the £17 000 owed by Gayle). He has never previously made a provision against debtors.

An analysis of Ulrich's debtors at 31 July 20X1 shows the following:

	£
Outstanding for one month or less	169 930
Outstanding for between one month and three months	143 370
Outstanding for over three months	67 400
Gayle Associates	17 000
	397 700

How will debtors be presented in Ulrich's balance sheet at 31 July 20X1? What is the effect of bad and doubtful debts on Ulrich's profit for the year?

8.18A   Umberto makes a provision of 1.5% against his total debtors each year. In the year to 31 August 20X7 he has used up £650 of this provision because a debtor has gone out of business. Umberto's debtors at 31 August 20X6, before provision, were £366 000. At 31 August 20X7 debtors before provision are £390 000.

How are debtors presented in Umberto's balance sheets at 31 August 20X6 and 31 August 20X7? What is the effect of the provision for doubtful debts on Umberto's profit and loss account for the year ending 31 August 20X7?

8.19   Ursula is a wholesaler trading in stationery supplies. She sells to offices and shops around the country and at any one time has up to 350 debtors due to pay her. She allows 30 days credit but finds that her bigger customers are quite likely to exceed this limit.

At 31 December 20X2 Ursula has the following balances in her accounts:

	£
Assistant's wages	10 008
Fixed assets	23 360
Opening stock at 1 January 20X2	31 090
Discounts allowed	1 046
Creditors	25 920
Discounts received	361
Electricity	4 850
Business and water rates	3 899
Warehouse rental	11 070
Telephone	2 663
Debtors	50 354
Opening capital at 1 January 20X2	70 219
Cash at bank	361
Insurance	3 414
Delivery costs	4 490
Drawings	33 988
Administration charges	3 242
Purchases	239 285
Sales	326 620
Closing stock at 31 December 20X2	30 048

Note the following additional information:

1. Ursula has recently been informed that a debtor of hers, Wainwright, has left the country owing large amounts of money. Ursula is relieved that the outstanding debt is no more than £672 because, in the past, she has sold large quantities of stationery to Wainwright. Ursula is advised by her accountant that the debt should be treated as completely irrecoverable, and should be written off.

2. At 31 December 20X2 there are accrued charges for electricity of £338.

3. The accountant's fees in respect of the year are likely to be in the region of £700. This amount should be accrued.

4. Two debtors are giving Ursula some cause for concern. Wilson has been owing £398 for almost six months. Wilson assures Ursula via frequent phone calls that the payment will be made when he gets back on his feet after a devastating fire at his offices. And £700 is owed for stationery supplies to a friend of Ursula who started a new business a few months ago. The friend assures Ursula that the bill will be paid, but Ursula knows from mutual friends that the new venture is not going well. Ursula decides to make a provision against both of these amounts.

5. Of the insurance balance of £3414, £622 relates to the next accounting year and should be treated as a prepayment.

Prepare a profit and loss account for Ursula for the year ending 31 December 20X2, and a balance sheet at that date, incorporating all the adjustments noted.

Answers to exercises

8.1   **Oscar: Extract from profit and loss account for year ending 31 December 20X1**

	£	£	£
Sales			72 411
Less: returns			(361)
Cost of sales			72 050
Opening stock		4 182	
Add: purchases	53 005		
Less: returns	(1 860)		
		51 145	
		55 327	
Less: closing stock		(5 099)	
			(50 228)
Gross profit			21 822

Therefore the correct answer is a).

8.3   **Omar: Extract from profit and loss account for year ending 30 April 20X7**

	£	£	£
Sales			347 348
Less: returns			(2 971)
Cost of sales			344 377
Opening stock		43 730	
Add: purchases	240 153		
Add: import duties	6 043		
Less: returns	(1 800)		
		244 396	
		288 126	
Less: closing stock		(41 180)	
			(246 946)
Gross profit			97 431

Therefore, the correct answer is a).

8.5   **Poppy: Profit and loss account for the year ending 28 February 20X2**

	£	£	£
Sales			220 713
Less: returns			(3 997)
			216 716
Cost of sales			
Opening stock		7 140	
Add: purchases	123 057		
Add: import duty	9 911		
		132 968	
		140 108	
Less: closing stock		(7 393)	
			132 715
Gross profit			84 001

Expenses

Rental	17 211
Staffing costs	9 777
Insurance	8 204
Delivery van expenses	2 107
Discounts allowed	716
Telephone charges	1 227
Electricity	1 604
Marketing	1 888
Administrative expenses	922
	43 656
Net profit	40 345

8.7   a) Electricity: £6464 + £2350 = £8814. Telephone: £3118 + 420 + 300 = £3838.

b) Total accrual = £2350 + 420 + 300 = £3070.

c) The accrual will be shown as part of current liabilities, generally immediately following trade creditors.

8.8   Telephone expense for inclusion in Pookie's accounts to 31 August 20X8:

	£
1/3 x £9 760 relating to September 20X7	3 253
October–December 20X7	12 666
January–March 20X8	8 444
April–June 20X8	9 530
July and August 20X8: (9 760 + 12 666 + 8 444 + 9 530) × 2/12	6 733
	40 626

Therefore, b) is the correct answer.

8.11   The prepayment at 28 February 20X7 is 7/12 × 644 = £376. The prepayment at 28 February 20X8 is 7/12 × 796 = £464
Therefore b) is the correct answer.

8.13

Simon: Profit and loss account for the year ending 31 July 20X4

	£	£	£
Sales			317 342
Cost of sales			
Opening stock		38 888	
Purchases		230 133	
		269 021	
Less: closing stock		(39 501)	
			229 520
Gross profit			87 822
Discounts received			377
Income from curtain making service		6 519	
Costs of curtain making service		(2 797)	
			3 722
			91 921

Expenses

Shop rental		18 750
Assistants' wages	22 379	
Add: accrued commission	3 173	
		25 552
Business rates		3 510
Insurance	4 478	
Less: prepaid	(501)	
		3 977
Electricity	2 064	
Add: accrual	377	
		2 441
Telephone		1 035
Travelling expenses		603
Delivery expenses		2 490
Trade subscriptions		165
Charitable donations		500
Accountant's fees		800
Legal fees		350
		(60 173)

Net profit		31 748

Total accruals:

	£
Assistants' commission	3 173
Electricity	377
Accountant's fees	800
Legal fees	350
	4 700
Prepayment: insurance	501

8.15   **Sharon: Profit and loss account for the year ending 31 August 20X1**

	£	£	£
Sales			464 714
Cost of sales			
Opening stock		45 517	
Add: purchases		224 069	
		269 586	
Less: closing stock		(46 522)	
			(223 064)
Gross profit			241 650
Discounts received			1 808
Interest received			460
			243 918

Expenses

Premises rental (including business and water rates)		68 000
Property services charge	17 004	
Add: accrual	1 307	
		18 311
Electricity	5 337	
Add: accrual	1 107	
		6 444
Assistants' wages		38 830
Phone – shop	3 234	
Add: accrual	200	
		3 434
Mobile phone		766
Insurance	5 237	
Less: prepayment	(465)	
		4 772
Administration expenses		8 219
Sundry expenses		1 007
Subscriptions to trade association		818
Bank charges		1 830
Accountant's and solicitor's fees		2 070
Travelling expenses		3 600
		(158 101)
Net profit		85 817

Sharon: Balance sheet at 31 August 20X1

	£	£
Fixed assets		27 662
Current assets		
Stock	46 522	
Prepayment	465	
Cash at bank	18 712	
	65 699	
Current liabilities		
Creditors	24 165	
Accruals (£1307 + £1107 + £200)	2 614	
	26 779	
Net current assets (£65 699 – £26 779)		38 920
Net assets		66 582
Capital		
Opening capital balance 1 September 20X0	42 065	
Add: net profit for the year	85 817	
	127 882	
Less: drawings	(61 300)	
Closing capital balance 31 August 20X1		66 582

Sharon's gross profit margin is: $\frac{241\,650}{464\,714} \times 100 = 52\%$

Her net profit margin is: $\frac{85\,817}{464\,714} \times 100 = 18.5\%$

Business performance has been better than usual in the year to 31 August 20X1. Gross profit margin is generally expected to be 50% but this year it has improved to 52%. Net profit margin is expected to be 16.3% but this year has improved to 18.5%.

8.16   **Ted: Extract from profit and loss account for the year ending 31 December 20X5**

	Closing stock at cost	Closing stock at cost/net realisable value
	£	£
Sales	599 790	599 790
Cost of sales		
Opening stock	49 071	49 071
Add: purchases	379 322	379 322
Less: closing stock	(62 222)	—
Less: closing stock*	—	(50 472)
	366 171	377 921
Gross profit	233 619	221 869
Gross profit margin	38.9%	37.0%
*Closing stock at cost	62 222	
Less: pink items at cost	(17 750)	
Add: pink items at net realisable value	6 000	
Closing stock adjusted to net realisable value for pink items	50 472	

8.17   Ulrich will require a general provision of 1% of debtors outstanding for over three months: $1\% \times £67\,400 = £674$.

The debt due from Gayle will be treated as irrecoverable and will no longer appear in debtors. Debtors will be stated at $£397\,700 - 17\,000 = 380\,700$.

Extract from Ulrich's balance sheet at 31 July 20X1:

	£
Debtors	380 700
Less: provision	(674)
	380 026

Ulrich's profit for the year is reduced by (a) the amount of the bad debt = £17 000; and (b) the provision made for the first time this year = £674. In total, Ulrich's profit is reduced by £17 674.

8.19 **Ursula: Profit and loss account for the year ending 31 December 20X2**

	£	£	£
Sales			326 620
Cost of sales			
Opening stock		31 090	
Add: purchases		239 285	
		270 375	
Less: closing stock		(30 048)	
			(240 327)
Gross profit			86 293
Discounts received			361
			86 654
Expenses			
Warehouse rental		11 070	
Business and water rates		3 899	
Electricity	4 850		
Add: accrual	338		
		5 188	
Insurance	3 414		
Less: prepayment	(622)		
		2 792	
Assistant's wages		10 008	
Telephone		2 663	
Delivery costs		4 490	
Administration charges		3 242	
Bad debt written off		672	
Provision for doubtful debts		1 098	
Accountant's fee accrual		700	
Discounts allowed		1 046	
			(46 868)
Net profit			39 786

Ursula: Balance sheet at 31 December 20X2

	£	£	£
Fixed assets			23 360
Current assets			
Stock		30 048	
Debtors*	49 682		
Less: provision	(1 098)		
		48 584	
Prepayment		622	
Cash at bank		361	
		79 615	
Current liabilities			
Creditors		25 920	
Accruals		1 038	
		26 958	
Net current assets (79 615−26 958)			52 657

Net assets		<u>76 017</u>
Capital		
Opening capital balance 1 January 20X2	70 219	
Add: net profit for the year	<u>39 786</u>	
	110 005	
Less: drawings	<u>(33 988)</u>	<u> </u>
Closing capital balance 31 December 20X2		<u>76 017</u>

*The bad debt of £672 disappears completely from the records. Debtors in the accounts list were £50 354 but are reduced for presentation in the balance sheet to £49 682 (i.e. £50 354–£672).

9

ADJUSTMENTS TO THE PROFIT AND LOSS ACCOUNT AND BALANCE SHEET: 2

AIMS AND LEARNING OUTCOMES

Aim of the chapter

To enable students to understand the use of adjustments for depreciation and amortisation and their effect on the profit and loss account and balance sheet of sole trader businesses.

Learning outcomes

After reading the chapter and completing the related exercises, students should:

- Understand the need for depreciation and amortisation in financial statements.
- Understand the distinction between tangible and intangible fixed assets.
- Be able to incorporate adjustments for depreciation and amortisation into a profit and loss account and balance sheet.

Depreciation and amortisation

In Chapter 8 we examined the matching (also known as accruals) convention in accounting. It is important to set off against sales for an accounting period all the expenses which have contributed to making those sales. We looked at examples of the adjustments for prepayments and accruals which are necessary to ensure that matching is done as precisely as possible. There is one further important category of adjustment that must be made under the matching (or accruals) convention: adjustment for the **depreciation** or **amortisation** of fixed assets.

Fixed assets are purchased for use in the business; they are used in the ordinary activities of the business to generate sales. For example, a business that delivers goods to its customers needs delivery vans. The vans are fixed assets in that they are used within the business over a long period of time. However, they do not last forever; eventually they will accumulate a high mileage and will become unreliable. It is likely that, before this point is reached, the business will dispose of them and buy new replacements.

The costs of running the fleet of delivery vehicles must be matched against the sales generated in an accounting period. Some of the costs are obvious: there is fuel, insurance, service and repair to consider. However, in order to fully meet the obligation to match costs against sales, it is conventional in accounting to include in costs an estimate of how much of the value of fixed assets has been used up in an accounting period. The next example illustrates how such an estimate would be arrived at in practice.

Example 9.1 Quickwash is a commercial laundry service used, principally, by hotels and restaurants. Dirty towels, sheets, tablecloths and so on, are collected in one of the Quickwash fleet of delivery vans, and are taken to the laundry on an industrial estate where they are washed, dried and pressed. The clean items are then delivered by van to the client, usually within 24 hours.

The delivery vans are essential to the running of the business. Experience has shown that even the high quality vans used by the business tend to start needing replacement parts after three or four years. The laundry business is highly competitive and Quickwash cannot afford to upset customers by being late with deliveries because a van has broken down. Therefore, Quickwash's management has a policy of replacing the vans every three years.

At the beginning of January 20X1 Quickwash buys a van at a cost of £20 000. Management's policy means that the van will be used for no more than three years. It will be sold second-hand and replaced in January 20X4. As explained in earlier chapters, the cost of the van will be included in the fixed assets section in the balance sheet. Initially, the amount included will be £20 000. However, by the end of the first year, some of that value has been used up in the course of Quickwash's business activities. Depreciation is a measure of the amount of value used up.

How do we calculate depreciation?

It is important to realise that depreciation is an estimate, not an exact figure. Quickwash's management knows the exact amount spent to acquire the van, and also knows that the van will be kept in the business for three years. However, they do not know exactly how much the van can be sold for at the end of the three-year period. Suppose that, based upon past experience, it is expected that the second-hand van can be sold for approximately £5000 at the end of the three-year period. What is the total value used up over three years?

	£
Cost of van	20 000
Expected proceeds from sale after three years	5 000
Value used up over three years	15 000

So £15 000 represents an estimate of the van's depreciation over a three-year period. This is a cost of running the business which, in order to comply with the matching convention, should be set off against the sales that are generated over that period.

How is depreciation spread over the three-year period?

A straightforward way of spreading depreciation is to split the total figure equally over the accounting periods that benefit from the use of the fixed asset. This approach would produce an annual figure for depreciation on this van of £5000. There are other ways of spreading the cost of depreciation, and later in the chapter we will examine one other popular method.

The equal split of depreciation over accounting periods is known as the **straight-line method** of depreciation. It is the most commonly used method in the UK.

Self-test question 9.1 (answer at the end of the chapter)

This question tests understanding of the process involved in estimating depreciation.

Salvatore runs a small haulage business. The business owns two heavy goods vehicles, one driven by Salvatore himself and the other by his assistant, Ginette. Business is booming and Salvatore decides to buy a new HGV, and to employ another driver. On 1 January 20X4 he spends £65 000 on a new vehicle. He plans to use it for four years and then to sell it. He hopes to be able to sell it for approximately £25 000.

Estimate the annual depreciation charge for the new vehicle using the 'straight-line' method of depreciation.

Impact of depreciation on the accounts

In order to apply the matching convention, the annual charge for depreciation must be set off against sales in the accounting period. In the profit and loss account, therefore, depreciation is shown as an expense.

Depreciation, however, also has an impact upon the value of fixed assets shown in the balance sheet. Over time, the value of fixed assets is depleted as they are used up in the course of business. Depreciation is, therefore, deducted from the initial cost of the asset each year.

Example 9.2 Using the information in the Quickwash example above, we will look at the impact on the profit and loss account and balance sheet of the business in the three years of the life of the asset. Quickwash's accounting year ends on 31 December.

Year 1

The asset is acquired on 1 January 20X1 at a cost of £20 000 paid out of the business bank account. Quickwash reduces the current asset of cash at bank and fixed assets are increased by the same amount. (Remember the accounting equation that was explained in Chapter 6.)

At 31 December 20X1 the van has been in use for one year. In Example 9.1 we estimated an annual depreciation charge of £5000 per year. So, in Quickwash's profit and loss account for the year ended 31 December 20X1 an expense of £5000 will be included. The inclusion of this amount reduces profit by £5000.

In the balance sheet at 31 December 20X1 the van is recorded at its value after taking into account the depreciation charged:

	£
Van at cost	20 000
Less: depreciation	5 000
Net book value of van	15 000

Some points to note:

1. It is conventional to show the original cost value of fixed assets, less a deduction for depreciation.
2. Cost less depreciation is described as 'net book value'.
3. Quickwash owns several vans; the cost and depreciation of this particular van will be included in an overall total for vans.
4. The value of the van in the balance sheet has been reduced from £20 000 to £15 000. At 31 December 20X1 it might be possible to sell the van on the open market for more or less than £15 000. Net book value is not the same as market value.

Year 2

At 31 December 20X2 the van has been in use for two years. The profit and loss account should include the amount of depreciation for the year; this is the amount that has to be matched against sales. An expense of £5000 is therefore included in the total expenses, while profit, as in the previous year, is reduced by £5000.

In the balance sheet at 31 December 20X2 the net book value of the van has reduced, as more of its value is used up in the course of the business activities.

	£
Van at cost	20 000
Less: depreciation	10 000
Net book value of van	10 000

Note that after each year of use in the business the net book value of the asset diminishes.

▶

Year 3

At 31 December 20X3 the van has been in use for three years. The profit and loss account should include the amount of depreciation for the year; this is the amount that has to be matched against sales. An expense of £5000 is therefore included in the total expenses, while profit, as in the previous year, is reduced by £5000.

In the balance sheet at 31 December 20X3 the net book value of the van has reduced, as more of its value is used up in the course of the business activities.

	£
Van at cost	20 000
Less: depreciation	15 000
Net book value of van	5 000

At this point in time the van is ready for disposal. It is shown in the balance sheet at a net book value of £5000, which is the value that Quickwash's management originally estimated it could be sold for after three years. It is unlikely that their estimate would turn out to be precisely correct; later in the chapter we will examine what happens when a fixed asset is sold for more or less than the original estimate.

Summary

For each year that the van is used in Quickwash's business a charge of £5000 is made to the profit and loss account. This charge reduces profit by £5000 and represents an estimate of the depletion in value of the van each year.

In the balance sheet at each year-end the following values are included:

	20X1	20X2	20X3
	£	£	£
Van at cost	20 000	20 000	20 000
Less: accumulated depreciation	5 000	10 000	15 000
Net book value	15 000	10 000	5 000

Note that the total for depreciation increases each year as the asset is used up. The net book value decreases by a corresponding amount.

Intangible assets and amortisation

At the beginning of the chapter the term 'amortisation' was introduced. Amortisation works in the same way as depreciation but is applied to **intangible fixed assets**, rather than **tangible fixed assets**.

So far, the examples in this book have mostly used tangible fixed assets. 'Tangible' means capable of being touched; it is a piece of accounting terminology used to refer to assets that have a physical presence, such as the vans in the Quickwash example earlier. 'Intangible' refers to assets that have a value to the business, but which do not exist physically. Examples of tangible fixed assets include land and buildings, plant and machinery, office equipment, vans, lorries and cars, and computer equipment. Examples of intangible fixed assets include brands, mineral extraction rights, patents and licences, lease premiums on property and newspaper titles.

The examples of tangible fixed assets probably need no further explanation. The intangible fixed assets are, perhaps, less familiar, and so brief explanations follow.

Brands

Brands can be immensely valuable to the business that owns them. Examples of world famous brands include Coca-Cola, Microsoft, Hoover and McDonald's. Brand names can be bought and sold; there are firms of specialist valuers who can assist in fixing an appropriate price. If a business buys a brand name it is buying an intangible asset that is likely to produce income for the business over a long period.

Mineral extraction rights

Where a piece of land contains valuable minerals, its owner may make profits by extracting the ores, processing and selling them. Alternatively, the owner may licence another firm or person to extract the ores over a period of time by granting a licence over the extraction rights. The purchaser of the licence is buying a fixed asset, although it is not tangible. The asset consists of the transfer of certain rights over a piece of land, not the land itself.

Patents and licences

The inventor of a useful and potentially money-making process may decide to set up a manufacturing business to exploit the value of the process (think, for example, of the Dyson bagless vacuum cleaner). The inventor lays claim to ownership of the knowledge by registering a patent which affirms his or her rights over the knowledge. Rather than setting up in manufacturing, however, he or she may grant the right to use the process to a manufacturer in exchange for cash. The manufacturer in this case is buying the rights of access to the inventor's knowledge; such rights are often known as patent rights.

Lease premiums on property

Lease premiums are another example of rights of access. Where a business buys, say, shop premises or a warehouse on a freehold basis, it acquires tangible assets. However, it may instead choose to invest in a lease of the premises instead. The lease represents the right to occupy the premises. Often in such cases a large sum of money must be paid over at the start of the lease and then, subsequently, regular rental is paid in addition. The large initial sum constitutes an intangible asset; rights of occupation have been purchased.

Newspaper titles

Newspaper titles are similar to brands, and can be very valuable assets. Such titles are a type of intangible asset in that they are usually very well known, with loyal readerships and with a reputation for a particular type of journalism. It is possible to buy and sell titles (sometimes known as 'mastheads'); if such a title is bought it constitutes an intangible asset.

Accounting for amortisation

The accounting procedure adopted in accounting for amortisation is identical to the procedure for depreciation, which we examined earlier in the chapter. Note, however, that amortisation is almost invariably estimated using the straight-line method. The following example will illustrate how to account for amortisation.

Example 9.3 Bright & Shoesmith is a pharmaceutical manufacturing business. It is not involved itself in pharmaceutical research and development; instead it buys rights, in the form of licences to manufacture medicines, from the large pharmaceutical development firms. On 1 January 20X4 it concludes its negotiations with Exnox Worldwide to buy a licence to manufacture Nox, a sleeping pill. The contract for the licence stipulates that it lasts for a period of four years and that a manufacturing royalty of 25.6p per packet of 20 pills will be payable over the whole period of the contract. An up-front payment of £3 600 000 will be paid by Bright & Shoesmith for the licence.

In this case, Bright & Shoesmith is acquiring an intangible fixed asset in the form of a licence for the sum of £3 600 000. It is clearly laid down in the contract terms that the licence will last for exactly four years. After four years, the intangible asset will be completely used up and there will be no value left in it. Over that four-year period, Bright & Shoesmith will receive revenue from the sale of the sleeping pills and this is the period over which the cost of acquiring the licence must be matched (in accordance with the matching convention).

Applying the straight-line method, amortisation of the licence fee amounts to £900 000 for each of the four years (£3 600 000/4). In each of the four years amortisation of £900 000 will be charged as an expense in the profit and loss account of Bright & Shoesmith.

Bright & Shoesmith's year-end is 31 December. The intangible fixed asset will appear as follows in the end-December balance sheets of the business:

	20X4	20X5	20X6	20X7
	£	£	£	£
Intangible fixed assets				
Licence at cost	3 600 000	3 600 000	3 600 000	3 600 000
Less: accumulated amortisation	(900 000)	(1 800 000)	(2 700 000)	(3 600 000)
Net book value	2 700 000	1 800 000	900 000	—

After four years the licence has no value remaining in the balance sheet. This is correct because, by that time, Bright & Shoesmith no longer has the right to manufacture the sleeping pills.

Note that part of the deal with Exnox is that a royalty must be paid on each packet of pills manufactured. This type of arrangement is quite commonly found in licence agreements. The royalty is part of the cost of manufacturing the pills, and it will be set off against revenue in arriving at a figure for profit. It has no bearing on accounting for the amortisation of the licence.

Another method of depreciation

We have examined the straight-line method of depreciation in detail in this chapter. Straight-line is the method of depreciation most often encountered in practice, and it is the method that is almost invariably adopted in accounting for amortisation. However, there are several other possible ways of estimating depreciation. The most common, apart from straight-line, is the **reducing balance method**. This method applies a given percentage to the net book value at each year-end to estimate the depreciation expense. This is illustrated in the following example.

Example 9.4 Boris runs a small manufacturing company that makes soft drinks and packages fruit juice for sale to supermarkets and other retailers. He runs a fleet of four delivery vehicles. At 1 April 20X1 he buys a new replacement vehicle at a cost of £15 000. Boris adopts the reducing balance method for depreciation on the vehicles, at a rate of 25% per annum. What is the depreciation expense for each of the three years to 31 March 20X2, 20X3 and 20X4, and what is the net book value to be included for this van at each year-end?

Year 1

The first year of ownership is the year to 31 March 20X2. The depreciation expense for the delivery vehicle is 25% of the original cost of the asset: 25% × £15 000 = £3750. This will be shown as part of the expense of depreciation in the profit and loss account.

In the balance sheet at 31 March 20X2 the vehicle will be included as follows:

	£
Vehicle at cost	15 000
Less: depreciation	3 750
Net book value of vehicle	11 250

Year 2

For the second year of ownership the depreciation expense for the delivery vehicle is 25% of the net book value at the beginning of the accounting year: 25% × £11 250 = £2813 (to the nearest £). This will be shown as part of the expense of depreciation in the profit and loss account.

In the balance sheet at 31 March 20X3 the vehicle will be included as follows:

	£
Vehicle at cost	15 000
Less: depreciation (£3750 + £2813)	6 563
Net book value of vehicle	8 437

Year 3

For the third year of ownership the depreciation expense for the delivery vehicle is 25% of the net book value at the beginning of the accounting year: 25% × £8437 = £2109 (to the nearest £). This will be shown as part of the expense of depreciation in the profit and loss account.

▶

In the balance sheet at 31 March 20X4 the vehicle will be included as follows:

	£
Vehicle at cost	15 000
Less: depreciation (£3750 + £2813 + £2109)	8 672
Net book value of vehicle	6 328

Summary

The depreciation charge to profit and loss for the vehicle is as follows for each of the three years:

20X2 = £3 750
20X3 = £2 813
20X4 = £2 109.

In the balance sheet at each year-end the following values are included:

	20X2 £	20X3 £	20X4 £
Vehicle at cost	15 000	15 000	15 000
Less: accumulated depreciation	3 750	6 563	8 672
Net book value	11 250	8 437	6 328

The following points should be noted:

1. Each year the depreciation charge to profit and loss falls. This may reflect the pattern of usage of the fixed asset more accurately than the straight-line method, depending upon how the asset is used up. Cars and other vehicles frequently lose a substantial amount of value in the first year of ownership from new, so the reducing balance method may be more realistic for such assets.
2. It takes many years of depreciation before the asset value is reduced to nil.
3. As with the straight-line method of depreciation it is possible to build in to the calculation the expected proceeds of sale at the end of the planned period of ownership. This requires the use of a mathematical formula. In this book none of the exercises will require use of the formula to calculate an appropriate rate of depreciation: the rate will be given in all cases.
4. Businesses may select a combination of methods for depreciating different types of fixed asset. Having selected a method, or methods, to apply to different assets it would be expected that the business would use the methods consistently. This is so that realistic comparisons between different years' results are made possible.
5. The cost in the balance sheet of £15 000 does not change.

Self-test question 9.2 (answer at the end of the chapter)

Silvio runs a mobile hairdressing business. His annual mileage is high and he expects to keep his car for no more than three years. On the advice of his accountant, Silvio applies the reducing balance method of depreciation to his car over the three years of ownership at a rate of 30% per annum. He buys a new car on 1 May 20X6, the first day of his accounting year, for £17 209. Calculate the depreciation on the car for Silvio's accounts for the three years ending 30 April 20X7, 20X8 and 20X9, and show how the car will appear in Silvio's business balance sheet on each of those dates. Calculate all figures to the nearest £.

Land and buildings

In almost all cases land is not subject to depreciation as it does not wear out. Only in exceptional cases is it necessary to charge depreciation on land. For example, land containing mineral deposits is likely to have an enhanced value. If the minerals are mined, the land will tend to lose value, and in this case it may be appropriate to reduce the value over time by charging depreciation.

Some buildings have a longer useful life than others, but all eventually wear out. Therefore, it is appropriate to charge depreciation, although it will usually be over a long period, such as 50, 75 or 100 years.

The role of judgement in estimating depreciation

In each of the examples used in the chapter up to this point we have referred to the need to 'estimate' depreciation. Depreciation is one of the many areas in accounting where precision is impossible. When an asset is purchased it is impossible to be precise about how long it will remain in use in the business. The longer the life of the asset the more imprecise the estimate will be. For example, a building estimated to last 75 years might last 102 years (or 78, or 93, etc.); in any case, the people who are making the estimates will probably not be around to answer for the quality of their judgement when the building eventually falls down.

Judgement is involved in estimating both the useful lifespan of the asset and any monetary value for which the asset could be eventually sold. As we have seen, depreciation has a direct impact on profitability. It is an aspect of accounting that is, consequently, subject to manipulation. A business that is going through hard times may wish to exaggerate the estimated useful lives of fixed assets so as to spread depreciation over a longer period (and thus minimise the impact on profits). It can be very difficult to challenge the judgements made by business managers in this respect.

Sale of a fixed asset

Upon sale, the fixed asset is exchanged for the asset of cash (or possibly a debtor if it is agreed that the cash does not have to be paid straight away). If the net book value of the asset is the same as the price agreed for the sale, then the exchange of one type of asset for another is straightforward. However, in most cases the net book value of the asset will be higher or lower than the cash price. In such cases, either a profit or a loss on sale will arise. Examples 9.5 and 9.6 illustrate the calculation of profits and losses on sale.

Example 9.5 Ibrahim runs a juice bar. His business is doing well and he has decided to buy a new improved juicing machine. He advertises the old machine in the paper for sale at £750. Takis, a restaurant owner, rings up and offers him £650 in cash for the old machine, an offer Ibrahim decides to accept. The net book value of the machine in the accounts is £475. What is Ibrahim's profit on sale, and how will the transaction be recorded in his accounts?

The profit on sale is the proceeds of £650 less the net book value of £475: i.e. a profit of £175. Tangible fixed assets are reduced by the net book value (£475) and cash at bank is increased by £650. The profit of £175 is shown in the profit and loss account, thus increasing Ibrahim's capital. In summary, in terms of the accounting equation, assets (overall) increase by £175, as does capital.

Note that the 'profit' is really just an adjustment reflecting the actual outcome of the judgements made about depreciation at the start of the useful life of the asset. 'Profit' in this context arises where the asset has been over-depreciated.

Example 9.6 Adebola's delivery service is run using two delivery vans. Her business policy is to replace the vans every four years. One of the vans, which was bought four years ago at a cost of £12 750, is due for replacement. Adebola depreciates the vans using the reducing balance method at a rate of 25% per annum. She accepts an offer of £3650 for the van. What is Adebola's profit or loss on sale of the van?

First, we must calculate the net book value of the van after four years:

	£
Van at cost	12 750
Year 1 depreciation (25% × £12 750)	3 188
Net book value at end of year 1	9 562
Year 2 depreciation (25% × £9562)	2 391
Net book value at end of year 2	7 171
Year 3 depreciation (25% × £7171)	1 793
Net book value at end of year 3	5 378
Year 4 depreciation (25% × £5378)	1 345
Net book value at end of year 4	4 033

The proceeds of the sale of the van are less than the net book value after four years. Therefore, Adebola makes a loss on sale of £3650 − £4033 = £383. Tangible fixed assets are reduced by £4033 and the asset of cash is increased by the sale proceeds of £3650. The loss of £383 is included in Adebola's profit and loss account for the year, thus decreasing her capital. In terms of the accounting equation, then, assets decrease by a net amount of £383 and capital is reduced by the same amount.

Note that the 'loss' on sale of the asset is really the amount by which the asset has been under-depreciated.

Self-test question 9.3 (answer at the end of the chapter)

Sergio sells one of the machines from his factory for £3010. The machine was bought new exactly five years ago for £15 000 and has been depreciated using the reducing balance method at a rate of 30% per annum. Calculate Sergio's profit or loss on sale of the machine.

Buying and selling assets during the year

In all the examples in the chapter up to this point it has been assumed that fixed assets are bought on the first day of the year and are held for an exact number of years. However, businesses may buy or sell assets at any time during the accounting period. Where this happens, a business must decide not only on the method of depreciation to be adopted but also on how the rate is to be applied in the year of acquisition or disposal of an asset.

Example 9.7 Angelina has a card shop that uses several display stands. She decides to replace all the stands at the same time as the shop frontage is refurbished as part of a new look for the shop. She spends £8780 on new stands on 1 May 20X3. Her accounting year-end is 31 December. The stands should last for five years before they require replacement and Angelina decides to apply the straight-line method of depreciation.

Her accountant advises her that she must decide on how she will apply the depreciation method in 20X3. She can either:

a) apply a policy of charging a whole year's depreciation in the first year of ownership, regardless of the actual date of acquisition of the assets; or
b) apply a policy of charging depreciation in respect of the number of months she has owned the assets.

What will be the difference in the depreciation charge under approaches a) and b)?

With a) – a full year's depreciation in the accounting year ending 31 December 20X3 – depreciation will be:

$$\frac{£8780}{5} = £1756$$

The balance sheet at 31 December would include the following:

	£
Display stands at cost	8 780
Less: depreciation	1 756
Net book value	7 024

Under approach b) depreciation would be charged for only eight months:

$$\frac{£8780}{5} \times \frac{8}{12} = £1171$$

▶

The balance sheet at 31 December would include the following:

	£
Display stands at cost	8 780
Less: depreciation	1 171
Net book value	7 609

Usually, businesses will seek to be consistent in the approach they adopt. So, if Angelina decides to adopt approach a) she should continue to do so. Also, businesses will adopt consistent approaches upon both acquisition and disposal of assets. So, if a full year's depreciation is charged as an expense in the year of acquisition, regardless of the actual date acquired, it would be consistent to charge none in the year of disposal. In answering questions on depreciation it is important to take careful note of how they are worded in order to adopt the correct approach.

So far, we have examined depreciation and amortisation calculations, and their presentation, in isolation. In Case study 9.1 we show how depreciation fits into the accounts as a whole.

The case study for Chapter 6 looked at a new business start-up – Buchanan International Designs, a retail business trading in rugs and carpets. The case study in this chapter looks at the business at the end of Isobel Buchanan's first year of trading. It is not necessary for students to look back to the details given in Chapter 6; the case study that follows can be worked through without reference to the earlier one.

CASE STUDY 9.1 Depreciation accounting

Buchanan International Designs is still in business at the end of the first year of trading. Initially the business was set up with £10 000 in cash contributed as capital by Isobel Buchanan. In addition, she received a loan of £40 000 from her Uncle Andrew and his wife Hannah. The loan was made at a commercial interest rate of 6%, with the agreement that it would be repaid at £5000 per year over eight years commencing on the 1 March 20X4. Andrew and Hannah would be willing to make a further £40 000 available in the form of a loan on similar terms if Isobel requires it.

Carpets and rugs are purchased in four sizes. Each size has a different purchase and selling price. The table below summarises the purchases, sales and closing stock at the year-end date, 28 February 20X2, together with the purchase and sales prices, which have remained at the same level throughout the year.

	Purchase price £	Selling price £	Number sold	Number in stock 28.02.X2
Small rugs	100	150	281	42
Larger rugs	300	420	103	8
Small carpets	750	1 035	16	6
Larger carpets	1 000	1 380	7	3

Isobel's best lines are undoubtedly the rugs. Carpet sales have been very disappointing. Although the carpets are useful for display purposes she has had very few customers who are prepared to spend over £1000 to buy one. A local businessman bought one of the larger carpets for his boardroom, and since then Isobel has been able to sell a few carpets on credit to other businesses. Isobel thinks it may be possible to expand this side of the business, but she would need to spend time away from the shop and this would mean employing a salesperson for the shop.

Isobel is concerned that she is not making sufficient profit on the carpets. Sales have been at a steady rate throughout most of the year and there is no indication that sales volumes are likely to increase very much; she has tried advertising in various outlets but without much obvious success. Most of her customers have come into the shop either because they were just passing or because they have heard about it from friends or colleagues. Isobel has added ranges of small bookcases, vases and ornaments to the stock in an attempt to increase sales. Sales of such items amounted to £3992 and related cost of sales was £2379. At 28 February 20X2 goods of this type in stock totalled £5300.

When the business started up Isobel took out a lease on shop premises for four years, paying a lease premium of £10 000. Annual rental, which covers rates and services charges, is £14 000 payable quarterly in arrears at the end of March, June, September and December each year. At 28 February 20X2 she had, therefore, paid four instalments, a full year's rental.

Isobel discovered shortly after setting up the business that many customers expected a delivery service to be available. She looked at the possibility of using commercial couriers but found that their charges were very high and that she was unlikely to be able to pass them on to her customers. Therefore, she has bought a second-hand van for £6500. Other fixed assets are display racks purchased in March 20X1 at a cost of £4500 plus sundry items of shop fittings, including a cash till, at a total cost during the year of £1630.

Andrew, who is a chartered accountant, suggests to Isobel that she should adopt the straight-line method of depreciation, with a full year's depreciation to be charged in the year of purchase of the assets. He tells her that the lease premium should be amortised over four years on the straight-line basis. Isobel decides that the other fixed assets, the display racks and other shop fittings, will probably last about five years, so she decides to apply a depreciation rate of 20% to them. She does not expect these assets to have any remaining value at the end of five years. On Andrew's advice Isobel decides to depreciate the van using the reducing balance method at 25% per year.

Other items for inclusion in the accounts to 28 February 20X2 are as follows:

	£
Interest received from the bank	651
Interest paid to Andrew and Hannah	2 400
Insurance paid	1 224
Electricity	1 681
Telephone charges	686
Staff (to cover Isobel's annual holiday)	300
Advertising	1 560
Motor expenses	551
Sundry expenses	3 446
Drawings	7 500

▶

	£
Cash at bank	13 323
Creditors for goods	6 327
Debtors	3 520

Of the insurance paid of £1 224, £507 relates to the year commencing 1 March 20X2. At the year-end Isobel has received an electricity bill for £665 up to 28 February 20X2. This is not included in the total in the list above.

You are required to prepare a profit and loss account for the year ending 28 February 20X2 and a balance sheet at the same date. Comment on the performance of the business in its first year and assess the probability of it being successful in the future.

Case study solution

A lot of information is presented in the case study, and it may seem quite confusing at first. In such cases it is best to deal with the information systematically.

Working 1: Financing
The first pieces of information provided in the question are about the financing of the business. We know that opening capital is £10 000 and that there is a long-term loan of £40 000. Interest is payable at 6% per annum and we can calculate that the amount due is therefore £2400 (6% × £40 000). The list of items for inclusion in the accounts shows that this amount has, indeed, been paid to Andrew and Hannah.

Working 2: Sales
Next, we are provided with some details about sales of rugs and carpets, purchase and sales prices and closing stock. (Because this is the first year of trading there will be no opening stock). From the information given we can calculate Isobel's sales, cost of sales and closing stock as follows:

	£
Sales	
Small rugs (281 × £150)	42 150
Larger rugs (103 × £420)	43 260
Small carpets (16 × £1035)	16 560
Larger carpets (7 × £1380)	9 660
Sales of other goods	3 992
Total sales	115 622

	£
Cost of sales	
Small rugs (281 × £100)	28 100
Larger rugs (103 × £300)	30 900
Small carpets (16 × £750)	12 000
Larger carpets (7 × £1000)	7 000
Other goods	2 379
Total cost of sales	80 379

	£
Closing stock	
Small rugs (42 × £100)	4 200
Larger rugs (8 × 300)	2 400
Small carpets (6 × £750)	4 500
Larger carpets (3 × £1000)	3 000
Other goods	5 300
Total closing stock	19 400

Working 3: Amortisation and depreciation

Amortisation and depreciation charges can be calculated from the information given. The lease premium of £10 000 was paid at the start of the lease for a four-year period. It will be amortised over four years using the straight-line method, i.e. at £2500 per year.

The lease amortisation will be included in the profit and loss account, and the intangible asset will be shown as follows in the balance sheet at 28 February 20X2:

	£
Intangible fixed asset	
Lease premium at cost	10 000
Accumulated amortisation	2 500
Net book value	7 500

The display racks cost £4500, and are to be depreciated over five years on a straight-line basis, with no estimated residual value. This produces a depreciation charge of £900 (i.e. £4500/5) per year.

Sundry fixtures and fittings cost £1630 and, because the policy adopted by Isobel is to charge a full year's depreciation in the year of purchase, the actual timings of the purchases are irrelevant. Depreciation is to be charged over five years on a straight-line basis, with no estimated residual value. This produces a depreciation charge of £326 (i.e. £1630/5) per year.

Finally, the van cost £6 500. The first year's depreciation will be 25% × £6500 = £1625.

Tangible fixed assets will be shown as follows in the balance sheet at 28 February 20X2:

	£	£
Tangible fixed assets		
Display racks at cost	4 500	
Less: accumulated depreciation	(900)	
Net book value		3 600
Sundry fixtures and fittings at cost	1 630	
Less: accumulated depreciation	(326)	
Net book value		1 304
Van at cost	6 500	
Less: accumulated depreciation	(1 625)	
Net book value		4 875
		9 779

Working 4: Insurance and electricity

Insurance paid in the year amounts to £1224. Of this amount £507 relates to the next financial year and so will be included in the balance sheet as a prepayment.

▶

The amount of insurance expense to be included in the profit and loss account is £1224 − £507 = £717.

Electricity paid in the year amounts to £1681. Isobel must also include the electricity bill she has received to 28 February 20X2 as an accrual. The accrual is £665 and the amount of electricity expense to be included in the profit and loss account is £1681 + £665 = £2346.

We can summarise all of the above information in a list of items for inclusion in the profit and loss account and balance sheet. Each item is identified as belonging in the trading account, the rest of the profit and loss account or the balance sheet.

	£	Category
Interest received from the bank	651	Profit and loss account
Interest paid to Andrew and Hannah	2 400	Profit and loss account
Insurance paid (working 4)	717	Profit and loss account
Electricity (working 4)	2 346	Profit and loss account
Insurance prepayment (working 4)	507	Balance sheet
Electricity accrual (working 4)	665	Balance sheet
Telephone charges	686	Profit and loss account
Staff	300	Profit and loss account
Advertising	1 560	Profit and loss account
Motor expenses	551	Profit and loss account
Sundry expenses	3 446	Profit and loss account
Drawings	7 500	Balance sheet
Cash at bank	13 323	Balance sheet
Creditors	6 327	Balance sheet
Debtors	3 520	Balance sheet
Sales (working 2)	115 622	Trading account
Cost of sales (working 2)	80 379	Trading account
Closing stock	19 400	Balance sheet
Lease premium at cost	10 000	Balance sheet
Lease premium: accumulated amortisation	2 500	Balance sheet
Lease premium: amortisation for the year	2 500	Profit and loss account
Display racks at cost (working 3)	4 500	Balance sheet
Display racks: accumulated depreciation (working 3)	900	Balance sheet
Display racks: depreciation for the year (working 3)	900	Profit and loss account
Sundry fixtures and fittings at cost (working 3)	1 630	Balance sheet
Sundry fixtures and fittings: accumulated depreciation (working 3)	326	Balance sheet
Sundry fixtures and fittings: depreciation for the year (working 3)	326	Profit and loss account
Van at cost (working 3)	6 500	Balance sheet
Van: accumulated depreciation (working 3)	1 625	Balance sheet
Van: depreciation for the year (working 3)	1 625	Profit and loss account
Rental of premises	14 000	Profit and loss account
Loan from Andrew and Hannah (working 1)	40 000	Balance sheet
Capital introduced (working 1)	10 000	Balance sheet

We can now prepare the profit and loss account and balance sheet at 28 February 20X2.

Buchanan International Designs: Profit and loss account for the year ending 28 February 20X2

	£	£
Sales (working 2)		115 622
Cost of sales		(80 379)
Gross profit		35 243
Interest received		651
		35 894
Expenses		
Rental	14 000	
Insurance (working 4)	717	
Electricity (working 4)	2 346	
Telephone charges	686	
Staff	300	
Advertising	1 560	
Motor expenses	551	
Sundry expenses	3 446	
Amortisation of lease (working 3)	2 500	
Depreciation of display racks (working 3)	900	
Depreciation of sundry fixtures and fittings (working 3)	326	
Depreciation of van (working 3)	1 625	
Interest paid	2 400	
		(31 357)
Net profit		4 537

Buchanan International Designs: Balance sheet at 28 February 20X2

	£	£
Fixed assets		
Intangible fixed assets (working 3)		
Cost	10 000	
Less: accumulated amortisation	(2 500)	
		7 500
Tangible fixed assets (working 3)		
Display racks at cost	4 500	
Less: accumulated depreciation	(900)	
		3 600
Sundry fixtures and fittings at cost	1 630	
Less: accumulated depreciation	(326)	
		1 304
Van at cost	6 500	
Less: accumulated depreciation	(1 625)	
		4 875
		17 279

▶

	£	£
Current assets		
Stock (working 2)	19 400	
Debtors	3 520	
Prepayments (working 4)	507	
Cash at bank	13 323	
	36 750	
Current liabilities		
Creditors	6 327	
Accruals	665	
	6 992	
Net current assets (£36 750 − £6 992)		29 758
		47 037
Long-term liabilities		
Loan		(40 000)
		7 037
Capital		
Capital introduced		10 000
Add: profit for the year		4 537
Less: drawings		(7 500)
		7 037

Note that in the above balance sheet fixed assets are disclosed in detail in order to assist understanding. Usually the information would be summarised into a total net book value for intangible fixed assets and tangible fixed assets, with more detailed information given in a note to the balance sheet.

Comments on the first year business performance

Starting on a positive note, we can see from the profit and loss account that the business has made a profit in its first year of trading, although the level of net profit looks rather modest at £4537. We can see from the balance sheet that Isobel has drawn £7500 out of the business for her living expenses – a figure which is not very extravagant, but is almost £3000 more than the business has generated in profit. Sole traders cannot continue indefinitely to draw more than the business is capable of generating.

We can use some of the techniques learned in earlier chapters to delve more deeply into profitability by calculating gross and net profit margins, as follows:

$$\text{Gross profit margin \%} = \frac{\text{gross profit}}{\text{sales}} \times 100$$

$$= \frac{35\,243}{115\,622} \times 100 = 30.5\%$$

$$\text{Net profit margin \%} = \frac{\text{net profit}}{\text{sales}} \times 100$$

$$= \frac{4\,537}{115\,622} \times 100 = 3.9\%$$

It is not, of course, possible to compare these figures to previous years, because this is the first year of the business. However, Isobel should have started the business with some idea of the level of profits she wished to achieve, and she would be able to compare these actual figures with her forecasts (we will look at forecasts in much more detail in Part III of this book).

Turning to the balance sheet we can see that the business has fixed assets at a total net book value of £17 279, and stocks of £19 400. Apart from these the principal asset in the balance sheet is the cash at bank balance of £13 323. This looks like a large sum, but we should remember that Isobel started the year with £50 000 in the bank. A net total of £50 000 less 13 323 = £36 677 has therefore been spent. It may be safe to assume that Isobel has by now purchased all the fixed assets that she will need in the business for the time being, and so the rate of spending in the second year of trading should not be so high. However, she is only two years away from having to start repaying the £40 000 loan from Andrew and Hannah. In three years time her lease will come to an end and she will have to negotiate a new lease, which may well cost more.

Although a profit has been made this year, in the longer run the future viability of the business looks questionable. What can Isobel do about it? Sales of the more expensive carpets have been disappointing. Isobel has begun to address the problem by starting to sell some of the more expensive items on credit to other businesses, and by adding ranges of smaller items to her stock. Sufficient information is given in the question to be able to examine the relative profitability of each of the ranges. We can work out gross profit margins on a single rug or carpet by calculating:

$$\frac{\text{Gross profit per item}}{\text{Selling price per item}} \times 10$$

For smaller rugs gross profit = 150 − 100 = 50. Gross profit margin equals:

$$\frac{50}{150} \times 100 = 33.3\%$$

For larger rugs gross profit = 420 − 300 = 120. Gross profit margin equals:

$$\frac{120}{420} \times 100 = 28.6\%$$

For small carpets gross profit = 1035 − 750 = 285. Gross profit margin equals:

$$\frac{285}{1035} \times 100 = 27.5\%$$

For larger carpets gross profit = 1380 − 1000 = 380. Gross profit margin equals:

$$\frac{380}{1380} \times 100 = 27.5\%$$

The other lines of vases, ornaments and so on produce an overall gross profit of £3992 (sales) − £2379 (cost of sales) = £1613 (gross profit). This gives a gross profit percentage of:

▶

$$\frac{1613}{3992} \times 100 = 40.4\%$$

We can see from this analysis that the best gross profit margins by far are obtained from the sale of these sundry other goods. However, total sales of these goods are relatively small. It looks as though Isobel should try to increase the sales of smaller items of stock. This will mean making an investment in a greater volume of stock but she has sufficient cash available to do this at the moment.

She should investigate further her idea of expanding sales to businesses. This would mean employing someone in the shop, at least on a part-time basis. Isobel needs to assess whether the likely increase in sales and gross profit arising from an expansion in sales on credit to businesses will adequately cover extra costs.

She could consider increasing selling prices. Carpets have the lowest gross profit margins and do not sell well in any case. Increasing the prices of carpets is not, therefore, likely to help her business much. Increasing the price of rugs may be a risky strategy. Increasing gross profit margin may be at the expense of a reduction in sales.

Isobel has tried advertising, without obvious success. This may mean that she has not succeeded in targeting her advertising to the right audience and she may need to rethink her strategy.

Is the business likely to be successful in the future?

Isobel's first year has not been a disaster. Nor, however, has it been a wild success. If the business is to survive and prosper she needs to take some tough decisions now about the right selling strategies. She still has cash left, but it will not last indefinitely, and she needs to think about how she is going to repay the loan from her relatives. A further loan of £40 000 is available to her, but if she is going to use this source of finance she needs a well thought out plan for the business over the next three to four years.

It is by no means certain that Isobel will be able to make a success of this business. Future success is dependent upon being able to make a sufficient volume of sales at the right prices. Other issues, such as controlling costs, are also important, but the key element is sales.

Chapter summary

This chapter has examined the accounting adjustments for depreciation and amortisation of fixed assets. The distinction between tangible and intangible assets was introduced, together with more detailed explanations of several examples of intangible assets.

The case study for the chapter incorporated adjustments for depreciation and amortisation into a set of financial statements comprising profit and loss account and balance sheet. The case study also involved the critical examination of a new business's first year accounts, with commentary about its performance and chances of future success.

The questions at the end of the chapter include several examples of isolated depreciation and amortisation calculations, progressing to examples that demonstrate the integration of the calculations into financial statements.

Answer to self-test question 9.1

	£
Cost of Salvatore's new vehicle	65 000
Estimated sales proceeds after four years of use	(25 000)
Estimated total depreciation over four years	40 000

Spread evenly over four years, this produces a straight-line annual depreciation charge of £10 000.

Answer to self-test question 9.2

Year ending 30 April 20X7: car depreciation expense in the profit and loss account will be £17 209 × 30% = £5 163. As regards the balance sheet:

	£
Car at cost	17 209
Less: depreciation	(5 163)
Net book value of vehicle	12 046

Year ending 30 April 20X8: car depreciation expense in the profit and loss account will be £12 046 × 30% = £3 614. As regards the balance sheet:

	£
Car at cost	17 209
Less: depreciation (5163 + 3614)	(8 777)
Net book value of vehicle	8 432

Year ending 30 April 20X9: car depreciation expense in the profit and loss account will be £8432 × 30% = £2530. As regards the balance sheet:

	£
Car at cost	17 209
Less: depreciation (5163 + 3614 + 2530)	(11 307)
Net book value of vehicle	5 902

Answer to self-test question 9.3

To calculate Sergio's profit or loss on sale of the machine, first the net book value after five years' depreciation must be calculated:

	£
Machine at cost	15 000
Year 1 depreciation (30% × £15 000)	4 500
Net book value at end of year 1	10 500
Year 2 depreciation (30% × £10 500)	3 150
Net book value at end of year 2	7 350
Year 3 depreciation (30% × £7350)	2 205
Net book value at end of year 3	5 145
Year 4 depreciation (30% × £5145)	1 544
Net book value at end of year 4	3 601
Year 5 depreciation (30% × £3601)	1 080
Net book value at end of year 5	2 521

Sale proceeds are greater than net book value and so a profit on sale has been made of £489 (£3010 − £2521 = £489).

Exercises

The answers to many of the exercises are set out later in this chapter. However, where the exercise number is followed by 'A' the answer is available only to lecturers. Remember that additional exercises (with answers) are available to students on the book's website.

9.1   Valerie runs a small delivery business. She has a van that she replaces every four years. On 1 January 20X3 she sells her old van for £2000 and buys a new one for £14 460. She expects to be able to sell it for approximately £4000 in four years time.

   Assuming that Valerie adopts the straight-line method of depreciation in her accounts what is her depreciation charge for the accounting year ending 31 December 20X3?

   a) £2 115

   b) £3 615

   c) £4 615

   d) £2 615.

9.2A   Victor adopts the straight-line method of depreciation in his accounts. He purchases a new machine on 1 June 20X4 for £13 750. He expects to keep the machine for approximately six years, at the end of which time it will have a scrap value of about £250. Victor prepares accounts to 31 December each year.

   What is the first year's depreciation charge, assuming that Victor charges a full year's depreciation in the year of acquisition of fixed assets and none in the year of disposal?

   a) £1 125

   b) £2 250

c) £2 292

d) £2 333.

9.3 Victoria owns a gym. In her financial year to 31 August 20X2 she buys a new exercise bike for £450. The date of purchase was 1 March 20X2. Victoria aims to keep gym equipment for three years. After three years she finds that the equipment is usually well worn and worth very little. She advertises old equipment to her members, and would usually expect to receive about £30 for an old exercise bike.

Victoria charges depreciation in her accounts on the straight-line basis, with a pro-rated charge in the first and final years of ownership, depending on the dates of acquisition and disposal. What is the depreciation charge in respect of the new exercise bike in the year to 31 August 20X2?

a) £70

b) £140

c) £75

d) £150.

9.4A Virginia runs a business that supplies food for office parties and similar functions. Food is delivered to the client's premises in vans which have been specially adapted to take shallow trays of food and which contain brackets for microwave ovens. The basic cost of a new van is £9570. When a new van is purchased Virginia sends it away for modification, which costs a further £1830. On 15 August 20X5 two new vans return with the modifications complete and Virginia puts them straight into service. Virginia expects to keep the vans for a period of six years. They are subject to severe wear and tear during their useful lives and she does not expect to get more than scrap value for them after six years. Therefore, she assumes a residual value of nil.

Her accounting year-end is 31 December. She charges depreciation on a straight-line basis. In the year of acquisition and disposal of fixed assets she charges depreciation for every full month of ownership in the accounting year. What is the depreciation charge (to the nearest £) for the two new vans in the year ending 31 December 20X5?

a) £1 267

b) £1 063

c) £1 329

d) £1 583.

9.5 Vinny is expanding his electrical components business. During his accounting year ending 31 December 20X6 he buys new machinery as follows:

● On 1 April a machine costing £10 300. The estimated useful life is five years, after which point Vinny expects that it will have a nil value.

● On 1 October a machine costing £8580. The estimated useful life is four years, and Vinny expects the machine to fetch £2000 on the second-hand market when the time comes to dispose of it.

Vinny charges depreciation in the accounts on the basis of the number of months of ownership of the asset in an accounting year. Working to the nearest £, what is the total depreciation charge for the new machines in the year ending 31 December 20X6?

a) £3705

b) £2081

c) £1956

d) £2779.

9.6   Having qualified as a mining engineer Violet decides that she would like to go into the gold-mining business. She spends a considerable period of time looking for mining opportunities. Finally she finds a piece of land in Wales that was formerly exploited for gold-mining. The activity had been abandoned some years ago because the yield was insufficient. However, Violet is convinced that the mine can once more be made profitable with the help of modern equipment and technology. She enters negotiations with the owners of the land. They refuse to sell it, but agree to grant Violet the rights for a three-and-a-half year period from 1 January 20X3. In exchange Violet agrees to pay £273000, plus a fixed fee per kilo of gold extracted.

How will the purchase of the mineral rights be reflected in Violet's accounts for the year to 31 December 20X3?

9.7   Vincenzo's balance sheet at 31 August 20X7 shows the following balances in respect of fixed assets:

	£
Buildings at cost	306000
Less: accumulated depreciation	(18360)
Net book value	287640
Motor vehicles at cost	48770
Less: accumulated depreciation	(16470)
Net book value	32300
Fixtures and fittings at cost	12720
Less: accumulated depreciation	(6360)
Net book value	6360

In the year ending 31 August 20X8 no purchases or sales of fixed assets are made. Vincenzo depreciates fixed assets as follows:

- Buildings at 2% per annum on cost on the straight-line basis.
- Motor vehicles at 25% per annum on the reducing balance basis.
- Fixtures and fittings (which were all purchased at the same time) over ten years on the straight-line basis.

First, calculate the total charge to Vincenzo's profit and loss account in respect of depreciation for the year ending 31 August 20X8. Secondly, show how fixed assets will be presented in Vincenzo's balance sheet at 31 August 20X8.

9.8A   Valda runs a marketing agency. She prepares her own accounts and is currently working on the profit and loss and balance sheet at 31 December 20X7. She purchased the freehold of a small office building on 1 January 20X2 for £364000. The land value included in the purchase price is estimated at £50000. Valda depreciates the buildings element of the freehold over 100 years, the expected useful life of the building.

Apart from the building, Valda's business owns fixtures and fittings that were purchased several years ago for £16 777. The fixtures and fittings are now fully · depreciated. Also, the business owns two cars used for staff visiting clients. One car was bought in the accounting year ending 31 December 20X5 for £15 300 and the other in 20X6 for £17 660. Valda depreciates the cars on a straight-line basis over their estimated useful lives of four years. Both cars have an estimated residual value of £5000.

a) Calculate the total depreciation charge to Valda's profit and loss account in respect of depreciation for the year ending 31 December 20X7.

b) Show how fixed assets will be presented in Valda's balance sheet at 31 December 20X7.

9.9   Wilma runs a wedding car service. Business is expanding and she is planning to buy a new vehicle. The basic list price of a new car is £24 400, but Wilma must pay an additional £800 for it to be sprayed white. She purchases the car on 1 March in time for the main spring and summer wedding season. Her year-end is 28 February. Wilma depreciates cars on the reducing balance basis at 15% per annum.

What will be the depreciation charge for the first year of ownership of the new car?

a) £3 660

b) £3 780

c) £3 540

d) £4 460.

9.10   At 1 January 20X3 William has the following balances in his books related to the fixed asset of cars:

	£
Cars at cost	38 370
Less: accumulated depreciation	(15 540)
Net book value	22 830

He acquires a new car on the same date for £14 447. No other cars are bought, or sold, during the rest of the accounting period which ends on 31 December 20X3.

William depreciates cars on the reducing balance basis at 25% per year. What is the total charge for depreciation on cars, to the nearest £, to be included in William's profit and loss account for the year ending 31 December 20X3?

a) £13 204

b) £9 319

c) £5 707

d) £9 592.

9.11A   Wally's business owns several machines that he depreciates on the reducing balance basis at the rate of 10% per annum. His balance sheet at 31 March 20X8 shows the following balances in respect of machines:

£

Fixed assets
Tangible fixed assets

	£
Machines at cost	288 994
Less: accumulated depreciation	(107 773)
Net book value	181 221

On 17 October 20X8 he buys a new machine for £14 800. There were no other additions or disposals of machines in the year. Wally's policy is to charge a full year's depreciation in the year of purchase of a new fixed asset, and none in the year of disposal. What is the charge for depreciation on machines (to the nearest £) to be included in Wally's profit and loss account for the year ending 31 March 20X9?

a) £28 899

b) £18 122

c) £18 739

d) £19 602.

9.12A Wilbur's celebration cake business is flourishing. He plans to move to new premises and to employ more staff. He finds a unit on an industrial estate with a seven-year lease, for which he is required to pay a lease premium of £21 000. The premium is paid on the date Wilbur and his business move to the new premises, 1 May 20X1. He is able to take quite a lot of equipment with him to the new premises, but needs to buy more. During the accounting year ending 30 April 20X2 he spend £8560 on new equipment. The cost of the equipment he transferred over to the new premises was £18 388, and its net book value at 1 May 20X1 was £7380.

Wilbur depreciates equipment on the reducing balance basis at 15% per year, with a full year's charge to depreciation in the year of purchase. The lease premium will be amortised over seven years on a straight-line basis. Assuming Wilbur has no other fixed assets, what amounts will be charged for depreciation and amortisation, to the nearest £, in Wilbur's profit and loss account for the year ending 30 April 20X2?

a) amortisation £3000 depreciation £2391

b) amortisation £1470 depreciation £4042

c) amortisation £3000 depreciation £4042

d) amortisation £1470 depreciation £2391.

9.13   Xenia no longer needs a second van in her business, and so she decides to sell it. The van originally cost £8300 and by Xenia's year-end of 31 March 20X4 depreciation had accumulated of £6330. She sells the van for £2380 on 1 April 20X4. What is the profit or loss on sale of the van?

9.14   Xanthe runs a florist's shop. Her assistant goes out every day in the van delivering flowers. The van accumulates high mileage quickly and Xanthe usually replaces it every three years. The van cost £10 100 on 1 June 20X1 and Xanthe has depreciated it on the reducing balance basis at 30% per year for three years. She sells it on 1 June 20X4 for £3000. What is the profit or loss on sale of the van?

9.15A Xavier depreciates his machinery over ten years using the straight-line method. On 31 December 20X7 he sells a machine that he has owned for exactly seven years. Its original cost was £73 730. The sale proceeds are £30 000. What is the profit or loss on sale of the machinery?

9.16A Xan has a machine at net book value of £13 338 in his accounts. If he sells the machine for £15 000 he makes a profit on disposal of £1662. Using the accounting equation, what is the effect on his assets, liabilities and capital?

a) assets increase; capital decreases; liabilities no change

b) assets decrease; capital increases; liabilities increase

c) assets increase; capital increases; liabilities no change

d) assets decrease; capital no change; liabilities decrease.

9.17 Ying runs a wholesale business supplying art equipment to retailers. She uses two computers to keep stock and other records – one in the office and one in the warehouse. In her accounting year ending 31 December 20X3 she decides to buy a new networked computer system, with terminals in both the office and warehouse. She is able to sell both of the old computers, one for £250 and the other, which is in slightly better condition, for £300. Both computers were bought on 1 January 20X1 for a total price of £3672. They have been depreciated on the straight-line basis over four years, with the assumption that their value will be nil at the end of the four-year period. Ying disposes of them on 1 July 20X3.

Ying charges depreciation for each full month of ownership of fixed assets. What is her profit or loss on sale of the computers?

9.18 Zoë starts up an independent fast food outlet on 1 January 20X4, trading as Zoë's Snacks. She has the following balances in her books at 31 December 20X4. Her accountant has advised her that she should depreciate her machinery and fixtures over a period of between four and seven years on a straight-line basis. Zoë, who is a keen amateur accountant, decides to prepare her profit and loss account and balance sheet on the basis of straight-line depreciation over a four-year period. However, she is also interested to see what difference it would make to her profits if she depreciated machinery over the maximum advisable period of seven years. Her books show the following list of balances (before any adjustment for depreciation):

	£
Sales	132 614
Staffing costs	15 030
Rental of premises	7 400
Purchases	83 430
Electricity	2 961
Phone	1 806
Insurance	1 437
Sundry expenses	981
Accountant's fees	600
Machinery and fixtures at cost	28 760
Stocks of food etc	1 209
Cash at bank	3 406
Creditors	1 650
Capital introduced by Zoë	20 000
Drawings	8 453

The following are required:

a) Draw up the profit and loss account and balance sheet for Zoë's Snacks at 31 December 20X4 making adjustments for depreciation of machinery and fixtures on the basis of the straight-line method of depreciation over four years, with an estimated residual value of nil.

b) Calculate the increase or decrease in net profit that would arise if Zoë depreciated the machinery and fixtures on the basis of the straight-line method of depreciation over seven years.

c) Calculate the net profit margin on the basis of i) depreciating the fixed assets over four years; and, ii) depreciating the fixed assets over seven years.

9.19A For several years Zak has run a contract office cleaning business. He employs several part-time staff who work at night and weekends. Zak has always run the business from rented premises; he has a small office to deal with the paperwork and a storage area where cleaning equipment and machinery is kept. He also runs three vans which deliver staff and their equipment to offices around the city.

Zak has the opportunity to buy the freehold office premises he currently occupies for £51 370. He would be able to obtain a commercial mortgage for £40 000 at a rate of 8% per annum. He would like some advice on whether or not to take out the mortgage to buy the premises.

Zak has the following balances in his books at 31 March 20X3:

	£
Capital at 1 April 20X2	21 410
Bank overdraft (note: overdraft limit £20 000)	10 447
Cleaning equipment at cost	6 400
Accumulated depreciation on cleaning equipment at 1 April 20X2	1 920
Office fixtures and fittings at cost	1 700
Accumulated depreciation on office fixtures and fittings at 1 April 20X2	1 660
Vans at cost	22 419
Accumulated depreciation on vans at 1 April 20X2	14 490
Debtors	13 796
Drawings	32 479
Creditors	1 624
Sundry stocks of cleaning materials	1 408
Sales	107 614
Premises rental	7 462
Electricity and other premises costs	2 444
Sundry office expenses	799
Staff costs	63 491
Accountancy and tax advice	1 200
Cleaning materials	5 177
Interest paid	390

Zak has not made any accounting adjustments in respect of depreciation in the above list of figures. He charges depreciation as follows:

● Cleaning equipment: straight-line basis over ten years. None of the equipment is fully depreciated at 31 March 20X3.

● Office fixtures and fittings: straight-line basis over ten years.

● Vans: 25% on the reducing balance basis.

There were no additions or disposals of fixed assets during the year ending 31 March 20X3.

a) Prepare Zak's profit and loss account for the year ending 31 March 20X3 and a balance sheet at 31 March 20X3

b) Advise him on whether or not, in your opinion, he should take out the mortgage and buy the premises.

Answers to exercises

9.1

	£
Cost of the new van	14 460
Less: expected sale proceeds in four years time	(4 000)
Depreciable amount	10 460

Spread evenly over four years this gives an annual depreciation charge of £10 460/4 = £2 615. The correct answer, therefore, is d).

9.3

	£
Cost of new exercise bike	450
Less: expected sale proceeds in three years time	(30)
Depreciable amount	420

Spread evenly over three years this gives an annual depreciation charge of £420/3 = £140. However, Victoria charges depreciation only for the period of ownership, which, in the year ending 31 August 20X2, is six months. The depreciation charge for the bike for this year is therefore £140/2 = £70. The correct answer, therefore, is a).

9.5   *Depreciation on machine one*:

$$\frac{£10\,300}{5} = £2\,060$$

This is a full year's depreciation, but Vinny would calculate depreciation only for the part of the year he had owned the asset. Therefore the charge for the year ending 31 December 20X6 would be:

$$£2\,060 \times \frac{9}{12} = £1\,545$$

Depreciation on machine two:

	£
Cost of new machine	8 580
Less: expected sale proceeds in four years time	(2 000)
Depreciable amount	6 580

Spread evenly over four years, this gives an annual charge of £6580/4 = £1645. However, the charge for the year ending 31 December 20X6 would be for the three months of ownership only:

$$£1\,645 \times \frac{3}{12} = £411 \text{ (to the nearest £)}$$

The total depreciation charge for these two assets is £1545 + £411 = £1956. The correct answer, therefore, is c).

9.6   Violet has purchased an intangible asset in the form of mineral extraction rights. She has a licence to extract gold (if she can find it) from the land for three-and-a-half years only. At the end of that period she has no further rights over the land unless she renegotiates them. The initial payment of £273 000 will be spread over the three-and-a-half year period of ownership of the rights. As noted in the chapter, amortisation is almost invariably calculated on the straight-line basis.

In the first year of ownership Violet will charge amortisation in her profit and loss account of:

$$\frac{£273\,000}{3.5 \text{ years}} = £78\,000$$

The balance sheet will show the following in respect of mineral rights:

	£
Fixed assets	
Intangible fixed assets	
Mineral rights at cost	273 000
Less: accumulated amortisation	(78 000)
Net book value	195 000

9.7   The total charge for depreciation for the year ending 31 August 20X8 is as follows:

	£
Buildings: £306 000 × 2%	6 120
Motor vehicles: £32 300 × 25%	8 075
Fixtures and fittings: £12 720 × 10%	1 272
	15 467

The presentation of fixed assets in Vincenzo's balance sheet at 31 August 20X8 is as follows:

	£	£
Fixed assets		
Buildings at cost	306 000	
Less: accumulated depreciation (18 360 + 6 120)	(24 480)	
		281 520
Motor vehicles at cost	48 770	
Less: accumulated depreciation (16 470 + 8 075)	(24 545)	
		24 225
Fixtures and fittings at cost	12 720	
Less: accumulated depreciation (6 360 + 1 272)	(7 632)	
		5 088
Total		310 833

9.9

	£
Basic cost of new wedding car	24 400
Additional cost of white spray	800
Total cost	25 200

The first year's depreciation on the reducing balance basis is £25 200 × 15% = £3 780. The correct answer, therefore, is b).

9.10

	£	£
Net book value of cars at 1 January 20X3	22 830	
Depreciation for the year: £22 830 × 25%		5 707
New car added on 1 January 20X3	14 447	
Depreciation for the year £14 447 × 25%		3 612
Total depreciation for the year		9 319

Another, quicker, way of doing the calculation:

	£
Net book value of cars at 1 January 20X3	22 830
Add: new car purchased on 1 January 20X3	14 447
Total depreciable value at 31 December 20X3	37 227

Depreciation: £37 227 × 25% = £9319. The correct answer, therefore, is b). Tutorial note: in William's balance sheet the presentation will be as follows:

	£
Fixed assets	
Tangible fixed assets	
Cars at cost (£38 370 + £14 447)	52 817
Less: accumulated depreciation (£15 540 + £9319)	(24 859)
Net book value	27 958

9.13

	£
Sale proceeds	2 380
The net book value of the van is £8300 − £6330 =	1 970
Profit on sale	410

Tutorial note: this is a profit on sale because Xenia receives more for the van than the value (net book value) at which it is recorded in her accounts.

9.14   First, we need to work out the net book value of the van at 1 June 20X4.

	£
Cost on 1 June 20X1	10 100
Year 1 depreciation: £10 100 × 30%	(3 030)
Net book value at 1 June 20X2	7 070
Year 2 depreciation: £7070 × 30%	(2 121)
Net book value at 1 June 20X3	4 949
Year 3 depreciation: £4949 × 30%	(1 485)
Net book value at 1 June 20X4	3 464

Comparing the net book value with the sale proceeds of £3000 results in a loss on disposal of £464.

9.17   By the time she disposes of them, Ying has owned the computers for exactly two years and six months (1 January 20X1 to 1 July 20X3). The annual charge for depreciation is: £3672/4 = £918. Two-and-a-half year's of charges = 2.5 × £918 = £2295.

The net book value of the computers at the date of disposal is:

	£
Cost	3 672
Less: accumulated depreciation	(2 295)
Net book value	1 377
Sale proceeds	550
Less: net book value	(1 377)
Loss on sale	827

In effect, Ying has underestimated the depreciation appropriate to these assets. Their value has dropped more quickly than she initially supposed.

9.18   *a) Working for depreciation*

Machinery at cost = £28 760. Straight-line depreciation over four years = £28 760/4 = £7 190.

Zoë's Snacks: Profit and loss account for the year ending 31 December 20X4

	£	£
Sales		132 614
Less: cost of sales		
Opening stock	—	
Purchases	83 430	
Less: closing stock	(1 209)	
		(82 221)
Gross profit		50 393
Expenses		
Staffing	15 030	
Premises rental	7 400	
Electricity	2 961	
Phone	1 806	
Insurance	1 437	
Sundry expenses	981	
Accountant's fees	600	
Depreciation (see working above)	7 190	
		(37 405)
Net profit		12 988

Zoë's Snacks: Balance sheet at 31 December 20X4

	£	£
Fixed assets		
Machinery and fixtures at cost	28 760	
Less: accumulated depreciation	(7 190)	
		21 570
Current assets		
Stock	1 209	
Cash at bank	3 406	
	4 615	
Current liabilities		
Creditors	(1 650)	
Net current assets		2 965
		24 535
Capital		
Capital introduced		20 000
Add: profit for the year		12 988
Less: drawings		(8 453)
		24 535

b) Depreciation over seven years

If Zoë used a period of seven years over which to depreciate the machinery and fixtures, the depreciation charge would be:

$$\text{Cost } \frac{£28\,760}{7 \text{ years}} = £4\,109 \text{ (to nearest £)}$$

Effect on profit:

	£
Net profit as stated in the profit and loss account above:	12 988
Add back: depreciation over four years	7 190
Net profit before depreciation	20 178
Net profit before depreciation	20 178
Less: depreciation over seven years	(4 109)
Net profit adjusted for change in depreciation	16 069

Net profit is £12 988 if machinery and fixtures are depreciated over four years. If the depreciation period is increased to seven years, net profit increases to £16 069 (an increase of nearly 24%).

c) Net profit margin

Net profit percentage is net profit as a percentage of sales. Net profit percentage with depreciation over four years:

$$\frac{£12\,988}{132\,614} \times 100 = 9.8\%$$

Net profit percentage with depreciation over seven years:

$$\frac{\pounds 16\,069}{132\,614} \times 100 = 12.1\%$$

Note that a change in the method of depreciation can make a large difference to net profit and to the net profit percentage.

10

THE ACCOUNTS OF MANUFACTURING BUSINESSES

AIMS AND LEARNING OUTCOMES

Aim of the chapter

To extend the knowledge and skills acquired in previous chapters to cover the preparation of a profit and loss account and balance sheet for a manufacturing business.

Learning outcomes

After reading the chapter and completing the related exercises, students should:

- Understand the distinctions between 'raw materials', 'work in progress' and 'finished goods' stock.
- Be able to calculate cost of sales for a manufacturing business.
- Be able to prepare the profit and loss account and balance sheet for a manufacturing business.

Manufacturing businesses

So far, in this section of the book, we have used examples of sole trader businesses engaged principally in selling goods or services. The accounts of businesses engaged in manufacturing are a little more complicated because such businesses typically buy in raw materials, put them through a manufacturing process and produce finished goods for sale. The calculation of cost of sales involves some additional steps in order to ensure that all costs are included. However, items of expenses deducted from gross profit are treated in the same way as for traders selling goods or services, so many aspects of the accounts preparation remain the same, and should be quite familiar by now.

First, we will look at an example of a manufacturing business in order to think through the processes involved and to become familiar with some of the terminology used in describing accounting in a manufacturing environment.

Example 10.1 Anna runs a small business making components for self-assembly furniture kits. She buys in **raw materials** in the form of different types and grades of wood, medium density fibreboard, hardboard and metals. Anna's employees then process the raw materials using various machines in order to produce **finished goods**, which she then sells to her customers. Her customers are mainly large retailers who source their flat-pack furniture from many different manufacturers. Anna herself does not sell directly to the public.

Anna's production falls into two categories. Most of her goods are produced to fulfil specific large orders from customers. However, she also keeps a finished goods stock of small components which are in general demand. Production for specific orders usually takes priority, but in slack periods Anna's small factory can be kept busy in the production of the smaller, generic components.

At any point in time, Anna's factory contains three categories of stock:

- **Raw materials**, which are waiting to enter the production process.
- **Finished goods**, either awaiting shipment to customers or kept in stock against possible future orders.
- **Work-in-progress**, which comprises partly processed materials.

Calculating cost of sales

In the examples provided so far in this book, cost of sales has been arrived at by the following calculation:

$$\text{Opening stock} + \text{Purchases} - \text{Closing stock} = \text{Cost of sales}$$

Where, as in the case of Anna's factory, there are three categories of stock, the calculation of cost of sales inevitably becomes more complicated. The valuation of raw materials stock is usually straightforward, and is based on the cost of the materials. However, once raw materials enter production, their value is increased by the various processes that they are subjected to. How is this additional value calculated?

In the next example, we will examine Anna's production process in more detail.

Example 10.2 Anna's factory contains several machines such as lathes, cutting machines and presses. She employs four members of staff to operate the various machines, and a production supervisor who is responsible for ensuring that production runs smoothly. What costs are involved in the production process? How do we arrive at the cost of finished goods?

1. *Materials costs*: the cost of raw materials put into the production process form part of the overall cost of the finished goods.
2. *Labour costs*: the cost of wages paid to the production workers forms part of the overall cost of the finished goods.
3. *Production overheads*: these comprise any additional costs of production, including such items as the cost of time spent in supervising production, the cost of electricity for running the factory, and the depreciation charges relating to the machinery used in production.

It is necessary to take all three categories of cost into account in order to calculate the overall cost of finished goods, and the cost of sales. (Note that in Part III of this book we will examine costing in much greater detail.)

In addition to these cost categories there are all the other costs that a business usually incurs: for example, administration costs such as phone bills, cost of employing office staff, accountancy and legal fees and salespersons' salaries. Such costs are not related to production; they are expenses that are deducted from gross profit.

Self-test question 10.1 (answer at the end of the chapter)

Billy has a factory that manufactures children's toys. Next door to the factory premises is a small office where Billy's secretary keeps the paperwork in order, and where the sales force of two people is based. Billy's business incurs costs in the following categories.

- purchase of wood for making toys
- depreciation of factory machinery
- employee costs – machine operators
- production supervisor's salary
- electricity bill for factory
- electricity bill for office
- depreciation of office equipment
- telephone bill
- delivery van expenses
- secretary's salary
- purchase of plastics for making toys
- purchase of paper for office computer
- purchase of toy packaging.

Place each item in one of the following categories:

- materials cost
- labour cost
- production overheads
- administration and selling expenses.

Direct and indirect costs

Direct costs are those costs that are clearly identifiable with the items produced. For example, Anna receives an order for 500 wardrobe door fittings, each to be packaged in its own plastic bag. In order to produce these she needs 16kg of metal that costs £5.00 per kilo, and 500 plastic bags at 0.25p each. The metal will be processed through a machine. To produce 500 fittings an employee will spend two hours on machine processing. The cost of employing one employee for an hour for this quite skilled work is £6.50. In addition, another employee, employed at £5.40 per hour, will spend one hour at the end of the process putting the goods into the plastic bags.

The material and labour costs involved are **direct costs** in that they are clearly linked to the number of items produced. If Anna received an order for 1000 wardrobe door fittings the overall direct cost could be expected to be twice as much as for 500 fittings. This can be demonstrated as follows:

	Direct costs for 500 fittings	Direct costs for 1000 fittings
Raw materials – metal	16kg × £5.00 = £80	32kg × £5.00 = £160
Labour – processing	2 hours @ £6.50 = £13.00	4 hours @ £6.50 = £26.00
Raw materials – packing	500 × 0.25p = £1.25	1000 × 0.25p = £2.50
Labour – packing	1 hour @ £5.40 = £5.40	2 hours @ £5.40 = £10.80
Total direct costs	£80 + £13.00 + £1.25 + £5.40 = £99.65	£160 + £26.00 + £2.50 + £10.80 = £199.30

The total figure for direct costs is commonly known as **prime cost**. The most commonly found direct costs are direct materials and direct labour. However, occasionally, other **direct expenses** are incurred.

Indirect costs are those that cannot be clearly linked to the items produced. For example, the cost of heating and lighting for the factory for one day remains the same regardless of how many items are produced during that day.

The value of finished goods stock contains a combination of direct and indirect costs. Work-in-progress stock is stock that is part way through the manufacturing process. Its value also contains a combination of direct and indirect costs, the amount of which depends upon how far it has proceeded through the production process. For example, suppose that at Anna's year-end, on 31 March 20X3, an order for 500 wardrobe fittings of the type shown in the example above had been partly completed. The fittings had been through the machine process but had not yet been packaged. The direct cost value of the work-in-progress would comprise only the cost of the metal raw material plus the cost of the labour to put it through the manufacturing process. Packaging material and labour costs would be excluded. The direct cost value would be (from the table above): £80 + £13 = £93 (for 500 wardrobe fittings). An additional estimate of indirect cost would also be added to arrive at a total value for the work-in-progress of wardrobe fittings.

The manufacturing account

In order to be able to calculate cost of sales in a manufacturing business it is necessary to work out manufacturing cost. A manufacturing account is used to calculated the total cost of producing finished goods during the accounting period.

A typical manufacturing account layout is shown below:

	£	£	£
Direct costs			
Direct materials			
Opening stock of raw materials	X		
Add: purchases of raw materials	X		
	X		
Less: closing stock of raw materials	(X)		
		X	
Direct labour		X	
Direct expenses		X	
Total direct costs (prime cost)			X
Production overheads (indirect costs)			
e.g. Depreciation of factory machinery		X	
e.g. Factory supervisor		X	
e.g. Factory rental		X	
e.g. Factory machinery repair and maintenance		X	
Total production overheads			X
Add: opening work-in-progress			X
Less: closing work-in-progress			(X)
Factory cost of finished goods			X

Note: it is important to remember to adjust the totals to take account of work-in-progress.

The next example shows the relevant figures for Anna's businesses and demonstrates how they are combined to form the manufacturing element of the accounts, and how that element fits together with the profit and loss account.

Example 10.3 Anna produces accounts to 31 March each year. At 31 March 20X3 she had the following balances relating to income and costs in her books:

	£
Depreciation of delivery vans	7 567
Office insurance	1 694
Factory workers' wages	47 350
Telephone	2 690
Accountancy and tax advice	1 500
Production manager's salary	16 750
Factory insurance	6 360
Office rental and business rates	7 520
Factory rental and business rates	30 610
Depreciation of office equipment	530

▶

	£
Maintenance and repair of machinery	1 750
Factory electricity	12 690
Secretarial costs	6 003
Delivery charges	16 760
Purchases of raw materials	91 004
Sales of finished goods	297 070
Office electricity	860
Sundry office expenses	2 034
Factory security services	2 166
Factory machinery depreciation	16 152

Opening stock at 1 April 20X2 was:

	£
Raw materials	7 593
Work-in-progress	1 675
Finished goods	16 240

Closing stock at 31 March 20X3 was:

	£
Raw materials	8 177
Work-in-progress	1 260
Finished goods	17 960

You are required to prepare a manufacturing account, and a profit and loss account for Anna for the year ending 31 March 20X3.

Step 1: Identify those items relating to the manufacturing account

In previous chapters we have allocated items in a given list of balances to trading account, profit and loss account or balance sheet. In this case we are not required to prepare a balance sheet, but we need to identify which items belong to the manufacturing account, and which to the trading account and profit and loss account. Remember that the costs for inclusion in the manufacturing account are those of direct materials, labour and expenses, and indirect production overheads. All costs relating to administration, selling and distribution are included in the profit and loss account.

	£	Category
Depreciation of delivery vans	7 567	Profit and loss account
Office insurance	1 694	Profit and loss account
Factory workers' wages	47 350	Manufacturing account – direct labour
Telephone	2 690	Profit and loss account
Accountancy and tax advice	1 500	Profit and loss account
Production manager's salary	16 750	Manufacturing account – indirect production overheads
Factory insurance	6 360	Manufacturing account – indirect production overheads
Office rental and business rates	7 520	Profit and loss account

	£	Category
Factory rental and business rates	30 610	Manufacturing account – indirect production overheads
Depreciation of office equipment	530	Profit and loss account
Maintenance and repair of machinery	1 750	Manufacturing account – indirect production overheads
Factory electricity	12 690	Manufacturing account – indirect production overheads
Secretarial costs	6 003	Profit and loss account
Delivery charges	16 760	Profit and loss account
Purchases of raw materials	91 004	Manufacturing account – direct materials
Sales of finished goods	297 070	Trading account
Office electricity	860	Profit and loss account
Sundry office expenses	2 034	Profit and loss account
Factory security services	2 166	Manufacturing account – indirect production overheads
Factory machinery depreciation	16 152	Manufacturing account – indirect production overheads

Step 2: Produce manufacturing account

Anna: Manufacturing account for the year ending 31 March 20X3

	£	£	£
Direct costs			
Direct materials			
Opening stock	7 593		
Add: purchases	91 004		
	98 597		
Less: closing stock	(8 177)		
		90 420	
Direct labour		47 350	
Total direct costs (prime cost)			137 770
Production overheads (indirect costs)			
Production manager's salary		16 750	
Factory insurance		6 360	
Factory rental and business rates		30 610	
Maintenance and repair of machinery		1 750	
Factory electricity		12 690	
Factory security services		2 166	
Factory machinery depreciation		16 152	
Total production overheads			86 478
Add: opening work-in-progress			1 675
Less: closing work-in-progress			(1 260)
Factory cost of finished goods			224 663

Note the adjustment for work-in-progress. Opening work-in-progress is a collection of costs brought into the current accounting period. Closing work-in-progress is the total of costs carried into the next accounting period.

Step 3: Produce profit and loss account, including trading account

Anna: Profit and loss account for year ending 31 March 20X3

	£	£
Sales		297 070
Less: cost of sales		
Opening stock of finished goods	16 240	
Add: factory cost of finished goods [from manufacturing account]	224 663	
	240 903	
Less: closing stock of finished goods	(17 960)	
Cost of sales		(222 943)
Gross profit		74 127
Expenses		
Depreciation of delivery vans	7 567	
Office insurance	1 694	
Telephone	2 690	
Accountancy and tax advice	1 500	
Office rental and business rates	7 520	
Depreciation of office equipment	530	
Secretarial costs	6 003	
Delivery charges	16 760	
Office electricity	860	
Sundry office expenses	2 034	
		(47 158)
Net profit		26 969

Improving presentation

The expenses in Anna's profit and loss account are listed in the same order as in the list of balances. However, it might be helpful to a reader of the accounts to have the expenses categorised in order to improve the quality of the information supplied. In this case, for example, two appropriate categories might be (a) selling and distribution expenses, and (b) administration expenses. Allocation to these two categories would give the following result:

Expenses	£	£
Selling and distribution		
Depreciation of delivery vans	7 567	
Delivery charges	16 760	
		24 327
Administration expenses		
Office insurance	1 694	
Telephone	2 690	
Accountancy and tax advice	1 500	
Office rental and business rates	7 520	
Depreciation of office equipment	530	
Secretarial costs	6 003	
Office electricity	860	
Sundry office expenses	2 034	
		22 831
		47 158

Note that the figures do not change at all, but there is an improvement in the presentation of the information.

Self-test question 10.2 (answer at the end of the chapter)

Ollie runs a small manufacturing business making components for the motor industry, trading as Brightwell Components. The following is a list of his account balances relating to income and costs for the accounting year ending 31 August 20X4.

	£
Depreciation of factory machinery	10 493
Accountancy and tax advice	1 200
Purchases of raw materials	78 439
Office insurance	3 442
Salespersons' salaries	24 410
Factory rental	23 700
Sales	341 115
Electricity and gas for factory	9 942
Office rental	6 344
Sundry selling expenses	827
Telephone – salespersons	2 492
Secretarial costs	9 314
Electricity – office	1 824
Factory insurance	3 773
Depreciation – factory computer	1 220
Repairs and maintenance to factory machinery	3 111
Production supervisory salaries	25 471
Delivery charges	17 270
Telephone – administration	1 720
Office sundry expenses	714
Factory sundry expenses	234
Factory wages	81 479

Opening stock at 1 September 20X3 was:

	£
Raw materials	13 210
Work-in-progress	2 511
Finished goods	26 700

Closing stock at 31 August 20X4 was:

	£
Raw materials	12 994
Work-in-progress	2 145
Finished goods	29 363

You are required to prepare a manufacturing account, and a profit and loss account for Brightwell Components for the year ending 31 August 20X4. Classify the expenses in the profit and loss account under two headings (a) selling and distribution expenses, and (b) administration expenses.

Manufacturing companies – including the balance sheet

The case study for this chapter provides a comprehensive example of accounting for a manufacturing concern, including the preparation of the manufacturing account, the profit and loss account and the balance sheet. All of the adjustments encountered in previous chapters – for example, accruals and prepayments, depreciation and amortisation, and adjustments for sales and purchases returns – are likely to occur in manufacturing accounts. The example in the case study includes several categories of adjustments. It may, therefore, look complicated at first sight, but there is no new material in it and students who have understood the book up to this point should have no difficulty in following the example.

CASE STUDY 10.1   Using accounts to give advice

Atul left university with a first class degree in chemistry. He had been particularly interested in plastics, and continued to study in his spare time after he started his career as an industrial chemist. He discovered a new way of laminating cloth, which produced a very durable, heat-resistant and fireproof result. He registered the patent for his method and decided to leave work and set up a manufacturing business to exploit the technology he had discovered. Atul's father, a businessman himself, advanced an interest-free loan of £15 000 to help get the business started. Atul was able to set up in a small unit on an industrial estate with the help of a low rental deal provided by the local authority.

Five years after setting up, Atul is still in business, trading as Belle Vue Laminates. He employs seven people full-time in the factory – six machine operatives and a production progress chaser. In the office there are a secretary, an invoicing clerk and a part-time bookkeeper. He has built up the sales order book himself and prospects are looking reasonably bright. However, Atul recently attended a seminar for young business people entitled 'Expanding your business'. He has felt for several months now that his business is in danger of stagnating and that he needs to increase the volume of sales. So far, Atul has done virtually all of the sales development work himself, although his father has helped by introducing him to some of his business contacts. He enjoys selling, and feels that he could increase sales volumes substantially if he spent more time out of the office. A recent article in the business press on export opportunities in Europe has encouraged him to think about potential markets overseas.

Atul has arranged a meeting with a small business development adviser to discuss an idea he has had to facilitate expansion of the business. He would like to explore the idea of employing a graduate in business studies with the intention of delegating quite a lot of the responsibility for day-to-day running of the factory and administration to the new employee. Atul estimates that he currently spends about three days per week running the factory and dealing with administrative queries, but problems keep building up and there have been some customer complaints about quality in recent months. (The rest of his working week is spent on the road visiting customers and seeking out new selling opportunities.) Atul's plan is that the new employee should spend, on average, three days per week supervising all aspects of production (including the implementation of proper quality control systems) and a further two days in improving the business administration. Atul realises that he will have to be prepared to pay a reasonably good salary to be able to employ a person with sufficient initiative to run the factory effectively in his absence, and he is prepared to pay up to £25 000 per year for the right person. However, he feels confident that he can increase sales substantially if his time is freed up to explore new selling opportunities.

Atul currently still has the £15 000 loan from his father, and has negotiated a flexible overdraft facility of up to £10 000 with the bank manager.

Atul's accountant, Shona, prepares his accounts annually up to his year-end of 30 September. It is now 15 October and Atul is due to meet the business adviser on 31 October. He asks Shona to quickly prepare a draft manufacturing account, profit and loss account and balance sheet from the list of balances and notes on adjustments given below.

Requirements are:

1. To prepare the profit and loss account for the year ending 30 September 20X2 and the balance sheet at that date for Belle Vue Laminates.

2. To advise Atul on the possible effects on his business of employing a graduate on £25 000 per year, examining both financial and non-financial potential impacts.

	£
Office salaries	21 560
Import duties on raw material purchases	3 370
Raw materials purchases	72 444
Accountancy and tax advice	1 150
Plant and machinery at cost	109 300
Accumulated depreciation on plant and machinery at 1 October 20X1	14 620
Debtors	29 930
Bank overdraft	2 495
Production progress chaser's wages	12 071
Factory electricity	7 474
Office electricity	950
Office insurance	1 879
Loan from Atul's father	15 000
Factory insurance	6 467
Distribution costs	9 308
Interest paid	951
Fixtures and fittings at cost	10 750
Accumulated depreciation on fixtures and fittings at 1 October 20X1	3 012
Maintenance of plant and machinery	3 060
Factory rental	20 792
Office telephone	2 145
Entertaining expenses	1 280
Creditors	12 790
Capital at 1 October 20X1	116 409
Office sundry expenses	963
Office rental	2 944
Bad debts written off	1 200

▶

	£
Travelling expenses	8 963
Factory wages	70 493
Factory sundry expenses	1 409
Sales	302 240
Sales returns	3 780
Charitable donations	300
Drawings	28 000
Opening stock at 1 October 20X1:	
Raw materials	6 888
Work-in-progress	3 131
Finished goods	23 614
Closing stock at 30 September 20X2:	
Raw materials	12 941
Work-in-progress	2 968
Finished goods	29 497

Note the following:

1. £584 of the office insurance balance of £1879 relates to the period after 30 September 20X2.

2. The last quarter's telephone bill of £703 was received on 8 October 20X2 and is not included in the figures above.

3. Atul has just discovered that a customer has gone into liquidation. The customer owes Belle Vue £400, but there is very little likelihood of ever receiving the money. Therefore, Atul decides to write off the bad debt.

4. Adjustments for depreciation have not yet been made. Plant and machinery is depreciated at 10% on cost. None of the plant and machinery is fully depreciated. Sundry fixtures and fittings are depreciated at 20% on the reducing balance basis.

Step 1: Allocate balances

The first step is to allocate balances to the manufacturing account, the trading account, the profit and loss account or to the balance sheet.

	£	Category
Office salaries	21 560	Profit and loss account
Import duties on raw material purchases	3 370	Manufacturing account – direct materials
Raw materials purchases	72 444	Manufacturing account – direct materials
Accountancy and tax advice	1 150	Profit and loss account
Plant and machinery at cost	109 300	Balance sheet
Accumulated depreciation on plant and machinery at 1 October 20X1	14 620	Balance sheet
Debtors	29 930	Balance sheet
Bank overdraft	2 495	Balance sheet
Production progress chaser's wages	12 071	Manufacturing account – indirect production overheads

	£	Category
Factory electricity	7 474	Manufacturing account – indirect production overheads
Office electricity	950	Profit and loss account
Office insurance	1 879	Profit and loss account
Loan from Atul's father	15 000	Balance sheet
Factory insurance	6 467	Manufacturing account – indirect production overheads
Distribution costs	9 308	Profit and loss account
Interest paid	951	Profit and loss account
Fixtures and fittings at cost	10 750	Balance sheet
Accumulated depreciation on fixtures and fittings at 1 October 20X1	3 012	Balance sheet
Maintenance of plant and machinery	3 060	Manufacturing account – indirect production overheads
Factory rental	20 792	Manufacturing account – indirect production overheads
Office telephone	2 145	Profit and loss account
Entertaining expenses	1 280	Profit and loss account
Creditors	12 790	Balance sheet
Capital at 1 October 20X1	116 409	Balance sheet
Office sundry expenses	963	Profit and loss account
Office rental	2 944	Profit and loss account
Bad debts written off	1 200	Profit and loss account
Travelling expenses	8 963	Profit and loss account
Factory wages	70 493	Manufacturing account – direct labour
Factory sundry expenses	1 409	Manufacturing account – indirect production overheads
Sales	302 240	Trading account
Sales returns	3 780	Trading account
Charitable donations	300	Profit and loss account
Drawings	28 000	Balance sheet
Opening stock at 1 October 20X1:		
Raw materials	6 888	Manufacturing account – direct materials and balance sheet
Work-in-progress	3 131	Manufacturing account – adjustment and balance sheet
Finished goods	23 614	Trading account and balance sheet
Closing stock at 30 September 20X2:		
Raw materials	12 941	Manufacturing account – direct materials and balance sheet
Work-in-progress	2 968	Manufacturing account – adjustment and balance sheet
Finished goods	29 497	Trading account and balance sheet

▶

Step 2: Deal with adjustments

1. A prepayment of £584 will be recorded in the balance sheet in respect of the office insurance paid in advance. The office insurance in the profit and loss account will be £1879 − £584 = £1295.

2. An accrual of £703 will be recorded in the balance sheet in respect of the telephone bill received after the year-end. In the profit and loss account office telephone charges will be £2145 + £703 = £2848.

3. There is already a balance of £1200 in respect of bad debts written off. This will increase by £400 to £1600 to reflect the additional write-off. Debtors in the balance sheet will reduce by the same amount and will be stated at £29 930 − £400 = £29 530.

4. Plant and machinery depreciation for the year will be £109 300 × 10% = £10 930. This becomes an expense in the manufacturing account, where it is included under indirect production overheads, and accumulated depreciation in the balance sheet increases to £14 620 + £10 930 = £25 550. Depreciation on fixtures and fittings is charged at 20% on the reducing balance basis. The net book value brought forward is £10 750 − £3012 = £7738. The depreciation charge for the year is 20% of that net book value: £7738 × 20% = £1548 to the nearest £. There will be a charge of £1548 to the profit and loss account, and accumulated depreciation in the balance sheet increases to £3012 + £1548 = £4560.

Step 3: Produce manufacturing account

	£	£	£
Direct costs			
Direct materials			
Opening stock	6 888		
Add: purchases	72 444		
+ import duty on purchases	3 370		
	82 702		
Less: closing stock	(12 941)		
		69 761	
Direct labour		70 493	
Total direct costs (prime cost)			140 254
Production overheads (indirect costs)			
Factory rental		20 792	
Depreciation of factory plant and machinery		10 930	
Maintenance of plant and machinery		3 060	
Production progress chaser's wages		12 071	
Factory electricity		7 474	
Factory insurance		6 467	
Factory sundry expenses		1 409	
Total production overheads			62 203
Add: opening work-in-progress			3 131
Less: closing work-in-progress			(2 968)
Factory cost of finished goods			202 620

Step 4: Produce Profit and loss account

Belle Vue Laminates: Profit and loss account for the year ending 30 September 20X2

	£	£
Sales		302 240
Less: returns		(3 780)
		298 460
Less: cost of sales		
Opening stock of finished goods	23 614	
Add: factory cost of finished goods [from manufacturing account]	202 620	
	226 234	
Less: closing stock of finished goods	(29 497)	
Cost of sales		(196 737)
Gross profit		101 723
Expenses		
Office salaries	21 560	
Office rental	2 944	
Office electricity	950	
Office insurance	1 295	
Office telephone	2 848	
Distribution costs	9 308	
Travelling expenses	8 963	
Entertaining expenses	1 280	
Depreciation of fixtures and fittings	1 548	
Interest paid	951	
Bad debts written off	1 600	
Accountancy and tax advice	1 150	
Charitable donations	300	
Office sundry expenses	963	
		(55 660)
Net profit		46 063

Step 5: Produce balance sheet

Belle Vue Laminates: Balance sheet at 30 September 20X2

	£	£
Fixed assets		
Plant and machinery at cost	109 300	
Less: accumulated depreciation (£14 620 + £10 930)	(25 550)	
		83 750
Fixtures and fittings at cost	10 750	
Less: accumulated depreciation (£3012 + £1548)	(4 560)	
		6 190
		89 940

	£	£
Current assets		
Stocks:		
Raw materials	12 941	
Work-in-progress	2 968	
Finished goods	29 497	
Debtors	29 530	
Prepayment	584	
	75 520	
Current liabilities		
Bank overdraft	(2 495)	
Creditors	(12 790)	
Accrual	(703)	
	(15 988)	
Net current assets		59 532
		149 472
Long-term liability: loan		(15 000)
		134 472
Capital		
Capital at 1 October 20X1		116 409
Add: profit for the year		46 063
Less: drawings		(28 000)
		134 472

Advice to Atul

Atul's proposal to employ a graduate at a salary of £25 000 involves some risks. There will be an additional charge on the business profits, which for this year are just over £46 000. The risk is that employing another person will not yield any benefits to the business, but will substantially increase its costs and reduce its profits. There is the additional major risk of employing the wrong person. It seems that Atul wants to use the opportunity to travel widely in order to increase sales, especially export sales. In doing so, he would not be able to supervise the work of the new employee closely. He takes the risk of incurring substantial damage to the business if he does not make the right appointment.

However, there are indications from the accounting figures drafted above that the business may lack sufficient effective supervision. There have been problems with quality, perhaps evidenced by the sales returns figure. Also, stock has built up substantially during the year: total stock at the beginning of the year was £6888 + £3131 + £23 614 = £33 633 and by the end of the year it had reached £12 941 + £2968 + 29 497 = £45 406. The percentage increase in total stocks over the year is 35%). The build-up of stock may be planned, but it may, on the other hand, indicate insufficient control over the business. The business has run into overdraft, and may need tighter controls over spending and collecting cash from debtors. A new employee in a supervisory role could make significant improvements in the control of the business.

If the new employee proved to be effective, and Atul was able to expand the order book, the business could potentially grow and become more profitable. However, Atul needs to be fully aware of the risks he takes in delegating so much responsibility to an employee who is likely to be relatively inexperienced. It might be possible to reduce the risk by easing the new employee gradually into his or her role. Atul could plan to spend more time on the premises at first, before gradually increasing the time he spends away from the factory in expanding sales.

All growing businesses reach a point where their proprietors have to seriously consider recruiting at a managerial level. The decision about how best to do this is never easy. Employing the wrong person at this stage could be disastrous. Atul might consider using the services of a professional agency to help in the recruitment process. This would not guarantee a successful appointment, but would probably make success more likely.

Chapter summary

This chapter has introduced some new accounting terminology relating to stocks and manufacturing businesses. The layout of a typical manufacturing account has been introduced, and a comprehensive example and Case study 10.1 show how the account integrates with the profit and loss account.

The case study incorporates both accounting for a manufacturing business and several of the accounting adjustments that have been covered in recent chapters. The details of the case required advice about employment of staff, which involves consideration of finance, personnel and general business issues.

A manufacturing account is a relatively complex statement, and practice will be needed before students can feel secure about their ability to prepare and understand one. The questions that follow in the 'Exercises' section include many examples of manufacturing accounts involving progressive degrees of difficulty.

Answer to self-test question 10.1

Billy's costs are categorised as follows:

- Purchase of wood for making toys = Materials cost.
- Depreciation of factory machinery = Production overheads.
- Employee costs – machine operators = Labour cost.
- Production supervisor's salary = Production overheads.
- Electricity bill for factory = Production overheads.
- Electricity bill for office = Administration and selling expenses.
- Depreciation of office equipment = Administration and selling expenses.
- Telephone bill = Administration and selling expenses.
- Delivery van expenses = Administration and selling expenses.
- Secretary's salary = Administration and selling expenses.
- Purchase of plastics for making toys = Materials cost.
- Purchase of paper for office computer = Administration and selling expenses.
- Purchase of toy packaging = Materials cost.

Answer to self-test question 10.2

Step 1: Identify those items relating to the manufacturing account

	£	Category
Depreciation of factory machinery	10 493	Manufacturing account – indirect production overheads
Accountancy and tax advice	1 200	Profit and loss account
Purchases of raw materials	78 439	Manufacturing account – direct materials
Office insurance	3 442	Profit and loss account
Salespersons' salaries	24 410	Profit and loss account

	£	Category
Factory rental	23 700	Manufacturing account – indirect production overheads
Sales	341 115	Trading account
Electricity and gas for factory	9 942	Manufacturing account – indirect production overheads
Office rental	6 344	Profit and loss account
Sundry selling expenses	827	Profit and loss account
Telephone – salespersons	2 492	Profit and loss account
Secretarial costs	9 314	Profit and loss account
Electricity – office	1 824	Profit and loss account
Factory insurance	3 773	Manufacturing account – indirect production overheads
Depreciation – factory computer	1 220	Manufacturing account – indirect production overheads
Repairs and maintenance to factory machinery	3 111	Manufacturing account – indirect production overheads
Production supervisory salaries	25 471	Manufacturing account – indirect production overheads
Delivery charges	17 270	Profit and loss account
Telephone – administration	1 720	Profit and loss account
Office sundry expenses	714	Profit and loss account
Factory sundry expenses	234	Manufacturing account – indirect production overheads
Factory wages	81 479	Manufacturing account – direct labour

Step 2: Produce manufacturing account

Brightwell Components: Manufacturing account for the year ending 31 August 20X4

	£	£	£
Direct costs			
Direct materials			
Opening stock	13 210		
Add: purchases	78 439		
	91 649		
Less: closing stock	(12 994)		
		78 655	
Direct labour		81 479	
Total direct costs (prime cost)			160 134
Production overheads (indirect costs)			
Factory rental	23 700		
Depreciation of factory machinery	10 493		
Repairs and maintenance to factory machinery	3 111		
Production supervisory salaries	25 471		
Electricity and gas for factory	9 942		
Factory insurance	3 773		
Depreciation – factory computer	1 220		
Factory sundry expenses	234		
Total production overheads			77 944
Add: opening work-in-progress			2 511
Less: closing work-in-progress			(2 145)
Factory cost of finished goods			238 444

Step 3: Produce profit and loss account, including trading account

Brightwell Components: Profit and loss account for the year ending 31 August 20X4

	£	£	£
Sales			341 115
Less: cost of sales			
Opening stock of finished goods		26 700	
Add: factory cost of finished goods [from manufacturing account]		238 444	
		265 144	
Less: closing stock of finished goods		(29 363)	
Cost of sales			(235 781)
Gross profit			105 334
Expenses			
Selling and distribution expenses			
Salespersons' salaries	24 410		
Delivery charges	17 270		
Telephone – salespersons	2 492		
Sundry selling expenses	827		
		44 999	
Administration expenses			
Secretarial costs	9 314		
Electricity – office	1 824		
Telephone – administration	1 720		
Office rental	6 344		
Office insurance	3 442		
Office sundry expenses	714		
Accountancy and tax advice	1 200		
		24 558	
			(69 557)
Net profit			35 777

Exercises

The answers to many of the exercises are set out later in this chapter. However, where the exercise number is followed by 'A' the answer is available only to lecturers. Remember that additional exercises (with answers) are available to students on the book's website.

10.1   Amber runs a small factory making hats. She employs several people who are directly engaged in hat production, as well as a supervisor and a couple of clerks who deal with sales orders, invoices and related paperwork. Amber's business includes costs in the following categories:

- purchase of felt for hat-making
- factory rental payments
- factory supervisor's wages
- clerk's wages
- depreciation of sewing machines used in hat-making

- telephone bill
- factory electricity bill
- employee costs – hat-makers
- purchase of feathers, beads and sequins for trimming hats
- depreciation of office computer
- factory insurance
- delivery costs.

Place each of the above items in one of the following categories:

- direct materials
- direct labour
- production overheads
- administration and selling expenses.

10.2A Alice runs a sweetie factory, manufacturing a wide range of sweets that are sold to retailers ready packaged in plastic bags. The following list includes some of the costs that she incurs:

- factory electricity and gas bills
- purchase of sugar
- salary of production supervisor
- oil for use on machines
- secretary's salary
- purchase of plastic bags for packing sweets
- factory cleaner's wages
- machine operators' wages
- salespersons' commission
- maintenance of factory security system
- purchase of paper for use in office computer
- factory insurance
- office insurance
- salespersons' mobile phone bills
- delivery van depreciation
- depreciation of machine used in toffee production
- factory canteen costs.

Place each of the above items in one of the following categories:

- direct materials
- direct labour
- production overheads
- administration and selling expenses.

10.3 Bob runs a manufacturing business. Included in his books are the following balances relating to the costs of running his business for the year ending 30 November 20X4:

	£
Raw materials purchase	26 540
Depreciation of plant and machinery	4 333
Factory supervisor's salary	12 004
Factory rental	8 327
Opening stock of raw materials	3 433
Closing stock of raw materials	3 221
Electricity – factory	3 522
Machine operatives' wages	19 366
Factory insurance	4 002

What is the total prime cost for inclusion in Bob's manufacturing account for the year ending 30 November 20X4?

a) £45 906

b) £57 910

c) £58 122

d) £46 118.

10.4A Brett's factory manufactures parts for bicycles. The balances in his books at 31 December 20X6 include the following items of cost:

	£
Depreciation of factory	1 200
Production supervisor's salary	11 690
Factory cleaning	8 818
Depreciation of office equipment	2 120
Administrative staff salaries	12 420
Purchase of rubber for inner tubes	18 280
Purchase of metal for spoke manufacture	12 992
Purchase of oil for oiling plant and machinery	986
Electricity supply to factory	6 469
Business insurance*	3 948
Depreciation of plant and machinery	5 888
Payment of wages to machine operators	26 969
Maintenance and repair of machinery	3 438
Opening stock of raw materials	3 307
Closing stock of raw materials	2 983

* The business insurance charge of £3948 covers both the factory and the administration office. Two-thirds of the charge relates to the factory.

1. What is the total prime cost for inclusion in Brett's manufacturing account for the year ending 31 December 20X6?

   a) £58 241

   b) £70 255

   c) £58 565

   d) £59 551.

2. What is the total for indirect production overheads for inclusion in Brett's manufacturing account for the year ending 31 December 20X6?

a) £41 121

b) £29 431

c) £55 661

d) £68 090.

10.5   Carrie runs a shoe factory and is about to prepare a manufacturing account for the month of May 20X6. The following balances are relevant:

	£
Production supervisor's salary	15 760
Maintenance of factory machinery	2 994
Purchase of raw materials	76 892
Machine operatives' labour costs	93 330
Factory cleaner's wages	7 400
Depreciation of freehold factory building	5 600
Stock of raw materials at 1 May 20X6	7 492
Stock of raw materials at 31 May 20X6	8 441
Stock of work-in-progress at 1 May 20X6	1 101
Stock of work-in-progress at 31 May 20X6	1 004
Factory insurance	4 654
Electricity for factory	10 333
Sundry factory costs	1 808
Depreciation of machinery	6 667

Prepare Carrie's manufacturing account for May 20X6.

10.6A   Curtis has a chewing gum factory. A manufacturing account is required for the year ending 31 December 20X4. Curtis has listed the following relevant balances from the accounting records of the business:

	£
Factory wages*	118 377
Purchase of gum	171 430
Purchase of flavourings	6 433
Purchase of chewing gum wrappers	8 989
Opening stock of gum	15 444
Opening stock of flavourings	737
Opening stock of chewing gum wrappers	981
Closing stock of gum	14 983
Closing stock of flavourings	1 317
Closing stock of chewing gum wrappers	890
Depreciation of machinery	9 818
Sundry maintenance materials	652
Factory cleaning	2 988
Factory canteen costs	9 883
Factory rental	29 380
Factory insurance	8 800
Opening work-in-progress	286
Closing work-in-progress	173

*Note: Machine operatives do not spend all their time directly engaged in production; they are also responsible for carrying out basic maintenance operations and cleaning.

The total for factory wages of £118 377 includes £17 465 for the factory supervisor's salary. Of the remainder 80% is classed as direct wages, and the remaining 20% as indirect production overheads.

Prepare Curtis's manufacturing account for the year ending 31 December 20X4.

10.7 Cornelius runs a small factory that manufactures artists' watercolours. He employs two staff. Maisie is engaged full-time in production, whereas Maggie spends 75% of her time in production and the remaining 25% in production planning and general maintenance activities. Cornelius draws up a manufacturing account monthly. For the month of April 20X1 he has the following relevant balances:

	£
Maisie's wages	1 370
Maggie's wages	1 448
Opening stock of raw materials	86
Closing stock of raw materials	77
Purchase of pigments and binders	1 883
Purchase of tins and plastic paint containers	800
Depreciation of paint mixing vats	70
Depreciation of factory building	100
Depreciation of other factory equipment	87
Electricity and gas supply to factory	177
Water rates – factory	97
Cleaning wages	130
Factory insurance	71
Sundry factory expenses	51
Opening work-in-progress	93
Closing work-in-progress	64

Prepare Cornelius's manufacturing account for April 20X1.

10.8 Dilip has run a successful umbrella manufacturing business for several years. His gross profit margin has remained constant at around 34%, and his net profit margin is usually between 14% and 15%. However, Dilip is concerned because he thinks that his business has underperformed in the current year. He presents you with the following list of balances for the year ending 30 September 20X8 and asks you to: (a) prepare a manufacturing account and a profit and loss account; and (b) calculate gross and net profit margins for the year. (Note that the profit and loss account is to show expenses under two main headings: selling and distribution; and administration.)

	£
Depreciation of factory machinery	6 696
Sundry administration costs	3 289
Raw materials purchases	112 787
Production supervisory salaries	24 690
Telephone charges – sales department	3 608
Administration office rental	13 374
Office insurance	2 401
Factory cleaning	8 792
Depreciation of office fixtures and fittings	1 895

	£
Salespersons' salaries	28 660
Salespersons' commissions	2 811
Sales	449 760
Sales returns	1 560
Depreciation of delivery van	2 180
Electricity charges – administration office	2 780
Factory insurance	4 393
Depreciation of fittings in factory	2 200
Telephone charges – administration	1 603
Accountancy and tax advice	2 500
Sundry distribution and selling costs	906
Secretarial and administrative salaries	23 749
Depreciation of office computer	2 060
Wages of factory machine operators	99 270
Light and heat for factory	9 222
Factory rental	28 700
Sundry factory expenses	1 861
Factory canteen costs	2 189
Factory repairs and maintenance	3 730
Opening stock at 1 October 20X7	
Raw materials	12 705
Work-in-progress	3 879
Finished goods	37 222
Closing stock at 30 September 20X8	
Raw materials	13 573
Work-in-progress	2 693
Finished goods	39 470

10.9A Debra is in business producing household linen. She buys in plain fabrics, dyes them and makes them up into table and bed linen. Her small factory employs six people, five of whom are directly involved in dyeing and stitching. The sixth splits her time evenly between administration and production supervision. Her wages of £9210 are split 50:50 between administration expense and production supervision expense.

Last year Debra's business made a net profit margin of 14.6% on turnover of £217 414. For this year, the year to 31 March 20X5, Debra knows that she has made slightly more in sales, but suspects that her net profit margin percentage has fallen.

From the list of relevant balances given below, prepare a manufacturing account and a profit and loss account for Debra's business for the year ending 31 March 20X5. Calculate the net profit margin percentage, and the percentage change in net profit from 20X4 to 20X5.

	£
Administration/production supervision wages	9 210
Purchases of fabrics	65 069
Purchases of dyes, ribbons and other trimmings	7 821
Purchases of packaging materials	6 988
Factory rental	13 750
Factory cleaning	3 700
Secretarial salary	7 935
Sundry factory expenses	2 475

	£
Sales	218 930
Rental of office and other premises costs	6 339
Electricity – offices	990
Factory heat and light	4 655
Factory wages – direct labour	42 373
Factory security services	1 250
Office telephone charges	1 576
Travelling expenses	1 653
Distribution expenses	4 772
Stationery and office supplies	871
Accountancy, tax and legal advice	1 350
Sundry office expenses	378
Opening stock at 1 April 20X4	
Raw materials: fabrics	5 900
Raw materials: dyes, ribbons, etc.	1 360
Raw materials: packaging	936
Finished goods stock	16 330
Closing stock at 31 March 20X5	
Raw materials: fabrics	8 208
Raw materials: dyes, ribbons, etc.	1 241
Raw materials: packaging	1 407
Finished goods stock	15 212

The following should be noted:

1. Debra makes sure that there is no work-in-progress stock in the factory at the accounting year-end.

2. The business has machinery at cost of £44 200. A depreciation charge of 10% on cost is to be included in the accounts for the year ending 31 March 20X5.

3. The business owns factory fixtures that cost £11 500. A depreciation charge of 10% on cost is to be included in the accounts for the year ending 31 March 20X5.

4. The business owns a van that is depreciated on the reducing balance basis at the rate of 25% per annum. The net book value of the van at 1 April 20X4 was £9788, and an adjustment for van depreciation will be required in the accounts for the year ending 31 March 20X5.

5. An electricity bill for office electricity consumption for the three months to 31 March 20X5 must be accrued. The bill is for £330.

10.10 Ermintrude makes components for the motor industry, buying in plastic and metal raw materials from the UK and overseas. Her factory contains mostly quite old machinery, some of which is fully depreciated. She incurs relatively high labour and maintenance and repair costs. Ermintrude would like to borrow more money from the bank to invest in new plant and machinery so as to bring the production processes up to date and reduce labour costs. The bank manager has told her, however, that she must take steps to reduce her overdraft before he will consider lending any more money.

    The following is Ermintrude's list of balances at 31 December 20X8 together with some notes that will help in preparing the accounts. You are required to:

a) Prepare a manufacturing account for Ermintrude for the year ending 31 December 20X8

b) Prepare a profit and loss account for the year ending 31 December 20X8 and a balance sheet at that date.

c) Advise Ermintrude on how she can help to reduce her overdraft and borrow more money for investment in new plant and machinery.

	£
Sales	337 570
Capital at 1 January 20X8	114 560
Fixed assets at cost:	
Land	13 850
Buildings	50 000
Plant and machinery	93 450
Motor vehicles	39 822
Office equipment	13 000
Accumulated depreciation at 1 January 20X8:	
Buildings	9 000
Plant and machinery	87 482
Motor vehicles	17 422
Office equipment	2 600
Opening stock:	
Raw materials	15 250
Work-in-progress	6 440
Finished goods	39 451
Purchases of raw materials	97 010
Import duties on purchases of raw materials	1 570
Direct labour costs	79 690
Factory supervisor's salary	14 771
Factory electricity	7 898
Factory insurance	5 790
Sundry factory expenses	1 770
Machinery repairs and maintenance	8 599
Factory cleaning	5 777
Closing stock:	
Raw materials	16 333
Work-in-progress	6 693
Finished goods	39 750
Debtors	46 242
Bank overdraft	28 411
Creditors	24 459
Bank loans (long term)	10 000
Drawings	39 511
Secretarial and clerical staff	12 760
Business rates	6 769
Electricity and gas	2 819
Office telephone	4 644
Delivery van expenses	3 890
Sales staff costs	17 231
Sundry administration and selling expenses	1 670
Interest paid	1 830

Note the following:

1. The depreciation charge for 20X8 in respect of plant and machinery has been calculated at £3130.

2. Depreciation is charged on the cost of buildings at 2% per annum on the straight-line basis. The charge is split between the factory (80%) and the administration office (20%).

3. Depreciation is charged on the motor vehicles at the rate of 25% per annum on the reducing balance basis.

4. Depreciation is charged on the cost of the office equipment at 10% on the straight-line basis.

5. A bill for office electricity for the period ending 31 December 20X8 was received after the year-end. The amount of the bill is £917 and it has not been recorded in the balances above.

6. Ermintrude's accountant advises her to include an accrual for his fees of £1300.

Answers to exercises

10.1   Amber's costs are categorised as follows:

- Purchase of felt for hat-making = Direct materials.
- Factory rental payments = Production overheads.
- Factory supervisor's wages = Production overheads.
- Clerk's wages = Administration and selling expenses.
- Depreciation of sewing machines used in hat-making = Production overheads.
- Telephone bill = Administration and selling expenses.
- Factory electricity bill = Production overheads.
- Employee costs – hat-makers = Direct labour.
- Purchase of feathers, beads and sequins for trimming hats = Direct materials
- Depreciation of office computer = Administration and selling expenses.
- Factory insurance = Production overheads.
- Delivery costs = Administration and selling expenses.

10.3   Prime cost is the total of direct costs. Bob's balances include two categories of direct costs: direct labour and direct materials. Total prime cost is worked out as follows:

	£	£
Direct materials		
Opening stock of raw materials	3 433	
Add: purchases of raw materials	26 540	
Less: closing stock of raw materials	(3 221)	
		26 752
Direct labour: machine operatives' wages		19 366
Prime cost		46 118

The correct answer, therefore, is d).

10.5

Carrie: Manufacturing account for May 20X6

	£	£	£
Direct costs			
Direct materials			
Opening stock	7 492		
Add: purchases	76 892		
	84 384		
Less: closing stock	(8 441)		
		75 943	
Direct labour		93 330	
Total direct costs (prime cost)			169 273
Production overheads (indirect costs)			
Production supervisor's salary		15 760	
Maintenance of factory machinery		2 994	
Factory cleaner's wages		7 400	
Depreciation of freehold factory building		5 600	
Factory insurance		4 654	
Electricity for factory		10 333	
Sundry factory costs		1 808	
Depreciation of machinery		6 667	
Total production overheads			55 216
Add: opening work-in-progress			1 101
Less: closing work-in-progress			(1 004)
Factory cost of finished goods			224 586

10.7

Cornelius: Manufacturing account for April 20X1

	£
Working – direct labour comprises:	
100% of Maisie's wages	1 370
75% of Maggie's wages: £1448 × 75%	1 086
Total	2 456

	£	£	£
Direct costs			
Direct materials			
Opening stock	86		
Add: purchases (£1883 + £800)	2 683		
	2 769		
Less: closing stock	(77)		
		2 692	
Direct labour (see working above)		2 456	
Total direct costs (prime cost)			5 148
Production overheads (indirect costs)			
Indirect wages (Maggie: 25% × £1448)		362	
Depreciation of paint mixing vats		70	
Depreciation of factory building		100	
Depreciation of other factory equipment		87	
Electricity and gas supply to factory		177	

	£	£	£
Water rates – factory		97	
Cleaning wages		130	
Factory insurance		71	
Sundry factory expenses		51	
Total production overheads			1 145
Add: opening work-in-progress			93
Less: closing work-in-progress			(64)
Factory cost of finished goods			6 322

10.8

Dilip: Manufacturing account for the year ending 30 September 20X8

	£	£	£
Direct costs			
Direct materials			
Opening stock	12 705		
Add: purchases	112 787		
	125 492		
Less: closing stock	(13 573)		
		111 919	
Direct labour		99 270	
Total direct costs (prime cost)			211 189
Production overheads (indirect costs)			
Depreciation of factory machinery		6 696	
Production supervisory salaries		24 690	
Factory cleaning		8 792	
Factory insurance		4 393	
Depreciation of fittings in factory		2 200	
Light and heat for factory		9 222	
Factory rental		28 700	
Sundry factory expenses		1 861	
Factory canteen costs		2 189	
Factory repairs and maintenance		3 730	
Total production overheads			92 473
Add: opening work-in-progress			3 879
Less: closing work-in-progress			(2 693)
Factory cost of finished goods			304 848

Dilip: Profit and loss account for the year ending 30 September 20X8

	£	£	£
Sales			449 760
Less: returns			(1 560)
			448 200
Less: cost of sales			
Opening stock of finished goods		37 222	
Add: factory cost of finished goods [from manufacturing account]		304 848	
		342 070	
Less: closing stock of finished goods		(39 470)	
Cost of sales			(302 600)
Gross profit			145 600

	£	£	£
Expenses			
Selling and distribution			
Telephone charges – sales department	3 608		
Salespersons' salaries	28 660		
Salespersons' commissions	2 811		
Depreciation of delivery van	2 180		
Sundry distribution and selling costs	906		
		38 165	
Administration			
Administration office rental	13 374		
Electricity charges – administration office	2 780		
Telephone charges – administration	1 603		
Secretarial and administrative salaries	23 749		
Depreciation of office computer	2 060		
Depreciation of office fixtures and fittings	1 895		
Office insurance	2 401		
Accountancy and tax advice	2 500		
Sundry administration costs	3 289		
		53 651	
			(91 816)
Net profit			53 784

Margins

Gross profit margin for the year:

$$= \frac{145\,600}{448\,200} \times 100 = 32.5\%$$

Net profit margin for the year:

$$= \frac{53\,784}{448\,200} \times 100 = 12\%$$

10.10 *Workings*

1. Depreciation on buildings at 2% on cost: £50 000 × 2% = £1000. 80% of this charge (i.e. £800) will be included in indirect production overheads and the remaining 20% (i.e. £200) will be charged to profit and loss account.

2. Depreciation on motor vehicles: net book value at 1 January 20X8 is cost less accumulated depreciation to that date: £39 822 − 17 422 = £22 400. Depreciation is, therefore, 25% × 22 400 = £5 600.

3. Depreciation on office equipment is 10% × cost of £13 000 = £1300.

4. The office electricity and gas charge recorded in the list of balances is £2819. This will be increased by the accrual of £917 to £3736.

5. An accrued expense of £1300 for accountant's fees will be included in profit and loss account.

6. The total for accruals in the balance sheet will be £917 + £1300 = £2217.

a) Manufacturing account

Ermintrude: Manufacturing account for the year ending 31 December 20X8

	£	£	£
Direct costs			
Direct materials			
Opening stock	15 250		
Add: purchases	97 010		
Add: import duty on purchases	1 570		
	113 830		
Less: closing stock	(16 333)		
		97 497	
Direct labour		79 690	
Total direct costs (prime cost)			177 187
Production overheads (indirect costs)			
Depreciation – plant and machinery		3 130	
Factory supervisor's salary		14 771	
Depreciation – building (working 1)		800	
Factory electricity		7 898	
Factory insurance		5 790	
Sundry factory expenses		1 770	
Machinery repairs and maintenance		8 599	
Factory cleaning		5 777	
			48 535
Add: opening work-in-progress			6 440
Less: closing work-in-progress			(6 693)
Factory cost of finished goods			225 469

b) Profit and loss and balance sheet

Ermintrude: Profit and loss account for the year ending 31 December 20X8

	£	£
Sales		337 570
Cost of sales		
Opening stock of finished goods	39 451	
Add: factory cost of finished goods [from manufacturing account]	225 469	
	264 920	
Less: closing stock of finished goods	(39 750)	
Cost of sales		(225 170)
Gross profit		112 400
Expenses		
Depreciation – building (working 1)	200	
Secretarial and clerical staff	12 760	
Business rates	6 769	
Electricity and gas (working 4)	3 736	
Office telephone	4 644	
Delivery van expenses	3 890	

	£	£
Sales staff costs	17 231	
Depreciation – motor vehicles (working 2)	5 600	
Depreciation – office equipment (working 3)	1 300	
Accountant's fees (working 5)	1 300	
Sundry administration and selling expenses	1 670	
Interest paid	1 830	
		(60 930)
Net profit		51 470

Ermintrude: Balance sheet at 31 December 20X8

	£	£	£
	Cost	Depreciation	Net book value
Fixed assets			
Land	13 850	—	13 850
Buildings	50 000	10 000	40 000
Plant and machinery	93 450	90 612	2 838
Motor vehicles	39 822	23 022	16 800
Office equipment	13 000	3 900	9 100
	210 122	127 534	82 588
Current assets			
Stocks:			
Raw materials	16 333		
Work-in-progress	6 693		
Finished goods	39 750		
		62 776	
Debtors		46 242	
		109 018	
Current liabilities			
Bank overdraft		28 411	
Creditors		24 459	
Accrual (working 6)		2 217	
		55 087	
Net current assets			53 931
			136 519
Long-term liability: loan			(10 000)
			126 519
Capital			
Capital at 1 January 20X8			114 560
Add: profit for the year			51 470
Less: drawings			(39 511)
			126 519

c) Advice

Although Ermintrude's business is profitable it is short of cash. Her overdraft and long-term borrowings from the bank total £38 411. It would be necessary to know more about the way her business works in order to be able to give her detailed advice. However, a brief review of the balance sheet suggests that a lot of cash is tied up in stock – over £60 000. Ermintrude could review her production process and order book, to see if the total can be reduced. Also, there may be scope to reduce debtors by reminding them to pay more promptly.

The business owns its own property. It appears from the depreciation accumulated that it was bought about 10 years ago. It may now be worth more than the net book value at which it is stated in the balance sheet. The bank might agree to advance Ermintrude a mortgage loan, secured on the value of land and buildings. Investment in new and up-to-date plant and machinery could help to increase profitability and it may well be worth borrowing money to do this. Ermintrude needs to carry out a thorough analysis and to calculate forecast savings in order to assess whether or not the investment is worthwhile.

Forecasting and appraisal of capital investment projects are covered in detail in Part III of this book.

CASH FLOW

AIMS AND LEARNING OUTCOMES

Aim of the chapter

To understand the importance of cash in business, and to deepen understanding of the distinction between profit and cash.

Learning outcomes

After reading the chapter and completing the related exercises, students should:

- Understand the important role that cash plays in business.
- Understand the distinction between profit and cash.
- Be able to draw up a simple cash flow statement for a sole trader business.

The role of cash in business

Cash is the fundamental business resource. Without the availability of cash to pay creditors, to buy up new stock and invest in fixed assets, any business will, sooner or later, fail. Sources of cash include the following:

- Cash resources placed in the business by its owner.
- Cash borrowed from individuals, other businesses or lending institutions.
- Cash generated by the business itself.

All profitable businesses ultimately generate cash. However, a business can be profitable but, nevertheless, suffer potentially devastating shortages of cash. Later in this chapter we will examine how this apparently paradoxical position can arise.

In a well-managed business sufficient (but not too much) cash circulates as demonstrated in Figure 11.1. The upper part of the diagram shows the **working capital cycle**. **Working capital** comprises the rapidly changing items of stock, debtors, creditors and cash. There are, of course, other cash inflows and outflows in a business and these are shown in the lower part of the diagram.

It is important to keep working capital in a business tightly under control. What are the consequences if the components of working capital are mismanaged? In the next section of the chapter we will look at the problems that can arise when the individual components of working capital are not at optimal levels.

Mismanagement of working capital

In the following sub-sections we consider some of the consequences in cases where working capital is not managed properly.

Figure 11.1

The movement of cash around the business

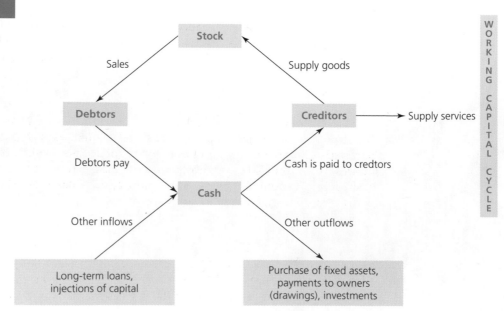

Too much stock

A fairly common error in business is to tie up too much cash in the form of stock. This can lead to some of the following problems:

- If the stock comprises items that rapidly go out of fashion, the stock may lose most or all of its value before it can be sold.
- If the stock is perishable it may reach the end of its shelf life before it can be sold.
- It costs money to store stock safely. Additional costs may be incurred for no obvious benefit.
- If too much cash is tied up in stock it is not available for investment elsewhere in the business.

Too little stock

There may not be sufficient stock to fulfil orders; customers may therefore go elsewhere.

Debtors too high

Where a high level of debtors exists, the business is not collecting cash quickly enough. There may be a bottleneck in the working capital cycle which causes a shortage of cash, with knock-on effects on other parts of the business.

Creditors too high

If creditors are not paid reasonably promptly there may be a consequent loss of goodwill towards the business. In extreme cases, suppliers may refuse to supply any further goods or services on credit, and will demand cash payments in advance or on delivery.

Creditors too low

Creditors like to be paid in good time. However, they usually offer credit terms such as 'payment within 30 days following receipt of invoice'. It usually makes good business sense to pay towards the end of the time allowed and thus to take advantage of what is, effectively, a source of interest-free credit.

Cash too low

If the stock, debtor and creditor elements of working capital are mismanaged, the consequence may be that the cash level in the business is too low. It may become necessary to borrow cash, and borrowing, of course, costs money in the form of interest. Unauthorised overdrafts, in particular, can be very expensive, and good cash management involves anticipating any cash shortages and making appropriate arrangements in advance.

Cash too high

It may seem surprising that a business can suffer from the problem of too much cash, but it can happen. One of the reasons people go into business is to make profits in the form of a return on their investment. The return (or 'profit') made out of the initial investment in the business has to be greater than the return that can be made by leaving the money in a simple bank deposit account. Putting money into a bank account is easy, and requires virtually no effort on the part of the investor; by contrast, starting up a business requires a great deal of effort, and the investor expects a much greater reward.

If there is surplus cash in the business, what can be done with it? The simple, short-term answer is to place the money on deposit where it can earn interest. However, this is unlikely to represent a sufficient return, and the business owner will look for other opportunities for investment. Sometimes it makes sense to return the money in the form of a repayment of capital, so that the owner can invest in, for example, another business venture or a personal pension fund.

The distinction between profit and cash

In the long run, a profitable business will increase its supply of cash. However, and especially in the short term, profits are not the same as cash.

In Chapter 8 we looked at the concepts of recognition and realisation and concluded that accounting income is not the same as cash received, and accounting expenditure is not the same as cash paid. The matching (or accruals) concept requires that costs are matched against the income that they help to generate. In some cases this results in the recognition of income and costs that have not been received/paid in the form of cash. Annual charges for depreciation and amortisation, for example, are set against profits, but these charges do not involve any movement in cash.

Cash can be depleted or increased by transactions that do not affect the profit and loss account; for example, the purchase of fixed assets. When an item of machinery, for example, is purchased for use in the business, the asset of cash is replaced by a fixed asset. There is no immediate impact on profits, although they will be depleted over a period of time while the asset is depreciated. Table 11.1 sets out looks at the implication for cash and profits of various transactions. Only in the case of the fourth transaction in the list – the sale for cash of £1600 – is the impact on cash and profit identical and simultaneous. All other cases result in a mismatch between cash and profit.

Self-test question 11.1 (answer at the end of the chapter)

What is the effect on cash and on profit of the following business transactions?
1. Purchase of raw materials for cash of £1800.
2. Sale of old delivery van for £360.
3. Long-term loan from brother of £5000.
4. Payment of interest on bank overdraft of £150.
5. Amortisation charge of £8000 relating to patent rights.

Table 11.1 The impact of transactions on cash and profits

Transaction	Impact on cash	Impact on profits
Borrowing £10 000 at an annual interest rate of 10%. Loan to be repaid after five years.	Cash and long-term liabilities are both increased in the balance sheet by £10 000. After five years the loan will be repaid; cash and long-term liabilities will both be reduced by £10 000.	No immediate impact on profits. Each year for five years there will be an annual interest payment of £1000. This will decrease both cash and profit.
Purchasing a new car for £8000. The car is to be depreciated on the straight-line basis over four years, with the assumption of no residual value at the end of four years.	Cash is reduced and fixed assets are increased by £8000.	No immediate impact on profits. Each year for four years there will be a depreciation charge of £2000 (£8000/4), but this has no effect on cash.
Drawings of £3500.	Cash and capital are both reduced by £3500.	There is no impact on profit. Effectively, the owner is taking £3500 of his/her capital out of the business.
Sale for cash of £1600.	Cash is increased immediately.	The sale is recognised immediately, and sales in the profit and loss account are increased by £1600.
Sale on credit for £1600.	Debtors are increased immediately. Provided that the debtor pays up, cash will be increased at some point in the near future.	The sale is recognised immediately, and sales in the profit and loss account are increased by £1600.

Preparing a cash flow statement

So far in this section of the book we have examined the preparation of the profit and loss account and the balance sheet for sole trader businesses. It is also possible, and may very well be useful, to prepare a **cash flow statement**. This statement summarises the inflows and outflows of cash for an accounting period, usually of one year. Because, as we have seen, cash and profit are not the same, a cash flow statement can provide useful additional information that assists in understanding the performance and position of the business. Note that, except for some larger businesses (see Chapter 12 for more information), there is no absolute requirement to prepare a cash flow statement. However, it can provide some very useful information about a business that is not immediately obvious from a profit and loss account or balance sheet.

The procedures involved in preparing a cash flow statement will be illustrated first by reference to a new business start-up. Example 11.1 revisits the case of Isobel Buchanan, whose new business start-up was examined first in Chapter 6. Later, in Chapter 9 we examined the results of her first year in business. However, it is not necessary to revisit either of these chapters for information; the example sets out all the relevant details.

Example 11.1 Isobel's profit and loss account for her first year of trading, and her balance sheet at 28 February 20X2 are shown below. The expenses in the profit and loss account have been presented in a slightly different way in order to emphasise the totals for depreciation and amortisation, and for interest paid and received. Note that profit before interest is described as operating profit.

Buchanan International Designs: Profit and loss account for the year ending 28 February 20X2

	£	£
Sales		115 622
Cost of sales		(80 379)
Gross profit		35 243
Expenses		
Rental	14 000	
Insurance	717	
Electricity	2 346	
Telephone charges	686	
Staff	300	
Advertising	1 560	
Motor expenses	551	
Sundry expenses	3 446	
		(23 606)
Net profit before depreciation, amortisation and interest		11 637
Amortisation of lease	2 500	
Depreciation of display racks	900	
Depreciation of sundry fixtures and fittings	326	
Depreciation of van	1 625	
		(5 351)
Operating profit		6 286
Interest paid		(2 400)
Interest received		651
Net profit		4 537

Buchanan International Designs: Balance sheet at 28 February 20X2

	£	£
Fixed assets		
Intangible fixed assets		
Cost	10 000	
Less: accumulated amortisation	(2 500)	
		7 500
Tangible fixed assets		
Display racks at cost	4 500	
Less: accumulated depreciation	(900)	
		3 600
Sundry fixtures and fittings at cost	1 630	
Less: accumulated depreciation	(326)	
		1 304
Van at cost	6 500	
Less: accumulated depreciation	(1 625)	
		4 875
		17 279
Current assets		
Stock	19 400	
Debtors and prepayments	3 520	
Prepayments	507	
Cash at bank	13 323	
	36 750	
Current liabilities		
Creditors	6 327	
Accruals	665	
	6 992	
Net current assets (£36 750 − £6992)		29 758
		47 037
Long-term liabilities		
Loan		(40 000)
		7 037
Capital		
Capital introduced		10 000
Add: profit for the year		4 537
Less: drawings		(7 500)
		7 037

Isobel started in business on 1 March 20X1 by putting cash into a new business bank account. The total cash deposited was £50 000, comprising a £40 000 loan from her uncle and aunt, and £10 000 of her own money. One year later we can see from her accounts that, although she has made a small profit of £4537, her bank balance has dwindled to £13 323, representing a drop of (£50 000 − £13 323) £36 677.

What has happened to the cash?

Isobel's balance sheet and profit and loss account convey a great deal of useful information, but are not obviously helpful in providing answers. A cash flow statement helps to answer the question by isolating the principal movements in cash.

Preparing a cash flow statement

Step 1

By convention, the first section in a cash flow statement examines profits adjusted for movements in working capital apart from cash (remember: working capital comprises items of stock, debtors, creditors and cash).

The starting point is operating profits. Isobel's operating profit (i.e. profit before interest) is £6286. This has been arrived at after deducting various items of depreciation and amortisation, which, as we saw earlier in this chapter, do not involve any movements in cash. Therefore, to get closer to a true cash figure, we add back those items that do not involve movements in cash:

	£
Operating profits	6 286
Add back: depreciation and amortisation	5 351
	11 637

Next, we adjust for investments in working capital in the form of stock, debtors and creditors:

- *Stock*. At the year-end of 28 February 20X2 Isobel has stock of £19 400. This will be converted into cash when sold, but that has not yet occurred. At 28 February 20X2 it represents a depletion of cash resources.
- *Debtors*. These are items that are waiting to be turned into cash; at the year-end £3520 of potential cash resource is locked up in debtors.
- *Prepayments*. These are amounts already paid for in cash, but for which services have not yet been received.
- *Creditors and accruals*. These are amounts yet to be paid by the business. Goods and services have already been received but have not yet been paid for. Cash balances will be lower once these amounts have been paid, but at the year-end point in time the cash to pay them has not yet left the business.

We add the following adjustments in respect of investments in working capital to the first section of the cash flow statement as follows:

	£	£
Operating profits		6 286
Add back: depreciation and amortisation		5 351
		11 637
Investment in working capital		
Stock	(19 400)	
Debtors	(3 520)	
Prepayments	(507)	
Creditors	6 327	
Accruals	665	
Net investment in working capital		(16 435)
Net cash outflow from operating activities		(4 798)

Step 2

The next step is to take into account all the other payments that have been made but which do not relate to changes in working capital:

1. *Interest received and paid*. Interest is separated out in a cash flow statement because it relates to financing, not operating activities. Interest received is £651 and interest paid is £2400.
2. *Capital expenditure*. In the first year in business, as is typically the case, Isobel has invested quite large sums in fixed assets. The total cash outflow relating to the investment of cash in fixed assets is:

	£
Intangible asset	10 000
Display racks	4 500
Sundry fixtures and fittings	1 630
Van	6 500
Total	22 630

The cash outflow is shown separately in the cash flow statement.

3. *Other* items. Looking through the balance sheet at this point in the calculations we can see that most items have been taken into account in the cash flow statement. The only items remaining are the long-term loan (which involved a cash inflow of £40 000), Isobel's capital (a cash inflow of £10 000) and Isobel's drawings for the year (a cash outflow of £7500).

Step 3

We can now bring all the cash inflows and outflows together in a cash flow statement, as follows:

Buchanan International Designs: Cash flow statement for the year ending

28 February 20X2

	£	£
Operating profits		6 286
Add back: depreciation and amortisation		5 351
		11 637
Investment in working capital		
Stock	(19 400)	
Debtors	(3 520)	
Prepayments	(507)	
Creditors	6 327	
Accruals	665	
Net investment in working capital		(16 435)
Net cash outflow from operating activities		(4 798)
Interest		
Interest received (cash inflow)	651	
Interest paid (cash outflow)	(2 400)	
		(1 749)
Capital expenditure (cash outflow)		(22 630)
Proprietor's drawings (cash outflow)		(7 500)

▶

◀◀◀

	£	£
Loan (cash inflow)		40 000
Capital introduced (cash inflow)		10 000
Net cash inflow		13 323
Cash balance at 28 February 20X2		13 323

Comments on cash flow statement

What additional information is provided by the cash flow statement? The aim of the cash flow statement is to provide explanations for the overall movement in cash in the accounting period. Neither the profit and loss account nor the balance sheet provide that information. In the cash flow statement presented above we isolate the major movements in cash. The outflow of cash into investments in various types of fixed asset is shown to have accounted for a substantial proportion of total spending. Also, we can see that operating activities and the movement of cash round the working capital cycle resulted in a net cash outflow. Both of these substantial outflows (i.e. on fixed assets and on investments in working capital) would be quite normal in the first year of a business.

The business does not have an immediate cash shortage, but it will need to generate cash (and profits) in the longer term in order to survive.

Direct and indirect approaches to cash flow

The example above shows the so-called 'indirect' approach to preparing cash flow statements. The first part of the statement prepared under the 'indirect' approach shows the cash flows derived from operating activities by taking profit and adjusting for non-cash items (in this case, depreciation and amortisation) and for investments in working capital.

There is an alternative: the so-called 'direct' method. This takes receipts from sales less payments for costs and expenses to arrive at a net cash flow from operating activities. This method is probably simpler to understand. However, in practice, businesses often use the 'indirect' method because the figures can be derived directly from the profit and loss account and balance sheet.

The 'direct' method explained

In the next example, we will present cash flow information for the first year of Isobel's business using the 'direct' method of preparing a cash flow statement.

Example 11.2 Isobel's total receipts of cash from sales in the year were £112 102.

Total payments for stock and the various categories of expenses (but excluding depreciation and amortisation, of course, because these do not involve any cash movement) were £116 900. The cash flow statement prepared under the 'direct' method is as follows:

Buchanan International Designs: Cash flow statement for the year ending

28 February 20X2

	£	£
Receipts from operating activities		112 102
Payments in respect of operating activities		(116 900)
Net cash outflow from operating activities		(4 798)
Interest		
Interest received (cash inflow)	651	
Interest paid (cash outflow)	(2 400)	
		(1 749)
Capital expenditure (cash outflow)		(22 630)
Proprietor's drawings (cash outflow)		(7 500)
Loan (cash inflow)		40 000
Capital introduced (cash inflow)		10 000
Net cash inflow		13 323
Cash balance at 28 February 20X2		13 323

Note that it is only the upper part of the statement that changes. All the information relating to cash flows on capital expenditure and so on remain exactly the same.

Cash flow statements in an established business

The case study for this chapter shows how a cash flow statement is prepared for an established business. In such cases, the information required is:

The opening balance sheet
The profit and loss account for the year
The closing balance sheet.

CASE STUDY 11.1 Advising using cash flow statements

Delroy Desmond has run a pizza restaurant for several years, trading as Dezzie's. He also provides a pizza delivery service to homes and a lunchtime delivery service to local offices, some of whom are supplied on credit terms. In the year ending 31 March 20X4 he has opened a new branch in another town, obtaining a mortgage loan to purchase freehold premises and to pay for some alterations to the premises. Delroy did not spend much on fixtures and fittings; he had some unused tables, crockery and so on in the store room of the existing premises and he transferred these over to the new branch.

Delroy is keen to expand the business further and would like to draw up a formal expansion programme. He has commissioned a market research survey of a representative sample of his customers from a firm of consultants. The survey report quotes some of the more negative reactions of the customers:

- 'Not enough staff on at weekends.'

- 'I had to wait almost two hours for my pizza delivery last week.'

- 'Great pizzas – shame the restaurant's so tatty.'

- 'You'd never think it was a brand new restaurant – it looks like it could do with a refit already.'

- 'That manager was so rude, I didn't go back for six months.'

- 'The delivery man said his bike had broken down; that's why the pizzas were stone cold when I got them.'

The consultant concludes that, although the standard of the product is high and there are many satisfied customers, there are quite a lot of staffing and premises-related problems. He recommends re-equipping the restaurants and replacing the existing managers with higher paid staff. Delroy accepts both the criticisms and the recommendations but realises that he probably does not have enough cash to address all the problems straight away. Delroy has asked his accountant to prepare a cash flow statement in addition to the usual accounting statements. Details of his profit and loss account for the year ending 31 March 20X4 and his balance sheets at 31 March 20X4 and 31 March 20X3 are supplied below.

The following is required: prepare the cash flow statement (using the indirect method) for Dezzie's for the year ending 31 March 20X4; and summarise for Delroy the key points that emerge from the cash flow statement, advising him, as far as possible from the information given, on the financial implications of following the consultant's advice.

Dezzie's: Profit and loss account for the year ending 31 March 20X4

	£	£
Sales		341 077
Less: cost of sales		
Opening stock	5 630	
Purchases	91 889	
	97 519	
	(6 186)	
Cost of sales		(91 333)
Gross profit		249 744
Expenses		
Restaurant heat and light	18 450	
Premises costs	18 295	
Salaries and wages	78 904	
Delivery expenses	6 411	
Telephone charges	6 349	
Advertising and marketing	6 904	
General administration expenses	5 966	
Consultants' fees	12 500	
Insurance	3 690	
Accounting and taxation advice	3 850	
Legal fees	1 000	
Sundry expenses	775	
Depreciation on buildings	2 000	

Depreciation on fixtures and fittings	1 829
Depreciation on delivery vehicles	4 763
Profit on disposal of delivery vehicle	(520)
	(171 166)
Operating profit	78 578
Interest received	(280)
Interest paid	4 617
	(4 337)
Net profit	74 241

Dezzie's: Balance sheets at 31 March 20X4 and 20X3

	20X4 £	20X4 £	20X3 £	20X3 £
Fixed assets				
Land and buildings	147 900		44 900	
Less: accumulated depreciation	(11 140)		(9 140)	
		136 760		35 760
Fixtures and fittings	18 290		16 251	
Less: accumulated depreciation	(12 419)		(10 590)	
		5 871		5 661
Delivery vehicles	21 603		12 920	
Less: accumulated depreciation	(8 313)		(8 450)	
		13 290		4 470
		155 921		45 891
Current assets				
Stock	6 186		5 630	
Debtors and prepayments	5 914		7 419	
Cash at bank	3 240		15 160	
	15 340		28 209	
Current liabilities				
Creditors and accruals	8 510		6 340	
Net current assets		6 830		21 869
		162 751		67 760
Long-term liability				
Mortgage loan		(73 750)		—
		89 001		67 760
Capital				
Capital brought forward		67 760		50 816
Profit for the year		74 241		59 444
Drawings		(53 000)		(42 500)
		89 001		67 760

Notes on the balance sheet

Land and buildings

Movements in the year ending 31 March 20X4 on land and buildings at cost and on accumulated depreciation are as follows:

	£
Cost	
Land and buildings at cost 1 April 20X3	44 900
Additions at cost	103 000
Land and buildings at cost 31 March 20X4	147 900

	£
Depreciation	
Accumulated depreciation 1 April 20X3	9 140
Depreciation for the year	2 000
Accumulated depreciation 31 March 20X4	11 140

Net book value at 31 March 20X4 is £147 900 − £11 140 = £136 760.

Fixtures and fittings

Movements in the year ending 31 March 20X4 on fixtures and fittings at cost and on accumulated depreciation are as follows:

	£
Cost	
Fixtures and fittings at cost 1 April 20X3	16 251
Additions at cost	2 039
Fixtures and fittings at cost 31 March 20X4	18 290

	£
Depreciation	
Accumulated depreciation 1 April 20X3	10 590
Depreciation for the year	1 829
Accumulated depreciation 31 March 20X4	12 419

Net book value at 31 March 20X4 is £18 290 − £12 419 = £5 871.

Delivery vehicles

Movements in the year ending 31 March 20X4 on delivery vehicles at cost and on accumulated depreciation are as follows:

	£
Cost	
Delivery vehicles at cost 1 April 20X3	12 920
Disposal of vehicle*	(6 500)
Additions at cost	15 183
Delivery vehicles at cost 31 March 20X4	21 603

	£
Depreciation	
Accumulated depreciation 1 April 20X3	8 450
Disposal of vehicle*	(4 900)
Depreciation for the year	4 763
Accumulated depreciation 31 March 20X4	8 313

*The vehicle was sold for £2120. The net book value at the point of sale was £6500 − £4900 = £1600. Profit on sale was, therefore, £2120 − £1600 = £520. (Note that this is included in the profit and loss account for the year.)

Net book value at 31 March 20X4 is £21 603 − £8 313 = £13 290.

Case study solution

The cash flow statement is set out immediately below, followed by detailed notes on its preparation.

Dezzie's: Cash flow statement for the year ending 31 March 20X4

	£	£	Note
Operating profit		78 578	1
Add back: Depreciation on buildings	2 000		1
Depreciation on fixtures and fittings	1 829		1
Depreciation on delivery vehicles	4 763		1
Profit on sale of delivery vehicle	(520)		1
		8 072	
		86 650	
Changes in working capital			
Stock (£6186 − £5630) (cash outflow)	(556)		2
Debtors (£5914 − £7419) (cash inflow)	1 505		2
Creditors (£8510 − £6340) (cash inflow)	2 170		2
Net change in working capital		3 119	
Net cash inflow from operating activities		89 769	
Interest			
Interest received (cash inflow)	280		3
Interest paid (cash outflow)	(4 617)		3
		(4 337)	
Capital expenditure (£103 000 + £2039 + £15 183) (cash outflow)	(120 222)		4
Sale of delivery vehicle − sale proceeds	2 120		4
		(118 102)	
Proprietor's drawings (cash outflow)		(53 000)	5
Mortgage loan (cash inflow)		73 750	6
Net cash outflow		(11 920)	
Change in cash balance			
Cash at 1 April 20X3		15 160	7
Cash at 31 March 20X4		3 240	7
Decrease in cash − net cash outflow		(11 920)	7

Notes on preparation of the cash flow statement

1. The starting point, as in the case of Isobel's business, is operating profit. We must then add back all the items in the profit and loss account that do not involve cash movements: in Dezzie's case these are the depreciation charges for buildings, fixtures and fittings and delivery vehicles. We must also adjust for the profit on the sale of the delivery vehicle of £520. (Note that there is a cash movement involved in the sale of the vehicle but we will take that into account – at the value of the cash actually received – later on in the cash flow statement.)

2. The changes in working capital must be calculated and recorded in this part of the statement. Comparing the working capital (i.e. current assets and current liabilities sections) in the two balance sheets we can see that:

   a) Stock has increased by £6186 − £5630 = £556; there has been an additional investment in working capital in respect of this item.

   b) Debtors have decreased by £5914 − £7419 = £1505; this means that the business has less capital tied up in debtors and there has been a release of cash (effectively, a cash inflow).

   c) Creditors have increased by £8510 − 6340 = £2170. This means that the business is managing to obtain a slightly increased level of finance from its creditors; this is equivalent to an inflow of cash.

   Note that this section of the cash flow statement often causes the most difficulties in understanding for students. For this reason, there are several short exercises at the end of the chapter that deal specifically with movements in working capital.

3. Interest paid and received: these figures are taken from the profit and loss account.

4. The total cash outflow on fixed assets is calculated by taking the actual capital expenditure from the notes on movements in fixed assets. Actual capital expenditure was:

	£
Land and buildings	103 000
Fixtures and fittings	2 039
Motor vehicles	15 183
Total	120 222

   These are outflows of cash from the business. The sale of an asset, on the other hand, produces an inflow of cash to the business. The correct amount to include in the cash flow statement is the actual proceeds of sale received; in this case, £2120.

5. Drawings are an outflow of cash from the business.

6. The mortgage loan received is an inflow of cash into the business in this year.

7. The net inflow or outflow of cash that is calculated in the cash flow statement should equal the change in the balance of cash between the two year-ends. In Dezzie's case there has been a net outflow of cash of £11 920. The final section of the cash flow statement 'proves' this figure by calculating the difference between cash at bank at 1 April 20X3 and at 31 March 20X4.

Advice to Delroy Desmond

Delroy's business has suffered a net outflow of cash in the course of the year. The cash flow statement shows where the outflows have occurred. The principal items of outflow are, of course, the expenditure on new fixed assets. Delroy obtained a mortgage loan for some of the major expenditure on new premises, but financed part of it (£103 000 − £73 750 = £29 250) from the business's own resources. In addition, over £15 000 was spent on acquiring new delivery vehicles and a further £2000 on fixtures and fittings. The second largest item of cash outflow is Delroy's own drawings, which have increased substantially (£42 500 increasing to £53 000).

However, Delroy's business is profitable (net profit margin for the year ending 31 March 20X4 is 21.8%), and it has generated net cash inflows from operating activities of £89 769.

Delroy accepts the consultant's analysis of the operating problems the business faces. The accounting information suggests that Delroy is happy to make investments in bricks and mortar, but is prepared to skimp on the furnishing of his restaurants. We can see from the figures that the fixtures and fittings are quite old (this shows up in the relatively high figures for accumulated depreciation), and that only around £2000 was spent on new fixtures and fittings. Customers have obviously noticed Delroy's cheapskate approach to these matters and are not happy about the appearance of the restaurants.

It appears that Delroy will be obliged to invest more money in restaurant fit out – new tables and so on – in order to keep the customers happy. He should be advised to do a thorough appraisal of the restaurant fittings and decoration, possibly in conjunction with an interior design expert (given that Delroy obviously has a blind spot in all matters relating to the appearance of his restaurants).

Over £15 000 has been spent on new delivery vehicles; this investment may address some of the problems noted by the customers of bikes breaking down and long waits for delivery. However, there could also be a problem with staffing, and it certainly appears to be the case that Delroy's managers are less effective than they should be. Delroy will have to arrange to employ higher paid staff. The obvious implication for cash and profits is that staffing expenses will increase. Also, he may have to spend extra cash on making existing staff redundant and could face legal problems if the staff consider themselves to have been unfairly dismissed.

However, if Delroy can sort out his staffing problems there are potential gains to be made in:

- increased customer satisfaction (leading to word-of-mouth recommendations, and an increased rate of return visits);
- better control of the delivery service, resulting in fewer complaints; and
- improved quality of service within the restaurants.

All of these factors could lead to increased turnover, and/or reduced costs.

Delroy's restaurants are profitable and bring in substantial sums of cash. The second restaurant has been open for only part of the year (we do not know from the details how long it has been open), and it could be expected to produce higher turnover and profits in the year ending 31 March 20X5. Delroy should prepare forecasts for at least the next following year, to show how much cash is likely to be available for spending on restaurant improvement and additional/replacement staffing.

The high profit/no cash paradox

In this chapter we have seen that profitability and availability of cash do not necessarily go hand in hand in the short term. The dislocation between profits and cash can create major short-term problems, even for very successful businesses.

Example 11.3 Adèle sells computer equipment, trading as Business Computer Specialist. She started in business six years ago and has done well, making a profit each year. However, about 18 months ago her business was the first in the UK to be granted the franchise to sell the XBS 0980, a specialist business computer system. She has become established as the principal supplier of the XBS 0980 and is likely to be supplied first with the XBS 0990 when it becomes available in the UK in the spring of 20X7.

Despite more than doubling her sales and nearly doubling net profits, Adèle's business is short of cash. During her accounting year to 31 December 20X6 she had to negotiate an overdraft of £20 000 with the bank, the first time since starting the business that she had done this. Later in the year, the overdraft facility was increased to £40 000 and Adèle is concerned that if things don't improve she will need to borrow more money. She has spent a total of £89 950 on new fixed assets during the year. Two new sales reps needed company cars, a lot of additional fixtures and fittings were required in the larger rented offices the business moved to, and the nearby warehouse, which is owned by the business, was extended to house all the additional stock.

The business profit and loss accounts for the years ending 31 December 20X5 and 20X6 are shown below, as are balance sheets at both dates.

Business Computer Specialist: Profit and loss accounts (summarised) for the years ending 31 December 20X5 and 31 December 20X6

	20X6 £	20X6 £	20X5 £	20X5 £
Sales		895 755		401 003
Less: cost of sales				
Opening stock	35 901		32 412	
Purchases	597 136		252 499	
	633 037		284 911	
	(78 700)		(35 901)	
Cost of sales		(554 337)		(249 010)
Gross profit		341 418		151 993
Expenses	204 016		82 278	
Depreciation	13 700		7 796	
		(217 716)		(90 074)
Operating profit		123 702		61 919
Interest received		—		988
Interest paid		(2 709)		—
Net profit		120 993		62 907
Gross profit margin		38.1%		37.9%
Net profit margin		13.5%		15.7%

Business Computer Specialist: Balance sheets at 31 December 20X6 and 20X5

	20X6 £	20X6 £	20X5 £	20X5 £
Fixed assets				
At cost	218 420		128 470	
Less: accumulated depreciation	(44 620)		(30 920)	
		173 800		97 550

	20X6 £	20X6 £	20X5 £	20X5 £
Current assets				
Stock	78 700		35 901	
Debtors and prepayments	95 514		34 996	
Cash at bank	—		12 804	
	174 214		83 701	
Current liabilities				
Bank overdraft	33 679		—	
Creditors and accruals	65 490		24 399	
	99 169		24 399	
Net current assets		75 045		59 302
		248 845		156 852
Capital				
Capital brought forward		156 852		120 945
Profit for the year		120 993		62 907
Drawings		(29 000)		(27 000)
		248 845		156 852

From this information we can draw up a cash flow statement for the year ending 31 December 20X6. This will help us to analyse the problems that Adèle currently faces.

Business Computer Specialist: Cash flow statement for the year ending 31 December 20X6

	£	£
Operating profit		123 702
Add back: depreciation		13 700
		137 402
Changes in working capital		
Stock (£78 700 − £35 901) (cash outflow)	(42 799)	
Debtors and prepayments (£95 514 − £34 996) (cash outflow)	(60 518)	
Creditors (£65 490 − £24 399) (cash inflow)	41 091	
Net change in working capital		(62 226)
Net cash inflow from operating activities		75 176
Interest paid		(2 709)
Capital expenditure (cash outflow)*		(89 950)
Proprietor's drawings (cash outflow)		(29 000)
Net cash outflow		(46 483)
Change in cash balance		
Cash at 1 January 20X5		12 804
Overdraft at 31 December 20X5		(33 679)
Decrease in cash – net cash outflow (£12 804 + £33 679)		(46 483)

Capital expenditure: We are told in the introduction to the case study that Adèle has spent £89 950 on new fixed assets. It is also possible to work the figure out from the accounts, as follows:

▶

	£
Fixed assets at net book value 31 December 20X5	97 550
Reduced by annual charge for depreciation in 20X6	(13 700)
	83 850
Fixed assets at net book value 31 December 20X6	173 700
Difference = purchases of fixed assets	89 850

The cash flow statement shows the principal causes of the decrease in cash/increase in overdraft. The business is expanding very fast, needing more fixed assets; nearly £90 000 has been spent in the year in acquiring new fixed assets. The next largest item has been the investment in working capital necessary to cope with the very rapid increase in sales. More sales means more stock on hand, and consequently, higher debtors and creditors. If the expansion continues at its present rate the business may need further overdraft facilities and possibly longer-term loans to fund the acquisition of more fixed assets.

It can be very difficult in practice to manage businesses that are expanding as fast as Business Computer Specialist. The problems such businesses encounter include:

- Need to take on more staff very quickly. Poor quality personnel decisions may be made when management is under pressure to employ more people in a hurry.
- Insufficient management time. Where small businesses grow very fast, the original proprietor is often swamped by the sheer weight and pace of decision making. Usually, in such circumstances, it is necessary to employ staff at managerial levels, but it can be difficult to get staff of the right calibre into positions quickly enough.
- Loss of control over costs and stock. A consequence of rapid expansion is often that costs get out of hand, because the business does not have systems in place to control them properly. In the case of Adèle we can see that her net profit margin has, in fact, fallen between 20X5 and 20X6 although gross profit margin has remained more or less constant. This suggests possible difficulties in controlling costs.
- Failure to control debtors. Debtors should convert into cash quite easily but some debtors need chasing to make them pay up. Where management time is short, amounts owed by debtors may be allowed to build up to unacceptable levels.
- Chronic shortage of cash to fund additional working capital and new investment in fixed assets.

Business success brings its own problems. Where businesses expand very rapidly they can become victims of their own success, and may even fail. Growing businesses may need to have controls over expansion to ensure that it does not happen too quickly. In Adèle's case, she needs, as a matter of some urgency, to prepare forecasts for the coming year in order to see just how much of a problem shortage of cash is likely to be. It may be time for her to consider recruiting a qualified accountant to the management team. She probably also needs to consider employing other specialists in areas such as sales and personnel.

In Part III of the book we will examine in detail the preparation of forecast information to assist business managers.

Chapter summary

This chapter introduced the role of cash in business by, firstly, examining the operation of the working capital cycle, and the problems that can occur when working capital is mismanaged. It emphasised the important distinction between cash and profits. Because of the operation of the matching (or accruals) principle, accounting income is not the same as cash received, and accounting expenditure is not the same as cash paid.

The chapter proceeded to examine the preparation of a third important accounting statement: the cash flow statement. The cash flow statement for the first year of trading in a new business was demonstrated, and then the case study for the chapter examined the preparation of the cash flow statement in an established business.

The final example in the chapter highlighted the problems that can occur where a profitable and successful business expands very quickly. The cash flow statement for such a business provides answers to the very basic question: 'where has all the cash gone?'

Students often experience some difficulty in understanding the preparation and significance of cash flow statements. By carefully working through the examples in this chapter, and then applying their knowledge to the questions at the end of the chapter, students should find that they are equipped with all the necessary skills to understand the cash flow statement.

Answer to self-test question 11.1

Transaction	Effect on cash	Effect on profit
Purchase of raw materials for cash of £1800.	Cash is immediately reduced by £1800.	No immediate effect on profit. Raw materials go into stock, and at some point will enter the production process. After conversion to finished goods a sale of those goods will probably take place at which point the value of the raw materials is set off against sales in the form of cost of sales.
Sale of old delivery van for £360.	Cash is immediately increased by £360.	A profit or loss on sale (see Chapter 9) will be calculated by setting off the proceeds of sale (£360) against the written down value of the asset. The effect on profit would be £360 only if the written down value of the asset was nil.
Long-term loan from brother of £5000.	Cash and long-term liabilities are both immediately increased by £5000.	The loan itself has no effect on profit. Any interest paid on the loan will reduce profits.

Transaction	Effect on cash	Effect on profit
Payment of interest on bank overdraft of £150.	Cash is reduced by £150 (or, more likely, the overdraft is increased by £150).	The interest paid reduces profits.
Amortisation charge of £8000 relating to patent rights.	No effect on cash.	Profits are reduced by £8000.

Exercises

The answers to many of the exercises are set out later in this chapter. However, where the exercise number is followed by 'A' the answer is available only to lecturers. Remember that additional exercises (with answers) are available to students on the book's website.

11.1   Fergus's business enters into the following transactions in the year to 31 December 20X2:

- Fergus introduces additional capital of £10 000 in cash.
- Purchase on credit of goods for resale for £8000.
- Payment received from debtor for £1800.
- Purchase of a new machine for use in the business. The machine costs £12 000 and will be depreciated over ten years on the straight-line basis, assuming no residual value, with a full year's depreciation in the year of acquisition.
- Sales returns of £1000 in exchange for a cash refund.
- Drawings of £1300.

For each transaction show the impact on cash, other assets and liabilities, and the impact on profits.

11.2A Flynn's business enters into the following transactions in the year to 31 March 20X5:

- Purchase of stock for cash of £1300.
- Sale of a fixed asset with a written down value of £300. The sale proceeds are £900.
- Sale on credit for £3500.
- Payment made to creditor for electricity bill of £6350.
- Drawings of £800.
- Purchase of a motor vehicle for use in the business. The vehicle costs £10 000 and is to be depreciated, with a full year's depreciation in the year of acquisition, at 25% per annum.

For each transaction show the impact on cash, other assets and liabilities, and the impact on profits.

11.3 Gilbert's business sells a fixed asset for cash proceeds of £1300. The asset originally cost £20 700, and accumulated depreciation at the point of sale was £18 210. Three of the following six statements are correct:

1. Profits increase by £1190.

2. Profits decrease by £1190.

3. Cash increases by £1300.

4. Cash increases by £1190.

5. The net book value of fixed assets decreases by £2490.

6. The net book value of fixed assets decreases by £1300.

Which statements are correct?

a) 1, 3 and 6

b) 2, 3 and 5

c) 1, 4 and 5

d) 2, 4 and 6.

11.4A Grant's business makes an operating profit of £16 632 in the year ending 30 April 20X1. One of the deductions in arriving at operating profit was depreciation of £6650.

At 30 April 20X1 the balance sheet showed stock of £26 750, debtors and prepayments of £12 704 and creditors of £11 667. On 30 April 20X0 the corresponding figures were: stock £27 997; debtors and prepayments £11 940; and creditors £9975.

What is the net cash inflow from operating activities to be included in Grant's cash flow statement for the year ending 30 April 20X1?

a) £21 107

b) £18 807

c) £22 073

d) £25 457.

11.5 Gaston's business prepares accounts to 31 December each year. In the year ending 31 December 20X4 stock, debtors and creditors are shown in the balance sheet, with comparative figures at 31 December 20X3, as follows:

	20X4 £	20X3 £
Stock	37 669	31 470
Debtors and prepayments	21 777	19 303
Creditors and accruals	18 250	16 264

Gaston's net profit for the year ending 31 December 20X4 is £36 790, after adding interest received of £763 and deducting total depreciation charges of £4585.

What is the net cash inflow from operating activities for inclusion in Gaston's cash flow statement for the year ending 31 December 20X4?

a) £47 299

b) £29 340

c) £33 925

d) £34 688.

11.6A Gunter's business sells an item of machinery for £2660 on 30 June 20X6. The balances at the beginning of the accounting year (1 January 20X6) for the asset were: cost = £17 700; accumulated depreciation = £15 930.

Gunter charges depreciation on this class of asset at the rate of 10% per annum on cost, with a month's depreciation charged for each full month of ownership in the year of disposal. He has assumed a nil residual value for this asset.

Two of the following eight statements are correct:

1. Profits decrease by £890.

2. Profits increase by £890.

3. Profits increase by £1775.

4. Profits decrease by £1775.

5. Cash increases by £2660.

6. Cash increases by £1775.

7. Cash decreases by £2660.

8. Cash decreases by £1775.

Which statements are correct?

a) 1 and 7

b) 4 and 6

c) 2 and 8

d) 3 and 5.

11.7 Henrietta runs a business, trading as Spicer & Co. She prepares accounts to 31 March each year. By the year-end 31 March 20X4 the business has run into overdraft. Henrietta asks you to prepare a cash flow statement for the business for the year ending 31 March 20X4 and she provides you with the following information:

Spicer & Co: Profit and loss account (summarised) for the year ending 31 March 20X4

	£
Sales	598 731
Less: cost of sales	(430 131)
Gross profit	168 600
Expenses excluding depreciation	(79 633)
Depreciation	(12 471)
Operating profit	76 496
Interest paid	(230)
Net profit	76 266

Spicer & Co.: Balance sheets at 31 March 20X4 and 31 March 20X3

	20X4 £	20X4 £	20X3 £	20X3 £
Fixed assets				
At cost	175 630		128 547	
Less: accumulated depreciation	(67 248)		(54 777)	
		108 382		73 770
Current assets				
Stock	40 747		36 600	
Debtors and prepayments	50 661		48 730	
Cash at bank	—		7 423	
	91 408		92 753	
Current liabilities				
Bank overdraft	1 348		—	
Creditors and accruals	36 644		35 191	
	37 992		35 191	
Net current assets		53 416		57 562
		161 798		131 332
Capital				
Capital brought forward		131 332		111 335
Profit for the year		76 266		61 297
Drawings		(45 800)		(41 300)
		161 798		131 332

Note: There were no disposals of fixed assets during the year.

You are required to prepare a cash flow statement for Spicer & Co. for the year ending 31 March 20X4.

11.8A Hamid prepares his business financial statements to 31 May each year. Because he attended an accounting course at college he knows how to prepare profit and loss accounts and balance sheets. However, the course did not include the preparation of cash flow statements and Hamid asks you to prepare a cash flow statement for his business for the year ending 31 May 20X2. He supplies you with the following information:

Hamid: Profit and loss account (summarised) for the year ending
31 May 20X2

	£
Sales	437 500
Less: cost of sales	(298 423)
Gross profit	139 077
Expenses excluding depreciation	(62 505)
Depreciation	(7 662)
Operating profit	68 910
Interest received	634
Interest paid	(506)
Net profit	69 038

Hamid: Balance sheets at 31 May 20X2 and 31 May 20X1

	20X2 £	20X2 £	20X1 £	20X1 £
Fixed assets				
At cost	82 610		38 750	
Less: accumulated depreciation	(21 462)		(13 800)	
		61 148		24 950
Current assets				
Stock	26 980		27 420	
Debtors and prepayments	44 349		42 760	
Cash at bank	5 354		6 642	
	76 683		76 822	
Current liabilities				
Loan	—		5 000	
Creditors and accruals	23 730		28 459	
	23 730		33 459	
Net current assets		52 953		43 363
		114 101		68 313
Capital				
Capital brought forward		68 313		33 766
Profit for the year		69 038		63 291
Drawings		(23 250)		(28 744)
		114 101		68 313

Note the following:

1. There were no disposals of fixed assets during the year.

2. Following your request Hamid supplies the following information relating to cash receipts and payments during the year: cash receipts = £435 911; cash payments = £365 217.

You are required to prepare Hamid's cash flow statement for the year ending 31 May 20X2 using a) the indirect method; and b) the direct method.

11.9 Horst is in business as a sole trader, trading under the name of Box Distributors. His accountant has prepared a profit and loss account for the business for the year ending 31 December 20X5 and a balance sheet at that date. Horst approaches you in your capacity as a small business adviser. He shows you the financial statements and says:

> I can't quite understand what's happened here. My sales for 20X4 were £600 227 and they've increased this year to £636 636. The business is really doing quite well. I had to replace one of the delivery vehicles during the year, because it was unreliable, but I thought I'd been quite sensible about covering that spending. I got £5200 for it and extended the long-term bank loan by another £5000 which should have more or less covered the cost of the new van, which was £10 660. I've made a big effort to control my own spending – I decided not to replace the BMW this year, and we went camping in France instead of going on that luxury cruise we'd planned. So, drawings are only slightly higher than they were in 20X4. Despite all this restraint the overdraft was almost £8000 at the year end. What's happened?

Horst's profit and loss account for the year ending 31 December 20X5 and his balance sheets at 31 December 20X5 and 20X4 are shown below.

Box Distributors: Profit and loss account for the year ending 31 December 20X5

	£
Sales	636 636
Less: cost of sales	(452 483)
Gross profit	184 153
Selling and distribution expenses (excluding depreciation)	(62 466)
Administration expenses (excluding depreciation)	(55 892)
Depreciation of delivery vehicles	(6 313)
Profit on sale of delivery vehicle	336
Depreciation of warehouse and machinery	(11 876)
Operating profit	47 942
Interest paid	(2 104)
Net profit	45 838

Box Distributors: Balance sheets at 31 December 20X5 and 31 December 20X4

	20X5 £	20X5 £	20X4 £	20X4 £
Fixed assets				
Delivery vehicles at cost	35 897		33 650	
Less: accumulated depreciation	(16 960)		(14 196)	
		18 937		19 454
Warehouse and machinery				
at cost	118 760		118 760	
Less: accumulated depreciation	(71 256)		(59 830)	
		47 504		59 380
		66 441		78 834
Current assets				
Stock	52 687		45 611	
Debtors and prepayments	78 490		65 442	
Cash at bank	—		371	
	131 177		111 424	
Current liabilities				
Overdraft	7 996		—	
Creditors and accruals	39 943		42 417	
	47 939		42 417	
Net current assets		83 238		69 007
		149 679		147 841
Long-term liability – loan		(15 000)		(10 000)
		134 679		137 841
Capital				
Capital brought forward		137 841		128 069
Profit for the year		45 838		58 222
Drawings		(49 000)		(48 450)
		134 679		137 841

A detailed analysis of the delivery vehicle accounts shows the following:

Cost	£
Delivery vehicles at 1 January 20X5	33 650
Disposal of vehicle	(8 413)
Addition of vehicle	10 660
Delivery vehicles at 31 December 20X5	35 897

Accumulated depreciation	
At 1 January 20X5	14 196
Accumulated depreciation on disposal	(3 549)
Depreciation charge for year (to profit and loss account)	6 313
At 31 December 20X5	16 960

You are required to prepare a cash flow statement for Horst's business for the year ending 31 December 20X5. Also, write a brief letter to Horst explaining the main reasons for the overdraft, offering advice on how he might go about eliminating it.

Answers to exercises

11.1   The following table details the impact of transactions on Fergus's business:

Transaction	Impact on cash, etc.	Impact on profits
Introduction of additional capital of £10 000 in cash.	Cash and capital are both increased by £10 000.	No impact on profits.
Purchase on credit of goods for resale for £8000.	Stock and creditors are both increased by £8000. There is no immediate impact on cash, but there will be an outflow of cash when the goods are paid for.	No immediate impact on profits. When the goods are sold, they will form part of cost of sales.
Payment received from debtor for £1800.	The asset of debtors is reduced by £1800 and there is a corresponding increase (inflow of cash) in cash of £1800.	No impact on profits. The sale to which the debtor relates would already have been recorded.
Purchase of a new machine for use in the business.	There is an outflow of cash of £12 000 and fixed assets are increased by £12 000.	No immediate impact on profits, but there will be an additional depreciation charge for the year of £1200 (i.e. £12 000 over ten years).
Sales returns of £1000 in exchange for a cash refund.	There is an outflow of cash of £1000.	Sales returns are increased by £1000. Sales returns are deducted from sales in the profit and loss account, and thus, reduce profit.
Drawings of £1300.	Cash and capital are both reduced by £1300.	There is no impact on profit. Effectively, Fergus is taking £1300 of his own capital out of the business.

11.3

	£
Fixed asset at cost	20 700
Less: accumulated depreciation	(18 210)
Net book value	2 490

The asset is sold for £1300; that is less than it is recorded at in the accounts. A loss is thus incurred on sale of £2490 − £1300 = £1190.

Profits are reduced by £1190 (statement no. 2), cash is increased by £1300 (statement no. 3) and fixed assets are reduced by £2490 (statement no. 5). The correct answer, therefore, is b).

11.5 The net cash inflow from operating activities in Gaston's business for the year ending 30 April 20X1 is calculated as follows:

	£	£
Operating profit (£36 790 − £763)		36 027
Add back: depreciation		4 585
		40 612
Changes in working capital		
Stock − increase (£37 669 − £31 470) (cash outflow)	(6 199)	
Debtors − increase (£21 777 − £19 303) (cash outflow)	(2 474)	
Creditors − increase (£18 250 − £16 264) (cash inflow)	1 986	
Net change in working capital		(6 687)
Net cash inflow from operating activities		33 925

The correct answer, therefore, is c).

11.7 **Spicer & Co.: Cash flow statement for the year ending 31 March 20X4**

	£	£
Operating profit		76 496
Add back: depreciation		12 471
		88 967
Changes in working capital		
Stock (£40 747 − £36 600) (cash outflow)	(4 147)	
Debtors and prepayments (£50 661 − £48 730) (cash outflow)	(1 931)	
Creditors (£36 644 − £35 191) (cash inflow)	1 453	
Net change in working capital		(4 625)
Net cash inflow from operating activities		84 342
Interest paid		(230)
Capital expenditure (cash outflow) (£175 630 − £128 547)		(47 083)
Proprietor's drawings (cash outflow)		(45 800)
Net cash outflow		(8 771)
Change in cash balance		
Cash at 1 April 20X3		7 423
Overdraft at 31 March 20X4		(1 348)
Decrease in cash − net cash outflow (£7423 + £1348)		(8 771)

11.9   **Box Distributors: Cash flow statement for the year ending 31 December 20X5**

	£	£
Operating profit		47 942
Add back: Depreciation of delivery vehicles	(6 313)	
Profit on sale of delivery vehicle	336	
Depreciation of warehouse and machinery	(11 876)	
		17 853
		65 795

Changes in working capital

Stock (£52 687 − £45 611) (cash outflow)	(7 076)	
Debtors and prepayments (£78 490 − £65 442) (cash outflow)	(13 048)	
Creditors (£39 943 − £42 417) (cash outflow)	(2 474)	
Net change in working capital		(22 598)

Net cash inflow from operating activities	43 197
Interest paid	(2 104)
Capital expenditure (cash outflow)	(10 660)
Proceeds of sale of fixed asset (cash inflow)	5 200
Proprietor's drawings (cash outflow)	(49 000)
Increase in loan (cash inflow)	5 000
Net cash outflow	(8 367)

Change in cash balance

Cash at 1 January 20X5	371
Overdraft at 31 December 20X5	(7 996)
Decrease in cash – net cash outflow (£371 + £7996)	(8 367)

Letter to Horst

Dear Horst

The attached cash flow statement summarises the movements in cash between 1 January and 31 December 20X5. As you will see from the lower part of the statement the overall net outflow of cash is over £8000. The principal cash inflows and outflows that have contributed to the increased overdraft are as follows.

A substantial investment in working capital of over £22 000. The total for debtors has increased by over £13 000, suggesting that the business has become significantly less successful at collecting money owed for credit sales. Stocks have also risen by a very significant amount.

The net cash inflow from operating activities is less than the total of drawings for the year. Drawings are therefore being removed from the accumulated capital of previous years.

Capital expenditure movements, as you have pointed out yourself, are not particularly significant in the year; the expenditure on the new vehicle is more or less covered by the proceeds of the sale of the old vehicle plus the increased borrowing from the bank.

The business is significantly less profitable in 20X5 than in the previous year. Net profit for 20X4 was £58 222 on sales of £600 227, a margin of 9.7%. The comparable margin for 20X5 is 7.2% (£45 838/636 636 × 100). This suggests the need for better control of costs.

As regards, reducing the overdraft, in the next accounting period the principal action points to address include the following:

- Control costs to improve the net profit margin.
- Reduce debtors by improving collection procedures.
- If possible, reduce the amount of drawings from the business.
- Reduce the amount of stock held so that less cash is tied up in this part of the working capital cycle.

I hope the analysis and suggestions for action are helpful to you. Please contact me if you would like further advice or information.

Yours sincerely

12

FINANCIAL REPORTING BY LIMITED COMPANIES

AIMS AND LEARNING OUTCOMES

Aim of the chapter

To understand the nature of company financial reporting, including an appreciation of the accounting regulatory framework applicable to companies.

Learning outcomes

After reading the chapter and completing the related exercises, students should:

- Understand in outline the regulations relating to accounting by companies.
- Understand the roles of directors in respect of company financial reports.
- Be able to draw up a set of financial statements for a simple limited company.
- Understand the need for additional financial and non-financial reporting by listed companies.

Introduction to accounting by limited companies

Some of the chapters in Part I of this book touched on various matters relating to limited companies. In Chapter 1 we considered the different forms of business organisation, including limited companies. In Chapter 4 we examined issues relating to financing of limited companies through the stock market, and Chapter 5 touched on the separation between the ownership and the management of capital that is characteristic of larger companies, and identified the principal users of the financial information produced by companies. Some of the information in these earlier chapters is reviewed in this chapter in order to provide a context for the examination of the regulation and practice relating to company financial statements, which is the principal focus of the chapter.

In this chapter we will examine in more detail the nature of limited companies and their accounting.

The limited company

The limited company has been an important form of business organisation since the middle of the 19th century in the United Kingdom. The need for this type of organisation developed as industrial organisations became larger, and as greater amounts of capital were required to fund the expansion of, for example, the railway system. It is unlikely that one single individual would be wealthy enough to fund a major institution like a railway or a bank, and so a legal mechanism that allows for ownership to be shared is very useful in the development of advanced economies. Most capitalist countries have adopted ownership vehicles akin to the UK limited company, and in most of Europe this development took place during the 19th century.

A company is a convenient form of organisation in that:

- It allows for investments of differing amounts to be made by a potentially very large group of individuals or organisations.
- In the form in which it is most commonly found in the UK and elsewhere, it offers investors the protection of limited liability. This useful mechanism ensures that investors are liable for no more than their original investment.
- A company is regarded as a 'person' in law. It can sue or be sued, can hold bank accounts and other forms of assets, and it can be named as a contracting party in legal contracts. The individuals investing in it are protected by the so-called 'veil of incorporation'.
- The structure of the capital of a limited company in the form of shares lends itself to shared ownership by many parties, and, in some cases, access to markets in which share capital can be easily exchanged for cash.
- It can offer certain tax advantages over sole trader and partnership forms of organisation.

Limited liability

Limited liability confers a great advantage upon investors in shares of companies. By contrast, a sole trader or a partner in a partnership is exposed to unlimited liability, to the extent of his or her own personal assets, in respect of business dealings.

There is, potentially, a corresponding disadvantage for the creditors of limited liability companies. Creditors of business organisations always face the risk that they will not be paid; but if a limited company fails to pay, the creditors may have very little chance of successfully pursuing an action against the company. If it has no assets, the creditors will simply not be paid. Consider the following example.

Example 12.1 On 1 June 20X4 Elba Limited places an order with a supplier, Tommy, to supply stock on credit to a value of £3000. Tommy supplies the goods, but then Elba goes out of business on 10 August 20X4, without having paid Tommy any of the money owing to him. Elba Limited has the following balance sheet at 31 May 20X4:

	£	£
Fixed assets		8 000
Current assets		
Stock	1 250	
Debtors	1 000	
	2 250	
Current liabilities		
Creditors	2 550	
Overdraft	6 300	
	8 850	
Net current liabilities		(6 600)
Net assets		1 400
Share capital		100
Accumulated reserves		1 300
Capital and reserves		1 400

By 10 August 20X4 Elba's position has deteriorated. The balance sheet shows the following position:

	£	£
Fixed assets		8 000
Current assets		
Stock	5 250	
Debtors	1 600	
	6 850	
Current liabilities		
Creditors	8 940	
Overdraft	8 300	
	17 240	
Net current liabilities		(10 390)
Net liabilities		(2 390)
Share capital		100
Accumulated losses		(2 490)
Capital and reserves		(2 390)

Elba's bank manager refuses to extend the overdraft any further and the company must cease to trade.

Where does Tommy stand as regards recovering the money due to him? In this case he may recover some of his money, but probably not all of it. In total, there are creditors of £17 240, of which Tommy's amount due is £3000. The balance sheet shows total assets of £14 850, a shortfall of £2390. However, the asset values may not be realistic estimates of the amounts that can be recovered by selling the assets.

Fixed assets, as we know, are presented in the balance sheet at cost less depreciation. The net book value may be higher than the amounts for which the assets can be sold. The debtors figure of £1600 may not be fully recoverable, and perhaps the stock could not be sold for the full amount stated in the balance sheet.

Suppose the assets of Elba could be liquidated as follows:

	£
Fixed assets in a forced sale	6 000
Debtors – amounts actually receivable	1 400
Stock in a forced sale	4 500
Total amount of cash that can be raised	11 900

Against total liabilities of £17 240 there is a shortfall of £5340, or just over 30%. The creditors cannot be repaid in full, and are likely to receive at most about 70% of the value of the sums due to them. In practice, this proportion will be reduced by accountants' fees for doing the work of winding up the company (yes: the accountants are paid before the other 'ordinary' creditors) and by any amounts due to the Customs and Excise and the Inland Revenue (who take precedence over other creditors). Note that the shareholders in Elba would lose the whole of their investment in share capital. However, the share capital amounts only to £100, and the loss is small compared to the loss that will be suffered by Tommy and other creditors.

Information needs

Information needs of company creditors

The situation outlined in Example 12.1 may seem very unfair to creditors. How could Tommy have avoided losing money? Well, if he had been aware of Elba's weak position he could have either refused to trade with the company, or he could have insisted on receiving the cash in advance. Either way, he would have been protected from loss.

It is partly to protect creditors like Tommy that regulation exists to ensure that companies are obliged to make certain financial details available to the public. If creditors are in possession of accounting information they are able to make better decisions. Even so, creditors like Tommy are rarely in possession of all the relevant facts. Companies are obliged to make information available within ten months of their year-end (seven months for some larger companies); by the time the information becomes available the company's position may have altered very significantly.

Information needs of company shareholders

Companies, especially larger companies, are sometimes owned and managed by different people. Where company directors and shareholders are two different groups of people (or two groups that overlap only partially), it is important that the directors are held to account for the way in which they have managed the shareholders' investments. (This accountability is known by the rather old-fashioned term **stewardship**.) Therefore, there are regulatory requirements to ensure that shareholders receive information in a standard form about the companies they have invested in. If the shareholders are unhappy about the way in which directors have managed the company, they can vote the directors out of office and replace them. Although there may be many shareholders, especially in very large companies, directors are voted out of office comparatively rarely.

Information needs of people other than shareholders and creditors

There are other groups of people who may be interested in the information made available by companies (see also Chapter 5). These include employees, customers, financial journalists, the government, academics and the general public.

In the next section of the chapter the nature of company regulation, especially in respect of accounting, is examined in outline.

Regulation of company accounting and other issues

There are few regulations governing accounting by sole traders. By contrast, accounting and financial reporting by companies is subject to comparatively heavy regulation. Some of the principal sources and features of company regulation will be explained in this section.

Companies Acts

Since the mid-19th century the conduct of companies has been subject to legal regulation in the form of Acts of parliament. Currently in the UK there are two Companies Acts in force: the Companies Acts 1985 and 1989. It is principally the earlier Act that concerns us.

The 1985 Companies Act contains many complex legal regulations relating to:

- formation of new companies and types of company
- company constitutional arrangements including the issue of shares
- role of directors
- the audit of companies
- publication and presentation of accounting information.

The 1985 Act introduced many aspects of European company law into UK legislation; in particular, standard formats for the presentation of company profit and loss accounts and balance sheets were introduced. These will be examined in more detail later in the chapter.

A major review of company law has taken place in the UK between 1999 and 2001. Company law as it stands has been criticised for retaining the same basic structure originally established in the Victorian era. It is argued that Victorian company law was appropriate for the 19th century but, as it now stands, it is an encumbrance to a modern economy. The proposals, many of which are radical, are currently under review and may well be considered by parliament in the near future. However, at the time of writing, company law in the UK retains many very traditional features. Some of the principal elements are discussed in the following sub-sections:

Company formation and types of company

Setting up a limited company is quite straightforward and is an inexpensive procedure (it can cost less than £100). It is usually handled by a professionally qualified accountant or solicitor, or by one of the specialist company formation firms. Certain forms have to be registered with Companies House, and there are provisions to ensure that a company is not registered with a name identical to that of an existing company.

There are two principal types of company under English law (note that English law applies to England and Wales, while arrangements in Scotland and Northern Ireland may differ):

1. *The private company*: this has a minimum of one shareholder, and one director. The word 'limited' is attached to the name of the company (in English or Welsh).

2. *The public limited company*: this must be described in its memorandum of association (see below) as a public company, its name must end in 'public limited company' or 'plc' (or the Welsh equivalents) and it must have a share capital of £50 000, at least 25% of which has been issued for cash.

Larger companies tend to be plcs. However, comparatively large businesses may be private companies. In order to be permitted to issue shares to the general public a company must be constituted as a plc. Only plcs may be listed on a stock exchange, but not all plcs are listed. (See Chapter 4 for further discussion of listing.)

Company constitutional arrangements including the issue of shares

There are formal arrangements in law for company meetings. An annual general meeting (AGM) must take place (although there are certain exemptions for very small companies), and shareholders must be permitted to vote democratically on resolutions at that meeting. The normal agenda for an AGM includes the following:

- acceptance of the directors' report and the financial statements
- authorisation for payment of dividend (and confirmation of dividends already paid)
- election of directors
- appointment of auditors
- any other business.

All companies are required to issue a **memorandum of association** and **articles of association**. The memorandum sets out the purposes for which the company is set up (usually framed in very broad terms) and the authorised share capital. The articles of association contain the company's internal constitution, including, for example, appropriate arrangements for appointment of directors, voting by shareholders, powers of directors and directors' expenses, pensions and remuneration.

Note that the **authorised share capital** is the quantity of shares that the company is authorised to issue. It does not have to issue all of the authorised capital, and, indeed, many companies do not. Therefore, **issued share capital** may be a lesser amount. The most common type of share capital is **ordinary share capital**. Each share carries the right to vote at the AGM and the right to receive a dividend (if any). Each ordinary share has a **nominal value**, which is commonly one of the following: 5p, 10p, 25p, 50p or £1.

Decisions on the amount of ordinary dividend to be paid are made by the company's directors. Ordinary dividends for an accounting year are often paid in two instalments: an interim dividend and a final dividend. At the year-end the final dividend may not have actually been paid out, and if so, it is included as a creditor in the balance sheet under current liabilities.

Some companies issue preference share capital. This differs substantially from ordinary share capital, in that preference shares carry a fixed rate of dividend (and are described as, for example, 8% preference shares), and have no vote at the AGM. Such shares are referred to as 'preference shares' because their dividends have to be paid out in preference to any dividend on the ordinary shares. Because there is a fixed rate of return on preference shares, they are really more akin to a long-term loan. Some preference shares are cumulative; that is, if the company does not pay the dividend on the shares the obligation to pay is carried forward to the next following year.

Example 12.2 Pauletta Limited has an authorised share capital of £40 000, split into shares of 25 pence each. Half of the shares are issued. In the year ending 31 December 20X4 a dividend of 4p per share is declared.
   Li Ming owns 5000 shares in Pauletta Limited:

a) What is the nominal value of the issued share capital of Pauletta Limited, and how many shares are in issue?
b) What is the total value of the dividend declared for the year ending 31 December 20X4?
c) What is the value of Li Ming's dividend for the year ending 31 December 20X4?

Answer

Pauletta Limited's authorised share capital, in terms of numbers of shares is £40 000 / 25p = 160 000. Half of those shares are in issue, i.e. 80 000. The nominal value of those shares is 80 000 x 25p = £20 000.

a) The dividend is 4p per share; total value is 4p x 80 000 = £3200.
b) Li Ming's dividend is 4p x 5000 (the number of shares held) = £200.

Example 12.3 Birch and Beech Limited has both ordinary shares and preference shares in issue, as follows:

● authorised and issued ordinary share capital: 30 000 £1 shares
● preference share capital: £50 000 7% preference shares.

The directors of the company declare an ordinary dividend of 5% of nominal share value in the year ending 31 December 20X1. The preference dividend is also paid.
   What is the total amount of dividend payable by Birch and Beech Limited for the year ending 31 December 20X1?

Answer

	£
Ordinary dividend: £30 000 × 5%	1 500
Preference dividend: £50 000 × 7%	3 500
Total	5 000

Role of directors

Company directors have important responsibilities under the law, and an appointment as a director is not to be taken lightly. Directors are required to act in good faith in the interests of the company (which may not be the same as the interests of shareholders). If a company loses money through the actions of directors, it may be able to reclaim the money from the directors even if they acted in what they thought were the best interests of the company.

In respect of accounting and related requirements, directors must:

- Keep adequate accounting records.
- Prepare accounts each year, which must be filed within certain time limits with the Registrar of Companies. The accounts must include a directors' report.
- Ensure that the company does not trade while insolvent (note that the example of Elba Limited used earlier demonstrates an insolvent company balance sheet at 10 August 20X4).

The accounts of a company must present a 'true and fair view' (this is a legal term which has existed in company law for over half a century) of the performance and state of affairs of the company. Although the directors themselves do not all necessarily take part in the preparation of the accounts (the task is often delegated to a finance director or company accountant) they nevertheless take complete responsibility in law for the preparation and filing of accounts. Fines are quite frequently levied on directors by Companies House in respect of late filing of accounts. Late filing is a criminal offence and guilty directors may end up with a criminal record.

Allowing a company to trade while insolvent can have very serious consequences for individual directors. Directors may be ordered by the courts to make contributions out of their personal resources if they have allowed the company to continue trading in circumstances where there is no reasonable prospect of avoiding liquidation. If it is proven that directors have deliberately defrauded creditors a criminal offence is involved; they may be disqualified as a director, fined or even imprisoned.

Claiming ignorance is no defence. If people are appointed directors they should fully understand their responsibilities and the possible adverse consequences of failing to meet those responsibilities. All members of the board of directors are equally responsible in law.

The audit of companies

Until a few years ago, all limited companies required a formal audit by a qualified chartered (or certified) accountant. The auditor examines the books and records of the business, and compares them to the final accounts. He or she issues an **audit report** addressed to the company shareholders, which states whether or not the accounts present a true and fair view.

Gradually, over the last few years, the requirement for company audit has been progressively restricted because it was felt that it was a bureaucratic burden for small companies. Where there are only one or two shareholders, who are probably the company directors, it seems a waste of resources to have a formal audit. Currently, small companies with a turnover of not more than £1 million and a balance sheet total of not more than £1.4 million are exempted from the audit requirement. Small companies can, of course, choose to have an audit if they wish to do so. If a small company, for example, wishes to borrow a large sum of money from a bank, it may assist the case if there is a set of audited accounts available to show the bank manager.

Publication and presentation of accounting information

As illustrated in Example 12.1, publication of financial information is of great importance to many interested parties. Companies are required to file their annual accounts at Companies House where they are available for inspection by any interested party. However, the meaning of 'annual accounts' varies depending upon the size of the company. Small and medium-sized companies are entitled to take advantage of exemptions that allow them to file a quite limited amount of information at Companies House. Small companies, for example, are not required to file a profit and loss account, and are entitled to restrict the amount of information they provide in the balance sheet and supporting notes. Medium-sized companies, while they are required to file a profit and loss account, are permitted to start the profit and loss statement with gross profit, so that they do not have to disclose turnover.

Note that the legal definition of a small company is a company that satisfies at least two of the following three criteria:

- Turnover not greater than £2.8 million.
- Balance sheet total (fixed assets + current assets) no greater than £1.4 million.
- No more than 50 employees on average.

The turnover and balance sheet total limits are changed from time to time.

The main reason for allowing small and medium-sized companies to file a reduced amount of accounting information is to ensure that competitors do not have access to information that may harm the interests of the business. The reduction in filing requirements does not save these companies much, if anything, in costs because a full set of accounts has still to be prepared for the shareholders.

Later in the chapter presentation requirements for company financial statements are examined in more detail.

Accounting standards

The Companies Acts contain various requirements as to the preparation and presentation of accounting information by companies. However, these requirements are often quite general in nature, and a need has emerged over the last 50 years or so for more detailed guidance on how specific accounting issues should be dealt with in the accounts of companies and other business organisations. The accountancy professional bodies have been responsible for providing an additional layer of accounting regulation in the form of accounting standards.

Before 1990 accounting standards were issued by the Accounting Standards Committee (ASC), which comprised senior members of the accounting profession. The ASC issued Statements of Standard Accounting Practice (SSAPs), some of which are still current (such as SSAP 9 dealing with the subject of accounting for stock).

Since 1990, accounting standards in the UK have been issued by the Accounting Standards Board (ASB), a more broadly based organisation that represents a wider constituency of interest groups than the accountancy profession. To date, 19 Financial Reporting Standards (FRSs) have been issued by the ASB. Many of these are on very complex topics beyond the scope of this book, but, for example, FRS 15 deals with accounting for fixed assets, including regulations relating to depreciation.

Accounting for limited companies

The basics of accounting remain the same, regardless of the form of organisation. The accounting equation, for example, which was explained in Chapter 6, holds good whether the accounting is for a sole trader, a partnership or a limited company. However, accounting for limited companies involves the introduction of some additional complexities into the profit and loss account and balance sheet.

Components of a set of limited company accounts

Under the law, a set of accounts for a limited company comprises the following:

- a profit and loss account
- a balance sheet
- notes to the accounts
- directors' report
- auditors' report (where applicable).

In addition, FRS1 requires the inclusion of a cash flow statement for companies that do not qualify as 'small' under the Companies Act.

The contents of the profit and loss account and balance sheet are dealt with in detail elsewhere in this chapter and in Part II of this book. Notes to the accounts can be highly complex in practice. They contain a great deal of supporting explanatory detail about the figures in the accounts, much of which is required by law or by various accounting standards. There are quite extensive requirements, for example, relating to the disclosure of directors' remuneration.

The directors' report is a quite formal document, which must contain explanation and comment on a range of items, including:

- description of the principal activities of the company
- review of the development of the business
- a note of political and charitable donations.

Presentation of accounting information

As noted earlier in the chapter, UK company law prescribes formats for the profit and loss account and balance sheet statements. There are two permissible balance sheet formats, and four profit and loss account formats. However, in the UK almost all companies adopt the same formats and these are shown, in outline, below.

Balance sheet

Fixed assets
   Intangible assets
   Tangible assets
   Investments
Current assets
   Stocks
   Debtors (including prepayments)
   Investments
   Cash at bank and in hand
Creditors: Amounts falling due within one year
   Bank loans and overdrafts
   Trade creditors
   Other creditors, including taxation and social security
   Accruals
Net current assets
Total assets less current liabilities
Creditors: Amounts falling due after more than one year
Capital and reserves
   Share capital
   Reserves

Note that the descriptions shown in bold type must, by law, be used where there are items falling under those classifications.

Profit and loss account

Turnover
Cost of sales
Gross profit or loss
Selling and distribution costs
Administrative expenses
Other operating income
Operating profit
Income from investments
Interest receivable and similar income
Interest payable and similar charges
Profit or loss on ordinary activities before taxation
Tax on profit or loss on ordinary activities
Profit or loss on ordinary activities after taxation
Dividends
Retained profit or loss

The following points should be noted concerning the balance sheet and profit and loss account formats:

1. None of the lines in the profit and loss account are specified in the legislation, and so it is not a legal requirement to adopt precisely these descriptions. However, the descriptions shown above are very commonly used in UK company accounting, and will be seen in most large company accounts.

2. In all the questions dealt with in earlier chapters in the book we have ignored the effects of taxation. Companies are subject to corporation tax and some of the examples in this chapter will include limited references to tax but no knowledge of corporation tax (or indeed any other tax) is required. In most cases, corpor-

ation tax will be a deduction from profit in the profit and loss account, with a corresponding liability in the balance sheet (corporation tax is payable nine months after a company's year-end, so the liability for tax is a current liability).

3. The formats for profit and loss account and balance sheet set out above are not complete; the Companies Act format contains more complex descriptions, some of which are beyond the scope of this book. Examples included in this and other chapters on company accounts will not usually contain any more complex descriptions than those set out above.

Accounting for share capital

As shown in the balance sheet format above, share capital is accounted for on a separate line. The amount shown is the nominal value of the share capital in issue (*not* the authorised share capital).

Example 12.4 Xenophon Limited has authorised share capital comprising 23 000 50p shares. Of these, 8000 have been issued. What is the amount of share capital to be shown in the balance sheet?

The nominal value of the issued share capital of the company comprises 8000 shares of 50p each: total value for inclusion in the balance sheet = £4000.

Self-test question 12.1 (answer at the end of the chapter)

Uppingham Telephones Limited has the following balances in its books at 31 March 20X2:

	£
Intangible fixed assets	35 866
Premises at net book value	65 700
Vehicles at net book value	44 430
Fixtures and fittings at net book value	17 260
Stock at 31 March 20X2	42 370
Debtors	82 026
Cash at bank and in hand	13 222
Trade creditors	39 210
Long-term loan	15 000
Share capital: 20 000 £1 shares issued	20 000
Reserves at 1 April 20X1	161 479
Sales	717 216
Cost of sales	509 582
Selling costs	63 477
Distribution costs	54 460
Administrative expenses	24 512

The chief accountant must allow for a corporation tax charge for the year of £19 500. Also, the finance director has told her that a dividend of 25p per share should be included in the accounts.

You are required to prepare the profit and loss account for the year ending 31 March 20X2 for Uppingham Telephones Limited, and a balance sheet at that date in a format that complies with Companies Act presentation requirements.

CASE STUDY 12.1 Figures in the boardroom

Joe Daley is the managing director of Daley Limited, which operates a small group of retail food stores in the West Midlands. Daley's was set up by Joe's father Edward and his uncle Eric several years ago; both have more or less retired from the business but each retain shareholdings of 15% and both remain directors of the company, although they rarely attend board meetings these days. Joe himself owns 34% of the shares. The remaining 36% not owned by Joe, his father or his uncle, are accounted for as follows:

Joe's sister Carol	10%
Carol's husband Nasser	7%
Eric's son Gervase	19%

Carol, Nasser and Gervase are all directors, although Carol rarely attends meetings as she is very busy with her own fashion design business, producing expensive designs in limited editions for the extremely rich. The normal business of Daley Limited is conducted by Joe, Nasser and Gervase; Joe takes overall control of the direction of the company, Nasser is principally responsible for purchasing and Gervase spends most of his time in day-to-day management of the retail outlets.

Generally, the directors work well together, although problems can arise when either Edward or Eric, or both, want to get involved in day-to-day business issues. The younger generation of directors feel that Edward and Eric have lost their grip on the business and don't understand current business issues. Edward and Eric, on the other hand, while they don't always agree with each other, are united in feeling that 'the youngsters' are too hasty in making important business decisions.

An important decision faces the board. Sales have remained strong but the profit margins of the business have dropped each year for the last five years. In the year ending 31 December 20X5 the operating profit margin (operating profit as a percentage of sales) had dropped to 21.3%. Joe has proposed that the retail units expand their range into clothing; this would entail transferring about one-third of the floor space in the stores from food to clothing. It would also mean borrowing money in order to lease additional storage facilities and to finance the investment in stock. He estimates that further borrowing of £200 000 will be required, which should be obtainable at 7% interest. He has sounded out the opinions of the other directors:

● *Carol*: 'Yes, great idea. I can use my contacts in the industry to get us some really good deals.'

● *Nasser*: 'Well, it's a risk, and I don't want to borrow money unless it's absolutely necessary, but Carol knows about the fashion business; it's not as though we don't have expertise on the board.'

- *Gervase*: 'I really don't think it can work for us. It's true that Carol knows about fashion, but she doesn't have experience of the type of clothing retailing we'd be doing. I'm very much opposed to going into an area where we have no experience. We could severely damage food sales if we get this wrong.'
- *Edward*: 'We should stick to what we know. Eric and I built this business up from scratch and this idea could ruin it. If you paid more attention to the core business instead of dreaming up daft ideas, we'd be able to keep the margins up.'
- *Eric*: 'You must be out of your mind . . .'

A board meeting is scheduled for Friday 16 January 20X6 to discuss the proposal. Each director has a single vote, and because there are six directors, there is always the possibility of deadlock. Where that happens, Joe, as managing director, can use a casting vote, but has never previously needed to do so; usually only he, Gervase and Nasser attend meetings and they tend to agree on most issues. It seems likely that all the directors will attend this meeting.

The company's year-end is 31 December, and draft figures are now available. Joe asks the company accountant, Estelle, to pull together some draft accounting data using the standard format for publication (so that the directors will be able to compare the figures easily to those of previous years).

The list of balances at the end of December 20X5 is as follows:

	£
Share capital: 150 000 £1 shares	150 000
Sales	2 793 800
Rental received from letting part of office building	29 350
Office building at net book value	423 751
Retail units at net book value	1 744 850
Vehicles, fixtures, etc. at net book value	404 470
Accumulated reserves at 1 January 20X5	1 788 208
Long-term loan	500 000
Creditors	106 309
Cash at bank	76 360
Opening stock at 1 January 20X5	263 404
Closing stock at 31 December 20X5	279 800
Directors' remuneration	69 550
Other administrative expenses	386 024
Selling and distribution costs	100 470
Purchases of goods	1 715 027
Interest payable	38 850
Dividends paid: interim	58 500
Debtors	86 411

Joe tells Estelle to include a final, proposed, dividend in the accounts of 50p per share. A provision for corporation tax payable is also required, and Estelle estimates this at £158 888.

The requirement is to prepare the draft financial statements, using the standard format for company profit and loss accounts and balance sheets, and to advise Joe on the key issues (both financial and non-financial) he needs to consider in preparation for Friday's board meeting, including an assessment of his position should he fail to convince a majority of directors to vote in favour of his proposal.

Case study solution

Workings comprise the following:

1. *Cost of sales*

	£
Opening stock	263 404
Add: purchases	1 715 027
	1 978 431
Less: closing stock	(279 800)
	1 698 631

2. *Administrative expenses*

	£
Directors' remuneration	69 550
Other administrative expenses	386 024
	455 574

3. *Dividends proposed*

150 000 shares @ 50p per share = £75 000.

Note: because this amount has not yet been paid it must be included in current liabilities in the company balance sheet.

4. *Tangible fixed assets*

	£
Office building at net book value	423 751
Retail units at net book value	1 744 850
Vehicles, fixtures, etc. at net book value	404 470
	2 573 071

5. *Other creditors*

	£
Creditor for corporation tax	158 888
Dividends payable (final proposed dividend)	75 000
	233 888

6. *Reserves*

	£
Accumulated reserves at 1 January 20X5	1 788 208
Profit for the year	237 237
Accumulated reserves at 31 December 20X5	2 025 445

The draft financial statements are as follows:

Daley Limited: Draft profit and loss account for the year ending 31 December 20X5

	£
Turnover	2 793 800
Cost of sales (working 1)	(1 698 631)
Gross profit	1 095 169
Selling and distribution costs	(100 470)
Administrative expenses (working 2)	(455 574)
Other operating income	29 350
Operating profit	568 475
Interest payable and similar charges	(38 850)
Profit on ordinary activities before taxation	529 625
Taxation	(158 888)
Profit on ordinary activities after taxation	370 737
Dividends:	
Paid	(58 500)
Proposed (working 3)	(75 000)
Profit for the financial year	237 237

Daley Limited: Draft balance sheet at 31 December 20X5

	£	£
Fixed assets		
Tangible assets (working 4)		2 573 071
Current assets		
Stock	279 800	
Debtors	86 411	
Cash at bank	76 360	
	442 571	
Creditors: amounts falling due within one year		
Trade creditors	106 309	
Other creditors (working 5)	233 888	
	340 197	
Net current assets		102 374
Total assets less current liabilities		2 675 445
Creditors: amounts falling due after more than one year		(500 000)
		2 175 445
Capital and reserves		
Share capital		150 000
Reserves (working 6)		2 025 445
		2 175 445

Advice

The draft accounts show that operating profit margin has dropped further this year, to 20.3% (£568 475/2 793 800 × 100), which may help to convince the other directors that radical action needs to be taken. The proposed scheme

◀◀◀

involves borrowing £200 000. At a 7% rate of interest this would increase interest charges by £14 000 per annum. The other directors need to be convinced that the proposal will increase profits by at least that much.

It seems likely from their initial response that Carol and Nasser will vote in favour of the proposal, but the other three directors appear to be very much opposed to it. It will almost certainly be very difficult to win them round. If the proposal is taken to a vote it seems probable that it will result in an even split of 3:3. Joe can use his casting vote, but this is likely to create a great deal of ill-feeling. The three directors most involved in the company's day-to-day running will be split (Joe and Nasser voting for the motion and Gervase against), and this may create further problems.

The continuing decline in profit margins probably means that something will have to be done soon, and it may be that a radical change, such as the one proposed by Joe, is called for. However, if effective change is to be brought about, any proposal really needs the active support of most, if not all, of the directors.

What is the relevance of the individuals' shareholdings? The directors each have an equal vote on the board, but their shareholdings are not the same (this is a quite common arrangement). The individuals' shareholdings could be significant in the annual general meeting where shareholders vote on reappointment of directors, because the proportion of shares held makes a difference to the voting. Suppose Gervase, Eric and Edward feel so strongly that Joe is taking the company in the wrong direction that they try to vote him off the board? (A simple majority – i.e. 50% – of votes is required to vote a director off the board.) Between them they hold 49% of the shares. Provided that Carol and Nasser will vote with Joe, his position is safe (just).

It may be relevant to query Edward's and Eric's retirement arrangements. How soon will they give up taking any active part in the business? Will they pass on their shares to their children? If they were to do this, presumably Eric would transfer all of his holding to Gervase, giving him a total of 34% of the shares, and Edward would split his holding equally between his children Joe and Carol (this would leave Joe with 41.5%, Carol with 17.5% and Nasser with his existing 7%). No one individual would control the company (although Joe and his sister would control a majority of the shares).

Joe is in a very difficult position. Unless he can persuade at least one of the dissenting directors to his way of thinking, the issue is likely to split the board and may leave a residue of ill-feeling, whether or not he exercises his casting vote. He may need to think of a less radical plan to take the business forward, or accept suggestions by other directors on how to address the problem of declining profitability. In the worst case scenario he may need to wait until he inherits sufficient shares to place him in a more secure position.

The case study illustrates a very typical family company scenario. The original founders of a business are often very reluctant to let go of a business that they have spent their working lives building up. Their children may become impatient and may try to reduce the parents' involvement. This type of business arrangement can lead to lasting conflict and very serious consequences at both a personal and business level.

The business illustrated is a limited company, with uneven shareholdings among six members of the same family. Democratic arrangements for voting at board level may not reflect percentage shareholdings. Some of the directors participate more fully in business activities than others. However, it is worth reiterating that all directors are equally responsible in law.

Accounting for listed companies: Additional requirements

Case study 12.1 features a company with six directors, who between them hold all the issued share capital. Listed companies, by contrast, may have thousands of shareholders, employees and creditors, and may be of interest to a very large group of people. The nature of the information published by such companies is clearly of great public significance. Listed companies vary greatly in size – some are surprisingly small – but all are subject to additional accounting requirements.

Listing regulations for quoted companies

Companies are described as 'listed' if they are quoted on a recognised stock exchange. Obtaining a quotation for a company opens up potentially vast sources of capital available through investment in the company's shares. The London Stock Exchange is a highly significant exchange. As well as listing UK based companies (just over 2400 of them at the end of January 2002), the London Stock Exchange has listings for many multinational companies (448 of them at the end of January 2002), such as Volkswagen, Volvo and Sara Lee.

In order to allow investors to trade in shares with a reasonable degree of security, stock exchanges tend to be highly regulated. The London Stock Exchange is no exception; for listed companies there are additional accounting and disclosure requirements beyond those that apply to companies in general. For example, listed companies in the UK are required to issue interim reports which follow six months after the principal annual accounts. A few companies are required to report quarterly (i.e. every three months). In the USA listed companies are required, as a matter of course, to produce quarterly reports. UK listed companies must also issue a preliminary announcement of annual results as soon as they have been approved by the board of directors.

Listed company regulation (the 'listing rules') are handled by the Financial Services Authority (FSA), which took over this responsibility comparatively recently in May 2000.

The annual report for a listed company

The annual report produced by a listed company is often a very long and complex document. It contains all the minimum annual accounting requirements under company law (the profit and loss account, the balance sheet and so on) but also a great deal of additional information. Some of the additional disclosures are voluntary and some are required by other regulations. The annual report is viewed by many listed companies as an important public relations vehicle, and a great deal of care is put into design and presentation. The report is often expensive to produce because of the high quality of paper, photography and graphics used.

Example: EMI Group

The annual reports of EMI Group plc are usually produced to a very high standard. The report for the accounting period to 31 March 2001 is no exception. Its cover is in grey suede-finish paper and it contains several glossy photographs of EMI's best-selling artists. The report is 77 pages long, broken down as follows:

	No. of pages
Highlights of the group's year	2
Chairman's statement	2
Glossy photographs	15
Graphs and general performance reviews	6
Financial review by finance director	2
Social responsibility section	2
Information about the board of directors	2
Directors' report*	1
Corporate governance	3
Remuneration report	5
Auditor's report*	1
Principal financial statements*	6
Notes to the financial statements*	26
Five-year summary of results	2
Investor information	1
Index	1

*Only these items are legal requirements.

Many items in the report are provided on a voluntary basis – for example, the photographs and the social responsibility section (some companies provide much more than others on issues such as social and environmental responsibility). Other items are required because EMI Group plc is a listed company. There are extensive additional disclosures on corporate governance and directors' remuneration. The background to these disclosures is explained in the next sub-section.

It should be noted that the annual report of EMI Group contains financial statements relating to all the companies in the EMI Group. Where a company owns several others it is usually necessary in law to prepare **consolidated financial statements**, which bring together the results and the assets and liabilities of all companies under common control. Therefore, the profit and loss account in EMI's accounts is referred to as a 'consolidated profit and loss account'.

Corporate governance requirements

Corporate governance is the system by which companies are directed and controlled. In the UK corporate governance of listed companies became the subject of much debate during the 1990s. The debate was provoked by several major company scandals that took place towards the end of the 1980s. Failures of governance were implicated in many of the scandals, and there was a general feeling that listed companies had to improve the way their boards were run.

Various reports and recommendations on corporate governance were issued (the *Cadbury Report* in 1992 the *Greenbury Report* in 1995 and the *Hampel Report* in 1998). Finally, in 1998 the London Stock Exchange published the final version of the various reports combined in *Principles of Good Governance and Code of Best Practice*, better known as the 'Combined Code'.

The detailed contents of the Combined Code are beyond the scope of this book, but broadly the Code addresses four areas:

- directors
- directors' remuneration
- relations with shareholders
- accountability and audit.

Each listed company is required to produce, as part of its annual report, statements on its corporate governance and on directors' remuneration.

Chapter summary

This chapter contains information about the nature of companies in the UK, shares, directors, financial statements and the general regulatory structures surrounding financial reporting by companies. There is a great deal of very detailed regulation pertaining to companies, and this chapter provides only an outline of it. Some of the website references listed below provide more information for those students who wish to obtain more details.

The need for publication of accounting information by companies was explained at the outset of the chapter as part of an introduction to limited liability companies. It was followed by an explanation of some of the key features of the legal requirements relating to companies, including the role of directors and the company audit. Accounting standards form part of the overall structure of regulation; they were mentioned briefly, but detailed consideration of their requirements is beyond the scope of this book.

Company law requirements for the presentation of financial information in the profit and loss account and balance sheet were outlined. The case study for the chapter demonstrated the preparation of the key financial statements in the form required for compliance with company law, in the context of a small family business whose board of directors face a difficult decision.

The final section of the chapter examined the additional regulation of accounting information required in the case of listed companies. Students should appreciate the reasons why the requirements relating to this class of company are so much more stringent than those that apply to smaller, less economically significant businesses.

It may take time to assimilate the information contained in the chapter. Students can increase their familiarity with company financial reporting by working through the exercises at the end of the chapter. However, reading the financial press will also help. Reading the *Financial Times* (FT) may present some challenges to understanding at first, but it will undoubtedly increase general business knowledge very quickly. A good way to start may be to read the *FT* once a week, or to start with the business pages of any of the broadsheet newspapers (e.g. *The Times, The Independent* or *The Guardian*).

Answer to self-test question 12.1

Workings for this question comprise the following:

1. *Selling and distribution costs*

	£
Selling costs	63 477
Distribution costs	54 460
	117 937

2. *Proposed dividend*. There are 20 000 shares in issue. A 25p dividend for each share gives a total of £5000 to be paid. Note that this will be included in current liabilities on the balance sheet.

3. *Tangible fixed assets*

	£
Premises at net book value	65 700
Vehicles at net book value	44 430
Fixtures and fittings at net book value	17 260
	127 390

4. *Other creditors*

	£
Creditor for corporation tax	19 500
Creditor for dividend	5 000
	24 500

5. *Reserves*

	£
At 1 April 20X1	161 479
Profit for the year	40 685
	202 164

Uppingham Telephones Limited: Draft profit and loss account for the year ending 31 March 20X2

	£
Turnover	717 216
Cost of sales	(509 582)
Gross profit	207 634
Selling and distribution costs (working 1)	(117 937)
Administrative expenses	(24 512)
Profit on ordinary activities before taxation	65 185
Taxation	(19 500)
Profit on ordinary activities after taxation	45 685
Dividends:	
Proposed (working 2)	(5 000)
Profit for the financial year	40 685

Uppingham Telephones Limited: Draft balance sheet at 31 March 20X2

	£	£
Fixed assets		
Intangible assets	35 866	
Tangible assets (working 3)	127 390	
		163 256
Current assets		
Stock	42 370	
Debtors	82 026	
Cash at bank	13 222	
	137 618	

Creditors: amounts falling due within one year
Trade creditors   39 210
Other creditors (working 4)   24 500
                                                                                           63 710

Net current assets   73 908
Total assets less current liabilities   237 164
Creditors: amounts falling due after more than one year   (15 000)
                                                                                                        222 164

Capital and reserves
Share capital   20 000
Reserves (working 5)   202 164
                                                                                                        222 164

Internet resources

The internet can be used to find out a great deal of information about UK companies and company law.

www.londonstockexchange.com – a very comprehensive site containing detailed information about share prices, stock exchange statistics and data relating to individual companies.

www.dti.gov.uk – this is the website of the Department of Trade and Industry. It contains detailed reports on the recent Company Law Review.

www.companieshouse.gov.uk – the website of Companies House. Some of the detailed information about individual companies is obtainable only upon payment of a fee, but there is some free information about companies. Also, the site contains a very good Frequently Asked Questions section and a lot of information about the law relating to companies.

www.hemscott.com – this is the website of the Hemmington Scott company information service. It is a very extensive resource that offers a large amount of free information about every UK listed company (but note that it does not include information about overseas companies listed on the London Stock Exchange).

Many individual listed companies, including practically all of the really large ones, have their own websites. Using a good search engine, such as Google, it is usually possible to find the website address. Alternatively, some companies have links through the Hemmington Scott website referred to above. One of the easiest and quickest ways to find out a company website address is to access the company phone number through Hemmington Scott and then ring up the company and ask for the address of the website.

Exercises

The answers to many of the exercises are set out later in this chapter. However, where the exercise number is followed by 'A' the answer is available only to lecturers. Remember that additional exercises (with answers) are available to students on the book's website.

12.1   Two of the following four statements are correct:

1. Directors must prepare the company's accounts themselves.

2. Directors take complete responsibility for the preparation of accounts.

3. Directors may be guilty of a criminal offence if the accounts do not present a true and fair view.

4. Directors may be guilty of a criminal offence if it is proven that they have defrauded creditors.

The correct statements are:

a) 3 and 4

b) 2 and 4

c) 1 and 2

d) 1 and 3.

12.2A   Three of the following six statements are correct:

1. The audit report of a company states that the accounts are correct.

2. A private limited company does not have to make any information available to the public.

3. A public limited company must have an authorised share capital of £50 000.

4. The minimum number of shareholders in a private limited company is two.

5. Each ordinary share carries the right to a vote at the annual general meeting of the company.

6. A company does not have to issue all of its authorised share capital.

The correct statements are:

a) 1, 3 and 5

b) 1, 2 and 4

c) 2, 4 and 6

d) 3, 5 and 6.

12.3   Bayliss Chandler Limited has an authorised share capital of £30 000, split into 50p shares. Two-thirds of the shares are issued. In the year ending 31 May 20X3 a dividend of 6p per share is declared.
      Ambrose owns 10% of the issued shares in Bayliss Chandler Limited. What is the value of Ambrose's dividend for the year ending 31 May 20X3?

a) £180

b) £120

c) £240

d) £360.

12.4A   Western Gadgets Limited has an authorised share capital of £24 000 denominated in 25p shares; 20 000 shares are issued. In the year ending 30 April 20X6 an interim dividend of 2p per share and a final dividend of 2.5p per share were paid.
      Joan owns shares in Western Gadgets Limited with a nominal value of £1500. What is the value of Joan's dividend for the year ending 30 April 20X6?

a) £270

b) £150

c) £225

d) £67.50.

12.5 Peachey plc has an authorised and issued share capital of £60 000 denominated in 25p shares. On 13 May 20X6 Carina, a shareholder, sells half of her total shareholding of 8000 shares to her sister Cathy.

Peachey's accounting year-end is 31 December. In the year ending 31 December 20X6 the company declares dividends of 10% of nominal value. Half the dividend is paid on 31 March 20X6 and the remainder on 30 September 20X6.

What amount of dividend do Carina and Cathy receive in the year ending 31 December 20X6?

a) Carina receives £600; Cathy receives £200

b) Carina receives £400; Cathy receives £400

c) Carina receives £100; Cathy receives £100

d) Carina receives £150; Cathy receives £50.

12.6A Parlabane Limited has an authorised share capital of 50 000 50p shares. Of these, 42 500 have been issued. In the year ending 31 December 20X4 a dividend of 2p per share is proposed, but it has not been paid by the year-end.

Jonah owns 13 000 shares in Parlabane Limited. What is the total dividend payable and how much is payable to Jonah personally?

a) Total dividend payable £850; payable to Jonah £260.

b) Total dividend payable £1000; payable to Jonah £260

c) Total dividend payable £425; payable to Jonah £130

d) Total dividend payable £500; payable to Jonah £130

12.7 Butterthwaite plc has issued share capital on 1 January 20X1, as follows:

● ordinary share capital: 68 000 £1 ordinary shares

● preference share capital: £20 000 6% cumulative preference shares.

On 31 January the company issued a further 12 000 £1 ordinary shares. The interim (paid 30 April 20X1) and final ordinary dividend amount to 5p per share in total. In 20X0 the company failed to pay its preference dividend, but in 20X1 finds that it can meet its obligations in full.

What is the total amount of dividend payable by Butterthwaite plc in respect of the year ending 31 December 20X1?

a) £5800

b) £5200

c) £6400

d) £4600.

12.8A Penge and Purley plc have in issue at 31 December 20X8:

● 138 000 ordinary shares of 50p each

● 40 000 8% preference shares of £1 each, issued on 1 July 20X8.

Derek owns 3250 ordinary shares in the company, and 1000 of the £1 preference shares. An interim dividend of 2.7p per ordinary share was declared and paid, and a final dividend of 3.7p per ordinary share was proposed. The preference dividend was also paid.

What is Derek's total dividend from the company for the year ending 31 December 20X8?

a) £184

b) £288

c) £144

d) £248.

12.9   The directors of Solar Bubble plc, a trading company, have asked the company's chief accountant to prepare a draft profit and loss account for the year ending 31 January 20X4 in time for them to discuss it at their board meeting on 15 February. The directors prefer to have the information presented in the same way as in the annual financial statements.

The chief accountant identifies the following relevant balances:

	£
Administrative expenses	73 959
Opening stock	51 240
Interest payable	1 977
Sales	975 420
Selling and distribution costs	80 714
Purchases	603 493
Closing stock	57 210

Note the following:

1. £6000 has to be accrued in respect of sales commission for the year ending 31 January 20X4.

2. The corporation tax charge for the year is estimated at £60 625.

3. A preference dividend on the £10 000 8% preference shares must be accrued, and also the directors have proposed paying a final dividend of 5p per share on the 100 000 ordinary shares in issue. No other dividends have been paid in the year.

4. Of the administrative expenses, £1270 relates to prepayment of insurance.

The chief accountant will be using the following format for the draft profit and loss account:

Turnover
Cost of sales
Gross profit or loss
Selling and distribution costs
Administrative expenses
Operating profit
Interest payable and similar charges
Profit or loss on ordinary activities before taxation
Tax on profit or loss on ordinary activities
Profit or loss on ordinary activities after taxation
Dividends
Retained profit or loss.

You are required to prepare the draft profit and loss account for Solar Bubble plc for the year ending 31 January 20X4.

12.10A Downside Green Limited has the following balances relating to its position at 31 December 20X5:

	£
Overdraft	7 746
Share capital	100 000
Loan repayable 31 December 20X9	100 000
Debtors	916 278
Cash in hand	260
Intangible fixed assets at net book value	80 000
Trade creditors	868 462
Reserves	1 850 824
Tangible fixed assets at net book value	1 082 184
Stocks	841 740
Fixed asset investments	24 860
Other creditors (all current liabilities)	18 290

The directors wish to see how the balance sheet will be presented when it is sent to shareholders. Downside Green's financial controller intends to use the following balance sheet format:

Fixed Assets
Intangible assets
Tangible assets
Investments
Current asssets
Stocks
Debtors
Cash at bank and in hand
Creditors: Amounts falling due within one year
Bank loans and overdrafts
Trade creditors
Other creditors
Net current assets
Total assets less current liabilities
Creditors: Amounts falling due after more than one year
Capital and reserves
Share capital
Reserves

You are required to prepare the balance sheet for Downside Green Limited for the year ending 31 December 20X5 in the format requested by the directors.

12.11 Brighton Magnets Limited has the following balances in its books at 31 August 20X9:

	£
Closing stock	186 420
Delivery vans at net book value	120 000
Secretarial costs	51 498
Electricity (admin. office)	12 491
Trade creditors	219 411
Factory and plant at net book value	2 518 000

	£
Reserves at 1 September 20X8	1 557 172
Share capital: £1 ordinary shares	800 000
Administration office: phone charges	6 964
Interest payable	1 207
Salespersons' salaries	64 299
Delivery van depreciation	12 000
Other selling and distribution costs	5 911
Office rental	42 704
Other administrative expenses	36 075
Sales	3 706 842
Interest receivable	644
Depreciation of office computer equipment	8 390
Salespersons' commission	12 270
Office manager's salary	21 704
Directors' remuneration	59 200
Delivery van expenses	24 470
Debtors	321 706
Office equipment at net book value	151 020
Cash at bank	18 290
Cost of sales	2 712 350
Other operating income	12 900

Adjustments are required as follows:

1. Corporation tax on the profits for the year is estimated at £216 470.

2. Dividends of 5p per share should be included in the accounts.

You are required to prepare a profit and loss account for Brighton Magnets Limited at 31 August 20X9 and a balance sheet at that date. Both financial statements are to be presented in an appropriate Companies Act format.

12.12 Two of the following statements are correct:

1. Listed companies are obliged to produce a social responsibility report as part of their annual report.

2. Consolidated financial statements bring together the results and assets and liabilities of all group companies.

3. Compliance with the requirements of the Combined Code is compulsory for listed companies.

4. Listed company regulation is handled by the London Stock Exchange.

The correct statements are:

a) 1 and 2
b) 2 and 3
c) 3 and 4
d) 1 and 4.

Answers to exercises

12.1 It is true that directors take complete responsibility for the preparation of accounts, but they do not have to actually prepare the accounts themselves.

They may delegate the preparation to others, but the directors take ultimate responsibility for ensuring that the accounts present a true and fair view, and that they are filed on time. It is not a criminal offence to produce accounts that fail to present a true and fair view. However, directors can be subject to criminal sanctions for failing to prepare and file accounts, and they may be guilty of a criminal offence if it can be proven that they have deliberately defrauded creditors. Statements 2 and 4 are, therefore, correct, so the answer is b).

12.3   Bayliss Chandler Limited has 60 000 authorised shares (£30 000 / 50p) – two-thirds of these are in issue, i.e. 40 000 shares. Ambrose owns 10% of the issued capital, i.e. 4000 shares. He is entitled to a dividend of 6p per share: 4000 × 6p = £240. The correct answer, therefore, is c).

12.5   A holding of 8000 shares in Peachey plc is equivalent to a nominal value of 8000 × 25p = £2000. The total dividend payable for the year is 10% of nominal value, therefore the holder of 8000 shares will receive 10% × £2000 = £200, half on 31 March 20X6 and half on 30 September 20X6.

At 31 March 20X6 Carina owns all 8000 shares and will receive £100 in dividend. At 30 September 20X6 Carina owns 4000 of the shares and her sister Cathy owns 4000. Therefore, they share the dividend, receiving £50 each. In total for the year, Carina receives £150 in dividend and Cathy receives £50. The correct answer, therefore, is d).

12.7   Butterthwaite plc

	£
80 000 ordinary shares × 5p per share =	4 000
Preference dividend for 20X1: £20 000 × 6%	1 200
Arrears of preference dividend for 20X0	1 200
Total	6 400

The correct answer, therefore, is c).

12.9   Workings comprise the following:

1. *Cost of sales*

	£
Opening stock	51 240
Add: purchases	603 493
	654 733
Less: closing stock	(57 210)
Cost of sales	597 523

2. *Selling and distribution costs*

	£
As stated in the list of balances	80 714
Add: accrued commission	6 000
	86 714

3. *Administrative expenses*

	£
As stated in the list of balances	73 959
Less: prepaid insurance	(1 270)
	72 689

Solar Bubble plc: Draft profit and loss account for the year ending

31 January 20X4

	£
Turnover	975 420
Cost of sales (working 1)	(597 523)
Gross profit	377 897
Selling and distribution costs (working 2)	(86 714)
Administrative expenses (working 3)	(72 689)
Operating profit	218 494
Interest payable and similar charges	(1 977)
Profit on ordinary activities before taxation	216 517
Taxation	(60 625)
Profit on ordinary activities after taxation	155 892
Dividends:	
Preference £10 000 × 8%	(800)
Ordinary 100 000 × 5p	(5 000)
Retained profit	150 092

12.11 Workings comprise the following:

1. *Administrative expenses*

	£
Secretarial costs	51 498
Electricity (admin. office)	12 491
Office rental	42 704
Administration office: phone charges	6 964
Depreciation of office computer equipment	8 390
Office manager's salary	21 704
Directors' remuneration	59 200
Other administrative expenses	36 075
	239 026

2. *Selling and distribution costs*

	£
Salespersons' salaries	64 299
Delivery van depreciation	12 000
Other selling and distribution costs	5 911
Salespersons' commission	12 270
Delivery van expenses	24 470
	118 950

Note: it is often a matter of judgement as to how expenses are allocated between selling and distribution cost and administrative expenses.

3. *Dividends payable*

800 000 £1 ordinary shares at 5p per share = £40 000

4. *Tangible assets*

	£
Factory and plant at net book value	2 518 000
Delivery vans at net book value	120 000
Office equipment at net book value	151 020
	2 789 020

5. *Other creditors*

	£
Taxation	216 470
Dividend	40 000
	256 470

6. *Reserves*

	£
Reserves at 1 September 20X8	1 557 172
Profit for the year	482 383
	2 039 555

Brighton Magnets Limited: Profit and loss account for the year ending 31 August 20X9

	£
Turnover	3 796 842
Cost of sales	(2 712 350)
Gross profit	1 084 492
Selling and distribution costs (working 2)	(118 950)
Administrative expenses (working 1)	(239 026)
Other operating income	12 900
Operating profit	739 416
Interest receivable and similar income	644
Interest payable and similar charges	(1 207)
Profit on ordinary activities before taxation	738 853
Taxation	(216 470)
Profit on ordinary activities after taxation	522 383
Dividends:	
Proposed (working 3)	(40 000)
Profit for the financial year	482 383

Brighton Magnets Limited: Balance sheet at 31 August 20X9

	£	£
Fixed assets		
Tangible assets (working 4)		2 789 020
Current assets		
Stock	186 420	
Debtors	321 706	
Cash at bank	18 290	
	526 416	
Creditors: Amounts falling due within one year		
Trade creditors	219 411	
Other creditors (working 5)	256 470	
	475 811	
Net current assets		50 535
Total assets less current liabilities		2 839 555
Capital and reserves		
Share capital		800 000
Reserves (working 6)		2 039 555
		2 839 555

12.12
- Statement 1 is false: listed companies are not obliged to produce a social responsibility report as part of their annual report.

- Statement 2 is true: consolidated financial statements do bring together the results and the assets and liabilities of all group companies.

- Statement 3 is true: compliance with the Combined Code is compulsory for all listed companies.

- Statement 4 is false: listed company regulation is handled by the Financial Services Authority (although until recently it was handled by the London Stock Exchange).

Statements 2 and 3 are correct, therefore the correct answer is b).

13

UNDERSTANDING FINANCIAL REPORTS: ANALYSIS OF TRENDS

AIMS AND LEARNING OUTCOMES

Aim of the chapter

To develop a range of skills that assist in the understanding of financial reports for various types of business.

Learning outcomes

After reading the chapter and completing the related exercises, students should:

- Understand the potential usefulness of financial reports to various interest groups.
- Understand the principal features of the analysis of trends in financial statements.
- Be able to perform an analysis based on horizontal and/or vertical analysis of financial statements.
- Understand the problems that can arise in comparing businesses with each other.

Techniques of analysis will be developed further in Chapter 14.

Introduction

Probably the most important aim of this book is to help students appreciate that financial information actually means something. The formal figures that are set out in reports may not look very interesting in themselves, but the underlying reality that the numbers symbolise is almost always fascinating, especially for those involved.

The case studies used in earlier chapters have all attempted to illustrate the fact that accounting information is actually used by real people as a means of understanding what is going on in business. For example:

- Jimmy Bowden, in the case study for Chapter 7, needed accounting information to help him understand how much a downturn in trade had affected his business profitability.
- Richard, in the case study for Chapter 8, was anxious to find out whether or not his business could survive his disastrous decision to trade with a man who would not, in the end, pay him.
- Joe Daley, in the case study for Chapter 12, was preparing accounting information in advance of a board meeting that promised to be very difficult and contentious.

This chapter and Chapter 14 look much more closely at the analysis of financial information as a route to understanding. The two chapters cover a range of techniques and calculations. However, those students who are less than totally confident about their numeracy skills should not be put off; none of the techniques covered in the chapters involves anything more difficult than simple arithmetical skills of the type already utilised. The important skill, in fact, lies in the interpretation of the results; this is a skill best achieved through practice.

In this chapter we will first briefly examine the various groups of people who are interested in accounting information, the reasons for their interest, and the aspects that might be particularly useful to them. Then the chapter proceeds to examine simple analytical techniques that compare one figure or group of figures with another. (Note that this chapter of the book considers the analysis of the formal financial reports covered in Chapters 6–12 inclusive. In the third and final part of the book (beginning with Chapter 15) attention will be turned to the type of management accounting information that is generated within a business for use by owners and managers in making plans and in controlling the business activities.)

Usefulness of financial reports to various interest groups

Owners and investors

Previous chapters have included several examples of sole trader owners using periodic financial information to inform them about the progress of their business. However, it must be recognised that most unincorporated business owners will have available to them other, more comprehensive, sources of information about their business performance. For example, an annual financial statement does not provide any information about the state of the business's order book, but the current levels of demand for products and services would be regarded by business owners as an absolutely vital means of assessing business prospects. So, although it is not unrealistic to suggest that owners of businesses use annual financial reports as aids to understanding, it should be recognised that they have other, potentially more useful, sources of information available to them.

The situation is rather different, however, for investors in limited companies. Unless they are also directors, they do not have any privileges of access to information beyond their right to receive the annual report and accounts. An investor who buys 100 shares in Marks & Spencer plc, for example (or any other listed company), obtains some rights (the right to receive a part of any dividend declared and the right to vote at the annual general meeting). However, he or she does not have the right to wander in off the street to the company's head office demanding to see the monthly accounts.

Investors in companies who do not have access to information other than the annual report and accounts are likely to be interested in the answers to some or all of the following questions:

- How is my investment doing?
- Should I buy more shares / sell the shares I've already got / hold on to the investment I've already got?
- Is the dividend likely to increase?
- What are the chances of the company going out of business?

Potential investors in a business

People who are thinking of investing in a business will usually take steps to obtain the most recent financial reports. If the company is quoted, access to this type of information is usually very easy. Most quoted companies have websites, and many of them contain the most recent published financial reports for the company; they may also contain other useful pieces of information like the preliminary announcement of results and the six-monthly interim reports. Unquoted companies, as we saw in Chapter 12, are obliged to file accounting information with the Registrar of Companies, and it is possible to obtain copies of this information fairly quickly in exchange for a fee of a few pounds.

It may, however, be impossible to obtain any financial information about other forms of business because sole traders and partnerships are not obliged to make information public, although if a business is interested in attracting buyers there is an incentive to provide recent, reliable financial information to potential investors. But it should be recognised that financial information such as the profit and loss account and balance sheet is essentially backward looking; these statements report events that have already occurred, and these may not be a reliable guide to what is going to happen in the future.

Potential investors tend to be looking for answers to some or all of the following questions:

- What are the risks involved in this business? How likely would I be to lose money? Would my investment be safe?
- How much can I make from investing in this business? Will the return be better than I could make if I were to put the money into some other business, or leave it in the bank, or risk it on a bet on the horses/dogs/a card game?
- What are my chances of getting seriously rich?

Creditors

In Chapter 12 (Example 12.1) we looked at the case of Tommy, who supplied goods on credit to a limited company but was unable to obtain payment for them before the company became insolvent. Businesses and individuals who supply goods on credit to limited companies take the risk that they will not be paid. As noted in the discussion in Chapter 12, one of the ways of reducing the risk is to examine the financial reports of a company to assess its financial condition.

Suppliers of goods and services, like anyone else, are entitled to obtain the financial information that is filed at Companies House (although remember that this information is quite limited in the case of small companies). Alternatively, they may prefer to use the services of a credit agency, which, for a fee, supplies a detailed report on the creditworthiness of a named company. (See, for example, the range of services offered by Dun and Bradstreet: **www.dnb.com**.)

In the case of sole traders and partnerships, there is no publicly available source of financial information, and suppliers must base their decision on whether or not to offer credit on other factors: they may, for example, ask the trader or partnership to supply references from some reputable person like a bank manager.

If a bank or other financial institution lends to a business it becomes a creditor, possibly for the long term. In such cases, the bank is usually in a position to demand financial information, regardless of whether the business is a sole trader, partnership or company, and indeed, this may be part of the lending deal.

When undertaking an analysis of financial reports, creditors are interested in obtaining answers to the following questions:

- How likely is it that I will be paid?
- How likely is it that I will be paid on time?
- Will my interest (where applicable) be paid regularly?
- Is there a risk that this business will go bust before I get paid?

Financial statements, especially those produced by limited companies, tend to be principally oriented towards the information needs of investors and owners. However, other interested parties such as creditors will also find a great deal of information that is relevant to their needs.

Analytical techniques: Changes in figures

The most straightforward analytical technique can be one of the most effective: comparing two or more figures with each other to assess the differences between them.

Example 13.1 Ilse is a sole trader who runs a shop selling imported fabrics and furnishings. Her sales figures for the three years ending 31 March 20X4 are as follows:

	20X4 £	20X3 £	20X2 £
Sales	217 300	209 220	204 240

It does not take a financial wizard to see that Ilse's sales have gone up between 20X2 and 20X4. Sometimes, this kind of straightforward pointing out of the obvious is all that's need in financial analysis. However, the analysis could be refined, without much additional difficulty, by calculating the percentage increase year-on-year, as follows.

Between 20X2 and 20X3

Sales have risen by £209 220 − £204 240 = £4980, which can be calculated as a percentage of the 20X2 figure, as follows:

$$\frac{4\,980}{204\,240} \times 100 = 2.4\%$$

Between 20X3 and 20X4

Sales have risen by £217 300 − £209 220 = £8080, which can be calculated as a percentage of the 20X3 figure, as follows:

$$\frac{8\,080}{209\,220} \times 100 = 3.9\%$$

What does this mean?

By calculating the percentage increases we have added a little to our slender stock of knowledge about Ilse's sales. If we know, for example, from local Chamber of Commerce information, that traders in Ilse's part of town have experienced an average annual growth in sales of 8% between 20X2 and 20X4 it suggests that Ilse's business performance is in relative decline.

In order to increase the value of the information about Ilse's sales, we need some point of comparison. The point of comparison may come from outside the business (e.g. the information provided by the Chamber of Commerce) or from inside the business. For example, suppose Ilse tells you, as her new financial adviser, that she invested a lot of additional working capital in a new line of stock during 20X2 and 20X3, expecting to boost sales by 20% per annum, you might well conclude that her efforts to expand the business had been relatively unsuccessful. A great deal depends upon the context of the financial information.

Analytical techniques: Horizontal and trend analysis

Horizontal analysis is a fancy piece of terminology describing, essentially, the type of analysis we carried out above on Ilse's sales figures. Where there are at least two years' worth of information, it is possible to conduct some type of horizontal analysis. In some cases several years' worth of information is available, and it becomes possible to carry out a **trend analysis**. This type of analysis includes figures over several years and attempts to track longer-term business trends.

Moving rapidly up the size scale from Ilse's business we will now consider the publicly available information provided by the EMI Group plc. Listed companies commonly provide five-year summaries of information (sometimes the summaries even extend to a ten-year period). In the next example, we will examine some elements of the five-year record of information for EMI.

Example 13.2 The following table shows extracts from EMI Group plc's financial statements for the year ending 31 March 2001.

	2001 £m	2000 £m	1999 £m	1998 £m	1997 £m
Turnover	2 672.7	2 386.5	2 373.5	2 352.7	2 511.5
Operating profit	332.5	290.6	269.7	340.9	374.8
Interest	103.0	73.7	72.0	64.3	19.0

This is just a small part of the information disclosed by EMI Group plc in its annual financial statements. What does it tell us?

Scanning the turnover line quickly we can tell that the business has improved its sales each year over the period since 1998. If turnover increases we could expect to see a corresponding improvement in profit figures. However, profitability is far more uneven than sales. The highest reported operating profit figure was in 1997, the earliest year reported. Interest charges over the period have risen steeply, with particularly sharp increases between 1997 and 1998 and between 2000 and 2001 suggesting that borrowings have increased substantially.

We can extend the horizontal analysis by calculating year-on-year percentage increases, in the same way as for Ilse's business. The percentage increases can be neatly presented in a table like this one:

Annual percentage increases (decreases) in a selection of key figures: EMI Group plc

	2001 %	2000 %	1999 %	1998 %
Turnover	12.0	0.5	0.9	(6.3)
Operating profit	14.4	7.7	(20.9)	(9.0)
Interest	40.6	2.4	12.0	338.4

The horizontal analysis using percentages highlights some of the general trends in the business. Although turnover has risen, most of the rise has been in the last year, and there is a general downward trend in profitability. Interest has risen very substantially, suggesting a large increase in borrowings over the period.

The chairman's statement for the year emphasises the positives (chairmen's statements usually do), but notes 'a weak worldwide music market' and that 'market conditions will remain highly competitive and somewhat unpredictable'. We can surmise from these statements, combined with an examination of some of the figures, that EMI Group plc is facing a difficult commercial environment with uncertain levels of demand for its products.

Self-test question 13.1 (answer at the end of the chapter)

Jamal is a sole trader selling a range of pre-packaged foods. He has a small food processing factory and employs several staff. Three years ago in 20X4 he made the decision to employ a full-time sales manager. The manager, Jared, claimed at the interview that he would be able to achieve 15% sales increases each year.

Jared is asking for a substantial increase in his annual salary effective from the start of 20X8. He tells Jamal that he thinks he's worth it because of the contribution he's made to the business. The final accounts for the year ending 31 December 20X8 have just been finished in draft form by the accountant. Jamal is now reviewing his annual sales figures, which are available as far back as 20X0 when he started the business. The following table shows sales for each year:

Year	£
20X0	250 031
20X1	347 266
20X2	441 179
20X3	531 150
20X4	523 622
20X5	545 331
20X6	590 942
20X7	679 244
20X8	771 485

Examine the horizontal trends in Jamal's sales figures and, briefly, advise him on whether or not Jared's claim for an increased salary appears justified.

Some problems with horizontal analysis

There are two principal problems which are likely to arise in respect of horizontal analysis, relating to changes in the business and the effects of inflation.

Changes in the business

Very rapid changes can take place in business. These may mean that figures are not really comparable over a period of years. Also, new accounting rules and standards may make a difference to the presentation of figures. The figures of the EMI Group plc that we examined earlier have been adjusted for these effects so that a proper and meaningful comparison can be made. In the case of unlisted companies and smaller businesses, which do not usually include five years' worth of comparative figures in their financial statements, the analyst must be careful to make any necessary adjustments.

Failure to take the effects of inflation into account

Although it is possible to adjust accounting figures for the effects of inflation, this is not usually done in UK accounting. In recent years the general rate of inflation in the economy has not been high, and its effects are often regarded as negligible. However, this can be misleading, as the following example shows:

Example 13.3 A five-year analysis of the sales of Trevor Fine Art Productions Limited shows the following figures:

	20X8 £	20X7 £	20X6 £	20X5 £	20X4 £
Sales	683 084	657 469	634 868	617 576	590 530
Percentage increase on previous year	3.9%	3.6%	2.8%	4.6%	—

Between 20X4 and 20X8 sales have increased in total by the following percentage:

$$\frac{£683\,084 - 590\,530}{590\,530} \times 100 = 15.7\%$$

Looking at the individual years we can see that there has been an increase each year. So far, so good, but if we take inflation into account the picture changes somewhat. Suppose that in each year between 20X4 and 20X8 the average rate of inflation in the economy has been 3% per annum. We can see that in most years the sales increases were only slightly above inflation and the increase between 20X5 and 20X6 was actually a little below the rate of inflation. The sales increases are not as impressive as they first appear to be.

Analytical techniques: Vertical analysis and common size analysis

Vertical analysis is a simple analytical technique that can be useful and informative. It involves expressing each figure in the profit and loss account and balance sheet as a percentage of one key figure (sales in the profit and loss account and – usually – net assets in the balance sheet). The next example explains the application of vertical analysis.

Example 13.4 Bore & Hole Limited makes mining equipment. The company profit and loss account and balance sheet for 20X6 are shown below, together with an extra column of percentage figures. In the profit and loss account all percentages are calculated by reference to the value of sales, and in the balance sheet by reference to the net assets total.

Bore & Hole Limited: Profit and loss account for the year ending 31 December 20X6

	£	%
Turnover	4 490 370	100.0
Cost of sales	(3 521 348)	(78.4)
Gross profit	969 022	21.6
Administrative expenses	(454 432)	(10.1)
Distribution and selling costs	(407 480)	(9.1)
Other operating income	16 210	0.4
Operating profit	123 320	2.8
Interest payable and similar charges	(33 900)	(0.8)
Profit on ordinary activities before taxation	89 420	2.0
Taxation	(26 461)	(0.6)
Profit on ordinary activities after taxation	62 959	1.4
Dividends	(40 000)	(0.9)
Retained profit for the year	22 959	0.5

Note that each item is calculated as a percentage of sales (to one decimal point): For example:

$$\frac{\text{Administrative expenses}}{\text{Sales}} \times 100 = \frac{454\,432}{4\,490\,370} \times 100 = 10.1\%$$

Bore & Hole Limited: Balance sheet at 31 December 20X6

	£	£	%
Fixed assets		3 975 750	99.1
Current assets			
Stock	586 404		14.6
Debtors	430 580		10.7
Cash at bank	10 110		0.2
	1 027 094		25.5
Creditors: amounts falling due within one year	(599 212)		(14.9)
Net current assets		427 882	10.6
Total assets less current liabilities		4 403 632	109.7
Creditors: amounts falling due after more than one year		(390 000)	(9.7)
		4 013 632	100.0
Capital and reserves			
Share capital		800 000	19.9
Reserves		3 213 632	80.1
		4 013 632	100.0

What does the vertical analysis statement tell us? It is a single period statement only, so its information content is limited. The percentage column is helpful in that it tends to draw attention to the relative size of the figures. For example, we can see from the statement that operating profit as a percentage of sales is only 2.8%, and that retained profit is a mere 0.5% of sales. These percentages suggest that the business is not performing well.

Turning to the balance sheet we can see that it is dominated by fixed assets; this is a manufacturing business, and fixed assets could be expected to be high. Cash is negligible and the business has long-term borrowings of almost 10% of the net asset value.

Common size analysis extends vertical analysis across more than one accounting period. In the next example we will build on our knowledge of Bore & Hole Limited by examining the vertical analysis percentages in the company's profit and loss account over four years.

Example 13.5 The profit and loss account in Example 13.4 shows vertical analysis of all the items, based upon sales, for the year ended 31 December 20X6. Below, the comparative vertical analysis figures are repeated for the 20X6 profit and loss account, and are set alongside the comparative figures for the previous three years.

	20X6 %	20X5 %	20X4 %	20X3 %
Turnover	100.0	100.0	100.0	100.0
Cost of sales	(78.4)	(78.3)	(77.2)	(77.0)
Gross profit	21.6	21.7	22.8	23.0
Administrative expenses	(10.1)	(7.3)	(7.4)	(7.2)
Selling and distribution costs	(9.1)	(10.0)	(9.3)	(9.7)
Other operating income	0.4	0.4	—	—
Operating profit	2.8	4.8	6.1	6.1
Interest payable and similar charges	(0.8)	—	—	—
Profit on ordinary activities before taxation	2.0	4.8	6.1	6.1
Taxation	(0.6)	(1.4)	(1.8)	(1.8)
Profit on ordinary activities after taxation	1.4	3.4	4.3	4.3
Dividends	(0.9)	(2.0)	(2.0)	(2.0)
Retained profit for the year	0.5	1.4	2.3	2.3

This statement is expressed entirely in percentages; it gives no indication as to the value of each component. However, the statement does help understanding by presenting the trends in the figures quite clearly. For example:

- *Gross profit* as a percentage of turnover has fallen in each of the four years. If this trend continues the business could ultimately fail.
- *Administrative expenses* have remained at a fairly constant level compared to turnover for three out of the four years reviewed. Suddenly, however, in 20X6 the percentage leaps. There could be many explanations for this change; for example, perhaps there has been a change of management and the new management are not controlling costs very well. Or, there may have been a major new investment in fixed assets on which related depreciation charges are shown as part of administrative expenses.
- *Interest payable* features for the first time in the 20X6 profit and loss account, suggesting that in previous years borrowings were either non-existent or negligible.
- *Dividends* have remained at a constant percentage of turnover in three of the four years, but the proportion has fallen in 20X6. The shareholders may lose confidence in the company's management if this trend continues.

Overall, although we have relatively little information about the company (compared, for example, with what is available in a full set of financial statements) the common size profit and loss statement does allow the analyst to draw some tentative conclusions about the performance of the business over time.

Comparing businesses with each other

So far in this chapter we have analysed single businesses, generally by reference to the increases and decreases in elements of accounting information over time. However, interested parties will often need to make comparisons between businesses. They can do this by: (a) comparing the results and balance sheets of two or more businesses; (b) comparing the results and balance sheets of a business with industry averages.

Problems in comparison

The regulation surrounding accounting, especially accounting by limited companies, goes some way towards ensuring that financial statements are prepared to the same set of rules and in the same way. The Accounting Standards Board, for example, sets out four key characteristics that accounting information should have:

- relevance
- reliability
- comparability
- understandability.

Comparability is accorded a great deal of importance precisely in order to allow meaningful comparisons between accounting statements. However, despite the best intentions of the regulators, there are often problems in ensuring that a valid comparison can be made. Some of these are briefly described in the following sub-sections.

Differences in accounting policies

Accounting policies are the principles of accounting applied in preparing the financial statements. Despite a fairly extensive level of regulation, there are many areas in which a business can make legitimate choices about the amounts at which items are stated, and the way in which those items are presented. The following example will illustrate the point.

Example 13.6 Spanners Limited and Gasket Limited operate within the same business sector. A financial analyst is examining the results of the companies on behalf of a client. Extracts from their profit and loss accounts show the following information (together with vertical analysis percentages):

	Spanners Limited		Gasket Limited	
	£	%	£	%
Turnover	984 742	100.0	1 096 880	100.0
Cost of sales	673 938	68.4	756 993	69.0
Gross profit	310 804	31.6	339 887	31.0

The companies appear to be similar in size in that they generate similar levels of turnover, and the percentage of gross profit to sales is close. It seems a fair conclusion, on the face of it, that their performance is virtually identical. However, the analyst finds out that the companies' policies on inclusion of costs in cost of sales are not the same. Specifically, Spanners Limited includes depreciation of vehicles within cost of sales, whereas Gasket Limited includes the same type of cost within selling and distribution costs. Gasket's vehicle depreciation is £28 977 for the year under review.

In order to compare like with like the analyst must make an adjustment to Gasket's cost of sales:

$$\text{Adjusted cost of sales} = £28\,977 + £756\,993 = £785\,970$$

Building this adjusted cost into the profit and loss analysis results in the following changes (vertical analysis percentages are recalculated for Gasket Limited):

| | Spanners Limited | | Gasket Limited | |
	£	%	£	%
Turnover	984 742	100.0	1 096 880	100.0
Cost of sales	673 938	68.4	785 970	71.7
Gross profit	310 804	31.6	310 910	28.3

The recalculation makes the comparison appear in a rather different light. Gasket's gross profit is 28.3% of sales, as compared to Spanners' at 31.6%.

Financial statement analysts have to be alert for this type of difference. As the example shows, application of different accounting policies can make a lot of difference. The example illustrates the point in relation to cost classification but there are many other potential areas of difference, including, for example, depreciation and amortisation methods.

Differences in business activities

No two businesses are entirely alike. Comparison of two apparently similar businesses can lead to incorrect conclusions if the differences between the two are not fully appreciated.

Example 13.7 A financial analyst is comparing the results of two companies for 20X7 and 20X6. Pool & Splash Limited and Dive & Float Limited are both involved in swimming pool installation and maintenance. The industry is prospering; a prolonged period of economic growth has led to many more people installing swimming pools in their own homes.

Sales figures for the two companies for 20X7 and 20X6 are as follows:

| | Pool & Splash Limited | | Dive & Float Limited | |
| | 20X7 | 20X6 | 20X7 | 20X6 |
	£	£	£	£
Sales	1 662 997	1 357 549	1 842 791	1 543 360

The analyst calculates that the sales of Pool & Splash Limited have increased by 22.5%, whereas Dive & Float Limited's sales have increased by only 19.4%. On the face of it, Pool & Splash appears to have performed better in terms of sales growth. However, the picture changes when we are supplied with information about the breakdown of sales. Pool & Splash Limited's sales and maintenance contracts are in respect of domestic sales only. Dive & Float Limited, on the other hand, undertakes contract pool maintenance for local authorities. A breakdown of the sales figures shows the following:

	Pool & Splash Limited		Dive & Float Limited	
	20X7	20X6	20X7	20X6
	£	£	£	£
Sales – domestic	1 662 997	1 357 549	1 430 111	1 135 910
Maintenance contracts – local authorities	—	—	412 680	407 450
Total	1 662 997	1 357 549	1 842 791	1 543 360

From the more detailed figures the analyst can calculate a more meaningful comparison. Dive & Float's domestic sales have, in fact, increased by 25.9% as compared to Pool & Splash's increase of 22.5%.

Industry averages may be misleading

Comparison of a single company against a range of industry averages may be misleading.

Example 13.8 Wellington Burke Limited and Ashington Smith Limited are two companies operating in the same industry, but in different parts of England. According to a recent trade survey, the average increase in sales in the industry in the year ending 31 December 20X5 was 13.8%. The two companies show the following levels of sales growth over that period:

- Wellington Burke Limited = 14.2%
- Ashington Smith Limited = 11.6%.

It appears as though Wellington Burke Limited is the clear leader in terms of sales growth. However, the average increase in sales published in the trade survey masks wide regional variations.

- average growth in the north of England = 9.7%
- average growth in the south of England = 17.9%.

If we know that Wellington Burke's operates in the Home Counties, while Ashington Smith is based in Yorkshire, the comparison starts to look different. It appears that, in fact, Ashington Smith Limited may have outperformed other northern based firms in the industry, whereas, relatively speaking, Wellington Burke has underperformed in terms of sales growth.

Comparisons between businesses, then, must be approached with caution, because apparently obvious facts may be misleading.

Self-test question 13.2 (answer at the end of the chapter)

Barnes & Jack Limited and Carleen Baker Limited are competitors in the aquarium supply business. Both companies supply, install and maintain aquariums. Sales figures for the two companies for 20X6 and 20X5 are as follows:

	Barnes & Jack Limited		Carleen Baker Limited	
	20X6	20X5	20X6	20X5
	£	£	£	£
Sales	2 044 032	1 743 906	1 850 490	1 564 774

a) Which company has produced the more impressive growth in sales (calculate growth to one decimal place)?
b) Does the answer differ with the addition of the following information about sales?

Barnes & Jack Limited's sales are principally to the domestic and pet shop market. However, in addition, the company sells to zoos. Sales growth in the latter area has been slow in recent years due to cuts in public funding. Carleen Baker Limited would like to break into the zoo market, but currently supplies only the domestic and pet shop market.

Barnes & Jack's sales to zoos were £450 800 in 20X5, increasing to £488 307 in 20X6.

CASE STUDY 13.1 Financial analysis: BAA plc

The case study for this chapter is relatively short; it is intended to demonstrate some aspects of the trend analysis of financial statements in the context of real company results. Note that many of the points covered in this chapter are also examined in the extended case study presented in Chapter 14.

This case study examines some information taken from the annual report of BAA plc for the year ending 31 March 2001. BAA plc owns and runs seven airports in the UK, and has stakes in several others around the world. The following table presents extracts in respect of the most recent five years from the ten-year financial summary provided in the 2001 annual report.

	2001	2000	1999	1998	1997
Passengers served (in millions)	124.7	117.8	112.5	104.5	98.0
	£m	£m	£m	£m	£m
Sales turnover	2 261	2 192	2 013	1 679	1 373
Profit on ordinary activities before taxation	530	494	507	472	444
Taxation	(129)	(115)	(115)	(203)	(111)
Profit before dividends	398	259	398	277	296
Fixed assets	6 883	6 467	6 457	5 995	4 963

Total assets less current liabilities	6 675	6 394	6 221	5 495	4 905
Creditors due after more than one year	(1 836)	(1 877)	(1 987)	(1 756)	(1 444)
Shareholders' funds [total net assets]	4 839	4 517	4 234	3 739	3 461

Tutorial notes:

1. Note the inclusion of non-financial information in the form of passenger statistics. Many companies include statistics to help to illustrate trends in their activities.

2. The very high taxation charge in 1998 is explained by the one-off charge to a windfall tax imposed by the government. (Of the £203 million tax charge, £102 was windfall tax.)

3. Not all of the lines from the profit and loss account and balance sheet are included in the summary information. Generally, companies include the key figures such as sales turnover and shareholders' funds.

Working to one decimal place for all percentages, the following are required:

1. Calculate and put into a table the percentage increases and decreases from year to year for each line of the figures presented above by BAA plc (i.e. conduct a horizontal trend analysis).

2. Calculate and put into a table common size statistics, as far as it is possible from the figures presented above. Exclude the passenger statistics. Base the profit and loss account common size percentages on sales, and the balance sheet common size percentages on shareholders' funds (net assets).

3. Comment on the fluctuations and trends revealed by the horizontal trends and common size statements.

Case study solution

Horizontal trend analysis

BAA plc: Horizontal trend analysis (% change on previous year) for a selection of key figures for the five years ending 31 March 2001

	2001 %	2000 %	1999 %	1998 %
Passengers served (in millions)	5.9	4.7	7.7	6.6
Sales turnover	3.1	8.9	19.9	22.3
Profit on ordinary activities before taxation	7.3	(2.6)	7.4	6.3
Taxation	12.2	—	(43.3)	82.9
Profit before dividends	53.7	(34.9)	43.7	(6.4)
Fixed assets	6.4	0.2	7.7	20.8
Total assets less current liabilities	4.4	2.8	13.2	12.0
Creditors due after more than one year	(2.2)	(5.5)	13.2	21.6
Shareholders' funds [total net assets]	7.1	6.7	13.2	8.0

Common size statistics

BAA plc: Common size statistics for the five years ending 31 March 2001

	2001 %	2000 %	1999 %	1998 %	1997 %
Sales turnover	100.0	100.0	100.0	100.0	100.0
Profit on ordinary activities before taxation	23.4	22.5	25.2	28.1	32.3
Taxation	5.7	5.2	5.7	12.1	8.1
Profit before dividends	17.6	11.8	19.8	16.5	21.6
Fixed assets	142.2	143.2	152.5	160.3	143.4
Total assets less current liabilities	137.9	141.6	146.9	147.0	141.7
Creditors due after more than one year	(37.9)	(41.6)	(46.9)	(47.0)	(41.7)
Shareholders' funds [total net assets]	100.0	100.0	100.0	100.0	100.0

Commentary on fluctuations and trends

BAA plc's statistics show a year-on-year increase in the number of passengers served, and also in sales turnover. The growth over the five-year period has been substantial. The horizontal trend analysis shows, however, that sales turnover growth has slowed during the five-year period and that growth from 2000 to 2001 was only 3.1%. This analysis shows that there have been considerable fluctuations in the profit before dividends figure; however, BAA plc has succeeded in making a profit before dividends in each of the five years examined.

Growth in net assets (shareholders' funds) has taken place each year, but has slowed towards the end of the five-year period. Long-term creditors, after substantial increases in 1998 and 1999, have reduced slightly in 2000 and 2001.

The common size statistics show that the business has become less profitable over the period. The percentage of profit on ordinary activities before taxation was 32.3% in 1997 but has dropped substantially since then. The abnormally high taxation charge because of the 1998 windfall tax has already been noted. Over the five-year period long-term creditors have diminished relative to net assets. Creditors due after more than one year reached a high of 47% of net assets in 1998 but dropped back to 37.9% by 2001.

In summary, BAA plc appears to be a profitable business that deals with increasing volumes of passenger traffic. However, it has been relatively less profitable towards the end of the five-year period from 1997 to 2001.

Conclusions

An analysis of the type provided above is just a starting off point in understanding the activities of a very large business such as BAA plc. The figures are extracted from an annual report of 76 pages, which contains large amounts of detailed information. In order to gain a full understanding of the activities of the business it is necessary to look in detail not only at a series of annual reports, but also press comment and reports about BAA's activities. Also, it is necessary to understand some of the wider issues that affect those activities. For example, the chairman's statement in the 2001 report refers to the increase in demand for airport services that is expected to take place in the future. BAA plc's future will be affected by this demand, but also by decisions on the building and siting of future airports and new runways. Environmental and social factors will also have a part to play in the government's decisions on expansion of airline services within the UK.

Chapter summary

In this chapter we first examined the usefulness of financial statements to certain interest groups: owners and investors, potential investors and creditors. The rest of the chapter was devoted to the study of a range of simple analysis techniques:

- *Horizontal analysis*: involving analysis of the financial statements of at least two consecutive accounting periods.
- *Trend analysis*: i.e. horizontal analysis taking place over several years.
- *Vertical analysis*: expressing figures in a financial statement as a percentage of one key figure (commonly sales in the profit and loss account and net assets in the balance sheet).
- *Common size analysis*: vertical analysis taking place over more than one accounting period.

We examined some of the problems of comparability that can arise when the analyst attempts to compare accounting information from two or more businesses:

- accounting policies may be different
- there may be differences between the activities of the businesses
- industry averages may be misleading.

The case study for the chapter involved the analysis of some data from a very large UK business. Effective analysis requires the consideration of not only financial data, but also a range of other factors that affect the operations of the business.

Answer to self-test question 13.1

Horizontal trend analysis: Jamal's sales 20X0–20X8

Year	£	Percentage increase (decrease) on previous year
20X0	250 031	—
20X1	347 266	38.9
20X2	441 179	27.0
20X3	531 150	20.4
20X4	523 622	(1.4)
20X5	545 331	4.1
20X6	590 942	8.4
20X7	679 244	14.9
20X8	771 485	13.6

Since the business started sales have increased each year, apart from 20X4 when there was a small drop. Jared claimed at interview that he would be able to increase sales by 15% each year, but it is only in 20X7 and 20X8 that the increase has approached 15%. The early years of the business were characterised by very rapid sales growth, but this had clearly stopped by the time Jared was appointed. It is possible that Jared has made a major contribution to the improvements in sales, but the figures alone do not prove this conclusively.

Jamal's decision on Jared's salary increase will depend on the answers to some of the following questions:

- To what extent has Jared been responsible for the recent improvements in sales trends?
- Are there other market factors at work (for example, has demand in the market for pre-packaged foods strengthened)?
- Has Jamal set performance targets for Jared, and have these been met?

Answer to self-test question 13.2

a) *Sales increase*
The increase in the sales figures for the companies are:

$$\text{Barnes \& Jack Limited} = \frac{(2\,044\,032 - 1\,743\,906)}{1\,743\,906} \times 100 = 17.2\%$$

$$\text{Carleen Baker Limited} = \frac{(1\,850\,490 - 1\,564\,774)}{1\,564\,774} \times 100 = 18.3\%$$

Carleen Baker's sales growth is slightly higher.

b) *Extra information*
The additional information allows for a more detailed breakdown of Barnes & Jack Limited's sales, as follows:

	Barnes & Jack Limited		
	20X6	20X5	Change
	£	£	%
Domestic and shop market	1 555 725	1 293 106	20.3
Zoos	488 307	450 800	8.3
	2 044 032	1 743 906	17.2

From this analysis, it appears that Barnes & Jack Limited have done slightly better in terms of sales growth than Carleen Baker Limited in the areas of their business that are directly comparable.

Exercises

The answers to many of the exercises are set out later in this chapter. However, where the exercise number is followed by 'A' the answer is available only to lecturers. Remember that additional exercises (with answers) are available to students on the book's website.

13.1   Ronald's trading business operates from a shop in a large city centre. Extracts from Ronald's most recent profit and loss accounts for 20X4 and 20X3 show the following key figures:

	20X4	20X3
	£	£
Sales	110 450	95 544
Cost of sales	(72 058)	(62 075)
Gross profit	38 392	33 469

Ronald belongs to a trade association that has recently carried out a confidential survey of its members. The survey found that between 20X3 and 20X4 the average increases in sales and gross profitability of the membership were:

- increase in sales = 12.6%
- increase in gross profit = 15.2%.

Which of the following is correct? A horizontal analysis of Ronald's sales and gross profit figures shows:

a) Higher than average increase in sales, and lower than average increase in gross profit.

b) Lower than average increase in sales, and lower than average increase in gross profit.

c) Lower than average increase in sales, and higher than average increase in gross profit.

d) Higher than average increase in sales, and lower than average increase in gross profit.

13.2A Rasheda's sales for 20X2 were £206 400, and for 20X3 were £214 656. Her gross profit margins were 20X2 = 36.3% and 20X3 = 36.4%. Rasheda expects sales in 20X4 to increase by the same percentage as between 20X2 and 20X3. Gross profit margin should improve to 36.5%.
What is Rasheda's expected gross profit in 20X4 (to the nearest £)?

a) £78 349

b) £78 135

c) £81 483

d) £81 363

13.3 Rory's profit and loss account statements show the following figures for the period 20X3 to 20X6 inclusive:

	20X6	20X5	20X4	20X3
	£	£	£	£
Sales	562 064	539 409	520 665	505 500
Cost of sales	(410 619)	(392 802)	(378 879)	(368 509)
Gross profit	151 445	146 607	141 786	136 991

Which of the following is correct? Analysed horizontally, these figures show:

a) A gradually increasing percentage of sales growth and a gradually increasing percentage of gross profit growth.

b) A gradually decreasing percentage of sales growth and a gradually increasing percentage of gross profit growth.

c) A gradually increasing percentage of sales growth and a gradually decreasing percentage of gross profit growth.

d) A gradually decreasing percentage of sales growth and a gradually decreasing percentage of gross profit growth.

13.4A Reva has a jewellery business in a well-established shop. Her most recent profit and loss accounts show the following key figures:

	20X5	20X4
	£	£
Sales	696 400	585 702
Cost of sales	(416 447)	(352 007)
Gross profit	279 953	233 695

A recent survey by the Jewellers' Guild shows that average jewellery sales increased by 17.3% in 20X5 over the previous year. Also, it was found that the average gross profit margin in 20X5 among the survey respondents is 38.3%. Which of the following is correct? An analysis of Reva's figures shows:

a) A higher than average increase in sales, and a higher than average gross profit margin.

b) A lower than average increase in sales, and a lower than average gross profit margin.

c) A higher than average increase in sales, and a lower than average gross profit margin.

d) A lower than average increase in sales, and a higher than average gross profit margin.

13.5 Inge Larsen is the principal shareholder in Larsen Locations Limited. Her company provides services to businesses that are in the process of moving from one location to another. Inge and her staff plan the moves in detail, ensuring that all arrangements are made and that the move goes smoothly. Lately, the company has itself moved into larger premises and has taken on more staff.

Tom Wilton runs The Wilton Group plc, of which he is the major shareholder; the company's principal activity is similar to Larsen's. He is considering making an offer to Inge to buy the business from her, so that he can consolidate Wilton's position as market leader in the region. He does not want Inge Larsen to know anything about his possible interest in her company until he has completed some basic financial analysis.

Tom obtains Larsen's company accounts for the last three years from Companies House. Some of the extracted profit and loss account information is summarised in the following table:

	20X8	20X7	20X6	20X5
	£	£	£	£
Sales of services	3 709 480	3 690 900	3 502 404	3 497 983
Administrative expenses	1 446 437	1 204 448	1 109 932	1 100 555
Operating profit	756 734	841 525	795 046	787 046

Over the period 20X5 to 20X8 The Wilton Group plc has experienced steady growth in sales, administrative expenses and operating profits of 2–3% per year.

You are required to analyse Larsen's sales, administrative expenses and operating profits horizontally, reporting briefly on how the trends in these items compare with those of The Wilton Group plc.

13.6A Isaac Prentiss Limited produces parts and components for ships' engines. The business requires a continuing investment in new machinery in order to keep production as efficient as possible. Isaac Prentiss is the founder and principal shareholder of the business, although he no longer takes an active part in management. Isaac is concerned because he feels that the business is borrowing too much.

Burgess, the managing director, assures Isaac that sales and operating profits continue to improve and that the borrowing is necessary to fund the general expansion of the business, including the acquisition of new fixed assets. In order to reassure Isaac, Burgess prepares the following statement of key extracts from the financial statements for the last five years:

	20X8 £000	20X7 £000	20X6 £000	20X5 £000	20X4 £000
Sales	1 635	1 421	1 254	1 181	1 133
Operating profit	303	254	223	203	199
Interest payable	(245)	(181)	(177)	(171)	(151)
Fixed assets	5 314	4 190	3 633	3 237	2 950
Borrowing	3 944	2 921	2 766	2 510	2 431

You are required to analyse the company's figures horizontally over the five-year period and write a brief report to Isaac on the results of the analysis. You should refer particularly to Isaac's concerns about the business borrowing.

13.7 Chapter Protection Limited is a security firm. Its profit and loss account for the year ending 31 December 20X2 is as follows:

	£
Turnover	188 703
Cost of sales	(115 863)
Gross profit	72 840
Administrative expenses	(14 260)
Distribution and selling costs	(20 180)
Operating profit	38 400
Interest payable and similar charges	(1 200)
Profit on ordinary activities before taxation	37 200
Taxation	(7 450)
Profit on ordinary activities after taxation	29 750
Dividends	(10 000)
Retained profit for the year	19 750

You are required to prepare a vertical analysis statement of Chapter Protection's profit and loss account on the basis that the sales figure is 100%.

13.8A Starkey Wilmott Limited has the following balance sheet at 31 March 20X3:

	£	£
Fixed assets		704 710
Current assets		
Stock	369 440	
Debtors	416 700	
Cash at bank	81 450	
	867 590	
Creditors: amounts falling due within one year	(390 900)	
Net current assets		476 690

	£	£
Total assets less current liabilities		1 181 400
Creditors: amounts falling due after more than one year		(200 000)
		981 400
Capital and reserves		
Share capital		50 000
Reserves		931 400
		981 400

You are required to prepare vertical analysis statements of Starkey Wilmott's balance sheet at 31 March 20X3 based upon (i) net assets = 100.0% and (ii) fixed assets = 100.0%.

13.9 The following is a simplified extract from the balance sheet of The Boots Company plc at 31 March 2001, with comparative figures for 31 March 2000.

	2001 £m	2001 £m	2000 £m	2000 £m
Fixed assets		2 258.1		2 002.5
Current assets				
Stock	646.7		689.5	
Debtors	497.8		408.5	
Investments, deposits and cash	148.0		422.2	
	1 292.5		1 520.2	
Creditors: amounts falling due within one year	(1 082.0)		(1 153.2)	
Net current assets		210.5		367.0
Total assets less current liabilities		2 468.6		2 369.5
Creditors: amounts falling due after more than one year		(451.9)		(489.2)
Provisions for liabilities and charges*		(39.8)		(26.8)
Net assets		1 976.9		1 853.5
Capital and reserves				
Share capital		224.9		224.8
Reserves and similar items		1 752.0		1 628.7
		1 976.9		1 853.9

*Provisions for liabilities and charges: we have not met this item previously. In this particular case the provisions relate to liabilities for future taxation.

You are required to prepare a common size statement showing the balance sheet items for 2000 and 2001 on the basis that net assets = 100.0%. Comment upon any significant changes that emerge from the analysis.

13.10 Causeway Ferguson plc is a trading company specialising in the supply of tea and coffee and related products. Jason has a small shareholding in the company that was left to him by a relative. He has never taken much interest in the company's activities but has noticed that the company pays a regular twice yearly dividend that never seems to vary much.

Jason has recently started reading the financial press on a regular basis and one day he finds a brief news item about tea and coffee suppliers. Causeway Ferguson is mentioned in passing: 'Causeway Ferguson, a fine old name in British tea supply, is quietly withering away. Its lacklustre management team has failed to tackle new competitors in the market – at this rate, it starts to look like a modest takeover target for one of the food industry big boys.'

Jason never throws anything away, and after a search, manages to dig out from a dusty pile of papers a set of unopened annual reports from Causeway Ferguson going back over four or five years. He gives the reports to his cousin, Jasper, who is a trainee accountant, and asks him to comment on the company's trading over the last few years.

Jasper extracts the following profit and loss account information from the annual reports:

	20X7 £000	20X6 £000	20X5 £000	20X4 £000	20X3 £000
Turnover	13 204	13 561	13 602	12 430	12 003
Cost of sales	(8 012)	(8 217)	(8 213)	(7 401)	(7 085)
Gross profit	5 192	5 344	5 389	5 029	4 918
Administrative expenses	(2 184)	(2 101)	(2 097)	(2 010)	(1 975)
Selling and distribution costs	(2 086)	(2 001)	(1 977)	(1 972)	(1 951)
Operating profit	922	1 242	1 315	1 047	992
Taxation	(277)	(373)	(395)	(314)	(298)
Profit on ordinary activities after taxation	645	869	920	733	694
Dividends	(250)	(240)	(240)	(230)	(230)
Retained profit for the year	395	629	680	503	464

The requirement is to prepare a horizontal trend analysis statement and a common size statement and to comment on the key features that emerge from the analysis of these statements. Does the newspaper report appear credible in the light of the analysis?

Answers to exercises

13.1   Ronald's percentage increase in sales is:

$$\frac{110\,450 - 95\,544}{95\,544} \times 100 = 15.6\%$$

His increase in sales is, therefore, higher than average. Ronald's percentage increase in gross profit is:

$$\frac{38\,392 - 33\,469}{33\,469} \times 100 = 14.7\%$$

His increase in gross profit is, therefore, lower than average.
The correct answer, therefore, is a).

13.3   Horizontal analysis of Rory's profit and loss account data shows the following
percentage changes (percentage increases over previous year)

	20X6 %	20X5 %	20X4 %
Sales	4.2	3.6	3.0
Gross profit	3.3	3.4	3.5

The sales growth percentage is gradually increasing, while the gross profit
growth percentage is gradually decreasing. The correct answer, therefore, is c).

13.5   **Horizontal analysis of selected items from Larsen Locations Limited's profit and
loss account 20X5 to 20X8**

	20X8 %	20X7 %	20X6 %
Sales of services	0.5	5.4	0.1
Administrative expenses	20.1	8.5	0.9
Operating profit	(10.1)	5.8	1.0

Larsen Locations has experienced more volatile change in sales, administrative
expenses and operating profit than The Wilton Group plc. Sales in 20X7
increased by a greater amount than Wilton's sales, but there was a negligible
rate of sales growth in 20X6 and 20X8. However, the most obvious difference is
in the greatly increased level of administrative expenses in Larsen Locations 20X8
accounts. Presumably this increase arises because of the move to larger premises
and taking on more staff. The increase in costs in 20X8 does not appear, as yet,
to have produced a similar level of increase in sales. The higher costs appear to
have resulted in a lower level of operating profit – a 10.1% decrease in 20X8
compared to the previous year.

13.7   **Vertical analysis: Chapter Protection Limited's profit and loss account for the year
ending 31 December 20X2**

	£	%
Turnover	188 703	100.0
Cost of sales	(115 863)	(61.4)
Gross profit	72 840	38.6
Administrative expenses	(14 260)	(7.6)
Distribution and selling costs	(20 180)	(10.7)
Operating profit	38 400	20.3
Interest payable and similar charges	(1 200)	(0.6)
Profit on ordinary activities before taxation	37 200	19.7
Taxation	(7 450)	(3.9)
Profit on ordinary activities after taxation	29 750	15.8
Dividends	(10 000)	(5.3)
Retained profit for the year	19 750	10.5

13.9 **The Boots Company plc: Common size balance sheet statements at 31 March 2001 and 31 March 2000**

	2001 £m	2001 £m	Common size %	2000 £m	2000 £m	Common size %
Fixed assets		2 258.1	**114.2**		2 002.5	**108.0**
Current assets						
Stock	646.7		**32.7**	689.5		**37.2**
Debtors	497.8		**25.2**	408.5		**22.0**
Investments, deposits and cash	148.0		**7.5**	422.2		**22.8**
	1 292.5		**65.4**	1 520.2		**82.0**
Creditors: amounts falling due within one year	(1 082.0)		**(54.7)**	(1 153.2)		**(62.2)**
Net current assets		210.5	**10.7**		367.0	**19.8**
Total assets less current liabilities		2 468.6	**124.9**		2 369.5	**127.8**
Creditors: amounts falling due after more than one year		(451.9)	**(22.9)**		(489.2)	**(26.4)**
Provisions for liabilities and charges		(39.8)	**(2.0)**		(26.8)	**(1.4)**
Net assets		1 976.9	**100.0**		1 853.5	**100.0**
Capital and reserves						
Share capital similar		224.9	**11.4**		224.8	**12.1**
Reserves and items		1 752.0	**88.6**		1 628.7	**87.9**
		1 976.9	**100.0**		1 853.9	**100.0**

Commentary

Fixed assets have increased during the year, while long-term liabilities have decreased. The component parts of working capital have altered; current asset investments, deposits and cash have decreased substantially and the amount of working capital tied up in stock has also reduced. Current creditors are also quite significantly lower.

It is difficult to identify trends from only two years' information, but it appears that liabilities may have been settled rather more quickly in the year ending 31 March 2001 than in the previous year.

13.10 **Causeway Ferguson plc: Horizontal trend analysis (% changes over previous year), of profit and loss statements 20X3–20X7**

	20X7 %	20X6 %	20X5 %	20X4 %
Turnover	(2.6)	(0.3)	9.4	3.6
Cost of sales	(2.5)	—	11.0	4.5

	20X7 %	20X6 %	20X5 %	20X4 %
Gross profit	(2.8)	(0.8)	7.2	2.3
Administrative expenses	4.0	0.2	4.3	1.8
Selling and distribution costs	4.2	1.2	0.3	1.1
Operating profit	(25.8)	(5.6)	25.6	5.5
Taxation	(25.7)	(5.6)	25.8	5.4
Profit on ordinary activities after taxation	(25.8)	(5.5)	25.5	5.6
Dividends	4.2	—	4.3	—
Retained profit for the year	(37.2)	(7.5)	35.2	8.4

Causeway Ferguson plc: Common size analysis of profit and loss statements, 20X3–20X7

	20X7 %	20X6 %	20X5 %	20X4 %	20X3 %
Turnover	100.0	100.0	100.0	100.0	100.0
Cost of sales	(60.7)	(60.6)	(60.4)	(59.5)	(59.0)
Gross profit	39.3	39.4	39.6	40.5	41.0
Administrative expenses	(16.5)	(15.5)	(15.4)	(16.2)	(16.4)
Selling and distribution costs	(15.8)	(14.7)	(14.5)	(15.9)	(16.3)
Operating profit	7.0	9.2	9.7	8.4	8.3
Taxation	(2.1)	(2.8)	(2.9)	(2.5)	(2.5)
Profit on ordinary activities after taxation	4.9	6.4	6.8	5.9	5.8
Dividends	(1.9)	(1.8)	(1.8)	(1.9)	(1.9)
Retained profit for the year	3.0	4.6	5.0	4.0	3.9

Commentary

The following key features emerge from the horizontal and the common size analysis:

1. In each of the five years from 20X3 to 20X7 there has been a fall in the gross profit percentage. The falls from year to year are not dramatic but decline gradually.

2. There was some growth in sales until 20X6. The last two years show decreases. The decline in sales together with the steady decline in gross profit margin suggest that the company has some problems to address.

3. Administrative expenses and selling and distribution costs have increased each year. Usually the increases are small, but they represent significant amounts over a five-year period. In 20X7 both categories of cost increased by over 4%, and contribute significantly to the overall substantial drop in operating profit for the year.

4. Dividends have increased twice over the five-year period but the increases have been small. A steady or gradually increasing dividend tends to reassure shareholders.

5. While it might be premature to announce the 'withering away' of the company, some aspects of its performance would cause concern to a shareholder. The fact that there are new competitors in the market would explain the declining sales performance of the last two years. The gradual decline in gross margin, however, goes right back to the beginning of the five-year period and could not be solely attributable to competitive effects if the competitors have emerged only recently.

UNDERSTANDING FINANCIAL REPORTS: USING ACCOUNTING RATIOS

AIMS AND LEARNING OUTCOMES

Aim of the chapter

To add to the range of skills developed in the previous chapter in order to understand financial reports for various types of business.

Learning outcomes

After reading the chapter and completing the related exercises, students should:

- Understand the usefulness of accounting ratios in financial analysis.
- Be able to calculate a range of accounting ratios.
- Be able to use their knowledge of accounting ratios to assist in the analysis of financial statements.

Financial ratio analysis techniques

The simple analysis techniques explained in the previous chapter can be of great assistance in understanding a business. Sometimes, however, it helps to build in some ratio analysis techniques.

There is nothing particularly remarkable about a ratio: it simply expresses the relationship between one quantity and another. Taking a very simple example: a basket of fruit contains eight apples and four oranges. The ratio of apples to oranges can be expressed in an arithmetical term as 8:4. It is common to reduce the smaller part of the ratio to one, so the ratio of apples to oranges is expressed as 2:1.

Not all of the techniques and calculations commonly included under the term 'financial ratio analysis' actually involve the calculation of a ratio of the 2:1 type calculated above. The same relationship could be expressed by a percentage (e.g. '33.3% of the fruit in this basket is oranges'). However, all of the techniques result in ways of expressing the relationships between two or more figures.

A typical set of financial statements contains many figures, and it is possible to calculate almost infinite permutations expressing their relative dimensions. Some, however, are very obviously of more use than others; it is important that the figures being compared do have some genuine relationship. In the rest of this chapter we will examine some of the more commonly considered relationships between items in the financial statements.

It can be helpful, when trying to understand accounting ratios to group the various categories of financial relationships together. We will examine ratios in five principal categories:

- *Performance ratios* – used to assess the relative success or failure of business performance.
- *Liquidity ratios* – used to assess the extent to which a business can comfortably cover its liabilities.
- *Efficiency ratios* – used to assess the extent to which asset and liability items are well utilised and well managed.
- *Investor ratios* – used to assess various items of particular interest to investors.
- *Lending ratios* – used to assess the relationship between financing via loan capital and financing via equity capital.

A word of caution about financial ratio analysis

Some of the ratio calculation techniques explained here may appear quite complicated, especially for students whose arithmetical skills are rusty. However, the purpose of their calculation, and the overriding purpose of this section of the book, is to assist in *understanding* financial information. Students often concentrate on trying to memorise the ratio formulae and either forget, or have never properly understood, what the relationship between the figures means. Therefore, in each example, we will search for the meaning in the expression of the relationship between figures.

Performance ratios

Students may be relieved to discover that they have already studied several aspects of the financial analysis of performance. Earlier chapters introduced the idea of a significant relationship between (a) sales and gross profit and (b) sales and net profit. In many examples and case studies used up to this point in the book, gross profit margins and/or net profit margins have been calculated, and students should by now be accustomed to the idea that these margin calculations can express financial relationships between sales and profits in ways that are actually quite helpful.

Return on capital employed

Return on capital employed (also known as ROCE) is widely used as a means of assessing the performance of a business. ROCE looks at the level of profits generated compared to the amount of capital invested in the business. Unfortunately, although the ratio is easy to calculate, it does present problems in that it can be difficult to decide what is included in 'return' and in 'capital employed'. An example should help to illustrate the issue.

Example 14.1 Bilton Burgess plc is a trading company occupying its own freehold premises. It has recently obtained a listing on a stock exchange. The company has the following summarised profit and loss account for the year ending 31 December 20X5 and balance sheet at that date:

Bilton Burgess plc: Profit and loss account for the year ending 31 December 20X5

	£000	£000
Sales		1 600
Cost of sales		
Opening stock	100	
Add: purchases	994	
	1 094	
Less: closing stock	(104)	
		(990)
Gross profit		610
Various expenses		(319)
Operating profit		291
Interest payable and similar charges		(80)
Profit on ordinary activities before taxation		211
Taxation		(64)
Profit on ordinary activities after taxation		147
Dividends		(40)
Retained profit for the year		107

▶

Bilton Burgess plc: Balance sheet at 31 December 20X5

	£000	£000
Fixed assets		1 813
Current assets		
Stock	104	
Debtors	170	
Cash	10	
	284	
Creditors: amounts due within one year	97	
		187
Net current assets		
Total assets less current liabilities		2 000
Creditors: amounts due after more than one year		(800)
		1 200
Capital and reserves		
Share capital: £1 ordinary shares		300
Reserves		900
		1 200

Return on capital employed measures the profit made by the business against the funds invested:

$$\frac{\text{Profit}}{\text{Investment}}$$

Which profit figure should be used? There are several to choose from:

- gross profit (£610 000)
- operating profit (£291 000)
- profit on ordinary activities before taxation (£211 000)
- Profit on ordinary activities after taxation (£147 000)
- Retained profit (£107 000).

And how much has been invested? Should we include total net assets/ shareholders' funds (£1 200 000) or total assets less current liabilities (which is the same as the total of shareholders' funds and loan capital) at £2 000 000?

There are no definitive right answers; it depends upon which ratio is the most useful for the analysis. For example, if the analyst is looking at a set of accounts on behalf of a shareholder, he or she will be most interested in the return made by the shareholders' total investment. However, it is important to make sure that the 'return' matches the 'capital employed'. And what are 'shareholders' funds'? Shareholders' funds are the sum of the amount of the original investment in share capital, plus the total of whatever profits have been retained in the business. In this example, £300 000 of share capital plus £900 000 of retained profits.

In the case of Bilton Burgess plc pre-tax ROCE (return on shareholders' funds) equals:

$$\frac{\text{Profit before taxation and after interest}}{\text{Shareholders' funds}}$$

$$= \frac{211}{1\,200} \times 100 = 17.58\%$$

The correct figure to use here is £211 000 because it is what is left to the shareholders after interest has been deducted from profit.

Post-tax ROCE might also be helpful in the analysis. Post-tax ROCE equals: (return on shareholders' funds)

$$\frac{\text{Profit after taxation and after interest}}{\text{Shareholders' funds}}$$

$$= \frac{147}{1\,200} \times 100 = 12.25\%$$

Both pre-tax and post-tax ROCE could be useful to shareholders in order to compare the return on their investment in Bilton Burgess plc with other possible investments.

A third possibility is to look at the overall return against total investment in the business. Total investment in the case of Bilton Burgess plc is the total of shareholders' funds and long-term loan capital. The matching profit figure is the operating profit before any deduction for interest. ROCE (on total capital invested) equals:

$$\frac{\text{Profit before interest and tax}}{\text{Shareholders' funds and long-term capital}}$$

$$= \frac{291}{2\,000} \times 100 = 14.55\%$$

This is a very useful measure of business performance because it focuses purely on performance rather than bringing in considerations related to the method of financing the business operations.

ROCE may seem rather confusing. Try to focus upon the objective of the analysis and, above all, ensure that, where comparisons are being made, the ratio is calculated on a consistent basis. Students sometimes want to know which of the calculations explained above is 'right'. The answer is that the ROCE calculations are tools to be used for the purpose of analysis. The 'right' ROCE in any given situation depends upon the focus of the analysis. It is important from the outset to try to focus on the meaning of the figures and remember that accounting is an art rather than a science.

Self-test question 14.1 (answer at the end of the chapter)

The following figures are extracted from Augustus Algernon Limited's profit and loss account and balance sheet for 20X4:

	£
Operating profit	186 000
Interest	(24 000)
Profit before taxation	162 000
Taxation	(48 000)
Profit after taxation	114 000

From the balance sheet:

	£
Share capital	120 000
Reserves	1 000 000
Long-term loan	480 000

Calculate the following:

- Pre-tax ROCE, where capital employed is shareholders' funds (i.e. share capital plus reserves)
- Post-tax ROCE, where capital employed is shareholders' funds (i.e. share capital plus reserves).
- ROCE on total capital invested, where total capital invested is shareholders' funds plus long-term loan.

Liquidity ratios

Liquidity ratios are used to assess the extent to which a business can comfortably cover its liabilities. The emphasis in this group of ratios is especially on current liabilities. Long-term liabilities, by definition, do not have to be settled in the immediate future. Current liabilities, on the other hand, have to be settled within, at most, one year of the balance sheet date, and usually much more quickly. If the business fails to settle its current liabilities it is in danger of failing altogether. Can the business meet its liabilities as they fall due? Two ratios are used to provide answers to this question: the **current ratio** and the **quick ratio**. We will use data from the Bilton Burgess plc accounts provided in Example 14.1 to illustrate the calculation of these important ratios.

Example 14.2

Current ratio

The current ratio assesses the relationship between current assets and current liabilities. If current liabilities had to be settled in full, would there be sufficient current assets to cover them? Bilton Burgess's current assets are £284 000 and its current liabilities are £97 000. The formula for the current ratio is:

$$\frac{\text{Current assets}}{\text{Current liabilities}}$$

$$= \frac{284\,000}{97\,000} = 2.93$$

It is customary to express this relationship in the form of a ratio – i.e. current assets: current liabilities – which in this case is 2.93:1. Current assets are 2.93 times as large, in total, as current liabilities. Another way of looking at this information is to say that, for every £1 of current liabilities that has to be met by the business there is £2.93 in current assets.

Does the current ratio for Bilton Burgess look reasonable? Well, the business does not appear to be in danger of going under because of inability to meet its current liabilities. If all the creditors were to arrive in a group on the company's doorstep demanding immediate payment, there is actually only £10 000 in the bank with which to pay them. However, this is an unlikely scenario. Given a month or so, many of the debtors will pay up in cash, and working capital will continue to cycle around the business as described in earlier chapters. It is reasonable to conclude that Bilton Burgess does not have any obvious liquidity problems.

Is there any 'gold standard' figure for the current ratio? Current ratios vary widely between industries, and there is no ideal figure (although some textbooks suggest that there is). It is best used as a point of comparison: for example, if we know that the current ratio for Bilton Burgess at 31 December 20X4 was 2.63, we can compare the two figures at consecutive year-ends and conclude that the current ratio has improved from 2.63 to 2.93.

Quick (acid test) ratio

The analysis of liquidity can be further refined by examining the quick ratio, which is also referred to as the **acid test ratio**. This works on the assumption that it takes longer to turn stock into cash, and so it leaves stock out of the analysis. The formula for the quick ratio is:

$$\frac{\text{Current assets} - \text{Stock}}{\text{Current liabilities}}$$

For Bilton Burgess plc:

$$= \frac{284 - 104}{97} = 1.86$$

Expressed in the form of a ratio this is 1.86:1. For every £1 of current liabilities there is £1.86 in cash or debtors available. If this ratio drops below 1:1 there may potentially be problems in meeting liabilities. However, it is difficult to generalise about this point. A business that generates cash quickly (like a food retailer, for example) can operate on a very low quick ratio. The quick ratio calculated for Bilton Burgess does not suggest that the company has any immediate problem in meeting its liabilities. As with the current ratio, the quick ratio is most informative when used in comparisons.

Self-test question 14.2 (answer at the end of the chapter)

Arbus Nugent Limited has the following figures for current assets and current liabilities in its balance sheets at 31 December 20X8 and 31 December 20X7:

	20X8	20X7
Current assets		
Stock	34 300	31 600
Debtors	42 950	42 610
Cash	10 370	640
	87 620	74 850

Creditors: amounts due within one year
Trade creditors   31 450   32 970

Calculate the current ratio and the quick ratio for Arbus Nugent for both years, working to one decimal place. Have the ratios improved or worsened?

Efficiency ratios

Efficiency ratios are used to assess the extent to which asset and liability items are well managed and well utilised. We will consider efficiency measurement related to four items: fixed assets, stock, debtors and creditors. The following example uses the Bilton Burgess plc data given in Example 14.1.

Example 14.3

Fixed asset turnover ratio

Fixed assets are employed in the business in order to generate sales and, ultimately, profits. It can be interesting and useful to gauge the success with which fixed assets are employed to produce turnover. The **fixed asset turnover ratio** examines the efficiency with which fixed assets have been utilised in the business. The formula is:

$$\frac{\text{Turnover (sales)}}{\text{Fixed assets}}$$

Applying the formula to the relevant figures for Bilton Burgess plc, fixed asset turnover equals:

$$\frac{\text{Sales}}{\text{Fixed assets}}$$

$$= \frac{1\,600}{1\,813} = 0.88$$

A helpful way of looking at this result is to think of it in terms of amount of sales generated per £ of investment in fixed assets. Each £ invested in fixed assets in Bilton Burgess plc produces, on average, sales of 88p.

Again, there is no 'gold standard' for this ratio. Businesses differ from each other in the extent to which they use fixed assets. Some businesses are largely people-based; because the value of people does not appear on business balance sheets, such businesses are likely to produce a high level of sales relative to very low investment in fixed assets. Bilton Burgess plc owns its own premises and therefore fixed assets are higher than in an equivalent business where the buildings are rented. When comparing the fixed asset turnover of two businesses, caution must be exercised to ensure that like is compared with like.

Stock turnover

Where stock is a significant factor in a business, its management is of prime importance. Holding too much stock costs money (because of storage costs, insurance, working capital tied up); holding insufficient stock may also lead to problems where there is a delay in supplying customer orders. The **stock turnover ratio** gauges the average length of time that an item of stock spends on the premises before it is sold. There are two related calculations:

$$\text{Stock turnover} = \frac{\text{Cost of sales}}{\text{Average stock}}$$

$$\text{Stock turnover in days} = \frac{\text{Average stock}}{\text{Cost of sales}} \times 365 \text{ days}$$

Extracting the relevant figures from Bilton Burgess's accounts, average stock is taken as the average of opening and closing stock:

$$\frac{\text{Opening stock} + \text{closing stock}}{2} = \frac{100 + 104}{2} = 102$$

The average could be more accurately calculated if more information were available; for instance, if monthly stock figures were available, a fairly accurate average stock figure for the year could be calculated by adding together the monthly figures and dividing by 12.

Bilton Burgess plc stock turnover ratio equals:

$$\frac{\text{Cost of sales}}{\text{Average stock}}$$

$$= \frac{990}{102} = 9.7 \text{ times}$$

This means that on average stock is replaced 9.7 times in a year. The additional calculation expresses the same information in a slightly different (possibly more helpful) way:

$$\text{Stock turnover in days} = \frac{\text{Average stock}}{\text{Cost of sales}} \times 365 \text{ days}$$

$$= \frac{102}{990} \times 365 \text{ days} = 37.6 \text{ days}$$

This means that, on average, an item of stock spends 37.6 days in Bilton Burgess's warehouse.

As with previous ratio calculation results, it is difficult to assess the significance of this figure without some point of comparison. If we know that in the previous year stock turnover in days was 32.7 days, we can conclude that the stock turnover ratio appears to have worsened. Also, much depends on the nature of the stock. If Bilton Burgess is in the fresh fruit supply business, 37.6 days would appear to be an excessive stock turnover; on the other hand, if it supplies electrical components, there is probably nothing out of the ordinary with a measure of 37.6 days.

▶

Debtors turnover ratio

The **debtors turnover ratio** assesses the length of time that debtors take to pay. The calculation of this ratio is as follows:

$$\text{Debtors turnover ratio} = \frac{\text{Average debtors}}{\text{Credit sales}} \times 365 \text{ days}$$

In the case of Bilton Burgess plc we have no data available about the opening figure for debtors. In such cases we can use the closing figure, but it must be interpreted with some caution.

Extracting the relevant figures from the Bilton Burgess accounts, and assuming that all sales are made on credit (i.e. there are no sales made for cash):

$$\frac{\text{Debtors}}{\text{Credit sales}} \times 365 \text{ days}$$

$$= \frac{170}{1600} \times 365 \text{ days} = 38.8 \text{ days}$$

(Note that this is sometimes referred to as the debtors collection period.) This figure would be useful for making a comparison over time; if we had sufficient information we would be able to say whether or not this was an improvement over the previous year's figure.

The length of time debtors take to pay is related to the business's policy on offering credit. Let's suppose that Bilton Burgess's sales invoices state: 'Payment must be received within 30 days of despatch of goods'. The debtors turnover ratio tells us that, on average, customers exceed the credit terms by 8.8 days. It may be that, by improving its credit control procedures, Bilton Burgess would be able to reduce its debtors turnover figure.

Creditors turnover ratio

The **creditors turnover ratio** measures the length of time, on average, that a business takes to pay its creditors. Its calculation is very similar to that used for the debtors turnover ratio:

$$\text{Creditors turnover ratio} = \frac{\text{Average creditors}}{\text{Purchases}} \times 365 \text{ days}$$

In the case of Bilton Burgess plc we have no information available about the opening balance of creditors. In such cases it is usually acceptable to use closing creditors, but the results of the calculation need to be treated with caution.

Extracting the relevant figures from Bilton Burgess's accounts we can calculate the ratio as follows:

$$\frac{\text{Creditors}}{\text{Purchases}} \times 365 \text{ days}$$

$$= \frac{97}{994} \times 365 \text{ days} = 35.6 \text{ days}$$

Given that many businesses stipulate payment within 30 days, Bilton Burgess is probably not taking an unreasonably long time to pay its creditors.

Where the creditors turnover ratio is very high, or where it has risen significantly over the previous period(s), it may indicate possible liquidity problems. To some extent, it is good management practice to take advantage of this source of interest-free credit. However, it must be kept within reasonable limits. If a business takes an unreasonably long time to settle its creditors, there may be a consequent loss of goodwill and the business may find it difficult to obtain supplies on credit.

Self-test question 14.3 (answer at the end of the chapter)

Armitage Horobin Limited is a trading company that makes all its sales on credit. Its profit and loss account and balance sheet for the accounting years 20X4 and 20X3 are as follows:

Armitage Horobin Limited: Profit and loss accounts for the years ending

31 March 20X4 and 20X3

	20X4 £000	20X4 £000	20X3 £000	20X3 £000
Sales		283.4		271.1
Cost of sales				
Opening stock	23.7		21.2	
Add: purchases	184.8		177.5	
	208.5		198.7	
Less: closing stock	(25.9)		(23.7)	
		(182.6)		(175.0)
Gross profit		100.8		96.1
Various expenses		(75.9)		(73.0)
Operating profit		24.9		23.1
Taxation		(4.9)		(3.7)
Retained profit		20.0		19.4

Armitage Horobin Limited: Balance sheets at 31 March 20X4 and 20X3

	20X4 £000	20X4 £000	20X3 £000	20X3 £000
Fixed assets		289.2		275.3
Current assets				
Stock	25.9		23.7	
Debtors	33.0		28.2	
Prepayments	1.0		1.5	
Cash at bank	6.0		4.2	
	65.9		57.6	

	20X4 £000	20X4 £000	20X3 £000	20X3 £000
Creditors: amounts falling due within one year				
Trade creditors	24.5		20.6	
Accruals	1.3		3.0	
	25.8		23.6	
Net current assets		10.1		34.0
Total assets less current liabilities		329.3		309.3
Capital and reserves				
Share capital		40.0		40.0
Reserves		289.3		269.3
		329.3		309.3

Calculate the following efficiency ratios:

- fixed asset turnover
- stock turnover
- debtors turnover
- creditors turnover.

In each case state whether the ratio shows an improvement or not.

Investor ratios

Investor ratios, as the name implies, are those ratios that are likely to be of particular interest to investors and potential investors. In Chapter 13 we identified some of the questions investors are likely to ask:

- How is my investment doing?
- Should I buy more shares/sell the shares I've already got/hold on to the investment I've already got?
- Is the dividend likely to increase?
- What are the chances of the company going out of business?

The group of accounting ratios classified in this section under the heading 'investor ratios' may help to suggest answers to some of these questions. Although the ratios covered in the section may be of particular interest to investors, they are likely also to provide information that is useful to other people who have some reason for wanting to know more about a business.

Note that several of the ratios that follow in this section can be calculated only for limited companies. They are not applicable to sole trader and partnership businesses.

As with the other main groups of ratios, we will use the information given for Bilton Burgess plc in Example 14.1 to illustrate calculations.

Example 14.4

Dividend per share

This ratio calculates the amount in pence of the dividend for each ordinary share:

$$\frac{\text{Dividend for the year}}{\text{Number of shares in issue}}$$

The relevant figures for Bilton Burgess are:

$$\frac{40}{300} = 13.3\text{p per share}$$

Note that, in this case, the number of shares is the same as the value in the balance sheet, because the shares are of £1 each. Care must be taken where the shares are, for example, 50p shares. In this example, if the shares were of 50p nominal value there would be twice as many to take into the calculation.

Dividend cover

Dividend cover calculates the number of times the current dividend could be paid out of available profits.

$$\frac{\text{Profits after tax attributable to ordinary shareholders}}{\text{Dividend}}$$

For Bilton Burgess:

$$\frac{147}{40} = 3.67$$

What does this mean? Remember that the directors determine the level of dividend payout; usually they will seek to ensure that it is comfortably within available profits and that a good proportion of profits is retained in the business. The dividend cover calculated for Bilton Burgess tells us that the directors could pay the current level of dividend 3.67 times out of available profits.

As with all ratios the dividend cover ratio is of limited use on its own. However, it does suggest, in this case, that dividend cover is comfortable. If dividend cover equals one it means that all available profits for the year are being paid over to shareholders in the form of dividends. This would be a matter of concern for two reasons: (a) no profit is being retained in the business; and (b) it may not be possible to sustain this level of payout in future years.

Earnings per share

The dividend per share is the amount that is actually paid out per share to investors in the company. Earnings per share is the amount that is theoretically available per share. It is calculated as follows:

$$\frac{\text{Profits after tax attributable to ordinary shareholders}}{\text{Number of shares in issue}}$$

This gives earnings per share (often abbreviated to eps) in pence.

▶

The relevant figures for Bilton Burgess are:

$$\frac{147}{300} = 49\text{p per share}$$

(Note that even where eps is greater than 99p the amount is always expressed in pence.) It is worth emphasising again that the eps of 49p per share does not end up in the pockets of the Bilton Burgess shareholders; it is a theoretical figure that expresses the amount of earnings available to shareholders. The amount that does end up in the pockets of the shareholders is (usually) a lesser amount: the dividend.

Price/earnings ratio

This is a very important stock market ratio. It expresses the relationship between earnings per share (which we have just looked at) and the price of the share. Because the calculation involves a share price, it can be performed only for companies listed on a stock exchange for which a share price is available. This ratio cannot, therefore, be calculated for most businesses, such as sole traders, partnerships and unlisted companies.

In order to calculate the ratio for Bilton Burgess plc (which, remember, is a listed company) we would need to obtain a current share price. Bilton Burgess plc is a fictional company; if it were a real UK listed company, a current share price could easily be obtained for it by looking in the companies listings in the *Financial Times* or by accessing the London Stock Exchange website.

Suppose that the current share price of Bilton Burgess plc is £6.40 per share. (Yes, these are £1 shares, but the value at which they are traded on the stock exchange depends upon the market's perception of the value and the prospects of the company.) The price/earnings (or P/E ratio, as it is often known) for Bilton Burgess is:

$$\frac{\text{Price per share}}{\text{Earnings per share}}$$

$$\frac{640\text{p}}{49\text{p}} = 13.1 \text{ (to one decimal place)}$$

So what does this mean? The P/E ratio for Bilton Burgess tells us that investors are currently prepared to pay 13.1 × the company's earnings for a single share. On its own, as with most ratios, it has little significance. However, it is very useful for making comparisons with other listed companies, and, especially, with companies in the same industry sector.

Suppose that Bilton Burgess's two main competitors are both listed companies, and that their P/E ratios are:

Abacus Casement plc = 18.4
Carew Grapeshot plc = 10.3

Investors are prepared to pay up to 18.4 × earnings for a share in Abacus Casement plc, which suggests that they regard the company more highly than Bilton Burgess. Carew Grapeshot plc, on the other hand, has a lower P/E than Bilton Burgess; investors are prepared to pay only 10.3 × earnings for a single share.

The P/E ratio is a measurement of the market's perception of a company's shares. A high P/E ratio suggests that the shares are regarded as highly desirable; this is often because they are perceived as relatively low risk. Low P/Es, on the other hand, suggest an unfashionable share that has been is downgraded by the market.

The following table shows a sample of real companies' P/E ratios in March 2002. All are 'household name' shares that appear under the 'general retailers' classification.

Examples of P/E ratios of companies listed on the London Stock Exchange

Company	P/E
Boots	14.1
Dixons	26.2
TJ Hughes	70.9
Marks & Spencer	34.8
Selfridges	14.7
Woolworths	10.1

The P/Es in the table demonstrate the very large range into which they can fall. Investor confidence in TJ Hughes and Marks & Spencer appears, from the P/Es shown, to be much higher than for many other retailers. However, appearances can be deceptive. A sudden fluctuation in share price can result in a significant change to the P/E so that at any point in time, the P/E may not be representative.

Market capitalisation

Market capitalisation is not a ratio calculation, but it is a piece of information that is likely to be of interest to investors and potential investors in a listed company. Market capitalisation is the current share price multiplied by the number of shares in issue. It provides a guide as to the market's view of the current value of the company. For Bilton Burgess:

$$\text{Price £6.40} \times \text{number of shares in issue 300 000} = \text{£1 920 000}$$

Self-test question 14.4 (answer at the end of the chapter)

Armley Regina plc is a listed company with a current share price at 31 December 20X3 of £5.08 per share. The company has 1 000 000 50p shares in issue. Other relevant data for the company at 31 December 20X3 is as follows:

	£000
Profit after taxation (all attributable to ordinary shareholders)	680
Dividends	(220)
Retained profit for the year	460

Calculate the following:

- dividend per share
- dividend cover
- earnings per share
- price/earnings ratio
- market capitalisation.

Lending ratios

Gearing

A **gearing ratio** expresses the relationship between two different types of financing of a company: (a) financing through equity (i.e. ordinary) shares; and financing through long-term loans, i.e. debt.

Equity is contributed to a company by its ordinary shareholders who are able to vote in the annual general meeting, and who have a right to a share of any ordinary dividend that is declared by the company directors. Any undistributed profits are regarded as part of equity financing.

Debt is finance in the form of loans. Lenders are usually entitled to interest at a fixed rate on the loans, but, unlike shareholders, they do not have a vote and are not entitled to any share of the dividend.

Note that in Chapter 12 we briefly looked at another type of capital: preference share capital. This is share capital that confers the right to a fixed rate of dividend (for example, 10% preference share capital). Preference shareholders do not have any right to a share of the ordinary dividend; even if the company does really well, and distributes a lot of money to its ordinary shareholders, the preference shareholders still receive only the fixed percentage to which they are entitled. Preference share capital has characteristics more akin to debt, and so for the purposes of the gearing calculation, it is usually regarded as debt.

Gearing has great significance for shareholders and potential shareholders. However, it is a ratio of general importance that is likely to be significant for many interest groups.

There is more than one way of calculating gearing:

$$\frac{\text{Debt}}{\text{Equity}}$$

or

$$\frac{\text{Debt}}{\text{Debt} + \text{Equity}}$$

The really important point in adopting one or other of these methods is to be consistent.

The effect of interest in the profit and loss account is measured by our last ratio: interest cover.

Interest cover

Interest cover is a measurement of the number of times interest could be paid out of available profits. Students who have understood the idea of dividend cover will recognise that interest cover performs a similar function. It is calculated as follows:

$$\frac{\text{Profit before interest and taxation}}{\text{Interest}}$$

As for previous groups of ratios we will use the Example 14.1 data from Bilton Burgess to illustrate the calculations.

Example 14.5

Gearing

The relevant figures for debt and equity for Bilton Burgess are:

- Debt (assuming that amounts due after more than one year all relate to long-term debt) = £800 000.
- Equity (share capital + reserves) = £1 200 000.

Gearing for Bilton Burgess is calculated as follows. Either:

$$\frac{\text{Debt}}{\text{Equity}}$$

$$= \frac{800\,000}{1\,200\,000} = 66.7\% \text{ (to one decimal place)}$$

or

$$\frac{\text{Debt}}{\text{Debt} + \text{Equity}}$$

$$= \frac{800\,000}{800\,000 + 1\,200\,000} = 40\%$$

Interest cover

The relevant figures for Bilton Burgess are:

$$\frac{291}{80} = 3.64 \text{ times}$$

The effects of gearing

Why are ordinary shareholders interested in gearing?

A high level of debt capital relative to equity capital (i.e. a high level of gearing) means that the company faces a relatively high interest charge. Interest must be paid out of the store of available profits. If the interest charge soaks up most of the available profit there will be very little left over for the ordinary shareholders. Therefore, an investment in a highly geared company is usually seen as relatively risky for equity shareholders. However, a great deal depends upon the level of profits generated.

The following example illustrates the potential impact of gearing.

Example 14.6 Two companies, Basket Rabbitts plc and Telford Barron plc, have very similar operations and are of very similar sizes. However, their financing varies: Basket Rabbitts is highly geared and Telford Barron is low geared. Their total capital is as follows:

▶

High gearing		Low gearing	
Basket Rabbitts plc	£	*Telford Barron plc*	£
Long-term debt finance		Long-term debt finance	
10% interest	40 000	10% interest	5 000
Equity finance	30 000	Equity finance	65 000
	70 000		70 000

Let's look at the effects of the gearing at three different potential levels of profit before tax:

	£
High level	12 000
Medium level	8 000
Low level	4 000

In all cases we will assume a tax rate of 30%.

1. High level of profit

High gearing		Low gearing	
Basket Rabbitts plc	£	*Telford Barron plc*	£
Profit before interest and tax	12 000	Profit before interest and tax	12 000
Less: interest £40 000 × 10%	(4 000)	Less: interest: £5 000 × 10%	(500)
Profit before tax	8 000	Profit before tax	11 500
Tax: £8 000 × 30%	(2 400)	Tax: £11 500 × 30%	(3 450)
Profit after tax attributable to ordinary shareholders	5 600	Profit after tax attributable to ordinary shareholders	8 050

Post-tax return on equity shareholders' funds:

$$\frac{5\,600}{30\,000} \times 100 = 18.7\%$$

Post-tax return on equity shareholders' funds:

$$\frac{8\,050}{65\,000} \times 100 = 12.3\%$$

2. Medium level of profit

High gearing		Low gearing	
Basket Rabbitts plc	£	*Telford Barron plc*	£
Profit before interest and tax	8 000	Profit before interest and tax	8 000
Less: interest £40 000 × 10%	(4 000)	Less: interest: £5 000 × 10%	(500)
Profit before tax	4 000	Profit before tax	7 500
Tax: £4 000 × 30%	(1 200)	Tax: £7 500 × 30%	(2 250)
Profit after tax attributable to ordinary shareholders	2 800	Profit after tax attributable to ordinary shareholders	5 250

Post-tax return on equity shareholders' funds:

$$\frac{2\,800}{30\,000} \times 100 = 9.3\%$$

Post-tax return on equity shareholders' funds:

$$\frac{5\,250}{65\,000} \times 100 = 8.1\%$$

3. Low level of profit

High gearing			**Low gearing**	
Basket Rabbitts plc		£	*Telford Barron plc*	£
Profit before interest and tax		4 000	Profit before interest and tax	4 000
Less: interest £40 000 × 10%		(4 000)	Less: interest: £5 000 × 10%	(500)
Profit before tax		—	Profit before tax	3 500
Tax		—	Tax: £3 500 × 30%	(1 050)
Profit after tax attributable to ordinary shareholders		—	Profit after tax attributable to ordinary shareholders	2 450

Post-tax return on equity shareholders' funds:

$$0\%$$

Post-tax return on equity shareholders' funds:

$$\frac{2\,450}{65\,000} \times 100 = 3.8\%$$

The example illustrates that returns to shareholders in a highly geared company are more volatile than returns to shareholders in a low geared company. Highly geared companies are, therefore, seen by ordinary shareholders as more risky.

CASE STUDY 14.1 Analysing financial statements

This is a long case study that brings together the analysis techniques covered in both Chapters 13 and 14. Students should work through it carefully to ensure that they understand all aspects of the calculations and discussions, before attempting the end of chapter questions.

Having qualified as a physiotherapist, Louise Donovan now has a job in the physiotherapy department of a large city hospital. She is very careful with money and has managed to pay off all her student loans, as well as saving almost £5000 towards a deposit to buy a house. Louise's boyfriend, Ben, is not so good with money. Ben is an insurance broker and he earns more than Louise, but she quite often has to help him out with cash towards the end of the month. Louise is in love with Ben and would like them to get married as soon as they've saved up enough to get the house.

A couple of months ago Louise's grandma died. No-one had realised until she died and the will was read that the old lady had also been a very efficient saver. She leaves Louise, her favourite granddaughter, £30 000. Louise is delighted by this unexpected piece of good news; now she has enough money for a deposit and she can go ahead and arrange the mortgage as soon as she and Ben have found the house they want. Ben, however, has other ideas. In his opinion, Louise should invest the money and he thinks he's found her a really good investment opportunity. Ben isn't too worried about buying the house; he's not sure that he's ready to settle down yet, and, besides, the way Louise has been saving, they'll have enough in another couple of years in any case. He occasionally feels guilty that he hasn't contributed any savings himself, but part of his salary is in commission, and he's planning to work really hard this year to find new clients.

▶

◄◄◄

The investment opportunity Ben has identified for Louise is in Fitton Parker Limited. Two brothers, Sam and Henry Fitton, and their friend Barney Parker started up the company six or seven years ago; they are all directors and each has a shareholding of 15 000 £1 shares. The company imports a basic range of sports clothing and footwear. It adds value to the range by imprinting logos and brand names, which it uses under licence, then re-sells to large retailers. Ben met Barney Parker by chance in a bar a few months ago, and Barney explained to him that the business is looking for some additional investors. The business has continued to be successful but is always short of cash. An additional infusion of cash would allow for the overdraft to be paid off (although the loan of £57 000 from Sam and Henry's father would have to remain for the time being) and would provide some additional cash for investing in new ranges and more effective advertising. There are several good opportunities that would be open to the business if only it had access to more ready cash. Ben was really impressed by the way Barney talked about the business, and promised to look round his own range of contacts to see if he could identify anyone who might be interested in this promising business opportunity.

Ben contacts Barney in November 20X4 to tell him that Louise may be willing to invest in Fitton Parker. Barney says that they've had some preliminary discussions with several potential investors, but that so far nothing definite has been decided. He tells Ben that Fitton Parker would issue a further 10 000 £1 shares to Louise in exchange for £30 000 in cash. As a result of the deal Louise would own just over 18% of the company (she would have 10 000 new shares and Barney, Sam and Henry would continue to own 15 000 each: Louise would therefore own 10 000 out of the total number of issued shares of 55 000). Barney, Sam and Henry do not want any new investors to take an active part in the business, but propose to pay a decent level of dividend once the business has really taken off.

When Ben explains the proposition to Louise she is unimpressed at first. However, after a while, he manages to sell her the idea of investing in shares rather than property. 'This is a great opportunity, Lou; you could end up owning 18% of a really major business; if the prospects are as good as Barney says, they might be floating on the stock market in five years time, and you could be a millionaire.'

Patrick Donovan, Louise's father, is a man of strong views. One of his strong views is that Ben is not nearly good enough for Louise: 'He's a parasite and a loser, and they'll get married over my dead body', as he tells a friend. When Patrick hears about the investment plan he is horrified, and tells Louise that 'it's just another one of Ben's stupid ideas' and that she might as well throw the money away. This has the effect of making Louise more determined to stand up for Ben, and she tells Patrick that she's made up her mind to go ahead. Patrick tells her that she must, at least, get hold of the business accounts for the last couple of years and have a financial adviser go through them. He tells her that, if she insists on investing in shares (and he doesn't advise it) she should at least invest in listed company shares, then she would be able to sell them at any time.

Ben explains to Barney that Louise's father is causing trouble but that he'll probably come round if he sees some figures. After a few weeks, Barney produces profit and loss accounts and balance sheets for Fitton Parker for the three years ending 31 March 20X3. He tells Ben that each year's accounts were audited and there were no problems. The figures provided by Barney are as follows:

Fitton Parker Limited: Profit and loss accounts for the years ending 31 March 20X3 20X2 and 20X1

	20X3	20X2	20X1
	£	£	£
Sales	596 860	491 383	415 985
Cost of sales	(402 964)	(325 089)	(271 588)
Gross profit	193 896	166 294	144 397
Selling and distribution costs	(76 990)	(60 930)	(52 538)
Administrative expenses	(33 750)	(31 695)	(32 772)
Directors' remuneration	(60 000)	(60 000)	(60 000)
Operating profit/(loss)	23 156	13 669	(913)
Interest payable and similar charges	(5 133)	(4 027)	(3 275)
Profit/(loss) on ordinary activities before taxation	18 023	9 642	(4 188)
Taxation paid	(3 350)	(2 406)	—
Retained profit for the year	14 673	7 236	(4 188)

Fitton Parker Limited: Balance sheets at 31 March 20X3 20X2 and 20X1

	20X3 £	20X3 £	20X2 £	20X2 £	20X1 £	20X1 £
Fixed assets		86 790		83 250		94 484
Current assets						
Stock	55 450		44 791		36 425	
Debtors	70 315		56 233		44 190	
Cash	—		806		—	
	125 765		101 830		80 615	
Creditors: amounts due within one year						
Trade creditors	47 491		34 750		31 418	
Overdraft	10 696		10 635		11 222	
	58 187		45 385		42 640	
Net current assets		67 578		56 445		37 975
Total assets less current liabilities		154 368		139 695		132 459
Creditors: amounts due after more than one year						
Long-term loan		(57 000)		(57 000)		(57 000)
		97 368		82 695		75 459
Capital and reserves						
Share capital £1 shares*		45 000		45 000		45 000
Reserves						
Profit and loss account brought forward		37 695		30 459		34 647
Profit/ (loss) for the year		14 673		7 236		(4 188)

▶

	20X3 £	20X3 £	20X2 £	20X2 £	20X1 £	20X1 £
Profit and loss account carried forward		52 368		37 695		30 459
		97 368		82 695		75 459

*Authorised share capital is 80 000 £1 shares. Issued share capital is £45 000 i.e. £15 000 of shares issued to each of the Fitton brothers and to Barney Parker.

As Louise's financial adviser analyse the financial statements of Fitton Parker and provide her with some advice on a recommended course of action. Include any reservations you may have about the information.

Horizontal trend analysis

Because there are three years of figures available it is possible to carry out, to a limited extent, horizontal trend analysis, as follows:

Fitton Parker Limited: Horizontal trend analysis for 20X3 20X2 20X1

	% change over previous year 20X3	% change over previous year 20X2
Sales	21.5%	18.1%
Cost of sales	24.0%	19.7%
Gross profit	16.6%	15.2%
Selling and distribution costs	26.4%	16.0%
Administrative expenses	6.5%	(3.3%)
Directors' remuneration	0%	0%
Interest payable	27.5%	23.0%
Fixed assets	4.3%	(11.9%)
Stock	23.8%	23.0%
Debtors	25.0%	27.3%
Trade creditors	36.7%	10.7%
Overdraft	0.6%	(5.2%)

The horizontal trend analysis show that there is a general trend towards increases in most items. The increase in sales is substantial but although there is a corresponding increase in gross profit, the increase is not as great. It looks as though gross profit margin may be declining.

Selling and distribution costs have risen a lot between 20X2 and 20X3 but administrative costs appear to be firmly under control. Also, the directors have not increased their own remuneration in the three-year period.

Investment in fixed assets has been modest, but all working capital items have increased substantially. The overdraft remains at a fairly constant level, but trade creditors have increased by a large percentage (over 36%) in 20X3, suggesting that the business is relying to an increasing extent on the interest-free source of credit offered by trade creditors. This is cheaper than increasing the overdraft (because interest has to be paid on an overdraft) but there is a danger of alienating suppliers if they are not paid promptly.

Vertical analysis

Vertical analysis of the profit and loss accounts is based upon sales = 100% and vertical analysis of the balance sheets is based upon net assets = 100%. The vertical analysis produces the following results:

Fitton Parker Limited: Vertical analysis of profit and loss account for the years ending 31 March 20X3 20X2 and 20X1

	20X3 £	20X2 £	20X1 £
Sales	100.0	100.0	100.0
Cost of sales	(67.5)	(66.2)	(65.3)
Gross profit	32.5	33.8	34.7
Selling and distribution costs	(12.9)	(12.4)	(12.6)
Administrative expenses	(5.7)	(6.4)	(7.9)
Directors' remuneration	(10.0)	(12.2)	(14.4)
Operating profit/(loss)	3.9	2.8	(0.2)
Interest payable and similar charges	(0.9)	(0.8)	(0.8)
Profit/(loss) on ordinary activities before taxation	3.0	2.0	(1.0)
Taxation	(0.6)	(0.5)	—
Retained profit for the year	2.4	1.5	(1.0)

Fitton Parker Limited: Vertical analysis of balance sheets at 31 March 20X3 20X2 and 20X1

	20X3 £	20X2 £	20X1 £
Fixed assets	89.1	100.6	125.2
Current assets			
Stock	57.0	54.2	48.3
Debtors	72.2	68.0	58.5
Cash	—	1.0	—
	129.2	123.2	106.8
Trade creditors	48.8	42.0	41.6
Overdraft	11.0	12.9	14.9
Creditors: amounts due within one year	59.8	54.9	56.5
Net current assets	69.4	68.3	50.3
Creditors: amounts due after more than one year	(58.5)	(68.9)	(75.5)
	100.0	100.0	100.0
Capital and reserves			
Share capital	46.2	54.4	59.6
Reserves	53.8	45.6	40.4
	100.0	100.0	100.0

The vertical analysis of the profit and loss account confirms the suspicion that the gross profit margin is declining. Administrative expenses are declining as a percentage of sales. This may be because of very good controls over costs and a deliberate attempt to keep administrative expenses to a minimum. However, savings on such costs can be taken too far, and the business may be operating at less than optimal efficiency.

The operating profit margin is low, as is the margin of retained profits to sales. Although there has not been a loss since 20X1 profits are not impressive, and even at their highest level in 20X3 there would not be much scope for paying a dividend.

Stocks and debtors have increased as a percentage of net assets, with a particularly large increase in debtors between 20X1 and 20X2. Trade creditors, as noted in the horizontal analysis, have also increased substantially.

Ratio analysis

Performance

Gross and operating profit margin were discussed in the vertical analysis section. Because Louise is looking to invest as an ordinary shareholder, she will probably be most interested in the return on shareholders' funds:

$$\frac{\text{Profit before tax, and after interest}}{\text{Shareholders' funds}}$$

	20X3	20X2	20X1
Return on shareholders' funds	$\frac{18\,023}{97\,368} \times 100$ $= 18.5\%$	$\frac{9\,642}{82\,695} \times 100$ $= 11.7\%$	$\frac{(4\,188)}{75\,459} \times 100$ $= (5.6\%)$

The overall return has increased rapidly.

Liquidity

Information is available to calculate two ratios: the current ratio and the quick ratio.

	20X3	20X2	20X1
Current ratio $\frac{\text{Current assets}}{\text{Current liabilities}}$	$\frac{125\,765}{58\,187} = 2.2$	$\frac{101\,830}{45\,385} = 2.2$	$\frac{80\,615}{42\,640} = 1.9$
Quick ratio $\frac{\text{Current assets} - \text{stock}}{\text{Current liabilities}}$	$\frac{125\,765 - 55\,450}{58\,187}$ $= 1.2$	$\frac{101\,830 - 44\,791}{45\,385}$ $= 1.3$	$\frac{80\,615 - 36\,425}{42\,640}$ $= 1.0$

Neither liquidity ratio appears to give any cause for concern. Although the figure for creditors is very much higher in 20X3 than it was in 20X2 it is covered quite adequately by current assets.

Efficiency ratios

Three will be calculated: fixed asset turnover, stock turnover (in days) and debtors turnover (in days). Creditors turnover cannot be calculated because no figures for purchases are available.

	20X3	20X2	20X1
Fixed asset turnover: $\dfrac{\text{Sales}}{\text{Fixed assets}}$	$\dfrac{596\,860}{86\,790} = 6.88$	$\dfrac{491\,383}{83\,250} = 5.90$	$\dfrac{415\,985}{94\,484} = 4.40$
Stock turnover: $\dfrac{\text{Stock}}{\text{Cost of sales}} \times 365$	$\dfrac{55\,450}{402\,964} \times 365$ $= 50.2$ days	$\dfrac{44\,791}{325\,089} \times 365$ $= 50.3$ days	$\dfrac{36\,425}{271\,588} \times 365$ $= 49.0$ days
Debtors turnover: $\dfrac{\text{Debtors}}{\text{Sales}} \times 365$	$\dfrac{70\,315}{596\,860} \times 365$ $= 43.0$ days	$\dfrac{56\,233}{491\,383} \times 365$ $= 41.8$ days	$\dfrac{44\,190}{415\,985} \times 365$ $= 38.8$ days

Fixed asset turnover shows an increasing rate. Stock turnover at 50 days may indicate that stock is being managed inefficiently, but we would need to know more about the business activities to be able to reach conclusions on this point. It is gradually taking the business longer to collect debtors, although even at 43 days (assuming that debtors are allowed 30 days to pay) there is unlikely to be a serious problem.

Note that the investor ratios are mostly irrelevant because of lack of information. No dividend has been paid in any of the years, and, of course, it would not be possible to calculate P/E ratio because the company is unquoted and so there is no market price for its shares.

Gearing

In the circumstances it is relevant to calculate gearing because the business has a long-term loan of significant size.

	20X3	20X2	20X1
Gearing: $\dfrac{\text{Debt}}{\text{Debt} + \text{Equity}}$	$\dfrac{57\,000}{57\,000 + 97\,368}$ $\times 100 = 36.9\%$	$\dfrac{57\,000}{57\,000 + 82\,695}$ $\times 100 = 40.8\%$	$\dfrac{57\,000}{57\,000 + 75\,459}$ $\times 100 = 43.0\%$

Although debt remains constant at £57 000, equity gradually increases because of retained profits, so debt becomes relatively less important. Nevertheless, it is still significant at 36.9%.

▶

General comments and advice

Ben asks Barney for the company figures towards the end of 20X4, but Barney is able to provide figures up to 31 March 20X3 only. Nine months or so after the year-end of 31 March 20X4 it would be reasonable to expect 20X4 accounts to be available. If they are not yet available it may indicate some serious administrative problems within the business. There would be good grounds for serious doubts if the accounts had been prepared but Barney was unwilling to provide them. The question could be easily resolved by checking the latest filing at Companies House. Also, the information Barney provides is limited to the basic profit and loss and balance sheet statements. Although he assures Ben that the audit report is fine, he does not include it in the information; nor are the notes to the accounts or the directors' report made available. This looks a little suspect.

The business appears to be growing fairly rapidly, with increasing sales and fixed asset turnover. Working capital is growing, but there do not appear to be any immediate liquidity problems. It is not a particularly profitable business, and Louise or any other potential investor would need to know a great deal more about the prospects for the business and the directors' plans for expansion. Louise is being invited to buy into about 18% of the shares of a business with net assets at 31 March 20X3 of £97 368. Her 'share' of net assets would be £97 368 × 18% – approximately £17 500, in exchange for £30 000 in cash. If the net asset value approximates at all closely to current values it does not appear to be a very good bargain. The directors would no doubt argue that she would be buying into their expertise and the future prospects of the business, but, again, Louise would need to know a great deal more about these factors before she could commit to the investment. The other directors are not offering Louise a directorship and she will not, therefore, have much control, if any, over her investment.

Finally, it should be pointed out to Louise that this type of investment is almost certainly not appropriate for someone in her position. Investing in shares is risky, and should really be undertaken only by people who are in a fairly sound financial position, and who could afford to lose all the money. Investment in a private limited company is especially risky. Usually, it is difficult, sometimes impossible, to get the money out again if it is needed for some other purpose. As Patrick points out, at least by investing in listed company shares Louise would be able to turn her investments into cash again comparatively easily (although she might well lose money on such investments).

It is up to Louise to make her own decision on the investment; she should try not to be influenced by either Ben or by her father.

Chapter summary

A great deal of useful material on financial ratio analysis has been covered in this chapter. The following ratios were examined within five major groups:

- **Performance ratios**
  - Gross profit margins
  - Net profit margins
  - Return on capital employed.
- **Liquidity ratios**
  - Current ratio
  - Quick (acid test) ratio.
- **Efficiency ratios**
  - Fixed asset turnover
  - Stock turnover
  - Debtor turnover
  - Creditor turnover.
- **Investor ratios**
  - Dividend per share
  - Dividend cover
  - Earnings per share
  - Price/earnings ratio
  - Market capitalisation.
- **Lending ratios**
  - Gearing ratio
  - Interest cover.

The case study for the chapter examined many aspects of the analysis of financial reports. Due to its complexity it will require time and careful study.

A large number of short questions are included in the 'Exercises' section at the end of the chapter, so that students can become accustomed to the calculation of ratios. But remember that the purpose in analysing accounting information is to understand it better. Ratio calculations can be a useful means to an end, but the key objective is to understand the meaning of the financial statements.

Answer to self-test question 14.1

Augustus Algernon Limited's pre-tax ROCE (return on shareholders' funds) equals:

$$\frac{\text{Profit before taxation and after interest}}{\text{Shareholders' funds}}$$

$$= \frac{162}{120 + 1000} \times 100 = 14.46\%$$

Post-tax ROCE (return on shareholders' funds) equals:

$$\frac{\text{Profit after taxation and after interest}}{\text{Shareholders' funds}}$$

$$= \frac{114}{120 + 1\,000} \times 100 = 10.18\%$$

ROCE (on total capital invested) equals:

$$\frac{\text{Profit before interest and tax}}{\text{Shareholders' funds and long-term capital}}$$

$$= \frac{186}{120 + 1\,000 + 480} \times 100 = 11.63\%$$

Answer to self-test question 14.2

$$\text{Current ratio} = \frac{\text{Current assets}}{\text{Current liabilities}}$$

$$\text{Quick ratio} = \frac{\text{Current assets} - \text{Stock}}{\text{Current liabilities}}$$

For Arbus Nugent Limited for 20X8 and 20X7:

	20X8	20X7
Current ratio	$\frac{87\,620}{31\,450} : 1 = 2.8{:}1$	$\frac{74\,850}{32\,970} : 1 = 2.3{:}1$
Quick ratio	$\frac{87\,620 - 34\,300}{31\,450} : 1 = 1.7{:}1$	$\frac{74\,850 - 31\,600}{32\,970} : 1 = 1.3{:}1$

Both the current ratio and the quick ratio have improved.

Answer to self-test question 14.3

Ratio	20X4	20X3
Fixed asset turnover	$\frac{\text{Sales}}{\text{Fixed assets}}$ $\frac{283.4}{289.2} = 0.98$	$\frac{271.1}{275.3} = 0.98$

Ratio	20X4	20X3
Stock turnover	a) *Stock turnover*: $\dfrac{\text{Cost of sales}}{\text{Average stock}}$ Average stock $= \dfrac{23.7+25.9}{2} = 24.8$ $\dfrac{\text{Cost of sales}}{\text{Average stock}}$ $\dfrac{182.6}{24.8} = 7.36$ b) *Stock turnover in days* = $\dfrac{\text{Average stock}}{\text{Cost of sales}} \times 365$ $\dfrac{24.8}{182.6} \times 365 = 49.6$ days	Average stock $= \dfrac{21.2+23.7}{2} = 22.5$ $\dfrac{175.0}{22.5} = 7.77$ $\dfrac{22.5}{175.0} \times 365 = 46.9$ days
Debtors turnover	$\dfrac{\text{Debtors}}{\text{Sales on credit}} \times 365$ $\dfrac{33.0}{283.4} \times 365 = 42.5$ days	$\dfrac{28.2}{271.1} \times 365 = 38.0$ days
Creditors turnover	$\dfrac{\text{Creditors}}{\text{Purchases}} \times 365$ $\dfrac{24.5}{184.4} \times 365 = 48.4$ days	$\dfrac{20.6}{177.5} \times 365 = 42.4$ days

- Fixed assets turnover has hardly changed.
- Stock turnover has worsened in that stock is now held on the premises for an average of 49.6 days compared with 46.9 days in the previous year.
- Debtors turnover has worsened in that it is now taking debtors, on average, 42.5 days to pay, compared with 38 days in the previous year.
- Creditors turnover has improved, in that Armitage Horobin is taking advantage of the interest-free credit offered by creditors to a greater extent than in the previous year. However, 48.4 days may be regarded as too long a period to wait, on average, for payment, and there may be a loss of goodwill on the part of creditors towards the company.

Tutorial note: average stock has been used in the calculations because there was sufficient data available. In the case of debtors and creditors there was insufficient data, and so closing debtors and creditors have been used in the calculations. Although, ideally, averages should be used in the calculations it is often not possible to obtain them.

Answer to self-test question 14.4

$$\text{Dividend per share} = \frac{220\,000}{1\,000\,000} = 22\text{p per share}$$

$$\text{Dividend cover} = \frac{680\,000}{220\,000} = 3.09 \text{ times}$$

$$\text{Earnings per share (eps)} = \frac{680\,000}{1\,000\,000} = 68\text{p per share}$$

$$\text{Price/earnings (P/E) ratio} = \frac{508\text{p}}{68\text{p}} = 7.5$$

$$\text{Market capitalisation} = £5.08 \times 1\,000\,000 \text{ shares} = £5\,080\,000$$

Exercises

The answers to many of the exercises are set out later in this chapter. However, where the exercise number is followed by 'A' the answer is available only to lecturers. Remember that additional exercises (with answers) are available to students on the book's website.

The following information is relevant to questions 14.1 to 14.3 inclusive. Extracts from Sigmund & Son Limited's financial statements for 20X4 show the following:

	£000
Gross profit	616.4
Various expenses	(313.6)
Operating profit	302.8
Interest payable	(35.0)
Profit on ordinary activities before taxation	267.8
Taxation	(80.0)
Profit on ordinary activities after taxation	187.8
Dividends	(100.0)
Retained profit	87.8
Share capital	500.0
Reserves	1 790.0
Long-term loan capital	350.0

14.1 Calculate the pre-tax return on shareholders' funds (to one decimal place). Is it:

a) 13.2%

b) 10.1%

c) 26.9%

d) 11.7%?

14.2 Calculate the post-tax return on shareholders' funds (to one decimal place). Is it:

a) 3.8%

b) 8.2%

c) 3.3%

d) 7.1%?

14.3 Calculate the return on total capital invested (to one decimal place). Is it:

a) 8.2%

b) 11.5%

c) 13.2%

d) 10.1%?

The following information is relevant to questions 14.4A to 14.6A inclusive. Extracts from Sinclair Salter Limited's financial statements for 20X3 show the following:

	£000
Gross profit	896.4
Various expenses	(606.8)
Operating profit	289.6
Interest payable	(93.0)
Profit on ordinary activities before taxation	196.6
Taxation	(60.0)
Profit on ordinary activities after taxation	136.6
Dividends	(40.0)
Retained profit	96.6
Share capital	100.0
Reserves	1 170.0
Long-term loan capital	900.0

14.4A Calculate return on total capital invested (to one decimal place). Is it:

a) 15.5%

b) 13.3%

c) 9.1%

d) 22.8%?

14.5A Calculate pre-tax return on shareholders' funds (to one decimal place). Is it:

a) 15.5%

b) 10.8%

c) 9.1%

d) 22.8%?

14.6A Calculate post-tax return on shareholders' funds (to one decimal place). Is it?

a) 15.5%

b) 9.1%

c) 10.8%

d) 6.3%?

14.7 Shania would like to invest in a company that will give her a good rate of return on her investment. She has collected information on four companies. Extracts from their most recent financial statements are given below:

	Ambit Ltd £000	Bolsover Ltd £000	Carcan Ltd £000	Delphic Ltd £000
Operating profit	983.6	647.8	726.8	1 061.4
Interest	(180.0)	(107.0)	(151.0)	(206.0)
Profit before taxation	803.6	540.8	575.8	855.4
Taxation	(240.0)	(160.0)	(170.0)	(250.0)
Profit after taxation	563.6	380.8	405.8	605.4
Share capital	80.0	95.0	86.0	60.0
Reserves	4 550.0	3 881.0	3 928.0	7 000.0
Long-term loans	2 400.0	1 250.0	1 820.0	2 500.0

Which company currently has the highest pre-tax return on shareholders' funds?

a) Ambit Limited

b) Bolsover Limited

c) Carcan Limited

d) Delphic Limited.

14.8A Shirley has been thinking for a while about investing some surplus cash in an unlisted company that organises lettings of holiday properties in France. The company is run by an old friend of hers who is looking for additional investors in order to fund a planned expansion of the business.

Shirley has received financial statements for the business for 20X6 and 20X5. The profit and loss accounts and extracts from the balance sheets are as follows:

	20X6 £000	20X5 £000
Sales revenue	976.9	899.6
Gross profit	377.6	360.9
Various expenses	(102.5)	(98.6)
Operating profit	275.1	262.3
Interest payable	(18.7)	(16.5)
Profit on ordinary activities before taxation	256.4	245.8
Taxation	(77.0)	(74.0)
Retained profit	179.4	171.8
Share capital	80.0	80.0
Reserves	1 465.0	1 285.6
Long-term loan capital	319.0	276.0

Calculate (to one decimal place) the following financial ratios for Shirley:

i) gross profit margin

ii) operating profit margin

iii) return on shareholders' funds

iv) return on total capital employed.

Comment on any apparent changes in business performance between 20X5 and 20X6.

14.9   Trixie Stores Limited has the following working capital items in its balance sheet at 31 December 20X4:

		£
Stock		18 370
Debtors		24 100
Cash in hand		70
Trade creditors		15 450
Bank overdraft		6 400

The current ratio (working to two decimal places) for Trixie Stores Limited is:

a) 1.95:1

b) 1.11:1

c) 0.51:1

d) 0.9:1.

14.10A   Tadcaster Terrier Limited has the following working capital items in its balance sheet at 31 May 20X1:

		£
Stock		88 700
Creditors		90 450
Debtors		85 210
Bank overdraft		16 790

The current ratio (working to two decimal places) for Tadcaster Terrier Limited is:

a) 1.62:1

b) 0.62:1

c) 1.9:1

d) 0.79:1.

14.11   Trimester Tinker Limited has the following working capital items in its balance sheet at 31 December 20X1:

		£
Stock		108 770
Debtors		94 300
Cash in hand		1 600
Trade creditors		110 650

The company belongs to a trade association that has recently published industry averages for key financial ratios based upon a survey of its members. The industry averages for current and quick ratios applicable to the business of Trimester Tinker Limited are:

Current ratio = 1.62:1

Quick ratio = 0.93:1

Which of the following statements is correct?

a) Trimester Tinker Limited's current ratio is higher than the industry average and its quick ratio is also higher.

b) Trimester Tinker Limited's current ratio is higher than the industry average but its quick ratio is lower.

c) Trimester Tinker Limited's current ratio is lower than the industry average and its quick ratio is also lower.

d) Trimester Tinker Limited's current ratio is lower than the industry average but its quick ratio is higher.

14.12A   Turnbull Taffy Limited's figures to 31 March 20X4 show the following working capital items:

	£
Stock	67 400
Debtors	42 660
Cash at bank	6 050
Trade creditors	58 760

The company's finance director is preparing a projected balance sheet for 31 March 20X5 as part of a package of information to be presented to a bank from which the company hopes to obtain a long-term loan. The finance director estimates that there will be the following changes to working capital between 31 March 20X4 and 31 March 20X5:

Stock will decrease by 10%

Debtors will decrease by 15%

Cash at bank will increase by 50%

Trade creditors will decrease by 5%.

Calculate (to two decimal places):

i)   The current ratio and the quick ratio at 31 March 20X4.

ii) The expected current ratio and quick ratio at 31 March 20X5 based on the finance director's estimates.

14.3   Upwood Sickert Limited has total sales in the year to 31 May 20X6 of £686 430. Extracts from the company's balance sheet at that date show fixed assets as follows:

	Cost	Depreciation	Net book value
	£	£	£
Plant and machinery	200 000	30 000	170 000
Vehicles	106 640	46 655	59 985

Calculate the fixed asset turnover ratio for the year (to two decimal places). Is it:

a) 2.24

b) 0.34

c) 0.45

d) 2.98?

14.14A Uriah Westwood plc is an advertising agency operating from rented offices in the West End of London. Ulverstone Thunderbird plc is a company engaged in heavy engineering. It owns all its own plant and equipment and a small factory site in the north of England. Both companies have recently reported sales in the region of £10 million. The fixed asset turnover ratio for one of the companies is 1.14 and for the other is 10.62.

From the brief descriptions given, which of the two companies is more likely to have the higher fixed asset turnover ratio?

14.15 A sole trader's stock at 31 December 20X7 is £405 000. By 31 December 20X8 stock has increased in value by 10%. Cost of sales for the year ending 31 December 20X8 is £1 506 700.

What is the business's stock turnover in days?

14.16A The following are extracts from the profit and loss accounts of a sole trader business for the years ending 31 December 20X8 and 20X7:

	20X8	20X7
	£000	£000
Opening stock	1 605.3	1 396.4
Purchases	19 360.4	19 568.9
Closing stock	(1 565.7)	(1 605.3)
Cost of sales	19 400.00	19 360.00

Calculate the stock turnover in days for both years. Has it improved or worsened in 20X8?

14.17 A company has debtors in its year-end balance sheet of £218 603. Sales for the year were £1 703 698; 70% of these were sales on credit. Debtor turnover in days is:

a) 46.8 days

b) 32.7 days

c) 66.9 days

d) 18.3 days.

14.18A Whybird, a sole trader, has been advised by his accountant to keep an eye on the number of days his debtors take to pay. The accountant has explained how to calculate the debtors turnover period but Whybird doesn't really understand. He asks you to do the calculation for him. Extracts from the last two years' accounts show the following figures:

	20X5	20X4
	£	£
Sales	180 630	178 440
Less: returns	(1 300)	(1 060)
	179 330	177 380
Debtors	20 982	21 117
Less: provision for doubtful debts	(306)	(297)
	20 676	20 820

Calculate the debtors turnover period for Whybird for both years to one decimal place. Has the debtors turnover period improved or worsened in 20X5?

14.19   The managing director of Winger Whalley Limited has just received a report from one of the accounting assistants employed by the business. The report shows key ratios and supplies explanations for any significant fluctuations.

The MD is concerned to find that the debtors turnover period has worsened significantly in the period from 20X2 to 20X3 (it was 36.4 days at the end of 20X2 and is 41.2 days at the end of 20X3). The accounting assistant has supplied the following reasons for the fluctuations:

1. The company's credit controller did a parachute jump for charity about three months ago. The parachute failed to open properly, and because of her injuries she was away from work in the last three months of 20X3. The temporary staff agency was unable to provide a suitable replacement for her, and during most of the three-month period her work was simply not done.

2. Sales have increased by 4% in the course of the year.

3. During 20X3 the board decided to introduce a system of early settlement discounts. Debtors paying within 30 days would receive a discount of 0.5% of the value of their invoices.

4. A new order of sales invoice stationery was received part way through the year. Usually the sales invoice stationery is printed with 'SETTLEMENT REQUIRED WITHIN 30 DAYS', but the printers had omitted this by mistake. The office general manager decided to use the stationery anyway.

Two of these reasons could be valid explanations for the increase in the debtors turnover period. The valid explanations are:

a) 1 and 2

b) 3 and 4

c) 1 and 4

d) 2 and 3.

14.20   A business has creditors at its year-end of £206 460. Purchases for the year are £1 952 278, of which 90% were made on credit. What is the creditors turnover period?

a) 42.9 days

b) 38.6 days

c) 34.7 days

d) 11.7 days.

14.21A Wiswell Limited is a trading company. Its year-end accounts for 20X4 and 20X3 include the following relevant details:

	20X4 £	20X4 £	20X3 £	20X3 £
Sales		1 936 000		1 877 200
Cost of sales				
Opening stock	145 550		136 200	
Add: purchases	1 042 255		1 025 666	
	1 187 805		1 161 866	
Less: closing stock	(160 370)		(145 550)	
		(1 027 435)		(1 016 316)

	20X4 £	20X4 £	20X3 £	20X3 £
Gross profit		908 565		860 884
Stocks		160 370		145 550
Debtors		226 485		209 063
Creditors		160 479		151 742

Calculate the following ratios for both 20X4 and 20X3:

i) stock turnover in days

ii) debtors turnover in days

iii) creditors turnover in days.

Comment briefly on the significance of the changes in the ratios.

The following information about Waldo Wolff plc, a quoted company, is relevant to questions 14.22–14.25 inclusive. Extracts from Waldo Wolff's accounts for the year ending 31 December 20X4 include the following useful information:

	£000
Operating profit	1 836.4
Interest payable	(220.0)
Profit before taxation	1 616.4
Taxation	(485.0)
Profit after taxation	1 131.4
Dividends	(300.0)
Retained profit	831.4

The company has 6 000 000 shares in issue. The shares have a nominal value of 50p each. The market price at 31 December 20X4 of a share in the company is £3.11.

14.22   The dividend per share is:

a) 10p

b) 5p

c) 50p

d) 100p.

14.23   The dividend cover ratio is:

a) 3.77

b) 5.39

c) 2.77

d) 6.12.

14.24   Earnings per share (in pence) is:

a) 18.86p

b) 26.94p

c) 13.86p

d) 37.71p.

14.25 What is Waldo Wolff plc's market capitalisation at 31 December 20X4?

14.26 At 30 April 20X6 Wilson Streep plc has a market capitalisation of £6 303 000 with 3 300 000 ordinary 50p shares in issue. The profit attributable to ordinary shareholders in its profit and loss account for the year ending 30 April 20X6 is £750 090. What is the company's P/E ratio?

    a) 16.1

    b) 4.2

    c) 8.4

    d) 3.8.

The following information about Worsley Bacup plc, a quoted company, is relevant to questions 14.27A–14.30A inclusive. Extracts from Worsley Bacup's accounts for the year ending 30 September 20X9 include the following useful information:

	£000
Operating profit	986.7
Interest payable	(106.0)
Profit before taxation	880.7
Taxation	(240.0)
Profit after taxation	640.7
Dividends	(250.8)
Retained profit	389.9

The company has 2 200 000 shares in issue. The shares have a nominal value of 25p each. The market price at 31 December 20X4 of a share in the company is £7.66.

14.27A The dividend per share is:

    a) 45.6p

    b) 11.4p

    c) 25.0p

    d) 29.1p.

14.28A The dividend cover ratio is:

    a) 3.51

    b) 1.55

    c) 3.93

    d) 2.55.

14.29A Earnings per share (in pence) is:

    a) 17.72p

    b) 29.12p

    c) 116.49p

    d) 70.89p.

14.30A What is Worsley Bacup plc's market capitalisation at 30 September 20X9?

14.31A Watkinson Chapel plc is a listed company with a market capitalisation of £3 430 000 at 31 August 20X7. It has in issue 1 000 000 £1 ordinary shares, and profits attributable to ordinary shareholders for the year ending 31 August 20X7 are £243 700. What is the company's P/E ratio?

a) 21.4

b) 4.1

c) 3.4

d) 14.1.

14.32 Brazier Barkiss plc has the following capital structure at 30 April 20X6:

	£
Ordinary share capital (£1 shares)	1 000 000
Reserves	2 739 400
Long-term loans (10% interest rate)	2 000 000

Profit before interest and tax for the year ending 30 April 20X6 was £646 750 and interest payable was £200 000. Calculate the following ratios:

i) gearing (on the basis of debt/equity)

ii) interest cover.

14.33A Better Belter Limited has the following capital structure at 31 October 20X7:

	£
Ordinary share capital (£1 shares)	80 000
Reserves	696 400
Long-term loans (8% interest rate)	300 000

Profit before interest and tax for the year ending 31 October 20X7 was £35 000, and interest payable was £24 000. Calculate the following ratios:

i) gearing (on the basis of debt/equity)

ii) interest cover.

14.34 The directors of the Cuttlefish Biscuit Corporation Limited have calculated a set of key accounting ratios for their biscuit manufacturing business. These are detailed in the following table, together with industry averages provided by the National Biscuit Manufacturers' Federation.

	Cuttlefish	Industry average
Gross profit margin	32.3%	31.6%
Operating profit margin	16.2%	17.1%
Debtors turnover (days)	36.0	38.4
Stock turnover (days)	48.7	47.4
Creditors (days)	31.4	39.6
Gearing (debt/equity)	18.7%	29.4%

Write a brief report to the directors of Cuttlefish comparing the ratios for their company with the industry averages. Identify any areas in which you think they could make improvements.

14.35   Cryer Roussillon Limited is a trading company. Shortly before the beginning of the 20X5 accounting year (which ends on 31 December) a new managing director was appointed. He made the strategic decision to alter the company's range of products. Previously, the company had concentrated on lower margin products within its industry, but the new MD decided to move into higher quality products which produce better margins. He has made several other changes to the company. He persuaded the board of directors that the company should invest in some badly needed new fixed assets, and the company took out a long-term loan to help finance the acquisitions. He has also obtained the agreement of the other directors (all of whom are shareholders) not to propose any dividend this year, so that profits can be retained in the company to help finance future growth.

The summarised financial statements for 20X5 and 20X4 are as follows.

Cryer Roussillon Limited: Profit and loss accounts for the years ending 31 December 20X5 and 31 December 20X4

	20X5 £	20X4 £
Sales	206 470	210 619
Cost of sales	(121 198)	(141 789)
Gross profit	85 272	68 830
Various expenses	(41 459)	(47 610)
Operating profit	43 813	21 220
Interest	(3 000)	—
Profit before taxation	40 813	21 220
Taxation	(8 100)	(3 180)
Profit after taxation	32 713	18 040
Dividend	—	(13 000)
Retained profit	32 713	5 040

Cryer Roussillon: Balance sheets at 31 December 20X5 and 20X4

	20X5 £	20X5 £	20X4 £	20X4 £
Fixed assets		129 490		68 750
Current assets				
Stock	14 278		14 550	
Debtors	20 693		29 420	
Cash at bank	10 792		640	
	45 763		44 610	
Creditors: amounts falling due within one year	15 470		16 290	
		30 293		28 320

	20X5 £	20X5 £	20X4 £	20X4 £
Total assets less current liabilities		159 783		97 070
Long-term loan		(30 000)		—
		129 783		97 070
Capital and reserves				
Share capital		20 000		20 000
Reserves		109 783		77 070
		129 783		97 070

The managing director has asked you, as the company's financial adviser, to write a confidential report to the board commenting upon items of significance in the accounts. He would like you to calculate any key ratios that you consider to be important, and to provide an assessment of how the company is doing.

Answers to exercises

14.1   Pre-tax return on shareholders' funds:

$$\frac{\text{Profit after interest and before taxation}}{\text{Shareholders' funds}}$$

$$= \frac{267.8}{2\,290} = 11.7\%$$

The correct answer, therefore, is d).

14.2   Post-tax return on shareholders' funds:

$$\frac{\text{Profit after interest and taxation}}{\text{Shareholders' funds}}$$

$$= \frac{189.8}{2290} = 8.2\%$$

The correct answer, therefore, is b).

14.3   Return on total capital invested:

$$\frac{\text{Profit before interest and taxation}}{\text{Shareholders' funds} + \text{Long-term borrowing}}$$

$$= \frac{302.8}{2\,290 + 350} = 11.5\%$$

The correct answer, therefore, is b).

14.7   The pre-tax return on shareholders' funds is calculated as:

$$\frac{\text{Profit before taxation and after interest}}{\text{Shareholders' funds}}$$

For each company:

Ambit Limited	Bolsover Limited	Carcan Limited	Delphic Limited
$\dfrac{803.6}{80.0 + 4550.0} \times 100 = 17.4\%$	$\dfrac{540.8}{95.0 + 3881.0} \times 100 = 13.6\%$	$\dfrac{575.8}{86.0 + 3928.0} \times 100 = 14.3\%$	$\dfrac{855.4}{60.0 + 7000.0} \times 100 = 12.1\%$

The company with the highest return is Ambit Limited, and so the correct answer is a).

14.9   Trixie Stores Limited:

Total current assets = 18 370 + 24 100 + 70 = £42 540
Total current liabilities = 15 450 + 6 400 = £21 850.

The current ratio equals:

$$\frac{\text{Current assets}}{\text{Current liabilities}} = \frac{42\,540}{21\,850} = 1.95:1$$

The correct answer, therefore, is a).

14.11   Trimester Tinker Limited:

Current assets = 108 770 + 94 300 + 1 600 = £204 670
'Quick' assets = 94 300 + 1 600 = £95 900
Current liabilities = £110 650.

$$\text{Current ratio} = \frac{204\,670}{110\,650} = 1.85:1$$

$$\text{Quick ratio} = \frac{95\,900}{110\,650} = 0.87:1$$

Trimester Tinker's current ratio of 1.85:1 is higher than the industry average of 1.62:1, while its quick ratio of 0.87:1 is lower than the industry average of 0.93:1. The correct answer, therefore, is b).

14.13   Upwood Sickert Limited's fixed asset turnover is calculated as follows:

$$\frac{\text{Sales turnover}}{\text{Fixed assets}}$$

The correct figure to take for fixed assets is net book value, i.e. £170 000 + £59 985 = £229 985.

$$\frac{686\,430}{229\,985} = 2.98$$

The correct answer, therefore, is d).

14.15   Key data for the sole trader is:

Opening stock = £405 000

Closing stock = £405 000 + 10% = £445 500.

Average stock for the year equals:

$$\frac{405\,000 + 445\,500}{2} = £425\,250$$

Stock turnover in days equals:

$$\frac{425\,250}{1\,506\,700} \times 365 \text{ days} = 103.0 \text{ days}$$

14.17   Only credit sales are taken into account when calculating the debtors turnover ratio. Credit sales for the year equal:

$$£1\,703\,698 \times 70\% = £1\,192\,589$$

Debtors turnover ratio:

$$\frac{218\,603}{1\,703\,698} \times 365 \text{ days} = 46.8 \text{ days}$$

The correct answer, therefore, is a).

14.19   Winger Whalley Limited:

1. The absence of the credit controller on sick leave is likely to result in a slowing up of debtor payments. Many debtors will pay on time as a matter of routine, but some always need chasing. Unless a credit controller is chasing this latter group for payment they will delay or defer settling their debts. This is a valid reason.

2. An increase of 4% in sales is not likely to make any difference to the collection of debts. A very large increase might put pressure on administrative systems, but 4% is not likely to matter.

3. Early settlement discounts should have the opposite effect: debtors should pay up more quickly in order to take advantage of the settlement discount.

4. It is important to state the company's terms on the invoice stationery. If this is not done, new and occasional customers will simply not know the terms of trade, and may be inclined to take longer to pay. Other debtors may use the absence of stated terms as an excuse to take longer to pay.

Reasons 1 and 4 could be valid explanations. The correct answer, therefore, is c).

14.20   The calculation of the creditors turnover period ratio should include only purchases made on credit. Purchases made on credit equals:

$$90\% \times £1\,952\,278 = £1\,757\,050$$

Creditors turnover in days:

$$\frac{206\,460}{1\,757\,050} \times 365 \text{ days} = 42.9 \text{ days}$$

The correct answer, therefore, is a).

14.22   Waldo Wolff's dividend per share:

$$\frac{\text{Dividend}}{\text{Number of shares in issue}}$$

$$\frac{300\,000}{6\,000\,000} = 5\text{p per share}$$

The correct answer, therefore, is b).

14.23   Wablo Wolff's dividend cover ratio:

$$\frac{\text{Earnings after tax attributable to ordinary shareholders}}{\text{Dividend}}$$

$$\frac{1\,131\,400}{300\,000} = 3.77$$

The correct answer, therefore, is a).

14.24   Waldo Wolff's earnings per share:

$$\frac{\text{Earnings after tax attributable to ordinary shareholders}}{\text{Number of shares in issue}}$$

$$\frac{1\,131\,400}{6\,000\,000} = 18.86\text{p per share}$$

The correct answer, therefore, is a).

14.25   Waldo Wolff's market capitalisation is the share price times the number of shares in issue:

$$£3.11 \times 6\,000\,000 = £18\,660\,000$$

14.26   Wilson Streep plc. First, calculate earnings per share:

$$\frac{\text{Earnings attributable to ordinary shareholders}}{\text{Number of shares in issue}}$$

$$= \frac{750\,090}{3\,300\,000} = 22.73\text{p}$$

P/E ratio = price divided by earnings per share:

$$\text{Price per share} = \frac{\text{Market capitalisation}}{\text{Number of shares}}$$

$$= \frac{6\,303\,000}{3\,300\,000} = £1.91$$

$$\frac{\text{Price}}{\text{Earnings per share}}$$

$$= \frac{191\text{p}}{22.73\text{p}} = 8.4$$

The correct answer, therefore, is c).

14.32   Brazier Barkiss Limited

i) Gearing ratio

$$\frac{Debt}{Equity}$$

$$= \frac{2\,000\,000}{3\,739\,400} = 53.4\%$$

ii) Interest cover

$$\frac{Profit\ before\ interest\ and\ tax}{Interest}$$

$$= \frac{646\,750}{200\,000} = 3.23\ times.$$

14.34   **Report to the directors of The Cuttlefish Biscuit Corporation Limited**

Gross profit margin for Cuttlefish is better than the industry average, but net profit margin is worse. This suggests that the business is incurring higher costs on average, such as administration, selling and marketing costs, than its competitors. There may be good reasons in the short term why this should be so, but if business costs continue at a relatively high level the directors may wish to consider a range of possible cost reductions. In the meantime, it would be helpful to examine costs in detail to identify areas where savings are possible.

The debtors turnover ratio shows that Cuttlefish collects its debts more quickly than average in the industry. Given that most businesses will automatically take 30 days credit, 36 days is very good. There may be room for some improvement, however, and the directors may wish to consider, for example, introducing discounts for early settlement if they have not already done so.

Stock turnover is slightly worse than the industry average. It may be advisable to look more closely at the level of stocks held in the business and look for ways of managing stock more efficiently.

On average the industry takes a lot longer to pay creditors than Cuttlefish: 31.4 days would usually be considered a low turnover ratio where the industry trading terms are settlement within 30 days. The directors might consider extending this period by a few days; it would release some cash into the operating cycle, and could probably be done without endangering relationships with suppliers.

Cuttlefish's gearing ratio is low, compared to the industry. No particular action is recommended on this point, but if directors are looking for long-term finance for business expansion they should bear in mind that the business is not currently regarded as highly geared. Further long-term loans, within reasonable limits, would therefore be an option for consideration.

Generally, Cuttlefish appears to be doing well compared to industry averages.

14.35 **Confidential report to the board of Cryer Roussillon Limited**

Executive summary

The implementation of the range of new strategies has been very successful. The company is now more profitable than it was a year ago, and its balance sheet is healthy. The company should now concentrate on consolidating its position and should seek to expand sales volume.

The appendix to this report sets out a set of relevant ratio calculations.

Detailed report

The company's sales have dropped by almost 2% since last year. However, gross profit has improved by almost 24%, and the gross profit margin is now 41.3% compared to only 32.7% in 20X4. The company's strategy of pursuing higher margin sales appears to have paid off. It should now concentrate on increasing sales volume in those higher margin products. Operating expenses appear to be well under control; some effective cost-cutting appears to have taken place in 20X5.

The company has made a major investment in fixed assets: net book value has increased by 88% in the year. It is possible that the benefits to be obtained from these assets have not fed through into sales volumes and profits yet. The fixed asset efficiency ratio is notably poorer in 20X5 but could be expected to improve in 20X6 as the assets are utilised throughout the whole year.

Liquidity is not a problem. Liquidity ratios in both 20X4 and 20X5 are good, and the amount of cash at bank has increased very substantially. The directors' decision not to propose a dividend has helped, and means that spare cash is now available for extra investment.

Stock turnover has worsened to 43 days (from 37.5 in 20X4). The company must ensure that it is not over-stocking, and controls over stock levels perhaps need further attention. Debtors, on the other hand, appear to be better controlled in 20X5: debtor turnover has reduced, and appears to be at a quite satisfactory level.

The company has taken on long-term debt resulting in a relatively modest level of gearing. The level of gearing does not appear to be a cause for any concern at the moment.

Appendix

	20X5	20X4
Performance		
Gross profit margin	$\frac{85\,272}{206\,470} \times 100 = 41.3\%$	$\frac{68\,830}{210\,619} \times 100 = 32.7\%$
Operating profit margin	$\frac{43\,813}{206\,470} \times 100 = 21.2\%$	$\frac{21\,220}{210\,619} \times 100 = 10.1\%$
Return on shareholders' funds	$\frac{40\,813}{129\,783} \times 100 = 31.4\%$	$\frac{21\,220}{97\,070} \times 100 = 21.8\%$
Liquidity		
Current ratio	$\frac{45\,763}{15\,470} = 2.96$	$\frac{44\,610}{16\,290} = 2.74$
Quick ratio	$\frac{20\,693 + 10\,792}{15\,470} = 2.04$	$\frac{29\,420 + 640}{16\,290} = 1.85$
Efficiency		
Fixed assets turnover	$\frac{206\,470}{129\,490} = 1.59$	$\frac{210\,619}{68\,750} = 3.06$
Stock turnover (days)	$\frac{14\,278}{121\,198} \times 365 = 43.0$	$\frac{14\,550}{141\,789} \times 365 = 37.5$
Debtors turnover (days)	$\frac{20\,693}{206\,470} \times 365 = 36.6$	$\frac{29\,420}{210\,619} \times 365 = 50.1$
Gearing		
Debt/equity	$\frac{30\,000}{129\,783} = 23.1\%$	Nil

III

MANAGEMENT ACCOUNTING

15

MANAGEMENT AND COST ACCOUNTING INFORMATION

AIMS AND LEARNING OUTCOMES

Aim of the chapter

To establish the need for accounting information geared towards users within the business, and to introduce some of the basic terminology and ideas such as planning, control and decision making.

Learning outcomes

After reading the chapter and completing the related exercises, students should:

- Appreciate the need to generate accounting information for use within the business organisation.
- Understand the range of uses for internal accounting information.
- Understand some basic terminology such as planning, control and decision making.

This is a relatively short chapter, which sets the scene for the areas considered in detail in subsequent chapters. Much of this chapter is taken up with the illustrative case study that helps to explain the need for accounting information within the organisation.

Contrasting financial accounting and cost and management accounting

Part II of this book was concerned with financial accounting for the results and position of business enterprises, and the regular reporting of this information via the profit and loss account, the balance sheet and the cash flow statement. As we have seen, this type of accounting is useful to a potentially wide range of users, including the managers and proprietors of businesses.

However, there are limitations in the usefulness of the periodic financial statements. These include:

● lack of timeliness
● orientation to past events.
● high levels of aggregation.

Lack of timeliness

It takes time to produce financial statements for external users; they may not become available until six months or so after the year-end. Most businesses produce financial statements only once a year. Taking these two factors together, it means that the most recently available financial statements may be up to 18 months out of date.

Orientation to past events

Conventional financial statements report on events in the past; they do not tend to look forward into the future, and rarely contain any element of forecast information.

High levels of aggregation

As we have seen in preceding chapters, the profit and loss, balance sheet and cash flow statements pull together a lot of information into relatively few descriptions and figures. For example, most of the costs between the gross profit and operating profit lines in the profit and loss account are pushed into two categories: selling and distribution expenses and administrative costs. It is not possible to tell much about the nature of the costs included under such broad general headings.

Most external users of the information (for example, creditors, customers and potential investors) have to resign themselves to these limitations. Even if they want more information, they are not usually entitled to it. Business managers are in a different position; they have the resources of the business at their disposal and consequently they have access to a great deal of potentially useful information that can be used to help them run the business.

Cost and management accounting refers to the provision of information resources that business managers can use to help run the business.

Some features of cost and management accounting

Lack of regulation

Cost and management accounting is accounting that is internal to the business only. The nature and content of financial reporting, especially for limited companies, is heavily regulated, but, by contrast, there are no regulations relating to cost and management accounting. Accounting information is generated for internal use in whatever form, and in whatever quantity, is most appropriate for the business.

Orientation towards past *and* future

We noted above that financial reporting information is oriented towards events that have already occurred. Cost and management accounting draws upon past events for information but is also oriented towards the future. It considers such questions as, for example:

- How much profit is the business likely to make next year?
- How much additional business are we likely to pick up if we lower our prices by 5%?
- Should we close down a part of the business that is making losses?
- We need a new machine in the factory. Should we buy it or lease it?
- How much does this product actually cost to produce?
- Which divisions in the business are, relatively speaking, more profitable?

Timely production

The overriding objective of the production of cost and management information is that it should be useful. Management can set up systems that produce useful information quickly. For example, in most businesses it will be useful to have monthly sales figures reported as quickly as possible. Such figures do not necessarily have to be completely accurate. Also, they do not necessarily have to be accompanied by other profit and loss information (which would probably slow up the production of information). There is no reason why simple sales figures could not be available a day or two after each month-end. Managers would thus be in a position to respond to changes in the figures very quickly, as illustrated in the following example.

Example 15.1 Duckworth Failsafe Limited produces household alarm systems in do-it-yourself installation kits. Until recently there have been two types: the Standard and the De-Luxe systems. This year, from 1 January, the company has introduced the Super-De-Luxe, which has much more sophisticated circuitry and an extra alarm box for external installation. The gross margins on the three types are 38%, 40% and 46% respectively, and the company is keen to promote sales of the higher specification products.

Each month the sales director holds a meeting with the sales force on about the fifth or sixth of the month. On 5 April 20X4 he holds a meeting at which he discusses the sales figures (in units) for January, February and March, which are as follows:

▶

	Standard	De-Luxe	Super-De-Luxe	Total
January	2 038	1 604	213	3 855
February	2 175	1 598	344	4 117
March	2 240	1 634	28	3 902

At the meeting he asks his staff why they think that sales of the Super-De-Luxe, after a promising start in January and February, have nosedived in March. A couple of the sales reps tell him that Duckworth's principal competitor has brought out a de-luxe system that is not only cheaper than Duckworth's but which also has some extra features. 'We can't compete with it on either price or quality' says one of the reps.

The sales director now has quite a lot of information to take with him to the next main board meeting: concrete evidence in the form of the sales figures of problems with the Super-De-Luxe sales, and some reasons for the drop in sales. The information he has available does not *solve* the problem, but the rapid provision of figures has at least allowed him to *identify* that a problem exists. It is then up to the board of directors to discuss the problem and possible solutions to it.

Frequent reporting

In Example 15.1, sales of alarm systems were reported internally once a month. This is clearly a much more frequent basis of reporting than the annual financial reporting undertaken by businesses. Indeed, it is common for businesses to organise their internal management reporting on a monthly basis; monthly management accounts are produced for distribution to directors and managers. However, it is possible to produce internal cost and management information as frequently as necessary. In larger businesses some elements of internal information may be reported as frequently as once a day. For example, very large retailers are likely to produce sales figures daily for the business as a whole, for individual stores and for regions or divisions.

Cost accounting and management accounting

Both **cost accounting** and **management accounting** are referred to in the context of the production of information for internal purposes. Is there a difference between cost accounting and management accounting?

- *Management accounting* describes the process of collecting, collating and reporting information that is of use to the managers of a business for making decisions, for monitoring past performance and for making the most efficient use of resources.
- *Cost accounting* describes the process of identifying and accumulating the costs of business operations in a way that is helpful in valuing stock and in identifying the costs and profitability of different departments or divisions of a business.

There is a considerable overlap in the terms, and indeed, they are often used interchangeably. In this book we will not attempt to demarcate the terms rigorously. 'Management accounting' will be used as a general term to cover the production and uses of information within a business, and to contrast with the financial accounting and reporting that was the subject of Part II of the book. We will refer to 'cost accounting' in areas where we are specifically considering the identification and accumulating of costs. However, there is no need to be concerned about precision in the usage of either term.

The purpose and uses of management accounting

The case study for this chapter sets the scene for considering the principal uses of management accounting information. Through consideration of the case study and the discussion of it we will identify some of the principal uses of information prepared for internal use within a business.

CASE STUDY 15.1 Management accounting – pros and cons

Eight years ago Paco set up a greetings card company, Calder Calloway Cards Limited. The company buys in card designs from freelance designers and then prints, assembles and packs the cards for sale to retailers. Paco started out on a small scale; he and his brother Pedro bought up some card designs at low prices from struggling art students, printed them in runs of about 1000 and then went round card shops selling them in small quantities. The business did very well, largely due to the brothers' flair in spotting good, commercial, card designs, and their abilities as salesmen.

Initially, Paco owned 60% of the company, Pedro owned 30% and the remainder of the shares were held by other family members. However, the company gradually needed more capital to expand and the brothers sold off some of their shares to a couple of wealthy private investors, Walter and Jennifer. Pedro, although he still owns some shares and remains as a director of Calder Calloway, has moved on to start another business in selling advertising space. The private investors do not take an active part in the management of the company, but they are both very experienced and Paco quite frequently uses them as sounding boards for new ideas. Over the last two years they have both tried to persuade Paco to hire some expert managers. About a year ago, Walter and Jennifer had a meeting with Paco which proved to be a turning point. Although Paco lost his temper and accused them of trying to ruin his business, he was eventually brought round to accepting that the company had grown too big for him to manage alone.

> *Jennifer*: Look, Paco, you're the boss, and we're not trying to dictate to you, but the company's just too big and complex now to be run by just one person. You need some help if you're going to be able to stay on top of things.

> *Walter*: And it *is* getting out of hand. I'm concerned to see that the gross profit margin for 20X6 has fallen yet again – that's the third year running. Just how are you planning to tackle that little problem?

During 20X7 Paco accepts the inevitable, and uses the services of a recruitment consultancy to appoint a sales director, Tracey, and a production director, Karim, both of whom have a lot of relevant experience. The first formal meeting of the new board is on 1 February 20X8, exactly a week after the two new directors took

◀ ◀ ◀

up their appointments. Paco's plan was that they would have a few days to settle into their new responsibilities and then the board would be in a position to have an effective formal meeting to discuss ideas about future plans for the company.

Both new directors have submitted details of some new ideas for consideration at the meeting. Tracey's list includes:

● Introduce a commission scheme for the sales force [who are currently on fixed salaries] based on the extent to which their actual performance exceeds budget performance.

● Concentrate sales efforts on the more profitable ranges of cards.

Karim's list includes:

● Invest in some new printing equipment. The existing equipment is out-of-date; it keeps breaking down and staff report that the printing is often of such poor quality that a lot of work-in-progress has to be simply thrown away.

● Employ some designers to work full-time for the company. This would help to ensure that the company had a constant stream of new designs, and would help to establish a corporate design approach, which is lacking under the present haphazard system of buying in designs.

The directors' discussion of these points proceeds as follows:

Paco: Well, this idea about the commission could work, but I don't quite see what you mean about actual performance as opposed to budget performance . . .

Tracey: I mean the sales budget in terms of the number of units you're budgeting to sell in a given period. You could break the overall number down into an expected sales volume for each person in the sales force; if he or she exceeds that they get rewarded by a commission. You can make the scheme as complex as you like, really. In one company I worked for they had a 'seller of the month' scheme. If you won it three times the company paid for a luxury weekend break . . . that kind of thing.

Paco: But we don't have a sales budget. . . . People just sell what they can . . . it's always worked that way in the past and we've done pretty well. . . .

Tracey: Well, I was wondering why I got blank looks when I asked to see the sales budget. . . . Are you telling me you don't set budgets?

Paco: This is a very successful company. We don't need to bother with a lot of extra paperwork.

Karim: Well, what about management information generally? Don't you have any management accounting systems at all?

Paco: Well, no, why would we? It would just mean employing a load of expensive beancounters. I've got no time for accountants. The bookkeeper does an excellent job and the accountant comes in to do the final accounts once a year, and keep us out of trouble with the Customs and Excise and the Inland Revenue. That's good enough for me.

Tracey: But if that's the case we really can't consider either of my suggestions, can we? I want to concentrate on selling the more profitable ranges of cards, but how am I going to find out which ones are more profitable if we don't have any information?

Paco: Er . . .

Karim: And what about production? I can't make a decision about buying a new machine unless I can compare projected costs of using the new machine with the costs of the existing set up. Please tell me, at least, that you monitor the design costs. If we're going to employ designers I need to compare the costs of employing them against the costs of buying in a lot of separate designs.

Paco: Oh, well, the annual costs are all included in the profit and loss account, you see. Here's the draft profit and loss account for 20X7 – the accountant's just finished it. He'll do a summary one to send to Companies House, but this one's really quite detailed – look, there's a figure for design costs – I'm not quite sure what's in it, but I expect it includes all the costs of paying for the designs.

Tracey: But what puzzles me is how you keep on top of what's going on in the business. How do you know what your production costs are? How can you tell if they're getting out of hand? Did you know, before Karim told you, that a lot of the production simply goes to waste?

Paco: Look, I know what you're saying. You want me to fill the place up with overpaid accountants who'll waste a lot of time and money telling me things I know already. . . . When you work in a business long enough you get a feel for what's going on. I don't need a lot of management reports to tell me that.

The meeting degenerates into a prolonged argument. Tracey and Karim try to persuade Paco that a business of the size of Calder Calloway needs a sound system of management information. Paco, on the other hand, is opposed to spending (he uses the term 'wasting') money on gathering information that won't tell him anything that he doesn't already know.

What are the arguments for and against the provision of management information for a company like Calder Calloway Cards Limited? What kind of management information is required? Why is it needed?

Case study solution and discussion

The situation outlined in the case study is by no means unusual. The founder of a company who remains in control through a period of growth is often unwilling to accept that the nature of the business has changed. The approach to business management, which worked so successfully when the business was small, may not be appropriate once it has grown past a certain point. The investors, Walter and Jennifer, have managed to persuade Paco to bring in additional management expertise, but the new directors clearly face a struggle if they are to bring Paco round to their way of thinking about management information.

Tracey and Karim's point of view

In order to illustrate the need for management information in the company we will look at the four proposals made by the new directors:

1. *Introduce a commission scheme for the sales force based on the extent to which their actual performance exceeds budget performance*. A system of commission to reward the sales force can often be an effective way of motivating staff to increase sales. However, management needs to be sure that the scheme is set up in such a way that it does not cost more than the additional profit that can be generated from extra sales, and that it is fair to all

staff and sets achievable targets (if the targets are too high staff are likely to be demotivated). This proposal will require a decision, based upon an informed analysis of the existing costs involved in running the sales force and upon future projected figures. Various types of commission scheme are possible, and a range of options could be considered.

2. *Concentrate sales efforts on the more profitable ranges of cards*. We know from the details in the case that the company's gross profit margin has been falling. It might make sense to concentrate on the more profitable ranges of cards, but, as Tracey points out, in order to do so the directors need to know which ranges are most profitable. There is no management information on this point, making it very difficult to plan and make realistic decisions for the future. This is a good example of the need for detailed costing information.

3. *Invest in some new printing equipment*. This is another proposal that involves a decision. There may be several possible courses of action here, and information will be needed on all of them before an informed decision can be made. The directors really need to know quite a lot about the costs of running the existing production facility; the extent and cost of the wastage that appears to be taking place; and the projected costs of alternative production facilities. Until and unless this type of information is made available, the directors will find it impossible to reach a properly informed decision.

4. *Employ designers to work full-time for the company*. This is another proposal that involves the directors in decision making. As Karim says, they need to compare the costs of employing designers with the costs of buying in work from freelance designers. There are several aspects to this type of decision, not all of which are related to cost. For example, employing a team of designers might lead to a stronger corporate approach to design. On the other hand, the designs might become predictable and repetitive over time if they are being produced by the same team.

These proposals all involve, to a greater or lesser extent, decision making. Managers and directors of businesses need relevant information to feed into the decision-making process, so that they can make fully informed appraisals of alternative courses of action. It is quite clear that the directors of Calder Calloway do not have information to hand that will permit them to do this. Their ability to plan and to control the business is severely constrained because of the lack of management information.

In short, management information can help managers in planning, controlling and decision making.

Paco's point of view

Is there anything to be said for Paco's point of view? He does not appear to accept the need for any formalised source of management information, and thinks he can continue to run the business by instinct as he did in its early days. This is not a realistic approach.

However, Paco's views have some validity in that the cost of provision of management information is an important factor. Managers need to have enough relevant information upon which to base their decisions, but the process of providing information must, itself, be controlled. Sometimes organisations are criticised for having excessive bureaucracies and too much paperwork. Sometimes, accountants get the blame for being responsible for pushing too much paper around the organisation.

Calder Calloway, however, is an organisation that clearly lacks relevant information, and Paco should be persuaded to implement some systems that will provide what is necessary in order to plan, control and make decisions effectively.

An important final point

In their enthusiasm to get started in their new jobs and to make a positive impact on the company, both Tracey and Karim have produced lists of ideas for consideration. This is premature; they are rushing into action without considering the longer-term strategy of the business. What are the objectives of the business? What are its priorities in the mid to long term? What strategic decisions need to be made in order to achieve the objectives? These issues need to be thrashed out and decided at board level – the directors are ultimately responsible for deciding on where the business should be going. Then, and only then, is it appropriate to consider the detailed aspects such as those suggested by Tracey and Karim.

Determining business objectives

Determining the overall objectives of a business is not necessarily a straightforward process. Naturally, all businesses within an essentially capitalist system need to make a profit (eventually, and preferably sooner rather than later), and profitability is likely to be an important objective for business managers. However, there are others. Objectives could be expressed in some of the following ways:

- 'We want to be the market leader in plumbers' fittings.'
- 'This company aims to be the best travel agent in the business.'
- 'We aim to operate according to the highest ethical standards at all times.'

Let's look at a few real-life examples of what companies say about their objectives:

- *GUS plc* (formerly Great Universal Stores): 'GUS is focusing its skills and resources on the three areas of consumer understanding, choice and service in order to satisfy an ever more discerning consumer.'
- *GlaxoSmithKline plc*: 'Our mission is nothing less than to improve the quality of human life by enabling people to do more, feel better and live longer.'
- *Pearson plc*: 'We want to make outstanding returns for our shareholders by creating, owning, applying and exploiting intellectual property. We want to do this in a way that is brave, imaginative and decent.'

Strategic decisions

Moving on a stage from the overall business objectives towards more detailed considerations, business managers need to make strategic decisions that will assist in attaining the objectives.

Examples of the type of strategic decision that needs to be made by senior management include:

- *Positioning in market*: should the business aim to go up-market or down-market in its provision of goods and services? For example, a supermarket business could aim to compete with the 'no frills' operators such as Aldi, Netto and Kwiksave, or could aim to provide expensive high margin goods in competition with Marks & Spencer.
- *Sourcing of goods*: a decision that often has to be made in business is where to locate production operations. Should they be moved overseas to locations where labour costs are lower?
- *Moving into international markets*: should a business that is based in one country's market take the risk of moving into other areas?

The management accounting process

The case study discussion earlier illustrated several key points about the process of management accounting, and its link with the functions of management. In this section we will summarise what we have learned so far about management and its need for information.

- *Setting business objectives*: The primary functions of management are: (a) to identify the objectives of the business; and (b) to direct the activities of the business so as to meet the objectives.
- *Assess alternatives and make decisions and make plans*: Management needs information about the alternative actions it could take. Having assessed the available information, management takes decisions and makes detailed plans for the future.
- *Monitoring outcomes*: Management uses information to assess the extent to which its plans have succeeded and its business objectives have been met.
- *Control and redefine objectives and plans*: On the basis of a comparison with planned and actual outcomes it may be necessary to redefine the overarching objectives of the business and the detailed plans that are geared towards achieving the objectives.

Management information is needed at each of these stages, to carry out the essential functions of planning, control and decision making.

Because this is not a textbook about management, we will not consider the setting of strategic objectives in the chapters that follow. We are principally concerned with accounting and finance in business and we will be looking at the provision of management accounting information to assist with planning, control and decision making.

Chapter summary

First, financial accounting and cost and management accounting were contrasted. Financial accounting is of limited usefulness as a source of management information because of factors such as:

- lack of timeliness
- orientation to past events
- high levels of aggregation.

Some of the key features of cost and management accounting were described. These include:

- lack of regulation
- orientation towards past *and* future
- timely production.

The case study for the chapter illustrated the need for management accounting information in a growing business. Management accounting should provide relevant information to feed into decision making, and should allow managers to plan effectively and to control the activities of the business.

Finally, the stages involved in the management accounting process were summarised. Decision-making, planning and control functions are undertaken by managers as part of their primary functions of identifying and meeting the overall objectives of the business.

Exercises

Note that because this chapter is a relatively short introduction to management accounting, there is only a limited number of end of chapter exercises. The intention is that the exercises should be answered in fairly general terms, drawing upon both common sense and imagination. Students have to try to think their way into the situations described in order to specify the kind of management information that would be useful. The objective behind the questions is to get students accustomed to thinking about typical decisions that have to be made in business.

If this book is being studied as part of a taught course, any of the questions that follow could be used as a basis for class discussion.

The answers to many of the exercises are set out later in this chapter. However, where the exercise number is followed by 'A' the answer is available only to lecturers. Remember that additional exercises (with answers) are available to students on the book's website.

15.1 Cueline Limited manufactures furniture at factory premises held on a lease. The lease is due to end next year, but it could probably be renegotiated. The company's directors are also considering the possibility of buying freehold premises. What items of financial information would be useful to the directors in reaching a decision?

15.2A Cyclostyle Limited makes metal parts for bicycles. The metal press machine, which has been used in the business for several years, is now reaching the end of its useful life. The directors are looking at two replacement options. One is a German machine at a cost of £54 000. The other is a British machine at a cost of £38 500.

What items of information, financial and non-financial, are likely to be useful to the directors in deciding between the two machines?

15.3 Putt plc owns several shops selling golfing and other sporting equipment. It operates principally in the area around London. The company's directors will be meeting next month to discuss a proposal for a major change in business strategy. The sales director has observed that gross margins on golf-related items are much higher than those on other stock lines, and he is proposing that the company should in future sell only golfing equipment.

What items of information, financial and non-financial, are likely to be useful to the directors in assessing the pros and cons of the proposed change in strategy?

15.4A Preedy Price Limited is a small fashion company run by two sisters, Anne Preedy and Amelia Price. They have been very successful in marketing a range of very exclusive and expensive knitwear through small specialist retail outlets. The company has been approached by a large retailer, Shield & Flagg plc, which would like to market a cut-price version of some of the sisters' exclusive designs. Shield and Flagg's buyer assures the sisters that this would be a very good opportunity for them to make high volume sales and to make a lot of money. She estimates that volumes of up to 35 000 garments per year are quite feasible. The maximum number of garments the sisters have produced and sold in one year to date is 5600.

Production could be handled by some of Shield & Flagg's regular knitwear production factories, or the sisters could set up their own large-scale production facilities. In order to make the launch of the new lines successful, however, stocks of around 20 000 items would have to be available in advance of the items going on sale in Shield & Flagg's 35 stores around the country.

What factors (both financial and non-financial) should the sisters take into consideration in deciding whether or not to take up this new opportunity?

15.5 Bulstrode, Barker and Bennett is a successful firm of solicitors operating in a small town. Bulstrode died some years ago, Barker has retired, but Dexter Bennett still works in the business as senior partner. There are three junior partners, and Dexter has called a meeting of the partners to discuss the decisions they should make on the following proposals:

a) The conveyancing department is very busy. Would it make economic sense for the firm to employ another solicitor in that department?

b) The firm currently specialises in conveyancing and litigation work. The town's principal specialist in divorce work has just retired, and Bennett thinks there is an opportunity to pick up some extra business. He knows a highly experienced divorce specialist who is currently working for a large firm in London. She could be persuaded to move if she were offered a position as a junior partner.

What information are the partners likely to need (both financial and non-financial) in order to reach the right decisions on these proposals?

15.6A Denver runs a restaurant business, operating from rented premises in the centre of a large town on the outskirts of London. His business has been relatively successful; he has succeeded in making a small profit each year, but he feels that he could do better if he expanded the business.

Denver is a sole trader and the only person with whom he can really discuss business strategy, in complete confidence, is his accountant, Dylan. He has arranged a meeting with Dylan to discuss possible future directions for the business. He starts the meeting by explaining some of the ideas he's had to improve the business:

> The fundamental point is that I need to expand the number of covers. I can't do this in my current premises at Hanover Road, and I would need to move. There's a freehold building for sale on Cross Street with a restaurant on the ground floor. If I bought that I could have half as many covers again as I have now. I could sell my house and then move into the upper part of the building. That would help to keep the mortgage down to a reasonable level.
>
> I've also been wondering about making some fairly major changes to the menu. My net profit margin, as you know from the annual accounts you've just prepared for me, is only about 6%. I would like to cut out the less profitable menu items. I think I know which ones are less profitable but I can't be sure.
>
> As you know, I'm open six evenings a week at the moment. I'm wondering about starting weekend lunches as well, but I don't know whether I could make enough money to justify keeping the place open.

Advise Denver on the type of information – financial and non-financial – he needs in order to make decisions on the three points above (the advice can be given in fairly general terms).

Answers to exercises

Note: the answers are guidelines only. There are many relevant points that could be made in respect of each of the questions, and they may not all be included in the answers given below.

15.1 Cueline Limited's directors are looking at two options: renewal of the lease and purchase of freehold premises. They need to examine projected financial information for both options in order to ensure that they reach the right decision.

Renewal of the lease

The following items of information would be useful:

- The estimated cost of any lease premium (a lease premium is a capital sum payable at the outset of a lease).
- The regular annual rental and any service charges that will have to be paid over the lease term.
- If a large sum has to be paid at the outset of the lease the directors need to examine financing options. Does Cueline Limited have the cash available? Will it need to borrow? If it does have the cash available are there better uses to which the cash can be put?
- If a loan has to be taken out, how much will the regular charge for interest be?

Purchase of freehold premises

The directors need to identify a range of possible properties for purchase by contacting local commercial agents. By doing this they will be able to estimate an approximate capital outlay for the purchase. They need to plan any necessary financing for the purchase, taking into consideration the following points:

- Will a mortgage loan be available for this type of property?
- What effect will a loan have on the company's gearing? (For an explanation of gearing see Chapter 14.)
- How much will the regular charge for interest be?
- What are the implications of the loan and interest repayments for the company's cash flow?

15.3   Putt plc's directors need to make a thorough assessment of the consequences of a change in strategy. They should obtain information on the following:

- The state of the market for golf-related items and the outlook for sales over the next few years. This may involve commissioning specific market research.
- An estimate of the impact of the change on the future performance of the company. How profitable is the company likely to be in the future? Will future performance be an improvement on past performance? How big a difference will the change in strategy make?
- An assessment of the competition. How successful have competitor businesses been in obtaining market share? Are there any new entrants to the market who are likely to pose a threat to Putt plc?
- The likely effects of the proposed change on the need for selling space. Would the existing shops expand their range of golf-related items if more space were to be made available? Would shops need to move (for example, nearer to golf courses)? Are there any implications for staffing (for example, would some staff need to be made redundant)?
- Disposal of existing non-golf stock items. Would these items need to be sold quickly, and would they have to be sold at a loss? If so, what is the projected effect on the company's profit and loss account?

15.5   Bulstrode, Barker and Bennett

a) Employing a new solicitor in the conveyancing department

The obvious financial impact of employing another member of staff is the cost of the salary, plus other costs such as employer's national insurance, employer's contributions to the pension scheme (if any) and any other incidental costs of employment such as health benefits. It would appear to make sense to employ another person if the department's income would, in consequence, increase by enough to cover the additional costs, and the partners would require information about the effect on both income and costs.

However, there are other relevant considerations. If the conveyancing department is genuinely short-staffed, either or both of the following effects could occur:

- Existing staff will be overworked and may become disgruntled. If sufficiently dissatisfied they may seek to change employment.

- There might be an adverse effect on quality. If a serious mistake is made in conveyancing the firm could lay itself open to legal action, or to criticism from regulators. If it acts inefficiently in dealing with clients' business, the consequence could be a loss of reputation. Prospective clients may take their business elsewhere.

b) Employing a specialist divorce solicitor

This involves a significant strategic decision. The existing partners will seek information on:

- The likely cost of bringing in another partner. The new partner would be entitled to a share of the profits of the business, although this could be made dependent upon performance to some extent. She would also expect the same range of benefits (health benefits, pension scheme and so on) as the existing partners. There would, presumably, also be other knock-on effects on staffing (for example, she would almost certainly need some secretarial assistance).

- The expected benefits in terms of increased fees. How much extra business could a divorce specialist be expected to generate? Would she be able to contribute any capital to the business?

- How many solicitors experienced in divorce law actually operate in the area? Is there really a gap in the market for another one? Are there any cross-selling opportunities (for example, people who are getting a divorce often sell joint property, and there may be new opportunities for generating extra conveyancing work)?

- It is important that partners (as joint proprietors of a business) are able to agree among themselves. Would the proposed new partner be an easy person to work with?

16

COSTING

AIMS AND LEARNING OUTCOMES

Aim of the chapter

To achieve an understanding of some of the principal components of cost in business, and of the terminology and classifications used in costing, and to be able to apply this understanding to numerical examples.

Learning outcomes

After reading the chapter and completing the related exercises, students should:

- Recognise and understand a range of basic costing terminology.
- Be able to classify costs into direct and indirect costs.
- Understand the build-up of materials, labour and production overheads into full production cost.
- Be able to apportion costs between cost centres.
- Be able to calculate and apply suitable overhead absorption rates.
- Understand the basic principles of activity-based costing.

Costing in business

Costs are incurred in obtaining goods or services that will be used for the benefit of the business in achieving its overall objectives. Traditional costing techniques were established from the time of the Industrial Revolution onwards in the context of large manufacturing organisations. Such organisations were typically engaged in 'heavy' industrial activities, exploiting large amounts of investment in machinery and using a lot of labour.

Nowadays, of course, the nature of many industries has changed radically. More efficient production methods have focused on reducing the element of labour required in production and in using labour more efficiently. Heavy industry is no longer so economically significant (a factor that is especially noticeable in the more developed economies of the world) and recent years have seen the rapid growth of service industries. Such industries do not use capital in the form of large factories full of machinery. They rely for their economic success on exploiting ideas, employing the time and energies of creative people. This element of 'human capital' has become increasingly important in all types of industry.

Contrast, for example, a steelworks and an advertising agency. The steelworks uses physical objects in the form of fairly simple tools and machinery located in a very large space, plus physical labour, to transform iron ore via physical processes into steel. The emphasis is on *physical* transformation. The principal costs involved in such a process are the costs of raw material, the depreciation charges for the physical assets consumed and the cost of employing people to do the work.

By contrast, the advertising agency is about the transformation of mental processes and ideas. A team of creative people work together to produce ideas. The more successful of the ideas will gain a kind of physical form in due course when they are turned into newspaper and television advertisements, but the physical processing of the ideas is likely to be done by other firms and individuals outside the agency. The advertising agency itself is primarily a medium for the generation and transmission of ideas. The labour involved is not physical but mental. The principal costs involved in running an agency are the costs of paying staff salaries and benefits and providing them with computers, telephones and other communication media. There are some costs related to physical assets consumed (for example, the people have to be accommodated; they take up physical space in buildings) but these are likely to be relatively insignificant in a 'knowledge' business like an advertising agency.

In this chapter we will examine some basic features of traditional costing techniques. Many of these are related to examples in manufacturing industry where the techniques were developed. However, costing and management accounting techniques are also useful in service and knowledge-based industries. Some of the examples in this chapter and subsequent chapters in Part III will illustrate the application of management accounting in non-manufacturing environments.

Cost classification: Direct and indirect costs

Earlier in the book (in Chapter 10) we examined the basic components of cost in a manufacturing environment in order to be able to prepare financial statements for a manufacturing business. We established three basic components of manufacturing cost:

- materials cost
- labour cost
- production overheads.

Materials and labour cost are both direct inputs into the manufacturing process. Production overheads are indirect inputs. They are costs involved in running a production facility but which are not themselves identifiable with individual items produced. These costs are often classified as direct (direct materials, labour and any other direct expenses) and indirect (overheads). If in doubt about whether a cost is direct or indirect, ask the question: 'Can this cost be traced directly to the product?'

The following example will help to illustrate the point.

Example 16.1 The case study for the previous chapter was set in a greetings card company. Think about what is involved in producing a greetings card:

1. A design is produced.
2. The design is printed on to card in a run of an appropriate size – say 1000 cards per production run.
3. The card is cut and folded.
4. Other processes such as embossing, gilding and over-printing may be required, depending upon the design.
5. The cards are matched with envelopes of suitable size.
6. Each card and envelope is individually packaged in a cellophane wrapper.

What are the direct and indirect costs involved in this process?

Direct costs

Direct materials

Materials costs include the cost of card, ink, possibly metal-leaf, envelopes and cellophane and, perhaps, a label.

Direct labour

Labour is required to set up and operate the printing machine (likely to be a computerised process, but one which will involve some input of time), to operate the machine that cuts and folds the card, and to package the card together with the envelope (this last may be a completely manual process)

Direct expense

There is another expense involved in the process: that of the card design. If this is outsourced (i.e. individual designs are bought in from freelance designers), as in the Chapter 15 example, there is a clearly defined direct expense. Suppose the company pays the designer £100 for the design under an agreement that allows it to produce 1000 cards from the design, each card bears a cost of 10p in respect of design costs.

Indirect costs

Indirect production costs (overheads)

Indirect production costs, as we observed in Chapter 10 in respect of financial accounting for manufacturing industries, include all of those costs of running the production facility that cannot be directly identified with units of production. These would include such items as:

- factory rental
- production supervisor's wages
- factory cleaning costs
- maintenance and repair of factory and machinery.

Other indirect costs (overheads)

As well as indirect costs incurred in running the production facility, there are many other costs involved in running a business, for example:

- administration salaries
- rental of the office
- depreciation of the office computer
- salespersons' salaries.

Total cost

All of the costs taken together add up to the total cost of running the business, summarised as follows:

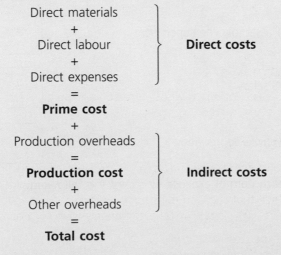

Note that the terms 'indirect costs' and 'overheads' mean the same thing. Either term can be used.

Self-test question 16.1 (answer at the end of the chapter)

Beeching Plumstead Limited has a factory which produces babies' pushchairs. The following is a list of some of the costs which the company incurs:

Canvas material

Metal spokes for wheels

Spare parts for sewing machine repairs

Advertising expenditure

Machine oil

Electricity bill for factory

Wages of assembly line workers

Wages of factory canteen staff

Wages of assembly line supervisor

Secretary's salary

Delivery vehicle depreciation

Classify each item of expense as one of the following:

● direct labour
● direct materials
● direct expenses
● indirect production overheads
● other indirect overheads.

In the next example, we will fit some figures into the structure.

Example 16.2 Julienne Jack Limited is a company that produces socks from a small rented factory space. In the month ending 31 August 20X4 it incurs the following costs:

	£
Depreciation of knitting machines	420
Knitting machine repair	68
Machine operators' wages	6 330
Wool	4 850
Sticky labels for socks	93
Plastic ties for sock pairing	133
Factory rental	1 230
Electricity costs – factory	216
Electricity costs – office	38
Part-time secretary's wages	540
Office stationery and supplies	21
Factory cleaner's wages	123
Telephone – office	83
Delivery costs	436
Other office costs	214
Other factory costs	130

Rearrange the information given above into a cost statement for August 20X4.

Julienne Jack Limited: Cost statement for the month ending 31 August 20X4

	£	£
Direct materials		
Wool	4 850	
Sticky labels for socks	93	
Plastic ties for sock pairing	133	
		5 076
Direct labour – machine operators' wages		6 330
Prime cost		11 406
Production overheads		
Depreciation of knitting machines	420	
Knitting machine repair	68	
Factory rental	1 230	
Electricity costs – factory	216	
Factory cleaner's wages	123	
Other factory costs	130	
		2 187
Production cost		13 593
Other overheads		
Electricity costs – office	38	
Part-time secretary's wages	540	
Office stationery and supplies	21	
Telephone – office	83	
Delivery costs	436	
Other office costs	214	
		1 332
Total costs		14 925

Cost classification: Product and period costs

Another way of looking at costs is to classify them as product or period costs.

- **Product costs** are those related to production of goods or services for sale by the business. Using the terminology we have already established, product costs include direct and indirect production costs.
- **Period costs** are those costs that are incurred in the period of account for example, salaries of sales and marketing personnel.

Note that the principle of accruals or matching operates in management accounting, just as in financial accounting. For example, cost of sales used in management accounting must be adjusted for opening and closing stock. In a manufacturing business, this means bringing forward opening stock and carrying forward closing stock, both valued at production cost. Next we will consider product costs in more detail.

Costing of products and services

In order to keep track of costs, to be able to plan and control business activity and to be able to value work in progress and finished goods stock, it is usually necessary, especially in manufacturing industries, to allocate costs to products. Work-in-progress and finished goods stock are carried forward to the next accounting period at production cost (i.e. including materials, direct labour and production overheads costs). This accumulation of costs is known as **absorption costing**.

Where the cost information relates to a single piece of work chargeable to one client the accumulation of costs may help in establishing the price at which the goods or services are to be invoiced. In costing terminology this is known as **job costing.**

Often in manufacturing industries goods of a generic type are produced to replenish general stocks of finished goods. Costing information is gathered for each type of product manufactured. In costing terminology this is known as **product costing**.

Sometimes in manufacturing industries it is appropriate to produce goods in batches or production runs of convenient sizes. Costs are allocated to each batch or run. In costing terminology this is known as **batch costing**.

All product and service costing involves the allocation of costs to cost units. A **cost unit** is an item of production or a group of products or a service for which it is useful to have product cost information. Three examples of cost units follow, each illustrating a different type of costing method.

Example 16.3 Gulam, a conveyancing solicitor, spends time on work for various different clients in the course of a day. Each piece of work for a client represents a cost unit. For example, Gulam's client, Maisie, is moving house and is also selling a commercial property. Each of these two matters represents a cost unit. Each of the matters Gulam deals with has its own unique code; for example, Maisie's house move is coded 0376 and her commercial property sale is coded 0375. During the

day Gulam keeps a time record of each unit of five minutes that he spends on each matter. On a particular day, extracts from his time records look like this:

Name: Gulam		**Date**: 14 October 20X4	
Time	*Time units*	*Client and code*	*Details*
2.05–2.15	2	Maisie 0376	Phone call to discuss possible completion dates
2.15–2.30	3	Bryan 0412	Dictate letter re Land Registry search
2.30–2.40	2	Maisie 0375	Dictate letter to commercial agents

This form serves as a computer input document. At the end of the day, all the solicitors in Gulam's firm submit their time sheets, and the details are input to the computer system. In respect of the day recorded above, two time units of five minutes each will be logged to each of Maisie's file codes. The time is costed by the computer at Gulam's charge-out rate – so, if his charge-out rate is £60 per hour, each file will receive a charge of £10 (i.e. 10 minutes at £1 per minute) in respect of the solicitor's time spent on 14 October 20X4. Other types of cost will be logged against the codes; for example, the cost of Land Registry searches and similar fees.

Once the conveyancing is successfully concluded Gulam will be able to generate an invoice to send to Maisie from the information that is logged on the computer.

This example illustrates **job costing** applied to a service environment.

Example 16.4 Peirce Waterworth Limited manufactures a range of components for the motor industry. The company keeps a constant stock of its 100 or so most popular lines so that it can respond immediately to orders. For example, once stocks of component XL046, an air filter, fall to 50 units, production is scheduled to replenish the stocks of the component. The input of materials is logged, and the number of hours and minutes that people spend operating the machines. These are charged to production of the XL046 and the stock value is built up by successive inputs of materials, labour and overheads.

This example illustrates **product costing**.

Example 16.5 In the example of the greeting cards company used earlier (see Example 16.1), a production run of 1000 cards was assumed. This is likely to be quite a reasonable size for a cost unit. Treating each individual card as a cost unit would involve a pointlessly detailed set of calculations. Given that the 1000 cards are identical and are all produced in one run, the cost unit in this case will be the run of 1000 cards. Having established the costs for the cost unit, the cost of an individual card is easily calculated by dividing total costs by 1000.

This example illustrates **batch costing**.

In the next three sections of the chapter we will examine the allocation of the three broad areas of cost – materials, labour and production overhead – to cost units. This is illustrated in the context of a manufacturing environment.

What follows may appear complicated. Students should try to bear in mind the overall objective of identifying the materials, labour and production overhead components of a cost unit.

Materials costs

Raw materials are bought in and a stock maintained as necessary in order to ensure that shortages, which would slow up production, do not occur. Direct materials are issued to production in appropriate quantities and the cost is allocated to the appropriate cost unit.

How do we establish the cost of raw materials transferred into production? The answer to this question is not, perhaps, as straightforward as it seems, especially where there is a fairly large volume of identical items moving in and out of stock, and where prices are changing. Businesses usually employ one of three principal valuation conventions in dealing with this matter: first in, first out; last in, first out; and weighted average cost.

- *First in, first out (FIFO).* This convention assumes that the items that have been in stock the longest are the first to move out into production. (Note that this is a theoretical assumption for valuation purposes only – it may not be borne out by the actual physical movements in stock.)
- *Last in, first out (LIFO).* This convention assumes that the items that have come into stock most recently are the first to move out into production. (Note that this is a theoretical assumption for valuation purposes only – it may not be borne out by the actual physical movements in stock.)
- *Weighted average cost (AVCO).* Under this convention the value of each individual item of stock is a weighted average of the value of all items in stock.

In practice in the UK, FIFO and AVCO are widely used. LIFO tends not to be used because it is an approach to valuation that is not approved by the accounting standards in the UK (although it is approved in some other parts of the world).

Example 16.6 Potts Pilchard Limited runs a business manufacturing pencils. These are placed in presentation boxes that hold 48 pencils. The boxes are purchased from the same supplier in batches of between 100 and 200. The stock record for February 20X3 shows the following details of deliveries into stock and transfers to production:

Date	Deliveries into stock
3 February	120 units purchased at £1.50 each
18 February	160 units purchased at £1.55 each

Date	Transfers to production
6 February	95 units
21 February	80 units
26 February	70 units

Stock at 1 February was 25 units which cost £1.50 each. Examining each of the three approaches to valuation in turn:

First in, first out (FIFO)

Date	Deliveries into stock			Transfers to production			Balance	
	Units	£	£	Units	£	£	Units	£
1 Feb							25	37.50
3 Feb	120	1.50	180.00				145	217.50
6 Feb				95	1.50	142.50	50	75.00
18 Feb	160	1.55	248.00				210	323.00
21 Feb				50	1.50	75.00	160	248.00
				30	1.55	46.50	130	201.50
26 Feb				70	1.55	108.50	60	93.00
Cost of transfers to production						372.50		

At the end of the month the closing balance of stock is 60 units. Because of the assumption that the first items to enter stock are the first to leave it, closing stock is valued on the basis of the latest price at which stock was purchased (in this case £1.55).

Last in, first out (LIFO)

Date	Deliveries into stock			Transfers to production			Balance	
	Units	£	£	Units	£	£	Units	£
1 Feb							25	37.50
3 Feb	120	1.50	180.00				145	217.50
6 Feb				95	1.50	142.50	50	75.00
18 Feb	160	1.55	248.00				210	323.00
21 Feb				80	1.55	124.00	130	199.00
26 Feb				70	1.55	108.50	60	90.50
Cost of transfers to production						375.00		

At the end of the month the closing balance of stock is 60 units (just as before). Because of the assumption that transfers to production are always of the most recently arrived stock, closing stock is valued on the basis of the earlier prices at which stock was purchased. Note that where prices are rising (as in this case) LIFO gives a comparatively lower closing stock value.

Weighted average cost (AVCO)

Date	Deliveries into stock			Transfers to production			Balance		
	Units	£	£	Units	£	£	Units	AVCO £	£
1 Feb							25	1.50	37.50
3 Feb	120	1.50	180.00				145	1.50	217.50
6 Feb				95	1.50	142.50	50	1.50	75.00
18 Feb	160	1.55	248.00				210	1.538	323.00
21 Feb				80	1.538	123.05	130	1.538	199.95
26 Feb				70	1.538	107.67	60	1.538	92.28
Cost of transfers to production					373.22				

At the end of the month the closing balance of stock is 60 units (as before), but the closing stock valuation is £92.28. It is usual to find that the AVCO value lies somewhere between the FIFO and LIFO value.

Summary

Method	Transfers to production £	Closing stock £	Total £
FIFO	372.50	93.00	465.50
LIFO	375.00	90.50	465.50
AVCO	373.22	92.28	465.50

Note that the total cost involved is identical in each case. What differs between the methods is the allocation of the total cost incurred between transfers to production and closing stock.

Why does the method of stock valuation matter? Remember the basic formula for cost of sales:

Opening stock
Add: purchases
Less: closing stock

If opening or closing stock values change, cost of sales changes, and so do the figures for gross or net profit. In a time of rising prices FIFO produces a higher profit figure than LIFO.

Self-test question 16.2 (answer at the end of the chapter)

Bryanston Buckley Limited is a manufacturing company. It buys in stocks of a component, X, which it uses in production. Stocks of component X at 1 March 20X6 were 55 units at £3 each. The following movements in stock took place in March: (a) on 10 March 160 units of X were purchased for £3.20 each; (b) 35 units of X were transferred to production on 12 March, and a further 70 were transferred to production on 25 March.

What is the closing stock value calculated under each of the following conventions?

a) FIFO
b) LIFO
c) AVCO.

Labour costs

Earlier, in Example 16.3, we looked at the case of a solicitor booking his time to various different jobs. In a production costing process direct labour time must also be booked to the production process. This is often a quite elaborate procedure involving careful observation and record-keeping. A production operative may work on a range of different cost units during a day, and a method must be found of ensuring that the work is accurately booked. If errors are made product costs will be misstated and incorrect decisions may result.

The following are some of the complexities that may arise in respect of the identification and allocation of direct labour:

● *Employee performs a combination of direct and indirect labour tasks*. An employee may spend part of his or her time on a production line engaged in specific aspects of production that can be allocated to cost units. However, in addition he or she may have more general tasks, such as cleaning machinery, sweeping up, engaging in routine maintenance and so on. Therefore, it may be necessary to allocate time between direct and indirect labour tasks.
● *Variation in methods of payment*. There are several ways of paying employees. Usually there is a basic rate element, but in addition there may be special payments for working overtime or unsocial hours. Sometimes, for example in garment production, direct labour employees are paid piece rates for work (a fixed amount, say, for each shirt sewn); in addition they may be paid a bonus for achieving a particularly high level of output.
● *Idle or non-productive time*. If a machine breaks down or there is some other kind of hitch in the production process employees may not be able to be employed in productive activity. This is sometimes known as idle time. Employees are entitled to be paid for the time, but how should it be treated?

It is often the case that the management accountant takes into account all of the complexities of labour costs, averages them, and produces an hourly rate for each grade of labour, which can then be applied to all direct labour time spent in production.

Example 16.7 This example demonstrates the allocation of direct material and labour costs to a particular job (remember the job costing method described earlier in the chapter).

Barker and Clyde Limited produce machine parts for the airline industry. They have an order from an aircraft manufacturer for 150 units of component BYA570. This work is assigned job code V477848. This involves the following transfers from stores:

650 kg of material V, valued at AVCO, which is currently £3.60 per kilo
125 kg of material G, valued at AVCO which is currently £5.50 per kilo.

Three grades of direct labour are involved:

Grade 7, which is to be recorded at the rate of £5.50 per hour
Grade 13, recorded at the rate of £7.60 per hour
Grade 14, recorded at the rate of £7.80 per hour.

The cost accountant collects information about direct labour time spent from the factory and summarises it on to computer input forms, which identify the job codes, labour grade and hours spent.

When the job is completed the computer record shows the following summary for prime cost:

Job No: V477848; Date: 12.11.X3 Component No: BYA 570; Supervisor: Ashton;

Quantity: 150 units

	£	£
Direct material		
Material V (650kg × £3.60)	2 340.00	
Material G (125kg × £5.50)	687.50	
		3 027.50
Direct labour		
Grade 7: 26.5 hours booked @ £5.50 per hour	145.75	
Grade 13: 12 hours @ £7.60 per hour	91.20	
Grade 14: 3.75 hours @ £7.80 per hour	29.25	
		266.20
Prime cost		3 293.70

This information allows us to calculate prime cost per component:

$$\frac{£3\,293.70}{150} = £21.97$$

Self-test question 16.3 (answer at the end of the chapter)

Harvey & Cork Limited produces photograph frames in batches of 500. The following materials and labour are booked to batch number 30453A:

● 100 kg of metal @ £4.50 per kilo
● Paint: 2 litres of blue @ £6.80 per litre
● Glass: 500 pieces at 30p each

- 22 hours of direct labour at A grade (charged at £4.80 per hour)
- 19 hours of direct labour at B grade (charged at £6.00 per hour).

Prepare a batch costing record to show the prime cost of batch no. 30453A. What is the cost per picture frame?

Production overheads

Allocation of production overheads is one of the most difficult problems for the management accountant. Production overheads are part of the overall production cost, and it is usually necessary to allocate them in order to produce useful information for management and for stock valuation. However, as we have seen, they are not directly identifiable with cost units. Where production goes through several stages, the first step in dealing with production overheads is usually to allocate them to cost centres.

Allocation to cost centres

Often, production is organised methodically into **cost centres** to which costs can be allocated. Cost centres are functions or areas into which costs can be organised.

Example 16.8 Choremaster Limited produces industrial cleaning machines. There are three distinct stages in the production process:

metal machining
brush fitting
paint and finishing.

The metal machining shop has its own full-time production supervisor. The other production supervisor employed by the company splits her time in a 60:40 ratio between the brush fitting shop and the paint and finishing shop. The cost of employing each supervisor, including benefits and employer's National Insurance, is £17 360 per annum. (Note that production supervisors' salaries are part of the company's indirect production overheads.)

What is the allocation of supervisors' salaries to each of the three production areas?

	£
Metal machining	17 360
Brush fitting (60% × £17 360)	10 416
Paint and finishing (40% × £17 360)	6 944

Apportionment to cost centres

In Example 16.8 the indirect cost of supervisors' salary could be allocated because precise information was available about the use of the supervisors' time. Where indirect costs cannot be allocated, they must be apportioned. Cost apportionment often involves some fairly arbitrary decisions about the split of costs between cost centres.

We will expand the Choremaster Limited example to illustrate what is involved in cost apportionment.

Example 16.9 Choremaster Limited incurs the following indirect production overheads in the year ending 31 December 20X7:

	£
Factory rent	33 970
Production supervisors' salaries	34 720
Canteen costs	13 440
Cleaning and other indirect labour	8 885
Factory rates	12 480
Insurance	8 760
Electricity – factory	10 770
Building maintenance	2 490
Machine maintenance and repair	3 423
Depreciation of machinery	12 220
Depreciation of canteen fixtures and fittings	1 792
Total	142 950

The indirect production overheads have to be apportioned between the three production areas: metal machining, brush fitting and paint and finishing.

Usually, different methods of apportionment are used depending upon the nature of the cost. Some common approaches to apportionment are listed below:

Type of cost	Typical method of apportionment
Factory rent, rates, insurance, building maintenance, electricity, indirect labour and cleaning	Floor area
Depreciation of machinery	Machinery value
Canteen costs	Number of employees
Machinery maintenance and repair	Number of call-outs
Production supervisors' salaries	Number of employees

It is important to note that these methods of apportionment do not constitute precise rules. Much depends upon the nature of the expense and the amount of detail that can be collected about how it is incurred. In the case of Choremaster Limited, for example, we know that the production supervisors' salaries can be allocated neatly across the three departments. In other companies, it might not be possible to make such an allocation, and a basis of apportionment (such as number of employees, as suggested in the table above) would be more appropriate.

We need some further information in order to be able to apportion Choremaster's costs. This is given in the table below:

		Cost centre		
	Total	Metal machining	Brush fitting	Paint and finishing
Floor area (sq metres)	10 000	6 000	2 000	2 000
Number of employees	28	17	6	5
Machinery value	122 200	103 000	8 400	10 800
Maintenance & repair call-outs	7	6	0	1

We can now apportion costs to each cost centre, as follows. Factory rent is apportioned to each cost centre on the basis of floor area. For example, the part of cost to be apportioned to the metal machining cost centre is:

$$\frac{6\,000}{10\,000} \times £33\,970 = £20\,382$$

Brush fitting:

$$\frac{2\,000}{10\,000} \times £33\,970 = £6\,794$$

Paint and finishing:

$$\frac{2\,000}{10\,000} \times £33\,970 = £6\,794$$

(Note that £20 382 + £6 794 + £6 794 = £33 970, i.e. all of the cost is apportioned.)
We can use the same approach to apportioning all the other costs:

			Cost centre		
	Basis	Total £	Metal machining £	Brush fitting £	Paint and finishing £
Factory rent	Floor area	33 970	20 382	6 794	6 794
Production supervisors' salaries	Actual	34 720	17 360	10 416	6 944
Canteen costs	Employees	13 440	8 160	2 880	2 400
Cleaning and other indirect labour	Floor area	8 885	5 331	1 777	1 777
Factory rates	Floor area	12 480	7 488	2 496	2 496
Insurance	Floor area	8 760	5 256	1 752	1 752
Electricity – factory	Floor area	10 770	6 462	2 154	2 154
Building maintenance	Floor area	2 490	1 494	498	498
Machine maintenance and repair	Call outs	3 423	2 934	—	489
Depreciation of machinery	Machinery value	12 220	10 300	840	1 080
Depreciation – canteen	Employees	1 792	1 088	384	320
Totals		142 950	86 255	29 991	26 704

Self test question 16.4 (answer at the end of the chapter)

Swift Metals Limited produces machine parts. Its factory space is divided into three areas: preparation, tooling and finishing. These three functional areas are used as cost centres. Swift's management accountant has asked you to prepare a schedule showing the apportionment of the company's production overheads between the three cost centres for the year ending 31 December 20X4.

The production overhead totals are as follows:

	£
Factory costs (rental, insurance, cleaning etc.)	700 000
Canteen costs	18 496
Machinery depreciation	17 650
Machinery maintenance and repair	2 961
Supervisory salaries	23 358
Total	762 465

- Factory costs are to be apportioned on the basis of floor area.
- Canteen costs and supervisory salaries are to be apportioned on the basis of number of employees.
- Machinery depreciation is to be apportioned on the basis of the net book value of machinery used in each cost centre.
- Machinery maintenance and repair is to be apportioned on the basis of the number of call-outs.

Relevant data is included in the following table:

		Cost centre		
	Total	Preparation	Tooling	Finishing
Floor area (square metres)	20 000	7 000	9 000	4 000
Number of employees	34	16	12	6
Machinery value	176 500	26 000	112 000	38 500
Maintenance & repair call-outs	9	2	6	1

Prepare the overhead apportionment schedule for the management accountant.

Overhead absorption

In the previous section of this chapter we examined the allocation and apportionment of costs to cost centres. This allows us to say, for example, that overheads of £29 991 were allocated to Choremaster's brush fitting cost centre, but we are no closer to identifying the total production overhead cost of an individual cost unit.

We need to find some way of transferring overhead costs to cost units. Traditionally, the way this has been done in manufacturing industries is via

overhead absorption, a method of allocating an appropriate portion of production overheads to cost units. A logical way of doing this might be on the basis of the number of units of production. Suppose that Choremaster Limited produces 5400 cleaning machines in the period during which it incurred total production overheads of £142 950. The total production overhead attributable to each cleaning machine could then be calculated as:

$$\frac{£142\,950}{5\,400} = £26.47 \text{ (to nearest penny)}$$

So £26.47 becomes the **overhead absorption rate** applied to each machine in respect of production overhead. It would be added to the materials and direct labour costs for each cleaning machine to arrive at a total production cost per machine. Note that this is a 'blanket' overhead rate; it is appropriate where a business produces only one product. Where there is more than one product the overhead absorption procedures become more complicated.

In this example, the information could only be calculated accurately once the accounting period was over and total costs could be summed and allocated to cost centres. Management accounting information, as we have seen, needs to be produced very quickly in order to be useful, and a retrospective exercise in overhead absorption is not likely to be very helpful. For this reason, overhead absorption is done in practice on the basis of figures budgeted in advance; a budgeted overhead absorption rate is calculated and then applied to production. (Note that we will examine budgeting in more detail in the next chapter.)

The next example will demonstrate some of the techniques involved in calculating overhead absorption rates and will examine three possible approaches to overhead absorption: number of units of production; machine hours; and labour hours.

Example 16.10 Rutland Stamp Limited produces large metal storage containers in one size only. The production process involves three stages:

1. *Cutting department*: large metal sheets are cut into standard sizes, and are shaped and drilled.
2. *Assembly department*: the standard pieces are attached together by screwing and welding.
3. *Painting and finishing*: the containers are smoothed down and spray painted.

Each department is treated as a cost centre.

The management accountant is working out appropriate overhead absorption rates for the next financial year (the year to 31 December 20X7). She estimates that total production overheads will be £136 000, allocated as follows between the cost centres:

	£
Cutting	£56 000
Assembly	£48 000
Painting and finishing	£32 000

Total production in units for 20X7 is estimated at 16 000 containers. The management accountant has also worked out budgeted materials and labour costs per container, as follows:

▶

Prime cost of container	£
Direct materials (metal, fixings, paint)	15.50
Direct labour	
Cutting: 10 minutes (@ £6 per hour)	1.00
Assembly: 1 hour 30 minutes (@ £6 per hour)	9.00
Painting and finishing: 20 minutes (@ £4.50 per hour)	1.50
Total prime cost	27.00

Note that the cutting department processes are mostly mechanised; there is a relatively low input of labour. Assembly processes, by contrast, are mostly manual. The extent to which processes are labour intensive influences the choice of overhead absorption method, as we will now see.

The management accountant now needs to work out an overhead absorption rate to be applied to each of the three cost centres. She will use three different rates, one for each department, and each worked out on a different basis.

Cutting department: Overhead rate per machine hour

Where manufacturing processes depend more upon machines than upon labour input, it is usually most appropriate to work out an overhead absorption rate based upon machine hours available. The number of machine hours is estimated by reference to factory working hours and number of machines. For example, in this case, suppose that the accountant estimates that a total of 16 000 hours of machine time will be available over the next year. The cutting department overhead for the year is estimated at £56 000. The estimated overhead absorption rate for the cutting department for 20X7 will therefore be:

$$\frac{56\,000}{16\,000} = £3.50 \text{ per machine hour}$$

For every machine hour used in production £3.50 will be charged in production overheads.

How many machine hours will be used to produce one container? Assuming that all of the available machine hours (16 000) are required to produce 16 000 containers, each cost unit uses up 1 machine hour, and therefore £3.50 will be included in the production cost of a container.

Assembly department: Overhead rate per labour hour

In this department the manufacturing processes are labour intensive. The accountant estimates that 24 000 direct labour hours will be used in this department in 20X7. The assembly cost centre overhead for the year is estimated at £48 000. The estimated overhead absorption rate for the assembly department for 20X7 will therefore be:

$$\frac{48\,000}{24\,000} = £2.00 \text{ per labour hour}$$

How many assembly labour hours will be used to produce one container? Each container requires 1 hour 30 minutes in labour time. Therefore 16 000 containers would therefore require 24 000 hours (which just happens to be the number of direct labour hours available in this department). The overhead to be absorbed in respect of assembly for each cost unit will be 1.5 × £2.00 – i.e. £3.00.

Painting and finishing: Rate per unit of production

The painting and finishing cost centre overhead for 20X7 is estimated at £32 000. This will be spread over an estimated 16 000 units of production (cost units). The estimated overhead absorption rate for the assembly department for 20X7 will therefore be:

$$\frac{32\,000}{16\,000} = £2.00 \text{ per unit}$$

Finally, we will work out an estimated total production cost per unit, as follows:

Production cost of container	£	£
Direct materials (metal, fixings, paint)		15.50
Labour:		
Cutting: 10 minutes (@ £6 per hour)	1.00	
Assembly: 1 hour 30 minutes (@ £6 per hour)	9.00	
Painting and finishing: 20 minutes (@ £4.50 per hour)	1.50	
		11.50
Production overhead		
Cutting	3.50	
Assembly	3.00	
Painting and finishing	2.00	
		8.50
Total production cost		35.50

Overhead absorption rates: Some other approaches

The example of Rutland Stamp Limited demonstrated the use of three different approaches to calculating overhead absorption rates: rate per unit, rate per machine hour and rate per labour hour. There are some other possibilities.

Percentage of direct labour

The overhead absorption rate would be calculated as follows:

$$\frac{\text{Production overheads}}{\text{Direct labour cost}} \times 100$$

The next example explains how the overhead absorption rate is calculated and applied on this basis.

Example 16.11 Suppose that the fabrications cost centre of Millom Sunter Limited uses two grades of direct labour. Grade A is paid at £6.70 per hour and

Grade B is paid at £5.90 per hour. The production estimates for the 20X8 accounting year require 30 000 hours of Grade A and 28 000 hours of Grade B labour. The management accountant has already carried out an allocation and apportionment exercise, which resulted in estimated production overheads of £208 000 for the fabrications cost centre in 20X8. What is the overhead absorption rate to be used for fabrications? Direct labour equals:

Grade A: 30 000 hours × £6.70 = 201 000
Grade B: 28 000 hours × £5.90 = 165 200
                                 366 200

Overhead absorption rate for fabrications:

$$\frac{\text{Total budget production overheads}}{\text{Direct labour cost}} \times 100 = \frac{208\,000}{366\,200} \times 100 = 56.8\%$$

(to one decimal place)

So, 56.8% of the direct labour charge for any batch, job or cost unit will be added to represent production overheads.

Taking the example a little further, Millom Sunter Limited manufactures components for the shipbuilding industry on a job costing basis. The job cost card for an order of 120 units of component 177Z2A is as follows:

Component No: 177Z2A; Quantity: 120 units	£	£
Direct materials		370.00
Direct labour		
Grade A: 25 hours @ £6.70	167.50	
Grade B: 39 hours @ £5.90	230.10	
		397.60
Prime cost		767.60
Production overheads		
56.8% × direct labour cost = 56.8% × 397.60		225.84
Total production cost		993.44

Percentage of direct materials cost

This approach to overhead absorption works in the same way as the percentage of direct labour cost. An overhead absorption rate is worked out in advance by using budget figures. Production overheads for an individual job, batch or product are then calculated by reference to the input of materials cost.

Both this method and the percentage of direct labour cost method can be particularly useful where a range of different products is made. It must be recognised, however, that there are no fixed rules about which method to use. The ultimate test to be applied to all management accounting information is whether or not it is useful in managing the firm. Management should use the methods and techniques that they find most efficient and effective in achieving the overall objectives of the business.

Many new techniques and ideas have been explored in this chapter. The case study brings together some of the key features of the material covered.

CASE STUDY 16.1 Dealing with overheads

Gemma Entwistle is the managing director of Entwistle Garden Equipment Limited. She inherited the business from her parents, Jeff and Hilda, when they retired two years ago, and she has put a lot of work into making improvements and in trying to improve efficiency. Jeff and Hilda manufactured a single product, a deluxe garden seat made of high quality hardwood, which has been a consistently good seller throughout western Europe. The company sells to garden centres and wholesalers.

Last year, after conducting some market research, Gemma made the decision to expand the range of products offered. When studying horticulture at college she developed a new mini-greenhouse design and she has decided to put that into production first because it uses the same range of production facilities as the garden seats. The two products use different wood qualities and the garden seats are much more carefully finished, but essentially the processes involved are very similar.

The factory facilities are split into two sections: (a) cutting and turning and (b) assembly and finishing. In the first section wood is cut by machine, drilled and shaped ready for assembly; most of the production activity is machine work. In the second section the pieces are assembled and fixed, the wood is polished and varnished and brass fixings attached. The range of tasks in this section is more diverse, and more labour intensive.

One of Gemma's innovations is to improve the quality of management information, which was generally more or less non-existent when her parents ran the business. She brought in a consultant to advise on systems developments and, following his recommendation, she now employs a part-time management accountant. Currently, towards the end of 20X1, the management accountant, Bernice, is looking at the likely costs for 20X2.

The basic prime cost structure for each of the two main products is as follows:

	Greenhouse £
Direct materials	12.00
Direct labour	
Cutting and turning dept; 1 hour @ £6.00 per hour	6.00
Assembly and finishing dept: 2 hours @ £7.00 per hour	14.00
Prime cost	32.00

Note that in the cutting and turning department two machine hours are required for each greenhouse, while in the assembly and finishing department 0.5 of a machine hour is required for each greenhouse.

	Garden seat £
Direct materials	15.00
Direct labour	
Cutting and turning dept: 1.50 hours @ £6.00 per hour	9.00
Assembly and finishing dept: 3 hours @ £7.00 per hour	21.00
Prime cost	45.00

▶

Note that in the cutting and turning department 2.5 machine hours are required for each garden seat, while in the assembly and finishing department 0.5 of a machine hour is required for each garden seat.

The greenhouses currently sell to retailers for £85.00 each and the garden seats sell for £103.00.

Bernice has estimated production overheads for 20X2. These have to be split between the two departments and she suggests to Gemma that the following bases of apportionment would be appropriate:

Overhead	Total for 20X2 £	Basis of apportionment
Factory rental	75 000	Floor area
Factory insurance	7 600	Floor area
Cleaning	8 900	Floor area
Canteen	11 100	Number of employees
Factory rates	9 500	Floor area
Electricity	22 500	Actual (because separately metered)
Machine maintenance	16 464	Number of call-outs
Machinery depreciation	30 000	Net book value
Canteen depreciation	3 500	Number of employees
Supervisors' wages	57 936	Actual
Other factory costs	23 000	Floor area
	265 500	

Bernice establishes the following information for the apportionment:

Basis of apportionment	Total	Cutting and turning	Assembly and finishing
Floor area (square metres)	5 000	3 500	1 500
Direct labour employee numbers	25	8	17
Electricity (actual)	22 500	15 200	7 300
Supervisors' wages (actual)	57 936	29 716	28 220
Machinery net book value	300 000	250 000	50 000
Maintenance call-outs	21	18	3

Bernice decides to calculate overhead absorption rates based upon (i) machine hours and (ii) direct labour hours. The totals anticipated for 20X2 for machine hours and direct labour hours by department are:

	Cutting and turning	Assembly and finishing	Total
Machine hours	22 500	5 000	27 500
Direct labour hours	12 500	25 000	37 500

Gemma aims to produce and sell 5000 units of each product in 20X2. Gemma and Bernice require the following information:

a) Totals for overheads apportioned to each department (cost centre).

b) Overhead absorption rates for each department based upon (i) machine hours and (ii) labour hours.

c) A calculation of the total amount of overhead absorbed using the two different methods if 5000 units of each product are produced and sold in 20X2.

d) A calculation of the gross profit for each greenhouse and garden seat on the assumption that selling prices remain the same, using i) the overhead absorption rate based on machine hours and ii) the overhead absorption rate based on labour hours.

e) A recommendation as to whether machine hours or labour hours should be used as the basis for overhead absorption.

Case study solution

a) Overhead apportionment

	Basis	Total £	Cutting and turning £	Assembly and finishing £
Factory rental	Floor area	75 000	52 500	22 500
Factory insurance	Floor area	7 600	5 320	2 280
Cleaning	Floor area	8 900	6 230	2 670
Canteen	No. of employees	11 100	3 552	7 548
Factory rates	Floor area	9 500	6 650	2 850
Electricity	Actual	22 500	15 200	7 300
Machinery maintenance	No. of call-outs	16 464	14 112	2 352
Machinery depreciation	Net book value	30 000	25 000	5 000
Canteen depreciation	No. of employees	3 500	1 120	2 380
Supervisors' wages	Actual	57 936	29 716	28 220
Other factory costs	Floor area	23 000	16 100	6 900
		265 500	175 500	90 000

The total production overhead apportioned to the cutting and turning cost centre is £175 500. The total production overhead apportioned to the assembly and finishing cost centre is £90 000.

b) i) Overhead absorption rate on the basis of machine hours

	Cutting and turning	Assembly and finishing
Production overhead	175 500	90 000
Machine hours	22 500	5 000
Overhead absorption rate	£7.80	£18.00

b) ii) Overhead absorption rate on the basis of labour hours

	Cutting and turning	Assembly and finishing
Production overhead	175 500	90 000
Labour hours	12 500	25 000
Overhead absorption rate	£14.04	£3.60

c) i) Machine hours

The details of the number of machine hours spent on each product are given in the case study (be careful not to get machine hours confused with labour hours).

Greenhouse		£
Department		
C&T	2 hours × £7.80	15.60
A&F	0.5 hours × £18.00	9.00
Total		24.60

Garden chair		£
Department		
C&T	2.50 hours × £7.80	19.50
A&F	0.50 hours × f18.00	9.00
Total		28.50

If 5000 greenhouses and 5000 garden chairs are produced and sold the total overhead absorbed will be:

$$£$$
Greenhouses: 5000 × £24.60 = 123 000
Garden chairs: 5000 × £28.50 = 142 500
265 500

c) ii) Labour hours

The labour hours spent in each department on greenhouses and garden chairs are given in the prime cost details in the case study.

Greenhouse		£
Department		
C&T	1 hour × £14.04	14.04
A&F	2 hours × £3.60	7.20
Total		£21.24

Garden chair		£
Department		
C&T	1.50 hours × £14.04	21.06
A&F	3 hours × £3.60	10.80
Total		£31.86

If 5000 greenhouses and 5000 garden chairs are produced and sold the total overhead absorbed will be:

$$£$$
Greenhouses: 5000 × £21.24 = 106 200
Garden chairs: 5000 × £31.86 = 159 300
265 500

This example demonstrates that, whichever method of overhead absorption is selected, the total amount of overhead absorbed remains the same. The only difference is the way in which the total overhead is allocated to products.

d) Gross profit

For this part of the case, we use the overhead absorption information calculated in part c) together with the prime cost information given in the case study.

Greenhouse (per unit)	Overhead absorption: machine hours £	Overhead absorption: labour hours £
Selling price	85.00	85.00
Less: prime cost	(32.00)	(32.00)
Less: overhead absorbed	(24.60)	(21.24)
Gross profit	28.40	31.76
Gross profit %	33.4%	37.4%

Garden seat (per unit)	Overhead absorption: machine hours £	Overhead absorption: labour hours £
Selling price	103.00	103.00
Less: prime cost	(45.00)	(45.00)
Less: overhead absorbed	(28.50)	(31.86)
Gross profit	29.50	26.14
Gross profit %	28.6%	25.4%

Discussion

It is very important to remember that there is no definitively correct way of absorbing production overheads. From the figures given above the greenhouses certainly appear to be relatively more profitable than the garden seats. However, the gross profit and gross margin per unit depend to some extent on the basis of overhead absorption used.

Because of this variability, figures based upon the absorption method of accounting (i.e. including production overheads) are not likely to be reliable for decision making involving questions such as:

● How much more profitable is one product than another?
● Which product should we concentrate on producing?
● How much of product X should we produce?

Later in this section of the book we will look more closely at techniques that allow us to provide better answers to such questions. For the moment, students should be aware that absorption costing, while it is useful for information and for stock valuation, should be treated with some caution as a tool for decision making.

e) Recommendation

The cutting and turning department relies more heavily on mechanised processes and for this reason it may be more appropriate to use an overhead absorption rate based on machine hours in respect of overheads allocated and apportioned to this cost centre. The assembly and finishing department, by contrast, is much more heavily reliant upon manual processes, and so the use of an overhead absorption rate based on labour hours may make more sense in this cost centre.

The effect on product cost would be as follows. Overheads absorbed, per unit of product:

▶

Greenhouse		
Department		£
C&T	2 machine hours × £7.80	15.60
A&F	2 labour hours × £3.60	7.20
Total		22.80

Garden chair		
Department		£
C&T	2.50 machine hours × £7.80	19.50
A&F	3 labour hours × £3.60	10.80
Total		30.30

Effect on total production cost per unit and on gross profit per unit:

	Greenhouse		Garden seat	
	£	£	£	£
Selling price		85.00		103.00
Prime cost	32.00		45.00	
Production overhead absorbed	22.80		30.30	
Production cost per unit		54.80		75.30
Gross profit		30.20		27.70
Gross profit %		35.5%		26.9%

If we compare these with the equivalent calculations in part d) we can see that using different overhead absorption rates for the two departments produces a gross profit per unit that lies between those calculated earlier. Because this approach steers a middle course by using machine hours for one cost centre and labour hours for the other, it may be most appropriate in the circumstances.

Activity-based costing (ABC)

As discussed at the beginning of this chapter, very significant changes have taken place in the business environment since the Industrial Revolution. Manufacturing industry has become relatively less important in the developed world, with service industries playing a correspondingly more significant part in economic development.

Traditional absorption costing techniques (which have been the subject of most of this chapter) are based upon a model of industry where the principal costs were associated with the employment of direct labour hours and/or machine hours. However, as industrial processes have become increasingly mechanised the prime importance of direct labour hours has been correspondingly reduced. Machine-based processes have, themselves, often become streamlined and more efficient, using less energy and other types of resource. There has been a consequent reduction in the input of machine hours in many types of process. At the same time, the relative importance of indirect overheads in many businesses' cost structures has tended to grow. So, increasing amounts of indirect overhead have been allocated to shrinking numbers of machine hours or direct labour hours. This results in questionable allocations of costs – if the overhead absorption rate is £60 per direct labour hour (not an unreasonable scenario, in practice), then every additional minute spent on the production of a cost unit will result in the burden of £1 extra in overhead allocation.

During the 1980s firms began to experiment with alternative approaches to costing. A very important alternative to traditional absorption costing has emerged – activity-based costing (ABC) – the adoption of which has been gradually spreading throughout the world. The basic principle of ABC is that cost units should bear the cost of the activities they cause. Costs are 'driven' by activities that take place in the business environment – activities which include, for example:

- ordering materials
- storing materials
- setting up production runs
- testing the quality of production
- organising production.

The next example illustrates ABC by contrasting it with traditional absorption costing.

Example 16.12 Sallis Weller Limited produces two products: product X and product Y. Until now, it has adopted traditional absorption costing techniques, transferring overheads to production via an overhead absorption rate based on direct labour hours. The company's managing director has recently read an article about ABC, a revolutionary costing technique. He asks the finance director to organise a comparison by applying ABC alongside normal absorption costing for a month.

Using absorption costing

During November 20X6 the company produces 2000 units each of product X and product Y, and incurs the following indirect production overhead costs:

	£
Factory cleaning	2 000
Power	16 000
Factory rental	23 000
Factory insurance	5 000
Supervisory salaries	12 000
Canteen charges	3 000
Machinery depreciation	21 000
Machinery maintenance	5 000
Production consumables	6 000
Other indirect labour costs	12 000
Other factory costs	8 000
Total	113 000

Total direct labour hours for the month are 5000, resulting in an overhead absorption rate of:

$$\frac{113\,000}{5\,000} = £22.60$$

Relevant details for the two products are as follows

	Product X	Product Y
Hours of direct labour (per unit)	1	1.5
	£	£
Direct materials (per unit)	17.50	12.00
Direct labour (per unit)	7.00	10.50
Prime cost	24.50	22.50
Overhead		
1 direct labour hour × £22.60	22.60	
1.5 direct labour hours × £22.60		33.90
Production cost per unit	47.10	56.40

Using ABC

ABC involves the identification of key activities and their drivers. The finance director carefully examines the activity bases of the factory operations and establishes five basic activities that take place:

machining
finishing
materials ordering
materials issue to production
scheduling, control and quality testing of production.

The fundamental cost driver for each activity, together with quantities, is established as follows:

Activity	Cost driver	Total	Product X	Product Y	£
Machining	Machine hours	3 000	2 000	1 000	45 000
Finishing	Direct labour hours	5 000	2 000	3 000	25 000
Materials ordering	Number of orders placed	25	16	9	4 000
Materials issue to production	Number of materials issues made	75	47	28	12 000
Scheduling etc.	Number of production runs	36	22	14	27 000
					113 000

This table shows that the production of X involves more activity in several respects than that of Y. Materials ordering appears more complicated (more orders have to be placed) and the number of production runs is far greater.

The final column of the table shows the results of the finance director's reclassification of the total of £113 000 indirect production overheads for the month. The individual items for rental, insurance, supervision, etc. have been apportioned between the five activities.

At this stage, all the information is in place to allocate overheads to each of the products by activity. An amount of cost per unit of cost driver can be calculated as follows:

Activity			Cost amount
Machining	$\dfrac{\text{Overhead}}{\text{Machine hours}} = \dfrac{45\,000}{3\,000}$		= £15 per machine hour
Finishing	$\dfrac{\text{Overhead}}{\text{Direct labour hours}} = \dfrac{25\,000}{5\,000}$		= £5 per labour hour
Materials ordering	$\dfrac{\text{Overhead}}{\text{Materials orders}} = \dfrac{4\,000}{25}$		= £160 per order
Materials handling	$\dfrac{\text{Overhead}}{\text{Issues to production}} = \dfrac{12\,000}{75}$		= £160 per issue
Scheduling etc.	$\dfrac{\text{Overhead}}{\text{Production runs}} = \dfrac{27\,000}{36}$		= £750 per run

Then the overhead is allocated between products X and Y:

	Product X		Product Y	
		£		£
Machining	2 000 × £15	30 000	1 000 × £15	15 000
Finishing	2 000 × £5	10 000	3 000 × £5	15 000
Materials ordering	16 × £160	2 560	9 × £160	1 440
Materials handling	47 × £160	7 520	28 × £160	4 480
Scheduling etc.	22 × £750	16 500	14 × £750	10 500
Total		66 580		46 420
Per unit	66 580/2 000	33.29	46 420/2 000	23.21
Prime cost per unit (as before)		24.50		22.50
Production cost per unit – ABC		57.79		45.71
Production cost per unit – traditional		47.10		56.40

The example illustrates the very large differences that can emerge when costing under the traditional method is compared with ABC. In this example, product Y appeared to cost more under the traditional method than product X. Following the application of ABC the positions reverse. Traditional methods of allocation ignore the detail of the activities that actually take place on the factory floor. Where production processes are more cumbersome because of, for example, the necessity for more frequent ordering of materials, such factors should be taken into account in costing.

It is argued that the application of ABC results in significant improvement in the quality of information obtained from the costing system, and consequently, in better control and planning of activities. However, as even this relatively straightforward example has shown, it is a system of considerable complexity. A great deal of information has to be collected and administered, and the system is costly to implement.

Chapter summary

This chapter has covered a great deal of ground and has introduced several new techniques and ways of thinking about business costs. It is important to work through the examples carefully, referring back to the content of the chapter where necessary.

First, we examined cost classification, classifying costs under the headings of direct material, direct labour, production overheads and other overheads. Some basic principles of costing of products and services were introduced, including examples of job costing, product costing and batch costing. The three basic elements of product cost – materials, labour and production overheads – were then dealt with in turn.

The principal issue with materials costs is the value at which they are allocated into production (and, in consequence, the closing stock value of unallocated items). Examples were used to demonstrate the first in first out (FIFO), last in, last out (LIFO) and weighted average (AVCO) methods.

Direct labour costs were then examined, and the application of direct labour hourly rates in job costing was demonstrated by means of an example.

The rest of the chapter was devoted to the complexities of accounting for production overheads within the costing systems of businesses. Detailed topic coverage included allocation and apportionment of production overheads to cost centres, and common methods of overhead absorption, including the calculation of overhead rates per machine hour, per labour hour, per unit of production, as a percentage of direct labour cost and as a percentage of direct materials cost. The case study for the chapter applied knowledge of overhead absorption to a detailed numerical example.

Finally, an alternative to traditional absorption costing methods was explained: activity-based costing (ABC). ABC is being adopted more widely now because of its superior information content. However, as the chapter example indicated, ABC is not without its problems; it can be complex and expensive to adopt.

Answer to self-test question 16.1

Cost	Classification
Canvas material	Direct materials
Metal spokes for wheels	Direct materials
Spare parts for sewing machine repairs	Indirect production overheads
Advertising expenditure	Other indirect overheads
Machine oil	Indirect production overheads
Electricity bill for factory	Indirect production overheads
Wages of assembly line workers	Direct labour
Wages of factory canteen staff	Indirect production overheads
Wages of assembly line supervisor	Indirect production overheads
Secretary's salary	Other indirect overheads
Delivery vehicle depreciation	Other indirect overheads

Answer to self-test question 16.2

a) FIFO

Date	Deliveries into stock Units	£	£	Transfers to production Units	£	£	Balance Units	£
1 Mar							55	165.00
10 Mar	160	3.20	512.00				215	677.00
12 Mar				35	3.00	105.00	180	572.00
25 Mar				20	3.00	60.00	160	512.00
				50	3.20	160.00	110	352.00

Tutorial note: the 110 items remaining in stock after the transfer to production on 25 March are all assumed to belong to the batch of items delivered on 10 March, and so are valued at £3.20 each (110 × £3.20 = £352.00).

b) LIFO

Date	Deliveries into stock Units	£	£	Transfers to production Units	£	£	Balance Units	£
1 Mar							55	165.00
10 Mar	160	3.20	512.00				215	677.00
12 Mar				35	3.20	112.00	180	565.00
25 Mar				70	3.20	224.00	110	341.00

Tutorial note: the 110 items remaining in stock are assumed to have been in stock the longest. Therefore closing stock comprises 55 units @ £3.00 each + 55 units (110 − 55) @ £3.20 each:

$$55 \times £3 \quad = 165.00$$
$$55 \times £3.20 = \underline{176.00}$$
$$\underline{341.00}$$

c) AVCO

Date	Deliveries into stock Units	£	£	Transfers to production Units	£	£	Balance Units	AVCO £	£
1 Mar							55	3.00	165.00
10 Mar	160	3.20	512.00				215	3.149	677.00
12 Mar				35	3.149	110.21	180	3.149	566.79
25 Mar				70	3.149	220.42	110	3.149	346.37

Answer to self-test question 16.3

Batch No: 30453A	£	£
Direct materials		
Metal: 100kg @ 4.50 per kilo	450.00	
Paint: 2 litres @ £6.80 per litre	13.60	
Glass: 500 pieces @ 30p per piece	150.00	
		613.60
Direct labour		
Grade A: 22 hours @ £4.80	105.60	
Grade B: 19 hours @ £6.00	114.00	
		219.60
Prime cost		833.20

Cost per picture frame equals:

$$\frac{£833.20}{500} = £1.67 \text{ (to two decimal places)}$$

Answer to self-test question 16.4

Swift Metals Limited: Apportionment of production overheads, year ending 31 December 20X4

			Cost centre		
	Basis	Total £	Preparation £	Tooling £	Finishing £
Factory costs	Floor area	700 000	245 000	315 000	140 000
Canteen costs	Employees	18 496	8 704	6 528	3 264
Machinery depreciation	Net book value	17 650	2 600	11 200	3 850
Machinery maintenance and repair	Call-outs	2 961	658	1 974	329
Supervisory salaries	Employees	23 358	10 992	8 244	4 122
Totals		762 465	267 954	342 946	151 565

Tutorial note: by contrast with the Choremaster example, note that supervisory salaries for Swift Metals are apportioned on the basis of the number of employees supervised. Remember, there are no fixed rules about the way in which costs are apportioned – the basis of apportionment is whatever is most appropriate for the business.

Exercises

The answers to many of the exercises are set out later in this chapter. However, where the exercise number is followed by 'A' the answer is available only to lecturers. Remember that additional exercises (with answers) are available to students on the book's website.

16.1 Paige Peverell plc produces plastic casings for telephones. The following is a list of some of the costs which the company incurs:

Plastic moulding machine depreciation	
Sales office fixtures and fittings depreciation	
Plastic materials	
Advertising expenditure	
Depreciation of factory building	
Electricity bill for factory	
Wages of assembly line workers	
Wages of factory canteen staff	
Wages of assembly line supervisor	
Secretary's salary	
Delivery vehicle depreciation	
Factory consumables	
Royalty payable per item produced to telephone designer	
Mobile phone bill – sales director	

Classify each item of expense as one of the following:

    direct labour

    direct materials

    direct expenses

    indirect production overheads

    other indirect overheads.

16.2A Monkseaton Purnell Limited produces motherboards for PCs from a range of bought in components. The following is a list of some of the costs that the company incurs:

Depreciation of factory work benches	
Bank interest charges	
Administration salaries	

Sundry factory expenses	
Factory insurance	
Supervisor's salary	
Assembly operatives' wages	
Managing director's salary	
Production office computer depreciation	
Purchase of silicone chips	
Factory rental	
Depreciation of sales representatives' cars	
Purchase of circuit boards	
Factory cleaning	

Classify each item of expense as one of the following:

    direct labour

    direct materials

    direct expenses

    indirect production overheads

    other indirect overheads.

16.3   ArtKit Supplies Limited manufactures metal paint tins for the artist's supplies industry. The company operates from a small rented factory unit. In the year ending 31 August 20X3 it incurs the following costs:

	£
Sundry factory costs	2 117
Hinge fittings for boxes	960
Secretarial and administration salaries	12 460
Delivery costs	1 920
Machine operators' wages	18 250
Machinery repair	176
Factory cleaning	980
Lacquer paint for boxes	1 600
Rental of factory	6 409
Finishing operative's wages	10 270
Sundry office costs	904
Salesman's salary	18 740
Metal	18 006
Electricity – factory	1 760
Office supplies	2 411
Depreciation – machinery	1 080
Office telephone	1 630

Rearrange the information given into a cost statement for the year ending 31 August 20X3.

16.4A Brisbane Melbourne Limited manufactures a range of containers for cosmetics in metal and plastic. In the year ending 31 December 20X4 the company incurs the following costs:

	£
Selling department sundry expenses	1 899
Metal	21 444
Depreciation of factory building	1 500
Factory cleaning	6 440
Metal moulding machine: operators' wages	12 222
Factory power	8 370
Finishing operative's wages	10 240
Sales department salaries	39 434
Security guard to factory	4 290
Dyes and paint	2 490
Sundry factory expenses	4 284
Depreciation of office building	1 100
Telephone charges	4 338
Factory canteen costs	12 234
Plastics	63 570
Distribution costs	18 777
Factory insurance	6 960
Plastics machine: operators' wages	15 249
Machinery depreciation	3 950
Administrative salaries	21 496
Stationery and other office admin. supplies	2 937
Other administrative expenses	6 422
Depreciation of office fixtures and fittings	1 929

Rearrange the information given into a cost statement for the year ending 31 December 20X4.

16.5 Porter Farrington Limited imports components for input into its production process. In May 20X4 the following deliveries into stock and transfers to production take place in respect of component PR430:

Date	Activity	Units
1 May	Balance of stock @ £3.00 per unit	30
2 May	Delivery of stock @ £3.30 per unit	50
18 May	Transfer to production	(40)
31 May	Balance of stock	40

What is the value of closing stock, assuming that Porter Farrington Limited adopts the FIFO convention?

a) £123

b) £126

c) £120

d) £132.

16.6A Wensleydale Woollen Waistcoats Limited (WWW Ltd) buys in wool to manufacture into waistcoats on its weaving machines. The stock card for wool code 78X4A shows the following movements in June 20X3:

Date	Activity	Kg
1 June	Balance of stock @ £2 per kilo	38
2 June	Issue to production	(8)
6 June	Delivery into stock @ £2.10 per kilo	50
20 June	Issue to production	40

There were no other transactions in the month.

What is the value of the issue to production on 20 June if WWW Ltd uses the AVCO stock valuation convention?

a) £82.50

b) £84.00

c) £80.00

d) £81.00.

16.7 Clement is a sole trader who owns a small factory. He and his team of skilled workers produce high quality furniture to order. He has been given an order for a set of 12 dining chairs by a luxury hotel chain. Clement keeps a job card record for each order on which he records prime cost details. This order (Code ref: 3223) has had the following materials and labour booked to it:

Direct materials	Booked
Mahogany	18 pieces
Seat padding	12 pieces
Leather cloth	6 metres

Direct labour	Booked
Grade 1	115 hours
Grade 2	86 hours

Mahogany is purchased at £36 per piece (average price), each piece of seat padding costs £3.50 and the leather cloth is £42.00 per metre.

Clement employs two grades of labour: grade 1, for which direct labour cost is £8.50, and grade 2, for which direct labour cost is £9.25.

Produce a job cost record for Job No. 3223 calculating: (a) total prime cost, and (b) prime cost per chair.

16.8A Ribble & Vance Limited produces components to order for specialist motor manufacturers. An order for 100 components (code 1187AB6) was received from one of Ribble & Vance's principal customers. A job code, X4721, was assigned and over the following month various items of direct material and labour were booked to the job:

Item	Booked
Material J	21.4kg
Material Q	3.7kg
Grade IV labour	16 hours
Grade VIII labour	8 hours

Material J was booked out of stores on 21 September 20X0. The store card for material J contains the following details for September 20X0:

Date	Activity	Kg
1 September	Balance of stock @ £14.30 per kg	28.7
8 September	Delivery of stock @ £14.20 per kg	30.0
18 September	Transfer to production job code X4692	(20.6)
21 September	Transfer to production job code X4721	(21.4)

Ribble & Vance Limited apply the FIFO method of stock valuation. Material Q costs £2.75 per kg. Grade IV direct labour cost equals £4.78 per hour and grade VIII direct labour cost equals £8.21 per hour.

Produce a job cost record for Job No. X4721, calculating (i) total prime cost and (ii) prime cost per component.

16.9 Jersey Brookfield & Co. Limited is a manufacturer of soap powders and detergents.

Each of the products moves through two stages: bulk production and then packaging. In the year ending 31 December 20X2 Jersey Brookfield incurred production overheads which it plans to allocate and apportion as follows between the two departments:

	£	Basis of apportionment
Factory building depreciation	5 670	Floor area
Factory rates	11 970	Floor area
Factory insurance	7 980	Floor area
Canteen costs	18 876	No. of employees
Supervisory salaries	29 480	No. of employees
Other indirect labour	18 275	Machinery net book value
Machinery depreciation	21 500	Machinery net book value
Cleaning	17 850	Floor area
Electricity	30 290	Actual
Building maintenance	5 040	Floor area
Total	166 931	

The following information is relevant for the apportionment of overheads:

	Total	Bulk production	Packaging
Floor area	10 500 sq. m.	6 000 sq. m.	4 500 sq. m.
Employees	22	10	12
Machinery NBV	215 000	146 000	69 000
Electricity	30 290	18 790	11 500

Produce a schedule apportioning the overheads between the two departments (cost centres).

16.10A Curtis Bedford is managing director of the family business, Bedford Bowler Limited. The company manufactures children's wooden train sets. Recently Curtis has been on a course about costing and he is keen to apply his new knowledge to the business. Thinking through the production process, he can identify three principal cost centres: machining, assembly and painting, and packaging.

Curtis's accountant supplies the following summary of production overheads incurred by the business to the most recent year-end, 31 December 20X6. Curtis adds a note of what he thinks is the most appropriate method of apportionment between cost centres.

	£	Basis of apportionment
Factory rental	21 105	Floor area
Packaging machine leasing charges	5 500	Actual (see note)
Cleaners' wages	17 991	1/3 to each cost centre
Factory rates	6 930	Floor area
Electricity – factory	8 280	Actual
Supervision	21 456	No. of employees
Machinery maintenance and repair	4 472	Call-outs
Machinery depreciation	12 250	Net book value
Total	97 984	

Note: the packaging machine leasing charges relate only to machinery used in the packaging cost centre. There is no other machinery in the packaging department.

The following information is relevant for the apportionment of overheads:

	Total	Machining	Assembly	Packaging
Floor area	6 300 sq.m.	2 500 sq.m.	1 700 sq.m.	2 100 sq.m.
Employees	18	5	9	4
Machinery NBV	61 250	35 000	26 250	—
Electricity	8 280	3 905	1 892	2 483
Call outs	8	5	3	—

Produce a schedule apportioning the overheads between the three departments (cost centres).

16.11   Barley Brindle Limited produces a single product, Product B. One unit of Product B has a prime cost of £6.20, which includes one hour of direct labour @ £6.20, and each unit uses 0.5 hours of machine time. Estimated production of B in 20X8 is 60 000 units and total production overheads are estimated at £218 000.

Calculate the overhead recovery rates (to the nearest penny) for 20X8, based on:

i)   direct labour hours

ii) machine hours

iii) units of production.

16.12A A manufacturing business, Oakshield Carver Limited, organises its production into four cost centres. In the coming financial year the company plans to produce 115 000 items of product. Further details of its plans are included in the following table:

Cost centre	Production overhead £	Machine hours	Direct labour hours
Machining	297 000	80 000	3 000
Assembly	136 000	20 000	6 000
Finishing	121 500	15 000	9 000
Packaging	76 000	5 000	2 000
Totals	630 500	120 000	20 000

Calculate the overhead recovery rate for each department on the following bases:

i) machining – machine hours

ii) assembly – units of production

iii) finishing – direct labour hours

iv) packaging – units of production.

16.13A The facts are as in Exercise 16.12A. The prime cost and timing details for one unit of production are:

	£
Materials	14.20
Direct labour	18.00
Prime cost	32.20

Each unit uses two hours of machine time in the machining department and 1.5 direct labour hours in the finishing department.

Calculate the total production cost for one unit of the company's product, using the overhead absorption rates calculated in Exercise 16.12A.

16.14 Washington and Middlewich Limited produce two types of metal shelving in their factory – one for domestic use, and one, which is produced to a higher quality standard, for commercial use (in factories and hotel kitchens, for example).

Each shelf unit passes through two processes: first, metal machining and second, painting and finishing (P&F). Commercial shelving is made of stronger material, has extra bracing bars and is given an additional coat of paint in the painting shop.

Cost structures for the two products are as follows:

Domestic shelves	Department	£
Materials	Machining	18.00
	P&F	3.30
		21.30
Direct labour	Machining 0.75 hours × £6	4.50
	P&F 1 hour @ £6	6.00
		10.50
Prime cost		31.80

Commercial shelves	Department	£
Materials	Machining	27.00
	P&F	4.60
		31.60
Direct labour	Machining 1 hour @ £6	6.00
	P&F 1.5 hours @ £6	9.00
		15.00
Prime cost		46.60

Production overheads are estimated at the following apportioned amounts for next year:

	£
Machining	172 490
Painting and finishing	116 270

The company plans to produce 6 000 units of each product next year.

Calculate overhead absorption rates based upon:

i) percentage of direct materials cost

ii) percentage of direct labour cost.

Discuss which basis of overhead absorption might be preferable for each cost centre.

16.15A Activity-based costing (ABC) is a costing system that was developed in the 1980s as a result of an increasing awareness in businesses of the deficiencies of traditional approaches to production overhead absorption.

i) Describe the principal deficiencies in the traditional product costing system that ABC seeks to correct;

ii) Describe the key features of ABC.

iii) Identify and comment upon a significant advantage *and* a significant disadvantage associated with the implementation of an ABC system.

Answers to exercises

16.1   Paige Peverell plc

Expense	Classification
Plastic moulding machine depreciation	Indirect production overheads
Sales office fixtures and fittings depreciation	Other indirect overheads
Plastic materials	Direct materials
Advertising expenditure	Other indirect overheads
Depreciation of factory building	Indirect production overheads
Electricity bill for factory	Indirect production overheads
Wages of assembly line workers	Direct labour
Wages of factory canteen staff	Indirect production overheads
Wages of assembly line supervisor	Indirect production overheads
Secretary's salary	Other indirect overheads
Delivery vehicle depreciation	Other indirect overheads
Factory consumables	Indirect production overheads
Royalty payable per item produced to telephone designer	Direct expenses
Mobile phone bill – sales director	Other indirect overheads

16.3

ArtKit Supplies Limited: Cost statement for the year ending 31 August 20X3

	£	£
Direct materials		
Metal	18 006	
Lacquer paint	1 600	
Hinge fittings	960	
		20 566
Direct labour		
Machine operators' wages	18 250	
Finishing operative's wages	10 270	
		28 520
Prime cost		49 086

	£	£
Production overheads		
Rental of factory	6 409	
Machine repair	176	
Depreciation – machinery	1 080	
Electricity – factory	1 760	
Factory cleaning	980	
Sundry factory costs	2 117	
		12 522
Production cost		61 608
Other overheads		
Secretarial and administration salaries	12 460	
Salesman's salary	18 740	
Office supplies	2 411	
Office telephone	1 630	
Sundry office costs	904	
Delivery costs	1 920	
		38 065
Total costs		99 673

16.5   Because Porter Farrington adopts a FIFO policy for stock valuation, the 40 items left in stock at the end of May 20X4 are deemed to be those most recently delivered. The most recent delivery before the end of the month was the 50 items delivered on 2 May at a cost of £3.30 per unit. The correct valuation is, therefore:

$$40 \text{ units @ } £3.30 = £132.00$$

The correct answer, therefore, is d).

16.7   Clement
Total prime cost:

Job No: 3223; 12 dining chairs	£	£
Direct materials		
Mahogany: 18 @ £36	648.00	
Seat padding: 12 @ £3.50	42.00	
Leather cloth: 6 metres @ £42.00 per m.	252.00	
		942.00
Direct labour		
Grade 1: 115 hours @ 8.50	977.50	
Grade 2: 86 hours @ 9.25	795.50	
		1 773.00
Prime cost		2 715.00

The prime cost total for 12 dining chairs is £2715. The prime cost per chair is:

$$\frac{£2\,715}{12} = £226.25$$

16.9   **Jersey Brookfield & Co. Limited: Apportionment of production overheads for the year ending 31 December 20X2**

	Basis	Total £	Bulk production £	Packaging £
			Cost Centre	
Factory building depreciation	Floor area	5 670	3 240	2 430
Factory rates	Floor area	11 970	6 840	5 130
Factory insurance	Floor area	7 980	4 560	3 420
Canteen costs	No. employees	18 876	8 580	10 296
Supervisory salaries	No. employees	29 480	13 400	16 080
Other indirect labour	Machinery NBV	18 275	12 410	5 865
Machinery depreciation	Machinery NBV	21 500	14 600	6 900
Cleaning	Floor area	17 850	10 200	7 650
Electricity	Actual	30 290	18 790	11 500
Building maintenance	Floor area	5 040	2 880	2 160
		166 931	95 500	71 431

16.11   *i) Overhead absorption rate based on direct labour hours*

Each unit uses one hour of direct labour; production of 60 000 units is planned, therefore 60 000 direct labour hours will be used.

$$\text{Overhead absorption rate} = \frac{£218\,000}{60\,000} = £3.63$$

ii) Overhead absorption rate based on machine hours

Each unit uses 0.5 hours of machine time. Anticipated total machine time is, therefore, 60 000 × 0.5 = 30 000.

$$\text{Overhead absorption rate} = \frac{£218\,000}{30\,000} = £7.27$$

iii) Overhead absorption rate based on units of production

$$\text{Overhead absorption rate} = \frac{£218\,000}{60\,000} = £3.63$$

(i.e. the same rate as calculated on the basis of direct labour hours).

16.14   Washington and Middlewich Limited

Totals for direct materials based on production of 6 000 of each product

	£
Metal machining department	
Domestic shelves: £18.00 × 6 000	108 000
Commercial shelves: £27.00 × 6 000	162 000
	270 000
Painting and finishing department	
Domestic shelves: £3.30 × 6 000	19 800
Commercial shelves: £4.60 × 6 000	27 600
	47 400

Totals for direct labour based on production of 6 000 of each product

	£
Metal machining department	
Domestic shelves: 0.75 × £6 × 6 000	27 000
Commercial shelves: 1 × £6 × 6 000	36 000
	63 000
Painting and finishing dept	
Domestic shelves: 1 × £6 × 6 000	36 000
Commercial shelves: 1.5 × £6 × 67 000	54 000
	90 000

i) Overhead absorption rates based on % of direct materials

$$\text{Metal machining department} = \frac{172\,490}{270\,000} = 63.9\%$$

$$\text{Painting and finishing department} = \frac{116\,270}{47\,400} = 245.3\%$$

ii) Overhead absorption rates based on % of direct labour

$$\text{Metal machining department} = \frac{172\,490}{63\,000} = 273.8\%$$

$$\text{Painting and finishing department} = \frac{116\,270}{90\,000} = 129.2\%$$

Materials are relatively much more significant than labour hours in the machining department. Therefore, it would probably make sense to use an overhead absorption rate based on the % of direct materials consumed.

By contrast, in the painting and finishing department, direct labour is relatively more important than the input of materials. Therefore, it would probably make sense to use an overhead absorption rate based on the % of direct materials consumed.

Because the machining department probably involves use of a relatively high level of machine hours it may be worth considering the calculation of an overhead absorption rate based on machine hours.

17

BUDGETING

AIMS AND LEARNING OUTCOMES

Aim of the chapter

To understand the reasons for, and the processes involved in, setting a budget in a business organisation, and to be able to prepare and evaluate budget statements.

Learning outcomes

After reading the chapter and completing the related exercises, students should:

- Understand the role of budgeting in planning and controlling business organisations.

- Be able to prepare straightforward budget statements for a small business.

- Know about the stages involved in setting a budget for a larger business organisation, and appreciate some of the behavioural issues that may arise.

- Be able to evaluate actual outcomes against budget plans.

What is a budget?

A budget is a plan, expressed in financial and/or more general quantitative terms, which extends forward for a period into the future. Budgets are widely used in organisations of all types and sizes. In this chapter we will concentrate on the use of budgets in profit-oriented businesses, but it should be recognised that budgets are used in all kinds of organisation, including, for example, schools, health trusts and charities. Also, it is possible (and often desirable) to prepare personal expenditure budgets to ensure that spending does not exceed income, or as a basis for negotiating borrowing such as a mortgage.

Budgeting forms part of a broader planning process. In Chapter 15 we examined the broad context of management accounting and its links with the functions of management. The summary from that chapter is repeated below:

- *Setting business objectives*: The primary functions of management are: (a) to identify the objectives of the business; and (b) to direct the activities of the business so as to meet the objectives.
- *Assess alternatives and make decisions and make plans*: Management needs information about the alternative actions it could take. Having assessed the available information, management takes decisions and makes detailed plans for the future.
- *Monitoring outcomes*: Management uses information to assess the extent to which its plans have succeeded and its business objectives have been met.
- *Redefine objectives and plans*: On the basis of a comparison with planned and actual outcomes it may be necessary to redefine the overarching objectives of the business and the detailed plans that are geared towards achieving the objectives.

The budgeting process falls largely into the second stage of the management process outlined above. Having established strategic objectives, management assesses the alternative actions that could be taken in order to meet those objectives. Having decided upon the action or actions that will best meet the objectives, taking into account any relevant constraints, managers must then formulate more detailed plans.

Often in larger organisations there will be a strategic (or long-range) plan reaching forward into the future over, for example, a three to five-year period. Within that plan, budgets are prepared, often on an annual basis, for the 12 months ahead. Example 17.1 illustrates the relationship between strategic objectives, long-range planning and an annual budget.

Example 17.1 Referring back to the Chapter 15 case study, let us reconsider Calder Calloway Cards Limited. To recap, the company, during its first eight or nine years of life, had had no formal management planning or control systems. With the appointment of two new directors it became clear that the haphazard approach to management that had been adequate in the early years would no longer suffice. During 20X8 Paco, the managing director, accepts the need for a more formal planning and management control process. He and his fellow directors meet several times with a view to deciding upon a set of strategic objectives for the business. They also decide to recruit a management accountant to help in the formal process of budget setting and evaluation.

The directors determine the following key strategic objectives:

- To grow the company to the point where it is a credible competitor with the largest producers in the greetings card market.
- To produce cards of high quality with a distinctive company design identity.

Out of these two key objectives a long-term plan develops. The directors decide that the plan should cover the next five years. It is a written document that identifies the strategy for achieving the key objectives. An extract from it includes the following principal actions (together with more detailed actions for achieving the key action):

- Increase sales by at least 30% per annum
  - Recruit new members of the sales team
  - Encourage and motivate by use of commission and reward schemes
  - Identify new outlets.
- Reduce unit costs and increase gross profitability to 45% within five years
  - Improve and expand production facilities by investment in 'state of the art' printing machinery
  - Implement a system of capital expenditure control and evaluation
  - Improve production logistics.
- Improve, and keep improving, the quality of the product
  - Recruit quality supervisor
  - Improve supervision
  - Implement a Total Quality Management system to motivate all staff.
- Create a distinctive design identity for the company's products
  - Recruit a design team under the strong leadership of a design director who will be a full member of the board of directors
  - Identify and recruit staff at an appropriate level and remuneration
  - Identify key elements of design policy in conjunction with design director.

Some of the points are likely to be acted upon within the next 12 months; others will produce action over the longer term.

The directors, working together with the new management accountant, will produce a budget for the next 12 months. This will identify financial and other quantitative measurements that represent the changes proposed. The immediate financial implications of the plan will be recognised in the budget. For example:

- *Personnel budget*: it seems likely that recruitment of the design team will take place within the next 12 months. Costs of recruitment and of the new salaries will be included in the budget. Consequential savings (for example, in respect of the payments made to freelance card designers) will also be estimated and their effect taken into account. The personnel budget will be expressed both in terms of numbers of staff and financial costs.
- *Capital expenditure budget*: a detailed budget taking account of the effects of likely short-term decisions will be required. For example, if the production director, Karim, decides that a printing machine should be scrapped and should be replaced during the year with a new machine costing around £20 000, the decision has an impact on production speed and quality, volume of production, cash (£20 000 has to be found) and depreciation.
- *Sales budget*: if the company aims to increase sales by at least 30% the budget should reflect this aim. The planned increase involves extra costs (for example, in recruiting additional staff, in creating and implementing a commission scheme and in planning a campaign to expand into new sales outlets).

All of these implications (and more) must be reflected in the budget for the following financial year.

Budgeting is not, as the example implies, a simple process. However, if the business sets its strategic objectives sensibly, the budget, to some extent, emerges naturally from higher level management decisions.

The budget process

In this section we will examine the kind of process involved in setting a budget for a medium to large-sized organisation that is organised into departments. Budget setting in a small organisation is likely to be more straightforward in that it involves communication between fewer parties. In a very small organisation it may be that only the proprietor of the business is involved in setting the budget. As usual, we will initially examine the process by means of an example.

Example 17.2 Arbus Arbuthnot plc manufactures and sells cosmetics and skincare products. It operates in a highly competitive market in which there is a culture of constant scientific development. The company's basic strategic objective is to improve market share by the development of improved products, innovating more quickly and effectively than the competition. Each year the research and development department finds new ways of improving products (for example, by changing the feel and consistency of a skin make-up).

Stage 1: Discussing the sales budget

The most important constraint on the company's activities is, generally, the level of sales. The sales budget is set first (as is the case in most commercial organisations operating in a competitive environment) and all other budgets are developed from it.

In June 20X3 the budget process gets under way to set the budget for the accounting year that runs from 1 March 20X4 to 28 February 20X5. The directors meet to talk about the sales budget. Their discussion is influenced by the fact that a new improved face cream has recently been introduced by a competitor. Arbus Arbuthnot has responded to this by changing the advertising and packaging of their equivalent product, emphasising the scientific soundness of the formula. The directors feel that the advertising is likely to prove fairly effective, and they are optimistic about the sales projections for the coming year. They agree that the budget volume of sales (i.e. number of items sold in the various categories of product) should increase by an average of 5%, and that prices can be increased by 3%. They are aware, however, that their competitors are working on anti-ageing products for both men and women; in order to keep up with the market Arbus Arbuthnot is going to have to increase its research and development activities.

Stage 2: The production budget

The next stage is that the detailed analysis of the sales budget is used to project production requirements. If sales volumes are expected to increase by 5% it is

▶

reasonable to suppose that a corresponding increase in production will be required. However, other factors can influence the production budget; for example, if a special product promotion is planned, linked to an advertising campaign, it will probably be necessary to plan for additional production.

Stage 3: Communication of budget guidelines

At this point it is probably appropriate to broaden the scope of the budget process. The directors have made the strategic decisions relating to objectives and they have decided upon the broad general approach to be taken in the next following year's budget (e.g. an increase of 5% in sales volume, some price increases and so on). Budgeting guidelines will then be communicated to the various departments around the company.

Stage 4: Submission of departmental budgets

Individual departments or divisions can now be asked to submit their budgets for approval. These should be prepared in accordance with the broad thrust of policy. The research and development department, for example, is clearly being directed to expand its activities; the head of R&D will probably revise personnel requirements and may start work on presenting a proposal for an expansion of laboratory facilities. The marketing department may respond to the call for a 5% increase in sales volume by planning additional marketing campaigns.

It is a generally accepted principle of budgeting that budgets are more likely to work if they involve the participation of all of the people who are expected to put them into operation. Such participation may involve a great deal of paper, meetings and discussion, but many organisations obviously feel that the process is worthwhile in order that participants feel that they can claim 'ownership' of the final budget.

Stage 5: Approval of budgets

A well-organised budget process will have a range of submission deadlines for parts of the budget. Once the departmental budgets have been submitted they can be coordinated and considered together to judge the extent to which they are reasonable and achievable given the inevitable operational constraints that apply to all businesses. For example, the head of R&D submits an ambitious budget based upon a planned expansion of numbers of personnel by 30%. He also requests capital expenditure of £1.5 million. These proposals may be quite reasonable in the context of management expectations (or perhaps the head of R&D is indulging in a spot of empire-building). Senior managers will accept, reject or modify such proposals and then return them to the originator. In some processes, budget proposals may be discussed and modified several times before the final budget is agreed.

Stage 6: Agreement of budget

Once the budget has been extensively negotiated and discussed, the final agreed version can be disseminated across the business and then people can get on with the business of implementing it. If the process has been genuinely participative and a feeling of 'ownership' has been achieved, the budget may prove to be a very useful co-ordinating and motivating tool. In the next section we summarise the benefits to be obtained from effective budgeting.

Benefits of effective budgeting

The principal benefits are summarised under the following four sub-headings.

Planning and coordination of operations and activities

Setting a budget concentrates the minds of all of the personnel involved on the objectives of the organisation and how they might best be furthered in the shorter term. This allows for coordinated, planned actions to take place, and should minimise the number of opportunities for 'off the cuff' decisions that are not necessarily in the best long-term interests of the organisation. The efficient coordination of activities becomes particularly important in a large organisation where individual departments or divisions may not have a sufficiently broad perspective on the overall objectives of the organisation. Decision making at a divisional level may make sense within the context of that individual division but may not be optimal within the context of the business operation as a whole.

Providing motivation

If the budget process is effective it may help to promote a sense of ownership of targets and objectives. Staff may feel motivated to work harder in order to achieve strategic and shorter-term objectives. However, if the budget process is not managed effectively the opposite effect can take hold. Some of the adverse effects of budgeting are discussed later in the chapter.

Control of operations and activities

Because a budget is (or should be) a carefully thought out plan, it should allow managers to control business activity. Once the budget has been set and approved it should be carefully monitored, with actual outcomes being compared to the budget. Where necessary, action should be taken, quickly, in order to correct any aspects of the operations that are not functioning as planned.

Basis for performance evaluation

A budget provides a yardstick by which group or individual performance can be judged. For example, each division in a major company may have sales targets set for it. Those divisions that regularly exceed targets may be rewarded by opportunities for new investment, by bonuses for staff, or at least by not being closed down or sold off. Individual performance may also be rewarded on the basis of evaluated budget out-turn. For example, a company where each division has a sales manager could reward the sales manager of the best performing division by means of an individual bonus or promotion.

Some problems with budgeting

The problems which are encountered with budgeting in practice are mostly linked to human behaviour. Some of the problems that can arise are highlighted in the following sub-sections.

Demotivational budgets

Although the budgeting process as described earlier in the chapter is intended, ideally, to encourage participation and 'ownership', the practical effect may not be as intended. If the budget process is essentially authoritarian with little or no effective participation, middle managers and staff may feel resentful and disinclined to work to budget.

Setting unrealistic targets

Unrealistic targets may add to the demotivational effect. If senior management set an over-optimistic budget for sales volume increases, staff may simply decide that it is not worth even trying to achieve the targets. Faced with an apparently hopeless task, they may withdraw their interest and enthusiasm and may even start to think about changing their employment.

Budgetary slack

Where managers and staff are closely involved in the budget setting process, they may try to give themselves an easy life by setting low targets for achievement. Senior managers need to be aware of the possibility that staff will attempt to build in **budgetary slack**.

An incremental approach

Often, in practice, **incremental budgets** are set. This would involve, for example, taking last year's total for each budget heading or the actual performance figures and adding 5%. This is a thoughtless and superficial approach to budgeting, which, usually, would fail to link the budget to strategic objectives of the business. (It also fails to recognise that not all costs increase at the same rate.) At its worst it positively encourages misuse of resources and overspending. If a department head knows that budgets are set by adding 5% to this year's actual spending, then he or she is much more likely to overspend in order to ensure a bigger allowance next year.

Use it or lose it

In many organisations managers feel it necessary to spend every last penny of budget allowance; they know that if they do not spend up to budget the unused allowance will be taken away from them in future years. This approach does not lead to the best possible strategic use of resources.

Name, blame and shame

It is important that responsibility for budgets and their outcomes is clearly identified. Managers should be answerable only for variations that are under their control. For example, sales figures are affected by sales returns. Failure to achieve target sales because of high levels of sales returns may or may not be the fault of the sales staff. If they have been selling too aggressively the high level of returns may be attributable to them. If, on the other hand, the goods are being returned because they are substandard as a result of a failure in the production quality inspection process, the responsibility does not lie with the sales staff.

Finally, it is worth noting that setting budgets is a costly process. Some organisations have dispensed with the type of traditional budgeting described in this chapter because the costs are perceived to outweigh the benefits gained.

The first case study for this chapter illustrates a budget process which could result in problems and less than optimal performance.

CASE STUDY 17.1 A budget dispute

Brunswick Carlton plc is a producer of domestic dishwashing machines. The company has gradually lost market share in recent years and its profitability has tended to decline, although it has not yet actually reported a loss. The chief executive has recently retired at the age of 70 and his successor, Clive Neil, has just been appointed. Also on the board is Shahera Patel, sales director, Bryn Edwards, production director and Clare Burnhope, finance director. At a recent meeting the directors agreed that the key strategic objectives for the business should be to regain lost market share and re-establish the company as an innovator and market leader.

The directors meet again to discuss the budget for the coming year. Shahera has just presented a proposal for the sales budget that includes a modest increase in machines sold; last year the actual number of machines sold, including export sales, was 164 000. She has had a meeting with the sales force, all of whom have worked for the company for many years and have a lot of experience of the market. They say that the market's very competitive at the moment and they don't feel that they'd be able to sell significantly higher volumes unless there was a real improvement in the product. On the basis of her discussions she has budgeted a sales volume of 168 000. She feels that selling prices should remain the same because of the level of competition in the market.

Clive does not respond well to the sales budget proposals:

Clive: We decided last week that we're going to reposition this company and regain the market share that's been dribbling away over the last five years. At a rate of an extra 4000 machines a year it'll take forever. Anyway, the size of the overall market is still increasing by about 8% a year, so we should be aiming higher than 4000 just to stand still. I'm sorry to say it, Shahera, but the trouble is that your sales people have grown complacent and lazy – they're just not prepared to put their backs into making new contacts. We need to set them a real challenge that they can get their teeth into and if they can't make their figures we'll recruit people who can.

Shahera: Well, fair enough, but what sort of figure did you have in mind?

Clive: If we said 200 000 machines next year, that'd be a bit over a 20% increase. It should be quite achievable given the 8% growth in the market that's forecast anyway. There's a lot of movement in the housing market, you know, and when people move house they often buy a new dishwasher. The sales are there for the asking.

Bryn: Yes, but if we sell 20% more we've got to produce 20% more, and I don't quite see how we can do that unless we can expand our production facilities. We're working flat out as it is on the shop floor, and we'd need to spend a lot more on product development to make any significant improvements to the product.

▶

Clare: And if we have to expand production facilities we'll need to finance additional capital expenditure and working capital.

Clive: It looks to me as if you've all become a bit complacent. What this place needs is a real shake-up – a culture change – I'm only interested in 'can do' and all you're giving me is a lot of reasons why we *can't* do things. We're going to play this one my way, whether you and the sales staff and the shop floor workers like it or not. I was brought in here to make changes and that's exactly what I'm going to do. We'll call it 200 000 in sales volume for next year, and that's final.

The case study requirement is to discuss the likely effects on the budget process and its effectiveness of Clive's decision to radically increase the sales volume budget for the next year.

Case study discussion

Clive is not encouraging a participative approach by his autocratic insistence on a very high sales volume target. The other directors are likely to feel resentful of the fact that he is disregarding their objections (which they may genuinely feel to be valid). However, Clive may not actually care very much about what the others think, especially if his hidden agenda is to drive them out of the company.

The orthodox approach to budgeting is that it should be participative in nature; people should be allowed their say and should be able to claim ownership of the agreed budget. Participation, it is argued, leads to higher levels of motivation and identification with the strategic objectives of the business. However, in this case, there may well be an element of complacency among the long-standing directors and the workforce. Market share and profitability have been decreasing over a long period, and it may be that only radical action will turn around the gradual decline.

Clive may be right; the sales force may indeed have become lazy. They may have been setting themselves easy targets for years, building in budgetary slack. However, presented with a budget of 200 000 units of sales, they may simply decide that it's not worth even trying to hit such a high target. Even if Clive is correct and this level of sales is achievable by the company in the short term, he and the other directors are probably going to have to work out a strategy for enthusing the sales team. Given that the sales director, Shahera, herself, is apparently happy with a very low target increase, Clive appears to be facing some major difficulties.

From the information given about the company, it seems that some fairly radical shake-up is required. However, Clive's abrasive and confrontational approach may not achieve the results he wants.

Preparing the budget: Principal types of budget

Budgets are often prepared for a budget period of one year. However, the budget period can extend over a shorter, or, occasionally, a longer period. Often, the annual budget is further split into quarters, months or even weeks.

Another, related type of budget is the **rolling budget**. The budget is initially prepared for an appropriate budget period (probably one year). With each month that elapses, another month is added on to the end of the budget, so that at any given time there is a full 12-month budget. For example, a company sets a budget for the 12 months between 1 September 20X3 and 31 August 20X4. At the end of

September 20X3 another month (September 20X4) is added on to the end of the budget. At the end of October 20X3 the budget for October 20X4 is added on, and so on.

As we have seen the starting point for most budgets is the sales budget. Within most businesses of any size, related budgets will be required for areas such as production, research and development, administration and capital expenditure. Once the budget process is complete a full set of interrelated budgets (the master budget) is available for use within the business.

Figure 17.1 sets out some of the principal budgets that will be required in a manufacturing business.

Figure 17.1 presents the sales budget in a central position, signifying its importance to all other budgets. The sales budget links in directly to the production budget, which, in turn, drives budgets for raw materials, direct labour and production overheads. The link with other costs is a little more tenuous, as denoted by the broken lines. However, all of these costs are related to some extent to the general volume of activity generated by the business. All functional areas in the business may have needs for capital expenditure, which is shown in the figure in a separate box below. Finally, all of the budget information (sales, production, expenses and capital expenditure) is brought together in the form of three principal budgeted statements: the budget cash flow statement; budget profit and loss account; and budget balance sheet.

Figure 17.1

Principal budget areas within a manufacturing business

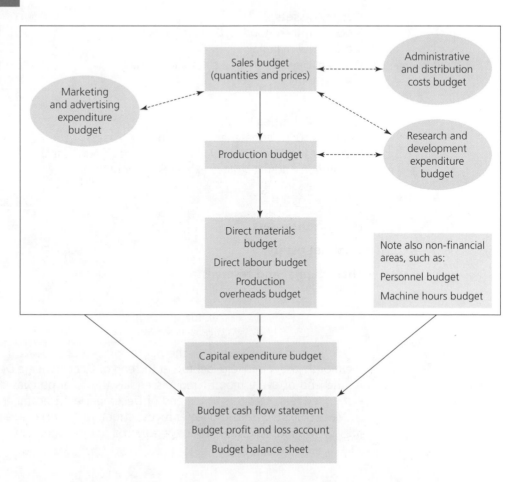

Setting the budget: A practical example

In this section we will examine the mechanics of budget setting using a simple example based on a company that manufactures only one product. Even though the setting is deliberately simplified the example produces many interlinked numbers. Students will need to work through it thoroughly in order to understand how the various elements fit together.

Example 17.3 Macey Nelson Limited manufactures a single product: vacuum cleaners. The company is in the process of preparing a budget for the six months ending 30 June 20X6. The balance sheet at 31 December 20X5 is as follows:

	£	£
Fixed assets		
Machinery at cost	96 000	
Less: accumulated depreciation	(38 400)	
		57 600
Office fixtures and fittings and computer	15 000	
Less: accumulated depreciation	(3 000)	
		12 000
		69 600
Current assets		
Stocks: finished goods (200 units)	15 000	
Stocks: raw materials	3 750	
Debtors (December 20X5 sales, all on credit)	40 000	
Cash at bank	8 000	
	66 750	
Current liabilities		
Creditors for raw materials (1 month's purchases)	10 000	
Creditors for production overheads (1 month's purchases)	9 000	
Creditors for administrative expenses (1 month's purchases)	4 000	
	23 000	
Net current assets		43 750
Total net assets		113 350
Share capital and reserves		
Share capital		20 000
Reserves		93 350
		113 350

At the end of every month the figure for debtors equals the total sales for the month just ended (e.g. debtors at the end of December are December's sales). At the end of every month creditors equals the total purchases for the month just ended (e.g. creditors at the end of December are December purchases).

Macey Nelson's selling price and cost structure for one vacuum cleaner is as follows:

	£
Selling price	100
Raw materials	25
Direct labour	20
Prime cost	45

The business uses full absorption costing based upon the number of units planned for production.

The company's sales director produces a forecast for sales (in units) for the first six months of 20X6 on the basis of discussions he has held with fellow directors and with his sales team. The production director then works out projected production in numbers of units. Projections for sales and production in units, together with opening and closing stocks of finished goods for each month are as follows:

Month	Opening stock in units	Number of units: sales	Number of units: production	Closing stock in units
January	200	250	300	250
February	250	280	280	250
March	250	280	330	300
April	300	300	350	350
May	350	300	350	400
June	400	300	350	450
Total		1 710	1 960	

Production in July is estimated at 350 units.

Production is planned in such a way as to build up stocks of finished goods towards the autumn; this is to ensure that the company has sufficient stock to respond to a potential increase in demand following a major advertising campaign that is planned for the latter half of the year. At the beginning of each month the production director plans to have half of the raw materials in stock which will be required for the coming month's production schedule. In order to simplify the budgeting exercise it is assumed that there is no work-in-progress at each month-end.

Production overheads forecast for the first six months of 20X6 are:

	£
Factory rental	16 000
Supervisory salaries	12 450
Other direct labour	6 250
Cleaning	3 900
Insurance	2 600
Power	5 800
Depreciation of machinery	4 800
Maintenance	1 000
Canteen costs	2 500
Business rates	2 800
Other factory expenses	700
Total	58 800

Production overheads accumulate evenly over the sixth-month period.

▶

Monthly administrative costs total £4000, plus £250 of depreciation of office fixtures and fittings and computer. Each month's expenses are paid in the next following month (remember that this does not include depreciation, which is a non-cash adjustment).

No capital expenditure is planned for the six months ending 30 June 20X6 and there will be no disposals of fixed assets.

The requirement is to prepare the following budgets for the first six months of 20X6:

a) Raw materials purchases budget.
b) Budget overhead absorption rate.
c) Budget profit and loss account for each of the six months ending 30 June 20X6 and a summary budget profit and loss account for the six-month period.
d) Budget balance sheet at 30 June 20X6.
e) Budget cash flow statement for each of the six months ending 30 June 20X6.

a) Raw materials purchases budget

Each unit of product uses £25 of raw material, and we need to ensure that raw material sufficient for half of each month's production is available in stock at the beginning of the month. We can work out the opening and closing stock for each month, the utilisation of raw materials in production and hence (by means of a balancing figure) the amount of raw materials purchases each month:

First, opening stock:

	Calculation of opening raw materials stock	£
January	Given in balance sheet at 31.12.X5	3 750
February	50% × 280 (Feb. production) × £25	3 500
March	50% × 330 (Mar. production) £25	4 125
April	50% × 350 (Apr. production) × £25	4 375
May	50% × 350 (May production) × £25	4 375
June	50% × 350 (June production) × £25	4 375

Each month's opening stock is the closing stock of the previous month. Closing stock in June is still required. We know that July production is estimated at 350 so the opening stock for July will need to be 50% × 350 × £25 = £4375 (remember that opening stock for July is the same as closing stock for June).

Utilisation of raw materials in production:

	Calculation of utilisation of raw materials in production	£
January	300 units × £25	7 500
February	280 units × £25	7 000
March	330 units × £25	8 250
April	350 units × £25	8 750
May	350 units × £25	8 750
June	350 units × £25	8 750

Bringing all this information together we can calculate the expected level of raw material purchases.

Opening stock + Purchases of raw materials − Raw materials used in production = Closing stock

This formula contains four pieces of information; we now know three of them so we can calculate the fourth. Purchases of raw materials is the balancing figure, which we can calculate for each month as follows:

Closing stock + Raw materials used in production − Opening stock

	Opening stock of raw material £	Purchases of raw materials £ (bal. fig.)	Raw materials used in production £	Closing stock of raw material £
January	3 750	7 250	(7 500)	3 500
February	3 500	7 625	(7 000)	4 125
March	4 125	8 500	(8 250)	4 375
April	4 375	8 750	(8 750)	4 375
May	4 375	8 750	(8 750)	4 375
June	4 375	8 750	(8 750)	4 375

b) Budget overhead absorption rate

Total production overheads for six months: £58 800
Total number of units to be produced: 1960.

Therefore the budget overhead absorption rate per unit is:

$$\frac{£58\,800}{1\,960} = £30 \text{ per unit}$$

We now know the total budgeted production cost per unit:

	£
Prime cost	45
Production overhead absorbed	30
Total production cost per unit	75

We need this information in order to calculate the budget profit and loss account for each of the six months in the budget period.

c) Profit and loss

Macey Nelson Limited: Budget profit and loss account for each month

January–June 20X6

	Jan £	Feb £	Mar £	Apr £	May £	Jun £
Sales	250 × £100 = 25 000	280 × £100 = 28 000	280 × £100 = 28 000	300 × £100 = 30 000	300 × £100 = 30 000	300 × £100 = 30 000
Cost of sales (= production cost)	250 × £75 = (18 750)	280 × £75 = (21 000)	280 × £75 = (21 000)	300 × £75 = (22 500)	300 × £75 = (22 500)	300 × £75 = (22 500)
Gross profit	6 250	7 000	7 000	7 500	7 500	7 500
Administrative expenses (incl. depreciation)	(4 250)	(4 250)	(4 250)	(4 250)	(4 250)	(4 250)
Net profit	2 000	2 750	2 750	3 250	3 250	3 250

▶

Macey Nelson Limited: Summary budget profit and loss account for the six months ending 30 June 20X6

		£
Sales	1710 units @ £100 each	171 000
Cost of sales	1710 units @ £75 each	(128 250)
Gross profit	1710 units @ £25 each	42 750
Administrative expenses	6 months × £4 250	(25 500)
Net profit		17 250

d) Budget balance sheet at 30 June 20X6

Workings are as follows:

1. Fixed assets

	At 31 December 20X5 £	Depreciation: six months to 30 June 20X6 £	At 30 June 20X6 £
Machinery			
Cost	96 000		96 000
Acc. depreciation	(38 400)	(4 800)	(43 200)
Net book value	57 600		52 800
Office equipment			
Cost	15 000		15 000
Acc. depreciation	(3 000)	6 × £250 = £1 500	(4 500)
Net book value	12 000		10 500

2. Stock

Raw materials closing stock at 30 June 20X6 has already been calculated at £4375. Finished goods closing stock in numbers of units at 30 June 20X6 is 450 units. The production cost of each unit is £75, therefore closing stock of finished goods is:

$$£75 \times 450 = £33\,750$$

3. Debtors

Debtors at the end of June 20X6 equal the amount of sales for June – i.e. £30 000.

4. Creditors

Creditors for raw material purchases at the end of June 20X6 equal the amount of raw material purchases for June – i.e. £8750. Creditors for expenses included in production overheads equal the production overheads incurred in June.

	£
Total production overheads for six months:	58 800
Less: depreciation (not a purchased item)	(4 800)
	54 000

$$\frac{£54\,000}{6} = £9\,000$$

Creditors for administration expenses at the end of June 20X6 equal the administrative expenses incurred in June, which will be paid in July 20X6 – i.e. £4000 (excluding depreciation, which is not a purchased item).

5. Reserves

	£
Reserves at 31 December 20X5	93 350
+ Budget net profit for six months to 30 June 20X6	17 250
	110 600

We do not know the figure for cash at bank (until we have done the cash flow budget which is the next stage), but we know all the other figures in the budgeted balance sheet at 30 June 20X6.

Macey Nelson Limited: Budgeted balance sheet at 30 June 20X6

	£	£
Fixed assets (working 1)		
Machinery at cost	96 000	
Less: accumulated depreciation	(43 200)	
		52 800
Office fixtures and fittings and computer	15 000	
Less: accumulated depreciation	(4 500)	
		10 500
		63 300
Current assets		
Stocks: finished goods (working 2)	33 750	
Stocks: raw materials (working 2)	4 375	
Debtors (working 3)	30 000	
Cash at bank (balancing figure)	20 925	
	89 050	
Current liabilities		
Creditors for raw materials (working 4)	8 750	
Creditors for production overheads (working 4)	9 000	
Creditors for administrative expenses (working 4)	4 000	
	21 750	
Net current assets		67 300
Total net assets		130 600
Share capital and reserves		
Share capital		20 000
Reserves (working 5)		110 600
		130 600

e) Budget cash flow statement for each of the six months ending 30 June 20X6

We have already calculated most of the information we need. However, we still require calculations for payments made in respect of direct labour. Each unit produced requires direct labour valued at £20. Therefore, for each of the six months, payments for direct labour will be made as follows:

Month	Production (units)	Production × £20
January	300	6 000
February	280	5 600
March	330	6 600
April	350	7 000
May	350	7 000
June	350	7 000

	Jan £	Feb £	Mar £	Apr £	May £	Jun £
Opening balance at bank	8 000	19 000	18 150	18 925	18 425	19 675
Add: sales receipts	40 000	25 000	28 000	28 000	30 000	30 000
Less: payments for raw materials purchases	(10 000)	(7 250)	(7 625)	(8 500)	(8 750)	(8 750)
Less: payments for direct labour	(6 000)	(5 600)	(6 600)	(7 000)	(7 000)	(7 000)
Less: payments for overheads	(9 000)	(9 000)	(9 000)	(9 000)	(9 000)	(9 000)
Less: payments for admin. expenses	(4 000)	(4 000)	(4 000)	(4 000)	(4 000)	(4 000)
Closing balance at bank	19 000	18 150	18 925	18 425	19 675	20 925

Notes:
1. Each month we start with the opening balance of cash at bank. On 1 January 20X6 this is the amount of cash at bank in the balance sheet at 31 December 20X5.
2. We add in sales receipts (which, in this case, are the amount of the sales made in the previous month).
3. We take away payments for direct labour (which are made within the month in which they are incurred so there is no opening or closing creditor balance in respect of this item).
4. We take away payments for overheads and administrative expenses, which, in this case, are the amounts from the previous month.
5. At the end of each month we can calculate a budgeted closing balance at bank. This, in turn, becomes the opening balance of cash at bank in the following month.

Discussion

This has been a very long, complicated example, with lots of calculations. Most students will need to work through this several times before they are completely familiar with the idea of the various budgets and the figures used to illustrate them.

The type of budget calculations shown can be done more easily and speedily on a spreadsheet, once a basic model is set up. Use of a spreadsheet facilitates 'what if' type questions, and allows budget setters to consider the effect of changes in assumptions. It is recommended that students set up the information above into a spreadsheet in order to understand the calculations and the way in which the figures work together.

There are some numerical examples of budget setting (none of them are as complicated as the Macey Nelson example) at the end of the chapter. Students can try these examples on paper, using spreadsheets, or, preferably, using both methods in order to gain understanding of the calculations.

Application of budgets to other types of business

The long example of Macey Nelson Limited above illustrates the budgeting process in a manufacturing business. However, it should be appreciated that the budget process is just as important in other types of business such as service and retailing. Exactly the same principles apply, but the process is likely to be somewhat more straightforward where manufacturing processes are not involved. Some of the end of chapter examples apply what we have learned about budgeting to non-manufacturing environments.

Monitoring outcomes

The summary set out at the beginning of this chapter links some of the key functions of management with management accounting. So far in this chapter we have looked at the role of management in setting business objectives, in assessing alternatives and making decisions, and in making plans (budgets). The next logical stage in the sequence is that of monitoring outcomes. Management uses information to assess the extent to which its plans have succeeded.

In order to be able to monitor outcomes accounting data must be gathered on a fairly frequent basis so that management is in possession of sufficient relevant information. Where the budget for a period of 12 months is divided up into 12 monthly budgets, it is likely that information about actual outcomes will be gathered and presented also on a monthly basis.

It is important that managers build into their work patterns a regular disciplined routine of monitoring outcomes and taking any necessary action. After all, as we have seen earlier in the chapter, building a budget requires a very significant input of people's time and energy. These would be wasted if management then fails to monitor outcomes thoroughly. It should be noted also that monitoring itself is a costly process because it uses expensive management time. Business organisations should ensure that the procedures involved do not get out of hand; managers may spend too much time looking backwards in order to provide explanations for what has already happened.

The second case study in this chapter examines the monitoring process in a very small business that has just recently started up. Many chapters ago (in Chapter 2 to be precise) we looked at the case of Pete, who started out in business in a very modest way. Having managed fairly successfully to combine a small, part-time business venture together with full-time employment, he had more or less decided by the end of the Chapter 2 case study to become self-employed on a full time basis, running a coffee bar.

This next instalment in the story of Pete does not require students to refer back to Chapter 2. In this case study we will look first at the budgeting Pete and his accountant do before the start-up of the business in order to support their application for borrowings. Then we will look at the actual outcome of Pete's first three months in business.

CASE STUDY 17.2 Business start-up: Budget vs. actual

Pete spends most of the 20X7 calendar year preparing to open his new business. Having identified premises that he can afford to rent, he then spends some time standing about outside counting the number of passers-by. The premises are on the edge of the main town centre, but are on a road that is used quite frequently by students going to college. Having studied the foot traffic, Pete is fairly confident that he will be able to attract passing trade. As regards competition, there are two other coffee bars in town. One is in the shopping centre, attached to a large department store. It attracts quite a high volume of business and always seems to be busy despite the fact that the coffee is really not very good. The other coffee bar is on the opposite side of town from Pete and he doesn't regard it as a serious competitor.

Pete's accountant, Norris, has been helpful in advising him on a business plan, and in forcing Pete to think carefully about costs. Norris helps Pete prepare a budget, based on a set of assumptions and estimates explained below:

1. Volume of trade: Pete reckons that trade will increase as people get to know about his coffee bar, and about the good quality coffee he plans to serve. He estimates that he should attract somewhere between 70 and 90 customers on an average day once the business gets established. To be on the safe side he estimates 70 customers per day for the first month, 75 per day for the second and third months of trading, 80 per day for the fourth and fifth months of trading, 85 for the sixth month of trading and 90 thereafter. Each month contains, on average, 26 days when the coffee bar will be open.

2. Average spend per person: Pete estimates that most people will buy at least one coffee plus a posh Italian biscuit or cake. Average spend is estimated at £2.50.

3. Gross profit percentage is estimated at 72%.

4. Pete and Norris establish a list of expenses that the business will incur in its first year, and the estimated timings of their payment:

Category	£	Estimated timing
Legal fees	1 000	To be paid in month 1
Launch party	2 300	To be paid in month 1
Advertising	1 600	£1000 in month 1, £400 in month 3 and £200 in month 6
Wages	2 800	£233 or £234 per month
Rental of premises	7 500	£1 875 in months 1, 4, 7 and 10
Business rates	2 600	£2 600 in month 3
Water rates	860	£71 or £72 per month
Power, heat and light	800	£200 in months 3, 6, 9 and 12
Phone charges	400	£100 in months 3, 6, 9 and 12
Insurance	500	£500 in month 1
Accountant's fees	800	£400 in month 5 and £400 in month 12
	21 160	

Wages are payable to an assistant who will help Pete out on two days per week for 50 weeks of the year. He or she will be paid for 7 hours per day at a rate of £4.00 per hour.

5. The shop needs some refitting and decoration. The costs will be kept as low as possible because Pete and his brother Dave will do a lot of the work themselves. Estimated costs to be incurred before opening are:

	£
Refurbishment and decoration	5 000
Fixtures and fittings (tables, chairs, cups, saucers etc.)	3 000
Coffee machine	5 000
	13 000

Pete will use savings of £2000 to meet part of these initial costs. Dave offers to do the work for free, and also amazes Pete by producing a cheque for £3000 out of his own savings to put into the business. Pete is touched and pleased that his brother is willing to support him by putting up some money, but he insists on treating it as a loan. Dave accepts this, but says that he definitely doesn't want any interest.

The costs of refurbishing the premises and buying essential equipment will be treated as fixed assets, to be depreciated on a straight-line basis over five years, and on the assumption that there will be no residual value at the end of that time.

Norris tells Pete that the next stage in planning is to establish a cash flow forecast for the first year of trading. Because a coffee bar is a cash business there will be no debtors. Also, the assumption is made that supplies (such as coffee) will be bought in and paid for straight away, so cost of sales can be assumed to be the same as payments for supplies.

Sales receipts can be estimated as follows from the information given in points 1 and 2 above:

Month	Calculation	£
1	70 customers per day for 26 days × £2.50 average spend	4 550
2	75 customers per day for 26 days × £2.50 average spend	4 875
3	75 customers per day for 26 days × £2.50 average spend	4 875
4	80 customers per day for 26 days × £2.50 average spend	5 200
5	80 customers per day for 26 days × £2.50 average spend	5 200
6	85 customers per day for 26 days × £2.50 average spend	5 525
7–12	90 customers per day for 26 days × £2.50 average spend	5 850

Cost of sales is, in each case, estimated at 28% of sales revenue (if the gross profit percentage is 72%, the cost of sales percentage is therefore 28%).

Norris points out to Pete that he had better make some allowance for drawings because Pete and his wife and children have no other regular income. After some discussion they fix upon £900 per month as being the minimum amount necessary to support the family.

At this point it is possible to prepare the cash flow forecast. It is assumed that all the set-up expenses will be incurred and paid for immediately before the start of business. Set-up expenses will amount to £13 000, but against that can be set off the contributions from Pete and his brother, totalling £5000, so the business will start off with a negative cash position of £8000. In order to keep things simple the cash flow forecast (see table) excludes the effect of any interest payable.

▶

Pete: Cash flow forecast for first year of trading

	1	2	3	4	5	6	7	8	9	10	11	12	Total
Month	£	£	£	£	£	£	£	£	£	£	£	£	
Receipts (sales)	4 550	4 875	4 875	5 200	5 200	5 525	5 850	5 850	5 850	5 850	5 850	5 850	65 325
Payments													
Cost of sales (28% × sales)	1 274	1 365	1 365	1 456	1 456	1 547	1 638	1 638	1 638	1 638	1 638	1 638	18 291
Legal fees	1 000	—	—	—	—	—	—	—	—	—	—	—	1 000
Launch party	2 300	—	—	—	—	—	—	—	—	—	—	—	2 300
Advertising	1 000	—	400	—	—	200	—	—	—	—	—	—	1 600
Wages	233	233	234	233	233	234	233	233	234	233	233	234	2 800
Rental	1 875	—	—	1 875	—	—	1 875	—	—	1 875	—	—	7 500
Business rates	—	—	2 600	—	—	—	—	—	—	—	—	—	2 600
Water rates	72	72	71	72	72	71	72	72	71	72	72	71	860
Power, heat, light	—	—	200	—	—	200	—	—	200	—	—	200	800
Phone charges	—	—	100	—	—	100	—	—	100	—	—	100	400
Insurance	500	—	—	—	—	—	—	—	—	—	—	—	500
Accountant's fees	—	—	—	—	400	—	—	—	—	—	—	400	800
Drawings	900	900	900	900	900	900	900	900	900	900	900	900	10 800
Total payments	9 154	2 570	5 870	4 536	3 061	3 252	4 718	2 843	3 143	4 718	2 843	3 543	
Opening balance	(8 000)	(12 604)	(10 299)	(11 294)	(10 630)	(8 491)	(6 218)	(5 086)	(2 079)	628	1 760	4 767	
Add: receipts	4 550	4 875	4 875	5 200	5 200	5 525	5 850	5 850	5 850	5 850	5 850	5 850	
Less: payments	(9 154)	(2 570)	(5 870)	(4 536)	(3 061)	(3 252)	(4 718)	(2 843)	(3 143)	(4 718)	(2 843)	(3 543)	
Closing balance	(12 604)	(10 299)	(11 294)	(10 630)	(8 491)	(6 218)	(5 086)	(2 079)	628	1 760	4 767	7 074	

From the information given it is also possible to calculate a budget profit and loss account statement for Pete's first year, and a budget balance sheet, again on the assumption of no interest charges and no loan apart from the £3000 from Dave.

Pete: Budget profit and loss account for first 12 months of trading

	£
Sales	65 325
Less: cost of sales	(18 291)
Gross profit	47 034
Expenses (excluding depreciation)	(21 160)
Depreciation: £13 000/5	(2 600)
Net profit	23 274

Pete: Budget balance sheet at the end of year 1

	£
Fixed assets at cost	13 000
Less: accumulated depreciation	(2 600)
Fixed assets at net book value	10 400
Cash at bank	7 074
	17 474
Loan: Dave	(3 000)
	14 474
Capital: Pete	2 000
Profit for year	23 274
Less: drawings	(10 800)
	14 474

The bottom line of the cash flow statement shows us the maximum amount that Pete would need to borrow (it is the largest of the figures in brackets). At the end of month one the business will be in a negative cash position of £12 604 before taking into account any interest.

Pete and Norris visit the bank manager with a business plan including these figures. After a long discussion the bank manager agrees to make an overdraft facility of £15 000 available at a rate of 10% per annum. Any unauthorised borrowing over this level will have interest levied on the whole balance outstanding at a rate of 20% per annum. However, the bank manager flatly refuses to make the overdraft available without security. Pete and his wife Angie rent their flat and have no property of their own. After consultation with members of his family, Pete persuades his mother to put her house up as security for the overdraft. If all goes according to plan, the overdrawn position will only last for a few months.

Pete signs a lease for the new shop, and he and Dave start work immediately. Angie has managed to get places for the twins in a nursery two days a week, and she starts attending college on a part-time basis to study accountancy. She was hopeless at maths at school so she wasn't expecting to find the course at all easy. However, she is staggered to find that, not only is it quite interesting, but that she has a clear aptitude for it. She starts keeping the books for Pete with enthusiasm.

▶

After three months it is clear that things are not going exactly to plan. Pete, Angie and Norris have a meeting to discuss the figures which Angie has prepared in the following schedule. For each month of trading the actual figure is shown next to the budget figure. These figures are all based on cash flows.

Actual and budget figures, months one, two and three

	1 Actual £	1 Budget £	2 Actual £	2 Budget £	3 Actual £	3 Budget £
Receipts (sales)	2 604	4 550	2 998	4 875	3 016	4 875
Payments						
Cost of sales	774	1 274	929	1 365	944	1 365
Legal fees	1 200	1 000	—	—	—	—
Launch party	1 907	2 300	—	—	—	—
Advertising	980	1 000	—	—	—	400
Wages	200	233	180	233	—	234
Rental	1 875	1 875	—	—	—	—
Business rates	—	—	—	—	2 600	2 600
Water rates	72	72	72	72	71	71
Power, heat, light	—	—	—	—	190	200
Phone charges	—	—	—	—	87	100
Insurance	505	500	—	—	—	—
Accountant's fees	—	—	—	—	—	—
Additional expenses	250	—	300	—	424	—
Drawings	900	900	900	900	900	900
Total payments	8 663	9 154	2 381	2 570	5 216	5 870
Opening balance	(8 325)	(8 000)	(14 384)	(12 604)	(13 767)	(10 299)
Add: receipts	2 604	4 550	2 998	4 875	3 016	4 875
Less: payments	(8 663)	(9 154)	(2 381)	(2 570)	(5 216)	(5 870)
Closing balance	(14 384)	(12 604)	(13 767)	(10 299)	(15 967)	(11 294)

Norris does some quick calculations and finds that actual sales are only 57% of budget in month one, 61% of budget in month two and 62% in month three. It looks as though Pete has significantly overestimated either the number of customers or the average amount spent per customer. Pete explains that he hasn't had quite as many customers as anticipated, but the real trouble is that they're not spending very much per head. He's succeeded in attracting student customers who like his easy-going style but the trouble is that they're all short of cash. They tend to buy a small coffee and a cheap chocolate biscuit, but the higher margin posh Italian biscuits and cakes have not sold well. Angie confirms that the gross profit margins have not turned out as well as expected, and says that she and the children have been eating a lot of expensive cake lately because it's past its sell-by date.

Each month there seems to have been some kind of unexpected expense. In the first month of trading a man came into the coffee bar and introduced himself as a representative from the Performing Rights Society (PRS). Because Pete plays the radio all day long, the PRS is entitled to a payment. Pete had no idea this might happen but he's checked with a friend who runs a pub, and found that this is a payment which has to be made where a radio is played in a public place. In the second month Pete discovered that the girl he's employed to help out two days a week had been stealing from the till. He worked out that she'd taken about £300. He sacked her straight away, and since then has managed without any extra help. Then, in the third month, he and neighbouring tenants discovered that there were rats in the back yard. Pete's share of the bill for employing ratcatchers came to £424.

Pete's tried hard to keep other expenses under control. He can't do anything about the drawings because he and Angie are having some difficulty managing on £900 a month, but he's cut back on advertising and has managed to keep the phone bills and electricity within budget.

By the end of March the business owes nearly £16 000 to the bank, against a budget overdraft figure of about £11 300. Pete rang up the bank manager a couple of weeks ago and persuaded him to stretch the overdraft facility to £17 000, but he knows that he can't keep on doing this.

Case study discussion and conclusion

When Pete and Norris negotiated the overdraft facility with the bank manager they did not allow for much leeway (or 'headroom' as it's sometimes referred to). Against a maximum requirement of £12 604 indicated by the budget they allowed a facility of £15 000. This means that, if performance was worse than expected, Pete was likely to hit trouble within a short period – and that's exactly what has happened. It appears that Pete has misjudged the market somewhat, and he is attracting customers who can't afford to spend very much. He may need to change the type of product he is offering if he wants to stay in business. Pete could have rehearsed a range of 'what if' scenarios relating to customer numbers and spending. If he had done this the failure of sales to meet expectations might not have come as such a shock.

Almost anyone who starts up in business will say that, no matter how careful the planning, unexpected expenses crop up, and Pete is no exception. He did not allow for any contingency for unexpected events in his business planning: with the benefit of hindsight he should really have put in an estimate for other expenses.

What is likely to happen to Pete and his business? After only three months it is hard to say. Pete is going to need both luck and skilful management to weather this current financial crisis. However, at least he has some accurate and timely management information available to help him make decisions about the future of the business. Many people starting up in business make the mistake of ignoring the need for information until it's too late.

Chapter summary

This chapter started off by looking at budgeting in the context of management activities and decision making. The need for strategic planning was briefly revisited, and an example illustrated the link between broad strategic planning and detailed actions leading to the construction of a budget.

Next, we examined the budget process by reference to a medium to large-sized organisation. The example in this section identified the crucial role of the sales budget and examined the way in which other budgets within a commercial organisation are linked to the sales budget.

The benefits of effective budgeting were discussed, and then various problems associated with budgeting were identified. The first case study for the chapter illustrated some of the tensions that operate at senior management level when there is disagreement about the budget.

The next section of the chapter was concerned with setting various linked budgets in the context of a manufacturing organisation. A comprehensive practical example was worked through to illustrate the practicalities of budget setting. Budgets were set for a six-month period, including budget cash flow statement, profit and loss account and balance sheet. The example demonstrated how all the figures fit together.

Finally, the last section of the chapter and the second case study examined some of the techniques and issues involved in monitoring outcomes. The case study reinforced the content of the earlier part of the chapter by providing an example of budget setting in a non-manufacturing context. Then the actual performance of the business was compared to budget and the principal reasons for the variation between actual and budget figures were discussed.

Exercises

The answers to many of the exercises are set out later in this chapter. However, where the exercise number is followed by 'A' the answer is available only to lecturers. Remember that additional exercises (with answers) are available to students on the book's website.

17.1   You are the newly appointed management accountant of Brewster Fitzpayne Limited, a small manufacturing company. The management accounting information used in the company has previously been at a low level in terms of both quantity and quality. The finance director of the company was himself appointed only a few months ago, and he has decided that, as a priority, the management information system should be improved. He is planning, with your assistance, to install a budgeting system, but he needs to persuade his fellow directors that this innovation will be of benefit to the company. He has asked you to draft a briefing paper to the board setting out the principal benefits of a system of budgetary control.

17.2A   It is widely recognised that budget setting can be mishandled in organisations and may result in some undesirable effects that work against an organisation's best interests.

Write a short report that describes potential problems that may arise if budgeting is not handled properly.

17.3 Buckle Purslane Limited uses a rolling budget system. The company's directors are currently preparing a sales and production budget for the month of March 20X7, which is just over one year away.

They have decided that sales of their single product should be budgeted at 12 000 units for March 20X7, with 14 800 units budgeted for April 20X7. The company's policy is to hold closing stock of finished goods at 75% of the next following month's sales level.

What is the production budget in units for March 20X7?

a) 8 100

b) 14 100

c) 9 900

d) 12 000.

17.4A Hillgate St. Martins Limited manufactures a single product. Its budget sales (in units) for December 20X4 are 9350. Opening stock of finished goods for the month is budgeted at 12 360 and closing stock is budgeted at 13 475.

Each unit of finished goods stock uses 2kg of a raw material that is forecast to cost £3 per kilo. Opening stock of raw material at the beginning of December 20X4 is forecast at 18 000 kilos, but closing stock for the month should fall to 16 000 units.

What is the budget amount in £s of purchases of this raw material for December 20X4?

a) £56 790

b) £68 790

c) £49 410

d) £55 410.

17.5 Luminant Productions Limited produces light fittings from a small factory unit. The company's directors have just met to discuss the sales budget and related matters for the next quarter, and have come up with the following figures for projected sales:

	Units
July 20X6	8 600
August 20X6	8 200
September 20X6	9 000

Opening stock of finished goods at 1 July 20X6 is expected to be 6000 units. The directors feel that they keep too many units in stock and they intend to reduce stock to more reasonable levels over the next few months. They plan to reduce opening stock by 500 units each month after July 20X6.

Each light fitting unit uses £2 of raw materials. Raw materials stock at 1 July is estimated to have a value of £2800. The directors wish to increase that stock level slightly over the next few months, as there is a danger of running out of stock to transfer to production.

	£
Opening stock at 1 August should be:	3 000
Opening stock at 1 September should be:	3 100
Opening stock at 1 October should be:	3 200

Calculate for each of the three months:

a) The production budget (in units).

b) The raw material purchases budget (in £s).

17.6A Colney Brighouse Limited makes office furniture. The company's directors are preparing sales and production forecasts for January, February and March 20X4. Sales forecasts in units for its two principal products, tables and office chairs, are as follows for the relevant months:

	Tables	Chairs
January 20X4	13 000	28 000
February 20X4	15 000	31 000
March 20X4	16 000	35 000
April 20X4	18 000	36 000

Opening stock at 1 January 20X4 is forecast at 7500 (tables) and 19 000 (chairs). The directors have decided to aim for closing stock at the end of each month amounting to exactly 50% of the following month's sales requirements. Prepare the production budget for tables and chairs for January–March 20X4 (inclusive).

17.7 Barfield Primrose Limited is the manufacturer of the renowned 'Primrose' ice cream maker, which retails at £199. Barfield Primrose sells to wholesalers at £145 per unit. The prime cost structure of the ice cream maker is as follows:

	Per unit
Direct materials	37.00
Direct labour	24.00
Prime cost	61.00

For the year ending 31 December 20X2, the finance director of Barfield Primrose estimates that production overheads will be incurred totalling £312 390. He plans to use an overhead recovery rate based upon budgeted machine hours. The budget for machine hours is 17 355 hours for the year, and each unit produced uses up 1.5 machine hours.

Administrative and selling cost budgets have been prepared and the directors have recently decided on the sales forecasts for the coming year. The forecasts for the first three months are as follows:

	Sales forecasts: units	Administrative and selling costs: £
January	620	18 400
February	610	19 250
March	640	18 900

Calculate a budget overhead recovery rate for use by the company during 20X2. Then prepare a budget profit and loss account for each of the three months January–March 20X2.

17.8A Corby Thirlwell Limited manufactures ornamental birdbaths made out of reconstituted stone. The company works on a rolling budget system, and its senior management is currently examining forecasts for the month of June

20X1. June is a big month for sales in the birdbath business, and the directors are optimistically forecasting sales of 3250 units. They intend to launch a sales incentive scheme to encourage the sales staff to sell more birdbaths; from the beginning of 20X1 each birdbath sold will result in a payment of £1.50 to the salesperson. The selling price of each birdbath is £65.

The production cost structure of one birdbath is as follows:

Per unit	£
Direct materials	18.00
Direct labour	12.57
Production overhead recovery	13.86
Production cost	44.43

Administrative overheads for June 20X1 are forecast at £12 479, and selling and distribution overheads (excluding the cost of commission) are forecast at £10 220.

Prepare a budget profit and loss account for the month of June 20X1.

17.9 Reinhart has his own wholesale business selling goods to retailers. His sales are made entirely on credit. In respect of the sales in any given month he expects 75% to be paid for in the next following month, and 25% in the month after that. (So, for example, sales made on credit in March would be paid for in April as to 75% and May as to 25%.)

Budget data relating to four months of Reinhart's sales are as follows:

	£
November 20X4	25 000
December 20X4	26 800
January 20X5	21 000
February 20X5	21 300

Reinhart is preparing his cash flow forecast for the month of February 20X5. How much should he include as sales receipts?

a) £21 000

b) £21 250

c) £22 450

d) £21 225.

17.10A Roxanne's budgeted year-end accounts at 31 December 20X4 include a figure for debtors of £23 600. This represents:

	£
20% of November sales of £28 000	5 600
60% of December sales of £30 000	18 000
	23 600

This calculation is based upon the normal pattern of receipts for the business: 40% of sales on credit are paid for within the same month, and 40% are paid for in the following month, with the remaining 20% paid for in the month after that.

If January 20X5 sales are budgeted at £28 000. How much will be included for sales receipts in the cash flow forecast in January 20X5?

a) £28 800

b) £23 600

c) £24 000

d) £19 520.

17.11   Skippy is about to set up in business as a tour operator, after several years of working in the travel industry. He is starting out on a small scale, working from a room in a friend's office. The friend has agreed to let him have the room rent free for six months in order to get him started.

In his first quarter of operations, January–March 20X4, Skippy plans two tours, both coach trips to Austria. He advertises the trips in November and December 20X3, paying the cost of £3000 out of his own money. He also pays £2000 for a computer. He intends that both of these amounts should constitute his initial capital contribution to the new business. The computer will be depreciated over its estimated useful life of five years on the straight-line basis.

The revenue and cost structure of each trip is as follows:

	£
The trip will cost £530 per person. The coach carries a maximum of 60 people and Skippy expects an 80% load factor – that is, 48 people. So 48 × £530 = sales revenue per trip	25 440
Hotel costs = £42.50 per person for 7 nights half board accommodation: 7 × £42.50 × 48	14 280
Coach travel costs	2 600
Insurance bond	1 500

The first trip is planned for 17 February, and the second for 15 March. The sales revenue from the trips will be received in advance – receipts from trip one will be received in January, and from trip two in February.

The hotel requires a non-returnable deposit of 50% in advance, with the remainder paid at the end of the stay. Advance payments for trip one will be made in January, and for trip two will be made in February.

The coach costs must also be paid in advance: trip one will be paid for in January and trip two in February. The insurance bond for both trips will be paid in January.

Other costs are: phone – the bill for an estimated £360 will be paid in March; and sundry office costs – £200 paid in cash each month.

Prepare for Skippy:

i) A budget cash flow statement for the three months of January, February and March 20X4.

ii) A budget profit and loss account for the three months ending 31 March 20X4.

iii) A budget balance sheet at 31 March 20X4.

17.12   Referring to the information given in exercise 17.11, at the beginning of April 20X4 Skippy reviews the past three months. Bookings on the first coach trip to Austria were not as good as planned: he sold only 42 places on the coach. However, the second trip was very popular with sales of 50 places. The hotel charged Skippy based upon the actual, not the budgeted number of people. Coach and insurance costs remained the same.

Actual office costs were higher than budgeted: in January Skippy paid £230, in February £350 and in March £270. The phone bill of £455 was paid in March.

Prepare a profit and loss account for the three months ending 31 March 20X4 showing columns for actual results, budgeted results and the variation between the two. Also prepare an actual balance sheet at 31 March 20X4 showing an extra column for the budgeted figures.

Has Skippy's business performed better or worse than budget, overall?

17.13A Silas is starting out in business on his own, running a shop selling scuba diving gear. He has gained a lot of free publicity for his new venture by writing articles in specialist trade and enthusiasts' magazines, and he is well known as a leading expert on scuba diving. He is therefore fairly confident that he will be able to start selling in reasonable quantities straight away.

Silas is renting shop premises, and his principal start-up cost has been the cost of equipping the shop with stock. He has also invested in an electronic till, a computer for keeping track of stock and dealing with correspondence, and some general shop fixtures and fittings. His expenditure just prior to start up is:

	£
Stock	42 000
Computer	2 500
Till	1 000
Fixtures & fittings	3 500
Total	49 000

Silas also transfers £6000 from his own bank account into a new business bank account. He has sold his house to finance the new venture and is currently living in the flat above the shop.

In his first year in trading Silas plans the following sales and purchases of stock:

	Sales	Purchases
	£	£
April	1 500	2 250
May	4 500	3 750
June	8 250	6 750
July	9 000	7 500
August	12 000	7 500
September	12 000	7 500
October	12 000	6 750
November	10 500	6 750
December	12 000	6 375
January	7 500	6 375
February	9 000	5 625
March	10 500	6 000
	108 750	73 125

It is expected that most sales will be for cash, but 25% are planned to be made on credit to scuba diving organisations. Credit sales are expected to be settled in full in the month after invoicing.

Purchases of stock will be on credit, with payment made in full in the month following purchase. Closing stock at the end of March is budgeted at £42 045.

Silas has budgeted for the following expenses:

Expense item	£	Payment details
Rent	6 000	Payable in quarterly instalments in April, July, October and January
Insurance	1 200	Payable in April
Phone	600	Quarterly bills of £150 to be paid in June, September, December and March
Water rates	750	Payable in May
Business rates	1 500	Payable in April
Wages	1 800	£150 to be paid each month
Subscriptions	300	£150 in May and £150 in November
Sundry admin and other expenses	2 400	£200 to be paid each month

Silas plans to draw £1000 from the business in cash each month.

The computer will be subject to depreciation on a straight-line basis over four years. Fixtures and fittings and the electronic till have an estimated useful life of 10 years and will be depreciated on a straight-line basis. No residual values are expected at the end of the assets' useful lives.

Prepare the following statements for Silas:

i) Budget cash flow statement showing the cash movement in each of the first 12 months of business.

ii) Budget profit and loss account for the 12 months ending 31 March.

iii) Budget balance sheet at 31 March.

17.14A Working with the information from 17.13A, put the cash flow information into a spreadsheet. Use the spreadsheet to perform 'what if' calculations to answer Silas's questions as follows:

i) 'What would happen to my estimated cash at bank balance at the end of March if my debtors took two months, instead of one month, to pay me? Would the bank account go overdrawn at any point in the year?'

ii) 'I think I may have underestimated my sundry admin expenses. What would happen to the cash at bank balance at the end of March if my expenses each month were £400 rather than £200?'

iii) 'What would happen to the end of March cash at bank balance if both of these things happened – i.e. debtors take two months to pay me, not one, and admin expenses increase to £400 each month? Would I have an overdraft at any point, and if so, what would be the maximum budget overdraft figure?'

Answers to exercises

17.1   Subject: Summary of the benefits of effective budgeting
To: the directors of Brewster Fitzpayne Limited
From: Management accountant

A budgeting system assists senior management in its tasks of planning and controlling business activity by ensuring that a detailed plan is laid out and quantified for a specified period (usually one year). The budget should help the company to attain its longer-term objectives, and it is important to ensure that there is a clear relationship between the budget and the longer-term business strategy determined by the directors.

Budgets allow for coordinated efforts on the part of all personnel and departments. Once the key elements of the budget have been determined (usually starting with the sales budget) budget guidelines can be issued to all departments and managerial staff. They will then be required to submit draft budgets for their own areas. Senior management must then ensure that these drafts are amended where necessary to ensure proper coordination of plans. Senior staff have an overview of the business objectives and should be able to ensure that individual budgets mesh together to achieve optimal outcomes.

If properly used, budgets can inspire and motivate staff to greater efforts. It is important that staff lower down the hierarchy feel a sense of 'ownership' of the budget so that they will be more inclined to make the extra effort to achieve targets.

It is important to ensure that actual business performance is monitored carefully against budget. If this is done properly and on a timely basis, senior managers are able to control operations much more effectively than is possible without a budget. Timely and effective control allows for higher quality decision making.

Finally, it is possible to use budgets as a basis for individual and group performance evaluation. For example, sales staff could be rewarded by means of bonuses or extra commission for exceeding budget targets. This use of budgets must be handled carefully, however. If targets for achievement are set too high then dissatisfaction and demotivation may well result.

17.3 Buckle Purslane Limited. The forecast for opening stock at 1 March 20X7 is 75% of forecast sales in March:

$$75\% \times 12\,000 \text{ units} = 9000 \text{ units}$$

The forecast for closing stock at 31 March 20X7 is 75% of forecast sales in April:

$$75\% \times 14\,800 \text{ units} = 11\,100 \text{ units}.$$

Transfers out of finished goods stock will be 12 000 units in March (i.e. the quantity sold), so production required is:

	£
Opening stock	9 000
Production (bal. fig)	14 100
Transfers out of stock	(12 000)
Closing stock	11 100

The correct answer, therefore, is b).

17.5 Luminant Productions Limited

a) Production budget July–September 20X6

	Opening stock: units	Production: units	Transfers out of production (for sales): units	Closing stock: units
July	6 000	8 100	(8 600)	5 500
August	5 500	7 700	(8 200)	5 000
September	5 000	8 500	(9 000)	4 500

b) Raw materials purchases budget: July–September 20X6

Closing stock + Raw materials used in production − Opening stock
= Raw materials purchases

	Opening stock of raw material £	Purchases of raw materials £ (bal. fig.)	Raw materials used in production f	Closing stock of raw material £
July	2 800	16 400	£2 × 8 100 = (£16 200)	3 000
August	3 000	15 500	£2 × 7 700 = (£15 400)	3 100
September	3 100	17 100	£2 × 8 500 = (£17 000)	3 200

17.7   Barfield Primrose Limited
Budget overhead recovery rate, based on machine hours:

$$\frac{\text{Budget production overheads}}{\text{Machine hours}} = \frac{312\,390}{17\,355} = £18.00 \text{ per machine hour}$$

The total production cost of one ice cream maker is, therefore:

	£
Prime cost	61.00
1.5 machine hours × £18.00 per hour	27.00
Production cost	88.00

Barfield Primrose Limited: Budgeted profit and loss account for three months ending 31 March 20X2

	Jan £	Feb £	Mar £
Sales	620 × £145 = 89 900	620 × £145 = 88 450	620 × £145 = 92 800
Cost of sales (= production cost)	620 × £88 = (54 560)	610 × £88 = (53 680)	640 × £88 = (56 320)
Gross profit	35 340	34 770	36 480
Admin and selling expenses	(18 400)	(19 250)	(18 900)
Net profit	16 940	15 520	17 580

17.9   In February Reinhart's budget sales receipts will be estimated as follows:

	£
In respect of sales made in January: 75% × £21 000	15 750
In respect of sales made in December: 25% × £26 800	6 700
Total	22 450

The correct answer, therefore, is c).

17.11   Skippy's tour operating business

i) Budget cash flow

Skippy: Budget cash flow statement for January–March 20X4

	January £	February £	March £	Total £
Receipts				
Trip 1	25 440	—	—	25 440
Trip 2	—	25 440	—	25 440
Total receipts	25 440	25 440	—	50 880
Payments				
Hotel: Trip 1	7 140	7 140	—	14 280
Trip 2	—	7 140	7 140	14 280
Coach	2 600	2 600	—	5 200
Insurance bond: 2 × £1 500	3 000	—	—	3 000
Phone bill	—	—	360	360
Office expenses	200	200	200	600
Total payments	12 940	17 080	7 700	37 720
Opening balance	0	12 500	20 860	
Add: receipts	25 440	25 440	—	
Less: payments	(12 940)	(17 080)	(7 700)	
Closing balance	12 500	20 860	13 160	

ii) Budget profit and loss

Skippy: Budget profit and loss account for the three months ending

31 March 20X4

	£
Sales	50 880
Expenses	
Hotel costs (£14 280 × 2)	28 560
Coach	5 200
Insurance bonds	3 000
Phone	360
Office costs	600
Advertising	3 000
Computer depreciation: £2 000 × 20% = 400 – for 3 months = £100	100
	40 820
Net profit	10 060

iii) Budget balance sheet

Skippy: Budget balance sheet at 31 March 20X4

	£
Computer at cost	2 000
Less: accumulated depreciation	(100)
Net book value	1 900
Cash at bank	13 160
	15 060
Capital introduced	5 000
Profit	10 060
	15 060

Note that capital introduced by Skippy consists of the advertising expenditure paid for before January 20X4 (£3000) and the computer (£2000).

17.12   Skippy's tour operating business

Working 1: Actual sales

	£
Trip 1: 42 × £530	22 260
Trip 2: 50 × £530	26 500
	48 760

Working 2: Hotel costs

	£
Trip 1: 42 × 7 nights × £42.50 per person	12 495
Trip 2: 50 × 7 nights × £42.50 per person	14 875
	27 370

Skippy: Actual and budgeted profit and loss account for the three months ending 31 March 20X4

	Actual £	Budget £	Variance* £
Sales (working 1)	48 760	50 880	(2 120)
Expenses			
Hotel costs (working 2)	27 370	28 560	1 190
Coach	5 200	5 200	—
Insurance bonds	3 000	3 000	—
Phone	455	360	(95)
Office costs (£230 + £350 + £270)	850	600	(250)
Advertising	3 000	3 000	—
Computer depreciation: £2000 × 20% = 400 − for 3 months = £100	100	100	—
	39 975	40 820	845
Net profit	8 785	10 060	(1 275)

* Variance is the term used in costing for differences between actual and budget figures. Adverse variances are shown in brackets in the comparison and favourable variances are shown without brackets. Variances are examined in more detail in Chapter 18.

Skippy: Actual and budgeted balance sheet at 31 March 20X4

	Actual £	Budget £
Computer at cost	2 000	2 000
Less: accumulated depreciation	(100)	(100)
Net book value	1 900	1 900
Cash at bank (see working 3)	11 885	13 160
	13 785	15 060
Capital introduced	5 000	5 000
Profit	8 785	10 060
	13 785	15 060

Working 3: Actual cash at bank

	£	£
Receipts (same as sales revenue)		48 760
Payments	39 975	
Less: depreciation (non-cash item)	(100)	
Less: advertising paid for by Skippy	(3 000)	
		(36 875)
		11 885

Overall, Skippy's business has performed slightly worse than budget: actual sales are 95.8% of budget, but there has been a related saving on hotel costs which helps to offset the variance. Office and telephone costs are higher than budgeted. However, overall, the differences are fairly minor and Skippy is likely to be quite pleased with his first three months in business.

18

STANDARD COSTING, FLEXIBLE BUDGETING AND VARIANCE ANALYSIS

AIMS AND LEARNING OUTCOMES

Aim of the chapter

To understand the nature of a standard costing system, the application of flexible budgeting in interpreting actual results against budgets and the detailed analysis of variances.

Learning outcomes

After reading the chapter and completing the related exercises, students should:

- Understand the use of a standard costing system in a manufacturing environment.
- Be able to compare actual results against flexed budgets.
- Be able to analyse and understand the range of possible reasons for the variances that emerge from comparison of actual with standard costs.

Identifying and attributing variances

In the previous chapter we examined the setting of budgets and the comparison of actual with budgeted results. Often the identification and analysis of the difference between actual and budgeted performance is quite straightforward. For example, suppose that a business budgets to spend £10 500 on business insurance on the basis that the previous year's charge was £10 000 and the general level of price inflation suggests that 5% would be a likely level of increase. The business's insurer's however, and in common with the rest of the insurance industry, raise charges by 10%. The actual bill for insurance totals £11 000, £500 more than was budgeted. Investigation of other insurers shows that it is not possible to obtain cover for less than £11 000. The **adverse variance** of £500 against budget in this case can be easily explained. It is a general price increase, not attributable to any internal factor such as poor purchasing or failure to control expenditure properly.

In practice, however, and especially in a relatively complex manufacturing environment, it can be difficult to track down the reasons for variances unless some quite detailed analysis is carried out.

Example 18.1 Sugden Harkness Limited, a manufacturing business, sets a budget based upon a sales forecast for July of 5000 units. Each unit of product is budgeted to use 3 metres of raw material (15 000 metres in total) at a cost of £4.20 per metre (15 000 × £4.20 = £63 000). The actual business performance statement for July shows that, although exactly 5000 units were sold, the total cost of the raw material element of cost of sales was £68 000. What has happened here? Clearly, raw material costs have increased; there is an adverse variance of £68 000 − £63 000 = £5000. The reasons, however, are not clear, unless further analysis is undertaken. It could be that:

- The price has increased to a level higher than the £4.20 budgeted.
- The production process has been less efficient than expected and has used more than 3 metres of raw material per unit of product.
- Both of these factors are present in some combination.

The management accountant of Sugden Harkness needs to be able to analyse the variance in more detail in order to be able to: (a) find out if there is a problem that needs attention; and (b) attribute responsibility for the adverse variance to the appropriate department or person.

The process of **responsibility accounting** ensures that problems are tracked to their source. Having correctly identified the source, it is then the responsibility of management to ensure that problems are dealt with via appropriate corrective action. As we saw in the previous chapter, one of the possible adverse consequences of a budgeting system arises where responsibility is incorrectly attributed, leading to resentment and demotivation. Sometimes, the reason for the occurrence of a problem seems obvious, but further investigation may be required to look beyond the apparently obvious and to uncover true causes and effects.

Taking the example of Sugden Harkness a little further, suppose that the adverse variance was found to be attributable to extra usage of the raw material. This looks, on the face of it, as though it should be the responsibility of the production manager and his team. It may well result from inefficiencies in the use of raw materials (too much wastage, for example). However, the picture changes if we find out that the regular supplier of the raw material had increased prices, and that, in response to the increase, the purchasing manager had purchased inferior quality material but at the budget price. The poorer quality resulted in more wastage as the material was put through the production process. The adverse variance now appears to be attributable to the purchasing manager rather than the production manager.

Despite problems of this type in attributing responsibility for variances, variance identification and analysis are very common procedures in manufacturing industry. Variances are often identified and quantified by using a **standard costing** system.

Standard costing

Standard costing is a system of costing that can be used in business environments where a repetitive series of standardised operations are carried out. In such systems each element of production involves a consistent input of resources at prices that can be predicted with a fair degree of accuracy.

Standard costs are the budgeted costs of individual units of production. The standard cost is compared with actual cost in order to calculate an overall variance. This overall variance can then be broken down further in order to identify:

● The effects of variation in volume of the resource inputs.
● The effects of variation in price of the resource inputs.

Standard costing and variance analysis are widely used in industries where mass production is carried out. Managers in such industries are frequently presented with financial reports including information about variances, and it is important even for non-financial managers to understand something about the fundamentals of standard costing systems.

Establishing standard costs

As we saw in the previous chapter, establishing budget information can be a time-consuming and potentially expensive task. Standard costs may also require a substantial investment of time in research and observation. For example, in order to establish standard costs for the direct materials component of a product, it is necessary to examine two aspects: (a) the purchase price of the material inputs; and (b) the expected rate at which material is used in the product.

The purchase price may be variable depending upon the supplier used, quantities available, movements on commodities markets and so on. The standard cost will probably reflect a price that can be obtained with a reasonable amount of effort on the part of those responsible for materials purchasing. If too low a standard price is set, purchasers will not have to make much of an effort to better it. On the other hand, if the standard price set would be obtainable only rarely, then purchasers may become demotivated. The motivational and behavioural factors for this type of budgeting, in fact, are the same as those we examined in Chapter 17.

Establishing the rate of usage will require careful observation of the manufacturing process, probably on a number of separate occasions. Again, the rate of materials consumption adopted as the standard is likely to reflect a realistic achievable target, set neither too low nor too high. However, standard cost setters need to be wary of relying upon too many established precedents and practices. There may be a need to challenge lax and wasteful production procedures in setting standards.

Each element of cost of production is broken down and costed. Even for an apparently simple product, there may be many different elements of cost. Take a tin of beans, for example. Materials input per batch includes: beans, tomatoes, salt, sugar, flavourings, tins and labels. Each part of the processing involves labour and machine times, which must be timed to the second in order to produce accurate costs and forecasts.

For each product a standard cost card is built up. A simple illustration is given in the following comprehensive example.

Example 18.2 We will use a comprehensive example to illustrate the application of variance identification in a standard costing system. Although the basic facts in the example are straightforward there are several calculations. The whole example takes up several pages, because each step is explained in full. Students should work through it slowly and ensure that each point is understood before moving on. It will seem difficult, if not impossible, at first, but it does all hang together quite logically. Don't give up!

Sherborne Suggate Limited manufactures a specialised metal component that is sold to manufacturers of heavy lifting machinery. The standard cost card for one component is as follows:

	£	
Selling price	150.00	Per unit
Costs		
Direct materials	35.00	7kg of metal @ £5 per kilo
Direct labour	15.00	3 hours @ £5 per kilo
Prime cost	50.00	

The company's budget for January 20X3 is as follows:

	£
Sales: 1000 units @ £150	150 000
Costs	
Direct materials: 1000 units × (7kg × £5)	(35 000)
Direct labour: 1000 units × (3 hours × £5)	(15 000)
Production overhead	(50 000)
	50 000
Selling and administrative overhead	(20 000)
Net profit	30 000

The production overhead, as we have seen in previous chapters, is usually absorbed via an overhead absorption rate. For the purposes of this particular demonstration we will assume that the overheads are simply recorded, and also, that they remain at the same level regardless of changes in the level of production, i.e. they are **fixed overhead costs**. Later in the chapter we will examine overhead variances in more detail, but for the moment, we will simplify the overheads aspects of the question.

Simple comparison of budget with actual results

After the end of the 20X3 financial year, the management accountant identifies the variances between the budget and actual results.
  Actual results are as follows:

	£
Sales: 1 100 units @ £145	159 500
Costs	
Direct materials: 1 100 × (7.5kg × £4.50)	(37 125)
Direct labour: 1 100 units × (2.8 hours × £5.50)	(16 940)
Production overhead	(52 000)
	53 435
Selling and administrative overhead	(21 250)
Net profit	32 185

A very brief comparison of the statements shows us that the company has produced higher profits than expected. Good news, surely? Well, yes, but has the business made as much extra profit as might be expected, given that it has sold an extra 100 components? The answer to the question is not immediately obvious; it requires further analysis of the variances.

Flexing the budget

One problem with comparing the two statements shown above is that we are not really comparing like with like. The initial budget was produced on the assumption that 1000 units would be sold. The actual outcome is that 1100 units were sold. In order to make a more useful comparison, we need to adjust the budget to reflect the additional volume of sales. This is known as flexing the budget.
  The flexed budget profit and loss account (flexed to reflect the actual level of activity of 1100 units sold) is as follows:

	£
Sales: 1100 units @ £150	165 000
Costs	
Direct materials: 1100 × (7kg × £5)	(38 500)
Direct labour: 1100 units × (3 hours × £5)	(16 500)
Production overhead	(50 000)
	60 000
Selling and administrative overhead	(20 000)
Net profit	40 000

The flexed budget shows the sales revenue that would have been expected from sales of 1100 units, and all the costs adjusted for the additional volume of sales.

Remember that we are working on the assumption that production overheads do not increase in line with the volume of sales. Selling and administrative overheads, also, are assumed not to increase in line with the volume of sales; they are also regarded as **fixed overhead costs**. (Note: The distinction between variable costs and fixed costs will be examined in more detail later in the chapter.)

We now have three profit and loss statements: the original budget, the flexed budget and the statement of actual results. It will help at this point to place them side by side:

	Original budget £	Flexed budget £	Actual £
Sales	150 000	165 000	159 500
Costs			
Direct materials	(35 000)	(38 500)	(37 125)
Direct labour	(15 000)	(16 500)	(16 940)
Production overhead	(50 000)	(50 000)	(52 000)
	50 000	60 000	53 435
Selling and administrative overhead	(20 000)	(20 000)	(21 250)
Net profit	30 000	40 000	32 185

Calculating variances

The original budget net profit was £30 000. Actual net profit is £32 185. The overall variance is a **favourable variance** of £2 185. We will break this figure down into its constituent variances which will allow us to identify possible problem areas.

Sales profit volume variance

A key element of the difference is the sale of more units than originally anticipated. This variance is the difference between the original budget profit and the flexed budget profit: £40 000 − £30 000 = £10 000. It is clearly in the interests of the company to sell more components, and so this is a favourable variance.

Sales price variance

The actual profit is affected by the fact that, although extra sales have been made, the selling price is actually lower than budgeted. This variance is calculated as follows:

	£
Actual volume of sales at actual selling price: 1100 × £145	159 500
Less: actual volume of sales at budget selling price:	
1100 × £150	165 000
Sales price variance	5 500

This represents an undesirable outcome for the firm; it would have been better to sell at the higher, budgeted price, so this is an adverse variance.

At this stage, refer back to the three statements presented side by side, and note that we are comparing the flexed budget statement with the actual statement in order to calculate this variance.

▶

Direct materials variances

Comparing the figure for direct materials in the flexed budget statement with the figure in the actual statement:

	£
Flexed budget for direct materials	38 500
Actual direct materials	37 125
	1 375

The actual amount is less than budget; this is a good outcome and so this is classified as a favourable variance.

We can analyse this variance further by looking at the budget input of resources against actual input. Management accountants are able to calculate two direct materials variances: direct materials price variance and direct materials quantity variance. These relate, respectively, to price effects and volume effects.

Direct materials price variance. We compare:

- The actual quantity of raw materials used at the price actually paid (actual price).
- The actual quantity of raw materials used at the price budgeted (standard price).

Using the same measure of quantity (actual) ensures that we isolate the price effect.

	£
Actual quantity at actual price	
7.5kg was used for each of 1100 components	
Actual quantity used is 7.5kg × 1100 = 8 250kg	
8250kg × price actually paid (£4.50)	37 125
Actual quantity at standard price	
8 250kg × standard price (£5.00)	41 250
Direct materials price variance	4 125

The business has paid less per unit for direct materials than it expected; this is therefore a favourable variance.

Direct materials quantity variance. We compare:

- The actual quantity of materials used at standard price.
- The standard quantity of materials used at standard price.

	£
Actual quantity at standard price	
Actual quantity used (already worked out) — 8 250kg	
Standard price per kg — £5	
Actual quantity at standard price = 8 250 × £5	41 250
Standard quantity at standard price	
Standard quantity: 7kg × 1 100 components = 7 700kg	
Standard price per kg — £5	
Standard quantity at standard price = 7 700 × £5	38 500
Direct materials quantity variance	2 750

The business has used more materials per component than budgeted; this is therefore an adverse variance.

In summary, the direct materials variances are:

	£
Direct materials price variance	4 125 (F)
Direct materials quantity variance	2 750 (A)
Direct materials variance	1 375 (F)

Note: 'F' stands for Favourable; 'A' stands for Adverse.

Direct labour variances

Comparing the figure for direct labour in the flexed budget statement with the figure in the actual statement:

	£
Flexed budget for direct labour	16 500
Actual direct labour	16 940
	440

The actual amount is more than budget; this is not a good outcome and so is classified as an adverse variance.

As with direct materials, we can break down this overall variance into two variances, one quantifying the price effect and the other quantifying the volume effect. These are traditionally known (respectively) as the direct labour rate variance and the direct labour efficiency variance.

Direct labour rate variance. We compare:

- The actual hours of direct labour used at the wage rate actually paid (actual rate).
- The actual hours of direct labour used at the wage rate budgeted (standard rate).

Using the same measure of hours (actual) ensures that we isolate the rate effect.

	£
Actual hours at actual rate	
Actual hours was 2.8 hours for each of 1 100 components:	
2.8 × 1 100 = 3 080 hours	
3 080 hours × rate actually paid (£5.50)	16 940
Actual hours at standard rate	
3 080 hours × standard rate (£5.00)	15 400
Direct labour rate variance	1 540

The business has paid more per hour for direct labour than it budgeted; this is therefore an adverse variance.

Direct labour efficiency variance. We compare:

- The actual hours of direct labour used at standard rate.
- The standard hours of direct labour used at standard rate.

	£
Actual hours at standard rate	
Actual hours used (already worked out) – 3 080 hours	
Standard rate per hour: £5	
Actual hours at standard rate = 3 080 × £5	15 400
Standard hours at standard rate	
Standard hours: 3 hours × 1100 = 3 300	
Standard rate per hour: £5	
Standard hours at standard rate = 3 300 – £5	16 500
Direct labour efficiency variance	1 100

The business has used fewer hours per component than budgeted; this is therefore a favourable variance.

In summary, the direct labour variances are:

	£
Direct labour rate variance	1 540 (A)
Direct labour efficiency variance	1 100 (F)
Direct labour variance	440 (A)

Production overhead variance

	£
Budget figure for production overhead	50 000
Actual figure for production overhead	52 000
Production overhead variance	(2 000) (A)

The company appears to have spent more than initially planned; therefore, this is an adverse variance.

Selling and administrative overhead variance

	£
Budget figure for selling and administrative overhead:	20 000
Actual figure for selling and administrative overhead:	21 250
Production overhead variance	(1 250) (A)

Having calculated this long list of variances, they can now be presented in the form of a standard cost operating statement, as follows:

Sherborne Suggate Limited: Standard cost operating statement

for January 20X3

	Total
	£
Original budgeted net profit	30 000
Sales profit volume variance	10 000
Flexed budget net profit	40 000

	Favourable £	(Adverse) £	
Other variances			
Sales price variance		(5 500)	
Direct materials price variance	4 125		
Direct materials quantity variance		(2 750)	
Direct labour rate variance		(1 540)	
Direct labour efficiency variance	1 100		
Production overhead variance		(2 000)	
Selling and administrative overhead variance		(1 250)	
Total	5 225	(13 040)	(7 815)
Actual net profit			32 185

What does this statement tell us? Remember that we started out with the simple observation that there was an overall favourable variance between budgeted profit and actual profit of £2185. The standard cost operating statement above allows us to identify the component parts of that overall variance, and to pinpoint the areas where problems may have arisen. There are several adverse variances:

- *Sales price variance.* Although the volume of sales has increased, the beneficial effect on profit is not as great as it might have been because the selling price has fallen. Of course, these two factors may very well be related; it could be that the company has made a deliberate attempt to boost sales by setting a lower selling price. If that was the intention, the objective appears to have been met.
- *Direct materials quantity variance.* It appears that the production process is less efficient in terms of usage of materials than was originally intended. There may be good reasons why this has happened; indeed, the problem may be that the original standard set for quantity was too ambitious. Further investigation of the variance would probably be necessary. This adverse variance, however, is more than offset by a favourable direct materials price variance. Perhaps a special purchase of materials has been made, but, of course, if the quality is slightly poorer, it may be more difficult to use the materials efficiently.
- *Direct labour rate variance.* Production staff appear to have been paid at a higher rate than allowed for in the standard cost calculations. If this is a permanent change, the standard cost needs changing. If it is a temporary change, the reasons for it should be investigated. It is noticeable, however, that the direct labour efficiency variance is positive; perhaps higher paid staff are working more quickly, or perhaps the supervision process is more effective than originally anticipated.

While the standard cost operating statement certainly provides management with more information than a simple statement like 'profits have gone up', it does not, clearly, answer all the questions. However, it serves a useful purpose in directing management's attention to areas that may require investigation and in suggesting the kind of questions that should be asked.

Before moving on, try this self-test question, which runs through the same variance calculations as the example above.

Self-test question 18.1 (answer at the end of the chapter)

Bridge and Blige Limited make metal casings for lawn mowers in one standard size. In February 20X6 the company's budget for sales and related costs is as follows:

	£
Sales: 800 units × £35	28 000
Costs	
Direct materials: 800 units × (2kg × £6)	(9 600)
Direct labour: 800 units × (1 hour × £7.50)	(6 000)
Production overheads	(4 000)
	8 400
Selling and administrative overheads	(2 300)
Net profit	6 100

The actual figures for February 20X6 are as follows:

	£
Sales: 900 units @ £36	32 400
Costs	
Direct materials: 900 units × (1.9kg × £5.50)	(9 405)
Direct labour: 900 units × (1.2 hours × £7.00)	(7 560)
Production overheads	(4 400)
	11 035
Selling and administrative overheads	(2 450)
Net profit	8 585

i) Prepare a flexed budget for 900 units for February 20X6.
ii) Calculate the full range of variances demonstrated in the Sherborne Suggate Limited example (Example 18.2).
iii) Prepare a standard cost operating statement that reconciles the difference between the budget net profit and the actual net profit figures shown in the statements above.

Overhead variances

The Sherborne Suggate example given above contained only very simple overhead variances. However, it can be useful to management to have access to rather more detailed analysis. It is customary in manufacturing businesses to draw a distinction between variable overheads and fixed overheads in the calculation of variances relating to production overheads.

Variable overheads are those that increase or decrease corresponding to increases and decreases in production. For example, the following costs would all tend to vary as production levels vary:

- machine cleaning and repair costs
- machine oil and consumables costs
- quality inspection costs.

Many overheads, however, will be fixed. A production supervisor's salary, for example, is likely to stay the same whether she is supervising the production of 100 units per day, or 95, or 105. It would be a different matter if production changed radically and the number increased to, say, 1000. More production supervisors would have to be employed. However, it is safe to say that, provided variations in production levels are relatively small, many costs remain the same.

In Example 18.3 we will examine variable and fixed overhead variances by means of a demonstration. It is possible to break down overhead variances for activity and expenditure effects (as for materials and labour) but such a level of complexity is regarded as being beyond the scope of this book. We will, therefore, calculate only one overall variance for variable production overheads and one overall variance for fixed production overheads.

Example 18.3 Goldman Le Saint Limited produces a single product. Its budget for March 20X7 is as follows:

	£
Sales: 1000 units @ £80	80 000
Costs	
Direct materials: 1 000 units × (4kg × £3)	(12 000)
Direct labour: 1 000 units × (3 hours × £5.00)	(15 000)
Variable production overheads: 1 000 units × (4 machine hours × £2.00)	(8 000)
Fixed production overheads: 1 000 units × (4 machine hours × £6.00)	(24 000)
	21 000
Selling and administrative overheads	(4 000)
Net profit	17 000

Note that in this example production overheads are split into variable and fixed production overheads – the first time that we have encountered such a split.

Both variable and fixed production overheads are recovered via overhead absorption rates based upon machine hours. The budget machine hours for March 20X7 are 4000 hours (1000 units × 4 machine hours per unit). The actual figures for March 20X7 are as follows:

	£
Sales: 900 units × £80	72 000
Costs	
Direct materials: 900 units × (4kg × £3.00)	(10 800)
Direct labour: 900 units × (3 hours × £5.00)	(13 500)
Variable overheads	(9 600)
Production overheads	(25 500)
	12 600
Selling and administrative overheads	(4 000)
Net profit	8 600

▶

The first stage in calculating variances, as before, is to flex the budget for the actual level of sales activity. Flexed budget for 900 units:

	£
Sales: 900 units × £80	72 000
Costs	
Direct materials: 900 units × (4kg × £3.00)	(10 800)
Direct labour: 900 units × (3 hours × £5.00)	(13 500)
Variable overheads: 900 units × (4 hours × £2)	(7 200)
Fixed production overheads: 900 units × (4 hours × £6)	(21 600)
	18 900
Selling and administrative overheads	(4 000)
Net profit	14 900

As in the previous example, it will be helpful to set the original budget statement, the flexed budget statement and the actual statement side by side:

	Original budget £	Flexed budget £	Actual £
Sales	80 000	72 000	72 000
Costs			
Direct materials	(12 000)	(10 800)	(10 800)
Direct labour	(15 000)	(13 500)	(13 500)
Variable production overhead	(8 000)	(7 200)	(9 600)
Fixed production overhead	(24 000)	(21 600)	(25 500)
	21 000	18 900	12 600
Selling and administrative overhead	(4 000)	(4 000)	(4 000)
Net profit	17 000	14 900	8 600

The overall variance is:

	£
Original budget net profit	17 000
Actual net profit	8 600
	8 400 (A)

Sales profit volume variance

This variance is the difference between the original budget profit and the flexed budget profit: £17 000–£14 900 = £2100 (A). The variance is adverse because the flexed budget profit is lower than the original budget profit.

Anyone who has managed to keep up so far will see that there are no variances for sales price, direct material, direct labour, and selling and administrative overheads. Once the budget is flexed, it becomes clear that sales prices, direct material and direct labour costs are exactly as would have been predicted if 900 units had been budgeted for. The example therefore isolates the changes in variable and fixed production overhead.

Variable production overhead variance

The variance can be calculated in the same way as, say, the total direct materials variance: by comparing the totals in the flexed budget statement with the actual statement:

	£
Flexed budget for variable overhead	7 200
Actual variable overhead	9 600
	2 400 (A)

Fixed production overhead variance

The overall variance can be calculated in the same way as, say, the total direct materials variance: by comparing the totals in the flexed budget statement with the actual statement:

	£
Flexed budget for fixed overhead	21 600
Actual fixed overhead	25 500
	3 900 (A)

We can now produce a standard cost operating statement for March 20X7:

Goldman Le Saint Limited: Standard cost operating statement

for March 20X7

	Total £
Original budgeted net profit	17 000
Sales profit volume variance	(2 100)
Flexed budget net profit	14 900

	Favourable £	(Adverse) £	
Other variances			
Sales price variance	—	—	
Direct materials price variance	—	—	
Direct materials quantity variance	—	—	
Direct labour rate variance	—	—	
Direct labour efficiency variance	—	—	
Variable overhead variance	—	(2 400)	
Fixed overhead variance	—	(3 900)	
Selling and administrative overhead variance	—	—	
Total	—	(6 300)	(6 300)
Actual net profit			8 600

Before moving on, try Self-test question 18.2, which isolates the calculation of the variable and fixed production overhead variances.

Self-test question 18.2 (answer at the end of the chapter)

Singh and Waterhouse Limited manufacture one style of storage shelving. The company's budget for April 20X8 is as follows:

	£
Sales: 1 800 × £45	81 000
Costs	
Direct materials: 1 800 units × (16 metres × £1.00 per metre)	(28 800)
Direct labour: 1 800 units × (2 hours × £5.00 per hour)	(18 000)
Variable production overheads: 1 800 units × (2 machine hours per unit × £1)	(3 600)
Fixed production overheads: 1 800 units × (2 machine hours per unit × £6)	(21 600)
Profit before other overheads	9 000

The actual figures for April 20X8 are as follows:

	£
Sales: 2000 units × £45	90 000
Costs	
Direct materials: 2 000 units × (16 metres × £1)	(32 000)
Direct labour: 2 000 units × (2 hours × £5.00)	(20 000)
Variable overheads	(3 800)
Production overheads	(23 400)
Profit before other overheads	10 800

You are required to:

a) Flex the budget for a sales level of 2000 units.
b) Calculate all variances.
c) Prepare a standard cost operating statement for the company for April 20X8.

Investigating the reasons for variances

Implementing a standard costing system represents a major investment of time and other resources for most businesses. The benefits of this investment will outweigh the costs only if full use is made by management of the information conveyed by variances. It is important, too, that the investigation of variances is carried out promptly. The examples in this chapter have all assumed that standard costs are being compared with actual on a monthly basis; this is a realistic assumption which reflects actual practice in industry. If the comparison were to be made annually or even quarterly, any underlying problems would persist for far too long. In order for management to be able to exert full control frequent and timely action is required.

Deciding which variances merit investigation

It is a matter of management policy to decide the level at which a variance becomes significant and worthy of further investigation. The following criteria will probably be important in deciding which variances merit investigation:

- *Significance in percentage or monetary terms*. For example, management may decide to investigate any variance, favourable or unfavourable, which is greater than 5% of the flexed budget total. Or they may use a monetary criterion, such as 'investigate any variance greater than £5000'.
- *Frequency of occurrence*. Variances may be individually minor, but cumulatively significant. For example, if there is a persistent adverse materials price variance across a range of different materials items, this may point to lax purchasing management.

Principal reasons for the occurrence of variances

Sales variances

Actual sales volume may differ from budget volume because of such factors as:

- greater than expected success of an advertising campaign
- improved efficiency and effectiveness of sales staff
- failure of a competitor
- entry of a new competitor into the market
- loss of sales staff, or loss of morale and motivation through poor management.

Sales prices may differ because of such factors as:

- lowering of prices to increase volume
- lowering of prices to respond to new competition
- increasing prices to take advantage of exit of competitor from the market
- fashion trends (it may be possible to charge higher prices for fashionable items).

Direct materials variances

Price variances may arise because of any, or a combination, of the following factors:

- successful negotiation for lower prices
- obtaining quantity discounts for large orders
- variation in material quality
- volatile market for material, leading to unexpected increases or decrease in price

Quantity variances may arise as follows:

- better or worse quality of material than expected
- employment of higher or lower skilled workers than anticipated
- level of supervision/number of quality checks
- poor functioning of machinery.

Direct labour variances

Rate variances may arise in the following circumstances:

- The mix of labour differs from plan; for example, using more higher paid staff in production because of under-employment elsewhere in the factory.
- Unexpected increase in rate arising from the conclusion of negotiations over wage levels.

Efficiency variances may arise as follows:

- better or worse quality of material than expected
- employment of higher or lower skilled workers than anticipated
- level of supervision/ number of quality checks
- poor functioning of machinery.

Overhead variances

Overhead variances may arise because of any of the following:

- non-controllable price changes because of events in the wider economy
- poor management control over costs
- improved management control over costs.

Last, but not least, variances may occur simply because the standard cost was incorrectly set. For example, if the standard cost for a particular item reflects the best possible cost achievable only in ideal circumstances, then it is unlikely to be met. The existence of variances may signal no more than the need to alter the standard cost. However, before this step is taken the variance should be thoroughly investigated to ensure that there is no other cause.

CASE STUDY 18.1 Variance investigation: A surprise result

Part 1

The case study for this chapter brings together all the different variance calculations in a comprehensive example.

Andrea Ellison is managing director of Francis & Follett Limited, an unlisted company that manufactures wooden bedframes. After a few difficult years in the last decade the company has managed to secure half a dozen contracts with major home furnishings retailers. This has significantly expanded the volume of trade and has allowed the company to repay its long-term loans. The company's accountant and business adviser suggested last year that it is now time to improve the quality of management control systems. Andrea and her brother, Phil, the sales director, are the two active directors in the business. In the past they have been able to keep tight control over the business by close supervision. However, as the business has taken on more staff, that kind of control has lessened.

Factory supervision is now under the control of a production manager, Faroukh, who was promoted to this position after several years as senior supervisor. The purchasing and stores function is managed by Perry, who has also been a trusted employee for many years.

A few months ago Andrea and Phil appointed a management accountant, Sylvie, who has worked hard to establish a budgetary control system in time for the start of the new financial year on 1 January 20X4. Sylvie has carefully monitored the production process with the help of Faroukh, and has established standard costs and times for all parts of the process. The annual budget is split into 12 monthly budgets, and actual performance is monitored each month. It is now the end of March 20X4 and the new system has been in place for three months.

The budget for March 20X4 is as follows:

	£
Sales: 1 600 units × £103	164 800
Costs	
Direct materials: 1 600 units × (12 metres × £2.50 per metre)	(48 000)
Direct materials: 1 600 units × 1 bag of metal components × £4.50	(7 200)
Direct materials: 1 600 units × 1 packaging box × £3.50	(5 600)
Direct labour: 1 600 units × (2.5 hours × £6.00 per hour)	(24 000)
Variable production overheads: 1 600 units × (1.5 machine hours per unit × £4)	(9 600)
Fixed production overheads: 1 600 units × (1.5 machine hours per unit × £10)	(24 000)
	46 400
Selling and administration overheads	(16 600)
Net profit	29 800

The pieces for each bedframe are flat-packed in the factory. Each pack contains the necessary metal components for assembling the bedframe. Francis & Follett Limited buys in the components ready packaged in plastic bags.

Production overheads are absorbed on the basis of machine hours. Machine hours for March are budgeted at 2400 hours. Actual figures for March are as follows:

	£
Sales: 1 650 units × £103	169 950
Costs	
Direct materials: 1 650 units × (12.2 metres × £2.70 per metre)	(54 351)
Direct materials: 1 650 units × 1 bag of metal components × £4.50	(7 425)
Direct materials: 1 650 units × 1 packaging box × £3.50	(5 775)
Direct labour: 1 650 units × (2.4 hours × £6.00 per hour)	(23 760)
Variable production overheads	(10 050)
Fixed production overheads	(23 960)
	44 629
Selling and administration overheads	(16 420)
Net profit	28 209

Sylvie has prepared a standard form for the monthly and quarterly reporting of variances. The form is set out below with the variances filled in for January and February and a space for the March figures.

Francis & Follett Limited: Standard cost operating statements for the quarter ending 31 March 20X4

	January £	February £	March £
Budget net profit (original)	28 350	29 800	
Sales profit volume variance	1 450	1 450	
Flexed budget net profit	29 800	31 250	

▶

	January £	February £	March £
Sales price variance	—	—	
Direct materials price variance	(3 904)	(3 934)	
Direct materials quantity variance	(360)	(413)	
Direct labour rate variance	—	—	
Direct labour efficiency variance	990	990	
Variable overhead variance	(592)	(460)	
Fixed overhead variance	776	750	
Selling and administration overhead variance	210	(26)	
Actual net profit	26 920	28 157	

Requirements are:

i) Prepare a flexed budget on the basis of sales and production of 1650 units for March 20X4.

ii) Calculate all relevant variances, and record them in the March column of the summary standard cost operating statement for the first quarter of 20X4.

Case study: Part 1 solution

i) Flexed budget for 1650 units for March 20X4

	£
Sales: 1 650 units × £103	169 950
Costs	
Direct materials: 1 650 units × (12 metres × £2.50 per metre)	(49 500)
Direct materials: 1 650 units × 1 bag of metal components × £4.50	(7 425)
Direct materials: 1 650 units × 1 packaging box × £3.50	(5 775)
Direct labour: 1 650 units × (2.5 hours × £6.00 per hour)	(24 750)
Variable production overheads: 1 650 units × (1.5 machine hours per unit × £4)	(9 900)
Fixed production overheads: 1 650 units × (1.5 machine hours per unit × £10)	(24 750)
	47 850
Selling and administration overheads	(16 600)
Net profit	31 250

The summary of original budget, flexed budget and actual statements is as follows:

	Original budget £	Flexed budget £	Actual £
Sales	164 800	169 950	169 950
Costs			
Direct materials: wood	(48 000)	(49 500)	(54 351)
Direct materials: components	(7 200)	(7 425)	(7 425)
Direct materials: packaging	(5 600)	(5 775)	(5 775)
Direct labour	(24 000)	(24 750)	(23 760)

Variable production overheads	(9 600)	(9 900)	(10 050)
Fixed production overheads	(24 000)	(24 750)	(23 960)
	46 400	47 850	44 629
Selling and administration overheads	(16 600)	(16 600)	(16 420)
Net profit	29 800	31 250	28 209

ii) Calculation of variances

Sales volume profit variance

	£
Flexed budget net profit	31 250
Original budget net profit	29 800
Sales volume profit variance	1 450 (F)

There are no variances for sales price or for direct materials (components and packaging).

Direct materials price variance

	£
Actual quantity at actual price	
12.2 metres was used for each of 1 650 units	
actual quantity used is 12.2 metres × 1 650 = 20 130 metres	
20 130 metres × price actually paid (£2.70)	54 351
Actual quantity at standard price	
20 130 metres × standard price (£2.50)	50 325
Direct materials price variance	4 026 (A)

Direct materials quantity variance

	£
Actual quantity at standard price	
Actual quantity used (already worked out): 20 130 metres	
Standard price per metre: £2.50	
Actual quantity at standard price = 20 130 × £2.50	50 325
Standard quantity at standard price	
Standard quantity: 12 metres × 1 650 units = 19 800 metres	
Standard price per metre: £2.50	
Standard quantity at standard price = 19 800 × £2.50	49 500
Direct materials quantity variance	825 (A)

There is no variance for direct labour rate (because the actual rate of £6.00 is the same as the budget).

Direct labour efficiency variance

	£
Actual hours at standard rate	
Actual hours used: 1 650 units × 2.4 hours = 3 960 hours	
Standard rate per hour: £6.00	
Actual hours at standard rate = 3 960 × £6.00	23 760

	£
Standard hours at standard rate	
Standard hours: 1 650 units × 2.5 hours = 4 125 hours	
Standard rate per hour: £6.00	
Standard hours at standard rate = 4 125 × £6.00	24 750
Direct labour efficiency variance	990 (F)

Variable overhead variance

	£
Actual expenditure	
Expenditure	10 050
Overhead absorbed at standard machine hours	
1 650 units at 1.5 hours of machine time (standard	
rate) = 2 475 hours	
At the absorption rate of £4.00 per hour: £4.00 × 2 475	9 900
Variable overhead variance	150 (A)

Fixed overhead variance

	£
Actual expenditure	
Expenditure	23 960
Expenditure absorbed	
Standard machine hours used in production x absorption	
rate: 1 650 × 1.5 machine hours × £10	24 750
Fixed overhead variance	790 (F)

Selling and administration overhead variance

	£
Actual expenditure	16 420
Originally budgeted	16 600
	180 (F)

We can now insert the variance figures for March into the quarterly statement:

Francis & Follett Limited: Standard cost operating statements for the quarter ending 31 March 20X4

	January	February	March
	£	£	£
Budget net profit (original)	28 350	29 800	29 800
Sales profit volume variance	1 450	1 450	1 450
Flexed budget net profit	29 800	31 250	31 250
Sales price variance	—	—	—
Direct materials price variance	(3 904)	(3 934)	(4 026)
Direct materials quantity variance	(360)	(413)	(825)

Direct labour rate variance	—	—	—
Direct labour efficiency variance	990	990	990
Variable overhead variance	(592)	(460)	(150)
Fixed overhead variance	776	750	790
Selling and administration overhead variance	210	(26)	180
Actual net profit	26 920	28 157	28 209

Part 2

Sylvie arranges a meeting with Andrea, Phil and Faroukh to discuss the first quarterly standard cost operating statement. The discussion runs as follows:

Sylvie: In each of the three months we've been using the standard costing system we've had better than budgeted sales, so the sales profit volume increase has been positive.

Phil: Yes, I think actually we were a bit on the cautious side in setting the sales budget; the market's looking good, and realistically I think we can expect to do better than budget for most of the rest of the year.

Sylvie: I don't see anything really to worry about in the overheads variances. Actual spend has been very close to budget levels across the various classes of overhead.

Faroukh: Yes, I think we're doing well on production overhead control. One of the cutting machines is getting a bit old and tired and I think we should be looking to replace it by the end of the year – it's causing a few problems on the shop floor. But, generally, morale is very good, especially now that everybody's had their annual bonus. That's why we're doing better than expected on labour efficiency.

Sylvie: The big problem area, as I'm sure you can see from the statement, is in direct materials. We've got smallish usage variances – no more than around 3% of flexed budget – and I actually now think we perhaps were a bit overambitious when we set the budget usage. But what about the price variance?

Faroukh: I had a word with Perry in January about this and he said that he's been using Lambert's almost exclusively for wood, because of delivery problems with the other suppliers. Unfortunately, Lambert's seems to charge more than the others.

Andrea: But I don't quite understand this – I met Chris Lambert at the Chamber of Commerce dinner the other night and he said the market for timber is very competitive and they've had to cut most of their prices to stay competitive.

Faroukh: It doesn't really make sense. I'll have another word with Perry and see if I can get to the bottom of the problem.

A few days after the meeting Faroukh asks Perry again about the raw materials costs. Perry gives him the same answer as before, but Faroukh is now sure that there's a real problem with the purchasing. He asks Perry for more detailed information, but Perry says that he'll discuss it further tomorrow – he has to leave early for a doctor's appointment.

Faroukh rings Chris Lambert to discuss pricing. Chris looks up the price of the timber and confirms that it has been steady at £2.50 per metre since the start of

▶

◀◀◀

the year. He has no immediate answer to the question of why Lambert's invoices to Francis & Follett show a price of £2.70 per metre, but he promises to look into it straight away. Two hours later Chris Lambert turns up in person holding a bundle of recent copy invoices, all showing a price of £2.50, and Faroukh realises that something is seriously wrong. His suspicions are strengthened when Perry does not come to work on the following day.

Upon further investigation, it emerges that Francis & Follett has been the victim of a purchasing fraud cooked up between Perry and his very close friend, Judith, who is Chris Lambert's office administrator. Judith, who deals with all the invoicing and receipts of cash, has also stopped turning up for work.

The operation of the fraud has been as follows: Perry has ensured that Lambert's receives a large number of the company's orders for timber. Judith has invoiced Francis & Follett for the correct quantities of timber, but at an inflated price. Copy invoices kept at Lambert's, however, show the correct price. When Francis & Follett pay their monthly timber bill, Judith pays all of their cheques into a bank account she has opened in the name of 'Lamberts' and writes out cheques for a lower amount to pay into the genuine Lambert's business account. Because she controls both paying in of receipts and invoicing, her boss is very unlikely ever to notice that anything is wrong. The proceeds of the scam, which, it emerges, goes back over several years, have been split 50:50 between Judith and Perry.

Case study: Part 2 discussion

The second part of the case demonstrates the importance of investigating all variances thoroughly, and of tracking variances from period to period to see if they indicate persistent problems. Francis & Follett has not previously had a standard costing budgetary system and it seems likely that the identification of this problem has only emerged because of the tighter control that is now being exercised over the company's activities.

Purchasing frauds, of the type described here, occur relatively frequently, but are difficult to detect. Because Judith is responsible for so many aspects of the administration of what is, presumably, quite a small business, she has been able to carry out the fraud successfully over a long period. Collusion between employees of different companies makes detection even more difficult. Also, from Francis & Follett's point of view, Perry has been an employee for a long time, and throughout a period of growth. It is quite likely that his activities are not tightly controlled and that he has had a high level of autonomy in decision making about purchases.

The costs of such a fraud can be substantial. In this case, 20p was added to the price of a metre of wood; each unit of product requires 12 metres, so the additional cost would be $12 \times 20p = £2.40$ per unit. Even though, presumably, not all of the timber would be purchased from Lambert's, the amount of cash siphoned off by the criminals could have been very significant indeed over a period of years.

In conclusion, the case study demonstrates how useful a system of full budgetary control can be, and how important it is for management to keep a tight control over the activities of the business.

Chapter summary

This chapter has dealt with several important aspects of budgetary control in practice. First, standard costing and responsibility accounting were described. Then the principal part of the chapter was devoted to a detailed description of variance analysis, and the mechanics of variance calculation and reporting. The variances discussed are summarised in Figure 18.1.

The chapter then proceeded to discuss the investigation of variances. Criteria for investigation were briefly described, and then some of the principal causes of the different variances were identified.

Finally, the case study for the chapter drew upon much of the chapter content in requiring both variance calculations and a consideration of the practical consequences of investigating variances.

Figure 18.1

Summary of variances covered in the chapter

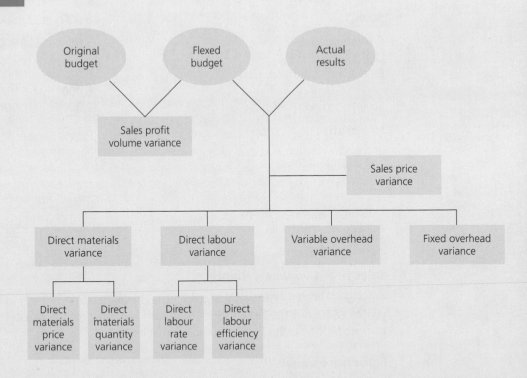

Answer to self-test question 18.1

i) Flexed budget for 900 units

	£
Sales: 900 units @ £35	31 500

Costs

	£
Direct materials: 900 units × (2kg × £6)	(10 800)
Direct labour: 900 units × (1 hour × £7.50)	(6 750)
Production overheads	(4 000)
	9 950
Selling and administrative overheads	(2 300)
Net profit	7 650

ii) Calculation of variances

Summary of budget, flexed budget and actual statements:

	Original budget £	Flexed budget £	Actual £
Sales	28 000	31 500	32 400
Direct materials	(9 600)	(10 800)	(9 405)
Direct labour	(6 000)	(6 750)	(7 560)
Production overhead	(4 000)	(4 000)	(4 400)
	8 400	9 950	11 035
Selling and administrative overhead	(2 300)	(2 300)	(2 450)
Net profit	6 100	7 650	8 585

The overall variance is:

	£
Original budget net profit	6 100
Actual net profit	8 585
	2 485 (F)

Sales profit volume variance

This variance is the difference between the original budget profit and the flexed budget profit: £6100 − £7650 = £1550. The flexed budget profit is greater than the original budget profit, so this is a favourable variance.

Sales price variance

	£
Actual volume of sales at actual selling price:	
900 × £36	32 400
Less: actual volume of sales at budget selling price:	
900 × £35	31 500
Sales price variance	900 (F)

Direct materials variances

Comparing the figure for direct materials in the flexed budget statement with the figure in the actual statement:

	£
Flexed budget for direct materials	10 800
Actual direct materials	9 405
	1 395 (F)

Direct materials price variance. We compare:

- The actual quantity of materials used at the price actually paid (actual price).
- The actual quantity of materials used at the price budgeted (standard price).

	£
Actual quantity at actual price	
1.9kg was used for each of 900 casings	
Actual quantity used is 1.9kg × 900 = 1 710kg	
1 710kg × price actually paid (£5.50)	9 405
Actual quantity at standard price	
1 710kg × standard price (£6.00)	10 260
Direct materials price variance	855 (F)

Direct materials quantity variance. We compare:

- The actual quantity of materials used at standard price.
- The standard quantity of materials used at standard price.

	£
Actual quantity at standard price	
Actual quantity used (already worked out): 1 710kg	
Standard price per kg: £6	
Actual quantity at standard price = 1 710 × £6	10 260
Standard quantity at standard price	
Standard quantity: 2kg × 900 casings = 1 800kg	
Standard price per kg: £6	
Standard quantity at standard price = 1 800 × £6	10 800
Direct materials quantity variance	540 (F)

In summary, the direct materials variances are:

	£
Direct materials price variance	855 (F)
Direct materials quantity variance	540 (F)
Direct materials variance	1 395 (F)

Direct labour variances

Comparing the figure for direct labour in the flexed budget statement with the figure in the actual statement:

	£
Flexed budget for direct labour	6 750
Actual direct labour	7 560
	810 (A)

Direct labour rate variance. We compare:

● The actual hours of direct labour used at the wage rate actually paid (actual rate).

● The actual hours of direct labour used at the wage rate budgeted (standard rate).

	£
Actual hours at actual rate	
Actual hours was 1.2 hours for each of 900 casings	
1.2 × 900 = 1 080 hours	
1 080 hours × rate actually paid (£7.00)	7 560
Actual hours at standard rate	
1 080 hours × standard rate (£7.50)	8 100
Direct labour rate variance	540 (F)

Direct labour efficiency variance. We compare:

● The actual hours of direct labour used at standard rate.

● The standard hours of direct labour used at standard rate.

	£
Actual hours at standard rate	
Actual hours used (already worked out): 1 080 hours	
Standard rate per hour: £7.50	
Actual hours at standard rate = 1 080 × £7.50	8 100
Standard hours at standard rate	
Standard hours: 1 hour × 900 = 900	
Standard rate per hour: £7.50	
Standard hours at standard rate = 900 × £7.50	6 750
Direct labour efficiency variance	1 350 (A)

In summary, the direct labour variances are:

	£
Direct labour rate variance	540 (F)
Direct labour efficiency variance	1 350 (A)
Direct labour variance	810 (A)

Production overhead variance

	£
Budget figure for production overhead	4 000
Actual figure for production overhead	4 400
Production overhead variance	(400) (A)

Selling and administrative overhead variance

	£
Budget figure for selling and administrative overhead	2 300
Actual figure for selling and administrative overhead	2 450
Production overhead variance	(150) (A)

iii) Standard cost operating statement

Bridge and Blige Limited: Standard cost operating statement for February 20X6

	Total £
Original budgeted net profit	6 100
Sales profit volume variance	1 550
Flexed budget net profit	7 650

Other variances	Favourable £	(Adverse) £	
Sales price variance	900		
Direct materials price variance	855		
Direct materials quantity variance	540		
Direct labour rate variance	540		
Direct labour efficiency variance		(1 350)	
Production overhead variance		(400)	
Selling and administrative overhead variance		(150)	
Total	2 835	(1 900)	935
Actual net profit			8 585

Answer to self-test question 18.2

a) Flexed budget for 2000 units

	£
Sales: 2 000 × £45	90 000
Costs	
Direct materials: 2 000 × (16 metres × £1)	(32 000)
Direct labour: 2 000 × (2 hours × £5.00)	(20 000)
Variable production overheads: 2 000 units × (2 machine hours per unit × £1)	(4 000)
Fixed production overheads: 2 000 units × (2 machine hours per unit × £6)	(24 000)
Profit before other overheads	10 000

b) Variance calculations

First of all, we will set the original budget, flexed budget and actual side by side:

	Original budget £	Flexed budget £	Actual £
Sales	81 000	90 000	90 000
Direct materials	(28 800)	(32 000)	(32 000)
Direct labour	(18 000)	(20 000)	(20 000)
Variable production overhead	(3 600)	(4 000)	(3 800)
Fixed production overhead	(21 600)	(24 000)	(23 400)
	9 000	10 000	10 800

The overall variance is:

	£
Original budget net profit	9 000
Actual net profit	10 800
	1 800 (F)

Sales profit volume variance

This variance is the difference between the original budget profit and the flexed budget profit: £9000 − 10 000 = £1000 (F). The variance is favourable because the flexed budget profit is higher than the original budget profit.

There are no variances for sales price, direct material, direct labour and selling and administrative overheads. Once the budget is flexed, it becomes clear that sales prices, direct material and direct labour costs are exactly as would have been predicted if 2000 units had been budgeted for.

Variable production overhead variance

The overall variance can be calculated in the same way as, say, the total direct materials variance — by comparing the totals in the flexed budget statement with the actual statement:

	£
Flexed budget for variable overhead	4 000
Actual variable overhead	3 800
	200 (F)

Fixed production overhead variance

The overall variance is calculated in the same way by comparing the totals in the flexed budget statement with the actual statement:

	£
Flexed budget for fixed overhead	24 000
Actual fixed overhead	23 400
	600 (F)

c) Standard cost operating statement

Singh and Waterhouse Limited: Standard cost operating statement for April 20X8

		Total £
Original budgeted net profit		9 000
Sales profit volume variance		1 000
Flexed budget net profit		10 000

	Favourable £	(Adverse) £	
Other variances			
Sales price variance	—	—	
Direct materials price variance	—	—	
Direct materials quantity variance	—	—	
Direct labour rate variance	—	—	
Direct labour efficiency variance	—	—	
Variable overhead variance	200	—	
Fixed overhead variance	600		
Selling and administrative overhead variance	—	—	
Total	800	—	800
Actual net profit			10 800

Exercises

The answers to many of the exercises are set out later in this chapter. However, where the exercise number is followed by 'A' the answer is available only to lecturers. Remember that additional exercises (with answers) are available to students on the book's website.

18.1   Denholm Pargeter Limited is an engineering company producing a wide range of component parts for the aerospace industry. Its component XP04/H has the following budget sales and prime costs for March 20X1:

	£
Sales: 1 200 units × £30 per unit	36 000
Costs	
Direct materials: 1 200 units × (3kg × £1.20)	4 320
Direct labour: 1 200 units × (2 hours × £8.50)	20 400
Prime cost	24 720

The production manager wishes to assess the change to the budget on the basis that 1300 units are produced and sold.

You are required to flex the budget for component XP04/H for 1300 units.

18.2A   Dorchester Slugg Limited manufactures plastic refuse bins. Its monthly budget for August 20X6 is as follows:

	£
Sales: 4 000 units × £18	72 000
Costs	
Direct materials: 4 000 (7kg × £1)	(28 000)
Direct labour: 4 000 × (0.5 hours × £6.00)	(12 000)
Production overhead	(10 000)
	22 000

	£
Selling and administrative overhead	(4 000)
Net profit	18 000

Dorchester Slugg does not absorb production overheads using an overhead absorption rate. It may be assumed that all of its overheads are fixed in nature. You are required to flex the budget for a sales and production level of 4500 units.

18.3   Darblay Harriett Limited produces a single product – a wooden cabinet. The company's budget for November 20X9 is as follows:

	£
Sales: 2 000 units × £19.50	39 000
Costs	
Direct materials: 2 000 × (2 metres × £2.00)	(8 000)
Direct labour: 2 000 × (1 hour × £6.00)	(12 000)
Production overhead	(10 000)
	9 000
Selling and administrative overhead	(3 000)
Net profit	6 000

Darblay Harriett does not absorb production overheads using an overhead absorption rate. It may be assumed that all of its overheads are fixed in nature. If the company flexes its budget for 2600 units, what will be the revised net profit figure?

a) £14 700

b) £8 700

c) £11 700

d) £17 700.

18.4A   Dillinger Thompson Limited produces a line of leather bags. Although they vary slightly in design the cost structure is the same for each bag. The company's budget for January 20X5 is as follows:

	£
Sales: 4 000 units × £22.00	88 000
Costs	
Direct materials: 4 000 × (1 square metre × £6.50)	(26 000)
Direct labour: 4 000 × (0.5 hours × £7.80)	(15 600)
Production overhead	(24 000)
	22 400
Selling and administrative overhead	(6 000)
Net profit	16 400

Dillinger Thompson Limited does not absorb production overheads using an overhead absorption rate. It may be assumed that all of its overheads are fixed in nature.

If the company flexes its budget for 3600 units, what will be the revised net profit figure?

a) £11 760

b) £17 760

c) £14 160

d) £7 600.

The following information is relevant for questions 18.5 to 18.10.

Edwards and Sheerness Limited is in the motor parts industry. Its budget for July 20X2 is as follows:

	£
Sales: 2 500 units × £29.00	72 500
Costs	
Direct materials: 2 500 × (3 kg × £3.00)	(22 500)
Direct labour: 2 500 × (1.5 hours × £4.40)	(16 500)
Production overhead	(17 000)
	16 500
Other overheads	(3 500)
Net profit	13 000

Edwards and Sheerness Limited does not absorb production overheads using an overhead absorption rate. It may be assumed that all of its overheads are fixed in nature.

The company's actual results for the month are as follows:

	£
Sales: 2 650 units × £28.00	74 200
Costs	
Direct materials: 2 650 × (2.8 kg × £3.30)	(24 486)
Direct labour: 2 650 × (1.7 hours × £4.20)	(18 921)
Production overhead	(16 900)
	13 893
Other overheads	(3 600)
Net profit	10 293

18.5   What is the sales profit volume variance for the month?

a) £2 707 (A)

b) £2 010 (A)

c) £2 707 (F)

d) £2 010 (F).

18.6 What is the sales price variance for the month?

a) £640 (F)

b) £640 (A)

c) £2 650 (F)

d) £2 650 (A).

18.7 What is the direct materials price variance for the month?

a) £2 226 (F)

b) £2 226 (A)

c) £2 385 (F)

d) £2 385 (A).

18.8 What is the direct materials quantity variance for the month?

a) £1 749 (F)

b) £1 749 (A)

c) £1 590 (F)

d) £1 590 (A).

18.9 What is the direct labour rate variance for the month?

a) £901 (A)

b) £795 (A)

c) £795 (F)

d) £901 (F).

18.10 What is the direct labour efficiency variance for the month?

a) £2 332 (F)

b) £2 332 (A)

c) £2 226 (F)

d) £2 226 (A).

The following information is relevant for questions 18.11A to 18.16A

Estella Starr Limited produces garden sheds that are sold direct to the public in kit form. March is one of the company's best months for sales, and in March 20X3 the directors have set some ambitious targets. These are summarised in the following budget for the month:

	£
Sales: 900 units × £217.00	195 300
Costs	
Direct materials: 900 × (16 metres × £4.00)	(57 600)
Direct labour: 900 × (4 hours × £6.30)	(22 680)
Production overhead	(62 300)
	52 720
Other overheads	(10 600)
Net profit	42 120

Estella Starr Limited does not absorb production overheads using an overhead absorption rate. It may be assumed that all of its overheads are fixed in nature. The company's actual results for the month are as follows:

	£
Sales: 830 × £214.00	177 620
Costs	
Direct materials: 830 × (15 metres × £4.10)	(51 045)
Direct labour: 830 × (4.1 hours × £6.00)	(20 418)
Production overhead	(61 400)
	44 757
Other overheads	(8 950)
Net profit	35 807

18.11A What is the sales profit volume variance for the month?

a) £6 313 (A)

b) £8 946 (A)

c) £8 946 (F)

d) £6 313 (F).

18.12A What is the sales price variance for the month?

a) £2 490 (F)

b) £2 490 (A)

c) £15 190 (F)

d) £15 190 (A).

18.13A What is the direct materials price variance for the month?

a) £6 555 (A)

b) £1 245 (A)

c) £6 555 (F)

d) £1 245 (F).

18.14A What is the direct materials quantity variance for the month?

a) £3 320 (F)

b) £3 320 (A)

c) £7 800 (A)

d) £7 800 (F).

18.15A What is the direct labour rate variance for the month (to the nearest £)?

a) £360 (A)

b) £360 (F)

c) £1 021 (F)

d) £1 021 (A)

18.16A What is the direct labour efficiency variance for the month (to the nearest £)?

a) £523 (A)

b) £523 (F)

c) £340 (F)

d) £340 (A).

18.17   Ferguson Farrar Limited is a manufacturing company. For the month of April 20X3 it budgeted for 4000 units of production, each to use 1.5 hours of machine time. Production overhead absorption rates were budgeted as follows:

Variable production overhead = £4 per machine hour.
Fixed production overhead = £8 per machine hour.

The actual level of production in the month was 4200 units. The original production overhead budget, the flexed budget and the actual expenditure are shown in the following table:

	Original budget £	Flexed budget £	Actual £
Variable production overheads	24 000	25 200	26 250
Fixed production overheads	48 000	50 400	48 750
	72 000	75 600	75 000

Calculate:

a) the variable production overhead variance

b) the fixed production overhead variance.

18.18A Feltham Finch Limited is a manufacturing company. For the month of August 20X4 it budgeted for 780 units of production, each to use four hours of machine time. Production overhead absorption rates were budgeted as follows:

Variable production overhead = £2.80 per machine hour.
Fixed production overhead = £7.60 per machine hour.

The actual level of production in the month was 760 units. The original production overhead budget, the flexed budget and the actual expenditure are shown in the following table:

	Original budget £	Flexed budget £	Actual £
Variable production overheads	8 736	8 512	8 476
Fixed production overheads	23 712	23 104	24 160
	32 448	31 616	32 636

Calculate:

i) the variable production overhead variance

ii) the fixed production overhead variance.

18.19   Grindleton Gears Limited is a manufacturing business that uses a standard costing system. If a variance exceeds 5% of the flexed budget total for that item, the management team investigates it, whether it is favourable or adverse. The company's flexed budget for February 20X4 is:

	£
Sales	123 470
Costs	
Direct materials	(28 250)
Direct labour	(29 900)
Variable production overheads	(8 640)
Fixed production overheads	(19 780)
Profit	36 900

The management team is presented with the following standard cost operating statement for the month:

	Total
	£
Original budgeted net profit	30 900
Sales profit volume variance	6 000
Flexed budget net profit	36 900

	Favourable	(Adverse)	
Other variances	£	£	
Sales price variance	1 030	—	
Direct materials price variance	—	(1 650)	
Direct materials quantity variance	—	(106)	
Direct labour rate variance	—	—	
Direct labour efficiency variance	200	—	
Variable overhead variance	1 400	—	
Fixed overhead variance	339	—	
Total	2 969	(1 756)	1 213
Actual profit			38 113

You are required to:

i) Using the company's own criterion, decide which variances should be examined.

ii) List reasons why the variances you have identified may have arisen.

iii) Calculate the actual figures for sales, direct materials, direct labour, variable overheads, fixed overheads and profit.

Answers to exercises

18.1 Denholm Pargeter Limited

March 20X1: Budget for XP04/H flexed for 1300 units

	£
Sales: 1 300 units × £30 per unit	39 000
Costs	
Direct materials: 1 300 units × (3kg × £1.20)	4 680
Direct labour: 1 300 units × (2 hours × £8.50)	22 100
Prime cost	26 780

18.3 Darblay Harriett Limited

November 20X9: Budget flexed for 2600 units

	£
Sales: 2 600 units × £19.50	50 700
Costs	
Direct materials: 2 600 × (2 metres × £2.00)	(10 400)
Direct labour: 2 600 × (1 hour × £6.00)	(15 600)
Production overhead	(10 000)
	14 700
Selling and administrative overhead	(3 000)
Net profit	11 700

The correct answer, therefore, is c).

Edwards and Sheerness Limited: General information for the answers to questions 18.5 to 18.10

The flexed budget for 2650 units is as follows:

	£
Sales: 2 650 units × £29.00	76 850
Costs	
Direct materials: 2 650 × (3 kg × £3.00)	(23 850)
Direct labour: 2 650 × (1.5 hours × £4.40)	(17 490)
Production overhead	(17 000)
	18 510
Other overheads	(3 500)
Net profit	15 010

Comparison of original budget, flexed budget and actual:

	Original budget £	Flexed budget £	Actual £
Sales	72 500	76 850	74 200
Costs			
Direct materials	(22 500)	(23 850)	(24 486)
Direct labour	(16 500)	(17 490)	(18 921)
Production overhead	(17 000)	(17 000)	(16 900)
	16 500	18 510	13 893
Other overheads	(3 500)	(3 500)	(3 600)
Net profit	13 000	15 010	10 293

18.5   Sales profit volume variance

	£
Flexed budget net profit	15 010
Original budget net profit	13 000
	2 010 (F)

The correct answer, therefore, is d).

18.6   Sales price variance

	£
Actual volume of sales at actual selling price: 2 650 × £28	74 200
Actual volume of sales at standard selling price: 2 650 × £29	76 850
	2 650 (A)

The correct answer, therefore, is d).

18.7   Direct materials price variance

	£
Actual quantity of materials used at actual price:	
2 650 × 2.8kg = 7 420 × £3.30	24 486
Actual quantity of materials used at standard price:	
7 420 × £3.00	22 260
	2 226 (A)

The correct answer, therefore, is b).

18.8   Direct materials quantity variance

	£
Actual quantity of materials used at standard price:	
7 420 × £3.00	22 260
Standard quantity of materials used at standard price:	
2 650 × 3.0kg = 7 950 × £3.00	23 850
	1 590 (F)

The correct answer, therefore, is c).

18.9 Direct labour rate variance

	£
Actual hours at actual wage rate: 2 650 × 1.7 hours	
= 4 505 × £4.20	18 921
Actual hours at standard wage rate: 4 505 × £4.40	19 822
	901 (F)

The correct answer, therefore, is d).

18.10 Direct labour efficiency variance

	£
Actual hours at standard wage rate: 4 505 × £4.40	19 822
Standard hours at standard wage rate: 2 650 × 1.5 hours	
= 3 975 × £4.40	17 490
	2 332 (A)

The correct answer, therefore, is b).

18.17 Ferguson Farrar Limited

a) Variable production overhead variance

	£
Actual variable production overhead	26 250
Flexed budget variable production overhead	25 200
	1 050 (A)

b) Fixed production overhead variance

	£
Actual fixed production overhead	48 750
Flexed budget fixed production overhead	50 400
	1 650 (F)

18.19 Grindleton Gears Limited

i) Significant variances

The variances that are regarded as significant according to the company's 5% criterion are:

● Direct materials price variance (£1650 (A): 5.8% of flexed budget).
● Variable production overhead variance (£1400 (F): 16.2% of flexed budget).

ii) Possible reasons for the variances

● Direct materials price variance
  – successful negotiation for lower prices
  – obtaining quantity discounts for large orders

- variation in material quality
- volatile market for material, leading to unexpected increases or decreases in price.
- Variable production overhead variance
  - price changes because of events in the wider economy
  - improved management control over costs.

It is also possible in this case (the variance being so large) that some items of expense have simply gone unrecorded.

iii) Actual figures

Actual costs can be derived from the information given by adding the flexible budget amount to the variances, as follows:

	£
Sales: £123 470 + £1 030	124 500
Direct materials: £28 250 + £1 650 + £106	(30 006)
Direct labour: £29 900 − £200	(29 700)
Variable production overheads: £8 640 − £1 400	(7 240)
Fixed production overheads: £19 780 − £339	(19 441)
Actual profit	38 113

19

MARGINAL COSTING FOR DECISION MAKING

AIMS AND LEARNING OUTCOMES

Aim of the chapter

To understand the key elements of marginal costing, including cost-volume-profit analysis and the use of marginal costing in making a range of business decisions.

Learning outcomes

After reading the chapter and completing the related exercises, students should:

- Understand the nature and classification of costs as variable, fixed or semi-variable.
- Be able to represent different types of cost in a graph.
- Be able to use cost-volume-profit analysis to establish a break-even point and to assist in business decision making.
- Be able to understand the figures and issues involved in making decisions about acceptance of contracts at special prices, extension of production capacity and prioritising of production in conditions where limiting factors exist.

Cost classification: Variable, fixed and semi-variable costs

It can be very useful for the purposes of decision making to classify costs according to their variability. Later in the chapter we will look at examples of business decisions, but for the moment we will simply consider the differences in cost behaviour between variable costs, fixed costs and semi-variable costs.

Variable costs

A fully **variable cost** is one that varies in line with the level of business activity. For example, direct materials costs tend to be fully variable.

Using a graph to show variable cost behaviour

Variable costs increase as the level of activity increases; the relationship between costs and activities is linear and can be plotted onto a graph, as shown in Figure 19.1.

As activity increases (e.g. the number of units of production) variable costs increase. The line on the graph begins at 0 because at this point zero activity = zero variable cost.

Figure 19.1	

Graph of variable cost behaviour

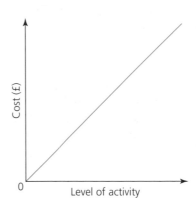

Example 19.1 Sparks Kitchenware Limited produces various types of kitchen equipment. A basic metal spatula requires 300 grams of metal at a cost of £1.00. The cost of metal to make two spatulas is exactly twice as much: 600 grams at a total cost of £2.00.

To make 10 spatulas, 3kg (300 grams × 10) of metal is required at a total cost of £10.00. For each additional spatula, the cost increases by £1 (i.e. the same amount every time). This is an example of a fully variable cost.

Earlier we noted that direct materials costs *tend* to be fully variable. When might they not be fully variable? Well, in practice, it is usually possible to obtain lower prices per unit of material as volumes increase. In the case of Sparks Kitchenware Limited, suppose that a quantity discount of 5% is available for purchases of metal in quantities over 100kg. This means that a higher volume of production will be relatively a little cheaper than a low volume. However, it is often quite realistic to make an assumption that direct costs are fully variable with the level of output.

▶

We can plot the variable cost data onto a graph similar to that in Figure 19.1. The variable materials cost of the spatulas produced by Sparks Kitchenware Limited is shown at three different levels of activity in the following table (and see Figure 19.2).

Number of units produced	Variable cost total (£1 x number of units produced)
0	0
10	£10
20	£20

Figure 19.2

Sparks Kitchenware Limited: Variable materials cost graph

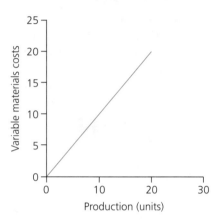

Fixed costs

A **fixed cost** is one that does not vary with the level of business activity.

Using a graph to show fixed cost behaviour

See the graph in Figure 19.3.

Figure 19.3

Fixed cost behaviour

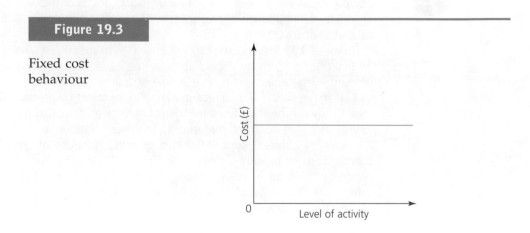

Example 19.2 Sparks Kitchenware Limited rents a factory unit. It pays rent of £28 000 per year for the unit, and insurance of £4360 per year. These are both examples of costs that do not vary with the level of output of the factory. Whether 1 or 1 000 000 metal spatulas are produced, the cost of factory rent and insurance remains the same.

We can plot the fixed cost of factory rental (£28 000) onto a graph (see Figure 19.4).

Figure 19.4

Sparks Kitchenware Limited: Fixed cost (factory rental) graph

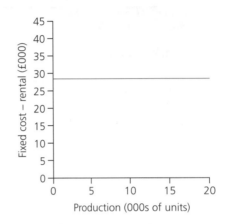

Of course, even fixed costs vary eventually. Suppose that the maximum number of spatulas Sparks Kitchenware can produce in its factory is 1 million per annum. If the business is successful and expands beyond this level of production it will need to obtain bigger production facilities – so factory rent and insurance would go up. It is only possible to describe costs as fixed within certain levels of activity.

Stepped costs

Where a business reaches the level of activity where a fixed cost must increase, the increase is sudden (see Figure 19.5).

Figure 19.5

Stepped cost behaviour

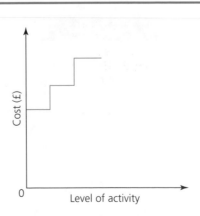

Example 19.3 Sparks Kitchenware Limited employs production supervisors at an annual salary cost of £12 500 each. The company's health and safety policy requires a certain level of supervision in the factory, and so the directors have decided that a supervisor must be employed for every 10 machine operators. So, if the number of machine operators is 50, 5 supervisors will be employed at a total cost of (5 × £12 500) £62 500. If the number of machine operators rises to 51 the company's policy requires that 6 supervisors will be employed. The total cost rises to (6 x £12 500) £75 000. We can plot this stepped cost onto a graph (see Figure 19.6).

Figure 19.6

Sparks Kitchenware
Limited:
Supervisors'
salaries cost graph

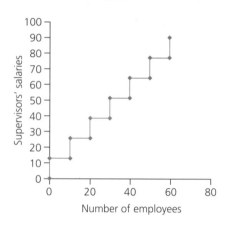

Semi-variable costs

A **semi-variable** cost is one that varies to some extent with the level of business activity; it has both fixed and variable elements.

For example, telephone bills have both fixed and variable elements. There is a line rental charge that is fixed; it remains the same regardless of the number of calls made. In addition to the fixed line rental, however, there is a variable element that depends upon the number of phone calls made.

Using a graph to show semi-variable cost behaviour

Figure 19.7 shows that, even at a zero level of activity, some cost is incurred; that is why the cost line starts part way up the vertical axis.

Figure 19.7

Semi-variable cost
behaviour

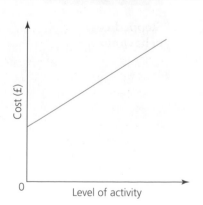

Example 19.4 Sparks Kitchenware Limited employs two sales staff. Each is paid a basic salary of £15 000 per year. In addition, each member of staff is paid a commission of 10% of sales value for every sale they make. Sales of £10 000, therefore, incur commission charges of £10 000 × 10% = £1000. Sales of £100 000 incur commission charges of £100 000 × 10% = £10 000.

Total sales salaries costs:

- Sales level of 10 000: £30 000 (basic salary) + £1000 (commission) = £31 000
- Sales level of 100 000: £30 000 (basic salary) + £10 000 (commission) = £41 000

We can plot the semi-variable cost of sales salaries onto a graph (see Figure 19.8).

Figure 19.8

Sparks Kitchenware Limited: Semi-variable cost (sales salaries) graph

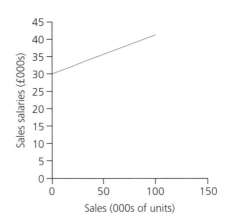

Typical cost behaviour in different business sectors

In some types of business there are few, if any, variable costs. Even in businesses where a substantial proportion of cost is apparently variable with levels of activity, the reality may be that the costs are fixed in nature. We will look at some examples to illustrate these points.

A manufacturer

Usually, the direct materials used in manufacturing production tend to be variable; a progressively larger amount of material is used as the level of activity increases. By the same token, we would expect direct labour to be a variable cost. However, in practice, an employer's obligations to employees under employment regulations are often such that the labour cannot necessarily be regarded as direct. In many of the examples in this section of the book we have assumed that the supply of direct labour, like water from a tap, can be turned on or off at the convenience of management. This assumption, in many circumstances, is unrealistic. While a long-term downturn in an industry is likely to result in reductions in employees, short-term reductions in activity do not result in workers being laid off.

Therefore, in determining whether or not labour is a variable cost, the circumstances must be examined carefully. For example, sometimes, especially in garment manufacture, workers are paid piece rates – i.e. a sum for each completed item. Where this forms the whole of a worker's pay, the cost is truly variable. In some cases, however, there will be a basic, fixed level of wages plus a piece rate. This arrangement constitutes a semi-variable cost.

A commercial airline

Very few of the costs involved in running a commercial airline are variable. There are some very significant fixed costs, though:

- depreciation of aircraft
- employment of pilots and cabin crew
- aircraft maintenance and safety charges
- airport charges
- interest costs (on borrowing money to finance the purchase or lease of the planes).

A commercial aircraft service running scheduled flights must run the advertised flights even if there are very few passengers (in fact, because the planes have to be in certain places at scheduled times, a plane is likely to make the flight even if there are no passengers at all).

Any variable costs are likely to be very minor indeed compared to the high level of fixed costs incurred. Variable costs would include, for example, the cost of drinks supplied free during flights (the fewer passengers the fewer the drinks served, by and large).

Restaurant

Running a restaurant usually involves incurring a high level of fixed costs. For example:

- premises rental
- cost of employing staff
- depreciation of equipment.

What about food costs? To some extent these are variable, but because of the perishable nature of many food items there may be a fixed element of cost involved. If food is not sold to customers it will have to be thrown away sooner or later.

Labour costs may be variable to some extent, depending upon the basis of employment. If the restaurant proprietor expects a quiet evening he may be able to reduce the level of waiting and kitchen staff to some extent, but he will have to schedule at least some staff. Even if no customers at all turn up, he will still have to pay the staff for their time, and this basic minimum of staff time would represent a fixed cost.

Holiday tour operator

A holiday tour operator incurs fixed costs such as rental of offices, employment of staff to take bookings and deal with ticket administration, and so on. However, some of the costs are likely to be variable with the level of bookings taken from the public. A total of 37 couples booking a resort holiday will require 74 flight tickets and 37 rooms. There could, however, be some fixed elements to these costs; for example, where the contract with a hotel owner stipulates that, say, a minimum of 30 rooms will be paid for each week by the tour operator, regardless of whether or not they are used. In a case like this, the tour operator is being obliged to share with the hotel owner the risk of unused rooms.

Clearly, categorising costs neatly into 'fixed' and 'variable' categories is not always as simple in practice as it may at first appear. In many businesses genuinely variable costs are rare.

Costing for decision making

In Chapter 16 we examined the features of absorption costing, and noted that this approach to costing, while useful for some aspects of planning and control, may be defective for decision making. We will re-emphasise this point by means of an example.

Example 19.5 Modena Mayhew Limited plans the following budget income and expenditure for May 20X7:

	£
Sales: 1000 units × £10 each	10 000
Costs	
Direct materials and labour	(4 000)
Production overheads, absorbed at £3 per unit	(3 000)
	3 000
Selling and administrative costs	(1 500)
Net profit	1 500

The business is not working to full capacity and it would be possible to produce more units of product. Modena Mayhew's sales director is approached by a contractor who wishes to order 100 units, to be produced and delivered in May; however, he wishes to negotiate a special price of £8.50 per unit. In order to help to decide whether or not to accept the order, the sales director needs information on the cost of a unit of product. What does it cost to produce one unit?

It might be tempting to take the total costs in the statement above (£4000 + £3000 + £1500 = £8500), divide by 1000 and come up with the figure of £8.50 per unit. However, this approach would be incorrect, unless *all* the costs were variable (and that is highly unlikely to be the case). Those costs that are fixed remain fixed unless the level of activity changes radically.

Really, the sales director needs to know the *additional cost* of manufacturing an extra unit of product. If we assume that all of the production costs and the selling and administrative costs are fixed (probably quite a reasonable assumption) and all the direct costs are variable, this means that the business is incurring £4000 of variable cost to produce 1000 units of product. Variable cost per unit of product is therefore:

$$\frac{4\,000}{1\,000} = \text{£4 per unit}$$

This is the additional cost that would be incurred by manufacturing the 1001st unit of product in May.

Comparing the two:

▶

	£
Total cost per unit of product	8.50
Variable cost per unit of product	4.00

If the sales director incorrectly calculated that the additional cost of the 100 unit order would be £850 (£8.50 × 100) he would conclude that it would not make sense to accept the order because the sales revenue from it would be no greater than cost. However, if he takes the variable cost per unit, he may conclude that the order should be accepted.

To prove that it would, indeed, increase profit to accept the extra order, we will look at the May budget statement revised to include the additional 100 units at a selling price of £8.50 per unit:

	£
Sales: 1 000 units × £10 each	10 000
100 units × £8.50 each	850
	10 850
Costs	
Direct materials and labour (at £4 per unit for 1 100 units) (*variable cost*)	(4 400)
Production overheads, absorbed at £3 per unit originally budgeted (*fixed cost*)	(3 000)
	3 450
Selling and administrative costs (*fixed cost*)	(1 500)
Net profit	1 950

The revised budget profit is £1950, that is £450 higher than the original budget profit figure. The figures show that extra profit can be made by accepting the order, even at a lower price.

Marginal costing

A **marginal cost** in economics is the cost of one additional item. In the example given above we looked at the cost of making the 1001st unit of product. This is a marginal cost. **Marginal costing** is a piece of accounting terminology describing an approach to costing that excludes fixed costs. As we have seen, marginal costing provides a much sounder basis for decision making than absorption costing.

In the rest of the chapter we will look at some important aspects of decision-making using marginal costing. First, it is necessary to introduce some more new terminology.

Contribution

Contribution refers to the amount that remains after variable costs have been deducted from sales. Referring back to the information in Example 19.5, the additional contribution per unit of product that would be made on the additional order for 100 units would be:

	£
Sales price per unit	8.50
Less: variable cost per unit	(4.00)
Contribution per unit	4.50

If contribution is a positive figure it contributes towards meeting the fixed costs of the business. Once sufficient contribution is made to cover all of the fixed costs, any remaining amount contributes to net profits.

Contribution can be calculated per unit, and can also be shown as a total (number of units sold × contribution per unit).

Break-even

The **break-even point** is the point at which no profit and no loss is made in a set of business transactions. For example:

	£
Sales: 10 000 units × £3	30 000
Less: variable costs: 10 000 units × £1	(10 000)
Contribution	20 000
Fixed costs	(20 000)
Net profit	Nil

Self-test question 19.1 (answer at the end of the chapter)

Brinn Bartholomew Limited sells municipal litter bins for £250 each. The bins cost £97 in direct materials (all variable cost) and £36 in direct labour (all variable cost). In June 20X9 the company plans to sell 1400 bins. Its budgeted fixed costs for the month are £120 400.

- What is the company's budgeted contribution for June 20X9?
- What is the company's budgeted net profit for June 20X9?

Cost-volume-profit analysis

It is important to understand the relationships between the level of business activity, the different types of cost and profitability. The analysis of the interaction of these factors is known as cost-volume-profit analysis (CVP analysis). We will examine CVP relationships further, firstly by charting cost, volume and profit in graphical form, and then by using formulae to express the relationships between the factors. We will look first at the construction of break-even charts.

Break-even charts

Step 1

Earlier in the chapter we constructed graphs for each different type of cost. Developing that approach further, we can show both fixed and variable costs on the same graph (see Figure 19.9). An alternative presentation is shown in Figure 19.10.

Fixed costs, as we have seen, are those that remain at the same level regardless of the volume of activity. Variable costs increase steadily as the volume of activity increases. Showing the two together on a graph gives the result illustrated. The upper sloping line represents total costs. Where there is zero activity (i.e. no production or sales) the only costs incurred are fixed costs (which is why the total cost line starts part way up the vertical axis). As activity increases, so do total costs.

Figure 19.9

Graph of total costs, split into fixed and variable

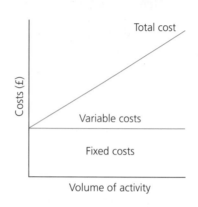

Figure 19.10

Graph of total costs, split into fixed and variable (alternative presentation)

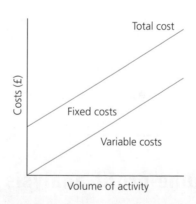

Self-test question 19.2 (answer at the end of the chapter)

Marshall Mexico Limited has the following cost structure for 20X7:

Fixed costs: £50 000 up to 10 000 units of production.
Variable costs: £5 per unit up to 10 000 units of production.

Using either graph paper or a spreadsheet program graphing facility, plot these costs onto a single graph, showing lines for fixed costs and total costs. Identify the areas of the graph that represent fixed costs and variable costs.

Step 2

We will now add a further line to the graph, this time for sales revenue (see Figure 19.11). The addition of this line produces a **break-even chart**, which provides useful information about the activities of the business.

The point at which the total revenue crosses the total cost line is break-even point. We can see that break-even point occurs where:

Total sales revenue = Total costs

By dropping a line down from the break-even point to the horizontal axis of the graph we can read off the volume at which break-even point occurs; this is shown as a vertical dotted line in Figure 19.11. Charting a line between the vertical axis and the break-even point, we can read off the sales value at which the break-even point occurs; this is shown as a horizontal dotted line on the figure.

Figure 19.11

Break-even chart

Self-test question 19.3 (answer at the end of the chapter)

The facts are the same as for self-test question 19.2. Marshall Mexico Limited sells its product at £15 per unit. Taking the graph drawn for self-test question 19.2, draw a total revenue line and establish the break-even point. Drop a line down to the horizontal axis and find out the volume of activity at which break-even point occurs. Draw another line from the break-even point to the vertical axis and find out the sales value at which break-even point occurs.

Break-even analysis using formulae

There are drawbacks to using graphs for establishing the break-even point of a business:

● The answer obtained tends to be approximate because of inaccuracies in drawing the graph.
● It would be unnecessarily time-consuming to have to draw a graph each time analysis of break-even was undertaken.

Instead, we can work out break-even points using the relationships between sales and costs that we established earlier.

Selling price per unit − variable costs per unit = Contribution per unit

Remember that contribution per unit contributes towards meeting the fixed costs of the business. The point at which all the fixed costs of the business are met is break-even point. Beyond break-even point, the contribution contributes towards the net profit of the business. So, break-even point occurs where:

$$\text{Sales revenue} = \text{Total costs}$$

And also where:

$$\text{Contribution} = \text{Fixed costs}$$

In order to calculate the number of units of sales required to break even, the following formula is used:

$$\text{Break-even point (in units)} = \frac{\text{Fixed costs}}{\text{Contribution per unit}}$$

The break-even point in sales value can be calculated by:

$$\text{Break-even point (in units)} \times \text{Selling price per unit}$$

Example 19.6 Mulberry Piggott Limited manufactures and sells raincoats. It sells each raincoat for £30.00. Variable costs are £10.00 per coat.

In the year ending 31 December 20X5 the company expects to incur fixed costs of £60 000. How many raincoats will it have to sell to break even?

Sales revenue per unit = £30.00
Variable costs per unit = £10.00

Contribution per unit is, therefore, £20.00 (sales minus variable costs).

$$\text{Break-even point (in units)} = \frac{\text{Fixed costs}}{\text{Contribution per unit}}$$

$$= \frac{60\,000}{£20} = 3000 \text{ units}$$

Break-even point in sales value:

$$3000 \text{ units} \times £30.00 = £90\,000$$

Self-test question 19.4 (answer at the end of the chapter)

Neasden Northwich Limited sells its products at £20 per unit. Variable costs per unit are £6. The company expects to incur fixed costs of £70 000 in 20X6. Calculate the break-even point (in units) for 20X6.

Further applications of break-even analysis

Target profit

The break-even point, expressed in numbers of units or sales value, provides management with valuable information. However, managers may also want to know how many units they will have to sell in order to reach a specified profit target.

We can apply marginal costing to this type of problem quite easily, as it is a logical extension to break-even analysis. Remember that, once sufficient contribution is made to cover all of the fixed costs of a business, any remaining amount contributes to net profits.

So, we can extend the break-even formula as follows:

$$\text{Target sales in units} = \frac{\text{Fixed costs} + \text{Target profit}}{\text{Contribution per unit}}$$

Example 19.7 Using data from the Mulberry Piggott example:

sales revenue per unit = £30.00
variable costs per unit = £10.00
contribution per unit = £20.00
fixed costs = £60 000

The company's directors would like to know how many units would have to be sold to reach their target profit of £307 000. Applying the formula:

$$\text{Target sales in units} = \frac{\text{Fixed costs} + \text{Target profit}}{\text{Contribution per unit}}$$

$$\text{Target sales in units} = \frac{60\,000 + 30\,000}{20} = 4\,500 \text{ units}$$

Expressed in terms of sales value:

$$4\,500 \text{ units} \times £30 = £135\,000$$

Showing profit on a graph

Up till now we have not focused specifically on the graphical representation of profit. Suppose that Mulberry Piggott can make and potentially sell up to 7000 raincoats per year without fixed costs changing. We can plot the following points on a graph:

Production level	Fixed costs £	Total costs £	Total revenue £
0	60 000	60 000	0
7 000	60 000	130 000	£210 000
		(£60 000 + 7 000 × £10)	(7 000 × £30)

This gives the result shown in Figure 19.12. The areas of profit and loss are marked on the graph. Beyond break-even point, as production increases, the area between the revenue and total costs lines is occupied by profit. The first dotted line shows sales in units and in revenue to produce profits of £30 000 (as calculated above). The second dotted line shows the maximum activity level that is possible at a level of fixed costs of £60 000. Profits at this level (the difference between the total revenue and total costs lines) would be much higher than at a level of 4500 sales; we can prove this by doing the calculation of profit at the maximum activity level of 7000 units:

	£
Sales (7000 × £30)	210 000
Variable costs (7000 × £10)	(70 000)
Contribution	140 000
Fixed costs	(60 000)
Profit	80 000

Margin of safety

Margin of safety is the excess of planned or actual sales above the break-even point. In Example 19.6 we calculated the Mulberry Piggott break-even point in units as 3000 raincoats. If we suppose that the sales of 4500 units targeted by the directors (as in Example 19.7) are a realistic target, the margin of safety, expressed both in units and in sales value, is as follows:

	Units of sales	Sales £
Actual sales estimate	4 500	135 000
Break-even point	3 000	90 000
Margin of safety	1 500	45 000

The margin of safety can also be expressed as a percentage of the sales estimate:

$$\frac{1\,500}{4\,500} \times 100 = 33.3\%$$

| **Figure 19.12** | |

Mulberry Pigott: Cost-volume-profit graph

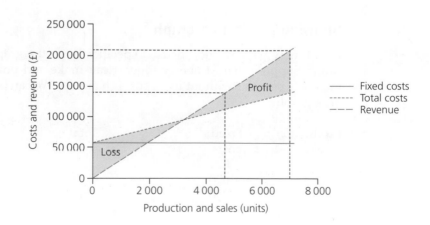

Special decisions: Accepting contracts

In this section we look more closely at business decisions involving acceptance or non-acceptance of contracts on special terms. Marginal costing analysis can be useful in reaching the appropriate decision.

If an order or contract at a special price would produce a positive contribution to fixed costs, then the business should accept the order. However, there may be other factors to take into consideration.

Example 19.8 Solidago Solanum Limited manufactures sofas. Although the design details and fabric coverings vary, the basic design of the sofas is the same and they all sell for £1500 each. The company's factory can produce up to 1000 sofas per month, but in fact, production rarely exceeds 700 per month.

The sales director has just received a query from a potential new customer, Cuttpryce Limited. Cuttpryce is opening a chain of discount furniture stores and is examining potential sources of supply. The purchasing director of Cuttpryce offers to buy an initial consignment of 300 sofas at a price of £1200 each. The potential discount of £300 per sofa is so great that Solidago's sales director is tempted to refuse the order straight away. However, he consults his fellow directors over the decision.

The latest set of monthly management accounts shows the following summary:

Solidago Solanum Limited: Management accounts for July 20X4

	£
Sales (655 × £1 500)	982 500
Variable costs (655 × £895)	586 225
Contribution	396 275
Fixed costs	304 000
Net profit	92 275

What should the directors' decision be? Applying the basic decision rule: would the contract make a positive contribution to fixed costs?

Under the proposed contract:

	£
Selling price per sofa	1 200
Variable cost per sofa	(895)
Contribution per sofa	305

The contribution per sofa is positive, and so it appears that the contract should be accepted.

However, there are likely to be other relevant considerations. If it becomes generally known that Solidago sofas are available from Cuttpryce at £300 less than the normal retail price, why should anyone pay £1500? Acceptance of this new contract could have a significant impact on the rest of the company's business. If the company has a reputation for exclusivity and high quality, it could be damaged by association with a discounter.

▶

The marginal costing analysis provides a useful starting point for discussion, but the decision made by the directors will have to involve many other relevant factors.

In industries where either the majority or all of the costs are fixed, the application of the decision rule explained above can lead to some apparently absurd prices. Where variable costs are virtually non-existent, selling price is more or less the same as contribution. This means that, potentially, even a very low selling price can make a positive contribution to fixed costs. This issue is explored in more detail in Chapter 20 which considers pricing decisions.

Special decisions: Major increases in activity levels

As we have seen, fixed costs remain fixed only up to certain levels of activity. If a business is considering major increases in levels of activity, it must take into account any likely increases in fixed costs.

Example 19.9 Spindrift and Schooner Limited is a small boat builder. It has operated successfully for many years from a boatyard that allows for production of 60 boats per year. In most years the company can sell all the boats it can produce. The selling price of each boat is £2600. Variable labour and materials costs are £985 per boat, and the fixed costs associated with running the business from the present boatyard are £48 200. Last year the company made a net profit of £48 700 on sales of £156 000.

The company's directors are meeting to discuss a proposal to increase the business's production capacity. A neighbouring property has become vacant and it would be possible to rent the additional space in order to produce more boats. The additional capacity in terms of production would be 20 boats. The sales director is confident that, with the growth in the leisure boating market, he will be able to sell the additional boats.

Variable costs per boat will remain the same. However, the expansion would produce an additional £26 500 in fixed costs. In a case like this, the increase in fixed costs has to figure in the decision making. The extra £26 500 is known as an *incremental* cost, and it must be compared with the *incremental* revenue that will be generated through higher sales. The basic decision rule is: if incremental revenue exceeds incremental costs, accept the project.

In this case we will assume that the sales director's confidence is justified and that he will be able to sell all of the additional 20 boats produced each year following the expansion:

	£
Incremental revenue	
Sales: 20 boats × £2 600	52 000
Incremental costs	
Variable costs: 20 × £985	(19 700)
Fixed costs	(26 500)
Incremental profit	5 800

Because the incremental profit is a positive figure it looks as though the business should increase its capacity. However, the directors might reflect that £5800 is a relatively small increase in net profit, and that the net profit percentage on these additional sales at 11.2% is substantially lower than the existing net profit percentage of 31.2%.

Special decisions: Limiting factors

So far, the only constraints on business activities which we have examined are the upper ceiling for production capacity and the restraint imposed by the market in terms of the amount of product or service that can be sold. However, there may be situations where other constraints operate. Such constraints are commonly known as **limiting factors**. For example, a product may require specialist labour for which there is a shortage, or a raw material which is in short supply.

Where a business produces more than one product, all of which require the input of resources whose supply is limited, management must come to a decision as to production priorities. The basic rule is that limited resources should be devoted to production of the products that produce the highest contribution per unit of limiting factor. This is not as complicated as it sounds, as Example 19.10 shows.

Example 19.10 Crosby and Crossthwaite Limited use the same production line to produce their three principal products, A, B and C. All three products use the same grade of labour, which is in short supply because of a booming local economy that has ensured virtually full employment.

The products have the following sales and variable cost values per unit sold:

	A	B	C
	£	£	£
Selling price	50	55	48
Variable costs	(28)	(28)	(24)
Contribution per unit	22	27	24

On the face of it, it would appear that the company should concentrate production on product B because it produces the highest contribution to fixed costs. However, the picture alters when we look at the input to each of the products of the scarce labour resource:

	A	B	C
Number of labour hours used	2	3	3
Contribution per unit	£22	£27	£24
Contribution per labour hour	£11	£9	£8

When we calculate the contribution per unit of limited resource, we can see that product A comes out ahead because it uses only two of the limited labour hours. The ranking of the three products is first A, second B and third C.

If there is sufficient demand for product A, it appears that the company should switch production entirely towards product A. However, demand for product A may be insufficient. We will examine the additional factor of demand in the next example.

Example 19.11 Using the same information as in Example 19.10, suppose that Crosby and Crossthwaite Limited can employ a maximum of 22 000 hours of labour in one year. Maximum annual demand for the three products is estimated at:

	A	B	C
Demand in units	8 000	6 000	8 000

How much of each product should the company plan to produce?

Taking product A first, 8000 units will use up 16 000 labour hours (at a rate of 2 hours per unit). The company should manufacture up to the maximum demand in respect of product A. This would leave 22 000 − 16 000 = 6000 labour hours available to manufacture something else. These hours should be used for the manufacture of product B, which is next in the limited resource rankings. Product B uses 3 labour hours per unit, so 6000 hours could produce 2000 units of product B.

The company's production plan is, therefore: product A 8000 units; and product B 2000 units.

Limitations of analysis based on marginal costing

Analysis based on marginal costing can be useful to management as a source of information for decision making. However, it has several significant weaknesses and limitations:

1. This type of analysis assumes that variable costs increase at a steady rate in line with activity. This assumption may not be valid in practice. As the level of business activity increases, variable costs per unit may tend to fall as the business takes advantage of discounts for purchasing larger quantities.

2. As we have seen, very few costs are truly variable. In some businesses only relatively trivial costs vary with the level of business activity. Providers of services, in particular, usually incur a mixture of principally fixed and stepped costs.

3. Fixed costs remain fixed only up to a point. Beyond a particular level of activity fixed costs will change. The level at which costs will change and the extent of that change may not be easy to estimate.

4. The examples used to illustrate the applications of cost-volume-profit analysis have all been based upon firms producing either a single product or a very limited range of products. In fact, most businesses provide a mixture of products or services. While it may be possible to identify variable costs for each product with a fair degree of accuracy, identification of fixed costs with a particular product is likely to be based upon quite arbitrary apportionment between products and activities.

5. All business decisions involve a complex range of factors. Marginal costing may help to point the way towards a decision, but there may be very good reasons in practice for ignoring the signposts offered by analysis based on marginal costing.

If the limitations of this type of analysis are not fully appreciated, it is possible for businesses to make serious mistakes in decision making.

CASE STUDY 19.1 Decision making and disagreement

Arthur Wright has owned and run a manufacturing business, A & A Wright (Ranges) Limited for many years. The business makes high quality, old-fashioned kitchen ranges. There has been a resurgence of demand in recent years as these ranges have become fashionable again, and the business has performed quite well both in terms of sales and net profits. Arthur set up the business originally with his brother Albert, but Albert died at a comparatively early age leaving his share of the business to his widow Ella. Ella takes no active part in the business, and until very recently, the major decisions have been left up to Arthur.

Arthur would like to retire early at around 55, and, as he is now in his early 50s, he is planning to hand over the business to his son, Vinnie. Vinnie is now 23; he left university with a degree in business studies a few months ago and since then has been working with his father in the company. Arthur and Vinnie get along reasonably well outside work, but there have been several disagreements over operational details within the business. Arthur realises that Vinnie has his own ideas about how he wants to do things and knows they won't agree about everything, but he's been making all the decisions for the business ever since Albert died and he's finding it difficult to let Vinnie have a say in running things. From his point of view, Vinnie finds it frustrating that Arthur won't listen to him properly. He's got a lot of ideas about improving the marketing and the financial management of the company, but Arthur really doesn't seem interested.

The latest disagreement is over a potential sales contract. Vinnie has been approached by Jay Johnson Kitchens Limited, a company that installs up-market kitchens. Jay Johnson wants to order, initially, ten ranges, but at a substantially discounted price. Wright's list price is £1300 per range; sometimes Arthur allows discounts to long-standing customers, but never more than around £50. On average, Wrights sell for £1280 per range. Jay Johnson wants to pay no more than £1050. Jay tells Vinnie that he should accept the order because 'there'll be plenty more business coming your way so long as we get a decent price. I often order 20 or 30 at a time, you know; even if I don't need to use them all immediately, it's good to have all the colours in stock to show people. Still, if you don't want the business, there are other suppliers who will.'

Vinnie did an accounting course at college, and he remembers the textbook chapter on marginal costing and decision making particularly well. One of the problems he has with his father's approach to business is that Arthur simply won't treat management accounting information seriously. Vinnie, on the other hand, would really like to get a proper budgeting and standard costing system going, but he hasn't made any progress in persuading his father that it would be a good idea.

The two men discuss the Jay Johnson order:

Vinnie: I really think we should go with this, you know. I've done the figures, and it's clear that even at a price of £1050 there'll be a positive contribution to fixed overheads.

Arthur: I'll take your word for it, but you know, it isn't all about figures. There are other things besides figures to consider. I've always been prepared to negotiate on discount, but £250 per range is just out of the question. Look at Leonard's Kitchens, for example; they've been buying from me for years so I give them £30 discount on each range. Leonard's happy with that; he knows it's as good as he'll get from anyone else.

▶

Vinnie: Yeah, but Leonard only orders three or four each month. Jay's asking for ten now, and who knows how many more he'll want if we give him the price he's asking for.

Arthur: But that's another thing. It's all very well getting the orders, but we've got a maximum production capacity in this factory of about 100 units a month. Sometimes, we're producing as many as 95. If we take this business and Jay starts ordering big numbers we'll not be able to do it.

Vinnie: Yes, well, I'm glad you've mentioned that, because I think we should be looking at increasing capacity anyway. This factory building's a disgrace – it's a nightmare trying to meet the health and safety regulations, and it costs a fortune to heat. We should be thinking about moving into one of those factory units they're building by the motorway.

Arthur: The trouble with you is you just want to change everything. All at once. No discussion. Your uncle Albert and I started with nothing, you know, and we built all this up ourselves. I'm still in charge here, and it'll be a while before I retire. Could be a very long while unless you develop a bit of common-sense.

Vinnie: 'You've never thought I was good for anything, have you? You don't want me to have this business, do you? You won't listen to any of my ideas, and anyway I'm sick to death of hearing about you and Albert. Give it a rest.

The discussion very rapidly degenerates into a nasty argument, the worst one yet.

Vinnie has prepared a brief summary of his costings. Establishing the average sales price was easy, but he's had to do a bit of guesswork on the variable costs. He meant to go through this calmly and rationally with Arthur, but that opportunity was lost when the discussion got out of hand. Here are Vinnie's figures:

A & A Wright Limited: Summary of 20X7 sales and costs

	£
Sales: 1 030 ranges at an average price of £1 280 per unit	1 318 400
Variable costs: estimated at £630 per unit	(648 900)
Contribution	669 500
Fixed costs: total costs of £1 240 300 less estimated variables of £648 900	(591 400)
Net profit	78 100

Contribution per unit on existing sales = 1 280 − 630 = £650.
Contribution per unit on Jay Johnson's order = £1 050 − 630 = £420.

Case study requirements

Discuss the following questions:

a) Are there any problems apparent from Vinnie's figures?

b) Is Vinnie correct in proposing to accept the Jay Johnson order? Is Arthur correct in wanting to refuse the order at such a low price? What about the other issues that Arthur and Vinnie raise in their discussion/argument?

Case study discussion: Question a)

In calculating contribution as the basis for making a decision on whether or not to accept an order, Vinnie's general approach to the business problem is fine, in principle. Because the business does not have costing systems it has obviously been difficult for him to establish totals for variable and fixed costs. In consequence, he has had to use estimates, and, of course, these may be quite inaccurate. His basic conclusion, that there will be a positive contribution to fixed overheads from the Jay Johnson contract, appears to be supported by the calculations.

The figures show that the business is certainly profitable, but not very profitable. Net profit as a percentage of sales is only about 6%. Also, the margin of safety at current level of sales appears small. It is possible to calculate an estimated margin of safety based on Vinnie's figures.

$$\text{Break-even point in units} = \frac{\text{Fixed costs}}{\text{Contribution per unit}}$$

$$= \frac{591\,400}{650} = 910 \text{ (to nearest unit)}$$

Actual sales in 20X7 were 1030 ranges, a margin of safety of 120 units, or 11.7% of actual sales.

Arthur and Vinnie should perhaps be looking at the overall profitability of the business as well as thinking about negotiating special prices on contracts. It may be that costs are not very well controlled. Costs are perhaps higher because of inefficiencies in the production process. Vinnie mentioned the very high cost of heating, and if the factory building is of a poor standard there may be other high costs in maintenance, cleaning and insurance.

Case study discussions Question b)

Although A & A Wright is clearly a profitable business, it appears to be facing several problems. Arthur plans to have Vinnie take over the business, but he is not finding it easy to let Vinnie have any say in running it. Arthur is probably going to find it harder than he anticipated to let his son take over completely. In family businesses like this one relationship problems can create major obstacles to the smooth running of the business. The case study describes a classic succession problem; the father unwilling to admit that his son may be right, and the son equally reluctant to concede that his father might just know a thing or two about running a business.

Is Vinnie correct? If we try to decode what Vinnie is saying, it's actually about a great deal more than the acceptance or non-acceptance of the contract; the sub-text is one of impatience with his father's approach to running the business. Vinnie wants to introduce a more systematic approach to management, using accounting figures to help make business decisions. He also sees, as perhaps his father can't, that the factory itself has become a liability. Because he has a business studies education he feels, rightly, that he knows a great deal and is capable of generating good ideas. What he obviously lacks is the experience of making real business decisions.

What about Arthur's view? Arthur is impatient with Vinnie's use of figures as an aid to decision making. He dismisses the notion of 'positive contribution to fixed overheads' with contempt. However, he does have a point: there are other factors apart from the figures to consider. If the business sells at such a large

▶

discount what impact will there be on other sales? If Leonard of Leonard's Kitchens discovers that Jay Johnson, a new customer, is getting a £250 discount, he will no doubt feel entitled to object to receiving a paltry £30 discount. Accepting this contract may mean a general drop in the selling prices that A & A Wright can command.

Suppose the order from Jay Johnson was accepted, and that it led to a general fall in selling prices to £1050 per range. What would be the effect on the business? Contribution would fall to approximately £420 per range, and the break-even point would become higher. We can estimate a new break-even point based upon lower contribution:

$$\text{Break-even point in units} = \frac{591\,400}{420} = 1408 \text{ units (to nearest whole unit)}$$

This level of sales is clearly impossible under current circumstances; even if 1408 sales could be sold in theory, the factory capacity at 100 units per month is a limiting factor. If the order were accepted, and if it led to a general fall in prices, the business could be in serious trouble, and might even go under.

Where do Arthur and Vinnie go from here? They have some major problems to tackle, none of which can be solved unless they can find some way of working harmoniously together. One approach would be to take some advice to help them build a strategy for the business that they can both agree on, perhaps by employing the services of a management consultant (but imagine what Arthur would say about that suggestion!). If they do not employ outside help they will have to solve the problems themselves. However, their relationship appears to be deteriorating fast and they may find themselves unable to resolve the problems on their own.

The case study illustrates the following points about decision making:

- Calculations of break-even, contribution and so on, can be very useful in providing input to business decisions.

- There are always other factors to take into account. The correct decision may seem obvious on paper, but matters are rarely so clear in practice.

- Making business decisions is really difficult, especially where human factors play a major role (and that is often the case).

Chapter summary

In this chapter we have explored costing for decision making. First we considered the nature of costs, and their classification. Using graphs we illustrated simple cost behaviour, classifying costs as variable, fixed or semi-variable. Cost behaviour in a range of manufacturing and service environments was examined to illustrate the point that categorising costs is by no means straightforward in practice.

Having established some basic cost classifications we proceeded to examine the use of marginal costing in decision making. Cost-volume-profit analysis and the calculation of the break-even point for a business were introduced and then applied in several examples covering break-even point, target profit and the calculation of the margin of safety.

Finally, we examined decision making in the following areas:

- acceptance of contracts at special prices
- increasing activity levels where fixed costs increase
- production plans where there are limiting factors.

The case study for the chapter emphasised the practical difficulties involved in making business decisions in the context of a family business. Decision making can be materially assisted by the provision of accounting information, but it is rarely, if ever, simply a matter of following the course of action suggested by the figures.

Answer to self-test question 19.1

Brinn Bartholomew Limited: Budget for June 20X9

	£
Sales: 1400 bins × £250 each	350 000
Variable costs	
Direct materials: 1400 bins × £97	(135 800)
Direct labour: 1400 bins × £36	(50 400)
Contribution	163 800
Fixed costs	(120 400)
Net profit	43 400

Answer to self-test question 19.2

The following points can be plotted onto the graph:

Level of production	Fixed costs £	Total costs £
0	50 000	50 000
10 000	50 000	100 000

We do not need to plot any other points in order to draw the graph, because variable costs increase at a steady rate in line with the level of production. The data produces the graph shown in Figure 19.13.

Answer to self-test question 19.3

From Figure 19.14 we can see that the break-even point is 5000 units. In terms of sales value this is between £60 000 and £80 000 on the vertical axis – probably at approximately £75 000.

We can check this answer by working out a profit statement at a production and sales level of 5000 units:

	£
Sales (5000 × £15)	75 000
Variable costs (5000 × £5)	(25 000)
Contribution	50 000
Fixed costs	(50 000)
	0

Figure 19.13

Marshall Mexico Limited: Total costs, split into fixed and variable, for 20X7

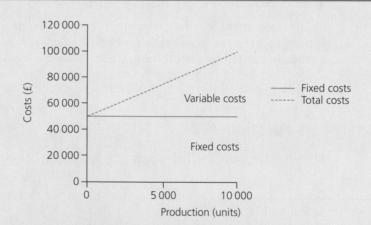

Figure 19.14

Marshall Mexico Limited: Break-even chart for 20X7

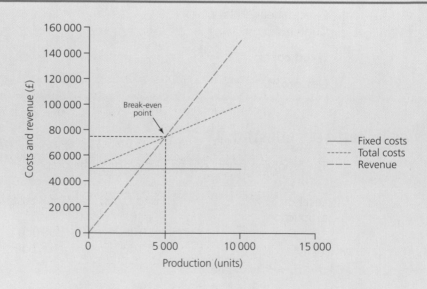

Answer to self-test question 19.4

Calculating Neasden Northwich Limited's break-even point (in units):

Sales revenue per unit = £20.00
Variable costs per unit = £6.00

Contribution per unit is, therefore, £14.00 (sales minus variable costs).

$$\text{Break-even point (in units)} = \frac{\text{Fixed costs}}{\text{Contribution per unit}}$$

$$= \frac{70\,000}{£14} = 5000 \text{ units}$$

Exercises

The answers to many of the exercises are set out later in this chapter. However, where the exercise number is followed by 'A' the answer is available only to lecturers. Remember that additional exercises (with answers) are available to students on the book's website.

19.1   Billericay Ashworth Limited makes tennis racquets. In an average month it produces about 3000 racquets. The following are some of the costs the company incurs:

● *Cost of raw materials.* Each racquet uses £13.00 of raw materials.

● *Factory insurance.* The cost for a month is £800.

● *Telephone charges.* The company has several telephone lines. Its line rental charges per month are £1000. If no calls are made, the call charge is £0. On average 500 calls cost a total of £250 and 1000 calls, on average, cost £500. In most months about 1500 calls are made in the company.

You are required to:

i)   Classify each of the above costs as one of the following:

● variable

● fixed

● stepped

● semi-variable.

ii) Using either graph paper or a spreadsheet program graphing facility plot each of these costs onto a separate graph. Activity levels should be on the horizontal *(x)* axis and costs on the vertical *(y)* axis.

19.2A   A tour operator, Colby Overland Limited, is organising a coach trip to Russia as one of its new season's forthcoming attractions. Two of the major costs incurred are described as follows:

i)   *Coach costs.* Each coach holds up to 40 passengers. The total cost of hiring a coach for the fortnight long trip is £14 000. The company will book only as many coaches as it needs. When the 41st holiday reservation is made, another coach is booked (and a further coach is booked upon receipt of the 81st holiday reservation, and so on). Because of constraints imposed by the limited availability of hotel rooms in Omsk, no more than four coachloads of passengers would be taken on the trip.

ii) *Hotel costs*. Each time a holiday reservation is made the company faxes the hotel in Omsk to make the extra booking. If no more rooms are available, the hotel refuses the booking and the tour is regarded as full. The hotel cost per passenger is £280.

Required:

i) Using either graph paper or a spreadsheet program graphing facility plot each of these costs onto a separate graph. The number of holiday reservations should be shown on the horizontal (*x*) axis and cost on the vertical (*y*) axis.

ii) Classify each of the costs as one of the following:
   – variable
   – fixed
   – stepped
   – semi-variable.

19.3   Classify each of the following costs as:

● variable
● fixed
● stepped
● semi-variable.

i) Sales staff members' mobile phone charges. There is a basic rental cost irrespective of the number of phone calls made, plus a charge for each phone call made, based on the number of minutes the call lasts.

ii) Factory machine oil.

iii) Metered water charges. The bill comprises a charge per unit for the number of units consumed.

19.4   For each of the following types of business, list at least two fixed and two variable costs that might typically be incurred:

● self-employed taxi driver
● solicitor
● shirt manufacturer
● beauty salon.

Try not to repeat the same examples of costs for the different businesses.

19.5A   For each of the following types of business, list at least two fixed and two variable costs that might typically be incurred:

● milk delivery business
● coffee bar
● stationery manufacturer
● cross channel ferry operator.

Try not to repeat the same examples of costs for the different businesses.

19.6 Porton Fitzgerald Limited manufactures wardrobes. The selling price of a wardrobe is £210. Each wardrobe costs £52 in direct materials (all variable) and £34 in direct labour (all variable). In April 20X4 the company expects to sell 450 wardrobes, and it has budgeted for fixed overheads of £43 200.

What is the company's budgeted contribution for April 20X4?

What is the company's budgeted net profit for April 20X4?

19.7A Vernon Xylophones Limited makes xylophones (no surprises there). The direct materials cost of a xylophone is £300; the direct labour process is intensive and costs £450 per xylophone. Both direct materials and direct labour are fully variable. Each xylophone sells for £1500. In August 20X2 the company expects to sell 120 xylophones, and it has budgeted for fixed overheads of £54 000.

What is the company's budgeted contribution for August 20X2?

What is the company's budgeted net profit for August 20X2?

19.8 Fullbright Bognor Limited, a manufacturing business, has the following cost structure:

Selling price per unit: £85

Variable costs per unit: £41

The company's directors expect to incur fixed costs of £62 000 in the year ending 31 December 20X1. The maximum level of production which the company can reach is 3000 units per year.
 You are required to:

i) Draw a break-even chart recording: fixed costs; total costs; total revenue.

ii) From the chart estimate the break-even point in units and in sales value for Fullbright Bognor for the year ending 31 December 20X1.

iii) Use the break-even formula to find the break-even point in units and in sales value for Fullbright Bognor for the year ending 31 December 20X1.

Remember that:

$$\text{Break-even point (in units)} = \frac{\text{Fixed costs}}{\text{Contribution per unit}}$$

19.9A Finch Fletcher Limited manufactures trumpets. Each trumpet sells for £350, and has variable costs of manufacture of £120. The company can produce no more than 1200 in a year. In the year ending 31 March 20X4 the company's directors expect to incur fixed costs of £172 000.
 You are required to:

i) Draw a break-even chart recording:
  – fixed costs
  – total costs
  – total revenue.

ii) From the chart estimate the break-even point in units and in sales value for Finch Fletcher for the year ending 31 March 20X4.

iii) Use the break-even formula to calculate the break-even point in units and in sales value for Finch Fletcher for the year ending 31 March 20X4.

19.10   Foster Beniform Limited makes mannequins for shop window displays. The company's directors are meeting to discuss sales budgets for 20X8. The business has struggled to make a profit in recent years, but the finance director has made strenuous efforts in the last year or so to reduce the level of fixed costs and the directors hope to be able to make a profit in 20X8. The production facilities can produce a maximum of 2000 mannequins per year.

The selling price of a mannequin is £55, with variable costs of production of £25 per unit. In order to be able to make plans for 20X8 the directors would like to know the break-even point in units if (a) fixed costs in 20X8 are £40 000; (b) fixed costs in 20X8 are £50 000.

You are required to:

i)   draw two break-even charts, one for each estimate of fixed costs, recording:

   – fixed costs

   – total costs

   – total revenue.

ii) From the charts estimate the break-even point in units and in sales value for Foster Beniform for 20X8 at each projected level of fixed costs.

iii) Use the break-even formula to calculate the break-even point in units and sales value at each estimated level of fixed costs for Foster Beniform for 20X8.

19.11A Fallon Frodsham Limited manufactures and installs small prefabricated building structures that are sold to people who want to establish a home office using part of their gardens. Each prefabricated building sells at £13 000, including installation costs. The variable costs of manufacture are £7300 per building. The company's directors have set a sales target of 150 buildings for the 20X5 accounting year.

i)   Using a break-even chart, estimate the maximum level of fixed costs the company can incur in 20X5 without making a loss, on the assumption that the sales target is met.

ii) Apply the break-even formula to calculate the maximum level of fixed costs.

Tutorial note: This question may require some thought. Known factors are total revenues (sales revenue per unit × number of units sold), and total variable costs (variable costs per unit × number of units sold). The point on the horizontal (x) axis at which break-even point is reached is also known (150 units). The line must be drawn from that point upwards to the point where it intersects with the total revenue line.

19.12   Gropius Maplewood Limited manufactures a single product that it sells for £150 per unit. Variable costs of each unit are £62, but are expected to rise at the beginning of 20X8 to £63; because of severe competition the company will not be able to pass on this increase in costs to its customers. Fixed costs for 20X8 are expected to be £90 000.

Break-even point for 20X8 is estimated (to the nearest whole unit) at:

a) 1 023 units

b) 1 429 units

c) 1 452 units

d) 1 034 units.

19.13A Gulf Gadgets Limited manufactures chess sets. Each chess set sells for £185. Variable costs of manufacture are £78. The company's directors are currently setting the budget for 20X9. Fixed costs are expected to be £65 000. The selling price of a chess set will rise to £187 and the variable costs of manufacture are expected to increase by 10%.

Break-even point for 20X9 is estimated (to the nearest whole unit) at:

a) 607

b) 655

c) 642

d) 596.

19.14   Gimball Grace Limited manufactures a single model of electric fan heater. Each heater sells for £21. Variable costs of manufacture are £7.50. Fixed costs of the business are estimated at £54 000 for the 20X3 financial year.

The net profit of the business in 20X2 was £36 500, and the directors hope to increase that by 10% in 20X3. How many fan heaters will they have to sell to reach their target net profit (to the nearest whole unit)?

a) 6 974

b) 4 000

c) 6 704

d) 7 374.

19.15A Gecko Grimsby sells specialist aquaria. In the 20X4 financial year each aquarium sold for £1320. The variable costs of manufacture were £321 per aquarium and the total fixed costs incurred were £85 750.

If the selling price, variable costs and fixed costs are all expected to increase by 10% in the 20X5 financial year, how many aquaria (to the nearest whole unit) will the company have to sell to make net profits of £50 000?

a) 131

b) 144

c) 136

d) 124.

19.16   Garbage Solutions Limited makes wheelie bins. In the 20X1 financial year each bin will sell for £25, with variable labour costs of £3.20 per bin and variable raw materials costs of £4.20. Fixed costs are budgeted at £178 900. The company's directors have budgeted net profit of £83 150 in 20X1.

What is the company's margin of safety in units (to the nearest whole unit)?

a) 10 165

b) 9 448

c) 5 441

d) 4 724.

19.17A Gospodin Grimshaw Limited manufactures hiking boots for sale which it sells principally in Russia and other parts of eastern Europe.

Each pair of boots sells for £15. Variable costs are £5.50 per pair. Fixed costs are budgeted at £87 900 for the 20X6 financial year. The company expects to sell 15 000 pairs of boots in 20X6. What is its margin of safety in £s (to the nearest £)?

a) £54 597

b) £86 205

c) £138 795

d) £62 520.

19.18   Harrison Haworth Limited makes rucksacks. It has developed and patented a highly effective waterproof material and a revolutionary design. These make the company's products very much sought after, and the rucksacks sell at a premium price of £68.50 to camping shops and hiking organisations. Annual sales are 20 000 rucksacks. Variable costs of manufacture are £29.00. The company's current level of fixed costs is £382 420.

Most of the company's sales are within the UK and Ireland, but there has been growing interest in Scandinavia and last financial year export sales to Norway and Sweden accounted for 10% of total sales.

The company has just received an enquiry from a Moroccan hiking organisation. The director of the organisation, Raoul, tried out one of the company's rucksacks on a recent hiking trip in the Atlas mountains, and is convinced that it's the best rucksack he's ever used. He would like to start supplying the rucksack in Morocco. However, he knows that there will be very few buyers in Morocco at the premium prices charged by retailers in the UK for Harrison Haworth's products. Raoul suggests that a reasonable price would be £50.00 and that the specification could perhaps be lowered, as the weather conditions are rather better in Morocco than in the UK and Scandinavia. He estimates that annual sales in Morocco would be around 1000 units. Harrison Haworth's production director modifies the design slightly, and estimates that the variable costs of the new design would be £26.30. You are required to advise the directors on whether or not they should accept the order, taking into consideration both financial and non-financial factors.

19.19   Inez & Pilar Fashions Limited is a fashion manufacturing and wholesale business operating from rented premises. The business is well established and has operated successfully for several years. However, Inez and Pilar, the company's directors, realise that they have reached maximum production capacity in their present building. They have an opportunity to expand into neighbouring premises. This would involve some minor reorganisation of production but could be achieved quite easily. Inez and Pilar have worked out that given extra production capacity their sales could increase, at an optimistic estimate, from the existing level of £310 000 per year to as much as £345 000. However, if there is a downturn in the economy the increase might be only £20 000.

Inez and Pilar estimate that variable production costs constitute 30% of sales value. If they take over the neighbouring premises there will be additional fixed costs of £15 000 per year.

You are required to advise Inez and Pilar on whether or not they should expand their production facilities, using calculations to support your arguments.

19.20A Ince Pargeter Limited manufactures padded carrying cases for laptop computers. The market is currently buoyant, and the company's factory is working to capacity. The company has been offered the opportunity to compete for a contract for 10 000 cases per year at a selling price of £15 per case. This is below the company's usual selling price of £17.25. Variable costs of manufacture would be the same as for existing cases, i.e. £5.63. However, in order to be able to take on the contract the company would need to expand its production facilities. For technical reasons it would be impossible to expand production to increase capacity to produce exactly 10 000 additional units. The expansion of facilities would increase capacity to the point where 20 000 additional units could be manufactured. Ince Pargeter's sales director thinks it is possible that he may be able to obtain additional orders that will use up the spare capacity. If production facilities were expanded, fixed costs would rise from £283 000 to an estimated £390 000.

You are required to advise the company on whether or not it should expand its production facilities.

19.21 Juniper Jefferson Limited manufactures two models of baby buggy: the De Luxe and the Super De Luxe. There is currently a shortage of the special grade of aluminium required for the buggy frame. This is unlikely to be a long-term problem, but it will affect production over the next three months.

The cost and selling price information for each model is as follows:

	De Luxe £	Super De Luxe £
Selling price	150	165
Variable cost of raw materials		
Aluminium (at £8.50 per kg)	38.25	42.50
Other raw materials	12.50	15.00
Variable cost of labour	13.65	15.60

The company has 350kg of aluminium in stock and expects to be able to buy no more than a further 1000kg per month for the next three months.

You are required to:

i) Calculate the contribution per unit of limiting factor for both models of buggy.

ii) Advise the directors on the production plan they should follow, assuming that:

a) demand for the De Luxe will be 800 units over the next three months, with demand for the Super De Luxe at 300 units over the same period; or

b) demand for the De Luxe will be 600 units over the next three months, with demand for the Super De Luxe at 400 units over the same period.

19.22A Jackson Demetrios Limited manufactures three different types of office desk. Type A has extra drawers, type B has a printer shelf and type C has a moveable footrest.

In the company's present factory, production facilities are limited and there is a restriction on the number of machine hours available. The directors have considered moving to larger premises, but they are unwilling to make the move just at the moment because of fears of a downturn in the office furniture market.

Cost and selling price information for each type of desk is as follows:

	Type A £	Type B £	Type C £
Selling price per unit	175	160	165
Variable materials costs			
Wood	37	35	35
Plastics	16	15	18
Screws and fixings	2	2	2
Variable labour costs	18	16	16
Machine hours required per unit	2.5 hours	2.0 hours	2.1 hours
Sales demand for 20X6	1 400	1 600	1 550

Machine hours available are 4000 hours during 20X6. You are required to:

i) Advise the directors on the most profitable production plan available to them without further expansion of the premises.

ii) Calculate the overall contribution to fixed costs (to the nearest £) if your recommended production plan is followed.

Answers to exercises

19.1   Billericay Ashworth Limited

i) Cost classification

The cost of raw materials is a variable cost; the cost of factory insurance is a fixed cost; telephone charges are a semi-variable cost.

ii) Graphs

For the graph of raw materials cost, two points are plotted:

● cost of raw materials at zero production: £0
● cost of raw materials at 3000 production level: $3000 \times £13 = £39\,000$.

Figure 19.15

Billericay Ashworth Limited: Raw materials cost

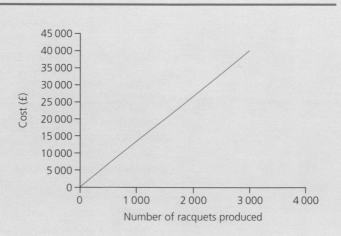

For the graph of factory insurance, two points are plotted:

- cost of factory insurance at zero production level: £800
- cost of factory insurance at 3000 production level: £800.

Figure 19.16

Billericay Ashworth Limited: Factory insurance

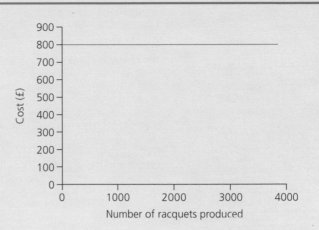

For the graph of telephone charges, three points are plotted:

- Telephone charges where no calls made: £1000 (i.e. basic rental charge).
- Telephone charges where 500 calls are made: £1250 (i.e. basic rental charge of £1000 + £250 in call charges).
- Telephone charges where 1000 calls are made: £1500 (i.e. basic rental charge of £1000 + £500 in call charges).

Figure 19.17

Billericay Ashworth Limited: Telephone charges

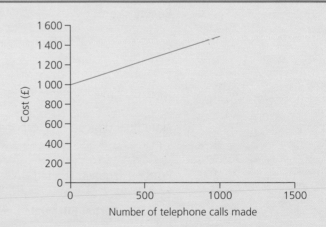

Note that the activity level in this case is the number of calls made: we have no information that links call charges with the level of production or any other measurement of activity.

19.3 Cost classification

i) Sales staff members' mobile phone charges: semi-variable cost.

ii) Factory machine oil: it depends! This would probably be a relatively minor cost and would, in practice, be treated as part of fixed factory costs. However, the more the machines are used, presumably the more oil they consume, so it could be argued that this cost is variable with production. It would depend upon the particular circumstances.

iii) Metered water charges: this is a variable cost based upon the number of units consumed.

19.4   Examples of fixed and variable costs

Type of business	Examples of fixed and variable costs
Self-employed taxi driver	*Variable costs* Petrol or diesel Replacement parts for cab
	Fixed costs Accountancy and tax advisory charges Cab licence
Solicitor	*Variable costs* Stationery costs (e.g. files for holding documents) Overtime payments to staff called out to attend clients in police custody
	Fixed costs Rental of office premises Employment costs of secretarial staff
Shirt manufacturer	*Variable costs* Cost of shirt material Labour costs (if variable such as piece rates)
	Fixed costs Sewing machine depreciation charges Factory heating charges
Beauty salon	*Variable costs* Cost of beauty products Stationery costs (e.g. cost of appointment cards)
	Fixed costs Staff salaries Business rates

Note how difficult it is, especially in service businesses, to think of significant variable costs.

19.6   Porton Fitzgerald Limited

Porton Fitzgerald Limited: Budget statement for April 20X4

	£
Sales: 450 wardrobes × £210 each	94 500
Variable costs	
Direct materials: 450 wardrobes × £52	(23 400)
Direct labour: 450 wardrobes × £34	(15 300)
Contribution	55 800
Fixed costs	(43 200)
Net profit	12 600

19.8 Fullbright Bognor Limited

i) Break-even chart

For the break-even chart for the year ending 31 December 20X1 the points plotted are:

Production level	Fixed costs £	Total costs £	Total revenue £
0	62 000	62 000	0
3 000	62 000	185 000	255 000
		(£62 000 in fixed costs + [3 000 × £41])	(3 000 × £85)

ii) Break-even point estimates

Reading from the chart, the break-even point in units lies somewhere between 1000 and 2000 units, at around 1400 to 1500 units. The sales value appears to be around £120 000. (Note: the larger the scale chosen for the graph, the more accurate the estimate of break-even is likely to be.)

iii) Break-even points at end-December 20X1

	£
Selling price per unit	85.00
Variable costs per unit	41.00
Contribution per unit	44.00

$$\text{Break-even point (in units)} = \frac{\text{Fixed costs}}{\text{Contribution per unit}}$$

$$= \frac{62\,000}{44.00} = 1409 \text{ units (to nearest whole unit)}$$

The break-even point in sales value = 1409 units × £85 = £119 765.

Figure 19.18

Fullbright
Bognor Limited:
Break-even chart

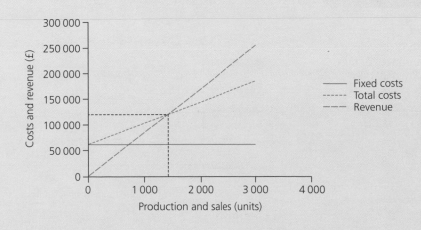

19.10   Foster Beniform Limited

a) Where fixed costs are £40 000

i) Break-even chart

For the break-even chart for 20X8 (fixed costs at £40 000) the points plotted are:

Production level	Fixed costs	Total costs	Total revenue
	£	£	£
0	40 000	40 000	0
2 000	40 000	90 000	110 000
		(£40 000 + [2 000 × £25])	(2 000 × £55)

ii) Break-even point estimates

Reading from the chart, the break-even point in units appears to be around 1300 units; the break-even point in sales value appears to be around £73 000.

iii) Formula calculations

	£
Selling price per unit	55.00
Variable costs per unit	25.00
Contribution per unit	30.00

$$\text{Break-even point (in units)} = \frac{\text{Fixed costs}}{\text{Contribution per unit}}$$

$$= \frac{40\,000}{30.00} = 1333 \text{ units (to nearest whole unit)}$$

Break-even point in sales value = 1333 units × £55 = £73 315.

Figure 19.19

Foster Beniform Limited: Break-even chart (fixed costs at £40 000)

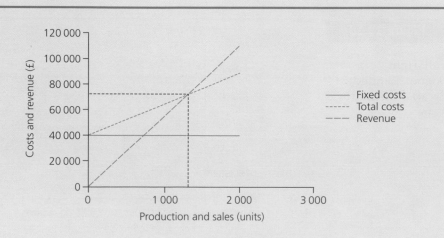

b) Where fixed costs are £50 000

i) Break-even chart

For the break-even chart for 20X8 (fixed costs at £50 000) the points plotted are:

Production level	Fixed costs £	Total costs £	Total revenue £
0	50 000	50 000	0
2 000	50 000	100 000	110 000
		(£50 000 + [2000 × £25])	(2000 × £55)

ii) Break-even point estimates

Reading from the chart, the break-even point in units appears to be around 1700 units; the break-even point in sales value appears to be around £90 000.

iii) Formula calculations

	£
Selling price per unit	55.00
Variable costs per unit	25.00
Contribution per unit	30.00

$$\text{Break-even point (in units)} = \frac{\text{Fixed costs}}{\text{Contribution per unit}}$$

$$= \frac{50\,000}{30.00} = 1667 \text{ units (to nearest whole unit)}$$

Break-even point in sales value = 1667 units × £55 = £91 685.

Figure 19.20

Foster Beniform Limited: Break-even chart (fixed costs at £50 000)

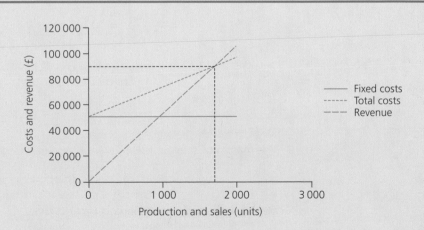

19.12 Gropius Maplewood Limited

	£
Selling price per unit	150
Variable costs per unit	(63)
Contribution per unit	87

$$\text{Break-even point (in units)} = \frac{\text{Fixed costs}}{\text{Contribution per unit}}$$

$$= \frac{90\,000}{87} = 1034 \text{ units}$$

The correct answer, therefore, is d).

19.14 Gimball Grace Limited

Target net profit for 20X3: £36 500 × 110% = £40 150.
Contribution per unit = £21.00 (selling price) − £7.50 (variable costs) = £13.50.

$$\text{Target sales in units} = \frac{\text{Fixed costs} + \text{Target profit}}{\text{Contribution per unit}}$$

$$= \frac{54\,000 + 40\,150}{13.50} = 6\,974 \text{ units}$$

The correct answer, therefore, is a).

19.16 Garbage Solutions Limited

Contribution calculation:

	£
Selling price per unit	25.00
Less: variable labour costs	(3.20)
Variable raw materials costs	(4.20)
Contribution per unit	17.60

$$\text{Break-even point} = \frac{\text{Fixed costs}}{\text{Contribution per unit}}$$

$$= \frac{178\,900}{17.60} = 10\,165 \text{ units.}$$

$$\text{Target sales in units} = \frac{\text{Fixed costs} + \text{Target profits}}{\text{Contribution per unit}}$$

$$= \frac{178\,900 + 83\,150}{17.60} = 14\,889$$

The margin of safety is the difference between target sales and break-even sales:

$$14\,889 - 10\,165 = 4724$$

The correct answer, therefore, is d).

19.18 Harrison Haworth Limited

The contribution per unit from the rucksack designed for the Moroccan market would be:

	£
Selling price per unit	50.00
Variable costs per unit	(26.30)
Contribution per unit	23.70

The contribution per unit is a positive figure, therefore the advice to management, based solely upon the accounting figures, would be to accept Raoul's order. This advice would be appropriate provided that spare production capacity was available and provided the level of fixed costs would not increase. What non-financial factors should be taken into consideration?

The sales of this special order are all to Morocco; therefore it is quite likely that UK and Scandinavian buyers would not find out that similar rucksacks were available at a substantially lower price. The fact that the specification is lower also helps; if UK or Scandinavian buyers were to ask why the rucksacks were priced so much lower in Morocco, it would be quite reasonable to point out that the product was of a different quality (although the difference in variable costs is only £2.70 between the two grades of product, suggesting that the quality difference is not very great).

Would the company suffer if it became known that it was offering a product of lesser quality? This is a factor that needs to be borne in mind by producers of high quality goods. However, as noted above, the quality differential is not likely to be very noticeable.

In the circumstances, the company should consider seriously accepting Raoul's order, although the sales director might like to investigate Raoul's assertions regarding the Moroccan market. Is it really true that there would be few buyers in Morocco at the company's normal prices? Or is Raoul just saying this to beat the company down on price?

19.19 Inez & Pilar Fashions Limited

Because fixed costs increase with the increase in production capacity, it is necessary to look at the level of incremental profits that could be made. We can examine these at two levels:

Optimistic incremental sales forecast

	£
Sales (£345 000 − 310 000)	35 000
Incremental variable costs: £35 000 × 30%	(10 500)
Incremental fixed costs	(15 000)
Incremental net profit	9 500

Pessimistic incremental sales forecast

	£
Sales	20 000
Incremental variable costs: £20 000 × 30%	(6 000)
Incremental fixed costs	(15 000)
Incremental net loss	(1 000)

Clearly, if the pessimistic forecast is accurate a net loss will be incurred by expanding the production facilities. However, at most levels of incremental sales some profit would be made. Unless the directors are very averse to taking risks, and/or they feel that the pessimistic forecast is the most likely outcome, it is probably worth expanding production facilities.

Other factors to take into account would be:

- Could the additional capacity be used to produce new product lines?
- Is the current constraint on production capacity causing problems with customers? (If customers are becoming impatient because of delays in production there may be a loss of goodwill; this could be an argument in favour of expanding the facilities even if there is a small risk of an incremental loss.)

19.21   Juniper Jefferson Limited

i) Contribution per unit of limiting factor

	De Luxe	Super De Luxe
	£	£
Selling price	150	165
Variable cost of raw materials		
Aluminium (at £8.50 per kg)	(38.25)	(42.50)
Other raw materials	(12.50)	(15.00)
Variable cost of labour	(13.65)	(15.60)
Contribution per unit	85.60	91.90
Kilos of material used		
De Luxe: £38.25/8.50	4.5	
Super De Luxe: £42.50/8.50		5
Contribution per unit of limiting factor	85.60/4.5	91.90/5
	= £19.02	= £18.38

ii) Production plan

The directors should follow a production plan that produces the De Luxe model in preference to the Super De Luxe, where possible.

The availability of the raw material in the next three months is:

	kg
Already in stock	350
3 month's purchases	3 000
	3 350

If all of this material were to be used in the production of De Luxe buggies, it would be possible to make 3350/4.5 = 744 De Luxe buggies (rounded down to the nearest whole number).

a) If demand for the De Luxe is 800 units, then it makes sense to turn production over completely to the production of the De Luxe (800 > 744).

b) If demand for the De Luxe is 600 units, then the maximum 600 should be produced. This would mean using 600 × 4.5kg = 2700kg of the scarce raw material, leaving 3350 − 2700 = 650kg for producing Super De Luxe buggies.

So 650kg would produce 650/5 = 130 Super De Luxe buggies at a rate of usage of 5kg per buggy. The production plan would thus be:

De Luxe = 600
Super De Luxe = 130.

20

PRICING

AIMS AND LEARNING OUTCOMES

Aim of the chapter

To understand the principal factors involved in setting selling prices by reference to a broad range of industry examples.

Learning outcomes

After reading the chapter and completing the related exercises, students should:

- Understand the interaction between supply and demand and the interdependence of price and quantity.
- Understand the various additional factors that play a part in pricing decisions.
- Understand the interface between pricing and costing, with especial reference to cost-plus pricing.
- Be able to apply knowledge of pricing issues across a range of industries and commercial activities.

The importance of pricing

So far, this part of the book has concentrated upon the various elements and classifications of cost with the aim of appreciating the importance of management accounting information that permits management to plan and control the business and make informed decisions.

In a commercial organisation, run with a view to profit, pricing is also of great importance. If prices are set too low to cover costs in the medium to long term, the business will suffer, and may even fail. In this chapter we will introduce some of the most important elements of decision making related to pricing.

The relationship between price and quantity

In fundamental economic terms, supply and demand are critical elements in the determination of prices. In a pure market environment, scarcity of supply of a commodity pushes up prices; lower available quantities command higher prices. Conversely, plentiful supply results in lower prices. There is, therefore, a theoretical interaction between quantity and price, which can be illustrated graphically (see Figure 20.1).

In the figure, two sets of lines have been drawn. Set #1 describes the supply of a lower quantity of goods; the relative scarcity is reflected in a higher price. Sets #2 and #3 describe a position of progressively higher supply which results in a relatively lower price. If a large number of price/quantity relationships are plotted the price/quantity relationship emerges. This is usually referred to as the **demand curve**.

The relationship described in the graph is an economist's representation of reality; it is an economic model of the relationship between price and quantity. How well does this neat graphical representation relate to reality? In practice, much depends upon the nature of the commodity traded, the degree of competition in the market and the context in which it is supplied. It is possible to observe, in general terms, examples of such a relationship in the real world. For example, in the United Kingdom the price of strawberries in the summer months (when strawberries grown in the United Kingdom are available in large quantities) tends to be lower than in the winter months when the supply is smaller (because the only available strawberries are imported). However, it is

Figure 20.1

Demand

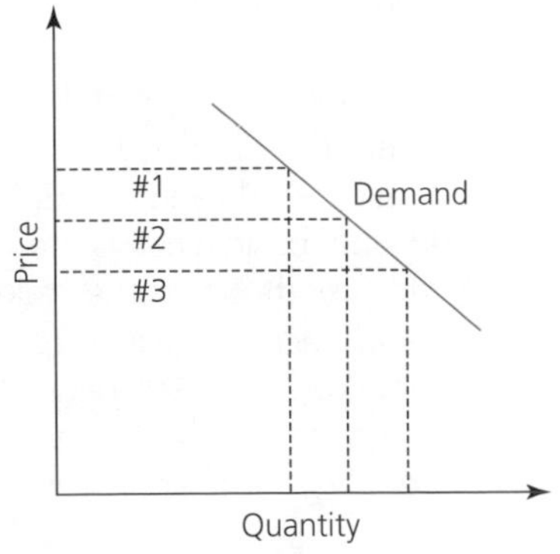

usually quite difficult to observe the classic relationship between price and quantity in operation.

Elasticity and inelasticity

Demand is described by economists as elastic where:

● Customers are relatively indifferent about the product (because, for example, there are many identical or close substitutes in the market).
● The demand is highly sensitive to changes in price.

By contrast, demand is inelastic where:

● Customers place a high value on the product.
● Demand is relatively insensitive to price (i.e. it takes a substantial increase in price to have any effect on demand).

Problems in applying the economic model to the real world

The model represented by the graph in Figure 20.1 takes account of only two variables – price and quantity. However, in the real world other complexities frequently come into play. For example, the effects of:

● *Advertising*. If advertising is effective it can affect both demand and the price that people are willing to pay for a commodity or service.
● *Novelty*. A new product on the market can often command higher prices initially simply because of its novelty value.
● *Fashion*. An item that is widely perceived as more fashionable may be able to command a premium price.
● *Reputation*. A good brand name may command a premium price.

Sometimes, in practice, several of these factors interact.

Example 20.1

The Skoda story

'Classic. Comfort. Elegance. It can only be Skoda. Pardon me? Skoda?' (from an article by Malcolm Baylis: 'Have I got the name right?' at **www.carkeys.co.uk**, 29 December 1999).

Skoda, a company based in the Czech Republic, for many years manufactured cars that sold principally in eastern Europe. Sales in western Europe were low, because the company was dogged by a reputation for unreliability and drab design. However, once Skoda joined the Volkswagen Group of companies, the situation started to change.

Volkswagen cars have acquired a reputation for quality and reliability over a period of many years. Many people are willing to pay relatively high prices for this particular brand. Volkswagen re-engineered a new line of Skoda cars, using the same basic chassis design as for other VW group members (Seat and Audi included). Since the redesigned models have come onto the market Skoda sales and prices have increased, and the cars hold their value well on the second-hand market. In 1999 the author of the article quoted above noted that 'Skoda is no longer the cheapo car. The sales pitch today is not the price but definitely the quality, with company chiefs confident that quality will eventually see off the

▶

public's jibes that still, sadly, accompany the Skoda name.' Since then, a series of adverts has employed humour in what appears to have been a successful attempt to challenge the brand name problems head-on.

So, the demand for these cars, and their prices, have increased because of the public perception of a real change in quality. Although the Skoda brand name is still a disadvantage, advertising has effected a change in attitudes towards the company's products. A complicated mix of advertising, fashion, price change, quality change and change in brand reputation has resulted in higher sales volumes in western Europe.

In addition to the complex combinations of factors that affect price, there are other problems that arise in real-world attempts to apply the simple economic model:

- *Lack of information.* In most cases, it is very difficult to obtain accurate information as to the effect on prices of a change in demand, because these are theoretical effects. The model may be useful in helping to broadly predict the direction of price movements, but it is difficult to know with any degree of precision how much a change in price, for example, will affect demand.
- *Product range.* As noted, it is very difficult to obtain accurate information about the interaction of price/quantity/demand. This becomes even more difficult where large numbers of products are concerned. Most businesses produce a range of products or services, some of which may differ only slightly from each other. Management, in most cases, will simply lack the huge resources that would be required to accurately estimate demand over a range of conditions.
- *State of competition in the market.* The number and nature of competitors in the market will affect prices. These effects are examined in more detail in the next sub-section.

Competition in the market

The more suppliers in the market, the more competitive the environment. In such conditions, a state approaching 'perfect competition' is likely to exist. Because there are many suppliers, no individual supplier can set prices at a significantly higher level. Prices and supplies will easily reach an equilibrium state in which dramatic movements are unlikely to take place.

There may be special competitive conditions, however, in the markets for some products.

Special competitive conditions

Monopoly

A **monopoly** exists where only one supplier supplies the market with a particular good or service. The monopolist can take advantage of this unique position in raising prices to a high level. Regulation by the state often seeks to ensure that a monopoly position cannot arise. For example, proposed mergers between businesses are often carefully examined by regulatory authorities who have the authority to block any merger that would lead to a single, monopoly supplier in a market.

Oligopoly

An **oligopoly** exists where there are few suppliers (between, say, three and five) in the market for the supply of a particular good or service, and where market shares are fairly evenly spread out. An example of oligopoly exists in the provision of accounting services. Although there is a proliferation of accounting firms in the UK and worldwide, most of them are very small practices. There are only four major international firms that can genuinely compete for the business of accountancy advisory services to multinational corporations. Where oligopoly exists, there is a danger of reduced competition in the market and stagnation of prices. Regulators often take a keen interest in oligopolistic market conditions and will carefully assess the competitive implications of proposed mergers between members of an oligopoly. Nevertheless, oligopolies are found in many industries.

Cartel

A **cartel** is a price-fixing arrangement where a few major suppliers in a market agree between themselves to keep prices high. This is widely regarded as anti-competitive and in most market economies regulations exist to outlaw cartels. Currently, in the UK the law allows for very substantial fines to be levied on companies involved in price-fixing arrangements, and the UK Treasury has recently proposed that those found guilty of operating cartels should be subject to the penalty of imprisonment.

In the UK the Competition Commission is the authority that examines cases of alleged anti-competitive practice, which is defined by several different pieces of legislation (for example, the Competition Act 1998). The work of the Commission is described in detail on the website at **www.competition-commission.org.uk**.

Price setters and price takers

The position of an individual business in the market may determine whether or not it has any control over prices. In an intensely competitive market, with many suppliers of goods or services, there may be little scope for an individual supplier to separate from the pack. Sometimes markets are dominated by a few large suppliers, trailed by a large number of smaller providers. In such cases, a small provider of goods or services is unlikely to be able to influence prices; this type of provider is known as a **price taker**; they have to take the prices determined by the more powerful players in the market. By contrast, a **price setter** does not have to accept the prices set by other people.

How do producers decide on prices?

As we have just seen, price takers have little scope for making decisions on prices. What about price setters? Theoretically, producers and suppliers of goods and services should have regard to demand and to market conditions. Some producers do examine the market. However, the practice of cost-based pricing is surprisingly common. In this section, we will first examine market-based pricing and then look at cost-based pricing.

Market-based pricing

If market information is available or can be obtained at relatively low cost, businesses should use it. Sometimes pricing is based upon perceptions (and experience) of market demand that have little, if anything, to do with costs.

Example 20.2

Merchandising at rock concerts

How do rock artists make money out of touring? A 2001 newspaper article explains that although ticket prices tend to be high, they are often not the principal source of revenue as far as the band itself is concerned. Costs of running tours and the high prices charged by the venues themselves often eliminate most, if not all, of the revenue from tickets. 'This is borne out by the price of merchandise. Programmes alone at Madonna concerts cost £25 each. At Iron Maiden concerts fans regularly pay £280 for branded jackets which are thought to cost less than one-fifth of that to produce' ('Rocking all the way to the bank', by John Cassy, *The Guardian*, 17 August 2001, page 24).

In each of the cases cited in the article, competition is not really a factor. The goods are unique. The Iron Maiden fan who pays for a branded jacket at the premium price of £280 is not concerned that he or she can buy a similar, unbranded jacket on the market for a great deal less. The brand is what counts.

In some circumstances, however, competition is important and pricing by competitors may be clearly visible. For example, supermarket businesses frequently compete with each other on price. It is, obviously, easy to determine what the competition is charging for a basket of products because prices are visibly displayed. There are relatively few supermarket businesses, and it is not clear that people will always go to the cheapest – other factors such as the range of goods on sale and the general brand identity matter, too. Nevertheless, the level of pricing in such markets is often an important factor in securing sales.

Cost-based pricing

Cost-based pricing, as the term implies, is the fixing of the price for a product or service based upon the cost of providing it. However, cost-based pricing cannot usually be undertaken without any reference at all to the market, especially in the longer term. If a cost-based price results in a product with a very much higher price than similar or identical products in the market, there is likely to be a problem. If the higher costs result from inherent inefficiencies or defects in the manufacturing process the business is likely to fail.

Sometimes international inequalities, very often in the price of labour, result in businesses either being priced out of a particular market, or having to change their source of supply. One of the reasons for the relative decline of manufacturing industry in the UK has been the availability of cheaper labour elsewhere. Firms have often moved their entire manufacturing operation into other countries where labour costs are lower.

Cost-plus pricing

As the name implies, this approach to pricing first establishes the cost and then adds on a 'plus' factor – the required level of profit.

Example 20.3 Binnie Fairweather Limited makes a range of commercial ovens for sale to hotels and restaurants. The company uses a cost-plus approach to pricing. Variable costs of producing an oven are:

	£
Direct materials	49.60
Direct labour	61.30
Other variable costs	21.50
	132.40

The company absorbs production overheads on the basis of machine hours used. Fixed production overheads for the current year are estimated at £695 000 and total machine hours are 25 000 for the year. Each oven uses 1.5 machine hours. Binnie Fairweather requires a profit of 25% on total cost.

The fixed production overhead absorption rate is:

$$\frac{695\,000}{25\,000} = £27.80$$

Selling price is calculated as follows:

	£
Variable costs	132.40
Fixed costs: fixed production overheads	
£27.80 × 1.5 machine hours	41.70
Total costs	174.10
Profit mark up: £174.10 × 25%	43.53
Selling price	217.63

Binnie Fairweather may be more or less flexible in relation to this calculated selling price. If the company looks around the other suppliers in the market it may see that selling prices for similar ovens are no more, generally, than £200. The company then has a choice: if it is in a price setting position it may decide to go ahead and market the product at approximately £218 or even higher, based upon factors such as:

● good brand name
● better quality (perceived or actual)
● a carefully targeted marketing campaign.

In fact, the selling price which is arrived at through application of cost-plus pricing may be simply a starting-off point in a long process of determining an appropriate price.

There are several disadvantages of cost-plus pricing:

● Absorption costing may not give a particularly accurate estimate of the fixed costs related to a product. As we have seen in previous chapters, allocation and apportionment of fixed costs can be quite arbitrary and may lead to incorrect decisions.

- The absorption rate is set in advance; it may prove to be quite seriously inaccurate, in which case pricing decisions based on full cost-plus calculations may prove, in retrospect, to be less than optimal.
- The emphasis on costs may result in firms failing to consider market conditions properly. Where the market is highly competitive, even a small price differential could result in a large fluctuation in sales. Fluctuations in volume of sales and production could result in significant misallocation of fixed costs, thus adding to the absorption costing problem already identified.
- In industries where cost-plus pricing is widely accepted as a basis for establishing contractual arrangements, inefficiency may actually be rewarded. Under cost-plus pricing arrangements, the higher the cost the higher the profit margin.

In order to address the problem of the unreliability of absorption costing for this type of decision making, the company could add a higher mark-up to the variable cost only.

Example 20.4 The directors of Binnie Fairweather have concluded that cost-plus pricing on the basis of total cost is simply too unreliable. They have therefore decided to use variable cost as a base, with a mark-up of 55% of the variable cost total.

This approach produces the following selling price:

	£
Variable costs	132.40
Add: profit mark up: £132.40 x 55%	72.82
Selling price	205.22

Whether or not this selling price is more realistic, given current market conditions for the company, would be a matter for the directors to decide. Again, this price might just be a starting point for the decision-making process.

Examples 20.3 and 20.4 illustrate cost-plus pricing in a manufacturing environment. This method is also commonly found in retail and service businesses. For example, a retailer may apply a standard mark-up to products in a particular category. In the case of service businesses a standard hourly charge is often applied to time spent on a particular customer's business. This is likely to be based upon an allocation of total costs of the business over the number of productive service hours available, plus a mark-up. Provided the resulting standard hourly charge is reasonably competitive, the cost-plus approach is likely to work well.

Variable cost-based pricing

We met this approach to pricing in Chapter 19; it is based upon the decision rule that an offer to buy at a given price should be accepted, provided that there is a positive contribution to fixed costs. This can, in practice, lead to the acceptance by businesses of some extremely low prices.

The information capability offered by the internet has allowed for a new type of purchasing and supply to arise in the case of certain goods and services. For example, hotels are businesses that incur high levels of fixed costs and relatively few variable costs. It is important for their continuing commercial viability that occupancy rates are as high as possible. Because of hotels' cost structure it is possible to sell at very low rates and still make a contribution to fixed costs. Late booking discounts, which can be widely advertised through the internet, allow hotels to sell some of their surplus rooms even if the prices obtained are low.

Example 20.5 A hotel in central London has 420 rooms. It regularly obtains occupancy rates of 80%. Recently, however, the hotel management has decided to advertise rooms via a late booking website. Most of the 420 rooms are double bedrooms with bath and shower; the normal price of an overnight stay, including breakfast, for two people is £165 each. Variable costs are £22.50 per person.

Using the basic decision rule, the position is clear: any price over £22.50 per person would theoretically be acceptable as it would result in a contribution to fixed costs. How low a price the hotel would actually accept in practice is, however, a different matter. If it lowers the price by too much it risks attracting the 'wrong' kind of customer, and thus damaging its reputation. Although the position in theory regarding contribution to fixed costs is clear, in practice the minimum selling price acceptable to the hotel is likely to be substantially in excess of £22.50.

Would the availability of the late rooms service damage the hotel's overall selling price? This would depend on the type of customer the hotel normally attracts. If the rooms are sold well in advance to travel agencies organising tours, for example, the rate offered to the agencies is likely to be very much lower than £165 per room in any case, and the people who occupy the rooms will not usually know how much the agency has paid for them. Business bookings could, however, be damaged; these would often be for only one or two people who would pay something close to the basic £165. If a business person is prepared to take the risk of leaving the booking to the last minute (the risk is that no rooms at all would be available in Central London on the date required) the room could probably be obtained at a substantially lower price.

Special cases

Tendering

Some types of commercial contracts for goods and services are arranged by tender. This is a process that involves several businesses competing for a contract; usually it involves the submission of sealed bids by a certain date and time. The customer opens the tenders on the same occasion, compares prices and conditions, and decides which tender to accept.

The sealed bid system is intended to allow for fair competition, and to give the customer the best opportunity of obtaining a fair price. In this situation, from the supplier's point of view, information about prices in the market is likely to be non-existent or limited (unless the suppliers have banded together in an illegal cartel to artificially adjust prices). Tendering is, therefore, likely to be done on the basis of a cost-plus approach, together with some guesswork about the prices likely to be offered by the competition.

The customer is not obliged to choose the lowest tender price. Sometimes, a supplier will submit a price that is obviously underestimated, perhaps because they wish to obtain the business at very low cost (this may be worth doing, for example, if labour is under-employed at a slack period). Alternatively, they may simply have underestimated what is involved in the contract.

Highly restricted supply of unique products

Some products do not fit particularly easily into either the market-based or cost-based approaches to pricing.

Example 20.6

Pricing original works of art

An original work of art is, by definition, unique. In a sense, each work of art creates its own demand because, until it is created, nobody can know with certainty that they want it or need it. However, once a certain class of works of art is established, a market of a sort may be created, and the market price is tied into intangible factors such as reputation and more obvious and quantifiable factors such as scarcity of supply. For example, the works of Vermeer, the 17th century Dutch artist, are so scarce (there are only 36 definitively attributed paintings) that prices become almost irrelevant; there is, effectively, no supply, although the demand would, presumably, be very high were one of his paintings to reach the market. Demand, in economists' terms, is highly inelastic.

The relationship between supply of works of art and prices does follow the classic economic model to some extent. When an artist with a reputation dies, the prices of his or her works will tend to increase because the supply has now definitively ceased.

Art pricing rarely has anything to do with cost, however great or small the reputation of the artist. A painting, for example, is a piece of stretched canvas, board or paper with pigments in some kind of medium applied to it; variable raw materials costs are unlikely in most cases to be very high. The labour required to produce it is rarely costed by the artist; if it were, the hourly rate would, in most cases, be laughably small. Cost-plus pricing in this case is hardly an option – information is lacking and the intrinsic cost of the product is rarely an issue in a decision to purchase in any case.

Target pricing

This approach to pricing turns cost-plus pricing on its head. A target price is established by reference to the market, not cost. Having set this, the firm will then deduct the desired profit margin on selling price. The residual amount then represents the maximum amount of cost that the firm can incur in producing the product or service. If this amount appears to be too small to accommodate all the associated costs, then the firm makes strenuous efforts to reduce those costs so that the target can be met. This may involve:

- Engaging in general cost reduction programmes to reduce fixed costs to a minimum.
- Re-engineering a product.
- Investing to create additional production efficiencies.
- Making compromises on quality of materials.
- Planning for additional volumes of production so as to reduce unit costs (by means of, for example, taking advantage of discounts for large-scale purchases).

Discounting

Many businesses will give discounts on selling price to reward customer loyalty or to ensure early payment for goods or services supplied on credit. Usually, such discounting reduces the supplier's profit margin by a small amount, but the reduction is balanced by a commensurate benefit.

However, sometimes a business may make a rational decision to sell goods or services at less than the cost of producing them. On the face of it this strategy appears foolish; it would clearly lead to the rapid downfall of the business if done too often over too wide a product range. However, it can make sense where:

- There is a large quantity of stock with a short shelf-life to clear.
- The goods or services are being treated as a loss leader.

Some stock is, by its nature, perishable: food and soft drinks, for example. In other cases, the life of stock is limited by fashion considerations. It usually makes sense for retailers to sell fashion items at the end of a season for whatever they can raise, so that room can be made for the new season's stock.

A **loss leader** product or service is used to attract customer attention to a range of goods or to a particular supplier. Although it does not make long-term sense to provide goods or services at less than cost, a loss leader may help a business to break into a particular market. This occasionally happens on a large scale, as demonstrated by the (fictional) Example 20.7.

Example 20.7 Mills Greaves plc is a supermarket group based in one of the English regions. It has turned in a high level of profits relative to other supermarket businesses, and is currently rich in cash. The company's directors are ambitious for the future of the group, and have planned in detail an expansion programme that will in due course mean that its supermarkets are found in all parts of England and Wales. The directors have targeted a series of smaller towns that do not currently have a supermarket. They will open relatively large premises and will provide a huge range of goods at extremely low prices. The company can afford to bear the losses because of its previous profitability, and, because it is mostly still owned by members of the Mills and Greaves families (most of the directors are family members and shareholders), it is not under pressure to pay a dividend. The strategy is fundamentally to drive out the competition by undercutting prices. Once competitors have been forced into closure, Mills Greaves will be able to raise prices in the new areas and return to previous levels of profitability.

The ethics of this type of business decision may cause some concern, especially because of the proposed scale of the operation. However, any new entrant to a market is likely to try a modified version of this approach, especially if price is the principal distinguishing feature in consumer choice.

Auction

Where prices are established at auction the seller abandons part of his or her control over price setting. For some types of commodity (e.g. art, antiques and certain categories of real estate) selling at auction is the accepted method of contracting; it would not normally apply for new goods. Usually the seller can stipulate a reserve price. For example, a seller sends an antique vase to auction, setting a reserve on it of £1500. This means that if the bidding does not reach that price, the item will not be sold by the auctioneer.

CASE STUDIES   Pricing in context

Rather than examining a single case study, this section of the chapter discusses pricing in the context of four very different cases. The cases illustrate some of the approaches to pricing explained earlier in the chapter.

Building contractor

Aziz & Sons Limited is a firm of building contractors. The company has just been invited to submit a tender for constructing a very large office building. Aziz & Sons would like to get the business, if possible. Although the directors do not know the names of the other contractors on the tender list, they are likely to be able to make an educated guess; there are relatively few competitors who have the capacity to take on a job of this size.

How does the company go about establishing a tender price? In practice, tendering for such contracts is an expensive and lengthy process. The cost of submitting the bid is wasted if the company does not obtain the tender; this is an operating cost that has to be accepted by such companies.

Aziz & Sons' management will have to study the architect's drawings in detail in order to understand what is entailed. They will have to cost raw materials, subcontracted elements of the work (such businesses rarely employ directly all the different trades they need), direct labour, managerial time and, probably, an element of fixed overhead recovery. An estimate of the time taken and a programme of works will also be required. Once the costs are established, a tender price can be discussed, based, probably, upon a cost-plus approach where a mark-up is added. At the end of the process an overall contract price is estimated. However, the senior management may feel at this point that the proposed bid price is simply too high: if it seems likely that competitors will bid less, the costs and the mark-up are likely to be re-examined. Sometimes, this may involve an element of target costing; working back from a bid price that seems feasible, management may look for ways of minimising costs.

In this type of case, establishing a price is a lengthy and expensive process. While the basic approach is likely to involve cost-plus calculations, the price that is finally submitted in the tender will usually have been influenced by market-based considerations as well.

Toothpaste manufacturer

Most people clean their teeth pretty regularly; therefore, toothpaste is a product that is sold in large quantities. It is a good example of a product to which people

◀◀◀

are relatively indifferent, in the sense that they give the purchase little thought. Demand is elastic because purchasers do not place a high value on the product, will accept substitutes relatively easily, and are really not very interested in it. (Contrast the purchase of a tube of toothpaste with the purchase of a new car, for example: which absorbs more of the purchaser's interest?)

Of course, we do not buy toothpaste direct from the suppliers, but almost invariably through the middleman, the retailer. As far as manufacturers are concerned their customers are retailers or wholesalers.

How, then, do manufacturers price their product? If there are many competitors in the market, prices are likely to be kept at a stable level through competition. The manufacturer may not be able to exert very much influence on price. Provided the selling price covers costs and provides some profit, the manufacturer will, presumably, continue to manufacture and sell the product. However, it may not charge the same amount to all customers. Powerful purchasers (like the large supermarket chains) are likely to be in a position to exert influence on the manufacturer's price and to demand discounts for bulk purchases. Smaller purchasers will probably have to pay more.

In the case of a bulk manufacturer of a product for which demand is elastic, price is determined by the market. Some sectors of the market, moreover, are likely to be in a position to demand lower prices; thus, different prices may be paid for the same product depending upon the power and influence of the customer. Although cost is important, in the sense that costs must be covered in the longer term if the manufacturer is to survive, they are less relevant to the pricing decision than in some other types of business.

Writer

Minnie Tanner has just finished her first novel, *Silver Moonlight*, a 'romantic tale of love triumphing over adversity'. Like most writers, Minnie's dream is to have her book published in numerous editions, translated into many languages, with worldwide sales in at least seven figures. Mostly, of course, the dream does not come true. Suppose, for a moment, that Minnie's book is publishable (unlikely) and that she finds someone willing to publish it (highly unlikely). How does Minnie set the price of the book?

The answer, of course, is that, although she is in a sense a producer, she doesn't set the price. In the unlikely event that a publisher accepts the manuscript, the firm will have control over all the details of production and pricing. Minnie's earnings (if any) will be in the form of royalties dependent upon sales, at a royalty rate determined by the publisher. Her only hope of varying this arrangement is if she becomes a really successful author with very high sales. In such cases, which are obviously rare, writers (or more likely, their agents) may be able to command large advances and better royalty deals. Minnie has a long way to go.

How does the publisher set the price of the book? The decision on pricing in this case, is likely to have a lot to do with the market. Romantic novels aren't exactly like toothpaste; there is more differentiation between products, but demand is relatively elastic. It becomes inelastic only once the author has established a faithful following of people who will go into a bookshop for 'the latest Minnie Tanner'; at that point demand for the specific product is assured. However, demand is only relatively inelastic; if the publishers double the price of the book the market probably will not respond by buying it, regardless of price.

Solicitors

Haringay, Fisker and Blott is a firm of solicitors, specialising in matrimonial and property conveyancing work.

How do solicitors establish their prices? Solicitors and other professionals such as accountants, surveyors and business consultants, usually establish charge-out rates, which are used to charge clients on the basis of time spent.

Haringay, Fisker and Blott are all partners in the business; they also employ four full-time solicitors and two legal executives to assist in the conveyancing side of the business – a total of nine fee-earners. Each year, the partners meet to discuss the charge-out rates to be employed in the practice in the coming year. The budget for 20X8 shows total costs of £625 000, which must be covered by income. In addition, of course, the partners wish to make a profit. Their desired mark-up on costs is 25%.

There are three grades of charge-out rate: for partners, staff solicitors and legal executives. During 20X7 the charge-out rates have been £90, £55 and £30, respectively. The partners work on the basis that they and staff are available for 46 weeks per year, 5 days per week, 7.5 hours per day. They aim to be able to charge 80% of available time to clients.

1. By what percentage do the partners need to increase charge-out rates for 20X8 to meet their desired mark-up?
2. What other considerations should the partners take into account in deciding whether or not, and by how much, to increase charge-out rates?

1. Percentage increase

At current rates, provided the estimates of time availability are accurate, accumulated charge-outs could raise the following fee income (based on) time available of 46 weeks × 5 days × 7.5 hours × 80% = 1380 hours per person):

	£
Legal executives: 2 × 1380 × £30	82 800
Solicitors (staff): 4 × 1380 × £55	303 600
Partners: 3 × 1380 × £90	372 600
	759 000

The target total for fees for 20X8 is the budget costs plus a mark-up of 25%:

$$[£625\,000 \times 25\%] + 625\,000 = £781\,250$$

The estimate of available fee income of £759 000 falls short of the target by (£781 250 − 759 000) £22 250. Charge-out rates would have to be raised by:

$$\frac{22\,250}{759\,000} \times 100 = 2.9\%$$

2. Other considerations

The partners would need to take into account the following factors in determining prices:

● *Recovery.* Although charge-out rates are very useful for management accounting purposes within many service businesses, they are sometimes used simply as a basis for establishing the amount of a bill. For various reasons, solicitors may not wish to charge the fees suggested by the bill, or may wish (and be able) to charge more. Usually, a percentage recovery figure will be calculated to indicate the extent to which the fees indicated by the charge-out rate have been recovered. If recovery falls much short of 100% the partners may need to rethink their rates.

- *Competition*. Traditionally, solicitors' fees have been shrouded in mystery. However, with the advent of advertising by solicitors (it used to be prohibited) and a greater willingness on the part of the public to challenge solicitors' bills, competition has become more of an issue. Word of mouth is an important factor for professional practices in gaining new business; if word gets round that Haringay, Fisker and Blott's bills are much higher than average, they could lose business. So, to some extent, price affects demand, and market conditions should be taken into account.

Chapter summary

The chapter began with a brief discussion of the classical economist's model of demand. Several additional factors that complicate the real-world application of the model were described.

The nature of competition was then discussed, and the special cases of monopoly, oligopoly and cartel were described. This was followed by more detailed consideration of market-based and cost-based pricing, including the technique of cost-plus pricing. Despite several disadvantages to the cost-plus approach, cost-plus pricing is widely used.

We considered a range of special cases of pricing:

- tendering
- pricing of unique products
- target pricing
- discounting
- auction.

Finally, a series of four mini-case studies were discussed, as illustrations of the range of pricing techniques and principles that may be adopted in practice. The cases were those of a building contractor, a toothpaste manufacturer, a writer and a firm of solicitors.

Pricing is a difficult area of management decision making. Despite the attractions of the simple demand model, in practice pricing in many industries is more of an art than a science.

Exercises

The answers to most of the exercises are set out later in this chapter. However, where the exercise number is followed by 'A' the answer is available only to lecturers. Remember that additional exercises (with answers) are available to students on the book's website.

20.1   The demand curve plots the relationship between:

   a) selling price and cost

   b) quantity and cost

   c) quantity and selling price

   d) selling price and discounts.

20.2   Demand is described as elastic where it:

   a) is highly sensitive to changes in price

   b) seldom increases or decreases

   c) cannot be met

   d) increases only where there is a substantial change in price.

20.3   An oligopoly exists in cases where:

a) one supplier controls the market

b) about three to five suppliers control the market

c) there are many suppliers of about equal size in the market

d) new suppliers enter the market frequently.

20.4   Auger Ambit Limited is a manufacturing company that sets prices based on total costs plus a mark-up. For the year ending 31 December 20X5 the company is forecasting total fixed costs of £788 000. Variable materials costs will be £18.00 per unit and direct labour costs will be £27.56 per unit. The company expects to produce 20 000 units, and normally looks for a profit mark up of 25%.

Suggest a suitable cost-based selling price per unit of product for 20X5.

20.5A   Ainsley Witt Limited manufactures old-fashioned dolls houses. The manufacturing process is labour intensive and involves a cost of £54 per house. Variable materials costs are £22 per house, and in addition the company pays a royalty per house manufactured of £1 to the designer.

The company's usual level of fixed costs is £125 000 per year. In an average year about 2400 dolls houses will be produced. Ainsley Witt's sales manager has suggested that the company should carry out an exercise to compare the current selling price of £150 for a dolls house with a cost-plus calculation, based upon a target mark-up on cost of 23%.

Calculate the difference between the current selling price and a selling price based upon the cost-plus calculation.

20.6   Belvedere, Bharat & Burgess are in partnership together as accountants. They have recently enlarged their practice and have taken on extra staff. The partners meet to discuss charge-out rates, which currently stand at £110 per hour for each of the three partners, £85 per hour for the five senior staff and tax specialists and £50 per hour for all other grades of qualified accountant (six employees). The partnership operates on the assumption that 75% of hours worked will be chargeable to clients as fees, and that a 43-week year is worked, at 8 hours per working day. Costs are expected to amount to £1 275 000 in the coming year, 20X6.

1. If the partners' assumptions are correct, how much in fees could the partnership expect to bill in 20X6?

2. If hours are worked exactly as planned, the average recovery rate on billing is actually 94%, and total actual costs are 1% above budget in 20X6, how much profit or loss would the partnership make?

20.7A   Burke and Harpur are solicitors who have recently set up in partnership together and are working hard to establish themselves in a town that already has several solicitors. Both have a charge out rate per hour of £65. They are preparing a bill for Mrs Henrietta Higgs, for whom they have recently drafted a will. The bill contains the following items:

	£
Fees for time: 43 hours @ £65	2 795
Taxation specialist's charges for advice	650
Other sundry charges	240
Total	3 685

The partners disagree about how much to charge. Burke thinks that £3685 is a ridiculously high amount to charge for drafting a will, and that if word gets out that the firm charges that much for the service it will badly damage their chances of increasing business. He says they should charge £1500 and be prepared to take the loss.

Harpur worked the majority of the 43 hours noted on the bill. He defends the high charge on the grounds that it is only so high because Mrs Higgs wasted such a lot of time changing her mind about who should inherit her considerable wealth. Also, because she is so rich, she should be able to afford the charges. He adds that he personally doesn't care if Mrs Higgs doesn't use their services again because she was so difficult to deal with.

Discuss the points of view of the two partners on this pricing problem. Which partner do you think is correct?

20.8   Discuss the key factors that would arise in determining selling prices for:

a garden centre

a small grocery store that is open for 24 hours.

20.9A   Discuss the key factors that would arise in determining selling prices for:

a plumber (sole trader)

a biscuit manufacturer.

Answers to exercises

20.1   The demand curve plots the relationship between quantity and selling price. The correct answer, therefore, is c).

20.2   Demand is described as elastic where it is highly sensitive to changes in price. The correct answer, therefore, is a).

20.3   An oligopoly exists in cases where about three to five suppliers control the market. The correct answer, therefore, is b).

20.4   Auger Ambit Limited

$$\text{Fixed costs per unit} = \frac{788\,000}{20\,000} = £39.40$$

Cost-plus calculation:

	£
Variable materials cost per unit	18.00
Variable labour costs per unit	27.56
Fixed costs per unit	39.40
Total costs per unit	84.96
Profit mark-up: £84.96 x 25%	21.24
Selling price	106.20

20.6   Belvedere, Bharat and Burgess

1. Fees billed

The partnership could expect to bill fees (based on time available: 43 weeks × 5 days × 8 hours × 75% = 1290 hours per person) as follows:

	£
Accountants: 6 × 1 290 × £50	387 000
Senior staff and tax specialists: 5 × 1 290 × £85	548 250
Partners: 3 × 1 290 × £110	425 700
	1 360 950

2. Recovery rate of 94%

If the average recovery rate on billing is 94% this means that the partnership has not been able to recover all of the hours charged by its staff and partners.

	£
Billed: £1 360 950 × 94%	1 279 293
Costs: £1 275 000 × 101%	1 287 750
Loss for 20X6	(8 457)

20.8   Selling prices

A garden centre

The managers of a garden centre will have regard to local competition in setting selling prices. If there is little competition it may be possible to charge higher prices. In the long run, of course, the business must be able to cover all of its costs. It would be normal practice for the management of such a business to apply a standard mark-up on cost.

Probably, cost-based pricing will be the principal price-setting strategy, but management will also keep an eye on the competition. Even if competitors are charging lower prices, management may feel justified in charging more if, for example, it offers complementary services such as garden design, a coffee shop and a bookshop.

A small grocery store, open for 24 hours

Generally, convenience stores are able to charge relatively high prices, simply because of the additional convenience they offer. Much depends upon the competition, of course. Now that many large supermarkets are offering 24 hour service, a small grocery store may find that it has to bring down prices in order to be able to compete.

There is a cost element to take into account in setting pricing; in a 24-hour business labour must be employed at highly unsocial hours, and there may be a wage premium to pay (although the extent of this depends upon the local employment market, availability of hard-up students to work through the night and so on). Additional costs have to be met either by increasing selling prices or reducing profit margins.

21

CAPITAL INVESTMENT DECISIONS

AIMS AND LEARNING OUTCOMES

Aim of the chapter

To investigate the techniques used by business managers to make decisions on capital investment.

Learning outcomes

After reading the chapter and completing the related exercises, students should:

- Understand the concept of capital budgeting and the need for control over capital investment decision making.
- Understand and be able to apply two simple methods of capital investment appraisal: payback and accounting rate of return.
- Understand the time value of money.
- Understand and be able to apply more complex methods of capital investment appraisal: net present value and internal rate of return.

What is capital investment?

Over the past few chapters we have examined many aspects of the control of costs, and we have examined short-term decision making involving contribution and pricing. Most businesses, however, are concerned not only with short-term costing decisions, but also with decisions that have an impact over the longer term. As well as expenditure on fixed and variable costs, business managers must make decisions about spending on capital items. Capital expenditure is expenditure on items such as fixed assets and investments in other businesses; its distinguishing feature is that it involves appraisal of profits and cash flows generated over more than one accounting period.

Capital expenditure includes, for example, purchase of land and buildings to be used for the business over several years, and purchase of plant and machinery, fixtures and fittings, computers and equipment that will be of benefit to the business over periods in excess of one year.

It is important to appreciate that the point of this type of expenditure is to generate extra profits for the business. If the expenditure does not contribute to business profitability it should not be made. Sometimes, it is not easy to see the connection; how, for example, does buying an extra filing cabinet for the accounts department contribute to business profitability? The argument for the purchase would probably be along these lines:

> A new filing cabinet will help the accounting department to keep its customer invoices in better order. Therefore, queries from customers can be answered more quickly and efficiently, and proper filing will ensure that copy invoices don't get lost so easily. If our response to customer queries improves, it makes it more likely that good relationships with customers will be maintained. The new filing cabinet therefore makes a positive contribution to the business.

And so on. Try arguing for the income generating potential of a new rubber plant or a coat stand for the reception area. (Be creative ...)

Capital budgeting

Capital expenditure can be of really significant proportions in a business, and it is important that it should be properly controlled. A decision to invest in a new building, for example, represents a major commitment of resources by the business and such a decision cannot be taken lightly.

The general principles of planning, control and decision making are by now familiar to us. In Chapter 15 we established the need for management to set business objectives and to assess alternatives and make decisions. Capital expenditure must also fit into the general framework of the business's strategy and objectives.

While it is obviously the case that larger investment decisions require more careful thinking and deliberation, many businesses in practice subject capital expenditure at all levels to scrutiny. It is often the case that even quite small amounts of capital expenditure require approval at high level. The reasons for such detailed scrutiny and approval include the following:

- Small items may appear individually insignificant, but taken together, may amount to a significant sum of expenditure;
- Managers at all levels are often quite keen to acquire small status symbols (a new printer, a desk, a comfy chair); unless these items are carefully controlled, the business may waste money.

Capital expenditure should always be geared towards meeting the strategic objectives of the business, and a capital budget should emerge as part of the overall budget procedures which we examined in Chapter 17.

Capital rationing

Businesses need to obtain the finance that is used to make capital investments. Finance may be available from the existing resources of the business. However, if available cash is employed for a capital investment project it cannot be used for anything else; managements need to be sure that the capital investment is the best available use of the resources. If the business has little cash, it may have to borrow in order to invest in capital assets and projects. Borrowing costs money in the form of regular interest payments and, of course, it cannot be infinitely expanded (there is a point, for both businesses and individuals, beyond which it is neither sensible nor practical to borrow more money). Whether finance comes from existing resources or from outside the business, management is likely to have to face difficult decisions about which assets and projects are to be preferred. In conditions of **capital rationing** it is important that management should have clear criteria, linked to overall strategic objectives, in order to make capital investment decisions.

Capital investment appraisal in practice

Most of the remainder of this chapter will be devoted to an examination of the principal techniques used by managers to make capital investment decisions in practice. We will examine four principal methods, all of which are widely used in practice:

- accounting rate of return (ARR)
- payback
- net present value (NPV)
- internal rate of return (IRR).

All of the methods involve assessing the initial investment required against future returns from the investment. Because investment appraisal looks forward into the future some elements of estimation and imprecision are unavoidable. Also, as in the case of short-term decision making, there are always other, unquantifiable factors to take into account. The calculations can never give a definitive answer; they merely provide input into the decision-making process.

In order to be able to compare the application of the four methods we will use a single, common example. First, the example will be explained in detail so that readers can understand how the figures are derived and estimated.

Example 21.1 Proctor Hedges Limited manufactures a wide range of gardening equipment. It has recently developed a new design of compost bin. A market research project costing £20 000 was undertaken in which the prototype was demonstrated to a large number of gardeners at show gardens around the country. Results of the market research have been very promising. In addition, the company's marketing director has used his contacts to have the new design prominently featured in a prime-time television gardening programme. The programme is due to appear in three months' time, and the company expects to receive a large number of orders very soon afterwards. The directors have decided that they must gear up production to be ready for the anticipated demand for the new product. The principal capital expenditure involved would be the purchase of an advanced plastics moulding machine. The existing factory site has ample spare room for the machine, and no significant additions to fixed costs are anticipated.

The production director has investigated the available machines, and has decided that the choice comes down to two alternatives, which he has imaginatively code-named Machine A and Machine B. Information about the two machines is as follows:

	Machine A	Machine B
	£	£
Capital outlay	450 000	600 000
Residual value at end of 5 years	50 000	100 000
Straight-line depreciation per year	80 000	100 000
Machine hours per year	80 000	120 000

Each compost bin takes two machine hours to manufacture; therefore the maximum capacity available is:

Machine A = 40 000 units per year
Machine B = 60 000 units per year.

The sales director estimates that demand will be greatest in the first couple of years. After that, it is likely that sales will tail off, as other new composting products are introduced to the market by competitors. After five years the product will probably have reached the end of its commercial life and will be discontinued. The machine could then be sold for its residual value, or, possibly, be transferred at net book value into some other line of production.

Demand figures are estimated as follows for the five-year production cycle:

Year	Demand
1	60 000
2	48 000
3	42 000
4	25 000
5	25 000

Machine A could not produce sufficient items to meet demand in the first three years. However, the directors decide that they would, nevertheless, like to consider the purchase of Machine A because it requires only three-quarters of the capital outlay of Machine B.

The costings prepared by the finance director show that compost bins produced by Machine A would be expected to make a profit per unit (before

▶

depreciation) of £4.00. Machine B is a more efficient user of raw materials and so would be expected to make a profit per unit (before depreciation) of £4.10.

Establishing relevant information for the appraisal

The basic requirement is that we assist the directors in making their choice between the two machines by use of investment appraisal techniques.

Even in a simple example like this one, there is a great deal of information. For investment appraisal purposes we need to take into account only relevant information. The cost of the market research project (£20 000), for example, is not information that is relevant to the decision. This may seem odd at first sight: why should it not be taken into account? The answer is that the costs have already been incurred and are therefore not relevant to the decision; they are known as **sunk costs**.

The directors must take into account only those costs and future revenues that are relevant to the decision between the machines – i.e. only incremental costs and revenues. Any costs or revenues that would have occurred in any case are irrelevant to the appraisal of the project. For each year of the life of the project the net cash inflow or outflow must be calculated. This involves adding together all the incremental revenues and taking away all the incremental costs.

In real life, taxation is often a significant item of cash inflow or outflow. In this chapter we will ignore the effects of taxation as being beyond the scope of this book. However, students should realise that if they encounter investment appraisal in practice, or go on to study accounting at a higher level, taxation will be an important element of appraisal calculations.

Timing

There are widely accepted conventions in respect of timing for capital investment appraisal.

The first event that would take place after the decision is made would be the outflow of cash to be spent in buying the machine. Capital investment appraisal techniques make the assumption that the cash is spent now, immediately, and 'now' is referred to as Time 0. The capital investment would generate costs and revenues in the future over a five-year (in this example) period. There is a further simplifying assumption that all costs and revenues are incurred on the last day of the year at Time 1, Time 2, Time 3 and so on.

These assumptions about timings are necessary in order to keep the calculations manageable, but it should be recognised that they introduce a further element of imprecision into the appraisal.

Assembling information for the appraisal

First, we will establish an estimated production and sales schedule for each of the two machines:

Year	Demand	Machine A production and sales	Machine B production and sales
1	60 000	40 000	60 000
2	48 000	40 000	48 000
3	42 000	40 000	42 000
4	25 000	25 000	25 000
5	25 000	25 000	25 000

Because Machine A has a maximum production capacity of 40 000 units per year, it cannot meet demand. It will produce up to capacity for the first three years (120 000 units as opposed to demand of 150 000). It is assumed that dissatisfied customers will not wait for a compost bin (people are not likely to put their name down on a waiting list for this type of product) and will simply buy another type.

Once we have established sales and production figures, we can estimate profits before depreciation for each of the five years, as follows:

Year	Machine A	Machine B
1	40 000 × £4.00 = £160 000	60 000 × £4.10 = £246 000
2	40 000 × £4.00 = £160 000	48 000 × £4.10 = £196 800
3	40 000 × £4.00 = £160 000	42 000 × £4.10 = £172 200
4	25 000 × £4.00 = £100 000	25 000 × £4.10 = £102 500
5	25 000 × £4.00 = £100 000	25 000 × £4.10 = £102 500
Total profit	£680 000	£820 000

Having tabulated this basic information we will now examine each of the capital investment appraisal techniques in turn.

Accounting rate of return

The accounting rate of return (ARR) method uses projections of accounting profit to calculate the expected rate of return on capital invested into an asset or project. It is calculated as follows:

$$\frac{\text{Average expected return (accounting profit)}}{\text{Average capital employed}} \times 100 = \text{ARR}\%$$

Calculating average expected return (accounting profit)

Accounting profit, as we have seen earlier in the book, takes depreciation into account. Therefore, we must deduct depreciation from each of the annual profit figures calculated earlier, before calculating the average profit over five years:

Year	Machine A £000	Machine B £000
1	160 − 80 = 80	246 − 100 = 146
2	160 − 80 = 80	196.8 − 100 = 96.8
3	160 − 80 = 80	172.2 − 100 = 72.2
4	100 − 80 = 20	102.5 − 100 = 2.5
5	100 − 80 = 20	102.5 − 100 = 2.5
Total profit	280	320

The average profit per year generated by Machine A is:

$$\frac{280\,000}{5} = £56\,000$$

The average profit per year generated by Machine B is:

$$\frac{320\,000}{5} = £64\,000$$

Calculating average capital employed

The capital employed figure to be taken into account is the capital employed by the project or investment (*not* the capital employed by the whole business).

In this particular example, because the straight-line method of depreciation is adopted, the capital investment is assumed to be depleted by the same amount each year (£80 000 for Machine A and £100 000 for Machine B). Therefore, we take initial capital employed (at Time 0) and capital employed by the end of the final year of operation (Time 5) and average the two figures, as follows:

Time	Machine A £000	Machine B £000
0	450	600
5	50	100
Average	$\frac{450 + 50}{2} = £250$	$\frac{600 + 100}{2} = £350$

We now have both elements necessary for the calculation (average accounting profit and average capital employed) of ARR. For Machine A:

$$\text{ARR} = \frac{56\,000}{250\,000} \times 100 = 22.4\%$$

For Machine B:

$$\text{ARR} = \frac{64\,000}{350\,000} \times 100 = 18.3\%$$

The ARR calculation shows Machine A as the better of the two options. Although Machine B is estimated to produce more profit, the average investment is considerably higher. If the directors were only to use this one method of investment appraisal they might very well opt for Machine A. Note, however, that the comparison of ARR ignores the fact that Machine B actually produces a higher absolute profit (£64 000) than that produced by Machine A (£56 000). This is a notable weakness of the ARR technique.

Students may well have spotted the similarity between the calculation of ARR and that of return on capital employed (ROCE) which was examined in Chapter 14. When calculating ROCE we looked at figures for the business as a whole. Proctor Hedges Limited will, of course, have a ROCE figure for the business as a whole. If ROCE is substantially in excess of the ARR of 22.4% the directors may wish to think again about the whole project. If a project is undertaken that produces an ARR that is lower than ROCE, the ROCE percentage will be reduced overall.

The Proctor Hedges example requires comparison between two investments. However, sometimes only one possible investment is appraised (because the choice is simply between making the investment and not making the investment). In such cases it is common to find ARR being judged against a yardstick or target return percentage. If the proposed investment's ARR is less than the target then the investment may well be rejected.

Payback

Payback is a simple investment appraisal technique that involves estimating the length of time it will take for cash inflows to cover the initial investment outflow. This can be a useful technique where one of management's principal criteria is the ability of a project to 'pay for itself' quickly, so that proceeds can be reinvested in other projects.

Note that payback appraises investments in terms of cash inflows and outflows. Because depreciation is neither an inflow nor an outflow (remember: depreciation is an accounting adjustment) it is not taken into account.

Payback is relatively simple to calculate:

Time	Machine A £000	Machine B £000
Initial outflow		
0	−450	−600
Inflows		
1	+160	+246
2	+160	+196.8
3	+160	+172.2
4	+100	+102.5
5	+100	+102.5
5*	+50	+100

*Note that at the end of year 5 the machine will be sold, or transferred into alternative production at net book value. An inflow of the amount of the net book value is therefore included.

Payback is calculated by taking cumulative cash flows into account, and identifying the point at which the net cumulative cash flow reaches zero. For Machine A:

Time	Cash flow £000	Cumulative cash flow £000
0	−450	−450
1	+160	−290
2	+160	−130
3	+160	+30
4	+100	+130
5	+100 + 50	+280

Cumulative cash flow reaches the zero position sometime during the third year. We can estimate a figure for payback expressed in years and months as follows:

Payback = 2 years + (130/160 × 12 months) = 2 years and 10 months
(to nearest whole month)

For Machine B:

Time	Cash flow £000	Cumulative cash flow £000
0	−600	−600
1	+246	−354
2	+196.8	−157.2
3	+172.2	15
4	+102.5	+117.5
5	+102.5 + 100	+320

Cumulative cash flow reaches the zero position sometime during the third year (as for Machine A). Estimating a figure for payback expressed in years and months:

$$\text{Payback} = 2 \text{ years} + (157.2/172.2 \times 12 \text{ months}) = 2 \text{ years and } 11 \text{ months}$$
$$\text{(to nearest whole month)}$$

Comparing the payback measures, we can see that Machine A pays back only slightly more quickly than Machine B. Payback, then, is unlikely to play a major part in this particular investment decision.

Payback is a popular method of appraisal in practice, but it has a major limitation in that it concentrates attention on only one important aspect – the ability of an investment to pay back quickly. As we can see from the Proctor Hedges example, cash flows beyond the point of payback are completely ignored. Surely these later cash flows should be taken into account in investment appraisal?

Net present value, which we examine next, does take into account all of the cash flows associated with an investment.

Net present value

In order to understand the net present value (NPV) technique of investment appraisal, we must first gain an appreciation of the importance of time in examining long-term investments.

The time value of money

The principle of the time value of money rests on the observation that £1 now is not the same as £1 in a month's time or a year's time or 10 years' time. The effect of interest is illustrated in the examples below.

Compounding

A saver puts £100 in the bank on 1 January 20X0. The bank's interest rate is 10% throughout the whole of the year which follows: when the interest is paid on 31 December 20X0 the saver now has £110 in the account. If £110 is kept in the account for the whole of the next year following – 20X1 – and the interest rate remains stable at 10%, by 31 December 20X1 the saver has accumulated:

$$£110 \text{ (at 31 December 20X0)} + \text{Interest for 20X1 } (10\% \times £110) = £121$$

Each year, provided the saver keeps both the original investment and the accumulated interest in the bank, the interest compounds. The amount of interest earned each year gradually increases. The five-year effect, assuming a constant interest rate of 10%, as follows:

Year	Balance at start of year	Interest for year	Balance at end of year
1	100.00	10.00	110.00
2	110.00	11.00	121.00
3	121.00	12.10	133.10
4	133.10	13.31	146.41
5	146.41	14.64	161.05

So, £1 at Time 0 (the beginning of year 1) is the equivalent of £1.61 at the end of year 5.

The compounding effect can be expressed via a formula derived as follows. Using 10% as an example:

$$£1 + (£1 \times 10\%) = £1.10$$

Removing the £ symbols:

$$1 + (1 \times 10\%) = 1.10$$

Simplifying:

$$1 + 0.1 = 1.1$$

So, the initial sum invested $\times$ (1 + the rate of interest) = amount at the end of year 1. That is:

$$1 \times (1 + i)$$

where i = the interest rate (expressed as a decimal, e.g. 0.10 rather than 10%).

Test this out by reference to the example of £100 invested at 10% for one year:

$$£100 \times (1 + 0.1) = £110$$

What about a formula for year 2? For the total at the end of year 2 we take the amount at the end of year 1 $\times$ (1 + the rate of interest) = amount at the end of year two. That is:

$$1 \times (1 + i) \times (1 + i)$$

Or:

$$1 \times (1 + i)^2$$

Test this out by reference to the example of £100 invested at a rate of 10% per year for two years:

$$£100 \times (1 + 0.10)^2 = £100 \times (1.21) = £1.21$$

The formula for year 3 adds another compounding factor:

$$1 \times (1 + i) + (1 + i) + (1 + i)$$

Or:

$$1 \times (1 + i)^3$$

And so on. The formula for the compounding factor is expressed as follows:

$$(1 + i)^n$$

where i = the rate of interest and n = the number of years. For each combination of interest rate and number of years, we can work out a compounding factor. For example, what is the compounding factor for £1 invested at a constant rate of 4% over 3 years? Answer:

$$(1 + 0.04)^3 = (1.04) \times (1.04) \times (1.04) = 1.125$$

So £1 invested at a constant rate of 4% over 3 years will result in a balance at the end of year 3 of £1.125.

Self-test question 21.1 (answer at the end of the chapter)

1. Write down the formula for £1 invested at a constant rate of 8% for 4 years and, using a calculator, work out the compounding factor.
2. Write down the formula for £1 invested at a constant rate of 7% for 5 years and, using a calculator, work out the compounding factor.
3. Write down the formula for £1 invested at a constant rate of 6% for 6 years and, using a calculator, work out the compounding factor.

Discounting

In the example and discussion of compounding we noted that, at a constant rate of 10%, £1 invested now (at Time 0) is the equivalent of £1.61 by the end of year 5. Conversely, we could say that £1.61 at the end of year 5 is the equivalent of £1 now. Also, we can say that £1.10 at the end of year 1 is the equivalent of £1 now. How can this be expressed in a formula?

Discounting formulae are the reciprocals of compounding formulae. So, we noted earlier that, at a constant rate of 10% the initial sum invested $\times$ (1 + the rate of interest) = amount at the end of year 1. That is:

$$1 \times (1 + i)$$

We can turn this round to discount back from the end of year 1:

$$\text{Amount at the end of year } 1 \times \frac{1}{(1 + i)} = \text{amount of the initial sum invested}$$

Similarly, taking the reciprocal of the year 2 compounding formula:

$$\text{Amount at the end of year } 2 \times \frac{1}{(1+i)^2} = \text{amount of the initial sum invested}$$

The formula for the discount factor is:

$$\frac{1}{(1+i)^n}$$

where i = the rate of interest and n is the number of years.

For each combination of interest rate and number of years, we can work out a discounting factor. For example, what is the discounting factor for £1 at the end of year 3, which has been invested since Time 0 at a constant rate of 4%? Answer:

$$\frac{1}{(1+0.04)^3} = \frac{1}{(1.04) \times (1.04) \times (1.04)} = 0.88$$

So, £1 at the end of year 3, which has been invested since Time 0 at a constant rate of 4%, is equivalent to:

$$£1 \times 0.88 = £0.88\text{p at Time } 0$$

So £0.88p is the **present value** of £1 at the end of year 3 at a discount rate of 4%.

A table showing the value of the discount factors at a range of interest rates and time periods is set out in the appendix at the end of the chapter. Make sure that you can understand how the figures are derived.

Self-test question 21.2 (answer at the end of the chapter)

1. Write down the formula to show the present value at Time 0 of £1 at the end of year 3 at a discount rate of 2%. Then, using a calculator, work out the discounting factor.
2. Write down the formula to show the present value at Time 0 of £1 at the end of year 5 at a discount rate of 4%. Then, using a calculator, work out the discounting factor.
3. Write down the formula to show the present value at Time 0 of £1 at the end of year 2 at a discount rate of 9%. Then, using a calculator, work out the discounting factor.

Applying the time value of money in investment appraisal

Using the technique of discounting we can express all future cash flows in the same terms, which allows us to take into account the time value of money and to compare like with like.

Before we can recalculate the cash flows for the Proctor Hedges example, we need to know the discount rate. Assume that the directors use a discount rate of 10% for investment appraisal (later in this section there will be a brief discussion of the factors managers must take into account in determining an appropriate discount rate).

In order to express all the cash flows in the same terms (i.e. in terms of the present value at Time 0 of future £s of cash flow) we take each anticipated cash flow for each of the machines and calculate present value using the appropriate discount factor.

Machine A

The first cash flow is assumed to arise at Time 0, i.e. the original investment of £450 000. Because this is already at Time 0 the effective discount factor is 1.

$$£450\,000 \times 1 = \text{cash outflow of }£450\,000\text{ at Time 0}$$

The next cash flow event is at the end of the first year. From the table in the appendix we can see that the discount factor at 10% for one year is 0.909. Applying the discount factor to the year 1 cash flow (remember that all of the cash inflow is assumed to arise at the end of year 1):

$$£160\,000 \times 0.909 = £145\,440$$

We continue to discount the cash flows using discount factors that decrease as the cash flow events recede into the future. Setting the figures out neatly in a table:

Time	Cash flow £	Discount factor (from table)	Discounted cash flow £
0	(450 000)	1	(450 000)
1	160 000	0.909	145 440
2	160 000	0.826	132 160
3	160 000	0.751	120 160
4	100 000	0.683	68 300
5	150 000	0.621	93 150
Total			109 210

The total of £109 210 is known as the **net present value** (NPV); it is the total of the cash inflows and outflows associated with the investment (hence 'net'), all discounted and expressed in terms of £s at Time 0 (hence 'present value').

Machine B

Time	Cash flow £	Discount factor (from table)	Discounted cash flow £
0	(600 000)	1	(600 000)
1	246 000	0.909	223 614
2	196 800	0.826	162 557
3	172 200	0.751	129 322
4	102 500	0.683	70 008
5	202 500	0.621	125 752
Total			111 253

The net present value of the investment in Machine B is estimated at £111 253. The basic decision rule that is employed in respect of NPV is:

If NPV > 0 accept the project or investment

Or, where there is more than one alternative project or investment:

Accept the project or investment with the larger (largest) NPV

In this case, Machine B produces a slightly larger NPV, and so looks preferable to the investment in Machine A. (Note that both ARR and payback indicate that Machine A is the better investment!)

Ratio of cash inflows to initial investment

In deciding between investment projects it can be helpful to look at the relationship between the discounted cash flows generated by a project against the initial outflow of cash.

Machine A

Total positive discounted cash flows generated = NPV + initial investment:

$$= £109\,210 + £450\,000 = £559\,210$$

(If this step seems complicated, just add up all the positive present values of cash flows from years 1 to 5 inclusive – it will give the same answer.) The ratio of the positive cash flows to the initial investment is:

$$\frac{£559\,210}{450\,000} = 1.24$$

Machine B

Total positive discounted cash flows generated = NPV + initial investment:

$$= £111\,253 + £600\,000 = £711\,253$$

The ratio of the positive cash flows to the initial investment is:

$$\frac{£711\,253}{600\,000} = 1.19$$

Machine A gives the higher ratio. This means that it produces more positive cash inflow relative to the initial investment. Although the NPV of Machine B is, overall, slightly higher, the calculation of this ratio points towards Machine A as a better investment.

Establishing a discount rate

Proctor Hedges Limited uses a discount rate of 10%. How have the directors arrived at this figure?

A rate of 10% represents an acceptable return for the activities in which the business is engaged. Suppose the general bank interest rate in the economy is 4%: why does Proctor Hedges expect to make more than that? The answer relates to risk. Investing in a business undertaking is a riskier venture than putting money in the bank. Normally, banks can be relied upon to survive and to carry on paying interest at the advertised rate; a normal savings account rate is more or less risk-free (there is always some level of risk; banks do occasionally fail, but this is an unlikely eventuality in most developed economies). A business investor is taking much more of a risk and therefore expects to be rewarded by a greater return in the form of interest or dividends. The 10% rate may be Proctor Hedges' best guess at the risk-free rate plus a premium for the level of risk actually incurred by the company.

Another helpful way of looking at the problem is to consider the alternatives. If Proctor Hedges invests in Machine A it needs to either borrow £450 000 or to take £450 000 out of existing resources. If there is an alternative use for that money that will yield 10% then the cost of the money is (at least) 10%. The cost of money for a particular business is known as its **cost of capital**.

Determination of the cost of investment for a particular company is one of the most complex problems in business finance. It is beyond the scope of this book to go into further detail, and in the exercises in the remainder of this chapter we will assume a discount rate without further discussion.

Internal rate of return

The final investment appraisal technique that we will examine is the internal rate of return (IRR). This technique is closely related to the NPV technique that we have just examined. The IRR of an investment or project is the expected yield (expressed as a percentage). IRR is the discount rate, which, applied to expected cash flows, produces an NPV of zero.

This can be quite hard to understand, so we will illustrate the point by means of a graph. Using the example of Machine A, we can see that at a discount rate of 10%, a positive NPV of £109 210 results. What happens if we calculate NPV using, say, 12%, 14%, 16%, 18% and 20%? The following NPVs have been calculated at each of these rates:

| | NPV |
Interest rate	£
10%	109 210
12%	82 790
14%	58 410
16%	35 960
18%	14 990
20%	(4 540)

Note: the workings for NPV at 10% are shown in the previous section of the chapter. The workings for the discount rates 12% to 20% are not shown. Use the tables to obtain the discount factors and calculate the NPV at each discount rate. Make sure that you can confirm the NPV results in the table above. (To save time, use a spreadsheet.)

We can see that, as the discount rate used in the calculation increases, the total NPV of the project decreases to the point where it becomes negative. The internal rate of return lies somewhere between 18% and 20%. Plotting these points onto a graph produces the result shown in Figure 21.1. The points plotted show a gentle curve. The point at which the curved line passes through the x axis (discount rate %) is the point of IRR. The graph confirms the observation we have already made from the figures: the IRR of Machine A lies just below 20%.

How can we arrive at a more accurate figure for IRR? There are two principal methods: (a) linear interpolation; and (b) using a computer.

Figure 21.1

Net present value of Machine A cash flows at various discount rates

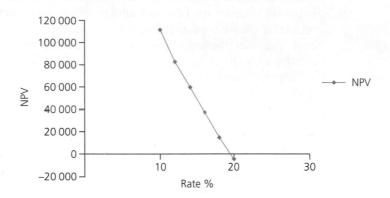

Linear interpolation

We take the two figures from the series that are closest to zero:

Using a discount rate of 18% NPV = £14 990
Using a discount rate of 20% NPV = (£4 540).

The total distance between these two figures is £14 990 + 4 540 = £19 530.
This total of £19 530 represents the whole range possible between 18% and 20%. Expressed diagrammatically:

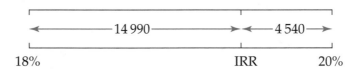

The distance between 18% and IRR is:

$$\frac{14\,990}{19\,530} \times 2\% = 1.54\%$$

The distance between IRR and 20% is:

$$\frac{4\,540}{19\,530} \times 2\% = 0.46\%$$

IRR is 18% + 1.54% = 19.54% (or alternatively: IRR is 20% − 0.46% = 19.54%: it amounts to the same).

Using a computer

This is so much easier than linear interpolation! IRR can be calculated easily via a spreadsheet program such as Excel.

List the times and cash flows in consecutive descending columns in the spreadsheet and then execute the IRR command. In Excel the command is:

$$= \text{IRR(Range)}$$

For the Machine A data, the IRR calculated by the computer is 19.53%. This is slightly different from the result arrived at by linear interpolation; usually there will be a small difference. However, where the estimation of cash flows into the future is so imprecise (and it always is imprecise) there isn't much point in getting too concerned about precision in calculating IRR.

Machine B

We will repeat all of the above steps for Machine B. The following NPVs have been calculated at each of the same discount rates as for Machine A:

	NPV
Interest rate	£
10%	111 253
12%	79 142
14%	49 093
16%	21 625
18%	(4 083)
20%	(27 989)

We can see that the IRR lies somewhere between 16% and 18%. Plotting these points onto a graph, Figure 21.2 confirms the observation we have already made from the figures: the IRR of Machine B lies about three-quarters of the way between 10% and 20%.

Linear interpolation: Machine B

We take the two figures from the series that are closest to zero:

Using a discount rate of 16% NPV = £21 625
Using a discount rate of 18% NPV = £4 083.

The total distance between these two figures is £21 625 + £4 083 = £25 708

This total of £25 708 represents the whole range possible between 16% and 18%. Expressed diagrammatically:

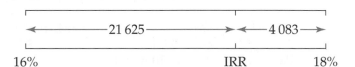

| 16% | IRR | 18% |

Figure 21.2

Net present value of Machine B cash flows at various discount rates

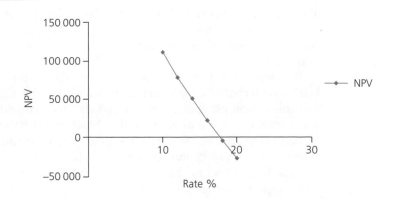

The distance between 16% and IRR is:

$$\frac{21\,625}{25\,708} \times 2\% = 1.68\%$$

The distance between IRR and 20% is:

$$\frac{4\,083}{25\,708} \times 2\% = 0.32\%$$

IRR is 16% + 1.68% = 17.68% (or alternatively: IRR is 18% − 0.32% = 17.68%: it amounts to the same).

Using a computer: Machine B

For the Machine B data, the IRR calculated by the computer is 17.68%.

Significance of IRR for decision making

Where IRR is greater than the business's cost of capital the project is acceptable. If, as in the example, a choice has to be made between two possible projects, the one with the higher IRR is preferable.

In the Proctor Hedges example, the Machine A project produces an IRR of 19.53%, whereas the Machine B project produces an IRR of 17.68%. Both are well in excess of the 10% used by the company and so both projects would be acceptable. However, Machine A produces the better IRR rate, and so is preferable.

Choosing between projects

The application of the four methods of investment appraisal to the example of Proctor Hedges produces the following results:

Method	Machine A result	Machine B result	Choice
ARR	22.4%	18.3%	Machine A
Payback	2 years 10 months	2 years 11 months	Machine A
NPV	£109 210	£111 253	Machine B
IRR	19.54%	17.68%	Machine A

Three out of the four sets of results point towards the choice of Machine A (but note that there is little to choose between them in terms of payback). NPV is the exception but in this case the results for the two machines are very similar.

It would seem that Machine A may be the better choice. However, as with all business decisions, the solution indicated by the figures may not be the more sensible once other factors are taken into consideration. A key point for consideration by the directors is that Machine A does not have sufficient capacity to meet demand in the first three years or so of the project. This means that a significant part of customer demand will be unfulfilled. Possible consequences include loss of customer goodwill, bad publicity and a knock-on effect on sales of the company's other products.

On the other hand, if demand for the compost bins proves to have been overestimated, Machine A will emerge, with the benefit of hindsight, as a very much better choice. None of the investment appraisal techniques we have examined in the chapter take account of the relative riskiness of the alternatives. This is a weakness that needs to be recognised by decision makers.

Which of the four techniques provides the most reliable results? The strengths and weaknesses of each of them are examined in the following section.

Strengths and weaknesses of the common investment appraisal techniques

There are some weaknesses common to all of four of the techniques examined. As noted above, the relative risk attached to future cash flows is not taken into account. Also, all of the appraisal techniques are based upon future estimates. As the estimates of cash flow recede into the future they become progressively less reliable. It is possible to accept, for example, that experienced managers are able to make a reliable prediction of the coming year's sales figures, but can they really predict sales figures five years from now with any degree of reliability? The imprecision that inevitably surrounds future figures means that they are open to manipulation by unscrupulous managers (the case study later in the chapter expands on this point).

A further problem about attaching apparently precise values to future predictions is that managers may give the figures more credence than they really merit. The figures can only ever provide a guide to decision making.

The principal strength of all of the techniques described is that they are better than nothing. Managers sometimes make decisions based on 'gut feeling' or 'instinct' or 'experience'. These may not be reliable qualities upon which to base decisions; at least by making some effort to formally appraise projects, managers may be able to avoid making really big mistakes.

In addition to these general points, each of the techniques has its own strengths and weaknesses.

Accounting rate of return (ARR)

Strengths

- Calculation of ARR is very straightforward.
- ARR is a widely used measurement (in the form of ROCE); it is easy to compare the ARR of a particular project with the overall ROCE for a business.
- It is a measurement that non-financial managers can readily understand.

Weaknesses

- ARR treats all future cash flows as equal in weight; it takes no account of the time value of money.
- ARR is calculated on the basis of accounting profits rather than cash flow. It includes the effect of depreciation, an accounting adjustment the nature and timing of which is determined by management.
- As noted earlier in the chapter, ARR fails to take into account the relative size of competing projects.

Payback

Strengths

- Calculation of payback is very straightforward.
- It can be useful where rapid recovery of funding is a priority.
- It is a measurement that non-financial managers can readily understand.

Weaknesses

- Payback treats all future cash flows as equal in weight; it takes no account of the time value of money.
- Where rapid recovery of funding is not a major priority, payback provides little useful information.
- All cash flows beyond the payback point are simply ignored.

Net present value (NPV)

Strengths

- NPV builds the time value of money into calculations.
- Unlike payback, NPV takes all of the future projected cash flows into account.
- NPV is very useful for ranking different projects as it deals in absolute values rather than percentages (which, as in the case of ARR, can give unreliable results).

Weaknesses

- It can be difficult to explain NPV to non-financial managers.

Internal rate of return (IRR)

Strengths

- IRR builds the time value of money into calculations.

Weaknesses

- It can be difficult to explain IRR to non-financial managers.
- Because IRR is expressed in percentage terms it ignores absolute values: 15% return on an investment of £100 000 is fine (£15 000), but not as good in absolute terms as a 12% return on £1 000 000 (£120 000).
- It is not always possible to calculate IRR.

The last point perhaps needs explanation. In the Proctor Hedges example, the pattern of cash flow was an initial major outlay of cash, followed by several years of inflows. Where the pattern of cash flows is more irregular (for example, a net inflow in years one and two followed by a net outflow in year three, followed by another inflow in year four) IRR cannot be used.

The best technique?

Of the four techniques examined in the chapter, NPV appears to have the fewest significant weaknesses and the most obvious strengths. All of the techniques described are used fairly extensively in practice, and many firms will routinely use more than one. The widespread availability of computers, and the fact that many business managers are now highly computer literate, means that the calculations of NPV and IRR no longer present any difficulties.

CASE STUDY 21.1 A competition for investment funding

The case study for this chapter examines the way in which investment appraisal techniques and estimates of future cash flows can be manipulated by managers in practice.

Lawson Pollard Packaging plc manufactures and sells a large range of packaging and office supplies. The company operates on a decentralised basis; its operations are split into three major divisions: cardboard, plastics and office stationery, each of which is responsible for most of its own administration and decision making. A small head office building houses the principal directors and some general administrative functions.

Although each division makes its own day-to-day operating decisions, responsibility for major capital investment decisions is in the hands of the directors at head office (all expenditure over £1000 must be approved by head office). As part of the budgeting process, each divisional management team must decide on how much capital investment they need to request for the coming year. The senior divisional manager prepares a detailed presentation for the directors that explains the purpose of the investment and justifies the amounts requested. On the basis of the presentation and the detailed working papers submitted with it, the directors decide upon whether or not they are going to fund the investment requested. The chief executive, Ernie Lawson, is very much in favour of competitive bidding for the available capital funds; if one of the divisions makes a better case than the other two it will get the lion's share of the capital funding. Ernie believes that the divisions should really have to fight for their funding; he thinks this will stop the management teams getting complacent and lazy and will ensure that funds are used in the most effective way possible.

Doug is the senior manager in charge of the cardboard division. It is now October 20X1 and he is working on the 20X2 budget with his management team. Doug and the cardboard division are having a hard time. Profitability has slipped over the last three years or so; almost half of the machinery used in the factory is fully depreciated, and is performing inefficiently. Production costs are therefore higher than they need to be; raw materials are used less efficiently, and expenditure on repairs and maintenance has shot up. The division is desperately in need of new investment.

Until a couple of years ago, Doug and the senior managers of the other two divisions had a useful informal arrangement that helped to get round Ernie's competitive approach to capital spending. The managers would get together once a year in secret to discuss their capital spending priorities, and would decide between them which bids were most important. The important bids would be polished up carefully and the others ranked as less important would be made to appear less attractive. This arrangement meant that sometimes Doug and the cardboard division got less in capital funding in one year, but Doug was happy enough because he knew that the other managers would let his bids take priority in the next year or two.

All this changed two years ago. Kamal, who had headed up plastics for years, retired and was replaced by a new appointment, Donna. Donna is not yet 30 and has an MBA from a leading business school. Doug has heard Ernie say that Donna's

▶

on the fast track for rapid promotion to the board, and that she could end up heading the whole company when he, Ernie, retires. Doug has never been on the fast track for anything in his entire life. He's in his late 40s and, until recently, has been quite happy at Lawson's. He knows that he's unlikely to get another job now if he leaves the company and he intends to stay put until he can retire.

In each of the previous two years Donna has made brilliant bids for new capital funding for the plastics division; she succeeded in convincing the directors that practically all of the capital spending should be devoted to plastics. Sales of plastics have grown by nearly 30% in each of the two years that she has been in charge and all the financial indicators show that the plastics side of the business is extremely strong.

Doug tentatively suggested to Donna recently that she might hold back on the capital bidding this year to let cardboard and office supplies get a share. Donna won't hear of it; she tells Doug that plastics is the future of the business and she, frankly, couldn't care less about the tribulations of the cardboard division. She is planning another major bid that will soak up practically all of the available funding for 20X2.

Doug is depressed; he can see that unless the cardboard division can make a really persuasive bid this year, a further year of declining sales and profitability will follow, and his personal reputation in the company will sink to an all-time low. He knows that he has to put together a great bid that will be more persuasive than Donna's. He decides to go for something really bold – nothing less than the replacement of the major part of the production line. This will involve purchasing the most up-to-date machinery and completely overhauling the organisation of production. Fewer production line workers would be required, raw materials would be used more efficiently and consequently contribution would increase. While there would be some increase in fixed costs, because of improved quality inspection and general supervision, some categories of cost (like maintenance and repairs) would be substantially reduced. Doug finds himself getting really quite enthusiastic about the plan; he suddenly realises that he's not been putting a lot of effort into the job recently, and that the division could actually perform a lot better if he could get the money to invest.

Doug and his team do some careful work on all aspects of the bid. Doug's assistant, Ron, summarises the work and prepares scenarios based upon two alternatives. The first supposes a modest rate of sales growth and improved efficiency in the factory. The second was specially requested by Doug; it assumes a high rate of sales growth between 20X1 and 20X2 (matching the 30% achieved by the plastics division), with regular increases in the following years, and a very substantial increase in efficiency. Doug examines the cash flows and tells Ron that he should concentrate from now on only on the optimistic scenario.

Ron: But the second one is really wildly optimistic – it assumes that our competitors will make no attempt to prevent us taking market share off them, and that everything will run perfectly in the factory at all times. I mean, how likely is that?

Doug: We've got to pull all the stops out with this one or we'll not get a penny. That pushy Donna wants all the money again this year and we've got to make sure she doesn't get it.

Ron: So, this time it's personal, eh? . . . But Ernie and the others are going to see through this if it looks too unrealistic.

Doug: Not if we do a really thorough job on the back-up. We want detailed sales projections, plans for seeing off the competition, lots and lots of impressive looking supporting graphs and charts and so on. You can manage that, can't you, Ron? I mean, it could make the difference between keeping the division going and us all losing our jobs. It's that serious.

Ron makes no further objections, and gets on with the work. The two sets of figures Ron has prepared are set out in the following table.

Year	Realistic £000	Optimistic £000
0	(7 800)	(7 800)
1	1 380	1 680
2	1 470	1 770
3	1 530	1 860
4	1 590	1 950
5	1 650	2 040
6	1 710	2 130
7	1 770	2 220
8	1 830	2 310
9	1 890	2 400
10	1 950	2 490
10 (sale of plant)	180	300

The company uses the NPV investment appraisal technique. The company's cost of capital is 12%.

The following is required:

i) Calculate the NPVs for the realistic and optimistic sets of figures, and comment on the results.

ii) Discuss the company's approach to appraising capital projects, identifying any particular strengths or weaknesses.

iii) Discuss Doug's plan for handling this year's bid for capital funds for the cardboard division.

Case study solution and discussion

i) NPV calculations

Year	Discount factors (12%)	Realistic £000	Discounted cash flows: realistic £000	Optimistic £000	Discounted cash flows: optimistic £000
0	1	(7 800)	(7 800)	(7 800)	(7 800)
1	0.893	1 380	1 232.34	1 680	1 500.24
2	0.797	1 470	1 171.59	1 770	1 410.69
3	0.712	1 530	1 089.36	1 860	1 324.32
4	0.636	1 590	1 011.24	1 950	1 240.20
5	0.567	1 650	935.55	2 040	1 156.68
6	0.507	1 710	866.97	2 130	1 079.91
7	0.452	1 770	800.04	2 220	1 003.44
8	0.404	1 830	739.32	2 310	933.24
9	0.361	1 890	682.29	2 400	866.40
10	0.322	1 950	627.90	2 490	801.78
10 (sale of plant)	0.322	180	57.96	300	96.60
Total			1 414.56		3 613.50

◀◀◀

Both the realistic and the optimistic projections produce a positive NPV. The realistic ratio of positive cash flows to initial investment is:

$$\frac{9\,214.56}{7\,800} = 1.18$$

The optimistic ratio of positive cash flows to initial investment is:

$$\frac{11\,413.50}{7\,800} = 1.46$$

The optimistic plan, naturally, produces a higher ratio than the realistic plan. However, would it be high enough? If Donna produces a better proposal for the plastics division it is likely to be preferred.

ii) Approach to appraising capital projects

The company's approach to capital investment decisions is highly competitive; it places divisional managers under a lot of pressure. Ernie, the chief executive, encourages this approach on the grounds that it acts as an incentive to management teams. This argument does have some force, and indeed, the circumstances in the case demonstrate a positive strength of the approach; Doug has been goaded by fear of competition into genuinely considering ways to improve the management and operational effectiveness of his division. However, there are several weaknesses in the approach:

- It may mean that one or two divisions are starved of capital funding simply because their managers have poorer presentational skills.
- It may encourage managers to exaggerate the figures in their bids in order to be able to compete with other divisions.
- It has led to collusion between divisional managers in the past; this type of collusion may not be in the best overall interests of the company.
- Senior management should really be looking at capital funding bids with a view to assessing the extent to which they address the strategic objectives of the business. The competitive bidding system may reward the best bids, but it has resulted in the cardboard division operating inefficiently with fully depreciated machinery and demoralised local management. Surely senior management did not intend this situation to develop?

iii) The cardboard division's bid

Doug is proposing to put forward a bid for funding based upon quite unrealistic estimates of future performance. Where local managers are placed under a great deal of pressure, they may react by exaggerating performance, both present and future. This is a step on the road towards outright fraudulent reporting; at the very least Doug's proposal might be regarded as somewhat unethical. Doug, himself, would no doubt argue that he has been forced into this position because of senior management's system of allocating capital funds. He might also argue that, in trying to secure funding for his division, he is ensuring that people keep their jobs (including himself, of course), and that 'the end justifies the means'.

In Chapter 17 we examined some of the adverse effects of budgeting. Capital budgeting is not exempt from these effects, and we can see the downside illustrated in this case study. A system of competitive bidding has resulted in a senior manager in the business trying to subvert the process by projecting figures that are unrealistically optimistic. This cannot be in the best long-term interests of the company. Senior managers should be wary of instituting systems that encourage this type of behaviour.

Chapter summary

This chapter has examined decision making for the longer term. It started by looking at capital investment and capital budgeting, and emphasised the need for capital expenditure to be congruent with the business's overall strategy and objectives. Businesses need to have clear criteria upon which to base capital investment decisions, especially in conditions of capital rationing.

Four appraisal techniques were examined within the context of a single detailed example:

- accounting rate of return (ARR)
- payback
- net present value (NPV)
- internal rate of return (IRR).

The concept of the time value of money must be understood if NPV and IRR are to make any sense. Compounding and discounting were explained at some length, including the use of formulae and the table of discount factors.

The basic decision rules for NPV and IRR were explained; however, it is also important to appreciate that the investment appraisal techniques explained in the chapter must be considered alongside other important factors. The formal appraisal techniques have some general drawbacks – notably, that they all involve the estimation of future cash flows and that they do not take risk into account, except in the general risk element incorporated in the cost of capital.

The strengths and weaknesses of each of the four techniques were listed and discussed. The general conclusion was that NPV is likely to be the most useful technique in practice; however, it was noted that all four are widely used.

The case study for the chapter examined a situation in which a company's system for evaluating capital projects results in some undesirable effects. A divisional manager is tempted to inflate future cash inflow figures in order to make a credible bid against stiff competition for limited capital funds.

In conclusion, we should note that non-financial managers will not often be called upon to make capital investment appraisal calculations. However, they are very often involved in decision making that rests, at least in part, on the application of investment appraisal techniques. Therefore, it is important that students should understand the rudiments of these techniques, and not least, the various weaknesses associated with them.

Answer to self-test question 21.1

1. Formula for £1 invested at 8% over 4 years

$$£1 \times (1.08)^4$$

Compounding factor $= (1.08) \times (1.08) \times (1.08) \times (1.08) = 1.360$

2. Formula for £1 invested at 7% over 5 years

$$£1 \times (1.07)^5$$

Compounding factor $= (1.07) \times (1.07) \times (1.07) \times (1.07) \times (1.07) = 1.403$

3. *Formula for £1 invested at 6% over 6 years*

$$£1 \times (1.06)^6$$

Compounding factor $= (1.06) \times (1.06) \times (1.06) \times (1.06) \times (1.06) \times (1.06) = 1.419$

Answer to self-test question 21.2

1. *Present value (PV) at Time 0 of £1 at the end of year 3 at a discount rate of 2%*

$$PV = £1 \times \frac{1}{(1.02)^3}$$

Discounting factor $= \dfrac{1}{(1.02)} \times \dfrac{1}{(1.02)} \times \dfrac{1}{(1.02)} = 0.942 = 94.2p$

2. *Present value (PV) at Time 0 of £1 at the end of year 5 at a discount rate of 4%*

$$PV = £1 \times \frac{1}{(1.04)^5}$$

Discounting factor $= \dfrac{1}{(1.04)} \times \dfrac{1}{(1.04)} \times \dfrac{1}{(1.04)} \times \dfrac{1}{(1.04)} \times \dfrac{1}{(1.04)} = 0.822 = 82.2p$

3. *Present value (PV) at Time 0 of £1 at the end of year 2 at a discount rate of 9%*

$$PV = £1 \times \frac{1}{(1.09)^2}$$

Discounting factor $= \dfrac{1}{(1.09)} \times \dfrac{1}{(1.09)} = 0.842 = 84.2p$

Exercises

The answers to many of the exercises are set out later in this chapter. However, where the exercise number is followed by 'A' the answer is available only to lecturers. Remember that additional exercises (with answers) are available to students on the book's website.

21.1   A business is considering whether or not to invest in a new factory building. The managers have incurred expenditure of £15 000 on an initial land survey. For capital investment appraisal purposes this expenditure is:

  a) a fixed cost

  b) a relevant cost

  c) a sunk cost

  d) an estimated cost.

21.2 Mellor & Ribchester Limited, a health drinks company, is considering whether or not to invest in a project to develop and sell a new range of fruit teas. Initial expenditure on a range of development expenses will be £150 000 at Time 0 to get the project up and running. Sales of the products will start in year 2, and it is anticipated that annual net cash inflows will be as follows:

	£
Year 2	68 000
Year 3	71 000
Year 4	54 000
Year 5	28 000
Year 6	10 000

Demand for the product is expected to decline after year 6 to the point where it will not be worth continuing production.

The £150 000 of initial expenditure is treated as a fixed asset, to be depreciated on a straight-line basis over 6 years, with an assumption of nil residual value at the end of 6 years.

i) Calculate ARR for the project.

ii) Calculate the payback period for the project.

21.3A Montfort Spelling Limited operates a chain of health clubs. Each year the company opens a club in a new location. For 20X6, the company is examining two possible locations: Broughton Town and Carey City. The directors have collected information about costs and local demographics, and have come up with the following summary of the initial investment required, and cash flows for the subsequent five years. The company's normal policy is to completely refurbish its clubs every five years; it remodels and redecorates the clubs and sells off all the old equipment.

Initial outlay includes the cost of taking out a five-year lease on premises, buying in all the equipment and paying architects and builders to remodel the premises. The net cash inflows from years one to five include estimated takings in annual subscriptions and joining fees, less the costs of employing staff, and various other fixed costs of running the club.

The table below summarises the costs for the two locations:

	Broughton Town £000	Carey City £000
Time 0: initial investment	(630)	(540)
Time 1: net cash inflows	250	242
Time 2: net cash inflows	275	250
Time 3: net cash inflows	280	260
Time 4: net cash inflows	295	270
Time 5: net cash inflows	310	280
Time 5: inflow from sales of equipment	35	30

The initial capital expenditure less the anticipated residual values is to be depreciated on a straight-line basis, in accordance with the company's policy, over five years.

      i) Calculate ARR for each project.

      ii) Calculate the payback period for each project.

      iii) Advise the directors as to which location should be preferred.

21.4 The compounding factor for an investment over 4 years at 3% per year is (to 3 decimal places):

    a) 0.888

    b) 1.093

    c) 0.915

    d) 1.126.

21.5A The compounding factor for an investment over 6 years at 8% per year is (to 3 decimal places):

    a) 1.587

    b) 0.627

    c) 1.595

    d) 0.630.

21.6 At the end of year 4, £312 invested now at an annual rate of 6% interest over 4 years will be worth (to the nearest £):

    a) £394

    b) £387

    c) £372

    d) £418.

21.7A At the end of year 6, £1900 invested now at an annual rate of 17% interest over 6 years will be worth (to the nearest £):

    a) £3 838

    b) £741

    c) £4 874

    d) £2 223.

21.8 The discounting factor for an investment over 3 years at 10% is (to 3 decimal places):

    a) 0.700

    b) 0.751

    c) 0.100

    d) 1.093.

21.9A The discounting factor for an investment over 5 years at 19% is:

    a) 0.419

    b) 0.190

    c) 0.950

    d) 0.810.

21.10 Assuming a constant discount rate of 12%, the present value of £1300 receivable at the end of year 5 is (to the nearest £):

a) £563

b) £520

c) £2 293

d) £737.

21.11A Assuming a constant discount rate of 14%, the present value of £85 000 receivable at the end of year 4 is (to the nearest £):

a) £50 320

b) £47 600

c) £49 045

d) £73 100.

21.12 Naylor Coulthard Limited is considering investing in a major advertising promotion of one of its skincare products. The advertising campaign would cost £250 000, all of which is assumed to be spent at Time 0. The effectiveness of the advertising would be short-lived; it would produce incremental cash inflows only in years 1 and 2. The year 1 net cash inflow is estimated at £196 000. The net cash inflow for year 2 is estimated at £168 000. After the end of year 2 another major advertising campaign would probably be needed to produce further incremental revenues.

The company's cost of capital is 9%. What is the NPV of the advertising promotion project? Does the NPV suggest that the project should be accepted or rejected?

21.13A Nuria Nailsworth Products Limited is a fashion clothing company. Nuria, the chief executive, regularly attends major fashion events in order to spot trends in the market. She has recently returned from a show that featured fake fur waistcoats and she thinks these could be next season's big fashion story. Unfortunately, fake fur tends to clog up the production machinery used in the company's factory, and it will be necessary to make an additional investment of £28 000 in new cutting and sewing machinery. Nuria thinks it quite likely that sales of 6000 waistcoats are achievable in the first year, and possibly up to 2000 in the second year. Her knowledge of fashion trends tells her that after that point the waistcoats will probably be unsaleable except at very heavy discounts. The first 5000 waistcoats will almost certainly sell at full price, and should produce a net cash flow of £4 each. The final 3000 of production may have to be sold at a discount and it is safest to assume that net cash flow will be only £3 per waistcoat. The machinery will be saleable at the end of the second year for around £10 000.

i) Assuming that the company's cost of capital is 13%, what is the NPV of the project?

ii) If Nuria's initial projections were wrong, and only 5000 of the waistcoats could be sold, all in the first year and producing net cash flow of £4 each, what would be the NPV of the project? Assume in this case that the machinery is saleable at the end of the first year for £13 000.

21.14 A company estimates the following net cash inflows and outflows for a capital investment project that is currently under consideration:

Time	£000
0	(680 000)
1	180 000
2	200 000
3	240 000
4	350 000

The company's cost of capital is 12%.

i) Calculate the NPV of the project.

ii) Calculate the IRR of the project.

21.15A A company estimates the following net cash inflows and outflows for a capital investment project that is currently under consideration:

Time	£000
0	(1 650 000)
1	480 000
2	450 000
3	390 000
4	360 000
5	450 000

The company's cost of capital is 8%.

i) Calculate the NPV of the project.

ii) Calculate the IRR of the project.

21.16 Outhwaite Benson Limited runs a chain of hairdressing salons. The company's directors, Linda Outhwaite and David Benson, are considering a proposal to add sunbed facilities to their salons. They have surveyed staff and customers and have found that 55% of their existing customers would consider using the facilities. On the basis of this finding they have constructed a set of costings and revenue projections. The sunbeds would cost £180 000 in total to buy and install; they would have an estimated useful life of 5 years after which they could be sold for £15 000 in total. Linda and David estimate that the net cash inflow arising each year from the sale of time on the sunbeds would be £46 000.

The £180 000 will be lent to the company by the two directors; it is the proceeds of sale of their second home in Italy. If the money is not put into the sunbed project it would be invested in the opening of a new salon. The average yield from a salon is 14% per year, and the directors decide to use this as the cost of capital in appraising the proposed sunbed investment.

i) Calculate the NPV of the sunbed investment project.

ii) Calculate the IRR of the sunbed investment project.

iii) Advise the directors on whether or not they should make the investment, considering any other relevant factors that might have a bearing on the decision.

21.17A Oppenheim Orgreave Limited sells sofas, armchairs and other furniture items from its premises in a retail park. Customers often ask for home delivery to be arranged, and the company has contracted out the service to a series of small delivery firms. The delivery services are of inconsistent quality; customers often ring Oppenheim's to complain that the delivery was late, or that the goods were damaged in transit. Oppenheim's directors have decided that the delivery problem must be properly addressed because the company is losing sales and acquiring a reputation for unreliability. The company's finance director has examined three options:

- *Option 1*. Buy three new delivery vehicles and employ full-time drivers. The initial outlay for the vehicles would be £76 000, and the annual incremental costs of employment, fuel and other motor expenses would be £82 000. At the end of their five-year useful life the vehicles could be sold for £9000.

- *Option 2*. Contract the service out to a single, high quality provider who would take on full responsibility for van purchase, maintenance and other costs, including the employment of drivers. Quotations for the service have been obtained; a good quality service can be purchased under a five-year contract for £105 000 per year.

- *Option 3*. Lease the three vehicles required for the service at a cost of £10 000 per year per vehicle for a term of five years. Fuel and other running costs, and the costs of employing three drivers, would be incurred direct under this option at a total cost of £77 000 per year.

The finance director estimates that an improved service would boost sales. Incremental sales of £113 000 per year would be made under all three options. Oppenheim's cost of capital is 12%.

i) Calculate the NPV for each option.

ii) Advise the directors on the most appropriate course of action, taking into account any other relevant factors.

Answers to exercises

21.1   The £15 000 spent on the initial land survey is irrelevant to the business decision because the expenditure has already been made. This is an example of a sunk cost; the correct answer, therefore, is c).

21.2   Mellor & Ribchester Limited

i) ARR calculations

$$\frac{\text{Average expected return (accounting profit)}}{\text{Average capital employed}} \times 100 = \text{ARR}\%$$

£150 000 of fixed asset expenditure, depreciated over 6 years on a straight-line basis, results in an annual depreciation charge of £150 000/6 = £25 000. This must be taken into account in calculating accounting profit.

Year	£000
1	0 − 25 = (25)
2	68 − 25 = 43
3	71 − 25 = 46
4	54 − 25 = 29
5	28 − 25 = 3
6	10 − 25 = (15)
Total profit	81

The average profit per year generated is:

$$\frac{81\,000}{6} = £13\,500$$

Time	£000
0	150
6	0
Average	150/2 = 75

$$ARR = \frac{13\,500}{75\,000} = \times 100 = 18\%$$

ii) Payback period

Time	Cash flow £000	Cumulative cash flow £000
0	(150)	(150)
1	0	(150)
2	68	(82)
3	71	(11)
4	54	43
5	28	71
6	10	81

Cumulative cash flow reaches the zero position sometime during the fourth year. Payback to the nearest whole month is:

3 years + (11/54 × 12 months) = 3 years and 2 months

Note that the cash inflows in this example do not start until the second year. This does not change the methods of working out ARR or payback.

21.4   The compounding factor for an investment over 4 years at 3% per year is:

$$(1.03)^4 = (1.03) \times (1.03) \times (1.03) \times (1.03) = 1.126.$$

The correct answer, therefore, is d).

21.6   The compounding factor is: $(1.06)^4 = 1.263$. To the nearest £:

$$1.263 \times £312 = £394$$

The correct answer, therefore, is a).

21.8   The discounting factor is:

$$\frac{1}{(1.1)^3} = 0.751$$

The correct answer, therefore, is b).

21.10 The correct discount factor (from tables) is 0.567. The PV of £1300 receivable at the end of year 5, assuming a constant discount rate of 12% is:

£1300 × 0.567 = £737 (to nearest £)

The correct answer, therefore, is d).

21.12 Naylor Coulthard Limited

Calculation of NPV of the advertising promotion project:

Time	Cash flow £	Discount factor (from table)	Discounted cash flow £
0	(250 000)	1	(250 000)
1	196 000	0.917	179 732
2	168 000	0.842	141 456
Total			71 188

The NPV is positive, which suggests that the project should be accepted.

21.14 NPV and IRR calculations

i) NPV at 12% cost of capital

Time	Cash flow £	Discount factor (from table)	Discounted cash flow £
0	(680 000)	1	(680 000)
1	180 000	0.893	160 740
2	200 000	0.797	159 400
3	240 000	0.712	170 880
4	350 000	0.636	222 600
Total			33 620

ii) IRR

12% cost of capital produces a positive NPV. The IRR (the point at which NPV = 0) must therefore be higher than this. Calculating NPV at 16%:

Time	Cash flow £	Discount factor (from table)	Discounted cash flow £
0	(680 000)	1	(680 000)
1	180 000	0.862	155 160
2	200 000	0.743	148 600
3	240 000	0.641	153 840
4	350 000	0.552	193 200
Total			(29 200)

IRR must, therefore, lie somewhere between 12% and 16%.

Using a discount rate of 12% NPV = £33 620
Using a discount rate of 16% NPV = (£29 200)

The total distance between these two figures is £33 620 + £29 200 = £62 820.
Expressed diagrammatically:

The distance between 12% and IRR is:

$$\frac{33\,620}{62\,820} \times 4\% = 2.14\%$$

IRR is 12% + 2.14% = 14.14%

(Note that the IRR according to computer calculation is 14.07%.)

21.16   Sunbed investment project

i) NPV at 14% cost of capital

Time	Cash flow £	Discount factor (from table)	Discounted cash flow £
0	(180 000)	1	(180 000)
1	46 000	0.877	40 342
2	46 000	0.769	35 374
3	46 000	0.675	31 050
4	46 000	0.592	27 232
5	46 000 + 15 000	0.519	31 659
Total			(14 343)

ii) IRR

14% cost of capital produces a negative NPV. The IRR (the point at which NPV = 0) must therefore be lower than this. Calculating NPV at 10%:

Time	Cash flow £	Discount factor (from table)	Discounted cash flow £
0	(180 000)	1	(180 000)
1	46 000	0.909	41 814
2	46 000	0.826	37 996
3	46 000	0.751	34 546
4	46 000	0.683	31 418
5	46 000 + 15 000	0.621	37 881
Total			3 655

IRR must, therefore, lie somewhere between 10% and 14% (but much nearer to 10% than to 14%).

Using a discount rate of 10% NPV = £3 655.

Using a discount rate of 14% NPV = (£14 343).

The total distance between these two figures is £3 655 + 14 343 = £17 998. The distance between 10% and IRR is:

$$\frac{3\,655}{17\,998} \times 4\% = 0.81\%$$

$$\text{IRR is } 10\% + 0.81\% = 10.81\%$$

Note that the IRR according to computer calculation is 10.77%.

iii) Advice

On the basis of the results of the NPV and IRR calculations it appears that the directors should not make the investment in the sunbeds. The company's cost of capital is 14% and this investment falls well short of that target. However, the directors may consider other factors in making their decision. For example:

- How important is it to the future of the business that it diversifies its range of services? Will the hairdressing business continue to produce strong returns? If there is some uncertainty, it may make sense to diversify.
- Are competitors offering sunbeds? If they are, the existing hairdressing business could be damaged if Outhwaite Benson Limited does not do the same.
- Is it possible that the provision of the sunbed service will attract new customers who may also use the hairdressing services? If so, has this potential for additional sales been taken into account in the projected cash flow figures?

Finally, how reliable are the estimates? If the projected cash flows are put into a spreadsheet the directors can perform a series of 'what if' calculations to test out various levels of projection (optimistic, pessimistic, average).

Appendix: Discount factors

The table gives the present value of a single payment received n years in the future discounted at x% per year. For example, with a discount rate of 7% a single payment of £1 in six years' time has a present value of £0.6663 or 66.63p.

Years	1%	2%	3%	4%	5%	6%	7%	8%	9%	10%
1	0.9901	0.9804	0.9709	0.9615	0.9524	0.9434	0.9346	0.9259	0.9174	0.9091
2	0.9803	0.9612	0.9426	0.9426	0.9070	0.8900	0.8734	0.8573	0.8417	0.8264
3	0.9706	0.9423	0.9151	0.8890	0.8638	0.8396	0.8163	0.7938	0.7722	0.7513
4	0.9610	0.9238	0.8885	0.8548	0.8227	0.7921	0.7629	0.7350	0.7084	0.6830
5	0.9515	0.9057	0.8626	0.8219	0.7835	0.7473	0.7130	0.6806	0.6499	0.6209
6	0.9420	0.8880	0.8375	0.7903	0.7462	0.7050	0.6663	0.6302	0.5963	0.5645
7	0.9327	0.8706	0.8131	0.7599	0.7107	0.6651	0.6227	0.5835	0.5470	0.5132
8	0.9235	0.8535	0.7894	0.7307	0.6768	0.6274	0.5820	0.5403	0.5019	0.4665
9	0.9143	0.8368	0.7664	0.7026	0.6446	0.5919	0.5439	0.5002	0.4604	0.4241
10	0.9053	0.8203	0.7441	0.6756	0.6139	0.5584	0.5083	0.4632	0.4224	0.3855
11	0.8963	0.8043	0.7224	0.6496	0.5847	0.5268	0.4751	0.4289	0.3875	0.3505
12	0.8874	0.7885	0.7014	0.6246	0.5568	0.4970	0.4440	0.3971	0.3555	0.3186
13	0.8787	0.7730	0.6810	0.6006	0.5303	0.4688	0.4150	0.3677	0.3262	0.2897
14	0.8700	0.7579	0.6611	0.5775	0.5051	0.4423	0.3878	0.3405	0.2992	0.2633
15	0.8613	0.7430	0.6419	0.5553	0.4810	0.4173	0.3624	0.3152	0.2745	0.2394
16	0.8528	0.7284	0.6232	0.5339	0.4581	0.3936	0.3387	0.2919	0.2519	0.2176
17	0.8444	0.7142	0.6050	0.5134	0.4363	0.3714	0.3166	0.2703	0.2311	0.1978
18	0.8360	0.7002	0.5874	0.4936	0.4155	0.3503	0.2959	0.2502	0.2120	0.1799
19	0.8277	0.6864	0.5703	0.4746	0.3957	0.3305	0.2765	0.2317	0.1945	0.1635
20	0.8195	0.6730	0.5537	0.4564	0.3769	0.3118	0.2584	0.2145	0.1784	0.1486
21	0.8114	0.6598	0.5375	0.4388	0.3589	0.2942	0.2415	0.1987	0.1637	0.1351
22	0.8034	0.6468	0.5219	0.4220	0.3418	0.2775	0.2257	0.1839	0.1502	0.1228
23	0.7954	0.6342	0.5067	0.4057	0.3256	0.2618	0.2109	0.1703	0.1378	0.1117
24	0.7876	0.6217	0.4919	0.3901	0.3101	0.2470	0.1971	0.1577	0.1264	0.1015
25	0.7798	0.6095	0.4776	0.3751	0.2953	0.2330	0.1842	0.1460	0.1160	0.0923
26	0.7720	0.5976	0.4637	0.3607	0.2812	0.2198	0.1722	0.1352	0.1064	0.0839
27	0.7644	0.5859	0.4502	0.3468	0.2678	0.2074	0.1609	0.1252	0.0976	0.0763
28	0.7568	0.5744	0.4371	0.3335	0.2551	0.1956	0.1504	0.1159	0.0895	0.0693
29	0.7493	0.5631	0.4243	0.3207	0.2429	0.1846	0.1406	0.1073	0.0822	0.0630
30	0.7419	0.5521	0.4120	0.3083	0.2314	0.1741	0.1314	0.0994	0.0754	0.0573
35	0.7059	0.5000	0.3554	0.2534	0.1813	0.1301	0.0937	0.0676	0.0490	0.0356
40	0.6717	0.4529	0.3066	0.2083	0.1420	0.0972	0.0668	0.0460	0.0318	0.0221
45	0.6391	0.4102	0.2644	0.1712	0.1113	0.0727	0.0476	0.0313	0.0207	0.0137
50	0.6080	0.3715	0.2281	0.1407	0.0872	0.0543	0.0339	0.0213	0.0134	0.0085

11%	12%	13%	14%	15%	16%	17%	18%	19%	20%	Years
0.9009	0.8929	0.8850	0.8772	0.8696	0.8621	0.8547	0.8475	0.8403	0.8333	1
0.8116	0.7972	0.7831	0.7695	0.7561	0.7432	0.7305	0.7182	0.7062	0.6944	2
0.7312	0.7118	0.6931	0.6750	0.6575	0.6407	0.6244	0.6086	0.5934	0.5787	3
0.6587	0.6355	0.6133	0.5921	0.5718	0.5523	0.5337	0.5158	0.4987	0.4823	4
0.5935	0.5674	0.5428	0.5194	0.4972	0.4761	0.4561	0.4371	0.4190	0.4019	5
0.5346	0.5066	0.4803	0.4556	0.4323	0.4104	0.3898	0.3704	0.3521	0.3349	6
0.4817	0.4523	0.4251	0.3996	0.3759	0.3538	0.3332	0.3139	0.2959	0.2791	7
0.4339	0.4039	0.3762	0.3506	0.3269	0.3050	0.2848	0.2660	0.2487	0.2326	8
0.3909	0.3606	0.3329	0.3075	0.2843	0.2630	0.2434	0.2255	0.2090	0.1938	9
0.3522	0.3220	0.2946	0.2697	0.2472	0.2267	0.2080	0.1911	0.1756	0.1615	10
0.3173	0.2875	0.2607	0.2366	0.2149	0.1954	0.1778	0.1619	0.1476	0.1346	11
0.2858	0.2567	0.2307	0.2076	0.1869	0.1685	0.1520	0.1372	0.1240	0.1122	12
0.2575	0.2292	0.2042	0.1821	0.1625	0.1452	0.1299	0.1163	0.1042	0.0935	13
0.2320	0.2046	0.1807	0.1597	0.1413	0.1252	0.1110	0.0985	0.0876	0.0779	14
0.2090	0.1827	0.1599	0.1401	0.1229	0.1079	0.0949	0.0835	0.0736	0.0649	15
0.1883	0.1631	0.1415	0.1229	0.1069	0.0930	0.0811	0.0708	0.0618	0.0541	16
0.1696	0.1456	0.1252	0.1078	0.0929	0.0802	0.0693	0.0600	0.0520	0.0451	17
0.1528	0.1300	0.1108	0.0946	0.0808	0.0691	0.0592	0.0508	0.0437	0.0376	18
0.1377	0.1161	0.0981	0.0829	0.0703	0.0596	0.0506	0.0431	0.0367	0.0313	19
0.1240	0.1037	0.0868	0.0728	0.0611	0.0514	0.0433	0.0365	0.0308	0.0261	20
0.1117	0.0926	0.0768	0.0638	0.0531	0.0443	0.0370	0.0309	0.0259	0.0217	21
0.1007	0.0826	0.0680	0.0560	0.0462	0.0382	0.0316	0.0262	0.0218	0.0181	22
0.0907	0.0738	0.0601	0.0491	0.0402	0.0329	0.0270	0.0222	0.0183	0.0151	23
0.0817	0.0659	0.0532	0.0431	0.0349	0.0284	0.0231	0.0188	0.0154	0.0126	24
0.0736	0.0588	0.0471	0.0378	0.0304	0.0245	0.0197	0.0160	0.0129	0.0105	25
0.0663	0.0525	0.0417	0.0331	0.0264	0.0211	0.0169	0.0135	0.0109	0.0087	26
0.0597	0.0469	0.0369	0.0291	0.0230	0.0182	0.0144	0.0115	0.0091	0.0073	27
0.0538	0.0419	0.0326	0.0255	0.0200	0.0157	0.0123	0.0097	0.0077	0.0061	28
0.0485	0.0374	0.0289	0.0224	0.0174	0.0135	0.0105	0.0082	0.0064	0.0051	29
0.0437	0.0334	0.0256	0.0196	0.0151	0.0116	0.0090	0.0070	0.0054	0.0042	30
0.0259	0.0189	0.0139	0.0102	0.0075	0.0055	0.0041	0.0030	0.0023	0.0017	35
0.0154	0.0107	0.0075	0.0053	0.0037	0.0026	0.0019	0.0013	0.0010	0.0007	40
0.0091	0.0061	0.0041	0.0027	0.0019	0.0013	0.0009	0.0006	0.0004	0.0003	45
0.0054	0.0035	0.0022	0.0014	0.0009	0.0006	0.0004	0.0003	0.0002	0.0001	50

Source: Drury, C. (2001) *Management Accounting for Business Decisions*, Second Edition, London: Thomson Learning.

GLOSSARY

Absorption costing The costing of products and services to include both direct and indirect costs of production.

Accounting policies Those principles of accounting that are selected by the managers of a business to be applied in the preparation of the financial statements.

Accounting standards Regulations containing detailed guidance and rules on the preparation of financial accounts. In the UK accounting standards are issued in the form of Financial Reporting Standards (FRSs) by the Accounting Standards Board (ASB).

Accruals An important accounting convention that involves the matching of sales and expenses, so that all of the expenses incurred in making a sale are deducted from it. Also referred to as matching.

Acid test ratio The ratio of current assets, excluding stock, to current liabilities (also known as the 'quick' ratio).

Adverse variance An unfavourable difference between a budget figure and an actual figure. (In terms of sales, an actual figure that is lower than budget; in terms of costs an actual figure that is higher than budget.)

Amortisation A measurement of the amount of fixed asset value that has been used up during the accounting period (the term usually relates to intangible fixed assets).

Articles of association A document, required by company law, which sets out the constitution of the company.

Assets Resources controlled by a business that it will use in order to generate a profit in the future.

Audit An independent examination by a properly qualified professional auditor of the records and financial statements of a business. (Note that in the context of this book the entity is a business enterprise, but audit of charities, local government and central government, for example, also takes place.)

Audit report The report by an independent auditor on the financial statements of a business.

Authorised share capital The number of shares that a company is authorised to issue (this is not necessarily the same number that has actually been issued).

Bad debt An amount owed to a business that cannot be recovered.

Balance sheet A statement of the resources owned and controlled by a business at a single point in time. Most businesses prepare balance sheets at least annually.

Batch costing The accumulation of costs relating to a batch of identical products.

Break-even chart A graph showing lines for costs and revenues, from which the break-even point can be estimated.

Break-even point The point at which neither a profit nor a loss is made – i.e. where total costs equal total revenues.

Budget A statement, prepared in advance, usually for a specific period (e.g. for one year), of a business's planned activities and financial outcomes.

Budgetary slack An adverse effect observable in some businesses where managers deliberately set themselves easily achievable targets.

Business entity concept The business is regarded as separate from its owner(s).

Business plan A detailed document produced to support an application for business finance.

Capital Amounts invested by the owners of the business to which they subsequently have a claim.

Capital introduced The resources in the form of money and other goods put into a business by its owner(s) when it starts up.

Capital rationing Where a shortage of capital available for investment requires prioritisation of investment projects.

Cartel A price-fixing arrangement where a few major suppliers in a market agree between themselves to keep prices high.

Cash flow The movement of cash in and out of a business.

Cash flow statement A statement prepared periodically that summarises the cash flows in and out of a business.

Chairman's statement A written statement by a company chairman that accompanies the annual financial statements of all companies in the UK listed on the London Stock Exchange.

Charge A legal arrangement for security for a loan. A lender puts in place a charge over specified property of the borrower. If the borrower fails to repay the loan, the proceeds of sale of the property are used to reimburse the lender.

Common size analysis The application of vertical analysis across comparable figures for more than one accounting period.

Consolidated financial statements The financial statements for a group of companies, which combine together the profit and loss accounts and balance sheets of all the companies in the group.

Contribution The amount that remains after deducting variable costs from sales revenue.

Cost accounting The process of identifying and summarising the costs associated with business operations.

Cost and management accounting Accounting oriented towards the provision of information resources that managers can use to run the business.

Cost centres Functions or areas into which costs can be organised.

Cost of capital The interest rate that is applicable to a particular business

Cost of sales The cost of buying in or manufacturing the goods that have been sold in an accounting period.

Cost unit An item of production or a group of products or a service for which it is useful to have product cost information.

Creditors Amounts owed by a business to other people or organisations.

Creditors turnover ratio Assesses the length of time, on average, that a business takes to pay its creditors.

Current assets Assets held in the business for a short period of time only (examples include stock, debtors and cash).

Current liabilities Amounts that will have to be paid by the business in the near future.

Current ratio The ratio of current assets to current liabilities.

Debentures Company bonds that entitle their holder to eventual repayment of the value of the stock plus a regular annual rate of interest (debentures are sometimes referred to as 'loan stock').

Debt Finance in the form of loans.

Debtors Amounts owed to a business by other people or organisations.

Debtors turnover ratio Assesses the length of time, on average, that debtors take to pay.

Demand curve An economic model of the relationship between price and quantity demanded.

Depreciation A measurement of the amount of fixed asset value that has been used up during the accounting period (the term usually relates to tangible fixed assets).

Direct costs Those costs directly associated with the manufacturing process.

Direct expenses – Direct costs other than direct materials and direct labour costs.

Directors The senior managers of a limited company. Directors have special responsibilities in law.

Dividend A payment periodically made by a limited company to its shareholders.

Dividend cover A ratio that calculates the number of times the current dividend could be paid out of available profits for the period.

Doubtful debt An amount owed to a business in respect of which recovery is doubtful.

Drawings The taking of cash (or other resources) out of an unincorporated business by its owner(s).

Equity The ordinary shareholders' interest in a company, comprising their original contribution in share capital plus any profits retained in the business.

Equity shares The share capital in a company that entitles its owner(s) to a share of the business's profits (in the form of dividend) and to voting rights.

Expenses The amounts incurred by the business in purchasing or manufacturing goods sold, and other expenditure on items like rent and telephone charges.

Factoring An arrangement to obtain cash from a factoring company in exchange for debtors of the business.

Favourable variance An advantageous difference between a budget figure and an actual figure. (In terms of sales, an actual figure that is higher than budget; in terms of costs an actual figure that is lower than budget.)

Financial accountants Specialists in the provision of financial information oriented towards interested parties external to the business.

Financial accounting The processes and practices involved in providing interested parties external to the business with the financial information that they need.

Financial reporting Reporting financial information to interested parties external to the business.

Finished goods Stock items that have been through a complete manufacturing process and that are now ready for sale

Fixed assets Assets that remain in the possession of the business over a long period of time, almost always in excess of one year.

Fixed asset turnover ratio Expresses the efficiency with which fixed assets have been used in a business to generate turnover.

Fixed overheads Those costs that do not tend to vary directly with increases and decreases in activity in a business.

Gearing The relationship between equity capital and loan capital in a company.

Gearing ratio The relationship between equity capital and loan capital expressed as a ratio.

Goodwill The intangible factors that add value to a business, such as brand names and customer loyalty.

Gross profit The amount of profit after deducting cost of sales from total sales.

Horizontal analysis Analysis of comparable accounting figures over a period of time.

Hostile bid A takeover bid which is not welcomed by the target company.

Income statement Profit and loss account (income statement is more widely used outside the UK).

Incorporation The process of setting up a limited company.

Incremental budgets Budgets that are set by taking a previous period's budget total and adding a standard percentage increase.

Indirect costs Those costs that are not directly identifiable with a unit of production.

Intangible fixed assets Fixed assets that do not have a physical presence.

Interest cover A measurement of the number of times interest could be paid out of available profits.

Interim financial statements Financial accounts issued half-yearly (or in rare cases in the UK, quarterly) by companies listed on the London Stock Exchange.

Inventory Items bought by a business to sell on to somebody else, or to process or transform in some way to make saleable goods (more usually known as 'stock' in the UK).

Issued share capital The number of shares actually issued by a company (it can issue a quantity of shares less than or equal to the amount of authorised share capital).

Job costing An accumulation of costs relating to one identifiable job or task.

Lease premium A substantial sum payable at the start (inception) of a lease.

Leasing A financing arrangement for obtaining the use of business assets without having to purchase them.

Lessee A person or business that obtains the use of an asset under a leasing arrangement.

Lessor A person or (usually) business that makes assets available to businesses under leasing arrangements.

Liabilities Amounts that the business is obliged to pay to other people or organisations.

Limited company A legal arrangement for regulating the ownership of business.

Limited liability The liability of the shareholders of a limited company is limited to the amount of their original investment.

Limiting factors Constraints on the level of business activity.

Loan stock Company bonds that entitle their holder to eventual repayment of the value of the stock plus a regular annual rate of interest (loan stock is sometimes referred to as 'debentures').

Loss The deficit that occurs when expenditure exceeds revenue.

Loss leader A product or service that is used to attract customer attention to a range of goods or to a particular supplier.

Management accountants Specialists in the provision of financial information for use within the business.

Management accounting Accounting carried out within a business for its own internal uses, to assist management in controlling the business and in making business decisions.

Marginal cost The cost of one additional unit.

Marginal costing An approach to costing that excludes fixed costs.

Margin of safety The excess of planned or actual sales above the break-even point.

Market capitalisation The total value obtained by multiplying the number of shares a listed company has in issue by the market value of one share.

Market value [of a share] The price at which the share can be traded on the stock market.

Matching An important accounting convention that involves the matching of sales and expenses, so that all of the expenses incurred in making a sale are deducted from it. Also referred to as accruals.

Memorandum of association A document, required by company law, which sets out the purposes for which the company is established, and its authorised share capital.

Monopoly A market condition where only one supplier supplies the market with a particular good or service.

Mortgage A loan secured on real estate.

Net present value The aggregate of a set of cash inflows and outflows forecast to take place at future dates, discounted to present values.

Net profit The amount of profit after deducting both cost of sales and other expenses from total sales.

Nominal value The basic denomination of a share – for example, 50p or 25p.

Offer for sale A general invitation to both the public and financial institutions to buy shares in a company.

Oligopoly A market condition where there are few suppliers (about three to five) of a particular good or service. Typically, the market shares between the suppliers are fairly evenly spread.

Ordinary share capital The shares in a company that confer the right to vote in company general meetings, and to receive a share of any dividend paid out by the company.

Overhead absorption A method of allocating an appropriate portion of production overheads to cost units.

Overhead absorption rate A rate used to estimate the amount of production overhead incurred in manufacturing.

Partnership A business that is run by two or more people with a view to making a profit.

Period costs Costs incurred during the accounting period.

Placing Offering a limited group of prospective buyers the opportunity to buy new shares in a company.

Prepayment An item of expense that has been paid in advance at the end of an accounting period.

Present value The discounted value at the present time (i.e. now) of a cash flow expected to arise in the future.

Price setter An influential supplier in a market with the power to influence the level of prices for a product or service.

Price taker A supplier in a market with little or no influence over the level of prices charged for a product or service.

Prime cost The total of all direct costs associated with manufacture.

Product costing The accumulation of costs relating to the production of a large number of identical units.

Product costs Those costs relating to the production of goods or services for sale by a business.

Profit The surplus that remains after deducting business costs from business income.

Profit and loss account A statement prepared by businesses of all sizes, at least annually, which shows the total business revenue less expenses. The net total is the profit or loss of the business.

Prospectus A document produced in accordance with (in the UK) Financial Services Authority regulation. It is prepared by a company which offers its shares for sale to the general public, and contains a large amount of information about the history and prospects of the company.

Provision (in respect of a doubtful debt) An amount recognised in the profit and loss of a business as a deduction from profit. It is included where the recovery of one or more debts is doubtful. It may be specific to a particular debt, or may be general, based upon an estimate of the proportion of debts that are doubtful.

Quick ratio The ratio of current assets, excluding stock, to current liabilities (also known as the 'acid test' ratio).

Raw materials Materials that are bought in by a business and then put through a manufacturing process.

Realisation Converted or capable of being converted into cash.

Recognition The inclusion of items of, for example, income and expense in the financial statements. Recognition is an important accounting convention.

Reducing balance method [of depreciation] A method of estimating depreciation which results in a higher charge in the earlier years of an asset's useful life, with the charge progressively reducing towards the end of the asset's useful life.

Registered auditors Professionally qualified auditors who are authorised to conduct the audits of businesses and other organisations.

Responsibility accounting Accounting within the business that identifies the person or department responsible for particular outcomes.

Retained profits The amount of profit left in a business (i.e. profit not distributed to the owners of the business).

Revenue The amount of goods and/or services sold in an accounting period by a business, expressed in terms of monetary amounts.

Rights issue An offer of shares made to existing shareholders in a company, in proportion to the number of shares already held (e.g. a one for seven rights issue involves offering one new share for every seven already held).

Rolling budget A budget that is updated on a regular basis as each period of time (usually one month) elapses.

Security An arrangement between a lender and a borrower where specified items of property can be used to meet the loan if the borrower defaults (i.e. does not repay the loan).

Semi-variable cost A cost that varies to some extent with the level of business activity; it has both fixed and variable elements.

Shareholders The investors in a limited company; each investor owns a share or shares in the company.

Sole trader A person who operates a business himself or herself, keeping any profits that are made.

Standard costing A system of costing that attributes consistent costs to elements of production.

Stewardship Taking responsibility for the management of resources on behalf of somebody else. (The principal example in this book is that of company directors managing a company on behalf of its shareholders.)

Stock Items bought by a business to sell on to somebody else, or to process or transform in some way to make saleable goods.

Stock turnover ratio Measures the length of time, on average, that an item of stock remains in the business before being sold.

Straight-line method [of depreciation] The method that charges depreciation evenly over all accounting periods that benefit from the use of a fixed asset.

Sunk costs Costs that are irrelevant to a capital expenditure decision, because they have already been incurred.

Takeover bid A move to take over a majority of shares in a target company so as to gain control of it.

Tangible fixed assets Fixed assets that have a physical presence (unlike intangible fixed assets).

Trade creditors Amounts owing to people or organisations that have provided goods or services on credit.

Trading account The upper part of the profit and loss account where gross profit is calculated.

Trend analysis The analysis of comparable accounting figures over a period of time sufficient to establish reliable tendencies and trends.

Variable cost A cost that varies in proportion to the level of business activity.

Vertical analysis An accounting analytical technique that involves expressing all of the figures in an accounting statement as proportions of a key figure (for example, sales).

Work-in-progress Items of part-completed stock.

Working capital The elements of financing required for investment in items that move rapidly in and out of the business, for example, stock.

Working capital cycle The movement of the elements of working capital (debtors, creditors, stock and cash) around the business.

INDEX